College Basketball Prospectus

2008–2009

College Basketball Prospectus

2008–2009

THE ESSENTIAL GUIDE TO THE MEN'S COLLEGE BASKETBALL SEASON

KEN POMEROY, JOHN GASAWAY,

AND THE AUTHORS OF

BASKETBALL PROSPECTUS

A PLUME BOOK

PLUME
Published by Penguin Group
Penguin Group (USA) Inc., 375 Hudson Street, New York, New York 10014, U.S.A.
Penguin Group (Canada), 90 Eglinton Avenue East, Suite 700, Toronto, Ontario, Canada M4P 2Y3
(a division of Pearson Penguin Canada Inc.)
Penguin Books Ltd., 80 Strand, London WC2R 0RL, England
Penguin Ireland, 25 St. Stephen's Green, Dublin 2, Ireland (a division of Penguin Books Ltd.)
Penguin Group (Australia), 250 Camberwell Road, Camberwell, Victoria 3124, Australia
(a division of Pearson Australia Group Pty. Ltd.)
Penguin Books India Pvt. Ltd., 11 Community Centre, Panchsheel Park, New Delhi – 110 017, India
Penguin Group (NZ), 67 Apollo Drive, Rosedale, North Shore 0632, New Zealand
(a division of Pearson New Zealand Ltd.)
Penguin Books (South Africa) (Pty.) Ltd., 24 Sturdee Avenue, Rosebank, Johannesburg 2196, South Africa

Penguin Books Ltd., Registered Offices:
80 Strand, London WC2R 0RL, England

First published by Plume, a member of Penguin Group (USA) Inc.

First Printing (2008–2009 edition), November 2008
10 9 8 7 6 5 4 3 2 1

ISBN 978-0-452-28987-1

Printed in the United States of America
Set in Garamond Book
Design by Jane Raese

Contents

AT A GLANCE

STATS

Introduction
How to Use this Book

Last February, when we were both grabbing anyone who would listen and insisting that then-unranked Louisville was one of the best teams in the country, the two of us agreed to write this book.

At the time, we set ourselves the goal of learning things we hadn't known about college basketball before and then sharing some of those finds in book form.

Such as ...

- Players shoot free throws about as well immediately after a time-out as in other situations.
- You know how you already knew that Michael Beasley was really good? He was actually even better.
- In terms of effective field-goal percentage, no major-conference team in the past three years has played better field-goal defense in-conference than did Georgetown last year.
- For the second year in a row, no NCAA tournament team scored a lower percentage of its points on three-pointers than North Carolina did.
- The Big Ten has been not just the slowest major conference but also the slowest conference in the entire nation over the past five seasons, in terms of possessions per 40 minutes in conference games.

Where do we come up with this stuff? Like you, we watch a lot of college basketball. But we've also been influenced greatly by illustrious hoops thinkers like former North Carolina coach Dean Smith and current NBA analyst Dean Oliver. They successfully deprogrammed both of us so that we really don't think in per-game terms anymore (points per game, rebounds per game, etc.). A team's per-game stats will be heavily influenced by pace—and a player's per-game stats will be influenced by both pace and playing time. So we try to control for all the above by instead looking at the game in tempo-free terms.

If you stopped by the Web site (Basketball Prospectus.com) during the season last year, you know the drill. We choose to bypass entirely the name-brand hoops groceries that offer aisle after well-stocked aisle of per-game stats, compiled by the NCAA and by the conferences. Instead, we both head directly to our favorite farmers market for the freshest organically grown box scores and play-by-play data. Then we go to our respective kitchens and cook up some weird and, we hope, wonderful tempo-free fare.

This book is the result of many such trips to the kitchen. Our fondest hope is merely that it imparts a little of the fun we've had learning, debating, pondering, and asking still more questions about college hoops.

A word on breadth. You hold in your hand but one book, there are but two of us, and there are 341 Division I teams. Preseason guides that cover more or even all of Division I call on the talents of many, many more writers—and we salute the good works done by these fellow lovers of hoops. We just wanted to toss some additional thoughts into the mix on a selected range of teams and topics.

One final note. We were right about Louisville back in February. Eventually, it took one of those snooty one-seeds, North Carolina, to knock the Cardinals out of the tournament. We were wrong about plenty of other things, of course, but last year was a lot of fun. We remember it quite well indeed.

Ken is still demanding congressional hearings because Butler's Mike Green, listed by his own school as 6-1 (and measured by the NBA as 6-1 without shoes), won the 2008 Frances Pomeroy Naismith Award, which, supposedly, is given annually to the nation's top senior no taller than six feet. John is still miffed that he didn't run with a tip he got last March 4th that Billy Packer was about to work his last Final Four and would be replaced by Clark Kellogg.

That was then. Bring on the new season.

Ken Pomeroy
John Gasaway
August 2008

THOUGHTS FOR A NEW SEASON

Arc Madness

KEN POMEROY

Every season, there's a significant newness to the college game. The typical team loses about a third of its previous season's roster. In a given season, about one in every six programs has a new head coach. This season, there's another change—the court will look different for the first time in over 20 years.

In May 2007, the NCAA Men's Basketball Rules Committee agreed to move the three-point line back a foot, to 20 feet, 9 inches, beginning this season, and ever since that announcement, there's been speculation on the impact the change will have on the game. Before we get to that, though, let's review how the game has evolved with the three-point line that has existed since 1987.

The aspect of the three-pointer that has been most predictable over time is its increasing frequency of use in each successive season. The trend has leveled off in the last decade, which is fortunate: Had it continued at the 1987-1995 rates, more shots would be three-pointers than two-pointers by now. The other dimension of three-point shooting—accuracy—has stabilized over the past 15 years at right around 35 percent. Here's what those trends look like in graphical form.

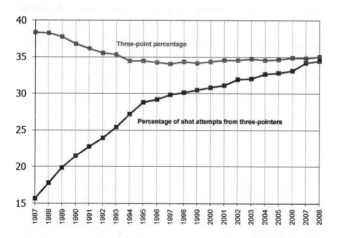

To put the explosion of three-point attempts since 1987 in perspective, consider that every team last season took 20 percent or more of its shots from beyond the arc, whereas the nationwide average was less than 20 percent in the shot's first three seasons of use. In 1987, Rick Pitino was considered a maverick when his Providence team rode the three-point shot to double-digit upsets over Alabama and Georgetown en route to a Final Four appearance as a six-seed. The Friars took 30 percent of their shots from long range in 1987, a figure that undoubtedly was one of the highest in the land that season, but would have placed a team on the timid side of the Division I average in 2008.

The 19-foot, 9-inch three-point shot has done a lot of growing up over its 21 years in the game. When the line reached adulthood, the rules committee decided to kick it out of the house. But don't expect any sort of sea change with the more distant line. The major adjustments to the three-point line took place in the 1980s. Changes occurring with the foot-long move will be almost imperceptible on a game-by-game basis, compared with what happened then, but there will be changes. So what can we expect?

The NCAA tends not to do anything too quickly, and such was the case with moving the three-point line. There were experiments with a similar three-point line during select preconference games in recent seasons. The latest effort took place in November and December 2004, when a 20-foot, 6-inch distance was used in 169 games. The results from that experiment give us a peek at what to expect this season.

Games in late 2004 were slower and lower scoring than games with traditional rules played at the same time. The experiment that season also included an expanded lane, which didn't help the offense's cause any and probably contributed as much to a lower two-point shooting percentage as the deeper three-point line did. It's not a surprise that both three-point accuracy and the frequency of the shot declined slightly with the more distant line.

Statistical differences between a 20-foot, 6-inch three-point line (experiment games) and a 19-foot, 9-inch one (regular games), November and December 2004

	Experiment Games	Regular Games
3P FG percent	33.7	34.8
3PA/FGA (percent)	31.7	32.8
2P FG percent	47.3	48.0
Poss/40 min	69.1	69.5
Pts/100 poss	96.9	98.6
Points/40 min	67.0	68.6

Before this 2004 experiment, a similar suite of rules changes had been used in 115 games at the beginning of the 2003-2004 season.

Statistical differences between a 20-foot, 6-inch three-point line (experiment games) and a 19-foot, 9-inch one (regular games), November and December 2003

	Experiment Games	Regular Games
3P FG percent	33.8	33.9
3PA/FGA (percent)	31.5	32.1
2P FG percent	45.0	47.9
Poss/40 min	69.9	70.4
Pts/100 poss	94.7	97.8
Points/40 min	66.2	68.9

The results were nearly identical to what occurred in 2004. The three-point percentage was almost unchanged, but the other trends are similar. Experiments in both seasons share a subtle decrease in pace and a more pronounced decrease in efficiency. When combined, the two changes resulted in a 2 to 4 percent decrease in scoring.

The focus of the permanent shift in the three-point line has been on how it will affect the distribution and accuracy of three-point shooting. But if the experiments of 2003 and 2004 are any indication, the effects of the change will transcend what happens beyond the arc. On average, teams will use a smidgen more of the shot clock to get a shot they're comfortable with. Although a reduction in pace should be minor, it isn't a welcome change in the current era. Over the last three seasons, the average pace of a college basketball game has been right around 67 possessions per 40 minutes, which is the slowest it's been for as long as people have been systematically recording stats in college hoops, or roughly the past 60 years.

Again, though, any adjustments will be slight and will evolve as the season unfolds. Which teams will benefit? The programs that need to adjust the least will be rewarded the most by the change. Even in previous seasons, teams benefitted from being able to extend the defense beyond the 19-foot, 9-inch three-point line. It's been a while since extending a defense meant merely hitting three-pointers. Players who could regularly hit 23-footers had the power to extend the defense more effectively than could a player who only hits shots from just behind the arc. Teams having more players with range have already enjoyed playing against an overextended defense, which in turn opens the floor for cutting lanes, with easier two-point shots being the result.

As for the long-term ramifications of the new distance, it's not hard to imagine that as players and coaches adjust, we'll eventually get back to last season's rate of three-point shots launched. The goal of this rule change was to spread the offense out more. And if the offense can make the long-distance shot as regularly as it did with the shorter line, then the defense will be spread out more. This may not happen in the first season of the deeper line, but when it does happen, the game will be more free-flowing, high-scoring, and faster-paced than before, because defenses have more ground to cover. If that happens by 2010 or 2011, a season or two of worse shooting and lower scoring will have been worth it.

Two Cheers for One-and-Done

JOHN GASAWAY

The one-and-done era began on July 29, 2005, when the NBA and the Players Association signed a new collective bargaining agreement (CBA). It will end on June 30, 2011, or perhaps on June 30, 2012, if the league exercises an optional one-year extension. Under the terms of the current CBA, eligibility is limited to players who are 19 or older during their draft year and who have been out of high school for a year.

One-and-done is often framed implicitly as a college basketball problem in need of reform when in fact it's an NBA rule of finite duration. It's here. It's not going anywhere for another three or four years, until a new CBA is signed. And then, one-and-done will quite possibly be gone.

Maybe the next system will go back to the old way of doing things, wherein high school seniors had the option of going straight into the NBA. Or maybe the new system will require two (two-and-through!) or even three (three-and-flee!) years to have passed since high school graduation before a player can be eligible for the NBA. Whatever the new number of required years is fated to be, however, it seems probable that the number will no longer be one. Meaning one-and-done is likely an interregnum. If so, the rule will be remembered as a specific, sharply delimited epoch, like John Wooden at UCLA or Larry Brown at wherever he is now.

For college basketball, the impact of one-and-done has been something of a spectacular trickle. In two seasons, there have been 20 players who played just one season of college ball and were then drafted:

2007

Greg Oden
Kevin Durant
Mike Conley
Brandan Wright
Spencer Hawes
Thaddeus Young
Javaris Crittenton
Daequan Cook

2008

Derrick Rose
Michael Beasley
O. J. Mayo
Kevin Love
Eric Gordon
Jerryd Bayless
Anthony Randolph
J. J. Hickson
Kosta Koufos
Donte Greene
DeAndre Jordan
Bill Walker

(Jordan and Walker are borderline cases. Both were drafted in the second round and therefore might have been better advised to stay in school. Moreover, in the 2008 draft, Walker was a freshman in name only, having played six games for Kansas State in December 2006 and January 2007 before suffering a knee injury and taking a medical redshirt.)

You hear a lot of plaintive either-or talk about one-and-done, of course. Either let "the kids" go directly from high school to the NBA or make them stay three years, "just like in baseball." It's a nice sound bite, one with the virtue of simplicity, but while college coaches may say the first part of that

5

sound bite, they don't really believe it. Or if they do, they have really short memories.

Allowing high school seniors to enter the NBA draft means that college coaches will unavoidably waste time on prospects who will eventually bypass college entirely to go pro. Worse, those coaches will waste time on prospects who will commit to their program, scare away other prospects at the same position, and then jump to the pros, leaving the coach with a gaping hole at that position. College coaches don't want to waste time, and they don't want gaping holes. Arizona coach Lute Olson can fume that one-and-done is a "farce" and a "terrible rule," but the truth is one-and-done gives college coaches at least a measure of peace of mind. They know they're recruiting against other schools and not the NBA.

Or they did, until Olson found he was recruiting in competition with Europe in the case of Brandon Jennings. I doubt that Jennings will be the last prospect to go directly from high school to Europe, but he may still turn out to be more of a news peg à la Maurice Clarrett than a true harbinger of things to come. Jennings would be more plausible as a harbinger if he'd been eligible to play Division I ball at the time he made his decision. He didn't choose Europe over Arizona; he chose it over Chipola or its ilk. Decry his example if you wish, but if I were faced with those alternatives, I'd take Rome in a heartbeat myself.

Then again, maybe I wouldn't. Maybe if I were fortunate enough to be advised by someone truly looking out for my best interests, I would have been told that signing with a European team (in Jennings's case, Pallacanestro Virtus Roma) simply burdens me with another mouth to feed. And that the European team is signing me to a multiyear contract in the expectation of not only a $500,000 buyout a year from now from the NBA (the maximum allowed), but perhaps even in anticipation of an additional buyout paid by me personally.

Seen in this light, O. J. Mayo stands accused of simply making a better deal than Jennings did: no buyouts, no need to leave the country.

Last May, when an ESPN investigation reported that Mayo received cash and gifts from runners acting on behalf of BDA Sports Management, the reaction from sportswriters was swift and severe. Part of that severity can be attributed to the depth of ESPN's investigation. The accusations leveled against Mayo by former associate Louis Johnson appeared to be backed by receipts, phone records, and the recollec-

tions of third parties (e.g., sales clerks at upscale menswear shops). If ESPN's reporting holds up, Mayo received under-the-table benefits not only as a freshman at USC, but also for years prior to that, perhaps even as far back as 2005. No wonder he was almost instantly adopted for use as a cautionary tale on the corrupting dangers of youth basketball in general and on the systemic flaws of one-and-done in particular.

There were two related yet distinct sources of outrage in this saga. The first was that Mayo allegedly got money. The second was that he couldn't have received much of an education at USC. I think the first issue is a relatively straightforward matter for the NBA. The second is a relatively straightforward matter for the rest of us.

Until the NBA, and more specifically the Players Association, polices its agents more effectively, college basketball programs that sign McDonald's All-Americans will be at risk for another Mayo. The Players Association has something called an Agent Regulation Program. If this had teeth, any firm found to have been fronting money or other benefits to a prospect (or, much more likely, to a runner who then passed the inducements along to the prospect) would lose its right to represent players to NBA teams.

You may scoff at the program and say that agencies will still find indirect ways of funneling money to recruits. Maybe. Still, announcing such a rule— even merely *reannouncing* one that's already on the books—would put the Players Association on record as being on the side of the angels here, and anyway, don't underestimate the competitive advantage that will accrue to agencies that blow the whistle on a competitor. (Question: Has the NBA inadvertently helped this problem along with its predetermined rookie-scale salaries? If you're a rookie about to enter the NBA, agency representation is a classic parity product: Your team will be paying you the same amount, no matter who your agent is. Maybe this state of affairs leaves agents to compete for players on the basis of inducements instead of based on—what a concept—the quality of their representation.)

From the perspective of college basketball, the Mayo accusations underscore what was surely already obvious: Freshmen who otherwise would have gone directly to the NBA comprise the at-risk group for under-the-table payments from agents. The saga that unfolded should have made it perfectly clear to every athletic director that these recruits need to be looked at very closely and even vetted. If I were an athletic director in the Age of Mayo, I'd have a procedure written up in advance for just such cases. (If the NCAA drafts a due-diligence protocol, all the better.)

In this case, it's said that Trojans coach Tim Floyd simply should have known better, given the history of Mayo associate Rodney Guillory. (A fixture in Southern California basketball circles, Guillory was found by the NCAA in 2001 to have been working as an agent's representative in fronting airfare to then-Trojan Jeff Trepagnier and to Tito Maddox of Fresno State.) Of course Floyd should have known better. I'd even be willing to guess that he *did* know better. But his crime here was that he signed a prospect who was then the top-rated player in the country and who was subsequently vouchsafed as eligible by the NCAA and the Pac-10 conference. Not too many Division I coaches would have done differently. It will be interesting and telling to see what the NCAA does, assuming USC is found guilty only of one count of "should have known better."

The second source of outrage in the Mayo saga is that one-and-done freshmen, even if they aren't being paid, can't possibly get much of an education. Such players need to keep their academic noses clean for just one semester. By the time their grades come in for work done (or not done) during the second semester, the athletes are already long gone.

Academically speaking, two years in college would clearly be better than one. (Of course, three or four would be better still.) Two years would require the most talented players to buckle down and stay eligible for three semesters instead of just one. Again, however, that's outside college basketball's control. NBA Commissioner David Stern in fact proposed a "two-and-done" system to the Players Association in 2005. One-and-done was a compromise arrived at in the face of player opposition to Stern's proposal.

As a result, the freshmen who play college basketball for just one year before going pro quite plainly constitute the least studious student-athletes in all of college sports. That's not a blanket academic dismissal of the players in question. Greg Oden by all accounts attended class and maintained a solid grade-point average at Ohio State. But the structural givens of this situation virtually ensure that academics are going to be an afterthought for the one-and-dones.

Of course, academics are occasionally an afterthought for other, even younger, athletes. Preternatu-

rally talented teenage golfers, tennis players, and, perhaps most famously, soccer players (Freddy Adu went pro at 14) have been known to pursue their professional careers on a schedule that nullifies the traditional academic progression. What's notable, then, is not that this happens in basketball as well (and has for decades: Moses Malone signed with the ABA as an 18-year-old in 1974), but rather that we're filled with horror only when it happens to take place on a college campus. Something about the ivied walls triggers the outrage.

I submit that this something is the student-athlete ideal. Worthy ideal, that: one that's exemplified by thousands of athletes nationwide, even in Division I, even in revenue-producing sports. Then again, college basketball is a hybrid, comprising not only thousands of true student-athletes, but also a tiny number of preemptively prominent athlete-athletes. As long as college basketball at its highest levels continues to function as a feeder system for the NBA, this hybrid quality will endure.

The key to making the hybrid work, however, is mere equity. Athlete-athletes have to be held to the same standards as true student-athletes. I can't force the athlete-athlete to take his education more seriously in his heart of hearts. But I can require him, and every other player on the team, to go to class, and I can discipline him when he doesn't. I can prohibit preferential treatment. Athlete-athletes have to be held to the same student-athlete standards.

Far-fetched? Too often coaches have thought so, but on this front, the fans may be way ahead of them. Look no further than Indiana, where new head coach Tom Crean simply jettisoned his best returning athlete-athletes for various behavioral and academic failings. Cleaning house means the Hoosiers will put little fear into opponents this coming year, yet the move has won almost universal acclaim from IU's notoriously dedicated fans.

As for Mayo, there was a palpable feeling of catharsis in many of the pieces written about him, pieces in which the student-athlete ideal was said to have been be rendered a "sham" by the one-and-done system. These writers see unsavory elements in youth basketball in the course of doing their jobs, I dare say, and the Mayo affair was the perfect occasion to condemn those elements.

My only question is whether in this case the perfect opportunity for catharsis was additionally any particular reflection on one-and-done per se. If ESPN is right, Mayo received benefits long before he arrived at USC. Moreover, Mayo was a one-and-done player, but not all one-and-done players are Mayos. The student-athlete ideal is certainly a sham on occasion. On some of those occasions, the player—whether or not he falls under the one-and-done heading—chooses to treat the ideal as a sham.

In the continuous and unruly discussion of college sports, our outrage has customarily been reserved for much less fortunate athletes, those who are used up but then do *not* make the pros and have not had much of an education. One-and-done turns that template upside-down. Players are referred to as one-and-done only when they're actually drafted by the NBA and, except for the odd cases of DeAndre Jordan and Bill Walker, making NBA money through the guaranteed contracts given to first-rounders. Assuming my call for equality of treatment is satisfied, we've reached a strange and rather peripheral moment in this discussion, surely, when the predominant object of our concern is the quality of instruction given over nine months to eight to 10 nascent millionaires per year.

The NBA draft is easily the most compelling and entertaining draft in sports. Baseball drafts have farm systems to populate and necessarily traffic in a cast of anonymous hundreds. The NFL draft is debilitated as spectator sport by its inherent apples-to-oranges nature. A professional football draft puts obscure 310-pound offensive linemen alongside wide receivers already bedecked with fame and cool hyphen-equipped nicknames and asks teams and fans to prioritize.

By contrast, the casual fan can easily attain a level of working knowledge sufficient to discuss the wisdom or folly seen in the 14 lottery picks of the NBA draft. And those 14 picks, while constituting just under 25 percent of the quantitative total, are likely to constitute something more like 75 percent of the qualitative total. I don't particularly follow the NBA, but its draft is the best draft in sports by far.

One thing I have to admit to liking about one-and-done, then, is that even if it lasts just six seasons, this will have been more than enough drafts under the bridge to yield some really interesting information on player evaluation. After all, one-and-dones will constitute the elite of the NBA from, say, 2010 to at least 2018 or so. What percentage of one-and-dones will pan out? Will we find that their performance during just one season of college ball was a good indicator of their performance as pros? No one really knows, but I'm interested in finding out.

From my chair, the one-and-dones in the 2008 draft to track from this point forward are Kevin Love, O. J. Mayo, and Anthony Randolph. I'm also adding Richard Hendrix to this list even though he was not a one-and-done player, and anyway, there's a distinct possibility that he won't see many minutes with Golden State. "Keeping an eye" on Hendrix might be difficult, but I still think he's an interesting example.

Kevin Love. As late as the first part of May, it appeared that the big man from UCLA was going to be my little secret: a player who won't make you shake your head in wonder at his athletic feats but who simply makes shots and gets defensive boards better than does any other player in the country not named Michael Beasley. Then a funny thing happened. About six weeks before the draft, Love started moving up the mock boards. On draft night, he was taken with the fifth pick by Memphis and then shipped to Minnesota in exchange for Mayo, who had been the third pick. In effect, the NBA came to a late decision that Derrick Rose and Michael Beasley were the only eligible players on the planet more promising than Kevin Love. My little secret no more. The NBA and I (gulp) agree. Will we be right?

O. J. Mayo. More than any other player taken in the first round, O. J. Mayo simply *looks* like an NBA player. I have little doubt that one day soon, he'll be playing in an All-Star game. By that, I mean simply that he'll be widely accepted as an elite player. He's got that star quality. My question with this particular star is whether purveyors of stats will be similarly impressed with his performance as a pro. Judging from his performance as a college freshman, the answer to that question may be no. Mayo certainly showed that he's a pure shooter, but beyond that, there's surprisingly little tangible supporting testimony from the hardwood for this phenom we've been hearing about since he was in the sixth grade. A lot may depend on Mayo's ability to enroll the cooperation of the refs in donning the mantel of Dwyane Wade 2.0: I drove into someone; therefore, I get free throws.

Anthony Randolph. The freshman from LSU may not be a big name to you, but to those of us who puzzle over college hoops Randolph looms as something of a legend, though for reasons he may not welcome. He merits an extended look—see below.

Richard Hendrix. As noted above, I'd be really interested to see what Hendrix could do with serious minutes in the NBA, but there's a chance I won't get to. One of the least discussed but most interesting questions left over from the past season in college basketball would be simply, Who was the best big man in the SEC? Your first clue is that, draft order notwithstanding, it was not Anthony Randolph. Personally, I'd go with Florida's oddly and severely underrated Marreese Speights, but the fact that a case can even be mounted for Alabama's Hendrix speaks volumes about the member of the Crimson Tide. Hendrix was too short (6-8 or 6-9, depending on who has the tape measure) and too old (21) to be of Randolph-level interest to the NBA, but he was dominant in the SEC for two years running. With the exception of free-throw percentage, he was superior—often dramatically so—to Randolph in every category playing against the same SEC competition. Yet on draft night, Hendrix's name went unspoken until he was finally taken in the middle of the second round by Golden State, the same team that had grabbed Randolph 35 picks earlier. Go fight City Hall.

Randolph and Hendrix personify a well-worn observation: Sometimes stats and scouts disagree. (It's true!) Then again, a lot of times stats and scouts agree …

Scouts' Evaluation

		Positive	Negative
Stats' Evaluation	Positive	Michael Beasley	Richard Hendrix
	Negative	Anthony Randolph	Me, Ken, everyone

Beasley is an obvious choice for that upper-left quadrant, but you don't need a Beasley-level phenomenon to trigger September 12–level consensus between scouts and stats. An even better example might be 2007 first-rounder Daequan Cook. Beloved by scouts and a huge name coming out of high school, Cook was seen in somewhat more diffident terms by the casual fan because he "didn't even start" for the Greg Oden/Mike Conley–led Ohio State team in 2007. Nevertheless, Cook looked excellent on paper, thanks to good three-point shooting and exceptional defensive rebounding.

And even though he's not in my nifty graphic, De-Andre Jordan has what can only be called paradigmatic value when it comes to player evaluation in the one-and-done era. Under the old rules, where players could go directly from high school to the NBA, Jordan would almost certainly have been a first-round draft pick in 2007 and indeed quite possibly a lottery pick. Instead, he was required to play one more year of pre-NBA ball and did so at Texas A&M. The NBA looked at that year—20 minutes a game and a limited role in the offense for a team that went 8-8 in the Big 12—and backpedaled politely but unmistakably, dropping Jordan to the second round. One-and-done gives NBA teams, for the first time, a usable past on these prospects, should the teams be so inclined to use it. That usable past cost DeAndre Jordan millions of dollars.

Stats can be dismissed, of course, as narrowly focused on performance when the business of sports and especially pro basketball is in truth rooted in the elusive chemistry of stars, charisma, and entertainment. But that's my point: The results of drafting based on a perception of the future were found wanting, precisely from an *entertainment* perspective. (If the NBA had given one-and-done its own logo, it would be a red circle and slash over a picture of Kwame Brown.) If you go out far enough, performance and entertainment align.

No player in the admittedly still young one-and-done epoch has so perfectly summed up the age-old dilemma of potential versus performance as has LSU's Anthony Randolph, who was selected with the 14th pick of the draft by Golden State. He is unquestionably blessed with tons of the former and demonstrably lacking in the latter. In the run-up to the draft, one analyst wrote that Randolph was "generating significant buzz from trusted NBA scouts." There's just one problem. Randolph wasn't a very good college basketball player.

To be fair, he happened to play his one year for a struggling (13-18) team that, Marcus Thornton notwithstanding, provided him with a comparatively middling supporting cast. What's more, that team endured no small measure of turmoil as its coach, John Brady, was dismissed in the heart of the conference season. All the above should be kept in mind as we look at Randolph's individual performance. The flip side of that coin, however, is that Randolph wasn't the only one-and-done player with non-Final-Four-level teammates, nor did every big man stuck with a tumultuous coaching situation necessarily see his own performance suffer. (See "White, D. J.")

Even though I'm drafting Randolph as a handy stats-versus-scouts wrestling mat, he actually had stats mostly to thank for his lofty position in the draft. Two stats in particular: He's listed at 6-11, and he was still 18 on draft day. So the question Randolph's situation actually poses with savory directness is *which* stats are more important: the ones that say what a player *is* (in this case, really young and really tall) or the ones that say what a player has *done*. Randolph is indeed strikingly long and athletic. He's also quite young, even by one-and-done standards. It's not unreasonable to look at that combination of attributes and expect improvement in the near term.

What is unreasonable, however, is to assume that Randolph belongs comfortably in the company of other long and athletic one-and-dones in terms of his performance in college. That's a dangerous assumption for an NBA front office to make.

Let's compare Randolph to a group I'll call *one-and-done big men*: Greg Oden, Kevin Durant, Brandan Wright, Spencer Hawes, Michael Beasley, Kevin Love, and DeAndre Jordan. I'll also toss in Tyrus Thomas because he was an old-school one-and-done, leaving LSU in 2006 after one year, when he'd had the opportunity to be drafted out of high school. Besides, I suspect that Randolph might have benefited from scouts' unconsciously projecting some of Thomas's abilities onto his successor in the paint in Baton Rouge.

In the weeks leading up to the draft, it was freely acknowledged that on offense, Randolph was no Michael Beasley. Actually, Randolph is no Kevin Love, either. Or Tyrus Thomas, Greg Oden, or any other frontcourt one-and-done. Simply put, for a 6-11 player to make just 48 percent of his twos and be drafted 14th is remarkable. Randolph displayed far and away the worst shooting of any one-and-done big man. Even more importantly for the purposes of NBA scouts, his struggles weren't purely a function of having to carry his team's offense—other one-and-done big men played equally large and even larger roles in their offenses and fared much better. This leads one to wonder if Randolph can be effective on offense in the NBA in 2009-2010, much less in 2008-2009. After all, Randolph wasn't terribly effective on offense in 2007-2008, even in a down-year SEC.

Which brings me to Gasaway's first law of player evaluation: *The competition has an upside, too.*

Going from the SEC one year to the NBA the next means, obviously, a huge difference in the level of competition. Young players get better, sure, but they need to get much, much better just to appear as good as they looked in college.

Given that Randolph had trouble getting the ball in the basket, you'd have to assume he's the world's greatest player at something else—defensive rebounding, maybe, or shot blocking. Something. That would be a faulty assumption. Among one-and-done bigs, only Brandan Wright was worse as a freshman on the defensive glass—and Wright even offset this by making an absurdly high proportion of his shots on offense. (True, as a freshman at Washington in 2007, Spencer Hawes was functionally equivalent to Randolph on the defensive glass. I don't suppose drafting Hawes with the 10th pick in 2007 was exactly a profile in sagacity, either, but my subject here is Randolph.)

Maybe Randolph's high draft position was due in part to the memory of another recent LSU freshman, one who also had an incredible wingspan and who always seemed to be swatting away shots. Randolph does indeed fare a little better in terms of blocks than he does on other metrics. Still, there was only one Tyrus Thomas, a player who was listed as only 6-9 but who inflicted an Oden-like level of disruption on opposing offenses. The team that drafts Randolph will get Randolph, not Thomas.

Stranger things have happened in sports and in life than Randolph someday blossoming into an NBA all-star, goodness knows. Nevertheless, with the current NBA eligibility requirements still in their infancy, we can hazard at least one sweeping pronouncement. Drafting Randolph with the 14th pick represented far and away the biggest risk of the one-and-done era.

Looking at a young kid playing basketball and then projecting the kid's performance out into the future is not only natural but unavoidable. If you don't think so, you've never been in a gym.

The pool I frequent in the summer is at the far end of a very long hallway between a rec center entrance and the locker room that opens out onto the pool. In between the entrance and the locker room are two large gyms. So as I make my way down that hallway, I see a steady stream of high school basketball players walking the other way. And my mind simply can't help but make scouting thumbnails: Man, look at those arms—that kid's going to grow another foot. Good grief, check out that moose—he can't possibly move his feet. Oh, he's way too thin, and those bones wouldn't support any meat, anyway.

Those thumbnails assert themselves as if against our will. Then we watch these same players in high school games against other players, and we learn even more. The visual narratives become longer and more detailed.

What the one-and-done system did was introduce additional information to put alongside the visual cues. With this additional information, we find that the amazing thing is not how often the visual assessments go awry but rather how often they're on the money. Michael Beasley really was as good as advertised—if anything, it takes some number-aided reflection to realize just how amazing he is. Player evaluation is often represented as a tug-of-war between scouts and stats, but the truth, as seen vividly in Beasley's case, is a lot of times, the stats and the scouts agree.

But acknowledging the consensus across evaluative styles on Beasley is quite different from an assumption that our visual thumbnails will always be right or will at least furnish the best available information. They don't, of course, any more than stats alone do. A team that understands this and, much more importantly, is bad enough for the next couple seasons to be positioned near the top of the draft could truly wreak some havoc in the NBA.

In any player's career, there comes a moment when the evaluations jump from the normative (he moves well, he has a quick release, he's got good footwork) to the comparative (he's less effective than player X). Right now, that initial comparative evaluation, for the most part, takes place in college basketball. When high school seniors can go directly into the draft, of course, that same moment is located in the NBA—at the league's peril. Trafficking in the normative is inherently ambiguous. So too, of course, is comparing players; it's just that the ambiguity here is rooted in our common quandary: We can't see the future.

As ambiguity increases, attempts to surmount it with precise language grow apace. Consider that hardy perennial of college basketball literature, the scouting report on the high school player. Like prose on architecture or wine, this mode of writing enjoys its own insularity, takes pleasure in its own peculiar argot, and, most crucially, is superseded completely once we've actually seen the building, tasted the wine, or watched a season of the player in Division I basketball.

Here's an actual post from a message board on an incoming recruit, whom I've taken the liberty of renaming:

John Doe is a very efficient player. He's a good shooter from range, plays with his head up all the time, which permits him to see the floor and pass extremely well, and can shot fake, take the ball to the hole, and use his body to shield defenders and finish against much bigger, more athletic kids. He's also a pretty good rebounder in traffic, and moves very well without the ball. The biggest problem John has, at this time, is not the athleticism thing—he's not fast, but he's not as slow as some have claimed—but rather lack of handling skills. He can put it on the floor to drive off the wing, but is not real good out front if pressured before he's comfortable with the ball and what he's going to do, and you wouldn't really see him as a guy who's going to be an extra handler against pressure. His shot release is decent, but not nearly as quick as [a teammate's]. Simply put, unless/until he gets better handles, he's a slightly undersized 3—really a point forward—with decent, but not great athleticism. I have no doubt that he can play in the conference because he is so fundamentally skilled and savvy, but to reach his potential, his ball handling needs to improve.

This writer obviously knows and, more importantly, loves their hoops. (Indeed, this kind of writing is more than an exchange of information. It's a ritual act of communion with something beloved.) My point is simply that if you applied the incredible diagnostic specificity of these statements to *yourself* as a player, their evanescence would quickly become apparent. Or if you no longer play hoops, imagine someone issuing an encyclical infused with this level of detail and finality about your job performance after he or she has watched you for a random two-hour period at your office.

It's good to know that a player is a certain height and weight, that he has a quick release, that he has a strong off-hand, and that he takes contact well in the lane. But if there's one irreducibly nonquantitative lesson taught by stats, it's that clichés about "heart" and "toughness" are sometimes borne out quite nicely by two players who have the same height, weight, release speed, off-hand strength, and contact readiness but who nevertheless differ dramatically in actual value to their team.

The NBA acknowledged as much when it decided that seeing prospects play a little college ball would help in their evaluations of these players. The striking thing about this realization, of course, is that it had to be formalized and implemented as a decree from the league. After all, if there's not enough information to go on when a player is coming out of high school, one would think the remedy here would be simply that teams would not draft that player. Instead, the NBA said, in effect, that general managers just can't be expected to act responsibly when presented with these tall and athletic 18-year-olds.

That's too bad, because on a number of levels, the best system for both college basketball and the NBA would be to allow players to enter the draft directly from high school *and* for the pro teams to be properly wary of these prospects. As my colleague Kevin Pelton has pointed out in his previous writing, there was once such a time: In the late 1990s, NBA teams largely stayed away from high school prospects. But when noncollegiate players like Kevin Garnett, Kobe Bryant, and Tracy McGrady started to show their undeniable worth, the teams that had passed on them kicked themselves and said, in effect, never again. Thus the high-school-heavy drafts of the early 2000s. In this sense, one-and-done was a correction to a correction.

So if the NBA decided to go back to the old system, I'd be fine with it. But if the league does the opposite and increases the number of post-high-school years required of prospects, I might be less sanguine about the change. Most notably, a system that required players to live their lives after high school for two full years before becoming eligible for the draft would force Michael Beasley to play college basketball this coming season, when clearly he doesn't belong there anymore. He belongs in the NBA. We didn't know that with certainty one year ago, but we do now. One-and-done was the correct timeline in his case, at least.

Besides, if we want to say it's wrong to deny high school seniors the "right" to enter the NBA draft (Oscar Robertson has memorably termed the current system "illegal," though truth be known, I am yet to find mention of high school seniors *or* the NBA draft in the Bill of Rights), how can we say it's fine to deny that right to college freshmen? And obviously, by these lights, requiring *three* years would be really odd. Imagine if we'd forced LeBron James and Amare Stoudemire to play three entire seasons of college (or European) ball. Why do that?

Mark me down, then, as a die-easy fan of one-and-done. It's probably doomed, it will probably be changed to something else, but I kind of like it. For one thing, it balances the league's wish for better information with the superstar's right not to be denied eligibility for a multiyear eternity when it's clear he can indeed play this game.

When one-and-done is done, there will be no utopia, just new laments. Whether the new required number of post-high-school years is two, three, or zero, there will still be athlete-athletes, there will still be bad draft choices, there will still be players entering the draft who should not do so, and there will still be agents slipping inducements to pre-professional players. One-and-done was born as a compromise, and goodness knows, compromises are hard to celebrate. No one wanted it, much less designed it, but it's what we have until at least 2011. Enjoy its peculiarities while they last.

Translating Success
Projecting College Players at the Next Level

KEVIN PELTON

EDITORS' NOTE: BasketballProspectus.com covers more than just the NCAA. Bradford Doolittle and Kevin Pelton cover the NBA online using many of the same statistical techniques employed by John Gasaway and Ken Pomeroy to analyze the college game. Here, Pelton takes a look at some of the top NBA prospects currently playing college ball.

We interrupt your regularly scheduled NCAA analysis for a brief digression about the NBA. That's right, the NBA. You know, the league that takes your favorite college stars and teaches them how to pound the dribble into the floor until forcing up a contested jumper to beat the shot clock, to never play any defense, and to complain about multimillion-dollar contracts.

In all seriousness, I hope Basketball Prospectus's in-depth analysis can help dispel some of the stereotypes that plague the NBA. Personally, I enjoy both the pro and the college games. While the NBA is my specialty, I appreciate the tradition and teamwork college basketball has to offer. There's an additional benefit to watching college games besides simply enjoying the action. I'm also looking to see how players will translate to the next level in preparation for upcoming NBA drafts.

Thanks to Chad Ford's prominent presence at ESPN.com and the emergence of draft sites, most notably DraftExpress.com and NBADraft.net, the draft is now a 365-day process for fans. As soon as the 2008 draft had concluded, those sites had already posted their mock drafts looking ahead to 2009. By combining the mock drafts from the two sites as well as Ford's 2009 Top 100, we can get a good idea of the consensus top prospects for next June.

This being the College Basketball Prospectus, naturally there's a statistical angle as well. Before the 2008 draft, I introduced the "Pelton Translations" on BasketballProspectus.com. Building on the theory of baseball's Davenport Translations, the Pelton Translations seek to convert a player's NCAA performance to an NBA equivalent, according to how players have made the transition to the professional game in the past.

My database includes nearly 200 players from the 2000-2007 drafts. Weighting by NBA minutes played, I've calculated the ratio of their NBA rookie performance to their last collegiate season in 14 statistical categories. It's important to look at each category individually, because the transition varies among different skills. For example, players tend to see their blocked-shot rate decline by more than half between the NCAA and the NBA, while they lose only about 10 percent of their rebound rate.

The other key factor, naturally, is strength of schedule (SOS). Using Ken Pomeroy's SOS numbers, I've also estimated the effect a player's level of competition has had on his transition to the NBA. This is crucial in leveling the playing field when comparing players from mid-major conferences to those playing top-tier schedules.

The last step is plugging the translated statistics into my Wins Above Replacement Player rating system, which estimates the winning percentage of a team made up of four average NBA players and the player in question.

Others, notably ESPN Insider's John Hollinger, have added other factors, including age, height, and weight, to a player's college statistics to come up with a single number estimating his NBA potential. I'd prefer to consider these factors subjectively alongside the numbers themselves. That has the side benefit of allowing these ratings to serve, to some extent, as schedule-adjusted NCAA player rankings. There's some shuffling because of the way different statistics translate, but for the most part, the highest-rated players are inevitably the most valuable college players.

Using the Pelton Translations, let's take a look at a few different groups. We start with the consensus top 10 returning NCAA prospects for the 2009 NBA Draft as picked out by their average placement between Ford's Top 100 and the NBADraft and Draft-Express mock drafts as of early July. Then we'll look at players whose translated statistics are better than their draft projections and vice versa, as well as a group that is barely on the radar of scouts but that has impressive translated numbers. Last, we'll look at the five freshmen likely to be this year's crop of one-and-done players. Because NBA potential is different from NCAA performance, the order is slightly different from John Perrotto's rankings of the top impact freshmen.

THE CONSENSUS TOP 10 RETURNING PLAYERS

1. Blake Griffin, Oklahoma
Sophomore
Avg. Position: 1.3
Translated Winning Percentage: .513

Year two of the NBA's age-limit era saw a record seven freshmen selected among the 14 lottery picks. Griffin surely would have joined that group had he opted to declare for the draft. After deciding to return for a second season at Oklahoma, Griffin is unanimously the top returning NCAA prospect and the odds-on favorite to be the top pick. The numbers agree: Griffin rates as the fourth-best prospect in terms of translated winning percentage. The only concern in Griffin's stat line is his 58.9 percent free-throw shooting, which hampers his True Shooting

Percentage (translated to 50.1 percent at the NBA level, compared with the league-average 54.0 percent).

2. Hasheem Thabeet, Connecticut
Junior
Avg. Position: 6.0
Translated Winning Percentage: .446

When he arrived on campus, Storrs figured to be little more than a way station for Thabeet on the way to the NBA. Instead, he's back for a third season, looking to translate his enormous shot-blocking potential into a complete game. Actually, on the strength of his 60.3 percent shooting from the field, Thabeet translates into a decent offensive player at the NBA level. On the other hand, his translated Defensive Rating is good but not great, largely because Thabeet projects to rebound just 13.2 percent of available defensive boards, very poor for any center, let alone one who is 7-3.

3. Austin Daye, Gonzaga
Sophomore
Avg. Position: 7.5
Translated Winning Percentage: .380

Daye's stock wobbled a bit in July, when he suffered a "minor low-grade tear" of his ACL at the LeBron James Skills Academy. The market correction might not be a bad thing. The strength of schedule adjustment takes a chunk out of Daye's freshman performance. In particular, he must improve his two-point percentage, which translates to a dismal 39.3 percent. Daye shows more potential at the defensive end, blocking a translated 2.4 shots per 40 minutes from the small-forward position. In the long run, Daye should be fine; just don't count on immediate NBA production.

4. James Harden, Arizona State
Sophomore
Avg. Position: 8.0
Translated Winning Percentage: .525

It was easy for Harden to get overshadowed in a Pac-10 that boasted five 2008 lottery picks and seven first-round picks. By returning for his sophomore season, Harden has guaranteed himself a brighter spotlight. In terms of translated winning percentage, he narrowly tops Tyler Hansbrough as the top returning prospect. Harden's game figures to translate easily to the NBA. He's a savvy scorer with three-point range and does a terrific job of playing the passing lanes.

5. Earl Clark, Louisville
Junior
Avg. Position: 8.7
Translated Winning Percentage: .423

A lanky athletic power forward in the mold of a Hakim Warrick or a Tyrus Thomas, Clark has budding perimeter skills, but should end up playing in the paint if he can add some bulk. Clark's numbers show he's ready to help a team on the glass (translated 14.3 percent rebound percentage) and as a shot blocker (translated 1.6 blocks per 40 minutes). He needs to show more consistency on offense, as he did in the NCAA tournament, averaging 14.5 points on 62.1 percent shooting as Louisville advanced to the Elite Eight.

6. Chase Budinger, Arizona
Junior
Avg. Position: 13.3
Translated Winning Percentage: .381

For a sophomore lottery prospect, Budinger's translated winning percentage is too low. From a statistical perspective, he doesn't have an NBA strength. The translations drag down his efficiency on offense, and scouts and the stats agree that Budinger is a liability on defense. Budinger's athleticism is obvious when we watch him play, but it doesn't really show up statistically. The hopeful perspective is that Budinger's progress was stopped by Arizona's chaotic season and that he'll rebound in 2008-2009.

7. Nick Calathes, Florida
Sophomore
Avg. Position: 15.0
Translated Winning Percentage: .428

Calathes is an interesting prospect—a big (6-5) pass-first point guard who can shoot the ball. There isn't really anyone like that in the NBA. Ford used Shaun Livingston as a comparison, but Livingston can't shoot. NBADraft went with Kirk Hinrich, who is a much better defender. Calathes translates to a strong passer (7.0 assists per 40 minutes) and an asset on the glass. The only thing holding him back is his 46.2 percent two-point shooting, which is much too low.

8. Ty Lawson, North Carolina
Junior
Avg. Position: 15.0
Translated Winning Percentage: .477

The top returning point guard in the country, Lawson looks like an underrated prospect, despite being considered a likely late-lottery or mid-first-round pick next June. It's difficult for point guards to put up strong translated numbers, because these players often struggle as NBA rookies. Lawson's numbers compare very favorably with the point guards taken in the lottery in June (Russell Westbrook, D. J. Augustin, and Jerryd Bayless). Though Lawson's height (5-11) is a legitimate issue, it is mitigated in the modern NBA, which favors quickness over size.

9. Gerald Henderson, Duke
Junior
Avg. Position: 15.5
Translated Winning Percentage: .364

Henderson inspires major disagreement. DraftExpress and NBADraft have him 13th and 18th, respectively, while Ford has him rated as the 64th-best prospect for next year's draft. The numbers tend to agree with Ford. Henderson just hasn't been efficient enough as a scorer. He has to develop his outside shooting, having made 31.7 percent of his threes last season, and he hurt his efficiency by hitting just 66.9 percent of his free throws.

10. Patrick Patterson, Kentucky
Sophomore
Avg. Position: 18.0
Translated Winning Percentage: .419

During his freshman season, Patterson was an offensive force at Kentucky, averaging 16.4 points on 57.4 percent shooting. That figures to translate to the pros; though Patterson is on the small side for an NBA power forward, his length and athleticism make up for it. The big concern for Patterson statistically is his poor defensive rebounding. His translated 11.7 percent rebound percentage is very low for a big man. Still, assuming the left-ankle stress fracture that ended Patterson's freshman season doesn't linger, he should be a mid-first-round pick.

THE STATS LIKE ...

DeJuan Blair, Pittsburgh
Sophomore
Avg. Position: 34.0
Translated Winning Percentage: .524

Blair is unlikely to enter next year's draft, so only Ford has him listed (as an early second-round pick; he's 44th in NBADraft.net's 2010 mock). Scouts question Blair's 6-7 height and think he could stand to shed more weight, having already slimmed down before starting at Pitt. Blair's terrific rebounding (his translated 18.1 rebound percentage is second among legit NCAA regulars, behind Washington's Jon Brockman) and his 2.4 steals per 40 minutes show great quickness for a big man. Look for Blair to be a second-round steal in the grand tradition of Paul Millsap, Carl Landry, and others.

Danny Green, North Carolina
Senior
Avg. Position: 47.5
Translated Winning Percentage: .458

As hard as it is to imagine a player at North Carolina being underexposed, Green might manage it because the team's depth limited him to 22.3 minutes per game last season. That and what is seen as limited upside make Green a likely second-round pick. The stats show him as a strong defender who can hit enough threes to keep a defense honest. It's easy to see him developing into a key role player on a contender.

Tyler Hansbrough, North Carolina
Senior
Avg. Position: 20.0
Translated Winning Percentage: .525

Hansbrough represents a case where the stats and scouts disagree, and frankly, I'm with the scouts. Hansbrough's NCAA résumé speaks for itself. Will it translate? What makes me dubious is that in the past, successful undersized big guys have tended to be either better athletes than Hansbrough or truer wide-bodies (Blair qualifies on both counts). Hansbrough could be vulnerable to shot blockers, and even his untranslated 54.0 percent two-point shooting is good, not great. All things considered, I think the late first round is about right for Hansbrough.

Jerome Jordan, Tulsa
Junior
Avg. Position: 13.0
Translated Winning Percentage: .438

Jordan's average position is misleading; Ford is the only one who lists him, while NBADraft has him as the 38th pick in 2010. As a second-round pick, Jordan would be a steal. His numbers compare very favorably with the defensive-minded big men taken in the first round in 2008 (Robin Lopez and JaVale McGee). Jordan's translated 3.4 blocks per 40 minutes are second among returning prospects. He's got all the physical tools, so expect his stock to rise.

Tyler Smith, Tennessee
Junior
Avg. Position: 18.3
Translated Winning Percentage: .483

Smith isn't exactly off the radar, rating just outside the consensus top 10. But with his numbers, he ought to vault over Budinger and Daye as the best collegiate small forward available. The numbers show Smith to be a highly versatile contributor: an above-average rebounder for his position at the NBA level and a terrific ball handler (his untranslated 1.54 assist-to-turnover ratio would be the envy of many point guards). The lone notable downside is that Smith is a year old for his class.

THE SCOUTS LIKE ...

James Anderson, Oklahoma State
Sophomore
Avg. Position: 8.0
Translated Winning Percentage: .326

Anderson is an odd case. NBADraft has him as a top-10 pick, Ford has him 68th, and DraftExpress does not have him coming out. The lottery would be a major reach. The scouts expect Anderson to develop into an NBA-caliber scorer, which is not unreasonable. He'll need to do so, because based on the numbers, he is highly one-dimensional. His upside is J. R. Smith.

Eric Maynor, Virginia Commonwealth
Senior
Avg. Position: 26.5
Translated Winning Percentage: .419

The scouts fell in love with Maynor during VCU's 2007 NCAA tournament run. The stats aren't entirely sold, as the adjustment for SOS (Virginia Commonwealth is rated 196th in the nation) knocks Maynor down to fringe territory. Is the adjustment too harsh? It didn't stop Jordan (SOS ranked 122nd) or Davidson's Stephen Curry (114th) from rating as first-round-caliber players.

DaJuan Summers, Georgetown
Junior
Avg. Position: 30.5
Translated Winning Percentage: .342

An NBA-caliber athlete, Summers has yet to turn that into big-time collegiate performance, especially in terms of efficient scoring. More than half of his shot attempts last season were threes, but Summers shot just 34.2 percent from downtown. At this point, the rest of Summers's game is not good enough to make up for the low shooting percentage.

THE SCOUTS AREN'T PAYING ATTENTION BUT SHOULD
(aka the Pomeroy/Gasaway Faves)

Luke Harangody, Notre Dame
Junior
Avg. Position: NR
Translated Winning Percentage: .452

The poor man's Hansbrough, Harangody developed into a 20-10 player as a sophomore. The major statistical difference between the two men is their two-point percentage; Harangody's subpar 50.0 percent mark hurts his translation. He figures to be a four-year player and should improve his draft stock over that time, though he's unlikely to ever get any higher than the second round.

Robbie Hummel, Purdue
Sophomore
Avg. Position: NR
Translated Winning Percentage: .486

As a freshman, Hummel was one of the most efficient offensive players in the NCAA last season. His translated Offensive Rating trails only Hansbrough. Hummel is unlikely to ever be a favorite of scouts; he is not an athlete, won't put up big scoring numbers, and is a weak defender. That aside, the rest of his game is highly versatile. He handles the ball well and is an above-average rebounder for a small forward.

Jarvis Varnado, Mississippi State
Junior
Avg. Position: NR
Translated Winning Percentage: .458

When it comes to blocking shots, Varnado stands alone. At a translated 3.9 blocks per 40 minutes, he's tops among returning prospects; only two players in my database (Joel Anthony and Justin Williams) had a better translated block rate. What's really impressive is that Varnado's blocks anchored an elite defense; Mississippi State allowed the lowest two-point percentage in the nation. Varnado is somewhat undersized and could definitely stand to improve his rebounding, but he's an interesting prospect, nonetheless.

TOP FRESHMEN

1. Demar DeRozan, USC
Avg. Position: 2.7

The NBA scouts love, love, love DeRozan's athleticism, making comparisons to Kobe Bryant and Vince Carter. Like Carter, DeRozan's pro potential is likely to exceed his production as a college player. The knock is that his focus and basketball IQ have a tendency to come and go, the hope being that this will fade with experience and maturity.

2. B. J. Mullens, Ohio State
Avg. Position: 3.0

The Buckeyes have made a tradition of one-and-done centers, with Kosta Koufos following Greg Oden into the NBA. Mullens could easily make it three straight years with an Ohio State center drafted in the first round. If he is a consistent force in college, Mullens will be a lottery pick and could potentially even join Oden as the number one overall pick.

3. Jrue Holiday, UCLA
Avg. Position: 8.0

Holiday could be compared to a more talented version of the player he will replace at UCLA, Westbrook. Considering Westbrook was the fourth pick of last June's draft, that's an impressive description.

Scouts love Holiday's ability at the defensive end and his well-rounded game. The biggest question is whether he can develop into a point guard—a question he may not be able to answer playing alongside Darren Collison.

4. Al-Farouq Aminu, Wake Forest
Avg. Position: 10.5
The kind of athlete who scouts have a tendency to fall in love with, Aminu has an athleticism that might take a little longer to be converted into production. As he did not turn 18 until September 2008, he is very young for a college player and something of a prospect at the NBA level.

5. Tyreke Evans, Memphis
Avg. Position: 16.3
Along with DeRozan and Mullens, Evans is the only freshman who NBADraft, Draft Express, and Ford all agree will go one-and-done. Where they disagree is in his potential. DraftExpress has him a top-10 pick, and NBADraft has him going late in the first round, with Ford splitting the difference. Not unlike O. J. Mayo a year ago, Evans will have to demonstrate that he can integrate his ability into a team setting to win over the scouts.

Ten Freshmen to Watch

JOHN PERROTTO

Last season's freshman crop in college basketball was one for the ages. The first three picks in the NBA draft were freshmen: Memphis's Derrick Rose, Kansas State's Michael Beasley, and Southern California's O. J. Mayo.

UCLA's Kevin Love and Indiana's Eric Gordon were two more freshmen who went in the top seven picks, while Arizona's Jerryd Bayless and Louisiana State's Anthony Randolph were selected in the first 15. North Carolina State's J. J. Hickson, Ohio State's Kosta Koufos, and Syracuse's Donte Greene were also first-rounders.

It is safe to say this season's freshman class won't have quite as many first-round picks. There is, however, a twist to this class: Point guard Brandon Jennings, who would have been number one on this list, decided to bypass college basketball entirely and instead play professionally in Europe for, he hopes and others expect, one year only. It will be most interesting to see if Jennings's unconventional move motivates other high school players to go overseas for a year before returning home to try the NBA.

Jennings, who lives in Los Angeles and played the last two seasons at Oak Hill Academy in Mouth of Wilson, Virginia, had signed with Arizona and was expected to replace Jerryd Bayless, who left for the NBA after one season, in the Wildcat's lineup.

Sans Jennings, here is a look at the top 10 freshmen for this season:

1. Samardo Samuels, Louisville
Position: Power forward
Ht./Wt.: 6-8, 240
Hometown: Newark, N.J.
School: St. Benedict Prep
PPG: 24.2

Also considered: Connecticut, Florida, North Carolina, Pittsburgh

Scouting report: Samuels has an outstanding inside presence and plays bigger than his size. He is an excellent finisher who is strong taking the ball to the hoop. He has the desire to dominate every game and he never takes a possession off on either offense or defense. A strong rebounder, Samuels is likely to average a double-double in college. Though he might give away a few inches to some other big men in college, his heart and intensity will make up for it.

How he fits the Cardinals: He will be the starting center after the graduation of David Padgett.

2. B. J. Mullens, Ohio State
Position: Center
Ht./Wt.: 7-0, 255
Hometown: Canal Winchester, Ohio
School: Canal Winchester High
PPG: 26.0

Also considered: Committed to Ohio State as a high school freshman in 2004

Scouting report: Mullen has outstanding size to play the pivot and the frame to put on a little more muscle without getting heavy. This versatile offensive player can step outside and hit the midrange jump shot while also using his size to score in the post. He struggled against bigger players in high school and needs to learn some countermoves. He also is an indifferent rebounder and defender at times.

How he fits the Buckeyes: He should move right into the starting lineup after center Kosta Koufos decided to jump to the NBA at the end of his freshman season.

3. Jrue Holiday, UCLA
Position: Shooting guard
Ht./Wt.: 6-3, 180
Hometown: North Hollywood, Calif.
School: Campbell Hall High

19

PPG: 24.2

Also considered: Washington

Scouting report: Holiday has an advanced feel for the game, which should make the mental transition to the college game smooth. He wins high marks for his character, work ethic, and desire to win and doesn't possess the attitude of many top high school players. He scores off a variety of slashing moves and is a good passer and defender. His jump shot needs more range, and he would add to his versatility if he learned to play the point.

How he fits the Bruins: Shooting guard Josh Shipp withdrew from the NBA draft to come back for his senior season, but there still figures to be playing time for Holiday after guard Russell Westbrook decided to leave for the pros with two years of eligibility remaining.

4. Tyreke Evans, Memphis
Position: Shooting guard
Ht./Wt.: 6-6, 190
Hometown: Aston, Pa.
School: American Christian School
PPG: 34.1

Also considered: Connecticut, Texas, Villanova

Scouting report: Evans is a big-time scorer who is a threat from all over the floor. He has outstanding range on his three-point shot, but can also create his own scoring opportunities from the wing with his slashing drives to the basket. He struggled to score off the dribble, though, and will have an adjustment period in trying to break down college guards. He is also prone to turnovers, doesn't like to mix it up on the glass, and is an indifferent defender.

How he fits the Tigers: Chris Douglas-Roberts's decision to forgo his senior season to enter the NBA draft leaves a need for backcourt scoring, a role that Evans will fill.

5. Demar DeRozan, Southern California
Position: Small forward
Ht./Wt.: 6-6, 180
Hometown: Compton, Calif.
School: Compton High
PPG: 30.6

Also considered: Arizona State, California, Florida State, UCLA, Washington

Scouting report: DeRozan is an outstanding athlete with plenty of raw ability. An explosive leaper, he plays with a great deal of flair, not to mention a penchant for spectacular dunks. He also has as much upside as does any player on this list; more than one talent evaluator believes he could have the best NBA career of anybody in his recruiting class. DeRozan has room to improve as a scorer, though, as he still struggles to get shots off the dribble and needs to improve the consistency of his jumper.

How he fits the Trojans: He will step right into the lineup after Davon Jefferson made the dubious decision of hiring an agent and entering the NBA draft after his freshman year. (Jefferson wound up not being selected.)

6. Scotty Hopson, Tennessee
Position: Small forward
Ht./Wt.: 6-5, 180
Hometown: Hopkinsville, Ky.
School: University Heights Academy
PPG: 24.2

Also considered: Cincinnati, Kentucky, Louisville, Mississippi State, Texas

Scouting report: Hopson is a very smart player who understands his opponents' strengths and weaknesses and how to break them down. He also loves to mix it up inside and is willing to hit the boards. With skills still somewhat raw, he figures to improve with his basketball savvy and desire. Hopson is prone to turnovers and needs to gain some consistency with his outside shot. His intensity tends to wane at times during games.

How he fits the Volunteers: Hopson is a little more raw than others on this list. He can be worked into the rotation slowly after small forward Tyler Smith decided to withdraw from the draft and return for his junior season.

7. Greg Monroe, Georgetown
Position: Power forward
Ht./Wt.: 6-10, 220
Hometown: Gretna, La.
School: Helen Cox High
PPG: 21.7

Also considered: Connecticut, Duke, Louisiana State, Texas

Scouting report: Monroe was considered the consensus top player in the nation before having a disappointing senior season, but still has great upside with an outstanding body that includes broad shoulders and long arms. Rebounding is his strong suit at this point, and he is particularly adept at taking the ball off the glass and making the outlet pass. He struggles to score in the low post at times and needs to develop some moves, but he has the athletic ability to do so.

How he fits the Hoyas: Monroe will get a chance to play right away, following the graduation of power forward Patrick Ewing Jr.

8. Jamychal Green, Alabama
Position: Power forward
Ht./Wt.: 6-7, 205
Hometown: Montgomery, Ala.
School: Saint Jude High
PPG: 29.4

Also considered: Auburn, Florida, Georgia Tech, Kentucky, Marquette, Mississippi, Virginia

Scouting report: The best defender on this list, Green loves to get after it on that end of the floor and uses his length to compensate for a lack of bulk. He has outstanding athleticism, highlighted by a springy set of legs that helps him finish off plays. He will need to get stronger in order to compete at the highest level of college basketball, however. Green also struggles to score away from the basket.

How he fits the Crimson Tide: There is a spot open inside after power forward Richard Hendrix left school a year early to go to the NBA, and Green will get the opportunity to fill it.

9. Tyler Zeller, North Carolina
Position: Power forward
Ht./Wt.: 6-11, 220
Hometown: Washington, Ind.
School: Washington High
PPG: 32.1

Also considered: Indiana, Notre Dame, Purdue

Scouting report: Zeller is a big man who moves like a guard; he can run the floor like someone 10 inches shorter. He is a much better offensive player facing the basket and is particularly adept at scoring on tip-ins. A highly intelligent player, he should quickly adapt to the mental aspect of the next level. Zeller is also rail thin, though, and could get pushed around by more physical big men. To combat this, he will need to add some inside moves to his game.

How he fits the Tar Heels: With consensus Player of the Year Tyler Hansbrough and Danny Green returning as the starters down low, Zeller can be worked into the rotation slowly.

10. Al-Farouq Aminu, Wake Forest
Position: Small forward
Ht./Wt.: 6-8, 195
Hometown: Norcross, Ga.
School: Norcross High
PPG: 22.1

Also considered: Georgia Tech

Scouting report: Aminu has the height of a power forward and the quickness of a point guard, which enables him to be creative on offense. The brother of Georgia Tech's Alade Aminu likes to stay on the perimeter and drive to the basket with a variety of moves. He has a decent midrange jump shot, but needs to add some more range. He has trouble scoring in the low post because of his lack of bulk and also tends to force passes.

How he fits the Demon Deacons: He should slot in the lineup next to promising sophomore power forward James Johnson to provide an athletic frontcourt duo.

Testing Hoops Axioms Using Play-by-Play Data

KEN POMEROY

When I watch games, I'm constantly questioning what I see and even more so what I hear. When an analyst makes a bold statement about the game or repeats a cliché, my natural inclination is to wonder whether the statement holds up against objective data. My interest in tempo-free statistics was the result of this skepticism. The most famous of these measures—offensive and defensive efficiency and tempo—have come in handy for determining the quality of a team's offense or defense or its pace of play. These measures showed us that Georgetown had a great offense in 2007, that North Carolina had a great defense in 2005, and that Illinois was a significantly slower-than-average team in 2005. All three conclusions tended to oppose popular thinking.

While the tempo-free processing of box-score stats tells us a lot about how the game is played, it's not good enough to test all the assertions you'll hear at one time or another this season. Fortunately, though, other data sets are becoming available and can help uncover additional nuggets about the game we become obsessed with during the winter.

Most prominently, play-by-play data recorded for nearly every Division I college game can be a tool to unravel many more mysteries about the game. For those who don't know, play-by-play data contains the details of every statistical action during a game. If Joe Hoopster grabs an offensive rebound at 14:05 of the first half, it's in the play-by-play. Not every athletic department makes this data easily available to the public, but many do, and I've been able to acquire over 5,000 games' worth of play-by-play information covering contests since the 2005 season.

Armed with this information, we can test a few of those statements that have always made me wonder. Let's start with this one …

First aphorism to be tested: *Three-pointers are more difficult than two-pointers for the defense to rebound.*

There is no doubt that long-distance shots tend to produce rebounds that are longer and more unpredictable. But are they truly more difficult for the defense to rebound than two-point attempts? We don't need to speculate anymore, because within the play-by-play data, there are over 300,000 reboundable shots to provide us with the answer. And the data says that this axiom, in general, isn't true.

Offensive rebounding percentage by shot type

Shot type	OR%
3-ptr	32.0
2-ptr	37.0
FT	17.8

The offense grabs about 32 percent of three-point misses compared with 37 percent on errant two-pointers. But in fairness to conventional wisdom, this doesn't tell the whole story. Every time Michael Beasley or Joey Dorsey was playing volleyball at the backboard, he was increasing the offensive rebounding percentage on two-point shots. Whether some big men are able to rebound their own misses on shots around the rim doesn't really speak to the ability of the defense to box out on two-point shots.

Because scorekeepers mark shots as either *jumpers* or *layups*, we can make an honest attempt to remove this effect. When looking solely at shot attempts recorded as two-point jumpers, 34.3 percent of misses were rebounded by the offense, which is still slightly higher than the rate on three-point misses.

One could give additional benefit of the doubt to the original statement by assuming that three-point shots tend to be taken more often by smaller, less athletic teams that might be poor rebounders, anyway. Still, it seems like a stretch to conclude that three-pointers are easier for the offense to rebound. Of course, because the percentages are somewhat close, there might be a few defenses that do rebound two-pointers better than three-pointers, and there surely are individual games where that happens. But that's almost entirely due to randomness. The general rule is that three-pointers are easier for the defense to rebound.

While we're on the subject of rebounding, here's an unrelated tidbit that I thought was worth checking: Blocked shots are rebounded by the offense an amazing 43.8 percent of the time. Yes, shot blocking is usually a defensive trait to be admired, and for good reason. There's an intimidation factor in play, even when an imposing big man isn't recording a block. But there's also an unspoken cost to the team's rebounding ability. This occurs both when a block is recorded and when a defender is unsuccessful on a block attempt, leaving at least one member of the defense out of position for a defensive rebound. Moving on …

Another idea that play-by-play might challenge: *It's a good idea to call a time out to try and ice a free-throw shooter.*

I'll attribute this one more to coaches than analysts. More frequently, it seems to me, a coach will use his time-out before an opposing player shoots a free throw rather than waiting until after the second attempt, when it may be advantageous to call a time-out to set up the offense, especially if that attempt is missed. Regardless, if a coach is calling a time-out expecting to significantly increase the shooter's chance of missing, it appears that he should think again.

Free throw percentage in final minute of regulation or overtime

Overall	72.2%
After a time out	71.0%

Again, keep in mind we're dealing with tons of data here. There were about 20,000 free throws overall, with 734 occurring immediately after a time-out. Given that both samples are limited to the final minute of play, I'd have to think that the average quality of the shooters in both cases is about the same.

Only one or two out of every 100 late-game time-outs has an impact. If you have a few time-outs to burn, then, of course, even the extremely slim chance of a payoff is worth it. But if there's a few seconds left and an opposing player is shooting two, save your last time-out until after the second shot, for other strategic purposes. It's your best hope.

Final common notion to study: *Shoot two-pointers first in a two-possession game.*

Specifically, there's the notion that a team trailing by four or five points shouldn't be shooting three-pointers initially, because the math doesn't add up. In both cases, whether a team scores two or three points on the first possession, the deficit is still no more than three, and thus a one-possession game. Because two-pointers are less difficult than three pointers, it would seem sensible to take the easiest route to a one-possession game.

Sensible, but incorrect. To test this theory, I looked at every game in which a team trailed by four points with 15 to 45 seconds left in the game. Then I looked at what type of shot the trailing team took first in that situation. A team trailing by four took a two-point shot as its first field-goal attempt 143 times. It would go on to win seven of those games (4.9 percent). Its first field-goal attempt was a three-pointer 120 times and resulted in a successful comeback 13 times (10.8 percent). Similar results follow in five-point deficits in which teams attempting a two-pointer first went 5-138 (3.5 percent) and teams taking a three first went 7-176 (3.8 percent). (However, five-point comebacks are so rare that the small difference between strategies isn't significant.) For clarification, I'm not looking solely at attempts that were made. I'm looking at all attempts, both makes and misses. Thus, the risk of each strategy is included in this analysis.

So it does appear that the more common strategy of trying to overcome a four-point difference using two-pointers isn't the way to go. This is probably because the trailing team doesn't play in a vacuum. It's true that 2 + 2 = 4, but this assumes that the opposing team isn't going to score, which is unlikely in late-game situations. Ergo, assuming the appropriate personnel is available and the defense permits a halfway decent look, the three-point strategy seems to be superior.

As stat tracking and data collection continue to get more sophisticated in college basketball, more of the game's tenets can be examined using objective data. As has been shown here, we can't always assume that the long-standing wisdom is true.

The Incredible Vanishing Turnover

JOHN GASAWAY

You would never know that college basketball passed an important milestone last year. After all, there was no ceremony to mark the occasion at the Final Four in San Antonio. No photos, no hand-shakes, no trophy—nothing. Nobody heard about it. In fact, I didn't even know about it myself until after the season had ended. That's when I had time to go back and look over some things that I track during the year.

It turns out that last year, in major-conference games, teams committed a turnover on less than one in five possessions.

Major-conference turnovers, 2006-2008
Conference games only: ACC, Big East, Big Ten, Big 12, Pac-10, and SEC
Turnover percentage

	2006	2007	2008
TO pct.	20.7	20.1	19.6

I realize a drop of roughly 1 percent in anything may not seem like a big deal. It certainly doesn't make for a splashy tabloid headline. ("X Drops 1 Percent in Three Seasons! Nation Abuzz!") But bear with me.

When we're talking about the cumulative results compiled by six conferences over the course of more than 1,800 games and something like 242,000 possessions spread across three seasons, a 1 percent drop does indeed mark a clear trend. That decline needs to be seen in the context of its surroundings.

In conference games last year, 69 of 73 major-conference teams posted turnover rates of between 16 and 24 percent. Against the backdrop of an 8 per-cent universe, a 1 percent decrease is actually a sig-nificant shift. Teams are simply taking better care of the ball.

To an extent, this trend appears to be correlated to the number of three-pointers that teams attempt.

Major-conference three-point attempts, 2006-2008
Conference games only: ACC, Big East, Big Ten, Big 12, Pac-10, and SEC
Three-point attempts as percentage of field-goal attempts

	2006	2007	2008
3PA/FGA (%)	32.9	33.6	34.0

As a general rule, teams that shoot more threes tend to hold on to the ball better. Such teams commit fewer charging fouls and are called for traveling less often. Moreover, the ball isn't as likely to be stripped from them out on the perimeter as it would be down in the paint.

My colleague Ken Pomeroy has already pointed out that moving the three-point line out a foot is likely to result in a small but still noticeable dip in the number of threes attempted this year. If the in-verse turnover-threes relationship holds steady, then we would expect that this year the downward trend in turnovers might flatten out temporarily.

Be that as it may, I wonder if we might be seeing a dawning realization that turnovers really are costly—more costly than we've been accustomed to believing. This realization could play out not so much for teams that commit fewer turnovers by shooting more threes, but rather for the exceptions to this rule. And as always, there are definitely exceptions to the rule.

Last year, for example, Iowa meddled with the primal forces of hoops nature big time, shooting a ton of threes *and* coughing up the ball an astounding 25 percent of the time in Big Ten play. Pity first-year coach Todd Lickliter, an uncommonly amiable and good-natured sort who nevertheless must have been tearing his hair out, if only metaphorically.

Recall that Lickliter was hired by the Hawkeyes on the strength of his famously efficient 2007 Butler team. That year, the Bulldogs also shot a lot of threes, but in this case, "a lot of threes" meant "no, really, *a lot*," because they committed turnovers on less than 16 percent of their trips. It's safe to say, then, that Lickliter isn't having any "dawning realization" where turnovers are concerned. He knows their true cost better than anyone. Now if he can just get his players in Iowa City to register that same understanding. (Prediction: He will, and soon.)

The exceptions, however, that I want to highlight here are at the opposite end of the spectrum from the Hawkeyes. These are teams that shoot very few threes yet also commit very few turnovers.

Exhibit A in this respect is—well, what do you know—your 2008 national champion, Kansas. In the Bill Self era, KU has shown significant year-to-year improvement in taking care of the ball. That's great news for Jayhawk fans, of course, but what makes Kansas particularly interesting for our purposes is that very little of that improvement would appear to have come from shooting more threes. Year in and year out, the Jayhawks just don't take many shots from beyond the arc.

Kansas: three-point attempts and turnovers, 2006-2008

Conference games only
Three-point attempts as percentage of field-goal
    attempts
Turnover percentage

	2006	2007	2008
3PA/FGA (%)	27.6	24.8	26.6
TO pct.	22.5	19.8	18.8

Maybe Self was lecturing his team daily on the importance of taking care of the ball and, in 2007 and especially 2008, those homilies finally bore fruit. Then again, maybe players like Brandon Rush and Mario Chalmers simply matured. Both their turnover rates showed a decline similar to that of their team over the same period.

Another factor that clearly came into play here was Darrell Arthur. You may remember him only as the unfortunate figure who was waiting around on draft night as team after team passed on him, but Arthur's prior experience should have given NBA teams plenty of cause to end his waiting a lot sooner. Most notably, he was very trustworthy with the ball in his hands. Where his teammates had to grow into that ability, Arthur displayed it even as a freshman. Self hopes some of this year's freshmen in Lawrence can show that same knack from day one.

Enough about last year's national champion. Say hello to a team you might hear a little bit about this year.

North Carolina: three-point attempts and turnovers, 2006-2008

Conference games only
Three-point attempts as percentage of field-goal
    attempts
Turnover percentage

	2006	2007	2008
3PA/FGA (%)	32.2	24.9	21.4
TO pct.	23.6	18.8	19.4

Every year, the Tar Heels shoot fewer and fewer threes, and (almost) every year, they commit fewer and fewer turnovers, thus standing our more-threes-fewer-turnovers "tendency" neatly on its head. True, Carolina's turnovers appeared to inch up in 2008, but believe me, Roy Williams will take a 19 percent turnover rate, plus or minus a fraction. His team's improvement in the area of turnovers the past three seasons has been pretty straightforward. It's been because of Tyler Hansbrough.

I'm oversimplifying, of course. Ty Lawson has been reliable with the rock, much more so than one might assume if your only acquaintance with him is seeing how unspeakably fast he is with the ball. And as always in Chapel Hill, stars have cycled in for short stints on their way to the NBA and done their share. In particular, Brandan Wright was tremendously efficient on offense in 2007. Yes, Hansbrough has had help.

Still, Psycho-T is truly a force of nature on offense. Williams has fed him possessions in mass quantities for three full seasons now, and the All-American has more than justified that confidence. Hansbrough's turnover rate started out small as a freshman and has since plunged to levels that are near microscopic. He simply never turns the ball over, he often makes his shots, he very often gets fouled, and he always makes the free throws. It's hard to envision any of the above changing in 2009.

So far, we've had a happy story to tell: Offenses are doing a better job holding on to the ball. In certain really prominent blue-chip instances, this has been true even over and above any gains achieved merely by shooting more threes. Offenses, take a bow.

But, of course, there's a corollary. If offenses are committing fewer turnovers, that must also mean that defenses are forcing fewer. Does that mean defense is on the decline in major-conference hoops?

Not necessarily. Let's look at the most extreme examples: Define *never* as less than 17 percent of the time. Now, what are the characteristics of defenses that never force turnovers?

Fewest opponent turnovers, 2006-2008

Conference games only: ACC, Big East, Big Ten, Big 12, Pac-10, and SEC
Opp. TO pct.: opponent turnover percentage
Opp. PPP: opponent points per possession

	Opp. TO pct.	Opp. PPP
Notre Dame, 2006	13.9	1.12
Cal, 2008	14.8	1.15
Boston College, 2008	15.4	1.11
Stanford, 2007	15.5	1.02
Oregon, 2008	15.6	1.10
Connecticut, 2008	15.7	1.02
Notre Dame, 2008	15.8	1.04
Mississippi St., 2008	15.8	0.96
Connecticut, 2006	16.3	0.96
South Florida, 2008	16.4	1.09

I love this list because it's so schizophrenic: It includes everyone from perhaps the most talented college team of the decade (Connecticut, 2006) to a team that went 3-15 in the Big East (South Florida, 2008). Clearly, a team can play very good, even great, defense without forcing turnovers. By the same token, it's obvious that many times, a total lack of forced turnovers should be a cause for concern.

A team that never forces turnovers usually falls into one of two camps. Either your defense has first-round NBA talent in the paint, or your defense is just plain bad, maybe even terrible. There's surprisingly little space in between those two extremes.

Actually, there was next to no space between the extremes until UConn and Mississippi State showed up last year. In Hasheem Thabeet, the Huskies definitely have their future first-rounder, but as shown in the table above, their defense last year was not up to the standard set in 2006. The Bulldogs are pretty much the exact opposite: excellent defense without (we think) that first-rounder. Whatever the future may hold for Jarvis Varnado, he's shown he's presently a phenomenal shot blocker and, more importantly, shot changer on the college level.

What about the other extreme? What if you don't have that disruptive shot blocker and instead you go all out to create turnovers? We're used to hearing about how an "aggressive" or even an "attacking" defense can in certain instances force more turnovers. Tennessee is usually the example invoked here, although if Matt Painter, Mike Krzyzewski, Tom Crean, Tubby Smith, Oliver Purnell, or Bill Carmody had ever taken off their shirt to attend a women's game at their school, maybe the college hoops world would know that in 2008, their team forced in-conference turnovers at an even higher rate than Bruce Pearl's Volunteers did.

As a group, these high-turnover defenses aren't as bipolar as their low-turnover brethren. Nevertheless, there are differences. Certainly, Tennessee, Duke, Purdue, Clemson, and Marquette all parlayed a lot of takeaways into very good defense. And while Minnesota turned those same takeaways into a defense that was just average, the rebuilding Gophers get extra credit for emerging from two seasons of unrelieved gloom and suddenly showing the life needed to create all those opponent turnovers.

That leaves Northwestern. As so often is the case, the Wildcats manifestly constitute their own analytic category: of major-conference teams, one of the best at extracting turnovers from opponents, yet also one of the worst defenses in the same population of teams. When NU's opponents did *not* commit a turnover in Big Ten play, they *averaged* over 1.5 points per possession. Again, this was a struggling defense in any case. But had the Wildcats' defense not bucked the national trend and recorded a lot of takeaways, the team would have set records—bad ones—that might have lasted for years or even decades.

Granted, there's a chicken-and-egg question in play here. Are fewer defenses choosing to play the "attacking" style, or are offenses simply committing fewer turnovers? To that, I answer with a resounding yes! We've already looked at teams that clearly took a hard look at themselves in the mirror, decided to take ownership of their offense, and started living life clean and (relatively) turnover free. But when a conference doesn't have even one team that at least occasionally goes for turnovers on defense, then, surprise, there won't be many turnovers. Look no further than the Pac-10 last year, where just 18 percent of possessions in conference games ended with a giveaway.

Turnovers can never vanish completely, of course, not even in the Pac-10. There's a demon in the sky out there at about 87 or 88 percent of major-conference possessions that even Tony Bennett can't get past without giving away the ball now and then. But it's much easier for a coach to work toward cutting down on turnovers, even just a little, than it is to wave a magic wand and make his players better shooters.

Football has probably done basketball something of a disservice when it comes to thinking about turnovers. In football, a team's first and only turnover in the game can, depending on the circumstances, be disastrous. We know that this is simply not the case in basketball, which is probably why the coaches in this sport don't sound like obsessive-compulsive maniacs, prattling on and on in pregame interviews about "winning the turnover battle."

No, a single turnover in hoops isn't the end of the world, but turnovers, plural, can be. Where turnovers in football are digital—present or absent, nothing in between—in basketball they're analog. They're always present, the only question being in what number. The higher that number becomes, the lower your point total will be. Possessions are finite, especially in the Big Ten, and turnovers rob you of possessions. Incredibly, it would appear that teams are acting accordingly.

At Cross-Purposes

The NBA, the NCAA, and the At-Risk Athlete

WILL CARROLL

I'm not much of a gambler. NCAA athletes shouldn't be, either, with continual reminders that everything on the spectrum, from point shaving to Internet poker, is against the "spirit of the student-athlete." Yet every time athletes take the floor in a game, the NCAA is forcing them to gamble with something more valuable than money—their future. A broken ankle? Lower-back problems? These are common injuries in the NCAA, and they represent the difference between being a first-round pick and a guy who might catch on with Unicaja Malaga.

The fact is that injuries can occur anytime. Kansas State had two solid draft prospects this year in Michael Beasley and Bill Walker. Walker injured his knee the day before the deadline to pull out of the NBA draft, whereas Beasley waited until his first practice after signing with the Heat. The difference? A couple million dollars in the bank. Walker was not a lottery pick, to be sure, but if the timing of the injuries had been reversed, what would the situation have been? Walker had been considered as high as the 17th pick, but ended up being selected with the 17th pick … of the second round. That difference is not only measured in dollars, but also in the guaranteed contract that comes with a first-round selection. Brandon Rush was in a similar situation in 2007, but decided to go back to school. By returning to Kansas, he picked up a national championship and rebuilt his draft stock, eventually ascending to the latter stages of the lottery.

The myriad of possibilities and real-world examples begs for a real solution. The NCAA has provided catastrophic insurance for athletes since 1991. The first billion-dollar television contract made the cash available for the NCAA to institute a policy that schools had long wanted to provide, but simply could not afford. There have been challenges to the program, mostly involving athletes who are not covered. Currently, only the "big money" sports of football, basketball, baseball, and hockey are covered, though women's basketball was added in 1998. Those Division III water polo goalies are still at risk, though legal challenges to the policy have occasionally come up.

Since the program's inception, participation by athletes has been low. According to the NCAA, only 100 to 150 athletes will participate in a given year. Most of those athletes are football and men's basketball players. Since it's an NCAA-funded loan that pays for the policy, the player must be projected to go in the first round of the NBA or WNBA draft, or in the first three rounds of the NFL draft. The loan must be repaid whether or not the athlete is actually drafted, and if the player is injured, the loan is repaid from the payout. The maximum payouts range from $4.5 million for basketball to $3.5 million in football. Payouts are significantly lower in other sports. Even with the reasonable maximum, the evaluation process will set the amount based on the projected draft position.

Sources within the insurance industry tell me that the maximum is almost never used, mostly for cost containment. "The premium on a lottery pick— a guy who comes into the season as a preseason All

American and is a no-doubter, especially the one-and-done guys—is likely to max it out," I was told. "The best example is Eric Gordon, who came to Indiana as one of the top recruits in the country and was widely expected to hit the NBA. His policy cost about $23,000 and gave him about $4 million in coverage. Once the Clippers picked him, the policy went to billing."

The experience (how insurance companies describe their payouts compared with expected results) has been positive for both the participating underwriters and for the NCAA. The best-known example of an athlete's endangering his draft position is former University of Miami running back Willis McGahee, who violently damaged his knee in the 2003 Fiesta Bowl national championship game against Ohio State, vividly exemplifying the risks athletes take on every play. McGahee's gruesome injury dropped him in the draft, but the policy never paid out. Why? He was drafted. The conditions of the protection are not only that a player lose value to injury, but that the person lose *all* value. McGahee, expected to be among the first players picked in that year's draft prior to his injury, fell only a bit, because the Buffalo Bills were willing to take a risk. Had he fallen all the way to the last pick, the policy would have only paid out a minuscule amount. It covers only a percentage of earnings potential.

Because of the limited nature of the program, which covers only the perceived elite athletes in the major sports, other athletes who could play their way into a payday have little or no protection. If a player isn't perceived as a top pick at the start of the season, coverage is likely to be denied out of hand. That leaves "risers" out in the cold. Moreover, new rules put in place requiring athletes to attend one year of college before being eligible for the NBA draft have also introduced new variables and expenses into the system.

One of the most interesting changes, especially with the one-and-dones, is a tendency for players to protect themselves in spite of the existence of the NCAA-funded insurance. Across the country, athletic trainers have seen an increase in the number of one-and-done players who sit on the sidelines, especially during practice. "There's no one-to-one connection I can show," said one trainer from a perennial powerhouse college, "but I see some of the guys sitting out with very minor injuries, even avoiding the training room. They think more about what might show up on a scouting report than what might be prevented." This sentiment holds true with many train-

ers, making some wonder what value the policies have beyond the financial. "I haven't seen any changes," said another trainer, who's been to the Final Four. "And where you think you would, you don't. The guys with policies aren't reckless, and the guys without them don't suddenly go into a shell."

The NCAA's system only covers earnings potential in a very limited "class," which is the universe of possible insureds. The system works by collecting premiums above and beyond the expected payoffs. The lack of payoffs and the limitation when it does exist have been seen as problematic to many. For better or worse, though, it's standard underwriting practice. The conditions necessary to gain a payoff were set up—correctly—by the NCAA to safeguard against only devastating injuries that remove or reduce an athlete's potential earnings. If Willis McGahee can't get a payout, you can imagine how difficult it is. When Florida State wide receiver De'Cody Fagg blew out his knee at the 2008 NFL Combine, he got nothing. Not only was he uninsured, but even if he had been, he was a consensus second-day pick. "It's tough," said a trainer, "to look at a kid and say, 'You weren't good enough,' but that's what this does." Thus far, no similar injuries at any of the predraft camps would make it into the catastrophic category, but it's easy to see how one bad step in Portsmouth or Orlando could change the future of a team. (While Len Bias's name comes up from time to time, that was clearly outside the scope of the policies.)

This has led to some abuses. Parents, often encouraged by agents, have tried to take out big-dollar policies outside the NCAA system. This is a near-impossible situation to track, and while many trainers and agents mentioned hearing of this practice, none could point to a single instance that they specifically knew of. With the costs involved, such a large, family-purchased policy seems unlikely. First, the cost of a policy outside the "class" would be prohibitive for an individual (or family). The premium on the NCAA-sponsored policies is held down because of the association's sponsorship and because it applies to a class. The same concept is at work in medical insurance—a policy issued under an employer's aegis is less expensive than one a person could get on his or her own. The employer-sponsored coverage spreads the risk across a class. The insurance industry calls it actuarial experience, but it's simple odds. An individual has his or her own risk, while a class of 10 can spread the risk further.

Beyond the catastrophic policies, the NCAA has ignored another significant issue. A student-athlete's medical insurance, surprisingly, is often obtained either entirely outside the school or merely as a school-sponsored supplement to an athlete's own personal insurance. The problem is that not all athletes are insured. This is a significant issue in college basketball, where lower-income and foreign athletes tend to be overrepresented and are the most likely to be uninsured. Many people are surprised that this insurance issue is not handled by the school or, at the very least, the athletic departments. Working at cross-purposes with the need to protect the athletes is the perception that any injury will be seen as a negative by the pro teams. Although injuries can have negative consequences in some scouting situations, injuries left untreated often end up being a bigger problem.

Insurance in college athletics isn't sexy or exciting. It is, however, a growing issue for college athletes and potentially for the colleges themselves or even the NCAA. An insurance executive I spoke with said of the uncertain situation: "It's a lawsuit waiting to happen, in one way or another. Either someone is denied a policy, is denied their claim, or falls outside the class and decides that their last meal ticket is the lawyer on TV telling them to sue." The NCAA's catastrophic policies were started after it scored the huge 1991 television contract, in part to deflect attention and show that the NCAA "cared." The dollars are up in revenue and in risk, but the NCAA is still not making progressive steps to protect the athletes.

Judging the Best Teams Without Judging

KEN POMEROY

I don't envy the job that the NCAA Basketball Committee has to do each March. Selecting the 34 best at-large teams and seeding the 65-team tournament field is always going to be second-guessed by somebody somewhere. While I'm not jealous of the committee, I do feel a certain kinship with its members. After all, the committee and I have the same interests—to determine which teams are the best.

This is a very difficult task, as evidenced by the observation that no two people seem to be able to agree on the issue. Any fan with a remote interest in the game has an opinion on it, and one person's opinion tends to differ with another's. That's the nature of opinions. The purpose of using a 10-member group of well-informed people deeply involved in collegiate athletics is to remove personal biases from the selection process and make a collective decision that is more objective than subjective come early March. The main difference between them and me is that I prefer to assess this throughout the season. My own desire to objectively rank teams has resulted in a fascination with automated ratings systems and with making one that truly measures what matters in identifying whether one team is better than another.

It makes sense that regardless of the reason for determining a team's true strength, any method should be grounded in truths repeatedly observed in the game. With that in mind, looking at how teams fare in their two-game series against conference opponents reveals some important ideas to consider.

Folks trying to rate teams have long known that the transitive property holds in algebra, but not college basketball. For those of you who slept through algebra class (or somehow avoided it entirely), the transitive property states that if A is greater than B, and B is greater than C, then A must be greater than C. In the sports world, this reduces to if Team A beats Team B and Team B beats Team C, then Team A is better than Team C. Plenty of examples every season turn this argument on its ear. In college hoops, the property doesn't even need three teams involved to be violated. Much evidence shows that just because Team A beats Team B, even by a lot, it doesn't mean that A is better than B.

The most extreme example of this occurred in early 2005. On January 29, Western Michigan hosted Central Michigan in a game that turned out to be the third-most-lopsided game played in any conference that season. The home-standing Broncos prevailed by a score of 84-39. Seventeen days later, the teams played the return game at Mount Pleasant, and astoundingly, Western lost.

The Broncos didn't just lose on some lucky shot at the buzzer, either; they lost rather convincingly, 84-74. Such a turnaround may seem stunning. And indeed, in the history of the game, you probably won't find too many other cases in which a team wins by 45 and promptly loses to the same team later in the season. Nevertheless, the general idea of a squad completely destroying its opponent only to have tense moments in the rematch is not as unusual as you might think.

On January 26 of that same season, Louisville beat Marquette by 47 at Freedom Hall. When the Cardinals visited Milwaukee on February 17, they beat the Golden Eagles by just three, scoring the game's last 14 points to do so.

And on January 18, 2005, Alabama destroyed Mississippi State in Tuscaloosa, 98-49. It was the Bulldogs' second-worst conference defeat since they joined the SEC in 1932. In the rematch in Starkville on March 5, the two teams were tied with 2:30 to go. The Tide pulled away from that point for a 68-63 win.

Perhaps 2005 was unusual by having three colossal mismatches turn into competitive contests when the venue was changed. But consider that over the past five seasons, teams that won a home game by 20-29 points were just 283-202 (.583) in the road rematch against the team they had previously clobbered. Teams winning a home game by 10-19 points were a pedestrian 781-759 (.507) in the return game.

The common thread here is that the lopsided games occurred at home. Just so you know, road teams that beat an opponent by 20-29 points were 141-35 (.801) in the home rematch, and those winning the first game by 10-19 were 670-176 (.792). The message is loud and clear: Big road wins deserve to be taken much more seriously, and a big home win means little in isolation. We can talk about match-ups all we want, but several factors produce a lopsided victory for the home team, and some of them have nothing to do with which team is truly better.

We've shown that a lopsided home win should be treated with a bit of caution when we are evaluating a team's season-long performance level. What about close wins? For a long time, I've been convinced that the outcome of close games can be chalked up to a combination of so many factors that winning close games is not a skill. For this reason, I assert that we can call a team's track record in close games "luck." Not luck in the sense that the players can stop trying and just leave it up to the alignment of the planets to determine which team prevails. I'm assuming both teams are trying their hardest to win. Certainly, players and coaches can commit blunders in the closing seconds of games—blunders that lead directly to a loss—but over the long haul, the tactical errors, like the clutch shots and favorable calls,

should even out. I'm not going to tell you that no team has the ability to consistently win tight games. I can't prove that. But I believe that very few teams possess that ability.

We can test this through a similar exercise to the one I just presented. Let's look at the teams that won one-point games and faced the same opponent later in the season. If a one-point win is a true measure of the better team, the winning team should be able to prove it when the two opponents square off again. Over the past five seasons, one-point winners have gone 209-193 in rematches. Their winning percentage of .520 suggests that the rematches were only a little more predictable than coin flips. This supports the notion that the initial contest did little to prove which team was superior.

Taking this one more step, I've long been curious if a one-point win at home is an indicator that the home team is actually worse than the road team if the two played elsewhere. The one-point winners at home were 57-110 (.341) when they had to play the same team again on the road. The home winners were outscored by an average of 5.3 points in the road rematches, a fairly significant indictment against the value of a close home win. By comparison, teams that *lost* at home by a single point were 55-126 (.304) in road rematches and were outscored by an average of 5.5 points. Basically, there's little predictive difference between a one-point win and a one-point loss. The outcome of a close game is less important than the fact that the game was close. And if the game *was* close, it usually suggests that the road team will be the better team in the long run.

If you're trying to determine the best teams in college hoops, whether you're on the selection committee or just somebody trying to create an automated ratings system, home-court advantage has to be considered. It's occasionally powerful enough to make a blowout nearly irrelevant and the outcome of a close game misleading.

Basketball off Paper

JOHN GASAWAY

I've never been comfortable with the term *best game I've ever seen.* I probably remember less than 1 percent of the college basketball games "I've ever seen," and anyway, *remember* is too strong a word for the elusive remnants I carry around even for that 1 percent. I don't remember individual plays so much as I've simply registered how the sum total of plays in a memorable game made me feel as they were unraveling.

For instance, though it represents far and away the most ubiquitous form of the sport, I find it's actually pretty tough for a regular-season game to elbow aside all the tournament classics already ensconced in my memory. The games of late March and early April carry the imprimatur of lasting verdicts. But as you rewind from that point back through February and the rest of the preceding season, the games, however good they were, lose their proximity to the final resolution of each one-season story.

So I'm a little surprised that one game I most certainly still remember is the one that Ohio State and North Carolina played in Chapel Hill in November 2006. This game was as entertaining and spectacular as any other regular-season game I can remember. The Buckeyes went into that game as both the top-ranked team in the nation and as an underdog.

North Carolina was headlined by Tyler Hansbrough, then a sophomore, and three eagerly awaited freshmen: Brandan Wright, Ty Lawson, and Wayne Ellington. After a "down" year in 2006 (these things are relative: UNC was a three-seed in the NCAA tournament that season), the Tar Heels were universally acknowledged as being back up to speed. They'd been ranked number two in the polls, behind defending champion Florida, until the night before Thanksgiving. That night, Carolina lost an eight-point game to Gonzaga in the preseason NIT in Madison Square Garden.

Actually, an odd dynamic was at work in the polls that November. Greg Oden's debut in Columbus had been delayed by a wrist injury, and consequently, Ohio State was being treated as if it was on a futures market, ranked as the new number two behind the Gators. Then, four days before the Buckeyes played in Chapel Hill, Florida lost in overtime to Kansas in Las Vegas. Thad Matta's team was number one.

I hadn't seen more than maybe 15 minutes of game time, total, of Ohio State's season to that point. They'd opened the year with a string of easy wins at home against unranked teams. Still, the numbers that freshman Mike Conley was putting up to my eyes would have been outlandishly impressive even if his team had played the Washington Generals six times. I agreed with everyone else in the country that the Buckeyes without Oden were not the number one team in the nation—but I thought this technically overrated team was actually being severely underrated. I thought the Buckeyes were much better than people realized.

Ohio State lost that night to North Carolina, of course, and the final margin was actually nine points. But this was one of those games whose final score was merely the beginning of the discussion. Both the Buckeyes and the Tar Heels showed me not only that they were as talented as advertised but also, more importantly, how seamlessly cohesive and even intelligent they could be at insanely high velocities on offense. I had to reach back to Illinois in 2005 to think of one offense that looked as good as *both* offenses looked that night. Hansbrough, along with players like Jamar Butler and Ron Lewis of OSU, we already knew. But players like Conley, Wright, Lawson, Ellington, and Daequan Cook were all effectively introduced to us that night, and they all looked preposterously good.

Even in the first half, the game had already reminded me of the 1999 national championship game in which Connecticut surprised favored Duke, the latter being the last team to have gone undefeated in ACC play (and a perennial entrant in "best team not to have won the national title" discussions). The parallel is not perfect, of course. Ohio State lost, UConn won. But in both games, I felt as if I saw an underdog spring on a favorite with sudden and unanswerable ferocity from the very first minute of the game. In both games, I thought I saw genuine surprise in the eyes of the favorite. North Carolina rallied and won in that situation. Duke did not.

There were some incredible numbers put up for offense in Chapel Hill that night, and even Roy Williams was quoted as saying, "You sit there and marvel at the level that kids are playing at offensively." But when I lavished praise on both teams in a day-after piece, I got some dissenting responses from readers who said, in effect, it wasn't good offense, it was bad defense from young players with no "fundamentals," and so on.

Later, I shared that feedback with a former player who, coincidentally, had won the defensive player of the year award in his conference. He'd also seen that game, and when I told him of the readers' objections, I thought I could actually hear him rolling his eyes over the phone. "People have no idea," he said, "what it takes to play that level of offense, how hard it is to make shots when you're running full speed for forty minutes."

There are other games that stay with me. Certainly, the 2007 regional final between Kansas and UCLA has. I doubt there's ever been a game where I expended more effort trying to see everything off the ball on every possession than I did while watching the two best defenses in the country collide in that final. By the same token, George Mason's epochal upset of Connecticut in the 2006 regional finals wasn't just a shocking outcome; it was an outstanding game, one that was closely played virtually throughout and where the Patriots plainly surprised and discomfited the Huskies by daring to take the ball right into the paint. And of course, the big comebacks stay with you. Not just Kansas over Memphis in the championship game last year, but also Illinois over Arizona in the regional final in 2005, or UCLA over Gonzaga in the Sweet 16 in 2006.

All these games that I've mentioned, including Ohio State at North Carolina in November 2006, have the same wind at their backs in terms of my memory. All had teams that went at least as far as the Final Four in those particular seasons. So why is it the game I've had stuck in my head from 2008 took place between two teams that didn't get anywhere near the Final Four?

The game that's stayed with me was the first-round Big Ten tournament contest between Indiana and Minnesota at Conseco Fieldhouse in Indianapolis. Actually, the *game* hasn't stayed with me. Just two amazing shots in the last four seconds of game clock: one from Indiana's Eric Gordon, the other from Minnesota's Blake Hoffarber. Respectively, the shots were the best intentionally missed free throw I've ever seen and a buzzer-beater that can at least be mentioned in the same breath as ones by Christian Laettner and Bryce Drew. Not a bad evening …

With 3.4 seconds left in the game and Indiana down 57-55, Gordon was at the line for two shots. Uncharacteristically, he missed the first one: down two with one free throw remaining, it was time for the play that in my experience non-basketball fans have the hardest time understanding, the intentionally missed free throw. A lot of players in this situation simply fling the ball at the rim and let fate take over, but I was interested to see what Gordon, an outstanding pure shooter mired in a terrible three-point slump, would do.

I wasn't disappointed. For a player trying to do something as uninteresting as making a shot, the basket presents a target that's a little more than 250 square inches. The back iron, by contrast, has only about 30 square inches of surface area. It's less than a third the size of the page you're reading right now.

Gordon hit it. Perfectly.

Then fate really did take over: Gordon had lofted a jewel of a sand wedge onto the back iron. It bounced on various parts of the rim no fewer than four times, more than enough time for D. J. White to get in position, grab the rebound, put the ball in the hole, and draw the foul. Tie game: 57-57, 3.1 seconds left. Give the credit to Gordon.

It's a mark of how eventful these final seconds truly were that I'm just going to skip ahead a second and a half, which was wild in its own right, and take you right up to 1.5 seconds remaining. Indiana now leads 58-57. Minnesota has called a timeout and will take the ball out under the Hoosier basket.

Hoffarber was supposed to be a decoy on the play. Tubby Smith actually had him running off screens in the hopes that Indiana would assume that anyone running off screens must be about to get the ball. It didn't work. Dan Dakich had his main defender, White, on the obvious candidate for the ball, Dan Coleman, the Gophers' undersized but hard-working senior.

The amazing thing about any full-court buzzer-beater comes not only at the end of the play, but also, and maybe even especially, at the beginning. The next time you're in a gym, try throwing an accurate pass—one that hits your teammate at the correct height without sailing over his head—from the baseline to the opposite free-throw line. The throw would be equivalent to about a 20-yard completion from the line of scrimmage in football. So Minnesota's Travis Busch can be forgiven for a lob that was off the mark. In fact, it died just past half-court and started coming down like a wounded quail.

Hoffarber stopped decoying and followed the flight of the ball. He was lucky. He had position on Jamarcus Ellis and jumped to catch the ball at the left end of the free-throw line, landing with his back to the basket. From there the left-handed Hoffarber spun right and, with a motion that was a cross between a push and a flick, shot a one-hander over IU's Armon Bassett.

Basketball's one of the few sports—hockey's another—that announces the end of a game with, for lack of a better term, a game-functional sound. The final gun in football is merely decorative, but in hoops the final horn is synchronized with the clock. In the case of Hoffarber's shot, the game-ending second went just the way such endings are imagined on driveways everywhere every day:

Release, horn, swish.

The Minnesota players flung themselves on top of Hoffarber and quickly formed a pile that spilled onto and under the courtside tables for the working press. Laptops were being bumped and jeopardized, and writers added to the confusion, lunging to save the company equipment from harm.

It didn't take place in an NCAA regional final, of course, but the play and most especially the shot did merit the inevitable comparisons to that holiest of college basketball highlight holies, Laettner. In the minutes following Hoffarber's shot, while the refs were reviewing the play, I actually did some quick math to see if the players on the floor had even been born when Laettner made his shot. Yes, they had been. In fact, in postgame interviews, Busch showed some impressive history chops by reaching even further back into the college hoops video canon: "I was thinking to myself, 'Hey, he can make this.' I started running and I was like 'Oh my God, he

did it.' I went nuts. I was like Jim Valvano looking for someone to hug."

With the publication of *Basketball on Paper* in 2004, Dean Oliver introduced prose to the lyric verse of basketball. You can still use verse. You *should* still use it. There are things it can say that prose can't. I use verse all the time—see above—and will continue to do so. But we also now have at least the option of prose for a sport that never had it before. My frustration with basketball talk pre-Oliver wasn't that it was conducted solely in verse, but rather that people occasionally *thought* they were speaking in prose when in fact they weren't.

Oliver's is a mode of expression that I'd struggled in odd moments to formulate, one that I was relieved to find had finally been perfected by someone, and one that I've happily added to my range of hoops dialects. I call this prose *tempo-free*, but that's just me. It's rare that something merits the label *entirely new*, but I think in Oliver's case, the words are justified, even if the word *unprecedented* may not be.

Although North Carolina coach Dean Smith tracked his team's performance on a possession-by-possession basis for decades, Oliver independently came up with a method of doing so for those of us who, unlike Coach Smith, can't call on a bench full of clipboard-wielding assistants. Before Oliver, looking at a team's performance in a way that held pace constant meant having an assistant coach manually count possessions during every game. Now I wonder if any team even does that anymore. It's much simpler just to grab the box score.

Basketball happens on the court, of course, not on paper. But the paper intrusion has been part of the sport from the very beginning. It happened when it was decided to track how many "points" are scored and to declare the team with the most points the winner. This ain't figure skating.

Points are the dispositive stat, but there are other stats, ones that, if you're interested in points, you need to know about. How often you make a shot, how often you miss a shot, how often you turn the ball over, how often you make a steal, how often you try a three instead of a two, how often you attempt a free throw, how often you commit a foul—they're all put on paper. That is, they're all recorded. But of course, being recorded is quite different from being *remembered*, the way I remember a few extraordinary games. For that you need verse, not the more literal prose of stats.

These are two different but I think complementary ways of appreciating and talking about the game, ways that I mix together and combine all the time. In fact, I don't find the realms of the recorded and the remembered to be in conflict all that often. When I've had a quibble with basketball stats, it has rarely been because I find them to be at odds with my eyes. Rather, it's because I occasionally find them to be superfluous.

While it's been heartening to see the enthusiastically rapid adoption of tempo-free stats by so many writers and by many more fans, having the data available has occasionally led to a reflexive assumption that we should start *any* discussion with that data. For my own consumption, when a team is really struggling, there's precious little enlightenment to be found two or three places to the right of the decimal. Our eyes can indeed tell us what we need to know: This team is too short, or too young, or too slow, or too undisciplined, or some combination thereof.

Nevertheless, on a few interesting occasions, eyes and paper are in greater or lesser degrees of conflict. What then?

Two or three seasons ago, I remarked that a particular team actually had a better offense than people realized. While that team operated at an exceptionally slow pace and didn't shoot particularly well, it nevertheless scored at an above-average per-possession rate simply because it never turned the ball over. After posting this piece, I was pleased that I'd added my small mite to hoops truth and enlightenment. Then I received an e-mail from a fan of that team saying, in effect, who cares if the offense is good? It's boring! He had it exactly right. My piece was correct as a work of hoops prose; his response had the unmistakable ring of truth and authenticity as a stanza of hoops verse.

I do find, however, that readers become more interested in the prose as the season gets closer to March. Past performance is the best predictor we have for the future. It's not perfect; it's just the best we have. I have more confidence in our descriptions of past performance in basketball now than I used to, thanks largely to Oliver's work. We can never know in advance who will be the national champion. But for this one specific and limited task, prose is more of an aid than is verse.

In fact, I think Oliver's work is far more powerful than has generally been recognized when it's applied to team performance. I think tempo-free stats are almost ideally well suited to the nature of basketball as a team sport. If so, it may be because of something I'm going to call play decisiveness.

Play decisiveness is simply the ratio between the number of points or runs scored on a winning team's most decisive single play in a game and that team's final score. Baseball has an extremely high level of play decisiveness; football a little less; basketball far, far less than the other two. And that has implications for the sovereign limits of analysis in each of the above sports when the subject under study is a team (though not when it's individual players).

In baseball there can be a level of play decisiveness as high as 1-to-1, say, in a pitcher's duel where one staff throws a shutout and the other yields only a two-run home run. That 1-to-1 ratio's possible but much less likely in football, where ratios more customarily range from 1-to-3 to 1-to-6. And then there's basketball: almost always somewhere between 1-to-18 and 1-to-30 for a three-point shot that's judged the single most decisive play of the game. We say a given three in basketball is a "dagger" but of course that's just a way of speaking. Pedants will always hustle forth to remind us with irritating correctness that the first basket of the game's as important as anything in the last two minutes. Behold the incorrigibly cumulative nature of hoops.

When it comes to scoring opportunities, Dr. Naismith's game is just, well, different from the other major team sports. In baseball, we're particularly interested and excited when there are runners "in scoring position." In football, we're particularly interested and excited when a team is "in the red zone." Of course, scoring can happen regardless in both sports, and the plays that make it so are all the more exciting. A home run's a big sudden deal even if no one's in scoring position. A long touchdown pass is a big sudden deal, especially because it takes place outside the red zone.

Basketball is another animal entirely. Made baskets from half-court or longer notwithstanding (and those are nine-tenths luck), you just don't get that sudden improbability. Basketball entertains through accretion, with momentum and sustained runs, as opposed to the searing, sporadic lightning strikes seen in baseball and football, which have true "big plays." The line drive that a pitcher gives up after a walk and an error is much more damaging than a line drive to start the inning. The same goes for turnovers deep in your own territory in football. But in basketball, alone among team sports, all scoring opportunities—possessions, in this case—are more or less created equal.

Of course, there's the occasional breakaway dunk off a steal or deflected pass, but each of those will account for about 3 or 4 percent of a team's points in a game. Contrast this to an interception returned for a touchdown, which will usually represent 20, 25, or even 50 percent of a football team's scoring in a game. And as for the three-run homer, that can be 100 percent of the team's total scoring output for the game, secured with but a single play and by a margin of millimeters.

Scoring opportunities in basketball all start out pretty much the same, but most crucially, each scoring opportunity arrives in the company of many others. Basketball's uniformity across frequent scoring opportunities means we can look at how well teams do per opportunity with an analytic confidence that's unusual for other team sports. The information to be gathered on how well a team does scoring and preventing points across a thousand-plus generally standard possessions achieves, by its very nature, a degree of pointillist specificity that's invaluable. Wins in basketball are the cumulative result of possessions, all of which are more or less equal in both degree of difficulty (minus the occasional steal and breakaway) and decisiveness. In this, basketball is markedly different from baseball or football.

In hoops, the truth about a team is gathered slowly and in accretion. The revolution wrought by Oliver, then, is that team stats in basketball have gone from being something we just *knew*, somehow, we shouldn't put too much stock in to something that borders on being startling in its analytic value. The statistical modeling done in any sport takes real-world stats and plugs them into simulated games to see who would win the most of, say, a thousand such contests. But when the unit of study is the college basketball possession, we already have a thousand of those to look at in the real world.

If this kind of possession-based information in college basketball is so invaluable, there is, of course, another sport that should yield even *better* information: pro basketball. Indeed, the NBA regular season offers almost three times as many possessions and, even more importantly, less than one-tenth as many teams. On paper, it's the perfect environment for a statistical theocracy.

Yes, but it's the NBA regular season we're dealing with here. It's an 82-game death march. Players have to "pick their spots" to simply survive the season.

And if you happen to be talking about a year in the NBA when there's an intact and still relatively youthful defending champion, forget it. You can make incredibly precise and meticulously detailed per-possession measurements of that team—measurements you can then throw out the window. Both the Bulls of the 1990s and the Lakers of the early 2000s successfully defended titles without home-court advantage in the playoffs. Their stats weren't as good as those put up by other teams during those regular seasons. Didn't matter. Stats are only trustworthy to the degree that player motivation is.

This particular chicken even came home to roost in college hoops for one year in the form of defending champion Florida in 2007. The Gators that year were actually outscored over the course of their last five conference games, a fact that didn't prevent them from winning their second national championship with somewhat disconcerting insouciance—never blowing any quality opponent out, really, but never lapsing into danger, either. Heed my words. Youthful and healthy defending champions are toxic to stats.

Before pulling the trigger on any statistical weapon, of course, you need to decide where you're going to aim it. Speaking in college basketball terms, there are several gradations of player motivation between the first exhibition game in November and the national championship game. Aim accordingly.

Tempo-free stats aren't objective. They're actually pretty comfortable in their manifest subjectivity and self-evident nonneutrality. They're fastened to just one criterion—points—which is far from being the only criterion we do or should use when savoring this thing called college basketball.

The subjectivity here is extensive and intractable; it should be on the warning label. If this subjectivity is a normative menace, however, it's also something of a comparative benefit. Its saving grace is that it visits a uniform level of mischief across hundreds of teams and thousands of players.

Now and then, these stats will have the impudence to dissent from the settled verdict of my eyes, just as that same verdict will sometimes be overturned entirely by a final score. So be it: These stats don't tell me what I "should" believe. They tell me how things look from one particular arbitrary and rather anodyne standpoint, that of scoring and preventing points.

But that's just one standpoint. There are, of course, many such …

Stats: Quantitative measures of performance are endlessly fascinating, even when used like a compositional grocery list in the assessment of a middling team. Whatever I say has happened with past teams will continue happening for all teams. If it doesn't, that doesn't mean I was wrong; it just means that this occurrence was an outlier. Refs and scouts are idiots.

Scout: The star player has a quick release and good range, but he needs to bulk up and work on his left hand. When assessing NBA potential, height is the equal of past performance. Height plus youth renders past performance irrelevant. Refs and coaches who don't listen to me are idiots.

College coach: Any development on our team needs to come from the players. My proximity to, and investment in, the situation is an unalloyed analytic good. I wince and stomp and hurl myself about ostentatiously when the players perform poorly. But if the players were to wince and stomp and hurl themselves about ostentatiously when I coach poorly, they would be showing me up. Refs and writers are idiots.

Working press: In tonight's game, the star of the team I cover needs to get 20 points. Players for the team I cover invariably mature as they play college basketball, and stories about that maturation are endlessly fascinating. The story of any college basketball player is a bildungsroman. Well, that is, except for the players on tonight's opposing team. Refs and bloggers are idiots.

Blogger: My snark is endlessly fascinating, as are embedded YouTube clips of coaches losing their temper or saying something dumb at press conferences. By the way, my commenters scare me. Don't tell them I said that. Refs and fans of my team's archrival are idiots.

Message board for an elite team: Our team is going to win the national championship. Writers who say otherwise haven't watched our team as much as we have. If the writers in question don't use stats, they're hacks and dinosaurs. If they do use stats, they don't really understand basketball. Either way, they're idiots, just like refs.

Message board for a nonelite team. Our coach is an idiot. Writers who say otherwise haven't watched

our team as much as we have. They're idiots, just like refs. And our coach.

But of course, no single standpoint can take in college hoops whole, whether it's supplied by stats, scouting reports, courtside seats, HD, blogs, mainstream analysts, message boards, or even coaches. Ask any player. He'll tell you his coach does not have a monopoly on knowledge …

Star: I need the ball more.

Nonstar starter: I need the ball more. I should be the star.

Reserve: I need the ball more. I should be starting.

I know how the reserve feels. The pinnacle of my playing career came as a sophomore at Springfield High School in Springfield, Illinois, when I scored a staggering eight points against visiting Urbana. I was a reserve on a team where reserves didn't see much time, but because this game was comfortably in hand, I was able to record a stellar 3-of-3 from the field and even a steady 2-of-2 from the line.

This performance earned me the ultimate honor. I was pulled from the game to make room for a reserve even *further* down the bench, meaning I was able to watch the rest of the game from the sidelines with the starters. For once happy to be on the bench, I took great care with my very body language to broadcast to everyone in the gym my conspicuous ease and thorough familiarity with this unprecedented turn of events that never happened again.

My clearest memory of that night, however, is what happened when I left the game. As I came off the court, my coach, Coach Barnes, gave me a hearty slap on the back and, drawing out my name in mock reverence, asked, "John Gas-a-way, where in the world did *that* come from?" Being a player and not a coach, I of course immediately thought, "What's he talking about? I can do that every time." (I was right.)

The thought emerged whole and unbidden from my inner primate brain, as inherent and hardwired as a circadian rhythm. If you're a player, the thought is just *there*. Every player since Dr. Naismith nailed his first peach basket to the wall has thought exactly what I thought that night: I need the ball more.

Now that I'm writing more often than playing, I know I shouldn't believe the player every time, of course. Nor should I believe the coach on every particular. Nor tempo-free stats, scouts, writers, bloggers, or even my own eyes, at least not implicitly and without further interrogation.

No, I should believe only the sudden yet seamless disbelief that the game keeps bringing my way, whether it arrives from Chapel Hill, Conseco Fieldhouse, or points as yet unknown. Disbelief outlives words and numbers. It erupts and endures entirely off paper.

2008–2009 PREVIEWS

Introduction

KEN POMEROY AND JOHN GASAWAY

The following pages contain our preview of the upcoming season. If you made it through Section I without many problems, then you should be able to easily negotiate our previews. Nevertheless, there are a few things you ought to know before reading further.

First, we play favorites. We approach things from the perspective of a general college hoops fan. Therefore, we don't follow IUPUI as closely as we do North Carolina. (Although if George Hill had not turned pro a year early, we would have had more to say about the Jaguars.) In the coming pages, you'll find in-depth team previews for each team in what have traditionally been the six best conferences in the nation this decade: the ACC, the Big East, the Big Ten, the Big 12, the Pac-10, and the SEC.

Within each of these team previews, we provide you with a few observations. First, we start things off on a positive note by telling you what the team did well. We can do this because every team did something well last season, even Oregon State! Ideally, this will be something that you didn't know the team excelled at. Next, we'll tell you something that we learned from the last season, because while we'd like to think we understand college basketball well, the game is constantly evolving and always provides us with increasing knowledge with each season. Finally, we'll give you an idea of what's to be expected this season. This section isn't going to tell you that the team will go 25-7 with a Sweet 16 appearance. We're not that good, and college hoops is not that predictable. What it will reveal is what's different about this team compared with last year (if anything).

We're not done, though. We give you a breakdown of each player who we expect to get meaningful playing time this season. For some teams, this is more difficult than others, but for the most part you won't see every scholarship player listed in this section—just the ones who will appear in the game plans of opposing coaches. To conclude, we give you a few sentences on where we think this team is headed for the upcoming season.

From there, we'll give you conference previews of four conferences that typically supply the NCAA tournament with at-large teams: the Atlantic 10, the C-USA, the Missouri Valley, and the Mountain West. The same principles apply regarding catering to the general hoops fan. We provide more details about teams that figure to have an impact on the national landscape (e.g., Memphis) than we do for those that don't (e.g., Saint Bonaventure).

After this, there are still 21 conferences left, so we're not done! We'll give you our read on which teams you'll be hearing about from these leagues heading into 2009, with special ink for teams like Gonzaga and Davidson. We admit there's a lot more to be learned about these teams than merely who might be "this year's Davidson," which is why you should be reading Kyle Whelliston.

Before you saunter off to check out what we say about your favorite conference, you should also understand that the language we use is different from what you'll see in any other preview publication. We judge a team's offense and defense in terms of its **points scored or allowed per possession**. In this way, we remove the corrupting influence of a team's pace from our judgment of its skills. We'll call these stats **offensive and defensive efficiency** from time to time. We tend to focus on how these measures look during regular-season conference games only to get the best estimate of how a team stacks up to its conference brethren. Occasionally, though, we'll refer to **adjusted efficiencies**, which includes all games played and accounts for schedule strength, among other things, to provide an estimate of how a team stacks up nationally.

We're also big believers in Dean Oliver's "Four Factors." For the uninitiated, nearly all of a team's offensive and defensive efficiency can be explained by its performance in four areas—shooting, rebounding,

43

turnovers, and free throws. With these things, too, we use different measurements from those you're used to seeing, unless you visited BasketballProspectus.com last season.

For shooting, we like to use **effective field-goal percentage** (typically shortened to eFG) in lieu of traditional field-goal percentage. The version we use gives 50 percent more credit for a made three-pointer, just as the scoreboard does. Thus, a player going 4-for-10 from the field while shooting all his shots from beyond the arc would have an eFG of 60 percent. His two-point-making counterpart would have an eFG of just 40 percent.

In the rebounding department, we also use a percentage. In this case, the number of rebounding opportunities is the divisor. When we talk about a **defensive rebounding percentage**, we mean the percentage of rebounds a defense grabbed among those available. The same principle applies for **offensive rebounding percentage**.

With ball security, we use **turnover percentage**. (Are you getting a theme here?) This is just the percentage of possessions on which a team commits or forces a turnover.

Finally, for free throws, we'll refer to something called **free-throw rate**, which is just free-throw attempts divided by field-goal attempts.

Those are the four factors. It's pretty easy once you get the hang of it. We use similar measures to de-fine a player's ability, also. You should become familiar with additional terms on the personal level: **offensive rating**, which is just the player version of offensive efficiency, and **usage** or **possessions used**, which describes how often a player did something statistically on the offensive end. This helps us distinguish the go-to guy from the screen setter.

You might wonder why we would use metrics that deviate from the long-established standard. Simply put, our measurements do a better job assessing the strengths and weaknesses of teams and players. Each of the stats we use is about fairness and opportunities. Teams that shoot a lot of three-pointers tend to have lower field-goal percentages than do teams that shoot fewer threes, but the three-point-shooting teams also have to make fewer shots to score the same number of points that two-point-shooting teams score. Effective field-goal percentage sorts this out.

Likewise, teams that make a lot of shots and play at a slow pace may appear to be poor offensive rebounding teams by more conventional measures. Offensive rebounding percentage allows us to compare the skills of this team with a fast-paced, bricklaying one in an equitable manner.

OK, you're now prepared to venture into the conference previews. We hope that once you're done, you'll be a more knowledgeable fan for the experience.

In-Depth

The ACC

Early Entrants Need Not Apply

KEN POMEROY

Last year was not a bad one for the ACC. It placed a team in the Final Four, had two teams ranked in the top five of the AP poll at some point during the season, had three teams get a five-seed or better in the NCAA tournament, and again dominated the ACC/Big Ten Challenge. But overall, the ACC did not have the impact on the national college basketball scene that it is accustomed to. For the second straight season, the conference sent only one team to the second weekend of the tournament. Prior to 2007, the ACC was in the habit of sending at least two teams to the Sweet 16. It had done so every year since 1980.

The ACC sent only four teams to the dance, but that wasn't historically low. That had happened three other times this decade, to go with another time (2000) that the conference was represented by just three teams. The ACC's prestige didn't take a hit solely with the sparse representation; it was the manner in which those teams performed that did it. Fifth-seeded Clemson was knocked off in the first round. Second-seeded Duke nearly suffered the same fate, before Gerald Henderson's last-second heroics prevented what would have been one of the signature first-round upsets in the 64-team era. Nevertheless, the Blue Devils lost decisively to West Virginia in the second round. Miami at least acquitted itself well with an easy first-round win over Saint Mary's and then used a frantic, late comeback to give second-seeded Texas a scare.

The conference was led, of course, by North Carolina. It was the top-ranked team in the AP's preseason poll, and last fall, few were debating whether it would win the ACC. The focus was on what needed to happen if North Carolina were to win a national title. The consensus turned out to be correct, although the conference race wasn't exactly boring. It wasn't decided until the final minute of the final game of the regular season in Durham, when UNC pulled out a 76-68 victory to beat out Duke by a game in the standings.

In the NCAA tournament, the Tar Heels did look like a national title contender for four games before getting run over by eventual national champion Kansas in the first 14 minutes of Final Four action. And with that, the ACC's season was over. For the second year in a row, the conference could be summarized succinctly as UNC and then a bunch of teams that didn't scare a whole lot of people once March rolled around.

The offseason treated the conference well, however. When it came time to put up or shut up about declaring for the NBA draft, the ACC had fewer players volunteer than any other power conference did.

Underclassmen declaring for the 2008 NBA Draft by conference

Pac 10	10
Big 12	8
SEC	4
CUSA	3
Big East	2
Big Ten	2
Atlantic 10	2
MWC	1
WAC	1
OVC	1
Summit	1
Community Colleges	1
ACC	**1**

Only NC State's J. J. Hickson went pro early last season, leaving the ACC with as few early entrants as the Summit League and the entirety of America's community colleges had. Of course, part of the reason for such a gap between the ACC (or other conferences with just one defector) and the Pac-10 and Big 12 is that there was a talent difference between those conferences. Among ACC players who elected to stay in college, only Ty Lawson and Tyler Hansbrough were considered possible first-round picks in 2008. But neither were all the Pac 10's and Big 12's early entrants first-round picks themselves. Nor were they even expected to be when they declared. Every year, a few players with good intentions declare for the draft, but aren't picked in the first round or at all. There are always guys like Davon Jefferson, Jamont Gordon, and Bill Walker who would just rather play pro ball anywhere than have to attend class for another season and not get paid. The ACC didn't have any players fall into that category, either.

The odd thing for the ACC is that few others were tempted to leave early. The Carolina trio of Lawson, Wayne Ellington, and Danny Green made news with their near simultaneous withdrawal from the draft, but the real news was that those three were the only players besides Hickson to even test the waters. It wouldn't have been crazy for Boston College's Tyrese Rice, Duke's Gerald Henderson or Kyle Singler, Maryland's Greivis Vasquez, Clemson's K. C. Rivers, or Wake Forest's James Johnson to at least float his name out there. But all of them are back, which means that the ACC's reputation should rebound this season. Especially when you consider that no seniors were taken with one of the first 40 picks in the draft. The talent that was in the league last season did not leave, nor did any of the 12 coaches.

Although the entire league is not back, if you want a handy reference on expectations for each of the ACC's teams, just get a sense for their accomplishment last season and bump it up a little. That assumption applies accurately to eight of the 12 members. UNC was a Final Four team last season, and now its reasonable goal is to win a national title. Duke had an outstanding season through February and then an ordinary one after that; it could expect to have finishing power in 2009. Miami, Wake Forest, and Virginia Tech all exceeded expectations last season, and an NCAA tournament appearance should be expected this time around. Florida State,

Boston College, and NC State may find themselves in the bottom half of the conference again this season because of the tide of the entire conference will rise in 2009. But all three should be better in terms of basketball ability than they were in 2008.

Not everyone in the conference will get better. Maryland and Virginia lost seniors who provided many of their teams' reasons for winning games. In Maryland's case, it was James Gist and Bambale Osby defending the basket. For Virginia, it was Sean Singletary scoring and distributing from the spot point guard spot. Both teams are going to struggle to find players to replace what was lost. Clemson, too, suffers serious senior losses between its athletic power forward James Mays and point guard Cliff Hammonds. But the Tigers were a five-seed last season, and with Rivers and Trevor Booker back to anchor the team, Clemson has enough firepower to return to the tournament.

There's reason to believe that the ACC will get back to the glory days of sending half its teams to the NCAA tournament, but that won't be enough to reestablish the honor of the conference. What the ACC really needs is for someone besides UNC to win some games in the tournament. It's difficult to say who those teams will be, and I don't think that's a cop-out. There isn't much difference between the tourney chances of Duke, Miami, Clemson, Wake Forest, and Virginia Tech (although that's how I'd order the respective teams' chances). There is strength in those numbers, though. When you have six teams that could realistically win a tournament game, chances are you'll have more than two that do.

	2008 Record	Returning Minutes (%)	2009 Prediction
UNC	14-2	85	14-2
Duke	13-3	84	11-5
Miami	8-8	79	10-6
Clemson	10-6	67	0-6
Wake Forest	7-9	97	10-6
Va. Tech	9-7	83	9-7
Boston Coll.	4-12	67	7-9
Ga. Tech	7-9	63	7-9
Florida St.	7-9	46	6-10
NC State	4-12	70	5-11
Maryland	8-8	70	4-12
Virginia	5-11	62	3-13

2008: 14-17 (4-12 ACC)
Lost to Clemson 82-48, ACC Quarterfinal
In-conference offense: 1.05 points per possession (6th)
In-conference defense: 1.12 points allowed per possession (11th)

What Boston College did well: *Block shots.*

For three seasons in a row, from 2005 to 2007, BC had one of the most feared shot blockers in the nation on its roster in Sean Williams. Granted, Williams never did play over half of BC's minutes in any year, but the Eagles generally had the reputation of blocking shots during that time. Last season, though, the Eagles blocked a higher percentage of opponents' two-point attempts than they did in any of Williams's years. That feat was entirely due to the work of Tyrelle Blair, the best shot blocker in the ACC in 2008. A year earlier, he had shown that he was a worthy replacement for Williams in that area. Blair is gone now, and looking at the Eagles' roster, one can safely assume that the fear of rejection will not be an issue for BC's opponents this season.

What we learned in 2008: *Al Skinner doesn't have mystical powers with marginal recruits.*

Boston College coach Al Skinner has made a living recruiting kids who schools of similar or higher stature don't think will cut it at the power-conference level. Along with that, he has a reputation for turning these marginal prospects into terrific players. Most recently, Craig Smith and Jared Dudley have led the Eagles to great things, but before them was Troy Bell, who ran the point guard spot for four years and was picked in the first round of the NBA draft in 2003.

Last season, the track record gave Skinner somewhat of a free pass on his incoming class, which did not get much acclaim from recruiting gurus. Because of Skinner's prior magic acts, the Eagles were given some benefit of the doubt heading into last season, despite the apparent offensive void left by the departure of Jared Dudley and Sean Marshall. It didn't quite work out, as the two freshmen who played the most, Rakim Sanders and Biko Paris, struggled adjusting to the college level.

What's in store for 2009

Turn on a BC game this season, and you're bound to see a lot of scoring by sophomores. Wing Corey Raji and center Josh Southern, two freshmen who saw less playing time than Sanders and Paris saw last season, immediately held their own against talented foes in 2008. All four of the rising sophomores should be in the top six in minutes played this season, and the Eagles add a sophomore newcomer in Joe Trapani, who will also get significant time.

So if youth alone is a reason for optimism, then Boston College has that in 2009. More substantively, one thing that needs to improve from the youngsters is offensive production. A team with a great point guard and no help is a team that can't compete at the power-conference level. Skinner's flex offense was so effective for three years running you could have called it Gonzaga East, but last season it was occasionally ugly. Pair that with a defense that was, as usual, lackluster, and you get a trip to the basement of the ACC. After a year in the Skinner system, BC fans must hope that the sophs step up and give Rice the necessary weapons for the team to score at will again.

MEET THE EAGLES

Tyrese Rice (6-1, 190, Sr.). Rice is following the career path of Virginia's Sean Singletary. He should be the second-best point guard in the conference, behind Ty Lawson, but he could use a lot more support from his teammates.

Rakim Sanders (6-5, 225, So.). Sanders presents an odd résumé. Had he turned 11 of his three-point misses into makes, he might have been the first player in history to be more accurate on threes than twos and more accurate on twos than free throws. Sanders shoots often enough and well enough (effective field-goal percentage of 51) that he could be a useful scoring threat. The problem is he rarely makes free throws, hitting just 30 of 65 (46 percent) last season. The percentage should go up at least a little: Players who shot at least 20 free throws and made fewer than 50 percent of them in 2007 averaged 56 percent from the line in 2008. (Shout out to Xavier's B. J. Raymond, who went from 9-of-22 in 2007 to 31-of-38 in 2008.) Sanders needs a boost in accuracy, but also an increase in frequency. There's little excuse for a player's taking more than 300 field-goal attempts, to only get to the line 65 times.

Corey Raji (6-5, 214, So.). Raji was sixth on the team in minutes played, which is a shame because he showed flashes of being the guy who could be headlining BC previews next season, when Rice is gone. At 6-5, Raji produced the stats of a player much bigger in two areas: He made over 60 percent of his two-point attempts and grabbed over 10 percent of his team's missed shots. No player as short as Raji and getting at least 20 minutes a game did that last season. He also didn't commit turnovers, despite his activity in the paint. Throw in a 9-for-25 effort from three-point range, and Raji is one of the most versatile players in the country.

Joe Trapani (6-8, 218, So.). Sophomore forward Shamari Spears, who was third on the team in minutes last season, transferred to Charlotte in the off-season. But BC gains a transfer in Trapani, who comes over from Vermont and should give the Eagles much of what Spears provided last season. He was a part-time starter in his freshman season with the Catamounts and was their most frequent shooter per minute. He deserved the green light, finishing the season with a 52 percent mark in effective field-goal percentage, aided by 40 percent accuracy on threes.

Josh Southern (6-10, 242, So.). Southern moves from third to first on the center depth chart this season, with both Blair and John Oates gone. It doesn't have to be a bad thing, either. He posted offensive numbers better than both players last season, and nearly all his minutes were in conference play. He won't block shots, however.

Biko Paris (6-1, 196, So.). Part-time shooting guard, part-time point guard, Paris struggled to get comfortable in Skinner's lineup last season. Paris's role is unlikely to change, so watch his turnover rate in season number two in Chestnut Hill. It has to drop some, but it would be nice if it dropped to acceptable levels, a change that would have to be considered a transformation if it occurred.

Reggie Jackson (6-3, 193, Fr.). It's another ho-hum recruiting class for BC, but Jackson could find that the minutes come easy if he's able to make plays without committing a bunch of turnovers.

Tyler Roche (6-7, 215, Jr.). Roche is primarily a three-point shooter, but he's surprisingly adept at setting up his teammates, too.

Evan Ravenel (6-8, 260, Fr.). Ravenel is a wide body from Florida.

Dallas Elmore (6-5, 205, Fr.). Another long-distance recruit for Skinner, Elmore, like Jackson, comes from Colorado.

Prospectus says
Boston College won just four ACC games, but deserved to win a couple more. Considering this plus the observation that the talent level on this year's team might be a notch higher, and the team's getting to the middle of the conference pack doesn't seem so crazy. Anything higher will require considerably better offensive contributions from somebody besides Rice.

CLEMSON

2008: 24-10 (10-6 ACC)
Lost to Villanova 75-69, NCAA first round
In-conference offense: 1.08 points per possession (3rd)
In-conference defense: 1.00 points allowed per possession (4th)

What Clemson did well: *Defend the three-point line.*
Few things are certain in the wacky world of college hoops, but for a while now, one constant has been that Duke will lead the ACC in three-point defense. At least what I would consider the best measure of three-point defense—the amount of points allowed on three-point shots. For some reason, while analysts define a team's defense by the number of points it gives up in a game, they define a team's three-point defense by the percentage of three-point shots its opponents make. But consider the case where a team allows its opponents to shoot very few three-pointers. Isn't that a sign of a good perimeter defense, also?

As a reader of *Prospectus*, you've evolved to using points per possession to evaluate the quality of a team's offense and defense. Now's the time to look past three-point percentage as the benchmark of defending the three-point shot. I prefer looking at the percentage of points allowed by the three-pointer. True, this measure also says a bit about a team's style. Perhaps opponents are able to feast on the interior and have no interest in shooting the three. But if you consider two teams that allow opponents to shoot a similar percentage from three-point range, the one allowing fewer attempts is likely to have the better three-point defense.

For the past five seasons, Duke opponents have scored only about 20 percent of their points from beyond the arc due to a combination of lack of accuracy and lack of opportunity. This figure has been among the national leaders and usually much lower than any other ACC team. That changed last season, when Clemson allowed its opponents to get just 21.7 percent of their points on threes, just 0.5 percent more than Duke allowed and the second-lowest non-Duke total in the past five seasons (surpassed only by the 2006 Tigers).

What we learned in 2008: *This team can get to the NCAA tournament.*

After a couple of seasons of having legitimate reasons to think a run at an at-large bid was possible only to be disappointed long before Selection Sunday, Oliver Purnell's team broke through in 2008. A few statistical indicators pointed to Clemson as being the third-best team in the league (by a wide margin over the fourth-best team) at the midway point of the conference season. And though it wasn't always pretty, the Tigers ended up third in the league standings and then won their way to the championship game of ACC tournament. Unfortunately, those ACC tournament wins would be their last.

Clemson earned a five-seed to the NCAA tournament, but failed to protect an 18-point lead against Villanova in the first round, losing 75-69. While it was a big step forward for the program to make its first NCAA tournament appearance since the Rick Barnes era, there has to be a little concern about whether Purnell's pressing defensive style is suited for a deep tournament run.

Actually, style has little to do with it. If Purnell could bring top-tier talent to Clemson, the hurdle would be overcome. This is precisely why Barnes was destined for prolonged success at Texas—if you can win tournament games at Clemson, then you can surely win games with *more* resources. The fact is, Purnell may not have had a single first-round NBA pick on his roster, but he guided the Tigers to a high seed. (Obligatory word of caution directed toward K. C. Rivers and Trevor Booker: They may well find themselves highly regarded by NBA scouts. It is difficult to predict these things a year or two out, as Russell Westbrook can attest to.)

What's in store for 2009

The Tigers lose of couple of significant contributors from last season's edition. Combo guard Cliff Ham-

monds and center James Mays finished their fourth seasons of eligibility in 2008. Both were cornerstones of what became an outstanding Clemson defense by their senior seasons. But the beauty of last season's team was that it had no star but six equally important contributors. Even the players occupying the seven through ten spots (from which senior Sam Perry has departed) on Purnell's deep bench were capable of making an impact at times. Don't expect much change in the level or style of play this season. The expectations for 2009 should be no different from 2008—get to the NCAA tournament, and do some damage while there.

MEET THE TIGERS

Trevor Booker (6-7, 240, Jr.). While Booker hasn't shot up any draft boards, he's a fine college player. Offensively, he uses his ability just as it should be used. He has some range, but it's rarely displayed simply because he is such an efficient scorer down low. Booker is also a nice rebounder on both ends of the floor and blocks a bunch of shots. The biggest knock against him is that he shot 57 percent from the free-throw line, which was nearly identical to his two-point percentage.

K. C. Rivers (6-5, 215, Sr.). Rivers gained fame in 2007 as the nation's best sixth man. It was a misplaced honor because Rivers was third on the team in minutes that season. That he began the game on the bench was irrelevant to his impact because he was on the floor at the end of games. So when he moved into the starting role last season, it wasn't a surprise that his performance and influence on the team were much the same. He's a ridiculously efficient player, due to excellent three-point accuracy and an insanely low turnover rate. He's not exclusively a spot-up shooter, either—he actually took more twos than threes last season.

Terrence Oglesby (6-2, 185, So.). Unlike Rivers, Oglesby was exclusively a jump shooter in his freshman season and one who deserved the attention of opposing game plans. He made 40 percent of his shots from downtown.

Demontez Stitt (6-2, 170, So.). Stitt's freshman season was about potential. He'll be the starter at point guard, and he showed he could get involved offensively. Last season, that involvement often ended in a missed shot or turnover, though.

David Potter (6-6, 205, Jr.). A role player off the bench, Potter gave fouls at the rate of 5.7 per 40 minutes. But that's the role of a Clemson reserve who plays just 16 minutes per game—be aggressive on defense.

Raymond Sykes (6-9, 220, Sr.). Sykes took 15 percent of his team's shots while he was on the floor, which actually was nearly double what he did in his previous two seasons. Considering the track record, you'd have to think he'll continue to be a defensive specialist. He's not a bad shot blocker.

Jerai Grant (6-8, 215, So.). In Grant's sparse minutes, he demonstrated that he's a solid rebounder. That's a skill Purnell could use in trying to replace Mays.

Tanner Smith (6-5, 190, Fr.). Smith is a lanky shooting guard who specializes in, well, shooting.

Andre Young (5-9, 180, Fr.). The diminutive point guard should get a few minutes behind Stitt.

Catalin Baciu (7-0, 225, Fr.). Hey, he's a seven-footer, and Purnell plays a lot of guys, so even with a limited offensive game, Baciu will get some time.

Prospectus says

Even with a few new faces, Clemson seems like a safe pick to get back to the NCAA tournament. Still, the inconsistency that has plagued this team under Purnell and is typical of pressing teams should continue. That 18-point lead against Villanova took 15 minutes to build and 12 minutes to evaporate. Those kinds of momentum shifts will again be common and prevent this team from getting too far north of .500 in conference play.

DUKE

2008: 28-6 (13-3 ACC)
Lost to West Virginia 73-67, NCAA second round
In-conference offense: 1.12 points per possession (2nd)

In-conference defense: 0.99 points allowed per possession (2nd)

What Duke did well: *Change its style.*

It's not unusual for a team to overhaul its offensive system, but these cases almost always involve a coaching change. One of last season's biggest transformations, however, took place in Durham under the guidance of the coach who currently holds the third-longest active tenure at his school. (Impress your friends by knowing that the two men currently ahead of Coach K are Jim Boeheim and Sacred Heart's Dave Bike.)

Last season, no power-conference team changed its tempo more than Duke, which added nearly eight possessions to its average pace in ACC games. Additionally, no team reduced its turnover rate more than the Blue Devils, who committed five fewer giveaways per 100 conference possessions. Sure, part of the change was driven by personnel, with a roster nearly devoid of big men. But it wasn't an obvious decision to go small. Mike Krzyzewski was giving a scholarship to 7-1 Brian Zoubek. Although Zoubek won't draw comparisons to Shelden Williams or Carlos Boozer, he's not a total project, either.

The up-tempo version of Duke struggled in the postseason, losing in the ACC tournament semifinals to Clemson and surviving a scare from 15-seed Belmont in the first round of the NCAA tournament before losing to West Virginia rather convincingly. But up to that point, Duke had put together a season that was as dominant as that of any other team that didn't get a one-seed.

What we learned in 2008: *Duke needs to change its dependence on the three-point shot.*

Given the consecutive first-week exits from the NCAA tournament, one has to wonder if this team has something fundamentally wrong that needs fixing before a Final Four appearance is a legitimate expectation again. In 2007, turnovers were the issue on both sides of the ball, but that leak was plugged last season with the smaller lineup. The lack of size naturally left a void in the rebounding department, especially on the defensive end. This was a weakness exploited religiously by West Virginia.

But what made Duke's trip through the postseason a risky one was its reliance on three-pointers. Of the teams seeded 12th or better, only these teams took a higher percentage of their shots from beyond the arc: Butler, Drake, Georgetown, Oregon, UNLV, Davidson, and Temple. Most of these teams were seeded worse than Duke, but even when considering seed, only Davidson was a success story.

What's in store for 2009

Barring a more prominent role for Zoubek, the rebounding problems aren't going away. The good news is the core returns from a team that went 28-6 and did enough good things on the floor to compensate for too frequently allowing second shots. The Blue Devils lose DeMarcus Nelson, who started 74 games in his four seasons in Durham, and Taylor King, a reserve swingman who transferred to Villanova after struggling to get minutes despite being a prolific scorer when he did play. This team should play similar to last season's, though the incoming trio of freshman should make Duke marginally less dependent on the long ball.

MEET THE BLUE DEVILS

Kyle Singler (6-8, 220, So.). As a freshman, Singler was right there with DeMarcus Nelson and Gerald Henderson as Duke's most consistent scoring threat. He's not going to impress anyone with his shooting accuracy—it was a mundane 53 eFG percent and 34 percent from three-point range. Singler's game is not reminiscent of someone you would call "big," but he was often the tallest player on the floor for Duke. His rebounding, however, is substandard for a power forward and especially a center, the two positions he was asked to play last season.

Gerald Henderson (6-4, 210, Jr.). Henderson took on the scoring load early in the season, but eventually came down to earth as the level of competition increased. After the December 20 loss to Pitt, Henderson had taken a whopping 18.8 shots per 40 minutes of playing time. For games played in calendar year 2008, that figure plummeted to 13.1.

Greg Paulus (6-1, 185, Sr.). Paulus gets a lot of credit for his leadership abilities from the point guard spot, but he doesn't get nearly enough credit for being one of the best three-point shooters in the college game. His 43.5 percent accuracy from long range over the last two seasons ranks him 17th out

of the 209 players who have taken at least 300 threes over that time.

Jon Scheyer (6-5, 180, Jr.). After Singler, Henderson, and Paulus, the rest of the returnees fall into the role-player category. Scheyer was an efficient fourth option for the Blue Devils. His midrange shooting is a bit suspect, but he gets to the line enough to make up for it.

Elliot Williams (6-4, 180, Fr.). Williams, regarded as the best player in Coach K's three-man incoming class, will get some of the minutes that DeMarcus Nelson leaves behind.

Miles Plumlee (6-10, 220, Fr.). Plumlee was originally headed to Stanford, but changed his mind after Trent Johnson took the head coaching job at LSU. With his size, he has a chance to get serious playing time, although he may need a year to add the muscle necessary to handle ACC centers.

Nolan Smith (6-2, 180, So.). As Duke's backup point guard, he got about 15 minutes a game last season. If Williams's game is as advertised, Smith's time is not likely to increase this season.

Lance Thomas (6-8, 220, Jr.). There was no ACC starter who shot less frequently than did Thomas. Despite being the team's best offensive rebounder, Thomas was a nonfactor on the defensive end. His sophomore season would have to be labeled a disappointment.

Brian Zoubek (7-1, 260, Jr.). Zoubek can grab offensive boards and block a few shots, but not enough to make up for his lack of footwork on the defensive end, which led to an astronomical foul rate. Still, for the second consecutive season, the stats suggested Zoubek deserved more than single-digit minutes per game.

Olek Czyz (6-7, 240, Fr.). Czyz is another freshman, and he'll be competing for bench minutes as a forward.

David McClure (6-6, 200, Sr.). A solid defensive and rebounding specialist during his sophomore season, McClure languished on the bench last season. When he did play, he shot even less often than Thomas.

Martynas Pocius (6-5, 190, Jr.). The Lithuanian took a redshirt last season after injuring an ankle in November. He played sparingly during his first two seasons, and there's no reason to think that will change this year.

Prospectus says

With everyone else back besides Nelson and King, the prognosis for 2009 is much like it was for 2008—Duke should finish in the top three of the ACC, but the prospects for a regular-season championship are a little worse, because of the lack of personnel changes at defending ACC champ UNC. Without a conventional presence at center, battling for a one-seed in March is probably a bit too much for this squad. Given what has happened in Durham the last two seasons, it's really not about what this team does between November and February, but whether the team's performance in March looks anything like it does in those other months.

FLORIDA STATE

2008: 19-15 (7-9 ACC)
Lost to Akron 65-60 (OT), NIT first round
In-conference offense: 1.00 points per possession (11th)
In-conference defense: 1.05 points allowed per possession (6th)

What Florida State did well: *Make free throws.*

For the second consecutive season, Florida State finished in the top 10 nationally in free-throw percentage. Last season, it made 77.3 percent of its attempts. The starting lineup was even better, with only Jason Rich (77.2) below 80 percent. Even with this demonstration of shooting touch, Florida State was merely an ordinary three-point shooting team in 2008. Two seasons ago, when the team shot 75.8 percent from the line, it was very accurate from beyond the arc.

The difference was not that Seminole players forgot how to shoot the three-ball, but that Al Thornton was no longer around to occupy the attention of opposing defenses and thereby create open looks for his teammates. No doubt, injuries and bad luck played a role in another mediocre season in Tallahassee, but the single most obvious reason for FSU's 7-9 season was a dip in its offensive efficiency.

And the reason for this was an increased dependency on the three-pointer which the Seminoles

made less often. The departure of the dynamic power forward is what started this chain of events in the first place. The ability to make free throws is merely window dressing for an effective offense. Ultimately, a team has to make shots from the field, and Florida State didn't do that nearly as often last season and they did in 2007.

What we learned in 2008: *Leonard Hamilton could use some good breaks.*

In 2007, Florida State may have ended an NCAA tournament drought that currently spans back to 1998 had Toney Douglas not suffered a wrist injury that forced him to miss five games in February. Four of those games were losses, three by a total of 10 points. It's possible FSU deserved to be in the tournament, anyway, but such is life on the bubble. Last season, the injury bug hit again late in the season, when starting guard Isaiah Swann tore his left ACL in early February. Hamilton also lost promising freshman center Solomon Alabi early in the season to injury. Who knows what would have happened with a healthy roster, but Seminole fans would have liked to have found out.

What's in store for 2009

Florida State loses three senior starters from last season's roster plus a key reserve in Julian Vaughn, so a few new faces are going to be making significant contributions this season. With that kind of turnover, one would have to consider it somewhat surprising if the Seminoles entered the at-large discussion this season. On the positive side, this season's team should feature the athleticism that has been a trademark of Hamilton's squads of late, but the basketball ability will probably need another season to develop to a level that can compete with the top teams in the ACC. While there is rising frustration among Seminole fans over the lack of an NCAA berth as Hamilton enters his seventh season in Tallahassee, remember that it took him eight seasons to get Miami to the tournament in his previous college coaching stint.

MEET THE SEMINOLES

Toney Douglas (6-1, 200, Sr.). Douglas has been the mark of consistency in his first three college seasons. He doesn't wow you in any particular category, but he does the things you expect out of a capable combo guard. He's a slightly above-average shooter and takes care of the ball pretty well. He got a steal about once in every 23 defensive possessions, which led the ACC.

Uche Echefu (6-9, 225, Sr.). Echefu is expected to exchange some of his minutes at center for time at power forward this season. He wisely took fewer three-pointers last season and in turn saw a rise in his appearances at the free-throw line, where he is remarkably accurate (81 percent last season) for a 6-9 player. He's an excellent finisher when he gets the ball close to the basket, but was more frequently a nonfactor against ACC competition.

Solomon Alabi (7-1, 241, Fr.). Alabi didn't see a minute of ACC action after being shelved with a stress fracture in his foot in December. In his 93 minutes of nonconference action, there's enough evidence to believe he has advanced beyond the project stage offensively. He blocked 11 shots during that time, and given his reputation as one of the more intimidating defensive big men out of high school, he'll be a capable eraser if he stays healthy.

Chris Singleton (6-9, 200, Fr.). This highly sought-after freshman should round out the front line. All accounts are that he has the athleticism to immediately compete at the ACC level.

Derwin Kitchen (6-4, 180, Jr.). Kitchen was one of the better juco prospects last season and will have a chance to start in the backcourt for Leonard Hamilton. He's not much of a three-point threat and is expected to end up being the third or fourth option on offense.

Ryan Reid (6-8, 237, Jr.). Reid was the team's best offensive rebounder, which was easily his most useful function offensively last season. He got to the free throw line a lot, considering he is usually the fifth choice on offense.

Xavier Gibson (6-11, 230, Fr.). Gibson is another big man who will give the Seminoles some athleticism up front.

Jordan DeMercy (6-7, 204, So.). DeMercy only got about 10 minutes per game last season as he struggled to adjust to the college game.

Prospectus says
Douglas is easily the most well-known quantity of this group, but he's going to need contributions from Singleton, Alabi, and Kitchen for the offense to improve to an acceptable level. So much of Hamilton's offense is dependent on players creating open shots off the dribble, and without an inside game to be respected, that will be difficult. On the other side of the ball, if Alabi can play a full season, the defense should remain in the middle of the ACC pack or perhaps even improve a little. Barring a couple of major surprises from the newcomers, this is a season that will require a fair amount of patience from 'Nole fans.

GEORGIA TECH

2008: 15-17 (7-9 ACC)
Lost to Duke 82-70, ACC quarterfinal
In-conference offense: 1.06 points per possession (5th)
In-conference defense: 1.06 points allowed per possession (8th)

What Georgia Tech did well: *Foul.*
It's not the most commendable trait, but fouling is what Georgia Tech excelled at. The Yellow Jackets gave 4.5 fouls per player minute, more than any other power conference team. (The national average is around 3.7.) They had a ways to go to reach national leader Texas State (5.46), but then again, the Ramblin' Wreck isn't playing at the breakneck pace the Bobcats are. Naturally, you can give a lot of fouls when you have a deep bench, which Paul Hewitt had last season. It looks as if he won't have this luxury in 2009, so the foul rate will have to drop.

What we learned in 2008: *One-and-dones can have a negative effect on a program.*
Think about it. Most programs that play the one-and-done game don't regret it. In hindsight, would Kansas State not go after Michael Beasley? Would Ohio State rather have done without Greg Oden (and Mike Conley, for that matter)? How about USC and O. J. Mayo? Most situations involving a one-and-done result in some kind of short-term boost to the quality of the program. That boost offsets whatever issues might arise as a result of an unexpected departure. (Of course, in truth, none of those departures were unexpected. But consider the pre-one-and-done-era example of LSU and Tyrus Thomas. Yes, John Brady ultimately lost his job within two years

of Thomas's leaving, but he got a trip to the Final Four that season, which probably would not have occurred otherwise.)

I will submit, though, that the experience of Georgia Tech with Thaddeus Young and Javaris Crittenton didn't turn out that well. With this duo leading the team through the 2007 season, Tech did get to the NCAA tournament, but only as a 10-seed, and it would lose its first-round game. The tandem's exit in the offseason left Hewitt scrambling to fill his backcourt last season and meant guys like Lewis Clinch suddenly had to fill a new role as go-to guy. There wasn't a short-term gain, and the roster changes caused at least a one-season setback in the quality of the program. The only benefit is that Hewitt can tell future recruits that he's coached a couple of guys in the NBA. It's something, sure, but it doesn't seem like enough.

What's in store for 2009

For every season but one of Paul Hewitt's tenure in Atlanta, the Yellow Jackets have ended the ACC regular season with between seven and nine wins. If that happens again, it would have to be considered a good season. Georgia Tech loses two of its best offensive players in Anthony Morrow and Jeremis Smith from last year's club. In addition, Ra'Sean Dickey, who took a redshirt last season after sitting out due to an academic suspension for the fall semester and an injured knee in the second semester, decided to play for pay in Europe rather than fight for playing time in a do-over of his senior year. Georgia Tech's strength should skew a little more defensive this season, although it's not as if the team will have no offensive weapons. Both point guard Maurice Miller and power forward Zack Peacock are capable scorers. Hewitt will depend on having much of the half-court offense go through them, along with sophomore center Gani Lawal.

MEET THE YELLOW JACKETS

Zack Peacock (6-8, 235, Jr.). He is one of the more likely breakout candidates in college hoops this season. Peacock didn't make a single start last year and didn't play much more than he did in 2007, but nearly every aspect of his game took a major step forward. Most importantly, he found a way to get his shot off more often. In fact, much more often. His increased accuracy in doing so indicates

that Peacock will be well suited to become Hewitt's go-to guy on offense in 2009.

Maurice Miller (6-1, 181, So.). If there was an obvious flaw to the Jackets offense last season, it was the turnover rate of the point guards. Between "Moe" Miller and his backup, senior Matt Causey, the Tech point men averaged four turnovers per game. Now, they also had the best assist rates in the conference, so it's not as if the point guards were incompetent. Given the losses of Anthony Morrow and Jeremis Smith, Miller will be counted on to play more minutes and provide more offense this season. He showed good shooting aptitude last season, and his decision making was acceptable, considering his youth.

Gani Lawal (6-8, 218, So.). Lawal was effective in his freshman season, showing the ability to grab offensive boards, get to the free-throw line, and block shots. He was an effective scorer, which is a little surprising for an undersized center. Holding him back from more accolades are poor free-throw shooting (just under 50 percent) and a high turnover rate. The latter should improve with experience.

Lewis Clinch (6-3, 195, Sr.). Getting his minutes at shooting guard, Clinch struggled with his shot last season, making just 27 percent of his three-point shots in ACC play and 33 percent overall. The big weakness in Clinch's game is an inability to score in traffic. Thus, he rarely gets to the free-throw line, even though he took half of his shots inside the arc.

D'Andre Bell (6-5, 210, Sr.). Bell's value is on the defensive end. He is generally the fifth option offensively when he's on the floor.

Iman Shumpert (6-4, 185, Fr.). Shumpert is the lone freshman on the squad this season and will be sharing time at the two-guard with Clinch, although Shumpert can play the point as well.

Alade Aminu (6-10, 225, Sr.). The tallest of the Yellow Jackets, Aminu brings to the table many of the same skills that Lawal does. Aminu's specialty is a low turnover rate, which is surprising for a big man who at first glance isn't the most polished on the offensive end.

Lance Storrs (6-4, 212, So.). Storrs was brought to Atlanta to make threes, but went just 4-of-24 in limited duty (about seven minutes per game) last season. He'll get a few more minutes this season.

Bassirou Dieng (6-9, 215, Sr.). Dieng transferred from a woeful Saint Francis (Pa.) team over the summer, and because of complicated NCAA academic rules, he earned a waiver to be able to play for Hewitt this season. Dieng will be the extremely rare case of a player suiting up for three Division I teams during his career. He played his freshman season at Norfolk State. At his previous two stops, he was a big-time foul magnet. His rebounding improved dramatically last season.

Prospectus says

Between Miller, Peacock, and Lawal, the lineup has enough guys who can provide offense. Lawal, in particular, is one to watch, having shown the unusual freshman attribute of taking on a heavy load offensively. If he can cut down on the turnovers and improve at the line, the offense won't be in bad shape.

MARYLAND

2008: 19-15 (8-8 ACC)
Lost to Syracuse 88-72, NIT second round
In-conference offense: 1.04 points per possession (7th)
In-conference defense: 1.04 points allowed per possession (5th)

What Maryland did well: *Defend the paint.*

The Terps didn't have twin towers in the traditional sense, but by playing James Gist and Bambale Osby side by side, Maryland did have twin towers functionally even though each player only measures 6-8. Both were among the best shot blockers in the conference, and as a team, Maryland blocked a higher percentage of opponents' twos than did all but seven other teams in the nation.

What we learned in 2008: *National titles create expectations that last a while.*

I got a little chuckle out of something Gary Williams said over the summer. After lamenting the sagas of a couple of would-be freshmen this season (more on that in a moment) in Maryland's student newspaper, the *Diamondback*, he also sort of lamented being a national champion: "You get judged here at Maryland if you win a national championship; at a lot of places your bar is set differently." I do believe

Williams was engaging in a bit of hyperbole here, but from the general vibe I get from Maryland fans, he's not far off. They may not expect national titles, but they'd like to at least consider the idea from time to time.

The facts speak for themselves, though. There have been 70 NCAA tournaments, and Maryland has won a total of one national title. Even if we don't take Williams's comment literally and do set the bar a little lower, the story isn't much different. Maryland has been to the regional finals just four times. (Granted, Lefty Driesell had a few pretty awesome teams that didn't even make the NCAA tournament in the days when all that mattered was winning three games in the ACC tournament to qualify. Everything else was irrelevant.)

The point is that Williams is the victim of his own success. Twenty years ago, he basically inherited a team that was banned from postseason play, and he eventually led the program to a national title. Now, the Terrapins are struggling even to appear in the NCAA tournament, let alone win games there. That trend will probably continue in 2009. Whether or not he's the person to run the program beyond that will be up for debate, but it figures that once you've managed a couple decades at one job in college basketball, you've done something right. And at that point, it takes more than a few mediocre seasons for an athletic director to take action.

What's in store for 2009

The anchors of the defense and, to some extent, the offense—Gist and Bambale—were seniors last season, and so Maryland will be going with a more inexperienced and less heralded lineup. It wasn't supposed to be this way, at least on the latter attribute. Williams was interested in juco point guard Bobby Maze but became skittish about academic issues. (Maze ended up at Tennessee.) Then Williams signed juco standout Tyree Evans, but once news of the shooting guard's criminal history (among other run-ins with the law, he once did time for possession of marijuana) was publicized and became a contentious topic in D.C.-area media outlets, Evans decided that attending Maryland wouldn't be a good idea.

Then there's the saga of Gus Gilchrist. The 6-9 player from suburban Maryland committed to the program last fall after being released from his letter of intent at Virginia Tech. He would have started once eligible, but even though he didn't play a game for the Hokies, he was still subject to ACC transfer rules, which required that he sit out the first semester. Once Gilchrist got wind of that, he decided that Maryland wouldn't be a good fit for him, either. Williams's recruiting class was severely damaged by those incidents, and in a season for which he needs to replace two critical starters, he suddenly finds his team to be very thin.

MEET THE TERRAPINS

Greivis Vasquez (6-6, 190, Jr.). Vasquez got less rest than any other player in the ACC last season, sitting about three minutes per game on average. Don't expect that to change this season. Nobody else on the roster can do what Vasquez does. He can play either guard position while using a lot of possessions fairly efficiently, and he's a solid defender. Maryland's three-point defense has improved greatly since Vasquez joined the program, and he has something to do with that. He's turnover prone and an average shooter, but on an offensively challenged team, he'll be better than the alternatives.

Sean Mosley (6-5, 210, Fr.). Mosley is the most accomplished freshman on the team and should move right into the starting lineup as a two-guard.

Eric Hayes (6-4, 184, Jr.). Hayes took over as a starter in the backcourt last season. He posted a 39 percent mark from three-point range in each of his first two seasons and takes most of his field-goal attempts from beyond the arc. Maryland's three most heralded players are guards, so Williams is expected to play a three-guard lineup often. Given the size of these guys, it's not a lineup that should be called small, though.

Landon Milbourne (6-7, 207, Jr.). Milbourne went from appearing solely in garbage time as a freshman to a starter as a sophomore. He was an offensive lurker as Vasquez, Gist, and Osby went about their business. He's going to have to improve his defensive rebounding this season.

Cliff Tucker (6-6, 190, So.). Tucker had a solid freshman season off the bench. He hit 55 percent of his twos in a limited role.

Braxton Dupree (6-8, 260, So.). Dupree was Williams's best offensive rebounder last season, and

of the three freshmen who saw significant playing time, he was the most likely to get involved in the offense. Sometimes, this was a problem since he only shot 38 percent on twos.

Adrian Bowie (6-2, 190, So.). Bowie is yet another sophomore who will have greater responsibilities in 2009. Though he doesn't take many threes for a guard, he made 61 percent of his twos, so more power to him. He has had a frighteningly high turnover rate.

Jerome Burney (6-9, 222, So.). Burney didn't see a lot of time last season, but he did get double-digit minutes in each of the Terps' last four conference games. It was a brief look, but Burney showed he could rebound and block shots. He may even be an effective scorer.

A player to be named later. With the offseason recruiting fiascos, Williams was more active than any other high-profile coach this summer, trying to fill scholarships for the upcoming season. Considering that his team likes to play at a very fast pace, it's possible another player or two will make contributions this season. Holdovers from last season include **Dino Gregory (6-7, 227, So.)** and **Dave Neal (6-7, 263, Sr.)**, but as of press time, Williams was also trying to bring in **Steve Goins (6-10, 250, Fr.)** and Korean-born **Jin Soo Kim (6-8, 180, Fr.)**, the latter freshman allegedly the first Korean to play Division I ball. Both Goins's and Kim's eligibility, however, is pending at press time.

Prospectus says

There are a lot of question marks for Maryland this season. Vasquez is steady, but he's going to need some help, and where that assistance is going to come from isn't clear. Terps fans who judge success in national titles will be disappointed this season. Patience will be required to get through the 2009 season without too much criticism of Williams.

2008: 23-11 (8-8 ACC)
Lost to Texas 75-72, NCAA second round
In-conference offense: 1.06 points per possession (4th)
In-conference defense: 1.08 points allowed per possession (9th)

What Miami did well: *Make free throws.*

Much like their ACC neighbors to the north, the Hurricanes were one of the best free-throw-shooting teams in the nation. Their starters were nearly automatic, making a phenomenal 84.7 percent of their freebies, leading the nation.

Top free-throw percentage by starters,* 2008

Miami FL	84.7
Houston	83.6
Cornell	83.4
Utah Valley St.	82.1
Missouri St.	81.2

*Starters defined as top five players by minutes played.

What we learned in 2008: *Frank Haith is a hell of a coach.*

Hypothetically, if you were the athletic director of a power-conference school and you had, say, a wealthy oil-magnate as your most prominent booster and he was willing to give you a blank check to hire a coach at an unprecedented salary, whom would you target? You *could* go after Bill Self, who just won a national title at Kansas, and if successful, you couldn't go wrong. I felt good for Self, who seemed to get unnecessary criticism of his coaching abilities because he didn't have a national title on his résumé. He's a great coach, for sure, but let's face it, at Kansas, he has more tradition and resources to work with than does just about any other college coach in America.

Then there's Frank Haith, who just took Miami to the NCAA tournament and even won a game there. In absolute terms, Haith's accomplishment pales to Self's. But in relative terms, considering the tradition and resources of Miami—this was a program that didn't exist for most of the 1970s and 1980s—there's not a huge difference. Miami fans, rare as they are, need to appreciate what they have. If he manages to lead the 'Canes to a single-digit seed this season, there should be a few prominent programs seriously considering him as their coach for 2010.

What's in store for 2009

Stability is the operative word in Coral Gables, where Miami brings back four starters and adds an impact freshman in DeQuan Jones. There's the potential here for the offense to be very good. Last season, the Hurricanes were ninth in conference play in effective field-goal percentage. That should improve,

if only because both departing seniors Anthony King and Raymond Hicks were below 50 percent in that category. With Jones and Dwayne Collins picking up most of the minutes that those two left behind, expect a significant improvement in shooting accuracy, especially inside the arc, which was the Hurricanes' primary weakness in 2008.

MEET THE HURRICANES

Jack McClinton (6-1, 185, Sr.). McClinton burst onto the national scene with a 38-point performance in a first-round tournament win over Saint Mary's. But McClinton's performance in his two seasons in the ACC has provided a steady track record to judge him on. He's a 40-plus percent shooter from three-point-land, and even though he's been more accurate from outside the arc than inside it, his penetration produces enough trips to the free-throw line, where he's a sure thing, that he's dangerous whether spotting up or attacking.

Dwayne Collins (6-8, 238, Jr.). Most Miami previews you'll read this fall are some variation of "Jack McClinton this, Jack McClinton that." My tea leaves tell me that if Miami gets to the NCAA tournament for the second consecutive season, pretourney previews will be more about Collins. Collins saw his playing time dip in his sophomore campaign as senior center Anthony King returned from injury to start every game last year. So Collins is still a pretty obscure player in the ACC, let alone nationally. Here's the thing—there was no Hurricane more productive per minute played than Collins. Either offensively or defensively. The good news for 'Canes fans is that Haith has no choice but to play him more this season. King is no longer around, and there's little competition for the center position. Collins could stand to improve his free-throw shooting—he made exactly half his attempts last season—because he will get fouled a lot. Just about everything else about his game is going to cause migraines for opponents.

DeQuan Jones (6-6, 190, Fr.). Jones figures to make a splash immediately as one of the nation's top-rated small forward recruits.

James Dews (6-3, 208, Jr.). Dews was the only player besides McClinton more likely to take a three than a two, and he also was quite accurate, making

37 percent. His offense is more limited to long-range shooting than McClinton's, however.

Brian Asbury (6-7, 223, Sr.). Asbury has a diverse offensive game, considering he doesn't take a ton of shots. He's a threat to score from anywhere on the floor.

Lance Hurdle (6-2, 181, Sr.). Hurdle was part of a three-guard lineup that Haith used frequently last season, especially down the stretch. With the addition of Jones, Miami should play bigger more often, which would mean that Hurdle and Dews won't be sharing the court as often. Hurdle made just 31 percent of his two-point attempts last season. Fortunately, he's a very good free-throw shooter.

Jimmy Graham (6-8, 251, Sr.). Graham is an outstanding rebounder who also has a penchant for getting to the free-throw line.

Reggie Johnson (6-9, 290, Fr.). A true center, Johnson should provide some rebounding help when he's in the game.

Eddie Rios (6-0, 193, So.). Rios is the closest thing to a pure point guard that Miami has. He was often overwhelmed during his freshman season, but did get 14 minutes a game to help his learning curve.

Cyrus McGowan (6-9, 235, Jr.). McGowan joins the team as a transfer from Arkansas. He's going to compete for bench minutes in the middle, also. He didn't play much at Arkansas, so don't expect him to have a huge impact in the ACC right away.

Julian Gamble (6-9, 242, Fr.). Gamble redshirted last season, but is in the wide-open battle for remaining minutes at center.

Adrian Thomas (6-7, 224, Jr.). Sadly, Thomas has played just eight games the last two seasons, missing the 2007 campaign with an abdominal injury and last season due to a torn ACL.

Prospectus says
About 99.5 percent of Division I teams would love to have an inside-outside combo like McClinton and Collins. And while the players around them have some questions, the fact that two guys should provide 50 percent of the offense when they're in the game, and do it efficiently, means that life will be that much easier for the supporting players. It's important to remember where this team is coming from, though. An impressive NCAA tournament appearance notwithstanding, this was an average ACC team in 2008. An improvement should be expected, and if Collins and Jones can play to their potential, double-digit wins in conference is realistic.

NORTH CAROLINA

2008: 36-3 (14-2 ACC)
Lost to Kansas 84-66, NCAA Final Four
In-conference offense: 1.14 points per possession (1st)
In-conference defense: 0.99 points allowed per possession
  (3rd)

What North Carolina did well: *Lots of things.*
Normally, this space is reserved for that single and often underappreciated trait that a team excelled at. In UNC's case, there really wasn't anything that slipped under the radar. What was underappreciated was that the Heels did everything well offensively, at least as far as the Four Factors are concerned. Most great offenses are kind of blah in one category, but not Carolina. The Tar Heels shot very well, didn't commit turnovers, grabbed more of their own misses than did any other team in the land, and made a bunch of free throws. It's no surprise, then, that their offense was arguably (with deference to Kansas) the best in the nation last season.

What we learned in 2008: *Ty Lawson is a necessary ingredient for UNC's offense to maintain greatness.*
UNC point guard Ty Lawson missed all or most of eight games due to injuries last season. Six of those were conference games, with the other two opponents being BYU and Ohio State, who it's safe to assume were ACC-level competition. Against conference opponents, with Lawson, UNC scored 1.15 points per possession. In those eight games without him, the figure dropped to 1.07. (Interestingly, UNC's defense improved without Lawson by nearly an equal amount.)

What's in store in 2009
I think this team will win a few games. It has some up-and-comers who are going to surprise some people. And watch this Hansbrough kid—he really plays hard.

OK, seriously, the Tar Heels have just about everyone back from a team that was a one-seed and advanced to the Final Four. All the other one-seeds from last season lost significant components of their success. I mean, I assume you didn't start reading this book to learn that Carolina should be the best team in the land this season. Note that this isn't the *exact* team from last season. Reserve forward Alex Stepheson transferred to Southern Cal in the offseason, and backup point guard Quentin Thomas was a senior. Those changes, combined with another highly rated recruiting class, mean that up to three freshmen will see a few minutes (or more) of playing time this season. It's not inconceivable that even with the Tar Heels maintaining their health, the first guy off the bench will be a freshman (most likely 6-10 Ed Davis).

MEET THE TAR HEELS

Tyler Hansbrough (6-9, 250, Sr.). It doesn't take long to get caught up in the repeated praising of Hansbrough's effort. Typically, when a player's most-noted ability is his effort, it means that he's not all that effective. That is not the case with Hansbrough. The primary source of his production is his ability to get to the free-throw line as frequently as anyone in the nation, even when you account for his large number of minutes on a team that plays at the fastest pace among power-conference teams. Throw in his ability to make 81 percent of those freebies and his miniscule turnover rate, and you have a recipe for a consistent scoring machine who shoots a good-but-not-amazing 55 percent from the field.

Ty Lawson (5-11, 195, Jr.). Of the three Tar Heels to float their names into the NBA draft last summer, Lawson had the best claim to keep his in. Some question his ability to finish, but he posted a 58 percent shooting mark from two-point range. Of course, many of those attempts were on the fast break and not the result of penetration from a half-court set, but regardless, no college player under six feet shot as well inside the arc while taking at least 100 attempts. (Players under six feet shot a collective 43 percent on twos last season.)

Wayne Ellington (6-4, 200, Jr.). As Lawson's side-kick, Ellington does the things you want your shooting guard to do. He made 40 percent of his threes, but didn't settle for the shot, taking over half his attempts from inside the arc. Again, the fast-break attempts skew this figure a little, but more detailed data indicates his midrange game is passable. Ellington gets to the line infrequently for someone who's not simply spotting up for threes all the time.

Danny Green (6-6, 210, Sr.). Green has sported an impressive combination of blocks and steals since his freshman season, but last season, his offensive game took a leap forward. He extended his range to beyond the three-point line, but there's still a significant hole in his game between the arc and layup-land. Still, if he manages to shoot 37 percent on three-pointers again, Carolina fans should be thrilled.

Deon Thompson (6-8, 240, Jr.). Thompson was pretty consistent all season. He's not going to be confused with the above four players in terms of offensive ability, but he held his own against other ACC big men. He's the team's best shot blocker, but a little foul prone, too.

Marcus Ginyard (6-5, 220, Sr.). Ginyard has developed a reputation as a defensive stopper. Offensively, he's usually the fifth option on the floor.

Ed Davis (6-10, 220, Fr.). With all the talent returning, Davis is a forgotten freshman. Still, he apparently holds the qualities to thrive in Williams's system, and he can block shots to boot. Seeing how Thompson averaged a little more than 20 minutes a game last season, there is playing to be had along the front line.

Bobby Frasor (6-3, 210, Sr.). Frasor is the lone Tar Heel whose main purpose is to shoot three-pointers. It's surprising, then, that he's only made 32 percent of his attempts in his career. Last season, he tore an ACL in a late December game against Nevada and didn't play again.

Tyler Zeller (7-0, 220, Fr.). Despite the lankiness, Zeller is touted as being able to keep up in a fast-paced system. His brother Luke plays at Notre Dame, which means that two UNC players have brothers playing for the Irish (along with Hansbrough's brother Ben).

Larry Drew (6-1, 180, Fr.). The third freshman expected to get playing time, Drew is going to get some minutes at least by virtue of his status as one of two true point guards on the roster.

Will Graves (6-6, 245, So.). Graves's playing time steadily increased last season, and he made good use of the opportunities by providing a rarely seen combination of three-point shooting touch (44 percent) and impressive rebounding from an undersized player.

Prospectus says

This is the best collection of talent in the game this season. But let's check the hype at the door for a moment. On paper, the Tar Heels don't seem to be as dominant as 2007 Florida or even 2005 UNC does. This team will lose some games, probably three or four. Collectively, the other 300-plus teams eligible for the national championship have a better chance of winning it all than Carolina. Still, there's no doubt that before a game is played, Carolina rightfully has the best chance of any team, and there's not a close second.

Most seasons, however, aren't like last year, when the October consensus of the four best teams makes it to the Final Four, or 2005, when the two best teams identified by January played in the final game. Most seasons contain surprises for college basketball's elite. There will be a lot of ups for UNC this season, but there will also be a few downs. When those downs occur will define how this season is remembered.

NORTH CAROLINA STATE

2008: 15-16 (4-12 ACC)
Lost to Miami (Fla.) 63-50, ACC first round
In-conference offense: 1.01 points per possession (10th)
In-conference defense: 1.15 points allowed per possession
    (12th)

What NC State did well: *Defend the three-point line.*

If you've read the ACC previews in order, then you already know that Duke and Clemson are the kings at making opponents score two at a time. The Wolfpack, though, was also one of the best in the country at preventing three-point attempts. The problem was that when teams did decide to shoot from long range, they were often successful, making a better-

than-average 37 percent of their attempts. This figure led many to lament NC State's inability to defend the three-point shot.

True, it would help to get more opponents' shots to miss. But State did about as well as it could to limit its opponents' opportunities, which is just as important, considering that the opposition made just 44 percent of its two-point attempts during the season. The real problem for Sidney Lowe's defense is that it rarely forces turnovers and it allows far too many second shots, especially for the team's size. These things need to improve if this team is to get its defense back to an average level.

What we learned in 2008: *Expectations can change in a hurry.*

The ACC media picked NC State to finish third in the conference before the season began. The national media ranked the Pack 21st in the preseason AP poll. It's fair to say that the consensus across the country was that this team was capable of making some noise. Yet sometime between early November and, oh, around mid-January, it became rather obvious that little noise would be made. To put it in perspective, State was the highest-ranked team in that preseason poll to miss postseason play. Actually, the next 19 highest vote getters after the Wolfpack would play in one of the postseason tournaments. So what went wrong?

Two things, J. J. Hickson and the need for a point guard. In fact, Hickson himself didn't go wrong. He was as good as advertised as a freshman. But it's difficult to think of another player so effective on both ends of the floor whose impact on the team was a net negative. Hickson scored most of his points in the paint, but was capable of scoring from anywhere. He rebounded very well on a team that desperately needed that. But both Brandon Costner and Ben McCauley, who had been the focal point offensively in 2007, saw their production drop dramatically. And thus as a team, NC State actually took a step back between 2007 and 2008.

What's in store for 2009

With Hickson joining the one-and-done crowd, the Pack will be without a true post man, as it was in Lowe's rookie season at the helm in 2007. Lowe has spoken of playing at a faster pace, but last season's team was only about a possession-and-a-half slower per game than it was in 2007, so there probably won't be a big change this season.

MEET THE WOLFPACK

Brandon Costner (6-9, 231, Jr.). Costner's junior-year productivity will probably be somewhere between his sophomore slump and his freshman freak-out. His shots were from farther away last season, but in any case, he shot worse, even accounting for that. Without Hickson, he'll get better shots and more of them. He came into last season out of shape after recovering from an offseason knee injury, which may have hampered his performance. Still, Costner's freshman season suggested he would be a first-team all-ACC type of player by his junior season, and given how sensitive he appears to be to his surroundings, those expectations are a little unrealistic.

Courtney Fells (6-6, 210, Sr.). Along with senior Gavin Grant, Fells was the only returning player who progressed in Hickson's presence. He made 39 percent of his threes and 57 percent of his twos. He should get more minutes as a small forward this season (he was almost exclusively a two-guard last year).

Ben McCauley (6-9, 237, Sr.). There were 753 players who took at least 100 two-point shots in both 2007 and 2008, and only one had a bigger drop in accuracy than did McCauley, who went from 59 percent to 44 percent. Part of the explanation, as with Costner, has to do with shot difficulty. McCauley got fewer bunnies than in 2007. But his midrange game fell apart. Expect it to improve, of course, but a return to flirting with the 60 percent mark is wishful thinking.

Farnold Degand (6-3, 185, Jr.). Degand is the de facto starter at the point. He struggled in the 10 games he played before the injury, but that wasn't shocking, considering he had little game experience coming into last season.

Julius Mays (6-2, 188, Fr.). Mays doesn't have the credentials of someone who is expected to be a starting point guard in this conference as a freshman. But given the Wolfpack's need for solid point guard play, if Mays progresses faster than expected, don't be surprised if he finds himself getting serious minutes during conference play.

C. J. Williams (6-5, 203, Fr.). Williams is a swingman who will fight for a few minutes among the numerous players on the squad with experience at the two or three spots.

Tracy Smith (6-8, 240, So.). Smith averaged less than nine minutes per game and didn't even appear in 11 games due to his coach's decision. Smith's stats during the limited time suggest he deserved better, especially since most of his time on the floor was during conference play. He is a reasonably accurate shooter, rarely commits turnovers, and gets to the line a lot. There has to be room for him near the top of Lowe's frontline rotation.

Trevor Ferguson (6-5, 190, Jr.). Ferguson is a three-point threat who made 14 of his 35 attempts (40 percent) last season.

Dennis Horner (6-9, 218, Jr.). Horner, a reluctant shooter from the small forward spot, takes about 40 percent of his shots from beyond the arc.

Javier Gonzalez (5-11, 172, So.). I'm not the first to suggest that an injury's effect on a team is usually short-term pain and long-term gain. Gonzalez wasn't ready to be a starting point guard in the ACC last season, but he got 15 starts as a result of Degand's injury. The statistical record confirmed Gonzalez's struggles, but perhaps the extra minutes against the likes of Ty Lawson, Sean Singletary, and Tyrese Rice accelerated his development. (Of note: NC State officially lists Gonzalez, Degand, and McCauley an inch shorter than last season. Here's hoping there's not an osteoporosis epidemic on campus.)

Johnny Thomas (6-5, 203, Fr.). Thomas was expected to contribute last season as a small forward, but severely injured a knee shortly after arriving on campus and didn't play.

Prospectus says

This team is essentially the 2007 team without Engin Atsur running the point. Atsur's presence was somewhat overrated in 2007. On the positive side, external expectations should be in check. If Lowe gets 2007 production from Costner and McCauley, this team could be in the at-large discussion. But while Hickson's loss might not be a bad thing for this team, the departure of forward Gavin Grant shouldn't be forgotten. He had become a reliable offensive player and wasn't affected at all by Hickson's arrival. The worst-case scenario is that Costner and

McCauley's slump had nothing to do with Hickson, and if that's the case, this team won't have a single dependable scorer.

VIRGINIA

2008: 17-16 (5-11 ACC)
Lost to Bradley 96-85, CBI semifinal
In-conference offense: 1.03 points per possession (8th)
In-conference defense: 1.09 points allowed per possession (10th)

What Virginia did well: *Get balance on offense.*

Sean Singletary gave the Cavaliers just about everything they had on offense last season. What was left over was spread out equally among the remaining players who shared the floor with him. This presents as interesting situation for the post-Singletary era. Who exactly will step forward to pick up all those possessions in which Singletary was so influential over the past three seasons? Based on last season's experience, it could be anyone. (OK, probably not Jerome Meyinsse.) Of course, it doesn't have to be a single player. There's no law in hoops that you have to have a star. The face of Virginia basketball must change this season, but it most likely will be a multifaced mosaic that defines what this team can do.

What we learned in 2008: *Great players can play for less-than-great teams.*

This doesn't come up in college hoops as much as in other sports, but it is an issue from time to time. The theory is that a player who doesn't lead his team to wins can't be that good. It says a lot about what Michael Beasley accomplished that he was even considered for national player-of-the-year honors while playing for a team that could grasp only an 11-seed in the NCAA tournament. Since tournament seeding began in 1979, the lowest-seeded team to produce an AP player of the year winner was the ninth-seeded Bradley team from 1988. That team had national scoring leader Hersey Hawkins, and it took 36.3 points a game for him to do it.

Anyway, *great player* in the context of the 2008 UVa basketball team, of course, refers to Singletary. The point isn't that he should have been national player of the year, but that his being overlooked for any All-American honors had more to do with his supporting cast than himself. The following point guards made one of the AP's first three teams: D. J. Augustin, Darren Collison, and Derrick Rose. If you replaced Singletary on the Virginia roster with any of those three, I have to doubt that the season would have turned out much differently.

They may have won two or three more conference games, but they weren't going to the NCAA tournament. Under that scenario, I don't think any of the three would have been an All-American, either. You look at what those three did on the floor, and it wasn't much different from what Singletary did. Singletary wasn't perfect, of course. He was notoriously poor at finishing in traffic. But he had just about every other trait you want in your All-American point guard.

What's in store for 2009

I would imagine most Virginia fans were not looking forward to the day they had to have someone running the point who would actually make mistakes and not be fully capable of carrying a team through the closing minutes of a close contest. But that day has arrived. The starting role figures to go to Sammy Zeglinski, who has just 62 minutes of college experience to rely on. He may turn into a solid point guard, and hey, it may even happen this season. But it's more likely that Virginia needs a lot more production from the other four positions to give its new point guard an easier transition to the college game.

MEET THE CAVALIERS

Mamadi Diane (6-5, 201, Sr.). Diane has progressed nicely in Charlottesville. His three-point percentage has gone from 24 to 35 to 41 in his three seasons. Extrapolate that trend for another season, and he should knock down about half his threes in 2009. OK, that's not how basketball really works. It's difficult to sustain 40 percent accuracy two seasons in a row. Regardless, Diane can shoot it and was second on the team in minutes, so he seems like the most likely player to lead the 'Hoos in scoring.

Mike Scott (6-8, 233, So.). Scott had an impressive freshman season in the rebounding department. He mainly stayed in the shadows on offense, although he did get to the line frequently and was rather sure-handed, considering his limited role.

Calvin Baker (6-2, 186, Jr.). Baker came over from William & Mary, and after shooting poorly in a starring role there, he was a nice spark off the bench with less pressure on him last season.

Sylven Landesberg (6-6, 209, Fr.). Just about every recruiting guru says Landesberg's best trait is his high "basketball IQ." It's almost as if there are Sylven Landesberg talking points floating around. If the game comes down to some sort of basketball SAT competition, then UVa will be in great shape. If it comes down to producing on the court, Landesberg appears to have the athleticism and body to provide quality minutes immediately.

Sammy Zeglinski (6-0, 175, Fr.). Zeglinski is following in Singletary's footsteps as point guard, which he's already done once before. Both attended the same high school in Philadelphia. Zeglinski played 62 minutes in eight nonconference games last season before undergoing ankle surgery. He's expected to be a pass-first (maybe pass-only) point guard in his first full season.

Jeff Jones (6-4, 193, So.). Jones struggled last season, but finished off the year with a 26-point/zero-turnover game in the CBI loss to Bradley.

Jamil Tucker (6-8, 241, Jr.). In Tucker's first two seasons, he's been a very good defensive rebounder and an efficient role player.

Raw freshmen big men and a do-over. Both **John Brandenburg (6-11, 225, Fr.)** and **Assane Sene (7-0, 226, Fr.)** bring size and perhaps some defense, but their offense is a work in progress. Although more experienced, any impact **Tunji Soroye (6-11, 252, Sr.)** will have will also be on defense. Soroye was granted a medical redshirt by the NCAA that allows him to have a do-over of his senior year after playing just two games last season due to a combination of knee and back injuries. All three will be suddenly thrust into a larger-than-expected role due to the August dismissal of Laurynas Mikalauskas, who figured to be a starter in the middle of the season.

Jerome Meyinsse (6-8, 245, Jr.). Meyinsse may be the team's second-best returning rebounder to Scott. He's limited on offense, though.

Prospectus says

This is Dave Leitao's first season in Charlottesville without one of the superguards (either Singletary or J. R. Reynolds) who he inherited from his predecessor, Pete Gillen. It's crucial that the Cavs play respectable defense because it's really hard to imagine where the points will come from. None of the returnees are skilled at creating their own shot. Landesberg could surprise, and Scott could blossom. That's the hope. But there have to be a lot more stops as well.

VIRGINIA TECH

2008: 21-14 (9-7 ACC)
Lost to Mississippi 81-72, NIT quarterfinal
In-conference offense: 0.99 points per possession (12th)
In-conference defense: 0.97 points allowed per possession (1st)

What Virginia Tech did well: *Defend.*
After losing Zabian Dowdell and Jamon Gordon to the professional ranks, I wouldn't have expected the Hokies to produce what turned out to be a dominant defense in 2008. Dowdell and Gordon were one of the best turnover-forcing duos in the game that season, and Tech had a good, but not great, defense. The simplest explanation for the lockdown defense last year is that freshman Jeff Allen's presence in the middle was a significant upgrade that more than offset what the senior guards brought to the table in 2007. But it seemed as if every frontline player who Seth Greenberg trotted out in a Hokies uniform was disruptive. Tech owned the paint. It forced a lot of two-point misses and grabbed the rebound when it did. It easily compensated for a small decrease in turnovers forced by the guards.

What we learned in 2008: *Replacing a senior backcourt with freshmen doesn't have to be the end of the world.*
Just about the entirety of Tech's backcourt minutes went to freshmen last season. The only significant exception was when junior A. D. Vassallo played the two. The seniors the younger players replaced weren't exclusively defensive stars. The freshmen

also led one of the steadiest backcourts in the game the previous season on a team that committed turnovers less frequently than all but three teams in Division I. There figured to be some transitional pains with the sudden lack of experience, but the season was far from a disaster.

The Hokies won nine conference games and bowed out of the ACC tournament in the semifinals only when Tyler Hansbrough hit a baseline jumper with under a second to go. Sure, it wasn't always pretty. In fact, it rarely was. The team's turnover rate ballooned, the offense suffered, and most of the credit for whatever success Virginia Tech achieved should certainly be given to the work done by the other three players on the floor. But the moral of last season's hoops story in Blacksburg was that you can replace senior guards with freshmen, even unheralded ones, and not necessarily have to wait until next year.

What's in store for 2009

The only loss from last year's team is Deron Washington, who won't be easy to replace. Washington was a disruptive defender in his own right and deserves almost as much credit as Allen does for the Hokies' defensive dominance. But while Washington was seemingly among the national leaders in highlight-reel dunks, he really struggled on offense in his senior season. Only his 219 free-throw attempts made him a marginally efficient player. Some combination of J.T. Thompson and Terrell Bell will pick up Washington's minutes, and seeing what the two sophomores did last season, they should be able to replace what Washington provided on both ends. Everything but the SportsCenter clips, that is.

MEET THE HOKIES

Jeff Allen (6-7, 240, So.). Allen's offensive game was difficult to watch at times last season. He doesn't have much touch and is a bit turnover prone. Still, the offense basically ran through him, especially when Vassallo was on the bench. Typically, players that involved will figure out how to score more efficiently. As mentioned above, Allen was a dominant defender. You won't see too many players as skilled at defensive rebounding, blocking shots, and grabbing steals as he was. In fact, there was only one player in this category last season who played at least half his team's minutes—Kent State defender extraordinaire Haminn Quaintance—but one could reasonably conclude that Allen did it against better competition. Allen gets in his share of foul trouble, as one might expect, but he was on the floor long enough to deserve a little more attention for his defensive impact.

A. D. Vassallo (6-6, 216, Sr.). Vassallo will never be described as a selective shooter. But it's for the best, as he's made 39 percent of his 468 three-point attempts during his three seasons in Blacksburg. He actually takes more twos than threes, but otherwise has all the characteristics of someone who shoots in bulk. He rarely commits turnovers, but also rarely attempts free throws.

Malcolm Delaney (6-3, 170, So.). As the starting two-guard, Delaney was a fine complementary player to the exploits of Allen, Vassallo, and Washington. He didn't shoot a lot, but he wasn't invisible, either, and he made 40 percent of his three-point attempts. He'll be asked to do a little more this season.

Hank Thorns (5-9, 160, So.). Thorns was the least frequent shooter among the starters, and for good reason, as he made less than 40 percent of his twos and less than 30 percent of his threes. He's a pass-first point guard who finished sixth in the ACC in assist rate but also struggled to avoid turnovers.

J. T. Thompson (6-6, 210, So.). The easiest way to describe Thompson is that he's a mini-Allen. He just does a little less than Allen in nearly every category you can think of.

Dorenzo Hudson (6-5, 220, So.). Hudson gained national notoriety by vomiting in the middle of a February game against Maryland. More relevant to this preview is that he was the third freshman guard on the team and one who struggled with his shot.

Victor Davila (6-8, 245, Fr.). Davila is expected to give the Hokies more depth up front.

Cheick Diakite (6-9, 217, Sr.). The long-armed Mali native has carved out a nifty role getting spot duty for three seasons now. His job: block shots. That's all he does, but he does it extremely well.

Terrell Bell (6-6, 205, So.). Bell averaged seven minutes a game last season at the wing, and he could stand to shoot it better if he'd like more time this season.

Lewis Witcher (6-9, 218, Jr.). For two consecutive seasons, Witcher has had a better rebounding percentage on the offense than defense. He's not too involved offensively, but he'll get his share of putbacks.

Prospectus says

An NCAA tournament appearance won't require that the offense get better, but it sure would help. Only two teams with a worse adjusted offensive efficiency than Tech's made the 2008 tournament field with a 12-seed or better. Of course, there's a difference between just making the tournament and having a team capable of winning a couple games in it. The latter will require a step forward on offense by the rising sophomores, especially Thompson and Delaney.

WAKE FOREST

2008: 17-13 (7-9 ACC)
Lost to Florida State 70-60, ACC first round
In-conference offense: 1.03 points per possession (9th)
In-conference defense: 1.06 points allowed per possession (7th)

What Wake Forest did well: *Have freshmen succeed.*
It's usually a good sign for your program when returning players get less playing time than they did the previous season. More precisely, it's a good sign if those returning players are actually working hard to improve their game, because it means that a newcomer has earned his minutes with his superior play.

Wake had not one, but two of those cases in 2008 with the arrival of shooting guard Jeff Teague and power forward James Johnson. L. D. Williams and Jamie Skeen were the players who saw their minutes drop as a result, but their team made an improvement. The situation could repeat itself in 2009 with two more positions on the floor being upgraded with new faces.

What we learned in 2008: *You can grow up in Wyoming and be a great basketball player.*
If James Johnson can develop a jump shot, the above statement will be true. Considering that a Wyoming native hasn't played in an NBA game in the last 40 years, this is no small accomplishment.

So, you kids in Casper, Afton, and Rock Springs, don't let your surroundings get you down. If you work hard enough and believe in yourself, you too can be a starter in the ACC. Of course, it would be nice if you were 6-8 and had some serious athleticism. Which partially describes what Johnson brings to the table. I'm a sucker for players who can grab offensive rebounds, block shots, and force steals, which is exactly what Johnson did as a freshman. When someone is doing those three things, chances are high he is doing other good things that don't show up in the box score.

But is my enthusiasm for Johnson justified? I decided to plug him into my database of players and find the freshmen who were most similar to him since 2005. The top five look like this: J. J. Hickson, Spencer Hawes, Brandon Costner, Trent Plaisted, and Wayne Chism. Hickson and Hawes both turned pro after their freshman season, and Costner is a special case discussed more in the NC State section of this publication. Plaisted and Chism do provide some insight into Johnson's future, as both guys are great athletes with little shooting touch, just like Johnson.

Neither of those two was able to improve his range in his sophomore season (or in the case of Plaisted, his junior season, either). The good news for Johnson is that both of those guys had a career free-throw percentage in the 50s. Johnson was around 69 percent last season, which means there's a little more hope he'll either develop some offense beyond 15 feet or that he already has it and simply had poor shot selection or was the victim of some bad luck in 2008.

What's in store for 2009

Except for one player (reserve forward Cameron Stanley), the Deacs are getting back everyone who had meaningful minutes last season. That in itself is reason for tremendous optimism. Only four teams in the top 11 conferences returned at least 90 percent of their minutes (and had those players make it to conference play) last season. One was UConn, which went from 6-10 in the Big East to 13-5 and a four-seed in the NCAA tournament. The others were Arkansas, Marquette, and Michigan State. None of them were huge success stories, but all improved their conference records in 2008. Without getting into detailed analysis, the continuity alone makes it seem as though Wake's 7-9 ACC record a year ago has a very good chance at flip-flopping, which would give the Deacons a good shot at their first NCAA bid since Chris Paul left.

MEET THE DEMON DEACONS

James Johnson (6-8, 235, So.). See above. Opposing defenses will do all they can to get Johnson to shoot three three-pointers a game again this season if he's only going to make 28 percent of them.

Al-Farouq Aminu (6-8, 205, Fr.). Aminu is expected to jump into a starting role in his freshman season at the small forward spot; no other freshman in the conference has more buzz surrounding him. Dino Gaudio also signed **Tony Woods (6-10, 230, Fr.)** and **Ty Walker (7-0, 220, Fr.)** to play this season, and both are considered ACC ready.

Jeff Teague (6-2, 175, So.). The other impact freshman Dino Gaudio had last season, Teague is a legit shooter on a team that doesn't have another one.

Chas McFarland (7-0, 225, Jr.). After playing just 81 minutes (13 in ACC games) as a freshman, McFarland was thrown into the starting role last season and was up to the task. Giving the appearance of a gangly big man, he was a very good rebounder and capable scorer. In addition, he quietly finished second in the conference to BC's Tyrelle Blair in block rate. Even with a couple of highly touted freshmen competing for his playing time, McFarland should get significant minutes. If he doesn't, it means the freshmen are ACC-caliber players, which isn't a bad scenario for Wake, obviously. It's possible no team in the nation is as deep at center as this one.

Ishmael Smith (6-0, 165, Jr.). Smith is an ultra-quick point guard who can't shoot. A point guard who shoots 29 percent from the free-throw line, as Smith did last season, is about as rare as one who blocks three shots a game. There are enough offensive options on the team to live with the deficiency,

but it's hard to imagine Wake becoming one of the top offensive teams in the ACC with this handicap.

L. D. Williams (6-4, 205, Jr.). If he ends up being the fifth starter, Williams will also be the fifth option offensively.

Harvey Hale (6-2, 190, Sr.). Hale has always struggled with his shot—for his career, he's a 31 percent on threes and 40 percent on twos. Nonetheless, he'll see some time at the two-guard.

Jamie Skeen (6-8, 245, Jr.). Skeen saw his minutes drop precipitously with the arrival of Johnson. He gives Wake some depth up front mainly as a rebounder, but his minutes should continue to dwindle with Aminu on the scene. He's on an academic-related suspension until mid-December.

David Weaver (6-10, 240, Jr.). Weaver is yet another big man. With the incoming freshmen, he too could be the victim of a shrinking rotation by January.

Prospectus says

If Aminu is as good as many are claiming, then third place in the conference and a decent seed in the NCAA tournament is a reasonable expectation. Outside of Carolina and Duke, no other team has as much going for it heading into the season. It must be remembered, however, that while the front line is loaded, the backcourt is somewhat suspect until it proves otherwise. Smith is difficult to contain, but opposing defenses did it often enough last season to make the Wake offense rather weak, by power-conference standards. The Deacs were outscored by 40 points in conference play, so they weren't a work of art in 2008. With the influence of freshmen this season, don't be surprised if they start slowly.

The Big East

The Accidental Super-Conference Comes of Age

JOHN GASAWAY

The Big East is different from other major conferences. It's bigger, it changes its composition when the seasons change from football to basketball, and there's a good chance that this year the Big East will become the first conference ever to send nine teams to the NCAA tournament. More on that magic number nine later. First, consider the unusual sequence of events that begat a conference poised to pull off the unprecedented.

If not an accident, the birth of the current Big East was at least something of an exercise in accelerated problem-solving. There was certainly no intent to pick up the fallen standard of the 16-team super-conference, an idea seemingly left in tatters by the WAC's implosion in 1998. Indeed, when the 16-team proposal was first floated in 2003, athletic directors at both Boston College and Syracuse reportedly threatened to resign their positions rather than watch the Big East suffer such a fate. Nevertheless, here we are. It went down like this . . .

In 2003, the ACC really wanted to burnish its football credentials. That year, the conference at long last succeeded in wooing Virginia Tech and, most crucially, Miami away from the Big East, leaving the latter conference with a rather basketball-heavy dozen teams: Boston College, Connecticut, Georgetown, Notre Dame (a Big East member for basketball but not for football, of course), Pitt, Providence, Rutgers, Seton Hall, St. John's, Syracuse, Villanova, and West Virginia.

Fine programs all, but there just wasn't enough there footballwise for a BCS conference, especially when later that same year the ACC voted unanimously to invite Boston College to relocate. So the Big East did what any league that's been raided by another conference would do. It raided another conference, namely, Conference USA. In addition to getting basketball-only members DePaul and Marquette, the Big East also picked up three basketball teams that kindly brought along football programs as well: Cincinnati, Louisville, and South Florida. These three schools were enough, along with a rechristened football program at Connecticut, to outfit an eight-team BCS football league.

The 16-team basketball conference? *Afterthought* is too strong a word, but this March, when you see Mike Tranghese proudly holding forth on how his conference saw all this coming, just remember that keeping eight Big East–member football programs in the league is the sine qua non here. By this calculus, South Florida football is well worth the South Florida basketball that comes with it. In effect, the Big East met its needs in football and was then faced with a choice between a 14- and a 16-team basketball conference. By extending invitations to non-football schools DePaul and Marquette, the league opted to go with 16 teams.

It's been that way for three seasons now, long enough to ask, how has this been working, basketballwise?

In the three-season history of the supersized Big East, the eight teams that made the tournament last year have performed at a level one notch above Syracuse, which, in turn, has clearly been a step or

Big East conference, 2006-2008

	Wins
Georgetown	38
Connecticut	33
Louisville	32
Pitt	32
Villanova	32
Marquette	31
Notre Dame	31
West Virginia	31
Syracuse	26
DePaul	20
Seton Hall	20
Providence	19
Cincinnati	18
St. John's	17
Rutgers	13
South Florida	7

two above the bottom seven teams of the Big East. Let's keep this in mind as a handy pocket sociology for this sprawling hoops populace. Most years, you've got your top half (the usual suspects), you've got Syracuse banging on that door, and then you've got everyone else (the usual suspects). The caveat being that, of course, you get an occasional outlier. DePaul finished three games ahead of Connecticut in 2007. Seton Hall went 9-7 in 2006. Heck, Rutgers went 7-9 in 2006.

And besides, that's all in the past tense. Programs rise and fall. It wasn't so long ago, after all, that now-mighty Georgetown was suffering through a five-year NCAA tournament exile. Nevertheless, in its first three years, the Big East hasn't exactly been what you'd call wild, especially not at the very bottom. South Florida has finished 16th, tied for 14th, and tied for 15th. St. John's has finished tied for 13th, 11th, and 14th. Rutgers has finished tied for ninth, tied for 14th, and tied for 15th. The Big East is a little like a black and tan poured by a rookie. The Guinness just lies there, unmixed, on top of the cheap beer.

What does this say about the conference's claim to being the nation's best league? This is in the eye of the beholder, of course. When this year's conference is praised as the "best" or "strongest" in the nation, I think what could truly be said is that the team that finishes eighth in the Big East is way better than the eighth-best team in any other conference. There's a heft to the league this year that's partly a

function of having so many teams but more importantly is the result of having so many good teams.

The Big East returns an unusually high number of its key players for a league that just put half its teams into the NCAA tournament the previous year. Eighteen of 26 players are back from last year's all-conference honorees (first and second teams and honorable mention recipients), including the conference player of the year, Notre Dame's Luke Harangody. This is a deep conference in what might be a comparatively thin year nationally, outside of Chapel Hill.

Still, if there's a recurring theme in my Big East previews this year, it's that this conference has at least eight exceptionally good teams but no truly scary ones, at least not yet. Maybe we were spoiled on this front last year—*scary* here meaning simply that a team is outstanding on both offense *and* defense. This description fit every 2008 Final Four team like a glove, and maybe it could even be stretched to include last year's Louisville and Georgetown teams as well. But I can't say with any confidence that it will apply to any Big East team in 2009. Who knows, it could describe the Cardinals, the Hoyas, or even West Virginia this year, but if so, some new players will have to come through. Georgetown and the Mountaineers lost NBA first-rounders (Roy Hibbert and Joe Alexander, respectively). Louisville lost its quartz mechanism on offense (David Padgett). But all the above schools have elite talent coming in this year, talent so elite that some of it may not be around long.

Meanwhile, very good teams like Connecticut, Notre Dame, and Pitt have pretty much everyone back, but their defenses ranked eighth, tenth, and 11th, respectively, in the Big East last year. Villanova also has mostly everyone back, but its offense ranked 12th in the conference in 2008. History says age alone usually ameliorates such deficiencies, but it can't obliterate them completely. Except obliterating deficiencies is exactly what happened in the case of Connecticut offense last year, a unit that went from substandard to outstanding in one season, with no appreciable changes in personnel. There's always room for surprises, of course; they just tend to be rare.

Marquette, too, is a very good team that has pretty much everyone back—except its coach. Tom Crean elected to start the rebuild at Indiana, and the Golden Eagles are now led by Buzz Williams. With four starters returning from an NCAA tournament team, the new coach will almost certainly stay the course stylistically, with good reason: This is a well-balanced team, albeit a little undersized.

No such stylistic restrictions apply at Providence, where any bold innovations from new coach Keno Davis will be more than welcome, even with a veteran roster. The Friars haven't won an NCAA tournament game since 1997, an improbable dry spell for a program that two decades ago showed the hoops world what could be done with this newfangled three-point shot. Davis has just one year of Division I head coaching under his belt, but last year, his Drake Bulldogs were known to shoot three every now and then themselves. With an experienced lineup long on perimeter players and short on size, Davis may well find he again has good reason to shoot threes, even if they are from a foot further out this season.

Another change that promises to be just as notable as the new three-point line is the new setup for the Big East tournament. For the first time, all 16 teams will participate, a salute to inclusion that will make the bottom four teams happy while adding another four games to the slate at Madison Square Garden. Note that in this new bracket, the bottom eight teams will play on the first day, with the four winners proceeding to a second round against seeds five through eight. It's therefore entirely possible that one or even two teams playing on that first day this year could still be nursing NCAA tournament hopes. Which brings us back to the matter of how the Big East will fare on Selection Sunday this season.

Last year, the Big East's number for tournament bids was an already hefty enough eight. (If you're keeping score at home: Georgetown, Louisville, Pitt, Connecticut, Notre Dame, Marquette, West Virginia, and Villanova.) The Rubicon to be crossed here in terms of conference heft, however, is actually nine bids.

For one thing, it would be a record. True, getting nine of your 16 teams into the tournament is, by a couple percentage points, less impressive than getting seven of your 12 teams in, as did the ACC in 2007. Still, an NCAA tournament with nearly 14 percent of its 65 teams coming from a single conference would be a sight, no two ways about it. You would also have the unprecedented specter of conference rivals colliding as early as the Sweet 16.

Nine Big East teams making the tournament is therefore likely to be a huge topic of discussion come February. There's a fair likelihood that the eight teams that played in the tournament last year

could all be invited again this year. Then it will be up to one additional team to get that fabled ninth bid: Syracuse, say, or Cincinnati. Maybe even Providence.

If that day comes and the 16-team superconference really does put nine of its teams into the NCAA tournament, I have my sound bite at the ready. Echoing remarks made by the ever eloquent President Nixon on the occasion of his visit to the Great Wall of China, I will solemnly intone: "It is indeed a super conference."

	2008 Record	Returning Minutes (%)	2009 Prediction
Louisville	14-4	74	14-4
Connecticut	13-5	77*	14-4
Marquette	11-7	81	13-5
Georgetown	15-3	53	13-5
Notre Dame	14-4	85	12-6
Pitt	10-8	66	12-6
Villanova	9-9	95	12-6
West Virginia	11-7	59	10-8
Syracuse	9-9	82	10-8
Providence	6-12	84	7-11
Cincinnati	8-10	57	7-11
St. John's	5-13	76	5-13
Rutgers	3-15	87	5-13
Seton Hall	7-11	52	5-13
DePaul	6-12	49	3-15
South Florida	3-15	58	2-16

*Does not include Stanley Robinson, whose status is unresolved as this book goes to press.

CINCINNATI

2008: 13-19 (8-10 Big East)
Lost to Bradley 70-67, College Basketball Invitational First Round
In-conference offense: 0.98 points per possession (14th)
In-conference defense: 1.03 points allowed per possession (9th)

What Cincinnati did well: *Start fast.*
Cincinnati turned a few heads at the start of the Big East season last year, when it posted a one-point win at Louisville. The Cardinals, it's true, were much more wobbly at the time than they'd prove to be later in the year. The Cincinnati game marked David Padgett's return from his six-week rehab of a broken

right kneecap. Still, the Bearcats had posted a win over Rick Pitino at Freedom Hall, after having gone 2-14 in the Big East the previous year.

When Mick Cronin's team followed that up with wins at home over Syracuse and Villanova, there was even some voguish talk in mid-January that the former bottom of the Big East was rising to the top: Cincy and DePaul both started 3-1 in-conference. The Blue Demons soon faltered, but Cincinnati kept chipping away, notching a home win against Pitt and even a road win at West Virginia. At 8-5 in the Big East, the Bearcats were still within shouting distance of the NCAA tournament bubble as late as February 23.

Then a funny thing happened. This team collapsed, losing its last five games in ways ranging from agonizing (an overtime loss at home against Providence) to humiliating (a 45-point season-ending loss at Connecticut). The problem was on defense: There was none, not over the last five games anyway . . .

Day into night: Cincinnati defense, 2008
Conference games only

	First 13 games	Last 5 games
Defensive rebound pct.	71.4	66.9
Opp. 2FG pct.	46.6	55.6
Opp. PPP	0.98	1.18
Record	8-5	0-5

Cincinnati's defense can't afford to take a night off, because its offense, while oddly consistent, has been weak for a while now, scoring a meager 0.98 points per possession against Big East opponents in each of the last two seasons. If Cronin can recapture the defense of those first 13 games, his team can go places in 2009. Relatively speaking.

What we learned in 2008: *Deonta Vaughn's a true "shoint guard."*
For most of basketball's 117-year history, of course, there were no such terms as *point guard* or *shooting guard*. There were merely *guards*.

Deonta Vaughn was such a guard last year. Very few UC field goals in 2008 didn't hit his stat sheet in some way, whether as a made basket or an assist. Never mind that the Bearcats had a "point guard" last year (Jamual Warren). The truth is, if you want to find the player who most closely resembles Vaughn,

you have to look at a "scoring point guard" like, say, D.J. Augustin, who played last year for Texas and will play this year for the Charlotte Bobcats.

Vaughn and Augustin, 2008

	ARate	%Poss.	%Shots	3FG pct.	2FG pct.	ORtng.
Vaughn	30.9	27.3	27.6	39.8	49.4	109.5
Augustin	30.5	27.9	26.0	38.1	47.1	115.5

Note the virtually identical assist rates and how each player accounted for a similar share of possessions and shots within his own offense. Not that Vaughn's the player Augustin was last year, of course. Augustin took much better care of the ball and got to the line much more often, thus accounting for his higher overall offensive rating. The similarity here is in method, not result. And categorical silos like *point guard* probably stand in our way when we try to understand these similarities.

Vaughn is a true shooting point guard. A shoint guard, if you will.

What's in store for 2009
Hopes are high for more scoring in Fifth Third Arena this season. Bearcat fans are expecting that the hard-working Vaughn will at last have some help on offense. "We're a lot better than we were two years ago," Cronin has said.

MEET THE BEARCATS

Deonta Vaughn (6-1, 195, Jr.). See above. Vaughn's a mensch who carried the UC offense, such as it was, last year. His turnovers are too numerous for a player who shoots many more threes than twos, but he has shown an ability to make his shots and to create opportunities for his teammates. If the newly arrived talent around Vaughn this season proves to be as good as advertised, this could be the season you hear a lot more about the young man from Indianapolis.

Mike Williams (6-7, 240, Jr.). Williams is about to make his long-awaited debut as a Bearcat. He must seem really old and scary to the freshmen. Williams was a McDonald's All-American in 2004, back when fellow honorees included current NBA graybeards like Dwight Howard and Al Jefferson. After transferring to Cincinnati from Texas after the 2006 season,

Williams sat out 2006-2007 and then was sidelined for the entire season last year with a torn Achilles tendon. He averaged 13 minutes per game for the 2006 Longhorns, a team that had LaMarcus Aldridge, P. J. Tucker, and Brad Buckman, and went on to earn a two-seed in that year's NCAA tournament. Technically, Williams has just one year of eligibility remaining, but Cincinnati lists him optimistically as a junior, and he will indeed have the option of petitioning the NCAA for an additional year after this season.

Yancy Gates (6-9, 255, Fr.). A highly touted local product from Withrow High School, Gates is billed as Big East ready in physique and in skills.

Cashmere Wright (6-0, 160, Fr.). Bearcat fans really want Wright to be the point guard who allows Vaughn not only to play, but also to thrive, "off the ball."

Steven Toyloy (6-8, 255, Jr.). A burly junior-college transfer, Toyloy averaged a double-double last year for Miami-Dade Community College.

Rashad Bishop (6-6, 220, So.). Bishop averaged 23 minutes a game as a freshman last year, functioning as a long body on defense and a pass-first wing on offense.

Larry Davis (6-3, 180, So.). Davis saw limited action as a freshman last year, but when he did get in the game, he was not shy about looking for his shot.

Anthony McClain (6-11, 245, So.). McClain showed hints of strong defensive rebounding and outstanding shot blocking during limited minutes as a freshman.

Prospectus says

The Bearcats' weakness last year was an inability to make shots, pure and simple. Whether from beyond the arc or in the paint, Cincinnati struggled to get the ball in the basket. Only Rutgers and St. John's fared worse from the field in Big East play. That's not going to be cured completely overnight, even with an infusion of new talent, but it can at least be improved. Average shooting, fewer turnovers, and, not least, a consistent level of defense throughout the entirety of the conference season should be Mick Cronin's goals for year three of his rebuild at Cincinnati.

CONNECTICUT

2008: 24-9 (13-5 Big East)
Lost to San Diego 70-69 (OT), NCAA First Round
In-conference offense: 1.11 points per possession (1st)
In-conference defense: 1.02 points allowed per possession (8th)

What Connecticut did well: *Transform.*
My personal choice for the most underreported college basketball story of 2008 would be the amazing change that took place at Connecticut from 2007 to 2008. In 2007, Jim Calhoun had no offense. None. The very next year, with pretty much the same group of players, he had the best offense in the 16-team horde known as the Big East.

Night into day: Connecticut offense, 2007 versus 2008
Conference games only

	2007	2008
2FG pct.	41.2	49.9
3FG pct.	31.3	35.9
Turnover pct.	21.8	19.1
PPP	0.94	1.11
Record	6-10	13-5

Seriously, this borders on a caterpillar-to-butterfly-level metamorphosis. Improvement exhibited by the same group of players is usually a slow and steady, multiyear Baylor kind of thing, not a lightning strike like this. If these two seasons were consecutive SATs taken by a prospect trying to qualify academically, the jump in performance would have been flagged immediately and the NCAA would be investigating. How did this happen? And why wasn't it a huge deal?

One key year-to-year difference was unquestionably a vastly improved A. J. Price. Every aspect of Price's game improved in 2008: two-point shooting, three-point shooting, free-throw shooting, assist rate, turnover rate—the whole deal.

Price's growth was impressive, but still, the improvement that Connecticut achieved on offense as a team was nothing short of remarkable. Maybe, every once in a great while, continuity is actually the best change agent. Consider what we saw here: same coach, same players (well, minus Marcus Johnson), same system (stylistic markers like pace and the ratio of twos to threes were unchanged from year to year)—really, nothing changed. Yet somehow everything changed. Coach Calhoun, whatever you did to these guys, bottle it. You'll sell out in no time.

And best wishes for your health, Coach.

What we learned in 2008: *Connecticut is a great defense trapped in the jerseys of an average one.*

For a team to hold its conference opponents to 41 percent two-point shooting and yet still give up more than a point per possession is pretty incredible. Connecticut did it last year. Great two-point field-goal defense is usually the bedrock of a great overall defense. Not for the Huskies in 2008, however, as they put a defense on the floor that was just barely better than the Big East average.

It begs the question as to whether "Connecticut defense" is simply Hasheem Thabeet's shot blocking, period. That's not an indictment of non-Thabeet Huskies alone. Thabeet himself has to answer for his share of a conundrum: How can it be that this tall, strong, and athletic team was merely the 13th-best defensive rebounding team in Big East play last year?

Goodness knows, a Calhoun-led Connecticut team will never lead the Big East in steals. And since its offense is already performing near peak efficiency, a few more defensive boards would go a very long way toward elevating this team's performance.

What's In store for 2009

I'm leading preseason appraisals of Connecticut by saying that the team will be better this year because newcomers like Kemba Walker and Nate Miles will give Calhoun more "creators" in the half-court offense. Maybe, but keep in mind that the air above the Huskies' offense is extremely thin. When you're already north of 1.10 points per trip, there's little room for improvement.

It just *looks* as if the Huskies can get better because last year they got so many of their points outside their half-court offense, specifically from the free-throw line. They were fouled often (Thabeet in particular was a human tackling dummy), and they hit 72 percent of their freebies last year. No major-conference team posted a higher ratio of made free throws to field-goal attempts. Free throws aren't glamorous, but last year they helped propel an outstanding Huskies offense, one that may change in appearance but will be hard-pressed to score more efficiently.

No, if UConn is indeed better this year, it will be because the defense is better.

MEET THE HUSKIES

A. J. Price (6-2, 180, Sr.). Price had surgery to repair a torn ACL on March 28 and is reported to be on track to return in time for the start of practice. As noted, in 2008 he had a year that few who saw 2007 could have anticipated. The lack of attention given to that year strikes me as a little odd. Price was the largest single factor behind a resurgent offense that single-handedly made Connecticut's season what it was last year. (I say "single-handedly": The defense played by the 13-5 team last year was actually worse than that played by the 6-10 team in 2007.)

Hasheem Thabeet (7-3, 265, Jr.). Calhoun may well have been surprised, albeit pleasantly so, by Thabeet's decision not to enter the draft, for the Huskies temporarily found themselves with more recruits than available scholarships. In any event, Thabeet made the right call. No prospect who plays such a tiny role in his team's offense can be drafted as anything other than a specialist on defense and multiyear project on offense. Sure, you can still be drafted on that basis, possibly even in the first round, but if he can show the same kind of progression on offense that Roy Hibbert displayed, Thabeet can improve his stock dramatically. In relation to field-goal attempts, no major-conference player in the country was sent to the line more often than Thabeet, who made 70 percent of his free throws. Oh, and did I mention he's pretty good on defense? Shot blocking might be the most binary stat in basketball: You either do it often enough to be feared, or you don't. Thabeet is feared, rightly. If he goes down for any amount of time, this defense is questionable, because even *with* him, it was middle-of-the-pack in the Big East last year.

Jeff Adrien (6-7, 245, Sr.). Adrien is well known to the college hoops world as the muscular dude who's always banging bodies down around the level of Thabeet's waistband. He led this team in minutes last year and made half his twos. Any improvement in foul shooting (62 percent last year) would be most welcome from a player who marches to the line as often as Adrien does.

Jerome Dyson (6-4, 190, Jr.). Dyson served a nine-game suspension in January and February last year after he and Doug Wiggins (who has since left the team) were ticketed by campus police in Storrs for possession of alcohol while being 20. On the court, Dyson's an excellent free-throw shooter who nevertheless struggled not only with turnovers last year but also with his shooting from the field in each of his first two seasons.

Craig Austrie (6-3, 175, Sr.). Austrie actually started more games (24) as a freshman for the fabled 2006 team than he did the past two seasons combined (22). (*Fabled* here meaning five of the team's players were taken in the first 40 picks of the ensuing NBA draft.)

Kemba Walker (6-0, 165, Fr.). A McDonald's All-American from the Bronx, Walker was named the MVP of the FIBA Americas Under 18 Championship played at Formosa, Argentina, in July.

Nate Miles (6-6, 170, Fr.). Miles turned 20 in March—he originally gave a verbal commitment to Xavier in June 2005. It took him a while to become eligible to play Division I ball, and rather than go the junior-college route, he prepped at the Patterson School in North Carolina. Now the Huskies have a 6-6 wing praised for his scoring and perimeter range.

Ater Majok (6-10, 215, Fr.). As a Sudanese player who prepped in Australia and is now in Storrs, Majok can surely boast of a multi-hemispheric ricochet that few of us will ever match. He's billed as an athletic and nimble big man.

Stanley Robinson (6-9, 200, Jr.). As this book goes to press, Robinson's status is up in the air. Calhoun filed paperwork for a medical redshirt in June, saying only that Robinson needs to deal with "personal" issues. At a minimum, Robinson will miss the first semester, but it appears that he might not return, period. "We don't know if he's coming back in January," Calhoun has said.

Prospectus says
Connecticut has the most feared shot blocker in all of college hoops and the best point guard in the Big East. They also have, even with this shot blocker, an average defense and an aforementioned point guard who's coming off knee surgery. I suggest we all just wait a bit on this team. If the defense improves and if that knee is healthy, we'll know very soon. Then the preseason expectations being heaped on this team will seem understated.

2008: 11-19 (6-12 Big East)
Did not make the field of 12 teams in the Big East Tournament
In-conference offense: 1.04 points per possession (7th)
In-conference defense: 1.12 points allowed per possession (16th)

What DePaul did well: *Prohibit Cliff Clinkscales from shooting.*
During his minutes on the floor last year, the now-departed Clinkscales took just 7 percent of DePaul's shots. Seven. A number so low I can spell it. That, my friends, is one seriously low shot percentage.

Clinkscales was no immobile seven-foot shot blocker, mind you. He was a 6-1 guard. Who, it's plain to see, was never allowed to shoot.

What we learned in 2008: *Defense really does matter.*
DePaul improved markedly on offense last year, but it was an exercise in futility because the Blue Demons were, suddenly, an absolute basket case on D.

Call them "ePaul," for there was no "D": *DePaul, 2007 versus 2008*
Conference games only
PPP: points per possession
Opp. PPP: opponent points per possession
EM: efficiency margin (PPP – Opp. PPP)

	2007	2008
PPP	0.99	1.04
Opp. PPP	0.98	1.12
EM	+0.01	-0.08
Conf. record	9-7	6-12

The 2007 team wasn't exactly filled with household names, but last year Jerry Wainwright found he couldn't replace players like Wilson Chandler and Marcus Heard, at least not on defense. Neither Chandler nor Heard were what you'd call spectacular defenders, but they were both pretty good on the defensive glass and both were capable shot blockers. Together they constituted what was a surprisingly good, if little-noticed, interior defense.

Last year was a different story. DePaul's defense deteriorated in every respect: two-point field-goal defense, three-point field-goal defense, defensive rebounding, opponent turnovers, everything. Wainwright suddenly had the worst defense in the Big East on his hands. (Yes, even worse than South Florida.) The low point came on March 2, when Notre Dame visited Allstate Arena and glided with apparent ease to 98 points in a game whose pace was merely average (69 possessions). The defense, more specifically the lack thereof, wrecked DePaul's season in 2008.

What's in store for 2009

Wainwright might want to look into his team's strength and conditioning regimen. Fatigue appeared to be a factor in last year's defensive collapse, as the Blue Demons allowed opponents to score an astonishing 1.18 points per trip over the second half of the conference season.

MEET THE BLUE DEMONS

Dar Tucker (6-4, 210, So.). For a freshman carrying a larger load on offense than any of his teammates, Tucker was rather startling in how well he held on to the ball. Indeed, this was the saving grace for a 6-12 Big East team: It did take good care of the ball, committing a turnover on just 17 percent of its possessions in-conference. Tucker couldn't get his threes to fall last year (and 63 percent free-throw shooting says that's not likely to change), but look at his work inside the arc: He made 54 percent of his twos. That's exceptional for a 6-4 freshman who's the main cog in his team's offense. It tells me that Tucker bears watching.

Mac Koshwal (6-10, 240, So.). A highly touted recruit who was a starter from day one, Koshwal actually played a surprisingly limited role in the DePaul offense as a freshman. His best chance to see the ball was often to get an offensive rebound—and he was excellent at doing so. Koshwal was also sent to the line more often than any other returning Blue Demon, but he made just 55 percent of his free throws. On the other end of the floor, he's an adequate defensive rebounder who's not much of a threat to block a shot.

Will Walker (6-0, 180, Jr.). Walker hit 44 percent of his rather infrequent threes last year. If he can follow that up, he should shoot more often from out there. I say "if" because Walker's 67 percent free-

throw shooting suggests fortune really smiled on him outside the arc in 2008.

Jabari Currie (6-4, 215, Sr.). Last year Currie had 10 starts and averaged 15 minutes per game as a pass-first option at point guard. He posted a nice assist rate but struggled mightily with turnovers.

Mike Bizoukas (6-1, 175, Fr.). Bizoukas missed most of last year due to mononucleosis and will seek a medical redshirt. He'll get a look at point guard.

Jeremiah Kelly (6-1, 165, Fr.). Still another candidate for minutes at the point.

Matija Poscic (6-10, 235, Sr.). Poscic played sparingly last year as a junior-college transfer, but he's the only returning player who can block an occasional shot.

Kene Obi (7-2, 260, Fr.). Obi redshirted last year and has reportedly been preparing for the rigors of life in the Big East.

Krys Faber (6-11, 245, Fr.). A late addition to the incoming class, Faber averaged the rare ascending-numbers double-double as a high-school senior: 16 points and 18 rebounds.

Prospectus says

The Blue Demons lose Draelon Burns, whose prominence in the offense was second only to Tucker's and whose efficiency was second only to Walker's. His departure leaves a decent-sized hole on offense. (Fun fact: No returning Blue Demon shot better than 67 percent from the line last year.) And we've seen that the defense is very much a work in progress. With what we know now, a lower-middle finish in the Big East would have to be classified a resounding success for DePaul in 2009.

GEORGETOWN

2008: 28-6 (15-3 Big East)
Lost to Davidson 74-70, NCAA Second Round
In-conference offense: 1.04 points per possession (8th)
In-conference defense: 0.92 points allowed per possession (2nd)

What Georgetown did well: *Force misses.*

If you've been reading along, you know that Ken and I start these previews with what a team did well the previous year. In this case, however, "well" doesn't do justice to reality. Georgetown's field-goal defense in 2008 was historic.

Best field-goal defenses, 2006-2008

Conference games only: ACC, Big East, Big Ten, Big 12, Pac-10, and SEC

Opp. eFG pct.: opponent effective field-goal percentage

Opp. PPP: opponent points per possession

	Opp. eFG Pct.	Opp. PPP
1. Georgetown 2008	41.9	0.92
2. Mississippi State 2008	42.1	0.96
3. Connecticut 2006	42.3	0.96
4. Connecticut 2007	43.3	0.96
5. Kansas 2008	43.5	0.92
6. Syracuse 2007	43.5	0.98
7. Kansas 2007	43.8	0.89
8. Stanford 2008	43.9	0.97

Given that the 2007 team's field-goal defense, while very good, was nowhere near this good, the question is simply, what did John Thompson III put in these guys' Gatorade?

The improvement here appears to have been an example of good old-fashioned maturation. If anything, the 2007 team actually played a little taller than its successors, with 6-9 junior Jeff Green in the starting lineup one year and 6-4 freshman Austin Freeman there (mostly) the next. Also note that last year, Roy Hibbert's block percentage went *down* slightly. Yet somehow, with a lineup that was, on average, shorter and with fewer blocks from Hibbert, this team inflicted unprecedented punishment on opponents who had the effrontery to attempt a shot.

The Georgetown team that went to the Final Four in 2007 was somewhat misunderstood, initially perceived as a reincarnation of the tough defensive units of the 1980s, when actually these particular latter-day Hoyas were merely "really good" on defense but "unbelievably outstanding" on offense. Last year, however, the common perception fit the team like a glove: Georgetown played superb defense in 2008.

What we learned in 2008: *Even successful coaches can change their spots, a little.*

Goodness knows, no one ever had less reason to change an offense than Thompson had coming off the 2007 season. That year, his team's offense was the best in the Big East by a strikingly large margin. (It missed out on its fair share of acclaim, though, because Georgetown's games were so slow and the point totals were thus relatively modest.) In the face of this kind of success, Thompson certainly could have been forgiven for standing pat in 2008, stylistically speaking.

Instead, he retooled, albeit selectively: The Hoya offense in 2008 was a little faster, shot way more threes, and recorded way, way, fewer offensive boards. By shortening possessions and shooting more threes, Thompson may have been trying to cut down on turnovers, which had been jarringly abundant in 2007.

Did the changes work? Well, define *work.* Turnovers did decline, a little. But, of course, no offense was going to replicate what Georgetown did in 2007. More specifically, replacing Jeff Green turned out to be no small task. The Hoyas' offense went from being possibly the best unit in the nation in 2007 to hovering right at the Big East average in 2008.

At least some of this—better defense and worse offense—may have come down to something as simple as a year-to-year increase in minutes for Patrick Ewing. In any event, the new and improved defense cushioned the blow inflicted by a decline in offense. Not many teams, surely, have seen their scoring drop off so precipitously and have still gone 15-3 in-conference.

What's in store for 2009

Fans with long memories who recall a time when Roy Hibbert was a slow-footed project on offense might be surprised to learn the extent to which the Hoyas' offense went through the big guy last year. Hibbert was actually a hair more prominent in that offense than DaJuan Summers. His departure leaves a hole, no doubt, on both sides of the ball.

MEET THE HOYAS

DaJuan Summers (6-8, 240, Jr.). If you drew a picture of the ideal dual-threat wing, the prototype would look a lot like DaJuan Summers: length, mobility, and strength. OK, *ideal* might be a bit much.

Summers is, after all, largely a stranger to assists, and he could stand to be more accurate on his threes. But last year, he was productive inside the arc and was the best defensive rebounder Thompson had—better even than Hibbert.

Jessie Sapp (6-3, 210, Sr.). In 2008, Sapp was Thompson's best source of assists; he made 41 percent of his threes after having suffered through a miserable year of 30 percent shooting from long range in 2007. On the other hand, his turnovers were a bit too numerous last year and his forays inside the arc were pretty unproductive. Sapp seems to have recognized this (or Thompson did, or both), as his shot selection shifted decidedly in favor of the threes.

Austin Freeman (6-4, 220, So.). Even though he arrived on campus as the much-heralded jewel of the recruiting class, Freeman last year largely left his shots on the table, so to speak, where they were scooped up obligingly by Summers and Hibbert. When he did pull the trigger, though, Freeman was outstanding, both on his twos and his threes. He would appear to be both a pure shooter and a scorer in the making, the logical choice for more touches this season. Many more touches.

Greg Monroe (6-10, 235, Fr.). Monroe is a McDonald's All-American out of Louisiana and is widely expected to be not only a starter but also a game-changer from day one.

Chris Wright (6-1, 205, So.). Wright was out for two months last year with an injured foot and returned to the lineup just in time for the Big East tournament. He picked up right where he left off, coming off the bench and functioning as a solid point guard, albeit one whose turnovers were a little too plentiful.

Henry Sims (6-10, 225, Fr.). Sims is a Baltimore product who figures to benefit not only from the graduation of Hibbert and Ewing but also from Vernon Macklin's decision to transfer out of the program. There will be minutes available, and Sims arrives touted as a formidable shot blocker.

Jason Clark (6-2, 170, Fr.). Clark, a shooting guard from Arlington, Virginia, has a reputation for excellent outside shooting and overall efficiency on offense.

Julian Vaughn (6-10, 245, So.). Vaughn played for Florida State last year before transferring to Georgetown to be closer to his family. He's been granted a waiver by the NCAA and is eligible to play for the Hoyas this season.

Prospectus says

Georgetown lost a lot, goodness knows, when it lost two starters like Roy Hibbert and Jonathan Wallace, not to mention a defender like Patrick Ewing. Still, if you had to chart out a situation in which a team was teed up to surprise people, it would look a lot like this. We know the Hoyas won't be as good as they were last year on defense, but there's room for improvement on offense. Better still, the biggest available improvement is the easiest one: fewer turnovers. For two seasons running, turnovers have been strangely frequent in what is, after all, alleged to be a Princeton-style offense. Simply bringing their turnovers down to the Big East average would be huge. Besides, for all the talk about a changing of the guard, this team does return three starters. So, yes, opponents will score more against Georgetown this year. But we may well look back at the end of the season and find that this team was underrated in the fall.

LOUISVILLE

2008: 27-9 (14-4 Big East)
Lost to North Carolina 83-73, NCAA Elite Eight
In-conference offense: 1.06 points per possession (5th)
In-conference defense: 0.91 points allowed per possession (1st)

What Louisville did well: *Shut down opposing offenses.*

If you're going through these Big East previews sequentially, you've just finished reading me praise the 2008 Georgetown defense to the skies. Well, guess what? The Hoyas *and* Louisville were in a class by themselves when it came to defense in the Big East last year. The Cardinals' defense in 2008 was every bit as good as Georgetown's, maybe even a hair better.

How can that be? I just got through saying that no defense in the past three years has made its major-conference opponents miss shots the way the Hoyas did last year.

True enough, but defense is more than forcing missed shots. It's also getting defensive boards, creating turnovers, and keeping your opponent off the line. As it happens, Louisville was as good as or better than Georgetown at all three.

Louisville and Georgetown on defense, 2008
Conference games only

	Louisville	Georgetown
Opp. effective FG pct.	44.3	41.9
Defensive rebound pct.	70.1	66.9
Opp. turnover pct.	20.7	20.4
Opp. FTA/FGA	0.32	0.40
Opp. PPP	0.91	0.92
Record	14-4	15-3

Both teams' opponents turned the ball over with virtually identical frequency, a little less than 21 percent of the time. So the fact that Louisville's defense was a tiny bit better than Georgetown's even though the Hoyas' field-goal defense was significantly superior to the Cardinals' speaks to the importance of taking care of the defensive glass and not fouling—mostly the former.

Defensive rebounding might be the single most underrated factor in basketball. In Big East conference games last year, it showed the same correlation to opponent scoring as did two-point field-goal defense. In other words, defensive rebounding is vital: It kills opponent possessions. Louisville, led by Earl Clark, was a very good defensive rebounding team in 2008.

What we learned in 2008: *David Padgett was sui generis.*
If you watched Louisville at all last year, you probably got used to hearing how vital David Padgett was to the team: what a heady leader he was, how the Cardinals struggled during his six-week absence in November and December, how Rick Pitino's offense really "went through" the 6-11 big man even though he didn't shoot all that often, compared with other big names, and so on.

I know my shtick is usually to dissent from such conventional wisdom, but from my chair I would agree with pretty much all the above. What's interesting about Padgett, though, is what a strange collection of traits he brought together in one player.

For instance, Padgett was highly efficient on offense despite being a poor (66 percent) free-throw shooter who was fouled often. Cardinal fans can thank Padgett's otherworldly shooting on his twos for this: He was actually more likely to make a shot while being defended than he was when given a freebie from the line. Then there's the fact that he was a good passer who was also fair on the offensive boards, yet he was a nonfactor on the defensive glass.

So what will Padgett's absence mean to this year's team? Hard to say, really, because his combination of skills was so unusual. It's as if the headiest drive-and-dish point guard you've ever seen, albeit one with no perimeter shot, was smuggled into a 6-11 body. No wonder he wasn't drafted. The NBA likes prior examples, and the only prior example for David Padgett the pro was David Padgett the collegian.

What's in store for 2009
Rick Pitino is a true original. He recruits on a par with programs like Kansas, North Carolina, and UCLA. Unlike those blue bloods, however, Pitino's teams customarily shoot a lot of threes. In effect, he has NBA prospects playing a style more familiar to scrappy mid-majors—on offense. On defense, conversely, Louisville is all about applying its athletic advantage to maximum effect. It makes for a very interesting and entertaining combination. More importantly, it should be a successful combination again this year.

MEET THE CARDINALS

Earl Clark (6-8, 220, Jr.). If you've seen Clark play, you might be surprised to learn that he's actually listed by Louisville as a "G/F." Indeed, he attempted no fewer than 66 threes last year—and made just 15. Pitino has won one more national championship than I ever will, but my unsolicited advice for the coach is that he nudge, cajole, or just plain force Clark into forgetting this "G" stuff entirely. For without question, Clark is one special "F." On the defensive glass, he's a beast who blocks shots and makes 54 percent of his twos. Clark's projected as a lottery pick in 2009.

Terrence Williams (6-6, 210, Sr.). Williams is not a shooter. In three seasons, he's made just 30 percent of his threes (and 59 percent of his free throws). But last year, he wisely cut down on his attempts from out there and thus improved to within shouting distance of the Division I average, making 34 percent of his treys. T-Will also posted a higher assist rate than that of any other Cardinal for the second consecutive season, and he's superb on the defensive glass.

Samardo Samuels (6-8, 240, Fr.). Samuels arrives from Jamaica by way of Newark with a bevy of honors, including McDonald's All-American status and selection as the *USA Today* national player of the year.

Jerry Smith (6-1, 200, Jr.). The best pure shooter on the roster, Smith's a perimeter threat who's opportunistic when inside the arc on offense and when guarding the ball on defense. He and Andre McGee both posted very good steal rates last year.

Andre McGee (5-10, 180, Sr.). McGee was the starting point guard for most of the season as a junior, though from time to time he sat and watched Edgar Sosa take the floor at tip-off. (McGee was given more starts, but Sosa logged more minutes.) When on the floor, McGee was a pass-first point who made 39 percent of his threes.

Edgar Sosa (6-1, 175, Jr.). Sosa played through some difficult stretches last year. Compared with 2007, his assist rate went down, his turnover rate went up, and, most damaging of all, he missed an unusually high number of twos. Pitino certainly doesn't need me to enumerate Sosa's struggles: The coach noted all the above last year and shaved about four minutes a game off Sosa's playing time, as the sophomore went from a full-time to an occasional starter.

Reginald Delk (6-4, 170, Jr.). A transfer from Mississippi State, Delk sat out last year. As a Bulldog in 2007, Delk fairly put the *narrow* in narrow specialization. That year, he existed only to attempt shots from the field, albeit both twos and threes. No rebounds, no assists, no steals, no free throws, no fouls. Just shots from the field, where Delk was OK on his threes and excellent on his twos.

Preston Knowles (6-1, 170, So.). In a summer update on his own Web site, Pitino had this to say about Knowles: "I hope he understands how competitive it will be for playing time next year." Point taken.

Terrence Jennings (6-10, 230, Fr.). If freshmen respond well to high expectations, Jennings should flourish: His new coach has compared him to Amare Stoudemire.

Jared Swopshire (6-7, 190, Fr.). Pitino is on the record as hoping Swopshire will bulk up for the rigors of Big East play.

Prospectus says

It comes as no surprise, of course, that Pitino can be counted among the acknowledged "system" coaches nationally, ones who can at least chuckle if not laugh in the face of modest attrition. So we find that even though Pitino lost Padgett and Juan Palacios to graduation—and Derrick Caracter to Derrick Caracterness—the common assumption among observers is that this season, Louisville will be just as good as if not better than it was in 2008. I look at this assumption with some qualifications (the Cardinals were much better last year than people realized), but it does represent a healthy instinct. The 'Ville should again be in the thick of it in a conference that's very thick when it comes to quality.

MARQUETTE

2008: 25-10 (11-7 Big East)
Lost to Stanford 82-81, NCAA Second Round
In-conference offense: 1.06 points per possession (6th)
In-conference defense: 0.98 points allowed per possession (3rd)

What Marquette did well: *Compensate.*

The Marquette offense in Tom Crean's final season last year was something of a wonder, not for its overall efficiency—it ranked a respectable but not stupendous sixth in the Big East—but rather for its ability to cover up what for other teams would be debilitating flaws. Simply put, the ability to score an above-average number of points when you can't make two-point shots and when you shoot a normal number of threes is something of a feat.

For two years running, the Golden Eagles have made 46 percent of their twos in Big East play. That may not be drop-dead awful (Rutgers' figure here last year was 42 percent), but it's oddly low for a team that fancies itself the rival of the Georgetowns and Louisvilles of the world, both of which made 53 or 54 percent of their shots inside the arc in-conference in 2008.

Offsetting its struggles close to the basket was the fact that in conference games last year, Marquette held on to the ball quite well while at the same time enjoying its best season of perimeter shooting since the Steve Novak days. Credit for the low turnover rate goes primarily to Dominic James, the Golden Eagles' quick yet sure-handed point guard who for three seasons has put rock-steady ball handling comfortably alongside incorrigibly unpredictable shooting. And the resurgent three-point shooting can be traced primarily to Lazar Hayward, who followed up on a promising freshman season with 45 percent shooting from outside the arc last year as a sophomore.

What we learned in 2008: *Fouls can be the price to be paid for steals.*

Tennessee under Bruce Pearl has won notoriety for its emphasis on wreaking havoc on opposing offenses with pressure defense and lots of steals. What's less well known, however, is that Marquette actually took the ball away more often in the Big East last year than did the Volunteers in the SEC.

The Golden Eagles' conference opponents turned the ball over on 24 percent of their possessions in 2008, a high figure that, along with outstanding perimeter field-goal defense, keyed the Marquette defense as a whole. No other Big East defense came close to Crean's team in terms of forcing opponent turnovers. So the scout on the Golden Eagles for opposing offenses is easy to state, but hard to execute: Take care of the ball and shoot twos. If you're not turning the ball over and you're not firing up threes, you're hitting this team where it hurts.

There's a cost, though, when you get this many steals, or at least there was for Marquette last year. This is one hack-tastic team: Conference opponents went to the line 453 times in 18 games in 2008. Few number pairings are more closely related than were a given team's fouls and its opponents' turnovers last year in the Big East. As the latter increased, so too did the former.

With many of the same players returning this year, it's tempting to say that we'll continue to see plenty of opponent turnovers and Marquette fouls in the Bradley Center in 2009. Then again, we can't be sure. There's been one significant change in personnel in Milwaukee this season . . .

What's in store for 2009

New head coach Buzz Williams takes over for the departed Crean, having served one season as an assistant on the Marquette staff. His only prior Division I head coaching experience came during one year at the University of New Orleans, a season blighted by litigation that Williams initiated against the school in the lingering chaotic aftermath of Hurricane Katrina. Williams's preferences and points of emphasis are thus as yet unknown, although to date he has said the right things about not fixing what ain't broke on an NCAA tournament team with four returning starters.

Besides, it's hard to envision what changes Williams *could* make with a very athletic yet somewhat undersized team. The style they play, particularly on defense, is what it is. For all we know, Williams yearns to someday emphasize Connecticut-style rebounding and shot blocking, but this isn't the roster for that particular preference.

MEET THE GOLDEN EAGLES

Jerel McNeal (6-3, 200, Sr.). McNeal is the Marquette steal/foul dialectic writ large. On the one hand, he's superb at sowing chaos in opposing offenses, posting a steal rate that was second only to that of Rutgers' Corey Chandler in the Big East last year. The downside, however, is that a 6-3 guard just shouldn't be in foul trouble this often. McNeal fouled out of four games and recorded four fouls 10 other times, one of those 10 being the season-ending one-point loss to Stanford in the NCAA tournament. (Granted, he was even more foul prone in 2007; maybe he's working on this.) McNeal's staying on the floor is important because he brings more than steals to the table: He's an able assist man who was also the only regular besides the now-departed Ousmane Barro to make more than half his twos last year.

Dominic James (5-11, 185, Sr.). James continues to be an outstanding point guard—as long as he doesn't shoot. He's a career 29 percent shooter outside the arc and 47 percent shooter inside it. (Strangely, his two-point percentage has gone down in each of his previous three seasons.) He doesn't swipe the ball away as often as McNeal does, but James does record a high steal rate in his own right.

More importantly, he does so at a much lower cost than McNeal: Where his teammate averages over four fouls per 40 minutes, James averages less than three. He's superb at dishing assists, and he takes very good care of the ball.

Lazar Hayward (6-6, 225, Jr.). Most of Marquette's shots last year were taken by McNeal, James, and Lazar Hayward. Of the three, Hayward is far and away the most efficient scorer. Unlike the other two, Hayward won't dish any assists, but he more than makes up for this by being the team's best defensive rebounder. There's just one major drawback with Hayward: Last year, he was even more foul prone than McNeal.

Wesley Matthews (6-5, 215, Sr.). The third member of the McNeal-James-Matthews guard trio that's been together seemingly for the past decade, Matthews got to the line last year far more often than any other returning regular did, and he made 79 percent of his free throws. In effect, he won back a little of what the Golden Eagles gave away with their high-volume fouling.

David Cubillan (6-0, 175, Jr.). Cubillan appears to be a good perimeter shooter who suffered through a mediocre season last year, hitting just 34 percent of his threes.

Maurice Acker (5-8, 165, Jr.). A former MAC freshman of the year, Acker transferred to Marquette from Ball State after just one season in Muncie. In averaging 13 minutes per game for the Golden Eagles last year, he showed flashes of good perimeter shooting but gave away too many turnovers.

Trevor Mbakwe (6-7, 240, So.). Mbakwe was sidelined until mid-February last year with a sprained knee ligament, and for some reason Crean chose to put him on the floor for nine minutes a game over the last 11 games instead of simply seeking a medical redshirt for his freshman. "It wasn't his call or my call," Crean told the *Milwaukee Journal Sentinel*. "It was the doctor's call. If he'd have been healthy all year, you'd be writing a lot about him."

Joseph Fulce (6-7, 205, So.). Fulce is a junior-college transfer with three seasons of eligibility remaining. Originally signed by Crean, Fulce has been touted for his rebounding and shot blocking.

Prospectus says

Marquette is athletic, fast, undersized, and not very productive when shooting twos. It's widely expected that because so many players are returning, the team will be better this year than it was last year. Maybe, but last year the Golden Eagles did just about as well as a team can do in some areas, namely, three-point defense (second in the Big East in 2008) and opponents' turnovers (first). Any backsliding there will have to be offset with improvement in other areas. Then again, we've seen that Marquette brings recent relevant experience to the table in the area of compensating for what other less resourceful teams would see as deficiencies.

NOTRE DAME

2008: 25-8 (14-4 Big East)
Lost to Washington State 61-41, NCAA Second Round
In-conference offense: 1.11 points per possession (2nd)
In-conference defense: 1.04 points allowed per possession (10th)

What Notre Dame did well: *Win more games despite having a weaker defense.*

Notre Dame last year had an outstanding offense and a defense that was a tiny bit worse than the Big East average. That translated into the numbers you see above, scoring 1.11 points per trip and allowing 1.04.

Funny thing is, winning 14 of 18 games while outscoring your opponents by 0.07 points per possession is pretty unusual. If Notre Dame were to post the same scoring margin again this season, the Irish would be much more likely to find themselves (a still very respectable) 12-6 come March. In terms of posting a won-loss record that's better than your scoring margin, only Kentucky, Penn State, Texas Tech, and Oklahoma were more fortunate in their respective conferences last year. In fact, on a possession-by-possession basis, the Irish's performance last year was surprisingly similar to that of the 2007 team.

Notre Dame, 2007 versus 2008
Conference games only
PPP: points per possession
Opp. PPP: opponent points per possession
EM: efficiency margin (PPP − Opp. PPP)

	2007	2008
PPP	1.09	1.11
Opp. PPP	1.01	1.04
EM	+0.08	+0.07
Record	11-5	14-4

It's not that last year's team was "lucky," per se. Actually, Notre Dame didn't see a lot of crunch time in Big East play: only one overtime game and just two other games decided by three points or less. (Yes, Notre Dame won all three.) No, it'd be more accurate to say simply that a team that loses four games by five, six, 19, and 26 points is very unlikely to go 14-0 in its other conference games. Go figure, the Irish did just that.

A more interesting question might be what can be done to improve the defense of a team that's been ranked in the top five nationally in some pre-preseason polls. The Irish field-goal defense in 2008 was pretty good, but the bang that ND got for its buck here was minimal, as this team was absolutely besieged by a never-ending barrage of opponents' shots. Possession after possession ended in still another field-goal attempt, as Notre Dame's Big East foes committed a turnover on less than 16 percent of their possessions—that is, *never*.

This team is built for offense, and mission accomplished, it excels at scoring points. It can improve on defense, of course, but we might more realistically view Notre Dame as something like a wayward SEC team that somehow landed in the Big East. The credo here: We'll outscore you tonight, take the win, and worry about the defense later. Purists may scoff, but that attitude won Florida a national championship in 2007.

What we learned in 2008: *Luke Harangody is a star.*
Long before I started watching basketball—I know not when, exactly—it became the custom to refer to a team not simply as, well, the team's name but rather as: "(Star) and the (team)." For instance, *I* might say simply "Notre Dame," but if you're seeing the game plugged on ESPN, you'd better believe it's going to be "Luke Harangody and Notre Dame."

Rightfully so. Michael Beasley was the only major-conference player in the country last year who played a more prominent role in his team's offense than did Harangody, who alone took about one-third of his team's shots during his minutes on the floor. Notre Dame's single-minded feed-Harangody compulsion on offense is surprising, imbalanced, and extreme. It also works beautifully.

The Irish came within a few baskets of beating out Connecticut for the title of best Big East offense in 2008. It's not that Harangody is another Beasley. Far from it: Beasley was vastly more efficient on offense last year while being even better than Harangody on the defensive glass. It's just that by assuming a role of Beasley-esque proportions (Mike Brey's workhorse attempted *509 two-point shots* last year), Harangody allows talented teammates the luxury of functioning as ruthlessly efficient supporting players.

Take away Harangody and 45 percent of Notre Dame's attempts from the field last year were threes. If you'll forgive the paradox, this is a perimeter-oriented team with a nonperimeter star absorbing the lion's share of the possessions. Basically, Harangody plus good three-point shooters equals a very tough challenge for any opposing defense—unless you happen to be Washington State, of course. The Cougars ambushed the fast-paced Irish with a 60-possession half-court quarantine. It worked. Big East take note.

What's in store for 2009
You'll note a decided lack of newcomers in the player descriptions below. Brey is riding this generational wave even as he uses an impending mass exodus of seniors as bait, landing transfers like Purdue's Scott Martin and Mississippi State's Ben Hansbrough, both of whom will be eligible next year. Nevertheless, the recruiting class that Brey signs this year is, obviously, huge for the future of Notre Dame basketball. I mean, just *look* at all these upperclassmen . . .

MEET THE FIGHTING IRISH

Luke Harangody (6-8, 250, Jr.). See above for my thoughts on Harangody's epochal importance on offense. As for the other side of the ball, Brey says he wants more from Harangody defensively. I know it's good motivation and standard practice for a coach to harp on the defensive shortcomings of his reigning conference player of the year and, granted, Harangody's no Hasheem Thabeet on defense. Still, there are plenty of coaches who would love to have a player who rebounds 24 percent of opponents' misses. Note to Brey: Harangody was second only to Kentrell Gransberry last year among Big East players in defensive rebounding. He was better on the defensive glass than Thabeet, Earl Clark, Roy Hibbert, Jeff Adrien, and DeJuan Blair. Your man Harangody may not look like the classic post defender, but he is in fact exceptionally effective at ending opponents' possessions. Give credit where due.

Kyle McAlarney (6-0, 195, Sr.). As already detailed, no one on this team shoots anywhere near as often as Harangody does. But among the non-Harangodys, no one shoots more than McAlarney, a spot-up shooter who's pretty hapless inside the arc but who made no less than 44 percent of his frequent threes last year. McAlarney thus belongs to that tiny and quixotic fraternity of players who actually shoot a higher percentage on their threes than on their twos. (For more on this rather odd group, see also "Collison, Darren" and "Paulus, Greg.") The senior from Staten Island is additionally a surprisingly good passer for a three-point master.

Tory Jackson (5-11, 195, Jr.). Jackson is an outstanding creator of assists, but he alone among the starters gives the ball away too often. What's more, he rarely shoots, a wise choice. Jackson's value on defense, however, is considerable: He records steals. If he didn't, it's conceivable that Notre Dame could have set a record last year for fewest opponent turnovers.

Ryan Ayers (6-7, 210, Sr.). Did I mention this team can make threes? Though he shoots even less than Jackson does, Ayers was even more deadly from outside than McAlarney last year, hitting 45 percent of his shots from beyond the arc.

Zach Hillesland (6-9, 235, Sr.). Hillesland is the only returning player not named *Harangody* who hauls in defensive rebounds. If he can merely fill the shoes of the now-departed Rob Kurz on the defensive glass, Hillesland will be making a big contribution to this team. He struggles a bit with turnovers, but then again, he has a weirdly high assist rate for a guy listed at 6-9 and 235.

Luke Zeller (6-10, 240, Sr.). Fated from this year forward to be known as the older brother of North Carolina freshman Tyler Zeller, Luke Zeller shot almost twice as many threes as twos last year and made 38 percent of his shots from three-point land.

Jonathan Peoples (6-3, 215, Jr.). Part of Brey's regular rotation, Peoples gives the guards a respite and appeared in all 33 games last year.

Prospectus says

Mike Brey is fast becoming the Rick Barnes of the Big East: Year after year, his teams score points in a highly efficient manner. Make no mistake, it's going to be tough for opponents to end Notre Dame's 37-game home winning streak. Then again, it's going to be tough for ND to duplicate last year's 14-4 record in this year's incredibly deep Big East. I think the best case for the Irish in 2009 is an offense that's even a little better than it was 2008 (no small feat, that) and a defense that allows about a point per trip. That would be one very good team—maybe not the national-title contender some have claimed to see here, but a very good team nonetheless, the best such seen in South Bend in a long while.

PITT

2008: 22-9 (10-8 Big East)
Lost to Michigan State 65-54, NCAA Second Round
In-conference offense: 1.09 points per possession (3rd)
In-conference defense: 1.05 points allowed per possession (11th)

What Pitt did well: *Laugh in the face of graduations and injuries—on offense.*

Entering last year, Pitt had bid farewell to three starters from the 2007 team that lost to UCLA in the Sweet 16: Aaron Gray, Antonio Graves, and Levon Kendall. Jamie Dixon's two returning starters were Mike Cook and Levance Fields. The two veterans, along with newly elevated starter Sam Young and a solid recruiting class headlined by DeJuan Blair, appeared to give the Panthers enough firepower to be a solid upper-tier Big East team.

Then things got interesting. Cook was lost for the season when he tore an ACL against Duke on December 20. Just nine days later, Fields suffered a fractured left foot against Dayton. At the time, it was thought he would miss up to 12 weeks. Dixon had lost his entire starting five from 2007, and the Panthers, if not written off entirely, were certainly consigned to the bin marked "tough luck" by most observers.

So what Pitt accomplished last year is a little astonishing: This was an outstanding team on offense, the third best in the Big East behind Connecticut and Notre Dame. Fields turned out to be a fast healer and returned to action on February 15, in time to guide the offense for the last seven games of the conference season. Interestingly, his return had little effect on the number of points being scored each trip down the floor: A good offense just kept being good.

The keys here were Young and Blair. Together they formed something of a two-point-making machine, a handy mechanism that not only made its shots but also took very good care of the ball. As a result, Pitt's turnovers were down and its two-point percentage was up in 2008 in Big East play. It also didn't hurt matters that Blair, though just a freshman, turned out to be one of the best offensive rebounders in the country.

What we learned in 2008: *Graduations and injuries can hurt your defense.*

Strange as it is to say of a Ben Howland legacy program, the weakness of Pitt last year was its defense. Even stranger, the weakness of that weakness was on the interior, where Big East opponents made more than half their twos. This marked the continuation of a mildly troubling three-season trend for Dixon's defense.

Pitt interior defense, 2006-2008
Conference games only
Def. reb. pct.: defensive rebound percentage
Opp. PPP: opponent points per possession

	2006	2007	2008
Opp. 2FG pct.	46.6	48.7	50.3
Def. reb. pct.	69.6	68.8	65.9
Opp. PPP	1.00	0.97	1.05
Record	10-6	12-4	10-8

Aaron Gray, who patrolled the paint for the Panthers through 2007, may have had his limitations, but you can say this for the big guy: He was seven feet tall. Levon Kendall, who played alongside Gray, may have been as quiet as a tomb on offense, but he was 6-10. Conversely, DeJuan Blair is indisputably a force of nature, one that helped propel his offense to unforeseen levels of efficiency as a freshman. But he's 6-7.

Last year the Pitt defense deteriorated as the Big East season progressed, reaching its nadir in the last seven games of the regular season. In fact, from Feb-ruary 12 to the start of the Big East tournament, no opponent failed to score at least 1.05 points per trip.

To be sure, Pitt put a positive spin on the year by winning the Big East tournament, beating three ranked teams in the process: Marquette, Louisville, and Georgetown. The impressive run in Madison Square Garden (where the Panthers always seem to play well) is what commentators apparently remember from 2008 when predicting that this team will go far in 2009. Perhaps Dixon can wring some additional motivation from his men, however, by also reminding them of the 3-4 finish to the Big East regular season or the 11-point loss to a five-seed (Michigan State) in the second round of the NCAA tournament.

What's in store for 2009
Pitt channeled the outstanding 2007 Georgetown offense a bit in 2008, scoring its points by making twos and crashing the offensive glass. In fact, the Panthers were the best offensive rebounding team in the Big East during conference play. There is at least one concern on offense for 2009, however. Two of Pitt's better perimeter shooters, Ronald Ramon and Keith Benjamin, have graduated, and the players who remain combined to shoot exactly 30 percent on their threes last year.

MEET THE PANTHERS

Sam Young (6-6, 215, Sr.). Young had a sweet run in the Big East tournament, scoring 80 points in four games and winning Most Outstanding Player honors. To date, he's functioned primarily as an undersized power forward, a very good one. Now he's reportedly slated to play a more suitable wing-type role for Dixon's team. Young is not going to lead your team in assists, but he has shown signs of being an honest dual-threat wing, hitting 38 percent of his threes and 54 percent of his twos last year. Indeed, the growth that all fans hope their team's players will achieve with the sheer passing of time actually seemed to take place with Young last year. In 2007, he averaged just 17 minutes a game and his shooting was so-so. Last year as a starter, his role in the offense grew, and so did his efficiency.

DeJuan Blair (6-7, 265, So.). As noted above, the Pitt offense, particularly during the 12 games that

Fields missed, very much went through Young and Blair last year. Blair in particular deserves all kinds of credit for carrying such a big load as a freshman in the Big East and doing so very effectively. During his minutes he rebounded almost 17 percent of his teammates' misses, an insanely high figure that was topped only by Nebraska's Aleks Maric among major-conference players last year. Blair is also excellent on the defensive glass, much more so than would be expected of a player listed at 6-7. And despite his 265 pounds, his team-leading steal rate says he's agile, never mind the body type. Blair is not the best foul shooter you'll run across, however.

Levance Fields (5-10, 190, Sr.). Fields missed a third of the season last year with his foot injury, but still played enough minutes to leave some impressive memories. Among Big East players, only A. J. Price posted a higher assist rate than Fields did in 2008. But what to make of his shooting? You know how, when a player is said to be "an erratic shooter," it's really a euphemism for "a bad shooter"? Not this time. Speaking literally, Fields is an erratic shooter. As a freshman in 2006, he made 43 percent of his threes. Swell, said Coach Dixon, here are some more touches. Unfortunately, with more touches came fewer makes, as Fields' three-point success dipped to 36 percent in 2007, before falling off the table last year to the tune of 28 percent. Yes, the injury may have continued to bother him after his return, but keep in mind that preinjury, he was just a 30 percent three-point shooter last year.

Gilbert Brown (6-6, 200, So.). Although he played for the Panthers in three games in November and December of 2006, Brown was given a medical redshirt. Last year, his minutes went up after his teammates went on the injured list, and he seemed to improve as the year went on. His 24 percent three-point shooting, however, suggests that he should probably stick to twos for the time being.

Tyrell Biggs (6-8, 240, Sr.). Still another very good offensive rebounder, Biggs played almost exactly half the available minutes for Dixon last year. Yet his defensive rebounding is oddly subdued, considering he was the tallest Panther to see regular minutes. Biggs is also foul prone, recording four fouls five times last year and never needing more than 26 minutes to do so.

Brad Wanamaker (6-4, 200, So.). Wanamaker ar-

rived last year as perhaps the most celebrated freshman recruit not named DeJuan Blair, but his first year featured many missed shots and turnovers. He will attempt to simply hit the reset button in his sophomore campaign.

Gary McGhee (6-10, 255, So.). McGhee barely got to 100 minutes total last year, but the talk is that he may see significant playing time this season as part of a go-big shift that will see Young playing more minutes as a wing.

Nasir Robinson (6-5, 220, Fr.). Touted as a tenacious defender who attacks the rim on offense, Robinson may see minutes at the wing or power forward positions, or both.

Ashton Gibbs (6-1, 175, Fr.). Even on a deep and experienced team, Gibbs could get a look as a freshman if he shows he can make his threes.

Prospectus says

No team in the country combines legitimately big names with legitimately big question marks like Pitt. Young, Blair, and Fields are all among the best in the Big East at what they do. Yet interior defense and perimeter shooting would, for an ordinary team sans big names, seem to be rather large question marks, no? If Pitt can surmount these obstacles as well as it overcame the ones that seemed to loom in their path last January, look out.

PROVIDENCE

2008: 15-16 (6-12 Big East)
Lost to West Virginia 58-53, Big East Tournament First Round
In-conference offense: 1.03 points per possession (10th)
In-conference defense: 1.08 points allowed per possession (13th)

What Providence did well: *Play Connecticut.*

If the Friars' schedule last year had consisted of 31 consecutive games against Connecticut, Tim Welsh would not only still be the head coach, but still be in line for a contract extension with a healthy bump.

If only all opponents were Huskies: Providence, 2008.

Conference games only

PPP: points per possession
Opp. PPP: opponent points per possession
EM: efficiency margin (PPP − Opp. PPP)

	Vs. Connecticut	Vs. rest of Big East
PPP	1.11	1.01
Opp. PPP	0.97	1.10
EM	+0.14	-0.09
Record	2-0	4-12

What's truly odd about Providence's apparent voodoo over the Huskies is that it was stylistically mobile. In the first meeting between the teams on January 17 in Hartford, the Friars won pretty much the way you'd expect a lesser team to win, by riding a wave of incredible (14-of-24) three-point shooting. In the rematch on March 6, however, Providence went to the other extreme. Doing a fair imitation of George Mason in 2006, Welsh's team took the ball right into the teeth of the UConn interior defense. That worked, too. *Everything* worked for the Friars in 2008 as long as the other jerseys said CONNECTICUT.

Alas, hegemony without mercy over just one team, even a team as good as Connecticut, wasn't enough to salvage Welsh's position as head coach. During the NCAA tournament, the Providence job was shopped without result to George Mason coach and Providence alum Jim Larranaga (who stayed put) and UMass coach Travis Ford (who went instead to Oklahoma State). As it happened, the job remained vacant for an entire nervous month before the Friars finally nabbed Keno Davis of Drake.

What we learned in 2008: *Herbert Hill's agent should use Providence's 2008 season to get his client a better contract.*

Man, does Herbert Hill look important in retrospect. Hill was the 6-10 senior who wrapped up his career at Providence in 2007 and was drafted late in the second round by Utah before promptly being traded to Philadelphia. Whether it was truly cause-and-effect I can't say, but with Hill gone last year the Friars' defensive rebounding collapsed rather spectacularly, fairly taking the whole defense and maybe even the coach's employment down with it. Only Seton Hall, barely, did a poorer job on the defensive glass in Big East play than did Providence. Or to put it another way (send the children out of the room), *even Northwestern* was a better defensive rebounding team in-conference than the Friars in 2008. Op-ponents' possessions just kept going and going, and Providence was utterly helpless to stop them.

What's in store for 2009
After last season, Providence sophomore Dwain Williams elected to transfer out of the program. (No one can accuse Williams of shying away from re-builds, surely. He left one high-major program that went 6-12 in-conference and transferred to another high-major program, Oregon State, that went 0-18 in-conference.) There have been and will be the usual good-riddance sentiments voiced on this front by PC fans, but the truth is Davis would have at least been interested in seeing what Williams could have done for him. In 2008, Williams's playing time was limited by injuries, and when he did play, he was unspeakably catastrophic in shooting twos. Then again, he did make 41 percent of his threes and 90 percent of his free throws. For Davis, who won national coach-of-the-year honors by spreading the floor with multiple three-point threats, those two numbers from Williams are enough to raise an eyebrow. In any case, he's gone, though the backcourt balance sheet at least evens out with the return of 2007 starting point guard Sharaud Curry, sidelined (virtually) all of last year with a stress fracture.

MEET THE FRIARS

Jeff Xavier (6-1, 185, Sr.). Xavier debuted with Providence as a junior last year, having transferred from Manhattan. He was a good addition who happened to arrive during a disappointing year. Xavier's steal rate was identical to that of renowned disrupter Jerel McNeal of Marquette. On offense, Xavier hit 36 percent of his shots from outside and preferred threes to twos at about a two-to-one ratio.

Weyinmi Efejuku (6-5, 210, Sr.). Last year was something of a struggle for Efejuku. After starting all 31 games as a sophomore in 2007, he found himself competing for minutes in 2008 with the since-departed Williams. The competition was settled in Efejuku's favor when Williams went down with an injury in mid-February, but seen as a whole, Efejuku's season was something of a surprise, and not in a good way. Most notably, he went from being very good inside the arc (53 percent in 2007) to very bad there (43 percent last year). On the bright side he made 38 percent of his threes.

Geoff McDermott (6-8, 235, Sr.). McDermott played through some injuries last year but over the past two seasons has shown that he comfortably combines two skills that, Joakim Noah notwithstanding, are rarely displayed by the same player: very good defensive rebounding and very good passing. His numbers in both areas are consistently high. Unfortunately, McDermott's turnover rate is also consistently high.

Sharaud Curry (5-10, 170, Jr.). Curry suffered a stress fracture before last season and, aside from eight foolhardy minutes against Sacred Heart in December, he sat the entire year. As the Friars' starting point guard in 2007, he made 37 percent of his threes and 90 percent of his free throws, though he also gave away too many turnovers. It was a solid but not spectacular season. Yet somehow today there seems to be a consensus that Curry's absence last year caused the Providence train to jump the track, so to speak. Perhaps the offense might have been more productive with him on the floor. But the Friars' largest issues by far in 2008 were on defense, and any help Curry could have provided here would have been indirect at best. Simply put, Providence's problems last year were much larger than the absence of Sharaud Curry.

Brian McKenzie (6-4, 205, Jr.). While the Friars' season was crashing around him, McKenzie quietly had a very nice year, scoring quite efficiently while attempting equal numbers of twos and threes.

Randall Hanke (6-11, 240, Sr.). If you like extremes, Hanke's the player for you. He's 6-11 but doesn't do defensive boards. He makes an incredible 63 percent of his twos and does so as an actual contributing member of the offense, not as a mere bit player. He recorded four assists in 519 minutes. OK, end of extremes: Hanke is also his new coach's best bet for an occasional shot block.

Jonathan Kale (6-8, 245, Sr.). An experienced workhorse who made nine starts last year, Kale is not averse to a little friendly contact under the boards, averaging a notably robust 5.4 fouls per 40 minutes.

Jamine Peterson (6-6, 225, So.). A high school teammate of Michael Beasley, Peterson arrived highly touted last year. Though he saw limited minutes as a freshman, he hoisted shots at a rate often seen from the highly touted and did OK. Peterson also displayed flashes of monstrous offensive rebounding. Stay tuned.

Bilal Dixon (6-9, 230, Fr.). Signed by Welsh and still coming to campus to play for Davis, by gar.

Prospectus says

If we can speak confidently of Keno Davis's "style" after he's coached just one year—albeit one spectacular year—we can say that he likes to shoot threes. In McKenzie, Efejuku, Curry, and Xavier, he has some decent perimeter threats. This team is also loaded with experience: The starting five will most likely be composed of three seniors and two juniors. And the fact that Providence's per-possession performance last year was actually a little better than its won-loss record means the Friars could probably improve their record by a game or even two this year simply by playing exactly as well as they did in 2008. All of which means there are a lot of signs pointing to immediate if modest improvement at Providence. Then again, the Friars have the singular misfortune to be rebuilding in a conference that's already ostentatiously built out. Move this team to the Big 12, and maybe you have a feel-good story on your hands this year. In the Hobbesian jungle known as the Big East, however, it's tougher to feel good in a hurry.

RUTGERS

2008: 11-20 (3-15 Big East)
Did not make the field of 12 teams in the Big East Tournament
In-conference offense: 0.88 points per possession (16th)
In-conference defense: 1.05 points allowed per possession (12th)

What Rutgers did well: *Recruit Jersey.*

Fred Hill is about to start year three of his rebuilding project at Rutgers, having arrived in 2006 largely on the strength of recruiting done as an assistant first at Seton Hall and then at Villanova. In his first recruiting class, Hill brought in a goodly sized name from nearby in the form of guard Corey Chandler of Newark. With this year's freshman class, Hill has continued his in-state foundation building, landing two Garden State products as highly touted as Chandler: big man Greg Echenique of Newark (a high school teammate of much-talked-about Louisville freshman

Samardo Samuels) and guard Mike Rosario of Jersey City, the first McDonald's All-American ever to choose Rutgers.

Granted, the actual results on the floor are still spotty—see below. But rebuilding a program at Rutgers, while no picnic, is hardly rocket science, either. This is a Big East school located in a state that's churned out a sizable number of top prospects over the past couple years, seemingly including the entire freshman class at Kansas this season. If Rutgers can get its fair share of the talent in its own backyard, this program can come back. So far, that's exactly what Hill is doing.

What we learned in 2008: *Solid recruiting doesn't always translate into wins right away.*

Last year, Rutgers had one of the worst offenses seen in major-conference basketball this decade, very nearly as bad as Oregon State's. Scoring less than 0.90 points per possession over the course of an entire conference season is exceptionally rare—OSU and Rutgers, both in 2008, are the only teams to have done so in the 219 seasons played by 73 major-conference teams over the past three years.

If you seek the problem here, just look around. In the Scarlet Knights' offense, one will observe, with the notable exception of perimeter shooting, chronic weaknesses as far as the eye can see. To think that one of the Knights' three victories last year was a 13-point (!) win on the road at Pitt fairly staggers the imagination.

Rutgers' most extreme liability in 2008 was a total lack of offensive rebounding. A low number of offensive boards need not be a problem, of course, if you're shooting a lot of threes and you're focused on getting back in transition in order to slow the pace of the game. None of the above applied with the Scarlet Knights last year, however, as Hill's men attempted an average number of threes and played at a pace that was much faster than in 2007.

Which brings me to the next glaring issue on offense: Much of that "faster" pace was in truth created by a sharp increase in Rutgers' turnovers. This team donated the ball to the opponent on 23 percent of its possessions in Big East play, a mark exceeded only by the even more charitable St. John's offense. Not that things went especially well on the other 77 percent of the trips, mind you. Even when they didn't turn the ball over last year, the Scarlet Knights couldn't make twos. No player with a contributing role in the offense made more than 46 percent of his two-point shots.

Of course, the very extremity of these problems suggests that things are almost sure to get better in 2009. But it would be remarkable if Rutgers' performance on offense rose merely to the level of the Big East average this season. There's so much distance to cover.

What's in store for 2009

Despite the 3-15 record, the Rutgers defense was actually within shouting distance of average last year, thanks largely to Hamady Ndiaye. The task at hand in year three of a rebuild, then, is more of the same on defense and a tourniquet for the profuse bleeding on offense. The Knights were adequate on their threes last year. Shooting more of them—even from a foot further out—plays to their strength, relatively speaking, and would also help limit the number of turnovers.

MEET THE SCARLET KNIGHTS

JR Inman (6-9, 220, Sr.). Since Quincy Douby left Rutgers in 2006, it's been Inman who's carried most of the load on offense for the Scarlet Knights. His assist rate has stayed amazingly constant at a very low level for three seasons, and he's never enjoyed much success in getting the ball into the basket: For his career, he's shot 45 percent on his twos. Then again, he's never exactly been blessed with a strong supporting cast.

Jaron Griffin (6-7, 210, Sr.). As a junior, Griffin had an absolute nightmare of a year shooting the ball. He was under the hoops equivalents of the Mendoza line on both twos and threes, shooting sub-40 percent on the former and sub-30 on the latter. His numbers for all the above were the same in 2007 as well. On the bright side, he's the least turnover-prone player who sees regular minutes. (I like to see the glass as half full.)

Anthony Farmer (6-1, 190, Sr.). Functions as a pass-first point guard for the Knights and earns his minutes by being one of the few players Hill can trust to hold on to the ball. On the rare occasions when Farmer did shoot from outside, he was successful. Maybe he should try it more often.

Hamady Ndiaye (6-11, 235, Jr.). Ndiaye might have been this team's most valuable player last year.

Without his shot blocking and defensive rebounding, Rutgers' defense would have been much worse than it was and you may well have been looking at a year of Oregon State–level futility. On offense, Ndiaye is rarely allowed to touch the ball—when he does, he often turns it over.

Mike Coburn (6-0, 195, So.). Hill obviously liked what he saw of Coburn as a freshman because he gave the young man 20 starts and more minutes than any other player except Inman and Farmer. Coburn peaked when his team did, scoring 23 and 17 points in late-January wins over Villanova and Pitt, respectively.

Corey Chandler (6-2, 190, So.). Chandler struggled with a foot injury as a freshman, but he still posted an outstanding steal rate, the best recorded by any Big East player last year. On the other side of the ball, he confidently assumed a leading role in the offense during his minutes but, much like Inman and Griffin, struggled mightily to make shots while turning the ball over even more frequently than they did.

Mike Rosario (6-1, 160, Fr.). Rosario committed to Rutgers in April of his junior year and then, as noted above, went on to earn McDonald's All-American honors as a senior. He's been praised by Hill as a great shooter who can do more than just shoot.

Greg Echenique (6-8, 240, Fr.). A native of Venezuela and a late addition to this class, Echenique arrives touted as an outstanding post defender.

Earl Pettis (6-5, 225, So.). Pettis had a night to remember on February 26 against Connecticut, scoring 18 points on 8-of-11 shooting. Unfortunately, over the course of the season, Pettis also had one of the highest turnover rates on a team that was itself turnover prone.

Prospectus says

The talent level is improving at Rutgers. The next step for this program is to win more games than it loses on its home floor against Big East opponents. If the offense improves significantly, this could happen as soon as this year.

SETON HALL

2008: 17-14 (7-11 Big East)
Lost to Marquette 67-54, Big East Tournament First Round
In-conference offense: 1.03 points per possession (11th)
In-conference defense: 1.09 points allowed per possession (14th)

What Seton Hall did well: *End the regular season memorably.*
It's bad enough, surely, to lose to Rutgers on your home floor, 64-61. But the actions of Seton Hall coach Bobby Gonzalez that day made a bad game even worse. In fact, the repercussions will still be felt this January, when the Pirates' coach serves a one-game suspension.

The game was won for Rutgers when JR Inman made a three with 1.2 seconds left on the clock. As soon as the shot went down, Gonzalez ran onto the floor demanding that the play be reviewed. As Gonzalez continued to yell toward the referees, a Seton Hall official attempted to come between the coach and the refs. It was reported that Gonzalez barked at the SHU staffer: "Get out of my face!"

Then, during the traditional coaches' handshake after the game, Gonzalez had a brief yet animated encounter with Scarlet Knights coach Fred Hill. Finally, Gonzalez used his postgame remarks to lambaste Big East referee Wally Rutecki, thereby violating the most black-letter no-no in the coaching book. The coach's actions earned him a one-game suspension to be served this year when the Pirates open Big East play. Those actions also brought forth a good deal of speculation that Gonzalez is rapidly painting himself into a corner at Seton Hall. Note that the suspension came not from the Big East office but from the school itself.

What we learned in 2008: *It's a long way from January to March.*
All was right with the Seton Hall world last January 30. The Pirates had just won at Rutgers in overtime, marking the team's fifth consecutive victory. At 5-3 in-conference and with a 10-point win over Louisville safely pocketed, SHU appeared to be on track for a solid middle-of-the-pack finish in the Big East and, more importantly, an NCAA tournament bid.

It wasn't to be. Seton Hall found February and March to be cruel indeed.

Seton Hall, 2008

Conference games only
PPP: points per possession
Opp. PPP: opponent points per possession
EM: efficiency margin (PPP – Opp. PPP)

	First 8 games	Last 10 games
PPP	1.08	0.98
Opp. PPP	1.05	1.12
EM	+0.03	-0.14
Record	5-3	2-8

This marks something of a worrisome trend for Gonzalez and the Pirates, for the team also collapsed in 2007, finishing 4-12 after a 3-2 start. The improvement seen in 2008 was that SHU's performance dipped after eight games instead of after five.

What's in store for 2009

Seton Hall finds itself in that most precarious of positions, that of the "rebuilding" program, which, at least on paper, has lost more talent than it's added from last year to this year. The Pirates bid farewell to Brian Laing and Jamar Nutter, two major contributors on offense. Their main addition is Duquesne transfer Robert Mitchell, who should likewise be a solid contributor. It'd just be nice if two or three more like him but of varying sizes were also arriving this year. Then again, if there's good news for the near future, it's that Seton Hall was absolutely killed by opposing teams' three-point shooting last year. Why is that good news? Nobody gets cooked like that on the perimeter two years in a row—it's just too far-fetched. Look at Cincinnati. The Bearcats played better-than-average three-point defense last year after virtually the same group of players allowed Big East opponents to make an astounding 43 percent of their threes in 2007. Gonzalez is hoping for a similar balancing of the perimeter karma for his team in 2009.

MEET THE PIRATES

Jeremy Hazell (6-5, 185, So.). Hazell had a 2008 debut that portends good things to come. His role in the offense was second only to that of Laing, yet Hazell was highly efficient on his many possessions.

The freshman recorded a turnover rate that's so low it looks like a typo, while he made 54 percent of his twos. Granted, those twos were sparse—Hazell much prefers threes, of which he made only 33 percent. But his good free-throw shooting gives reason enough for a continued, if provisional, green light from outside.

Eugene Harvey (6-0, 165, Jr.). It was a tough sophomore year for Harvey at the point. While his assist rate stayed robust, his turnovers were up and his shooting accuracy fell off dramatically. Nevertheless, Harvey helped his team by getting to the line often and making 73 percent of his free throws.

Paul Gause (5-11, 190, Sr.). Two years ago, Gause posted the highest steal rate in the nation. He might have repeated the feat last year if not for two separate injuries that sidelined him for 16 games.

John Garcia (6-9, 265, Jr.). Garcia is a very good defensive rebounder who touches the ball on offense only on put-backs, of which he gets many. Given this team's lack of size and chronic lack of defensive rebounding (last in the Big East in 2008), there is ample room in the Pirates' rotation for just such a player. Unfortunately, Garcia is almost comically foul prone, averaging over six fouls per 40 minutes as a sophomore. Against James Madison last year, Garcia fouled out in 10 minutes.

Robert Mitchell (6-6, 180, Jr.). A former A-10 rookie of the year and a transfer from Duquesne, Mitchell functioned as the focus of the Dukes' offense in 2007 and carried it off very efficiently. He's a good addition for this team.

Mike Davis (6-11, 255, So.). Gonzalez gave Davis very limited minutes last year, so it's tough to say what the young man can bring to the table. One thing we think we know: He can really block shots.

Augustine Okosun (6-11, 240, Sr.). Okosun saw even fewer minutes than Davis. He too is capable of blocking shots, but unlike Davis, he appears to be more at risk for turnovers on offense.

Prospectus says

For this year, Gonzalez's third at the Hall, the worries are the same as they were prior to each of his first two seasons: defense, rebounding, and whether the team will play well not only at the beginning of the conference schedule but also at the end. Under Gonzalez, the Pirates are 3-15 in Big East play in February and March.

SOUTH FLORIDA

2008: 12-19 (3-15 Big East)
Did not make the field of 12 teams in the Big East Tournament
In-conference offense: 0.99 points per possession (13th)
In-conference defense: 1.09 points allowed per possession (15th)

What South Florida did well: *Cut down on turnovers.*

The Bulls' offense last year didn't exactly strike fear into opponents, but any coach with a struggling team is going to focus on simply getting better. By this measure, Stan Heath deserves credit: In his first season at the helm, the USF offense took a big step forward in 2008, even though its shooting was actually a little bit worse than in 2007. More offensive boards helped, but the main difference from year to year was a huge drop in turnovers.

Largest declines in turnovers, 2007 to 2008

Conference games only: ACC, Big East, Big Ten, Big 12, Pac-10, and SEC
Turnover percentages

	2007	2008	Diff.
Duke	22.2	17.1	-5.1
South Florida	24.5	20.0	-4.5
Purdue	22.5	18.1	-4.4
LSU	22.3	18.4	-3.9
Baylor	20.5	16.6	-3.9

As I said, Heath deserves credit, but part of this result appears to have come from mere good timing. The Bulls lost at least one highly turnover-prone senior in 2007 and then welcomed freshman Dominique Jones to the program the following season. Jones played a big role in the offense and took excellent care of the ball last year. Kentrell Gransberry, of course, played an even larger role in that offense, but his turnover rate was dependably low from year to year: It was Gransberry's teammates who helped him out here.

What we learned in 2008: *The Bulls don't "do" threes.*

In 2008, only three major-conference teams in the country failed to make at least 30 percent of their threes in conference play: Virginia Tech, Oregon State, and South Florida. On paper, Dominique Jones and Jesus Verdejo appear to be respectable from the perimeter, but each saw his accuracy dip to about 33 percent from outside in Big East play—and these two players are the best options available for Heath. Last year's lack of success from the perimeter meant that opposing defenses were able to sag on Gransberry and limit his effectiveness. This year, Gransberry is gone: Continued struggles from outside for South Florida will be much tougher to offset with points in the paint.

What's in store for 2009

South Florida this year reminds me a little of Nebraska. Both teams have just said good-bye to big men—Aleks Maric for the Cornhuskers, Gransberry for the Bulls—who weren't judged worthy of even a second-round pick but who nevertheless absorbed a ton of possessions on offense and dominated the defensive glass. Both teams now face a lot of uncertainty.

Speaking of uncertainty, meet **Gus Gilchrist**, a player who hopes to take the floor for South Florida someday soon. The 6-9 Gilchrist originally signed with Virginia Tech in November 2006, but backed out of that commitment the following spring, when he reportedly evinced uneasiness about attending the Blacksburg campus in the wake of the tragic shootings of April 2007. Gilchrist then began attending classes at Maryland in January 2008, apparently unaware that strict ACC intraconference transfer rules would have required him not only to sit out a season but also to lose a year of eligibility. Once this became clear, he announced his intention to transfer to South Florida. As this book goes to press, Gilchrist's eligibility for this year is still in doubt. Little wonder—it's been an eventful couple years for the would-be Bull.

MEET THE BULLS

Dominique Jones (6-4, 205, So.). A freshman playing 87 percent of the minutes and carrying a large load on offense for a 3-15 team in the Big East would seem to be a recipe for a lot of turnovers and even more missed shots. Not for Dominique Jones last year. As noted above, he did an excellent job taking care of the ball while displaying average shooting on his threes and above-average success on his twos. Jones was also fouled with steady regularity and made 76 percent of his free throws—it was an excellent first season and one that can fairly be called a complete surprise. By my count, no fewer than 23 players signed by Big East teams in Jones's recruiting class were more highly rated coming out of high school. Yet it was Jones who, along with DeJuan Blair, Jonny Flynn, and Donte Greene, was a unanimous selection to the Big East's all-rookie team. He deserved to be there.

Mike Mercer (6-4, 190, Jr.). Mercer is a transfer from Georgia, where he was dismissed from the team by Dennis Felton last November. At the time, Mercer was serving a 15-game suspension for missing mandatory appointments with tutors. In taking the further step of dismissing Mercer from the team, Felton said his player had become a "disruption." Two weeks later, Mercer announced his decision to transfer to USF. He'll be eligible to play for the Bulls this season as of December 12.

Jesus Verdejo (6-4, 205, Sr.). As described above, Verdejo and Jones comprised much of the outside shooting threat for USF last year, with each hitting between 35 and 36 percent of his threes. Verdejo, however, doesn't fare as well inside the arc as Jones does.

Chris Howard (6-3, 200, Jr.). A classic pass-first point guard, Howard is excellent at delivering assists but is turnover prone. He is coming off a season of poor, if rare, shooting.

Ajayi Mobolaji (6-9, 225, Sr.). A freak of offensive rebounding nature, Mobolaji made 13 starts last year, but his playing time was limited by Heath and foul trouble in roughly equal measure.

Alex Rivas Sanchez (6-10, 230, Jr.). A junior-college transfer, Rivas Sanchez was brought to Tampa by Heath to give the roster some size and, hopefully, some post-Gransberry boards.

Eladio Espinosa (6-7, 220, Fr.). Espinosa has been praised by Heath as an athletic player who can function as either a power forward or a wing.

Prospectus says
This will be a transition year for USF, from the Gransberry era to whatever comes next. Landing Mercer helps in the short term, but the fundamental question with regard to South Florida is still in play. This is a team that's won seven conference games in three years. How long will it take South Florida to develop a Big East–caliber basketball program?

ST. JOHN'S

2008: 11-19 (5-13 Big East)
Did not make the field of 12 teams in the Big East Tournament
In-conference offense: 0.90 points per possession (15th)
In-conference defense: 1.02 points allowed per possession (12th)

What St. John's did well: *Post a winning record at home—sort of.*
Like Connecticut, St. John's is one of a tiny number of Division I teams that divvies up its "home" games between two venues. The Johnnies host visiting teams at both Carnesecca Arena in Queens and at Madison Square Garden on 7th Avenue in Manhattan.

Understandably, St. John's saves the marquee match-ups for the Garden. Last year, Georgetown, Marquette, West Virginia, Pitt, and Villanova came to MSG, whereas Cincinnati, DePaul, Providence, and Seton Hall were consigned to the 6,000-seat venue in Queens. In other words, every opponent at the Garden was an eventual NCAA tournament team. Carnesecca Arena was for everyone else.

The Johnnies went 0-5 against the cream of the Big East in Manhattan. But if you think of Carnesecca Arena as the true "home" venue, Norm Roberts's team defended its turf well, going 3-1 against conference visitors.

What we learned in 2008: *Defensive rebounding doesn't matter as much if your opponents don't miss.*
It went entirely unnoticed last year, but St. John's, a team that played a fair share of minutes without anyone taller than 6-9 on the floor, was the best defensive rebounding team in the tall and athletic Big East.

Big East defensive rebounding, 2008
Conference games only
Def. reb. pct.: defensive rebound percentage

	Def. reb. pct.
St. John's	72.0
Cincinnati	70.3
Louisville	70.1
West Virginia	69.1
Syracuse	69.0

Had the Johnnies not been so oddly exemplary on the defensive glass, things might really have gotten out of hand. Big East opponents feasted on pounding the ball into the paint against this defense, making almost 52 percent of their twos. I don't think I've ever seen a team with such a bad defense (12th in the Big East) do such an excellent job on the defensive boards.

This particular excellence was a true team effort, for Roberts's team had no players who were particularly good individual defensive rebounders. The potential exception here is Dele Coker, who will continue to be forbidden to touch the ball on offense but does at least show some promise at ending opponents' possessions after the first miss. This fact wasn't lost on Roberts. By the end of the year, Coker was starting, offense be damned.

What's in store for 2009

After last season, Larry Wright transferred to Oakland University to be closer to his family. Though Wright was given just 10 starts and averaged less than 20 minutes a game, it is said that his departure calls into question this team's perimeter shooting. It's true Wright was the best three-point shooter on the team, but it's equally important to note that St. John's last year was, remarkably, far worse when shooting twos than it was on its threes. *Both* kinds of scoring are likely to need help this season. If someone not named Anthony Mason steps into either void this year, it will almost certainly be a sophomore. Indeed, the St. John's rotation is pretty incredible, chronologically speaking. Mason and a couple incoming freshmen (**Quincy Roberts** and **TyShwan Edmondson**) notwithstanding, it's like a science fiction movie in which a ray gun fired from space has killed every earthling who's not a college sophomore . . .

MEET THE RED STORM

Anthony Mason Jr. (6-7, 210, Sr.) Mason had a tough time with ankle injuries last year and missed eight games between the start of the season and mid-February. When he was on the floor, though, he was the alpha and omega of the St. John's offense—for better or worse. Among Big East players, only Luke Harangody, Dar Tucker, and Corey Chandler accounted for a higher percentage of their teams' shots while they were in the game. Somewhat oddly, Mason simultaneously had the best year of his career shooting threes and the worst year of his career shooting twos. Though not much of a presence on the boards, he's also a very good passer for a player listed at 6-7.

Justin Burrell (6-8, 235, So.). If recruiting rankings are to be believed, the big catches in last year's giant haul of freshmen for St. John's were Coker and this young man, Justin Burrell. As it happens, however, Burrell had a rather rude introduction to college hoops, missing a high number of shots and committing a prodigious number of turnovers. Burrell's struggles were in large part his team's struggles, for in minutes played he led all players by a healthy margin.

Malik Boothe (5-9, 185, So.). Boothe will replace the now departed Eugene Lawrence at point guard. (Last year, Roberts deployed both Boothe and Lawrence as side-by-side starters against smallish opponents like Duke and Seton Hall.) As a freshman, Boothe posted a very nice assist rate, but like Burrell, he did battle with misses and turnovers and lost both fights. Unlike Burrell, Boothe shot very rarely.

D. J. Kennedy (6-6, 210, So.). Though listed at just 6-6, Kennedy was the best defensive rebounder among Johnnies who saw regular playing time. On offense, he was a supporting player and fared pretty well, making 49 percent of his twos. On this team, this qualified as positively stellar.

Dele Coker (6-10, 270, So.). As noted above, Coker gives hints of being a very good defensive rebounder. On the other end of the floor, Roberts may want to consider simply parking the lad on the weak-side low block for put-backs. Hey, it worked for Joey Dorsey.

Paris Horne (6-3, 180, So.). Horne averaged just 15 minutes per game last year, but he did post the best shooting from the field of anyone besides the now departed Wright. For what it's worth.

Sean Evans (6-8, 240, So.). Evans apparently exists

to foul and be fouled. He averaged more than five fouls per 40 minutes and was sent to the line himself with regularity. Unfortunately, he made just 35 percent of his free throws. (Not a typo: 35 percent.)

Rob Thomas (6-6, 235, So.). Thomas was academically ineligible until December last year, and, anyway, he was simultaneously rehabbing a knee injury. Big things are expected from the highly athletic Thomas if his health and eligibility ever fully align.

Prospectus says

It took a Rutgers offense of quite literally historic ineptitude (see the Rutgers preview) to deny St. John's the title of Big East's worst offense last year. In 2008, the Johnnies simply lacked ways to score—even when they didn't turn the ball over, which they did more often (23 percent of the time) than any other Big East team. A continuously healthy and full-speed Mason will help, but won't be enough by itself to solve the problem entirely.

SYRACUSE

2008: 21-14 (9-9 Big East)
Lost to UMass 81-77, NIT Quarterfinal
In-conference offense: 1.04 points per possession (9th)
In-conference defense: 1.02 points allowed per possession (6th)

What Syracuse did well: *Call accepted wisdom into question.*

You may have heard that Jim Boeheim likes to play zone defense. You may also have heard that playing a zone hurts your defensive rebounding because the defenders, watching the shot in flight, have trouble finding a man to box out. For years, the actual performance of Syracuse on the defensive glass has supported this article of faith.

Until last year, that is. Syracuse was a very good defensive rebounding team in-conference in 2008, one that secured no less than 69 percent of its opponents' misses. This is an abrupt departure from the recent past in the Carrier Dome, where 63 or 64 percent has been more like it when it comes to defensive boards. Syracuse fans, tip your orange caps toward Arinze Onuaku, the since-departed Donte Greene, and Paul Harris, in that order, for rather surprising services rendered.

This newfound ability was huge for the 'Cuse last

year—without it, the Orangemen could have been looking at some much more serious issues on defense. The 2007 team, the one that occasioned the o-the-humanity! hue and cry when it was left out of the NCAA tournament, very quietly played some unbelievable field-goal defense. (Syracuse fans, tip those same caps toward Darryl Watkins.) Last year, conversely, opponents had a much easier time getting the ball in the basket, particularly from inside the arc. If not for Syracuse's success at ending opponents' possessions after the first miss, this team would have looked a lot more like Providence on defense, for both teams played similar levels of field-goal defense. Strange as it sounds, rebounding made the difference for this zone defense.

What we learned in 2008: *Syracuse and its opponents played diametrically opposed styles.*

The Orangemen attempted far fewer threes last year than they had the previous two seasons. This wasn't some kind of stylistic epiphany experienced by Boeheim, of course, but was merely the consequence of losing both Andy Rautins in the preseason and Eric Devendorf in December to torn ACLs. Without Rautins and especially Devendorf on hand to wrest the ball away from Greene every now and then, this team shot twos.

So here's what you saw if you watched Syracuse play a conference game last year: The Orangemen would bring the ball up, and someone, often Greene, would shoot a two, usually against a man-to-man defense. (Only Connecticut devoted a smaller share of its shots to threes in-conference.) Then the opponent would bring the ball up and shoot a three, invariably against a zone defense. (No other team's opponents shot anywhere near as many threes as did the Orangemen's opponents in Big East play.) This sequence would then be repeated lots of times: Syracuse packed 71 possessions into every 40 minutes. Only Notre Dame played faster conference games.

I may ask Ken to do one of his patented archive dives, or I might just wax reckless and say flat-out in that Syracuse in 2008 was the first team in our planet's 4.5 billion years to combine all the following: zone defense, fast pace, lots of twos, and great defensive rebounding. It was a really odd combination, equal parts Boeheim, Bob Knight, and Mike D'Antoni.

What's in store for 2009

Greene is gone, drafted with the 28th pick of the first round by Memphis and then promptly traded to Houston. Devendorf and Rautins return, reportedly fully recovered from their respective injuries. This one-for-two exchange sums up pretty nicely what this year's team should look like: a little smaller, facing some questions on defense, but with some more potential from the perimeter, even with the line moved out a foot.

MEET THE ORANGEMEN

Eric Devendorf (6-4, 180, Jr.). Devendorf missed all but the first 10 games last year with a torn ACL, and for a player who's seemingly been around a long while, he's still surprisingly tough to gauge, at least for me. He had a sweet freshman year playing alongside Gerry McNamara in 2006, only to see his own efficiency inside the arc dip appreciably in 2007. (Devendorf did offset this to an extent with a dramatically improved assist rate.) If I'm a Syracuse fan, my worry for this season is that Devendorf will shoot around 250 twos. He shouldn't do that. Things didn't go well in 2007 when he did, and anyway, he has teammates who can put him to shame in this department (see below). On the other hand, if Devendorf is functioning on the perimeter as a second point-guard-level passer alongside Jonny Flynn and looking for his three, that sounds about right.

Paul Harris (6-5, 230, Jr.). Speaking of shot selection, I wouldn't be shocked to see Harris try more threes this year in a bid to boost his draft stock. To date, however, he's made his home largely inside the arc and done pretty well. Actually, his most effective tactic on offense is to make many visits to the free-throw line, where he shot 73 percent as a sophomore. Harris led the team in minutes last year and though his defensive rebounding was down from the impressive level seen in his freshman year, this feels to me like a contextual decline, one triggered by the arrivals of teammates like Onuaku and Greene. Until further notice, the assumption here is that Harris can still get it done on the glass.

Jonny Flynn (6-0, 185, So.). The Big East doesn't lack for undersized guards who are quick, well publicized, and fun to watch, but who can't really finish inside the arc. Flynn shatters that mold: As a freshman generously listed at 6-0, he made a sparkling 53 percent of his twos. He also fulfills the more traditional aspects of the job description, delivering plenty of assists while holding on to the rock. If not for A. J. Price, you could make a case that Flynn is already the best point guard in the conference.

Andy Rautins (6-5, 195, Jr.). Rautins spent the summer testing his knee by playing for Team Canada under the coaching of his father, former Syracuse player Leo Rautins. (Fun facts: Leo Rautins was both the first player ever to record a triple-double in Big East play and the first Canadian drafted by the NBA.) In 2007 for the Orangemen, Andy Rautins hit 36 percent of his threes while functioning mostly as a perimeter specialist, albeit one with a strange and incongruous ability to record steals.

Arinze Onuaku (6-9, 260, Jr.). Last year Onuaku made an eyebrow-raising 63 percent of his twos and, much more importantly, did so as an actual contributing member of the offense who really did attempt shots. Sure, some of those were put-backs, but not all of them. And anyway, put-backs count, too. As noted above, Onuaku was also the best defensive rebounder on a very good defensive rebounding team.

Scoop Jardine (6-1, 190, So.). As Boeheim cast about last year for a starting lineup sans Devendorf, he gave Jardine 10 starts. The freshman had a tough time holding on to the ball and, as if to atone, turned right around on defense and posted the team's highest steal rate. One more thing: For an 83 percent free-throw shooter Jardine was weirdly hesitant to shoot threes.

Kristof Ongenaet (6-8, 215, Sr.). Ongenaet got the nod as the fifth starter in late January and thereafter was given as many minutes as foul trouble would allow (he fouled out against South Florida in 10 minutes), furnishing Boeheim with another Greene-level defensive rebounder. Because of an apparent propensity for turnovers, the lanky Belgian is not allowed to touch, see, point toward, or think about the ball on offense, but he does make two of every three free throws when he's fouled, which is often.

Rick Jackson (6-9, 235, So.). Yet another member of last year's boisterous freshman class, Jackson saw limited yet consistent minutes off the bench and did his best work on the offensive glass.

Kris Joseph (6-7, 220, Fr.). A Canadian native, Joseph played his high school ball in Washington,

D.C., and arrives at Syracuse billed as a versatile wing who's also a good passer.

Mookie Jones (6-6, 210, Fr.). Jones is an athletic wing from Peekskill, New York. He rebuffed overtures from programs situated in warmer locales (e.g., Georgetown, Clemson, and Arizona State, from least to most salubrious) and instead elected to follow his hoops heart upstate.

Prospectus says

Syracuse's most prominent characteristic last year was poor perimeter shooting. The return of Devendorf and Rautins promises to take care of that. On the other hand, this team is still on the small side, and opponents should continue to fare well in the paint on offense. So the Orangemen won't lead the league in defense—but it is still likely that their two-year NCAA tournament exile will end in 2009.

VILLANOVA

2008: 22-13 (9-9 Big East)
Lost to Kansas 72-57, NCAA Second Round
In-conference offense: 1.00 points per possession (12th)
In-conference defense: 1.00 points allowed per possession (5th)

What Villanova did well: *Get into the NCAA tournament.*

The deliberations of the NCAA tournament selection committee are shrouded from public view, of course, and the comments made by the committee chair every year on Selection Sunday tend to stick to a reassuringly familiar script: most talented field ever, toughest decisions ever, outstanding work by the committee, the RPI (ratings percentage index) is just one tool of many, and on and on.

Still, looking at the actual results of those deliberations does give us some tea leaves to read. For instance, when a major-conference team makes the NCAA tournament as a 12-seed, as Villanova did last year and as Arkansas and Illinois did in 2007, you know that the team was either the last or second-to-last team given an at-large bid. In 2008, the Wildcats truly made the tournament by the very slimmest of margins.

For a while there, it didn't look as though Jay Wright's team would make it at all, as a 12-seed or any other seed. As late as February 8, it looked like a long shot: Villanova was 3-6 in the Big East. The Wildcats closed strong, however, going 6-3 over the last half of the conference season. The difference was much better field-goal defense, particularly on the perimeter:

Villanova defense, 2008
Conference games only

	First 9 games	*Last 9 games*
Opp. 2FG pct.	51.5	47.6
Opp. 3FG pct.	40.6	26.5
Defensive rebound pct.	64.8	68.6
Opp. PPP	1.07	0.93
Record	3-6	6-3

The Wildcats have made the dance now for four years running. If this turns into some kind of venerable Arizona-sized multidecade streak, just remember to give the credit to the defense played by 'Nova in February and March 2008. That defense was enough to keep the streak alive. Barely.

What we learned in 2008: *Villanova fouls opponents silly . . . or maybe that was then.*

You don't need any fancy-schmancy tempo-free stats to see that the undersized Wildcats were weirdly foul happy in 2008. Just look at the bottom line: Villanova's Big East opponents attempted 935 shots from the field and 468 free throws. Meaning there was one free throw for every two shots from the field, an extraordinarily high frequency of freebies. During the Wildcats' harrowing four-game losing streak spanning late January and early February, opponents *averaged* almost 38 free throws a game. No Big East team fouled at a higher rate in-conference.

Villanova's fouling in Big East play has increased steadily in each of the past three seasons, and bear in mind that the team's starting point was already above the conference average. Maybe that's about to change, though. Over the second half of the conference season in 2008, when, as we've seen, the Wildcat defense was at its best, the team's foul rate plummeted to the point where 'Nova resembled a normal Big East team. Perhaps this team has turned over a new leaf where fouling is concerned.

What's in store for 2009

It's common to say of a team that "everyone's back," particularly in the Big East this year. But for Villanova, it's almost literally true: Everyone's back. (The only exception here is Malcolm Grant, who started four games but transferred to Miami after logging a grand total of three minutes in the five Big East and NCAA tournament games.) Given this continuity, it'll be interesting to see if Wright stays with the rather novel rotation he put in place last year. Forget something as bourgeois as a starting five, the key numbers for Wright were two and six. The two constants on the floor were Scottie Reynolds and Dante Cunningham. Around those twin stalwarts there was a revolving cast of no fewer than six other players, all of whom saw roughly equal minutes.

MEET THE WILDCATS

Scottie Reynolds (6-2, 190, Jr.). There's a clear headliner in this post-Foye-Ray generation of Villanova hoops, and his name is Scottie Reynolds. He leads the team in minutes, and when he's in the game the possessions and shots are routed through him, especially if he's not sharing the floor with Corey Fisher. Last year Reynolds made 44 percent of his twos, which sounds low (OK, is low), but it did represent a significant improvement over his results inside the arc as a freshman. Besides, he made 38 percent of his threes and 78 percent of his (frequent) free throws. Reynolds has also shown, particularly in his freshman year, that he can deliver assists to open teammates.

Dante Cunningham (6-8, 230, Sr.). As noted above, Cunningham is the other indispensable cog in the machine Wright has built the past couple years, the only Wildcat of some size who the coach trusts enough to simply leave on the floor until fouls or fatigue intercedes. Cunningham plays a supporting role in the offense and his turnovers are a little too frequent, though on the rare occasions when he shoots, he is effective. Throughout his career he's been much more of a force on the offensive boards than on the defensive glass, yet the Wildcats as a team achieved defensive-rebound results that were right at the Big East average last year.

Corey Fisher (6-1, 200, So.). We know Wright thinks Fisher at least has potential because the coach gave him ostentatiously ample slack even during some truly epic on-floor struggles. See, for example, Fisher's 1-of-16 shooting from the field in the fated-to-become-infamous Georgetown game, a performance that surely left old-school purists from coast to coast good and riled. It is apparently hoped that Fisher will arrive someday soon as a scoring point guard in the D. J. Augustin/A. J. Price mold. The lad has the point-guard part mastered, having shown he can dish assists and take fairly good care of the ball. Perhaps the scoring part will follow, but the points Fisher scored last year were purchased at tremendous cost.

Antonio Pena (6-8, 235, So.). Along with Dwayne Anderson, Pena is the best defensive rebounder on the team. He also gets to the line regularly and makes 70 percent of his free throws, far and away the best offensive feature of a player who otherwise struggles with turnovers.

Shane Clark (6-7, 205, Sr.). Aside from the 29 percent three-point shooting, Clark looks pretty good on paper: a very good free-throw shooter who's adequate on the boards on both ends of the floor and who makes over half his twos as a bit player in the offense. The nice totals at the end of the year, however, kind of masked what was in fact a year of spurts for Clark. He started the season very well, tapered off a bit as the conference season progressed, and then came on strong again toward the end: See, for example, his 15 points on 7-of-11 shooting against South Florida on March 5.

Corey Stokes (6-5, 220, So.). In averaging 18 minutes a game, Stokes didn't leave much of a trace other than the 135 threes he attempted. Though he only made 40 of those, he may yet round into form on the perimeter. It's hard to gauge free-throw shooting when it's so infrequent, but still, hitting 88 percent from 15 feet says Stokes might find the range from 20 feet nine inches someday.

Dwayne Anderson (6-6, 215, Sr.). Anderson excels at taking the ball away from opposing offenses. As noted above, he also supplies the same level of defensive rebounding as did Pena, but with fewer turnovers.

Reggie Redding (6-5, 205, Jr.). The utility infielder, Redding does the necessary work wherever it needs to be done, including on the boards and, somewhat surprisingly, in the assist column. His value is plain to Wright, at least, for Redding was surpassed in minutes last year only by Reynolds, Cunningham, and Fisher.

Casiem Drummond (6-10, 275, Jr.). The ninth player in last year's eight-player rotation, Drummond returned from a foot injury suffered early in the season and actually started three games in February. After that, however, his minutes tapered off. Drummond continues to be something of a hovering mystery, like Ralph Nader or the future of newspapers.

Prospectus says
So many Big East teams are expected to improve this year because so many players in the conference are coming back. But of all the teams expected to be better than they were last year, Villanova may well have the best case for optimism—for the simple fact that it has the most room for improvement, specifically on offense. At just one point per possession in-conference, the Wildcats had the worst offense of any Big East team that made the NCAA tournament last year. (Actually, 'Nova had a worse offense than three teams that *didn't* make the tournament: DePaul, Providence, and Seton Hall.) Watch for both the Wildcats' perimeter shooting (14th in Big East play last year) and their turnover percentage (11th) to improve this season, bringing the offense and the team up with them.

WEST VIRGINIA

2008: 26-11 (11-7 Big East)
Lost to Xavier 79-75 (OT), NCAA Sweet 16
In-conference offense: 1.07 points per possession (4th)
In-conference defense: 0.99 points allowed per possession (4th)

What West Virginia did well: *Preserve the best of the old while welcoming the new.*
Bob Huggins's replacing John Beilein at West Virginia last year represented an abrupt shift in style for the Mountaineers. For instance, in Big East play WVU went from devoting a whopping 52 percent of its field-goal attempts to threes to a much more mainstream 35 percent.

Of course, *any* coach replacing Beilein would have represented an abrupt shift in style, for over the course of Beilein's career the current Michigan coach has worked up a system on offense that's anything but vanilla. The challenge for Huggins was to lay off what wasn't broke—this team had the fourth-ranked offense in the Big East in 2007—while getting his players to buy into changes that would lift the Mountaineers higher than an NIT title.

Mission accomplished. The offense last year was almost as good as in 2007, but the change that really propelled West Virginia in 2008 was a vastly improved defense.

West Virginia, 2007 versus 2008
Conference games only
PPP: points per possession
Opp. PPP: opponent points per possession
EM: efficiency margin (PPP – Opp. PPP)

	2007	2008
PPP	1.08	1.07
Opp. PPP	1.05	0.99
EM	+0.03	+0.08
Conf. record	9-7	11-7

Huggins has earned his chops on defense, no doubt, but he additionally benefited simply from finding key reserve Wellington Smith available and on hand. Though Smith averaged just 20 minutes a game and is listed at a mere 6-7, he proved to be an outstanding shot blocker. Smith alone wasn't sufficient, but he was probably necessary to catalyze the sudden and dramatic drop-off in two-point success enjoyed by the Mountaineers' Big East opponents in 2008. This, along with much better defensive rebounding, made the difference between NIT in 2007 and NCAA in 2008.

What we learned in 2008: *Joe Mazzulla is a very good hoops analyst.*
One of the toughest gigs for an upperclassman has to be when the local reporter comes calling to ask what you think of your sensational new freshman teammate. What are you supposed to say? "Yes! By all means, let's talk at length about my vastly more talented teammate, who hasn't done anything yet but is getting all this coverage! Yippee!"

Nevertheless, Joe Mazzulla managed to be pretty interesting when asked about his highly anticipated new teammate, freshman Devin Ebanks. Basically, Mazzulla told the *Charleston Daily Mail* that

Ebanks can be a one-and-done player if he listens to Huggins like Joe Alexander did—eventually: "Joe Alexander was obviously a great player and a great athlete, but he didn't completely listen to Huggs the first half of the season and sometimes it showed. . . . The last ten games of the season he looked Huggs in the eye every second and listened to everything he said. He and Huggs built that trust and you see what happened."

Sounds like standard-issue college hoops boilerplate, right? The talented but willful young scorer matures into a true team player, thanks to the blunt counsel of his crusty but wise coach. Throw a stick at any sports section, and you'll hit 10 such write-ups.

Maybe, but this one holds water. Not that I can vouch for the changing dynamics between Alexander and Huggins last year, of course. But in terms of results on the court, Mazzulla's version of events is remarkably accurate.

The epiphany for Alexander seems to have taken place in early February, after a miserable 2-of-11 performance from the floor at Pitt. Up to that point in the season, Alexander was a 46 percent two-point shooter. Over the Mountaineers' final 14 games, however, his role in the offense ballooned even as he became much more accurate on his shooting. In effect, Alexander made as many shots in the last 14 games as he did in the first 23. It was a spurt that landed him in the NBA.

What's in store for 2009

Huggins has said his team needs "to consistently score better." What's this? You don't want 1.07 points per trip, Coach? Hey, Jay Wright would kill to get that at Villanova this year. Maybe, even in 2008, coaches are still fooled by pace. If Coach Huggins is simply looking at point totals, he'll think West Virginia didn't score much last year, because it was the fourth-slowest team in the Big East. In terms of performance versus the conference average, however, the Mountaineers' offense was actually a tiny bit better than their defense. Be happy, Coach. You have one well-balanced team.

MEET THE MOUNTAINEERS

Da'Sean Butler (6-7, 225, Jr.). Alexander was clearly the Man in this offense last year, but Butler had an excellent season riding shotgun: sterling efficiency inside the arc, enough threes to keep de-

fenses honest, and zero turnovers. I don't want to jinx Butler or anything, but I can't help but note that his sophomore campaign was superior to the one Alexander had in 2007, albeit while carrying a little less of the load on offense than did the once and future Man. Butler is best when the clock is running, though. He shot just 64 percent at the line last year.

Devin Ebanks (6-8, 185, Fr.). Ebanks signed a letter of intent with Indiana in November 2007, but that was before (or, though we didn't know it, during) the Kelvin Sampson debacle. After attending the Big Ten tournament in March and stating his case in person, Ebanks was released from his commitment by IU. As discussed above, Ebanks is widely expected to be Joe Alexander 2.0 in 2009, but that might be a little too pat. What set apart phenoms like Durant and Beasley and was essential even for relative graybeards like Alexander was that they took on these absurdly outsized roles in their offenses and did it without turning the ball over. That was critical in the case of Alexander and the Mountaineers last year, because this was a relatively poor shooting team. Ebanks might do exactly that—Durant and Beasley have shown that freshmen can pull it off. In addition to watching Ebanks' point totals, then, keep an eye on his turnovers as well.

Alex Ruoff (6-6, 215, Sr.). Pick your favorite example of that most familiar of hoops characters, the lethally efficient role player. Lee Humphrey of Florida? Matt Lawrence of Missouri? Jonathan Cox of Drake? The short list should now include Ruoff. When you make 41 percent of your threes and 62 percent of your twos, life is good. If Ebanks is truly as diverting to opposing defenses as promised, Ruoff should again be able to thrive in the creases created by the freshman and by Butler.

Joe Mazzulla (6-2, 210, Jr.). It's strange to say this of a point guard, but one of Mazzulla's most vital contributions last year was his defensive rebounding. Only Joe Alexander rebounded a higher percentage of opponents' misses than did the 6-2 Mazzulla. Although Mazzulla also posted the team's highest assist rate, he shot just 65 percent on his free throws. Note also that his turnover rate was uniquely average on a team on which everyone else's number here was much better than average.

Wellington Smith (6-7, 215, Jr.). See above: Smith's shot blocking made itself felt on this team last year. Though he wasn't a starter, his playing time was limited by fouls far more than by Huggins.

John Flowers (6-7, 195, So.). Flowers averaged 12 minutes a game as a freshman and distinguished himself on the offensive glass and as a shot blocker.

Kevin Jones (6-8, 195, Fr.). In a normal recruiting class sans Ebanks, Jones would loom as a big name, billed as an all-around multiposition player, one who scores, defends, and rebounds.

Roscoe Davis (6-10, 220, Fr.). Davis has been praised by Huggins for his agility and ability to run the floor. "We will work with Roscoe to get the kind of strength he needs to excel in the Big East," Huggins has said.

Darryl Bryant (6-1, 185, Fr.). This point guard was recruited to help Mazzulla fill the void left by the departure of Darris Nichols.

Prospectus says

When the Mountaineers came together in February of last year, it was a sight to behold. Over the last half of the Big East season, only Louisville played better than West Virginia did. What this says is that Bob Huggins was able to compress a traditional transition year into something more like a transition three months. Now the transition has been made, and the team should have a collective memory of how to perform at an elite level in this conference. Yes, Alexander will have to be replaced, but Butler's no slouch, Ruoff's an assassin, and Ebanks doesn't have to be a savior, just good. The Big East this year won't be for the faint of heart, goodness knows, but the Mountaineers can again make their home in the conference's upper tier if they play the way they finished last year.

The Big Ten

Midwestern Exceptionalism at Its Finest

JOHN GASAWAY

When last we saw the Big Ten, its season was ending with exceptional quickness and severity.

On a Friday evening in late March, the Big Ten's best team, Wisconsin, clambered up onto the raised floor placed at the center of Detroit's Ford Field for its first Sweet 16 game in three years and got schooled 73-56 by the SoCon's best team, Davidson. Facing a defense that had held Big Ten opponents to an anemic 0.91 points per trip, the Wildcats were singularly unimpressed, blithely reeling off 73 points in just 54 possessions. As my colleague Ken Pomeroy noted aptly at the time, "No team has shredded a Wisconsin defense over the past two seasons like Davidson did last night."

Later that same Friday night, Michigan State clambered up onto the raised floor placed at the center of Houston's Reliant Stadium for its first Sweet 16 game in three years and was effectively euthanized inside of 20 minutes by Memphis. The 92-74 final score was a forgery, one that reflected either magnanimity or a mere loss of interest on the part of John Calipari's team, for the Tigers led the Spartans 50-20 at the half.

It was left to Ohio State to salvage some desiccated morsel of conference dignity by winning the NIT. Nevertheless, postseasons in even-numbered years have not been kind to the Big Ten of late: No Elite Eight entrants last year, no second-weekend teams at all in 2006. Odd-numbered years, conversely, have been much more gratifying: national runners-up in both 2005 and 2007, with three Elite

Eight teams and two Final Four teams in the earlier year.

This iambic quality to the conference's fortunes highlights a surprising feature. The Big Ten, that putative bastion of all that's Midwestern and mainstream, is actually quite exceptional. In a number of ways, the conference of middle America stands out as an extreme outlier . . .

Threes

The Big Ten shoots far more threes than any other major conference. Call this the Beilein-Lickliter effect.

Conference games only

Three-point attempts as percentage of field-goal attempts

Major-conference three-point attempts, 2008

Big Ten	37.9
SEC	35.8
Big East	33.2
Big 12	32.8
Pac-10	31.9
ACC	31.4

This year's new three-point line may cause a slight reduction in the number of three-point shots attempted across college basketball. But with teams like Iowa, Northwestern, and Michigan setting the standard, the Big Ten will almost certainly continue to be more three-happy than its peer conferences. In effect, the league as a whole has become a perimeter-oriented team, albeit a slow one.

Speed
The Big Ten is the slowest major conference in the country.
Conference games only
Possessions per 40 minutes

Major-conference tempos, 2008

ACC	70.8
SEC	67.5
Big East	66.9
Big 12	66.5
Pac 10	64.1
Big Ten	62.3

This disparity in velocities is no one-year blip. Looking at conference games played over the last five seasons, the Big Ten has been not only the slowest major conference but also the single slowest league out of the nation's 31 Division I conferences—see the statistical section that concludes this book.

Volatility
Illinois was in the national championship game in 2005 and went 5-13 in-conference in 2008. Last-place Purdue was 3-13 in 2006, then 15-3 in 2008. Iowa was in contention for the Big Ten title virtually throughout the 2006 season, then went 6-12 in 2008. Minnesota won as many conference games last year as it had in the previous two seasons combined. Ohio State was in the national championship game in 2007 and out of the tournament entirely the next season.

Sure, Wisconsin and Northwestern, in their diametrically opposed fashions, have had the temerity to rather churlishly buck this trend. But by and large, the Big Ten feels a little more yeasty than your other major conferences.

TV network
The Big Ten has one. Other conferences don't. Yet.

There was no shortage of skepticism greeting the arrival of the Big Ten Network in August 2007—with good reason. Unless you had a satellite dish, your chances of having the BTN piped into your home were fairly small. The network and the largest Midwestern cable carriers, Comcast in particular, were locked in a bitter, months-long dispute over BTN's price and placement (i.e., how much carriers would be charged and on which tier the network would appear). So it was big news in the heartland when Comcast and the Big Ten Network finally came to an agreement this summer. While still not available to every viewer in the Big Ten "footprint," the network appears to have navigated its way past the most perilous territory and gone from speculative venture to harbinger for other major conferences. Those conferences have been monitoring events on this front closely.

As to what viewers will actually be seeing on that network in the way of basketball this season, suffice it to say that player introductions will be watched more closely. Just one first-team All–Big Ten player returns this year: Robbie Hummel of Purdue. Hummel represents a team that returns virtually intact, but elsewhere in the conference the big names have largely moved on. For proof, look no further than the Boilermakers' in-state rival Indiana, which will be led by new coach Tom Crean. The team features an almost entirely new roster from top to bottom (Kyle Taber notwithstanding) and will even be overseen, as of January 1, by a new athletic director.

The Hoosiers figure to go through one year of ennobled struggle as Crean builds an entirely new edifice from the ground up on some of Division I's deepest and most storied foundations. In Minneapolis, by contrast, Tubby Smith has already graced his humble slab-on-grade with a comfortable first floor and is looking to add something even more luxurious this year. No team in major-conference basketball last year improved its per-possession performance in-conference as much as the Gophers did. It was a sterling first year for a coach and a team both looking for still more in 2009.

Smith took on a struggling program, of course, but he was nevertheless fortunate to inherit a particular team that returned 86 percent of its minutes from the previous season. His fellow new arrivals in the Big Ten coaching ranks in 2007 weren't as lucky. John Beilein and Todd Lickliter won a combined 11 games at Michigan and Iowa, respectively. Beilein at least returns his two main pillars on offense this year in Manny Harris and DeShawn Sims. But Ekpe Udoh's decision to transfer to Baylor will do the Wolverines' defense no favors. And in Iowa City, Lickliter will in some ways be undertaking his second consecutive rebuilding year. For better or worse (mostly the latter), his offense last year largely went through Justin Johnson and Tony Freeman, both of whom are now gone. The Hawkeyes will rise again, but in the near term nothing helps a new coach look better faster than a roster that's already been together a while.

Those aforementioned Wolverines did a good, if involuntary, deed last year, losing at home by two to Northwestern. By going 1-17, the Wildcats narrowly avoided becoming the first team to go winless over a Big Ten season since, well, Northwestern (in 2000). Bill Carmody's team was subpar on offense and much worse on defense. The return of all five players who were starting by the end of last season should help the former; Carmody hopes some added height that he signed in the spring can improve the latter.

Penn State also struggled on defense last year, a state of affairs that fell under the heading of really bad timing. The Nittany Lions needed every stop they could get: They were scoring fewer points after Geary Claxton was lost to a season-ending knee injury in January. Ed DeChellis's team also played most of the year with a hobbled Jamelle Cornley. This year Claxton is gone, but PSU fans hope Cornley has returned healthy—and that he gets some help this year, preferably tall help.

The Nittany Lions may have been porous on defense, but they were good enough to go 2-0 in the regular season against suddenly feeble Illinois. Indeed, the Illini missed the NCAA tournament for the first time in nine years and fell all the way to 5-13 in the Big Ten. Although a record like that offers Bruce Weber's team a lot of room for improvement, the real upswing in Champaign may still be a year out, when some eagerly awaited and highly rated recruits at last make their way to campus.

Having to wait patiently for coveted recruits is wholly unknown at Ohio State, already the only program in the country to have sent freshmen into the NBA in each of the one-and-done era's first two drafts. In fact it's possible that next June the Buckeyes will make it three in a row, with the potential ascension of B. J. Mullens to the proverbial "the next level." Even if it's for one year only, Mullens will be joined in Columbus this season by fellow McDonald's All-American William Buford. Every year Thad Matta trots out a new set of McDonald's All-Americans like a shark pushing forward its next row of teeth.

As for the two teams that closed out the Big Ten's season last March, both Michigan State and Wisconsin can legitimately greet the new season with high hopes. In Madison, the optimism is mere habit: The Badgers have never missed an NCAA tournament

since Bo Ryan started peddling his low-turnover no-foul brand of ball seven years ago. And in East Lansing, the raised expectations are a function of the personnel on hand. Every year, Tom Izzo lands still another outstanding freshman class. He did it again this year, and the cumulative result, albeit on paper, is the Big Ten's deepest and most athletic team.

Deepest and most athletic, yet not the favorite. Which brings us all the way back to Robbie Hummel and his Purdue Boilermakers. They went 15-3 last year and return all five starters. Go figure: Everyone's making the Boilers the preseason favorite in the Big Ten.

I am no exception.

	2008 Record	Returning Minutes (%)	2009 Prediction
Purdue	15-3	82	14-4
Michigan State	12-6	72	13-5
Wisconsin	16-2	65	13-5
Ohio State	10-8	46	12-6
Minnesota	8-10	75	11-7
Illinois	5-13	68	9-9
Michigan	5-13	72	7-11
Indiana	14-4	4	6-12
Penn State	7-11	77	5-13
Iowa	6-12	45	5-13
Northwestern	1-17	84	4-14

ILLINOIS

2008: 16-19 (5-13 Big Ten)
Lost to Wisconsin 61-48, Big Ten Tournament Final
In-conference offense: 0.99 points per possession (7th)
In-conference defense: 0.99 points allowed per possession (5th)

What Illinois did well: *Bottom out.*
Illinois went 16-19 last year, and Bruce Weber reportedly incorporated the numbers 16 and 19 in the door code at the practice facility so that his players would be continually reminded of this fact.

It was a fast escalator down from the national championship game in 2005 to 16-19. In retrospect, it's easy to see some things that few could have known when Weber was hired in 2003. Like the fact that in 2005, Illinois and Wake Forest would be blessed with two of the best point guards in recent college basketball history in subsequent Olympians Deron Williams and Chris Paul. With Williams absorbing more possessions than any other Illini player, talents like Luther Head and Dee Brown, who in any other year would have been burdened with being *the* star (as indeed Brown was in 2006), were given the luxury of functioning as absurdly efficient team players on offense. The stars truly aligned for Illinois that year.

Realignment ensued with a vengeance. In the parlance of human resources, there was no "backfill" even for the likes of James Augustine, much less for Head and Brown, and certainly not for Williams. Eric Gordon's announcing his intention to go to Indiana a full year after he'd given a verbal commitment to Weber certainly didn't help matters. But Gordon's change of heart can account for just one hole—shooting guards in the class of 2007—in the visibly pockmarked lunar surface that until recently comprised Illinois recruiting. In short, Gordon alone can't explain declines in performance at every position on the floor.

So there's considerable relief bordering on disbelief in Illini quarters now that Weber has hauled in verbal commitments from several highly rated prospects slated to arrive on campus in 2009, not to mention verbals from some even more highly rated prospects due to enter in 2010. As this book goes to press, that's all these are, of course: verbal commitments. But by the time you're reading this, signing day will either have happened or will be about to take place. If these 2009 commitments become letters of intent, there will be much rejoicing in the land of the orange and blue.

What we learned in 2008: *You can score about as many points as your opponents and still go 5-13.*

There was a yawning gulf last year between Illinois' performance on a per-possession basis (both scoring and allowing 0.99 points per trip in the Big Ten) and the 5-13 record that resulted. In fact, in the 219 conference seasons played by 73 major-conference teams over the past three years, only North Carolina in 2007 suffered from a larger discrepancy between its scoring margin and its wins.

The idea that the Illini scored and prevented scoring better than any other team in such a dire won-loss condition was actually circulated widely enough during the season last year to trigger something of a "Well, duh" reaction. Given that Illinois' foul shooting was awful and that the team most certainly

didn't have the proverbial "go-to scorer" you're supposed to have in "crunch time," it shouldn't come as any surprise, it was said, that this team can't win close games.

Certainly, the Illini's foul shooting was awful (332nd in the nation), and no one on this team last year could remotely be termed go-to. The thing is, all the above was true in 2007 as well. That year Illinois ranked 319th in the nation in free-throw percentage, and however much you may like Warren Carter he made no game-winning shots in-conference. Yet somehow that team's record matched its scoring margin. For whatever reason, there was added displeasure visited upon this team by the hoops gods last year.

What's in store for 2009

Illinois will be without the services of Jamar Smith. In 2007, the Illini guard was sentenced to two years' probation after a guilty plea on a charge of aggravated DUI. (That February the car he was driving slid off a snowy street, resulting in the hospitalization of passenger and then-teammate Brian Carlwell.) Then this past July, when the now 21-year-old Smith was spotted by police outside a campus bar, he reportedly acknowledged having had alcohol, a violation of his probation. Weber kicked him off the team for good. Before Smith's dismissal, the Illini coach had been quoted as being optimistic about his team's chances for improvement on offense. If that improvement is still going to happen, Illinois needs to commit fewer turnovers and make more of their threes, for those areas, along with their well-documented free-throw woes, constituted the two chronic weaknesses of the offense and indeed the entire team in 2008.

MEET THE FIGHTING ILLINI

Demetri McCamey (6-3, 205, So.). McCamey had the game of his young career against Purdue in the Big Ten tournament quarterfinals, shooting 6-of-6 on his threes and scoring 26 points as the Illini upset the Boilermakers in overtime. At least when it comes to perimeter shooting, the well-worn tale of freshman maturation held true in McCamey's case. Basically the more games he got under his belt the better his three-point percentage became until by the end of the year, he was right at the Division I average. No such good news obtained inside the arc, however, where McCamey's two-point percentage hovered right at a humble 40 for the better part of the season. In this respect his debut resembled the freshman year that Scottie Reynolds had for Villanova in 2007. As freshmen both players also posted excellent assist rates. That's where the similarities end, however. McCamey's struggles with turnovers last year were persistent, and they hurt an offense that, goodness knows, needed every shot it could get.

Alex Legion (6-4, 210, So.). Legion was a well-regarded shooting guard coming out of high school (rated at roughly the same level as Purdue's E'Twaun Moore and Michigan's Manny Harris, for what it's worth), but he played just 105 total minutes in his brief stint at Kentucky last year. Illinois fans love him already, though, because they trust he'll be a big improvement over the recent past. He'll become eligible for the Illini in December.

Trent Meacham (6-2, 195, Sr.). Meacham is rather notorious for an alleged inability to "create" his own shot. That may well be, but last year he, along with Shaun Pruitt, was one of the few players on this team whose shots went in occasionally, however they were created. Meacham made 40 percent of his threes and took good care of the ball—these two traits alone were enough to make him worthy of minutes on this team. Weber agreed: Only Chester Frazier logged more minutes last year.

Chester Frazier (6-2, 190, Sr.). As a sophomore in 2007, Frazier was given a shot at assuming a relatively normal-sized role in the offense. The results, if below-average, at least furnished grounds for further exploration along these lines. But as a junior last year, for whatever reason, Frazier took a big step back on offense in both prominence and effectiveness. Even as his role shrank to a size not seen since Dee Brown and James Augustine were still in residence, the historically turnover-prone Frazier posted the highest turnover rate of his career. Weber fed him team-leading minutes anyway, whether for Frazier's attitude and toughness on defense, a lack of viable alternatives, or all the above.

Calvin Brock (6-5, 200, Sr.). Brock started 16 games last year and was adequate on both his frequent twos and on his occasional threes. He was also the only Illini player who was any threat to record a steal.

Mike Tisdale (7-1, 215, So.). At this writing Illinois has yet to post its official roster for 2008-2009, but Tisdale has reportedly added a good deal of bulk since entering his freshman season listed at 215. If the new heft enables him to average about 27 minutes a game and get to 18 or 19 percent of opponents' misses during those minutes, that will be a huge service done for this roster full of guards and wings. Tisdale has already shown that he's a good but not great shot blocker. And in limited minutes as a spindly freshman, he was notably eager to shoot, making a respectable 52 percent of his twos.

Mike Davis (6-9, 195, So.). Like Tisdale, Davis can block a shot for you now and then. And though listed as four inches shorter, Davis actually achieved better results than Tisdale did on the defensive glass. Both players will be given every opportunity by Weber this year to show that they can clean up the misses that used to be hauled in by Pruitt.

Dominique Keller (6-7, 220, Jr.). A junior-college transfer, Keller averaged 25 points and nine rebounds last year for Lee Community College in Texas.

Bill Cole (6-9, 210, So.). Cole couldn't get on the floor as a freshman, but he should at least get a look early in the year with the departures of Pruitt and Brian Randle.

Prospectus says

The wildly varying fortunes of Illinois basketball over the past four seasons have perhaps given rise to the differing evaluations of this team by Illini fans. Orange-clad optimists can envision Legion being as good as advertised and McCamey, with large portions of the burden on offense removed from his still-developing shoulders, flourishing as a scoring point guard. Then again, the Block-I-sporting pessimists can just as easily imagine a continuing struggle with turnovers and even, as odd as this sounds for Illinois under Weber, the potential for weak rebounding. The truth might be somewhere in between. Last year, the Illini played well enough on a possession-by-possession basis to be a middle-of-the-pack Big Ten team. With a merely normal amount of luck, Illinois can give the appearance of significant improvement this year by simply repeating their 2008 performance.

INDIANA

2008: 25-8 (14-4 Big Ten)
Lost to Arkansas 86-72, NCAA First Round
In-conference offense: 1.08 points per possession (2nd)
In-conference defense: 1.01 points allowed per possession (6th)

What Indiana did well: *Rise and fall.*
Kelvin Sampson's brief tenure at Indiana has already been written off by some as simply a Faustian bargain that came due, one that IU entered into with its eyes wide open. Maybe, but while watching the saga play out in real time, the 23 months struck me as more interesting, more chaotic, and above all less formulaic than that. Indiana didn't sell its soul to win. It jeopardized its soul to hire a coach who might win.

Sampson was and is a good coach, capable of excellent, albeit phone-enhanced, recruiting. His 2006 recruiting class at Oklahoma would have included both Scottie Reynolds and Damion James had Sampson stayed put. But even with the benefit of players secured through promiscuous phone calling, he wasn't necessarily John Wooden II in terms of actual results.

Or maybe it was just that by 2006, when Sampson was hired at Indiana, the time for this particular misapprehension had passed. Sampson's perceived value as a potential hire peaked in 2003, when his Sooners followed up on their Final Four appearance the previous year with a one-seed in the East Regional. OU lost to Carmelo Anthony and Syracuse in the Elite Eight that year, but who could blame Sampson for losing to a team of destiny? No, this was his moment, and Sampson's name figured prominently when major-conference vacancies occurred that spring. One such vacancy was at Illinois, where interest in the Sooners' coach was keen enough to trigger speculation over whether Sampson, a Lumbee, would coach at a school that (then) had Chief Illiniwek.

From that point on, Sampson's Oklahoma teams made two tournament appearances over three seasons and won just one game. Sampson was good, but never soul-selling good. No coach is, of course, but if there's one who comes closest, it wasn't Sampson.

You know the rest. The last two schools to employ Kelvin Sampson have both been cited by the NCAA Committee on Infractions for failure to monitor. Sampson's stay at Indiana was so brief that it ended before the term of Oklahoma's probation had even expired.

Indiana's hiring of Sampson in 2006 was a mistake but it was also something worse because it was so needless. It was a hire made by a venerated program in a position to virtually have its pick of excellent coaches *not* under investigation by the Committee on Infractions. My understanding is that in 2006 one such coach was particularly eager to be considered for the Indiana job, even to the point of letting his eagerness be known. His name was Tom Crean.

What we learned in 2008: *Eric Gordon can play hurt—as long as his coach isn't embattled.*
Now a member of the L.A. Clippers, Gordon suffered through a miserable shooting slump over the last month of his only season as a collegian. That didn't hurt his draft stock—or if it did, the effect was minimal—because Gordon was widely seen as (1) injured, (2) playing for a program that was crashing to the ground around him, and (3) excellent all the while at getting to the foul line and making his free throws.

Gordon injured his left (nonshooting) wrist in practice on January 29. Still, the injury didn't seem to hurt his shooting. In his first four postinjury games, he made 44 percent of his threes (14-of-32). It turned out to be his last burst of effectiveness from outside the arc, however. The slump then truly arrived in mid-February, which, suggestively enough, was when the Sampson saga broke wide open.

In an interview after the season, interim coach Dan Dakich praised Gordon's perseverance and noted that the freshman just couldn't get any shots to fall: "That ain't quittin'," Dakich said, "that's just missin'." Dakich noted correctly that Gordon made just seven of 50 threes after Dakich took the reins. What's interesting, though, is that despite Gordon's slump, Indiana's struggles under Dakich actually had very little to do with offense (take a bow, D.J. White) and everything to do with defense. IU simply stopped playing any.

Sampson versus Dakich: Indiana in the Big Ten, 2008
Conference games only
PPP: points per possession
Opp. PPP: opponent points per possession
EM: efficiency margin (PPP – Opp. PPP)

	PPP	Opp. PPP	EM	Record
Sampson	1.08	0.96	+0.12	11-2
Dakich	1.08	1.12	-0.04	3-2
Overall	1.08	1.01	+0.07	14-4

True, Indiana in the short Dakich era may not have been quite as defensively deficient as these figures suggest. The numbers for five games are unavoidably skewed by one extreme game: the 103-74 mauling inflicted on the Hoosiers by Michigan State on March 2 in East Lansing. Then again, IU was last seen allowing an average Arkansas offense to score 86 points in just 66 possessions. Maybe the numbers had a story to tell after all.

What's in store for 2009

A cleansing breath.

Crean was hired April 2. On May 1, Eli Holman told his new coach that he wanted to leave the program and punctuated his point by throwing a flower pot—police were called. On May 2, Crean announced that he had dismissed DeAndre Thomas from the team and that Armon Bassett and Jamarcus Ellis, who had been kicked off the squad by Dakich back on March 31, would not be reinstated. On May 22, the coach showed Brandon McGee the door. And on June 11, Jordan Crawford informed Crean that he too would be leaving.

What you see below are the players brought in to replace all the above. On paper, the team that Indiana now most closely resembles is perhaps St. John's last year—except that even a hobbled Anthony Mason was most likely a more effective player for the Johnnies than anything Crean will have in uniform this season. But of course the home games should be irresistible Hoosier theater: "My team is on the floor," brought to real life. The seats will be filled with fans predisposed to take these players to heart, even with some losses—maybe especially with some losses. Opponents should prepare accordingly.

MEET THE HOOSIERS

Kyle Taber (6-7, 215, Sr.). Indiana's current players have between them started a total of four games as Hoosiers. Meaning, of course, that Taber started four games last year. He is the experience of this team, which is entirely appropriate because in truth he's paid some serious bench dues. In his first two seasons, Taber played a total of 14 minutes. Last year he peaked in Big Ten play, averaging 17 minutes a game in February and recording 10 boards in 31 minutes against Penn State in March.

Nick Williams (6-3, 185, Fr.). Williams originally signed to play at Marquette and then took a look at Arkansas when Crean switched jobs. In the end, though, Williams decided to follow Crean to Bloomington.

Tom Pritchard (6-8, 240, Fr.). Signed by Sampson as a complementary player in a class once populated by the likes of Devin Ebanks (now at West Virginia) and Terrell Holloway (Xavier), Pritchard now finds himself in line for some serious minutes in the paint right from the start.

Matt Roth (6-3, 175, Fr.). Roth and Pritchard are the only two recruits listed here who originally made their commitments to Sampson. Roth arrives with a reputation as an excellent shooter.

Verdell Jones (6-4, 180, Fr.). Jones is a point guard from Champaign, Illinois. He took a long look around before signing with the Hoosiers in May.

Devan Dumes (6-2, 195, Jr.). Another point guard, Dumes was the first recruit to sign with Crean.

Tijan Jobe (7-0, 255, Jr.). By late May, Crean really needed some size for this roster and he unearthed Jobe, a junior-college transfer, at relatively nearby Olney Central College. (That would be Olney, Illinois, home of the white squirrels.)

Malik Story (6-5, 220, Fr.). The last piece of the puzzle, Story is a wing from southern California who committed to the Hoosiers in June.

Prospectus says

Indiana's year is dedicated to foundation building, of course, but after that watch for good things packaged in an up-tempo pressing style, if Crean's years at Marquette are any guide. The new coach wouldn't be here at present unless he saw the Hoosiers' past as a means to achieve what he wants in the near future. Indiana is about to test the tensile strength of tradition.

IOWA

2008: 13-19 (6-12 Big Ten)
Lost to Michigan 55-47, Big Ten Tournament First Round
In-conference offense: 0.94 points per possession (11th)
In-conference defense: 1.02 points allowed per possession (7th)

What Iowa did well: *Change its style.*

Anytime a new coach is hired, and particularly when that coach brings with him a distinctive scheme, the question arises as to whether it's best to switch styles immediately or to wait until the new coach's own recruits start to come in. First-year Iowa coach Todd Lickliter opted for the former approach last year. He was hired away from Butler on the strength of a very slow but very efficient offense, one that featured an incredible number of threes.

Sure enough, the Hawkeyes slowed down last year (though truth be known, they weren't exactly the Phoenix Suns when it came to tempo under former coach Steve Alford). Averaging just 59 possessions per 40 minutes in Big Ten play, the Hawkeyes are now officially the slowest team in the slowest conference in the country. That may sound like it'd be dull to watch, but back in 2007 elite offenses like Butler and Georgetown made sub-60 speeds seem downright hip. Besides, the change in shot selection in Iowa City last year was even more dramatic. With Lickliter at the controls, almost half of Iowa's field-goal attempts in conference play were launched from beyond the arc in 2008.

The new coach is also a firm believer in the school of thought that says your defense begins the instant the shot leaves your hands on offense. Lickliter's teams never go after offensive rebounds (only Northwestern rebounded a smaller percentage of its own misses in Big Ten play last year), instead dropping back defensively to prevent any points in transition for the opponent.

There were, to say the least, some rough patches for the Hawkeyes in their new coach's first year. Perhaps most memorable was the November 30 loss at home to Louisiana-Monroe in Iowa's own annual Hawkeye Challenge, an event in which the Hawkeyes previously sported a record of 49-1. No one said change would be easy—and it hasn't been. But Lickliter already has his players going slow, shooting threes, and getting back on defense. It's a start.

What we learned in 2008: *Shooting better than your opponents doesn't matter if they get more shots.*

Iowa actually improved in some significant areas last year over 2007. Most notably, the Hawkeyes shot better from the field in-conference than they had the year before and they made their Big Ten opponents shoot worse. Yet the Hawkeyes went from 9-7 in the Big Ten in 2007 to 6-12 in 2008 for almost literally one reason alone: an imbalance in shots. Iowa shot far too rarely, and their opponents shot far too often.

The Hawkeyes turned the ball over on 25 percent of their possessions in-conference, while opponents gave the ball away less than 18 percent of the time. That was the worst such discrepancy in major-conference hoops last year.

Worst turnover margins, 2008

Conference games only: ACC, Big East, Big Ten,
  Big 12, Pac-10 & SEC
TO pct.: turnover percentage
Opp. TO pct.: opponent turnover percentage

	TO pct.	Opp. TO pct.	TO margin
Iowa	25.0	17.5	7.5
North Carolina State	23.8	16.5	7.3
Mississippi State	21.8	15.8	6.0
Boston College	21.2	15.4	5.8
Rutgers	22.8	17.8	5.0

In 2007, the bulk of Iowa's possessions went through Adam Haluska, who, as it happens, had one of the lowest TO rates in the nation. When the ball wasn't in Haluska's hands that year, it was often entrusted to current Tennessee Volunteer Tyler Smith, who was pretty reliable in his own right when it came to holding on to the rock. So increased turnovers were likely last year, no matter what. The problem is they didn't just increase; they exploded.

What's in store for 2009

Iowa is about to start its second consecutive clean-slate year on offense. Justin Johnson and Tony Freeman accounted for most of the shots in this offense last year. Now they're both gone: Johnson graduated, and Freeman elected to transfer to Southern Illinois. (After a standard year-end meeting with his coach, Freeman said he felt "unwanted.") Of course a clean slate might not be entirely bad, given Iowa's struggles to score points last year.

MEET THE HAWKEYES

Jake Kelly (6-6, 180, So.). Lickliter's system feeds a lot of threes to the guards and wings. As a freshman, Kelly showed signs that he can hold his own from the perimeter, making 43 percent of his infrequent threes.

Matt Gatens (6-5, 200, Fr.). The highest-rated recruit in Lickliter's incoming class, Gatens is a shooting guard from Iowa City and the reigning Iowa Mr. Basketball. He committed to the Hawkeyes after his freshman year in high school. His father, Mike, played for Lute Olson at Iowa.

Jeff Peterson (6-0, 185, So.). Peterson, a point guard from Washington, D.C., was recruited by Alford but was actually signed by Lickliter just days after the new coach arrived in Iowa City in 2007. Unfortunately, the freshman suffered through some epic struggles last year, particularly with turnovers. It's true he was thrown into action from day one, as Freeman was injured at the beginning of the year. Nevertheless, Peterson's turnover rate was stubbornly consistent even when Freeman returned and the freshman assumed more of a supporting role.

Jarryd Cole (6-7, 250, So.). As a freshman Cole had already become a starter by the end of November, but he was lost for the year on December 29, when he tore an ACL against Southeastern Louisiana.

Cyrus Tate (6-8, 240, Sr.). A wizened holdover from the Jeff Horner–Greg Brunner days, Tate saw his minutes rise after Cole went down. He is Iowa's most proven returning rebounder on both ends of the floor.

Anthony Tucker (6-4, 195, Fr.). Tucker was a four-year starter in high school and arrives billed as a pure shooter.

Jermain Davis (6-4, 205, Jr.). Davis is a transfer from Kirkwood Community College in Cedar Rapids.

Devan Bawinkle (6-5, 185, Jr.). Originally recruited to West Virginia by John Beilein, Bawinkle is a transfer from Highland Community College in Freeport, Illinois.

Andrew Brommer (6-9, 220, Fr.). Brommer is the first in what should be a long line of "versatile" forwards recruited by Lickliter, who likes players who can hit threes. Like Tucker, Brommer is a Twin Cities–area product.

Prospectus says

Iowa's defense was actually OK last year, performing close to the Big Ten average. It's the offense that needs help, and the turnaround on that side of the ball will probably take more than one season. One worthy goal for 2008 would be mere normality on turnovers: one in every five possessions instead of one in every four.

MICHIGAN

2008: 10-22 (5-13 Big Ten)
Lost to Wisconsin 51-34, Big Ten Tournament Quarterfinals
In-conference offense: 0.96 points per possession (9th)
In-conference defense: 1.04 points allowed per possession (9th)

What Michigan did well: *Set the bar low for Year 2 improvement.*

A year ago no one thought John Beilein's first season in Ann Arbor would be easy. In bidding farewell to Tommy Amaker, the Wolverines had also said goodbye to four starters from 2007. You knew going in that last year was going to be a struggle.

Turns out you didn't know the half of it. Michigan losing by 11 at Harvard will be remembered for years, and not only because the home team that night was coached by one Tommy Amaker. If the Crimson had been a tough Ivy League contender, à la Princeton or Penn teams of yore, that would be one thing. But Harvard went on to finish 3-11 in the Ivy, a mark that included home losses to the likes of Yale and Columbia. For a non-Northwestern Big Ten basketball program to lose that game by double digits was an affront to the laws of hoops gravity.

That loss put a stamp on this young Michigan team early in the season, and few people felt any need to come back around for a second look. After all, the Wolverines finished the year 10-22—what more was there to learn? Well, maybe a couple things.

Note, for example, that a team that loses by 11 at Harvard should ordinarily compile no better than, say, a 1-17 record in the Big Ten. Michigan instead went 5-13, a mark that included a 10-point win at home over better-than-commonly-supposed Ohio State. So this team did improve as the year went on.

And besides, there was improvement within the improvement. The Wolverines' defense was dramatically better over the second half of the Big Ten season, holding opponents to less than a point per trip. Granted, this was partly an artifact of having had to play far and away the conference's best team, Wisconsin, twice in the first half of the schedule. Even so, toss out this Badger effect and the trend line was still positive. Starting somewhere around the second week in February, Beilein's young charges learned how to play defense. If they can carry that lesson forward without having to relearn it, this will serve them in good stead in 2009.

What we learned in 2008: *If Michigan could make an occasional shot, it might actually be average.*

Michigan's shooting from the field last year was obviously painful to watch, but suffering Wolverine fans might be somewhat comforted to know that they weren't imagining things. It's been years since fans of any Big Ten team saw this many misses.

Worst Big Ten shooting, 2006-2008: effective field-goal percentage, conference games only

	eFG pct.
Michigan 2008	45.1
Illinois 2007	45.9
Northwestern 2007	46.1
Minnesota 2006	46.2
Minnesota 2007	47.8

The Wolverines were ineffective from everywhere on the floor, ranking 10th in the Big Ten in two-point accuracy in-conference and dead last on their threes. It was quite simply a ghastly performance, and it entirely negated Michigan's sudden and rather uncharacteristic adequacy in taking care of the ball, a Wolverine weakness seemingly from the dawn of time until the dawn of Beilein.

What's in store for 2009

Michigan last year looked a lot like the team and the season that Zack Gibson avoided by transferring to Ann Arbor: Rutgers in 2007. Both teams featured historically bad shooting by notably young players who just a year or two before had been somewhat highly touted high school recruits. If the comparison is apt, the example set by the Scarlet Knights last year isn't exactly encouraging for Wolverine fans looking ahead to 2009. Nor is the fact that after last season, Ekpe Udoh elected to transfer to Baylor. The core of Michigan's February defensive epiphany, alluded to above, was improved two-point field-goal defense. That fell squarely under Mr. Udoh's department.

MEET THE WOLVERINES

Manny Harris (6-5, 170, So.). No Big Ten offense last year went through one player more than the Michigan offense went through Manny Harris, who posted the highest percentage of possessions used that the conference has seen since Alando Tucker's star turn in 2007. (The next time Beilein approaches a Detroit-area high school scorer and promises to feature the kid, believe me, that kid should listen.) With said possessions, Harris shot and shot and shot—but just couldn't get the ball to go down. Beilein was giving a green light all the way but, wow, one player personally accounting for this many possessions and shooting just 41 percent on his twos and 32 percent on his threes? It was a sight. There was, however, a silver lining: Harris was fouled quite often and made 82 percent of his free throws. That was the strength not only of Harris's game but arguably of Michigan's entire offense last year. This accuracy on free throws also bodes well for future threes—or would if the line weren't being moved. Note as well that Harris is reportedly slated to move from shooting guard to wing this season.

DeShawn Sims (6-8, 225, Jr.). Let's start with a bouquet for Sims. It's been a very long time since a Michigan player absorbed so many possessions on offense while committing so few turnovers. De-Shawn, take a bow. Now, in other news: Sims was right there alongside Harris last year, firing up shots with extraordinary frequency in his own right. He was somewhat more successful than his teammate inside the arc, making 45 percent of his twos. But Sims was even less effective from the perimeter than Harris—and the troubling thought for Michigan fans here, of course, is that in Beilein's offense you know there will continue to be threes shot by Sims.

Kelvin Grady (5-11, 170, So.). Grady was given the keys to the Wolverine car, such as it was, when Beilein dismissed point guard Jerret Smith from the team last December. Now it is widely expected that Grady will himself be deposed when Arizona transfer Laval Lucas-Perry becomes eligible midseason. Lucas-Perry had better be as good as advertised, though, because Grady last year was a viable, if somewhat turnover-prone, pass-first option at point guard, one who fed assists to Harris and Sims and made 36 percent of his own rare threes.

Zack Gibson (6-10, 220, Jr.). A likely starter in the wake of Udoh's departure, Gibson is not averse to shooting threes. Moreover, while no one was going to look like a great shot blocker next to Udoh, of course, Gibson actually does block an occasional shot. He was virtually invisible on the defensive glass last year, however.

Anthony Wright (6-6, 235, So.). Wright is apparently going for a Daequan Cook-kind of thing: threes and defensive boards from a player who's 6-6 or thereabouts. He has the defensive glass part down—Wright is in fact Beilein's best returning defensive rebounder. But threes are another matter. Wright just kept firing them up last year, despite the nominally discordant fact that over 71 percent of them weren't going in.

Laval Lucas-Perry (6-3, 190, Fr.). Lucas-Perry will become eligible at the end of the first semester. At Arizona last year, the Flint native averaged 10 minutes a game for five games before deciding a return to more familiar, if less salubrious, surroundings was in order.

Jevohn Shepherd (6-5, 210, Sr.). The lone senior among the players listed here, Shepherd saw only a small increase in minutes last year, even though Michigan had just lost four starters.

Ben Cronin (7-0, 235, Fr.). Beilein has this to say of Cronin: "Given time and hard work we are confident he can really help us in the future."

Stuart Douglass (6-2, 180, Fr.). More from the Michigan coach: "The new three-point line will have no effect on Stu."

Prospectus says
Beilein has to be concerned about an interior defense that no longer has one of the best shot blockers in the nation. The Wolverine coach might similarly worry about a young team that shoots so poorly from the field and shoots so very many threes—in a year when the three-point line is being moved out a foot.

MICHIGAN STATE

2008: 27-9 (12-6 Big Ten)
Lost to Memphis 92-74, NCAA Sweet 16
In-conference offense: 1.06 points per possession (3rd)
In-conference defense: 0.97 points allowed per possession (4th)

What Michigan State did well: *Flip a switch.*
I don't know what Tom Izzo did on or around February 17, 2008. Maybe he hypnotized his team. Maybe he replaced his players with genetically engineered cyborgs. Or maybe he just got lucky.

One thing I do know. Starting in mid-February, Michigan State began taking care of the ball for the first time in many a moon.

Michigan State turnovers, 2007-2008:
turnover percentage, conference games only

	TO pct.
2007	26.0
2008 first 12 games	24.6
2008 last six games	16.6

The fact that for the past two seasons any discussion of Michigan State has needed to start with turnovers is actually something of a back-handed compliment to the Spartans. Even as they've struggled with turnovers, MSU has done just about everything else at least pretty well, and often very well. For example, this was both the best shooting and best offensive rebounding team in the Big Ten last year in conference play. State also made life miserable for opponents shooting threes, holding conference foes to under 32 percent from beyond the arc. There was a lot to like here.

For the better part of two years, Michigan State was a good team trapped inside its own inability to end possessions with shots instead of turnovers. It appears they may have at last turned that corner.

What we learned in 2008: *Drew Neitzel was more unusual than he looked.*

My colleague Ken Pomeroy has written previously on the overwhelming tendency toward continuity shown by players from year to year in terms of their role in their offense. Simply put, freshmen who are role players on offense tend to be role players even as upperclassmen. Freshmen who, for better or worse, are heavily involved in the offense are rarely busted down to role-player status as upperclassmen. All tendencies have exceptions, of course, but this one is surprisingly steady across thousands of Division I players each season.

Drew Neitzel, however, was indeed one of the exceptions. A big one.

It seems like ages ago but the now-departed Neitzel arrived in East Lansing four years ago this fall, widely hailed as the final piece in the puzzle of the Paul Davis–Mo Ager era at Michigan State: a "true" point guard. Though he played limited minutes as a freshman, he did indeed dish assists with true point guard frequency. He was also almost entirely a pass-first point guard, however, shooting next to never, even allowing for his sparse minutes. And he turned the ball over a lot on a Final Four team that for the most part did not. The following season, as a sophomore, Neitzel doubled his minutes and got his turnovers under control, but still deferred almost to a fault to his elders when it came to shooting the rock.

Then came Neitzel's junior year. With Davis, Ager, and Shannon Brown all departed to the NBA, Neitzel became The Man. Only Wisconsin's Alando Tucker and Iowa's Adam Haluska took a higher percentage of their teams' shots during their minutes than did Neitzel. It was an extraordinary year-to-year change, all the more so because Neitzel had blossomed not only into a frequent scorer but also into an efficient one. By the time he was a senior, Neitzel was actually in the position of trying to get his younger teammates more involved in the offense.

For his next act, Neitzel has signed a contract to play in Germany. This is an actual quote from his new coach, Thorsten Leibenath: *"Drew ist der combo-guard."* Ja, one who can assume many different identities in your offense.

What's in store for 2009

Michigan State is far and away the deepest team in the Big Ten. Indications are that Izzo will at least experiment with a smaller lineup, one with three guards, Raymar Morgan as the 4, and one big man, presumably Goran Suton. If so watch for pensive and habitual kvetching from Izzo (it's true!) about his team's lack of "toughness" and poor defense. But also watch for a lot of points to be put up by MSU. This should be a very good team, one with a really nice offense and an adequate defense that will be better than Izzo will make it sound.

MEET THE SPARTANS

Raymar Morgan (6-7, 225, Jr.). Morgan has a reputation for disappearing at times and his free-throw shooting is mediocre, but otherwise he's rather curiously underrated for a player who made 59 percent of his twos while functioning in a costarring role alongside Neitzel on offense. (And it was a relatively steady 59 percent throughout the season.) He's also a fair defensive rebounder—if Morgan does indeed see a lot of minutes as a 4 this year, he'll be expected to pitch in even more on the defensive glass.

Kalin Lucas (6-0, 180, So.). Back when Neitzel was a freshman point guard, he was reportedly hesitant to shoot because he was playing alongside Paul Davis, Mo Ager, Shannon Brown, and Alan Anderson. Well, last year as a freshman Lucas played at point guard next to Neitzel and Morgan and that didn't stop the young man from plunging right in and looking for his shot. Not at all. Lucas did OK in that department (45 percent on his frequent twos, 37 percent on his rare threes), but the most important talent he displayed was the ability to take care of the ball. That bodes well for this team.

Goran Suton (6-10, 245, Sr.). Suton arrived in East Lansing pegged in advance as one of those all-pass, no-bang Euro big men. Now as a senior he's the heart and soul of the rebounding for a coach whose very name is synonymous with the activity. Suton is excellent on the glass on both ends of the floor, particularly on the offensive boards.

Chris Allen (6-3, 195, So.). The likely starter at shooting guard, Allen wears the label of his position well: He is not shy about pulling the trigger on his shot. To date, he's a promising perimeter shooter who has had little success inside the arc. Then again, he suffered a bone bruise in his foot last December and missed four games.

Durrell Summers (6-4, 195, So.). Summers

logged fewer total minutes than even Allen did last year, and unlike his teammate Summers didn't miss four games. Nevertheless, he showed promise as a legitimate dual-threat wing in the making.

Travis Walton (6-2, 190, Sr.). The opponent's best perimeter player often finds himself guarded by Walton. On offense the senior is a pass-first point guard, one who struggled with turnovers last year.

Marquise Gray (6-8, 235, Sr.). Gray is roughly equivalent to Suton in rebounding both offensively and defensively, but last year, he posted the highest turnover rate of his career. He also averaged a notably exuberant 5.5 fouls per 40 minutes.

Delvon Roe (6-8, 220, Fr.). The highest-rated recruit in yet another highly rated recruiting class at MSU, Roe missed part of his senior season due to surgery on his right knee. Then in August, he had minor surgery performed on his left knee. As this book goes to press, MSU is saying Roe will be back in action in time for the start of the season. He had been compared, presurgeries, to Morgan by Izzo, "but may be more athletic in scoring around the basket."

Korie Lucious (5-11, 160, Fr.). Lucious is billed as a scoring point guard who's exceptionally quick.

Draymond Green (6-6, 220, Fr.). Green originally gave a verbal commitment to Kentucky when Tubby Smith was still in Lexington. When Smith moved to Minneapolis, Green turned down offers from Michigan and Indiana and chose MSU.

Prospectus says

The Spartans have made something of a habit of sabotaging how they're perceived. Consider the season they had last year. On a neutral floor last November, they led eventual Final Four entrant UCLA for most of the game before losing by five, a game in which Neitzel was weakened by flulike symptoms and didn't start. They beat eventual Elite Eight entrant Texas by six on a not very neutral floor at the Palace of Auburn Hills. And they went 12-6 in the Big Ten and made it to the Sweet 16. So why all the angst about this team? Scoring 36 points in a loss at Iowa didn't help matters. Nor did an offense that was singularly inconsistent, both statistically and visually. If Michigan State can continue to take care of the ball, its depth and quickness should serve it well in a league that looks potentially rather thin and deliberate.

MINNESOTA

2008: 18-12 (8-10 Big Ten)
Lost to Maryland 68-58, NIT First Round
In-conference offense: 1.01 points per possession (6th)
In-conference defense: 1.03 points allowed per possession (8th)

What Minnesota did well: *Resurrect.*

In 2006-2007, Minnesota played no fewer than 24 games—the balance of its season—with an "interim" coach, Jim Molinari. The team's performance on the court that year reflected the uncertainty surrounding the program. Then in March 2007, in the midst of that year's Sweet 16, came the stunning news that Kentucky's Tubby Smith had agreed to take over as head coach of the Gophers.

The change in fortunes that resulted last year was the season's largest improvement in major-conference basketball:

Improvement, 2007 to 2008

Conference games only: ACC, Big East, Big Ten, Big 12, Pac-10, and SEC
PPP: points per possession
Opp. PPP: opponent points per possession
EM: efficiency margin (PPP – Opp. PPP)
   See top of facing page.

Note that every team on this list had at least four starters returning from 2007. Smith was a good coach given a good situation. He was due one.

What we learned in 2008: *Shots can be made by the home team in "the Barn" after all.*

Minnesota's rise from its slumber last year was all the more remarkable because it was keyed by the offense. This despite Smith's reputation as a perfectionist on defense and despite the fact that *home-team offense* has been a self-evident oxymoron for years in Williams Arena.

Even the Gophers' surprising 2005 NCAA tournament team was offensively challenged and had a stellar (if little recognized) defense solely to thank for its relative success. But in 2008, the offense was the story in Minneapolis. Not only did it improve more than the defense did under Smith, but it was also simply better, in relation to the conference average, than said defense.

This team attempted threes somewhat rarely, at least by the lights of a fairly three-happy conference. Nevertheless, it was the strength of an offense that

	2007			2008			
	PPP	*Opp. PPP*	*EM*	*PPP*	*Opp. PPP*	*EM*	*Change in EM*
Minnesota	0.92	1.08	-0.16	1.01	1.03	-0.02	+0.14
Tennessee	1.07	1.05	+0.02	1.12	0.97	+0.15	+0.13
Baylor	1.03	1.14	-0.11	1.08	1.07	+0.01	+0.12
Connecticut	0.94	0.96	-0.02	1.11	1.02	+0.09	+0.11

was right at the Big Ten average: The Gophers made 38 percent of their threes (while also improving dramatically on the offensive boards). The sight of shots actually going through the net last year must have had the golden-clad fans rubbing their eyes. The 2006 and 2007 Minnesota teams were two of the worst-shooting teams in recent Big Ten annals.

This improvement on offense was crucial because Smith couldn't make his players any taller on defense. Conference opponents actually shot better against Minnesota in 2008 than they had in 2007, and the Gophers' defensive rebounding fell off to the point where only Northwestern was worse in-conference. The fact that this team still improved year-to-year on defense was due solely to a dramatic increase in takeaways. Only Purdue's Big Ten opponents committed turnovers more often.

What's in store for 2009

The first-year class that Smith brought in this year needs to be highlighted. Granted, it may not be the best such class in the Big Ten, but in terms of recent programmatic history in Minneapolis this class is an abrupt and even startling sea change. Smith landed the consensus national junior-college player of the year (Devron Bostick—watch for inevitable Vincent Grier comparisons), as well as high school recruits who said no to the likes of Connecticut, Kentucky, and Georgia Tech. It's been quite a change in a short time for Minnesota.

MEET THE GOLDEN GOPHERS

Damian Johnson (6-7, 195, Jr.). Johnson is a highly unusual force for good on defense, an undersized interior player who inflicts tangible and measurable pain on opposing offenses without getting many defensive rebounds. Last year he combined blocked shots and steals as well as any player in Division I. He's also a good offensive rebounder. On the other hand, he's a 56 percent free-throw shooter. And while this suggests Johnson's shooting stroke will not soon be confused with Stephen Curry's, he was somehow allowed to attempt no fewer than 40 threes last year. He made 10.

Lawrence Westbrook (6-0, 195, Jr.). Last year Westbrook played a lot of his minutes alongside the now departed Lawrence McKenzie. Both Lawrences were slightly turnover-prone combo guards who were adequate at dishing assists and good (Westbrook) or even very good (McKenzie) at hitting their perimeter shots. This year Westbrook figures to carry more of the perimeter shooting load as he may be logging more minutes alongside "true" point guard Al Nolen—see below.

Blake Hoffarber (6-4, 200, So.). Of all the college players in any sport in the United States, Hoffarber is the only one of whom it can truly be said that when he isn't nominated for an ESPY, he's had an off year. (If you're new to the phenomenon here, start with the young man's exquisitely Google-ready surname.) When not drawing millions of hits for YouTube, he functions almost exclusively as the designated shooter in the Minnesota lineup. Hoffarber made 43 percent of his threes as a freshman.

Al Nolen (6-1, 180, So.). Nolen excels at disrupting opposing backcourts, posting one of the highest steal rates in the nation last year. On offense he's a work in progress: He was excellent at delivering assists but had chronic turnover problems. Among Big Ten players who saw regular minutes last year, only Michigan State's Travis Walton took a smaller percentage of his team's shots during his minutes than did Nolen.

Devron Bostick (6-5, 210, Jr.). The aforementioned national junior-college player of the year, Bostick arrives billed as an athletic and prolific scorer.

Devoe Joseph (6-3, 170, Fr.). Joseph, an import from north of the border, tried out for Team Canada and has been touted for his ability to score both from the perimeter and from midrange.

Ralph Sampson III (6-11, 220, Fr.). Sampson is a highly rated freshman who has paradigmatic value beyond his famous name. When a coveted Atlanta-area recruit says no to Georgia Tech and Kentucky and chooses instead to *voluntarily* spend every September through May well north of Des Moines, it's officially time to start work on the Tubby Smith statue outside the Barn.

Colton Iverson (6-10, 235, Fr.). With Sampson and Iverson, Smith improved his roster's size dramatically, getting two highly touted and reportedly nonproject big men in the process.

Jamal Abu-Shamala (6-5, 210, Sr.). Abu-Shamala had a moment in the sun, as it were, in 2005-2006, when as a freshman walk-on he was promoted to the starting lineup. He saw his minutes decline last year, but he does give Smith a measure of experienced backcourt depth.

Jonathan Williams (6-9, 285, Sr.). Big men coming off the bench are, of course, expected to be "aggressive" (i.e., foul) and supply "energy" (foul some more). Still, at 6.3 fouls per 40 minutes, Williams is one of the most aggressive and energetic players you'll run across. Last year he functioned exclusively as a shot blocker.

Prospectus says

Suddenly the trend lines are all positive on offense. In fact, if Minnesota can simply learn to hold on to the rock (last year, the Gophers gave the ball away on 22 percent of their trips in-conference), look out. On defense, a lot will depend on the development of the freshmen in the paint, Sampson and Iverson. If one or both of them can get some defensive boards, they will have plugged the biggest defensive leak the Gophers had last year. This team should look pretty good in 2009. And don't even get me started about 2010. Fans of teams from Oregon State to South Florida must be looking at the programmatic insta-180 in Minneapolis and thinking, "Yes, we can!"

2008: 8-22 (1-17 Big Ten)
Lost to Minnesota 55-52, Big Ten Tournament First Round
In-conference offense: 0.95 points per possession (10th)
In-conference defense: 1.16 points allowed per possession (11th)

What Northwestern did well: *Evade infamy.*

Seeing a team go winless over the course of a major-conference schedule is unusual, even more so than you might think. Going into last year, it hadn't happened since 2004. So I have to admit that as the 2008 season unfolded I was watching with some level of morbid interest, for it looked exceedingly likely that *two* teams would post o-fers in-conference. Those two teams were Oregon State and Northwestern.

The ominous tone for the Wildcats' conference season was set right at the top, when their first four games included home losses to Penn State and Michigan by 11 and 10 points, respectively. Those were surely, I thought at the time, two of the best opportunities for a win that NU was going to get. With those two games already in the loss column, the possibility of a winless season in Evanston could therefore be raised by responsible adults as early as mid-January.

In the end, however, history's cruel grip was reserved solely for the 0-18 Oregon State Beavers. The 1-17 Wildcats wriggled out of Clio's grasp, albeit with a generous assist from a very young Michigan team. Visiting Crisler Arena on February 26, Northwestern led by 19 points in the first half and then held on for dear life in a 62-60 win.

Note that NU has now won a total of three conference games in the past two years, and oddly, two of those wins have come on the road: at Minnesota in 2007 and in Ann Arbor last year. Do lower-division teams actually play tight *at home* against the Wildcats because they sense (correctly) that apocalyptic pronouncements will be fastened upon them should they lose? Just asking.

What we learned in 2008: *There's a reason they don't call it the "Princeton defense."*

Northwestern famously plays a Princeton offense, a unique scheme with intricate sets, a colorful history, and even some notches in its belt. But to assume that we should start the discussion of any Princetoninflected team with that team's offense is, in the Wildcats' case, woefully incorrect. It's what's happening on the other side of the ball that's been truly unique and colorful of late . . .

Worst FG defenses, 2006-2008

Conference games only: ACC, Big East, Big Ten, Big 12, Pac-10 & SEC

Opp. eFG pct.: opponent effective field-goal percentage

	Opp. eFG pct.
Northwestern 2008	59.6
Auburn 2008	58.5
Penn State 2007	58.3
Miami 2007	57.2
Penn State 2006	56.9
Penn State 2008	56.2
Oregon State 2008	55.6
Florida 2008	54.1

Bill Carmody's team was exceptionally proficient at forcing turnovers last year, getting Big Ten opponents to give the ball away on almost 24 percent of their possessions. This was the only factor standing between the NU defense and a debacle of transcendent proportions—the difference between being merely the worst in the Big Ten and being plausibly adjudged the worst of the decade in major-conference basketball. When opponents didn't turn the ball over last year, it was if they'd been treated to a cup full of tokens at a North Carolina Tar Heels Offense simulator.

What's in store for 2009

Other things being equal, mere maturation usually improves an offense but tends to be much less helpful than simple height on defense. (Ask Ed DeChellis.) So during the spring signing period, Carmody shook the recruiting bushes with a vengeance and got some size for this year's incoming class. How that size performs will largely determine whether the Northwestern defense will improve (which sheer regression to the mean would seem to predict) or whether in fact it will be but more of the same. In what could be seen as an encouraging sign, Nikola Baran, who started 16 games for Carmody last year, took a look at the incoming class and apparently decided he would see more minutes by transferring to another program.

MEET THE WILDCATS

Kevin Coble (6-8, 190, Jr.). In one of the more challenging settings to be found in major-conference hoops, Coble does just two things and does them well: He shoots, and he gets defensive rebounds. There are some good things he never does (assists, offensive rebounds), and there are some bad things he never does (turnovers, fouls). His 81 percent foul shooting says he has a good stroke, and indeed, he hit 39 percent of his threes last year. As for his attempts from inside the arc, they were twice as numerous and he made 53 percent of those. So Northwestern's distinctive ways have probably occasioned some unneeded doubt as to where Coble ranks with respect to players in other, more common offensive systems. Forget the systems. Here's a 6-8 player who holds his own on the defensive glass and has three-point range. Ordinarily that would attract more interest and discussion than it has for Coble.

Craig Moore (6-3, 190, Sr.). Moore's been launching threes for three seasons in Evanston, and last year he finally found the range, as they say, hitting 40 percent of his shots from beyond the arc. This was huge for his congenitally perimeter-oriented team, which went from being the worst three-point-shooting team in the Big Ten in 2007 to attaining middle-of-the-pack normalcy in this endeavor in 2008.

Michael Thompson (5-10, 165, So.). Last year as a freshman Thompson was the starter from day one at point guard. He did surprisingly well, taking very good care of the ball and accounting for his fair share of assists in a system that spreads assists around. And if the two-point percentage recorded by a 5-10 freshman at Northwestern was predictably pedestrian, let us note that Thompson did hit 43 percent of his threes. (True, it'll be interesting to see if he can do it again with a new three-point line and, more importantly, off a 64 percent performance at the free-throw line.) It was a very auspicious debut during a very challenging year. Thompson, Moore, and Coble were the three mainstays on the floor for Northwestern last year once the conference season got under way.

Ivan Peljusic (6-8, 195, So.). Peljusic was promoted to the starting lineup in February as a redshirt freshman. The promotion came pretty late, but we can already say that Peljusic is comfortable looking for his shot. He might also turn out to be another Coble-level presence on the defensive glass, which Carmody would certainly welcome.

Sterling Williams (6-3, 190, Sr.). One of those proverbial glue guys you hear about, Williams was a starter yet was far less likely to shoot than any other Wildcat who averaged at least 20 minutes per game last year.

Kyle Rowley (7-0, 280, Fr.). Rowley was signed by Carmody in May and is expected to see quality minutes right away because, not to put too fine a point on it, he's very big. In the summer of 2007 he played for Trinidad and Tobago's Under-18 team.

Luka Mirkovic (6-11, 225, Fr.). After coming to the States from Serbia, Mirkovic played just one season of high school ball at LaPorte, Indiana (his coach was Delray Brooks), and put up numbers good enough for an offer from Northwestern.

Davide Curletti (6-9, 225, Fr.). Curletti was a high school teammate of Michigan State point guard Kalin Lucas.

Jeff Ryan (6-7, 190, Jr.). On a team that forces opponents into a lot of turnovers, Ryan stands out as the only player with something approximating a high steal rate.

Prospectus says

Northwestern improved its offense last year—thanks to better three-point shooting and fewer turnovers—but the defensive collapse negated any rewards to be yielded from something as peripheral as merely scoring more points. This year the bulk of the minutes return and Carmody did his best to make the roster a little bigger. Improvement is a safe enough forecast when the benchmark is 1-17, but the real question is how much this team will improve. The bet here: noticeably. A larger lineup will force fewer opponent turnovers, but should also allow fewer made shots while the Wildcats perhaps even (ultimate NU novelty) get a few defensive rebounds. There is a long, long way to go between where the Wildcat defense was last year and the midpoint that marks the Big Ten average. The 'Cats won't get there in one season, but they can move in the right direction.

OHIO STATE

2008: 24-13 (10-8 Big Ten)
Beat UMass 92-85, NIT Championship Game
In-conference offense: 1.02 points per possession (5th)
In-conference defense: 0.95 points allowed per possession (3rd)

What Ohio State did well: *Push around the little guys—when the little guys didn't push back.*

At first glance, Ohio State was manifestly the most underrated team in major-conference basketball last year. Thad Matta's men outscored their Big Ten opponents by a margin of 0.07 points per trip, yet they were unable to wrangle an invite to the NCAA tournament. (They went on to win the NIT.) As it happens, no fewer than 13 other major-conference teams secured at-large NCAA bids despite posting *smaller* per-possession scoring margins than OSU. Those 13 teams included not only bubble teams (e.g., Villanova and Kentucky) but also a five-seed (Notre Dame) and even two four-seeds (Pitt and Vanderbilt). What gives? Did the selection committee have it in for the Buckeyes?

Of course not. Ohio State was clearly better than people realized, but at the same time that made factors in play that made the Buckeyes *look* one way on paper and *feel* another way when you saw them.

It turns out that OSU compiled its impressive scoring margin almost exclusively through the medium of wins against inferior teams—assuming they won. This team, after all, dropped games at Michigan and at Iowa. (It's also a team, of course, that closed the year by beating Purdue in overtime and Michigan State at home.) But where the Buckeyes really excelled was in going for the proverbial kill when they led not very good opponents. In fact, in their eight wins against teams that finished below them in the standings, the Buckeyes were unbelievable.

Wins against inferior teams: top of the Big Ten, 2008
Conference games only
PPP: points per possession
Opp. PPP: opponent points per possession
EM: efficiency margin (PPP – Opp. PPP)

	PPP	Opp. PPP	EM
Ohio State	1.10	0.86	+0.24
Wisconsin	1.11	0.89	+0.22
Michigan State	1.11	0.90	+0.21
Purdue	1.06	0.89	+0.17
Indiana	1.11	0.97	+0.14

This table shows how the Big Ten's best teams performed last year in their conference wins against teams that finished below them in the standings. Clearly Ohio State mopped the floor with the conference little guys better than anyone else did—again, in their *wins*. The NCAA selection committee apparently looked at that record and decided that the ability to pummel inferior teams when you're not losing to them was intriguing and perhaps even admirable, just not enough for a bid.

What we learned in 2008: *Turnovers are more important than people know.*

Old-timers reading this book will remember a time long ago called 2007. Ohio State was led by Greg Oden and Mike Conley. The Buckeyes went 15-1 in the Big Ten that year and made it to the national-championship game before falling to Florida.

Then the seasons changed. Oden and Conley went to the NBA, along with Daequan Cook. Ron Lewis and Ivan Harris also departed. Kosta Koufos arrived. And these 2008 Buckeyes went 10-8 and didn't even get into the tournament. What changed?

In some surprisingly basic ways—making shots, preventing the opponent from making theirs—not much.

Ohio State, 2007 versus 2008
Conference games only
eFG pct.: effective field-goal percentage
Opp. eFG pct.: opponent effective field-goal percentage
Opp. PPP: opponent points per possession

	2007	2008
eFG pct.	51.0	51.1
Opp. eFG pct.	46.4	45.6
Opp. PPP	0.94	0.95

Obviously *something* changed last year, and the telling elisions in my table have probably already indicated to you what it was: offense. The Buckeyes continued to make shots at the same rate last year, but there's more to scoring points than making shots. Most importantly, there's getting the *opportunity* to make shots by not turning the ball over. Indeed, turnovers were the largest single difference between an NCAA championship runner-up (who turned the ball over on 17 percent of their trips in-conference) and an NIT champ (with a 21 percent turnover rate).

Ohio State last year wasn't *bad* where turnovers were concerned, mind you. It's just that the team was almost exactly average, while in 2007 it was superb in that department. Sometimes the biggest "problem" a team faces is being merely good in an area where it used to be great.

What's in store for 2009
I don't usually start these player profiles with two freshmen, but with the departures of Kosta Koufos and Jamar Butler, Ohio State has lost the two players who had absorbed the lion's share of this team's possessions on offense last year. Close readers of this book have already seen that, with the ridiculously flagrant exception of Drew Neitzel in 2006-2007, role players seldom shift gears and become focal points in the offense. That means there will be possessions and shots available for the incoming freshmen in Columbus. And this year it seems that Matta—prepare for a shock—has brought in something of a highly rated recruiting class. I know that sounds strange and off-kilter but it's true . . .

MEET THE BUCKEYES

B. J. Mullens (7-0, 275, Fr.). As this book goes to press, Mullens is projected as a top-five pick in the 2009 NBA draft by two mock boards of some repute. A McDonald's All-American, Mullens seems to attract superlatives in bulk: He's big, but he has quick feet and soft hands. He's a space eater, but he's a good athlete. Mullens was actually the first player to commit to Ohio State after Matta arrived in Columbus. The new Buckeye coach saw Mullens in the summer of 2004, when the young player had just completed the eighth grade. Matta offered him a scholarship. Here he is.

William Buford (6-5, 190, Fr.). Also a McDonald's All-American, Buford's been praised by Matta as "a long athletic wing" who "shoots the ball well from outside, drives and finishes around the basket and gets to the foul line." Buford must be encouraged by the featured role that Matta gave two years ago to another McDonald's All-American shooting guard from the state of Ohio, Daequan Cook. Even though he didn't start (with Conley, Butler, and Lewis all in residence, there was no room), Cook was fed shots in abundance from day one. Don't be surprised to see the same with Buford.

David Lighty (6-5, 220, Jr.). The lone holdover from the 2006 "Thad Five" class (which also included Oden, Conley, Cook, and Othello Hunter), Lighty has a reputation as a defensive specialist who's both long and quick. Note, however, that he's also working his way toward respectability as a perimeter shooter.

Evan Turner (6-7, 205, So.). Speaking of wings who are good on defense, Turner also has that square covered. And on a team where no one but Jamar Butler recorded assists, Turner, for what it's worth, posted the second-highest assist rate. On the flip side, he gave the ball away far too often as a freshman.

Jon Diebler (6-6, 205, So.). Diebler arrived last year billed as an unbelievable high school scorer, but for whatever reason he suffered through a terrible three-point-shooting slump as a college freshman. The end of the slump was oft proclaimed, and he did indeed have a nice five-game stretch in February. For the year, however, he made just 29 percent of his threes.

Dallas Lauderdale (6-8, 255, So.). Lauderdale couldn't get on the floor last year as a freshman, but the departure of Hunter should give him more minutes. He's shown hints of being one of those valued defenders who can both rebound and block shots. It appears, however, that Lauderdale also needs work on taking care of the ball.

Anthony Crater (6-1, 165, Fr.). A "true" point guard on a team that, unlike two years ago, doesn't have a lot of options in that department. Crater should get a long look.

Walter Offutt (6-3, 175, Fr.). Indianapolis product Offutt is, in Matta's words, "a tough combo guard."

Prospectus says

For three years in a row and with three vastly different groups of personnel, Thad Matta's Buckeyes have played very good defense. The variable has been offense. In Mullens and Buford, Ohio State has two freshmen used to carrying the offensive load. If they can do so efficiently in the Big Ten (made threes from Buford, Diebler, or someone would be a big lift), this team can be better than most people realize. If not, it'll be another middle-of-the-pack finish.

PENN STATE

2008: 15-16 (7-11 Big Ten)
Lost to Illinois 64-63, Big Ten Tournament First Round
In-conference offense: 0.98 points per possession (8th)
In-conference defense: 1.12 points allowed per possession (10th)

What Penn State did well: *Give the appearance of improvement.*

In 2007 Penn State went just 2-14 in the Big Ten. That record jumped all the way to a borderline respectable 7-11 last year. This improvement was mostly without Geary Claxton, who went down with a season-ending knee injury on January 15.

What we learned in 2008: *The appearance of improvement can be as much "appearance" as "improvement."*

The Nittany Lions were indeed better last year than they were in 2007. More specifically, their defense was better—enough so to offset a smaller drop-off in offense. (The offense was clearly hurt by the loss of Claxton.) But the really interesting thing about this team is how it somehow got much better results from slightly better performance.

Penn State, 2007 versus 2008

Conference games only
PPP: points per possession
Opp. PPP: opponent points per possession
EM: efficiency margin (PPP – Opp. PPP)

	2007	*2008*
PPP	1.02	0.98
Opp. PPP	1.19	1.12
EM	-0.17	-0.14
Conf. record	2-14	7-11

Looking at the six major conferences during the past three seasons, a team that's outscored by 0.14 points per trip over an 18-game conference schedule will typically go 3-15, with the next most likely record being 2-16. Instead, Penn State went 7-11, making its year perhaps the single most fortunate season in the 219 team-seasons played by 73 major-conference teams since 2006.

What made the Nittany Lions' record so much better than their per-possession performance? Little things, unremarkable at the time, that added up. Of their 11 losses, eight were by double digits and four were by at least 22 points. Conversely, of their seven wins, their largest margin of victory was 11 points. They won two one-point games and their only overtime game.

In Penn State's defense, to have that kind of year in the first place requires a particular kind of team in a particular kind of conference. To have that kind of year, it surely helps to be a below-average team in a conference with a small number of quality teams that will beat you soundly and, conversely, a few teams that are really struggling that you will beat five times by between one and 11 points. (The Nittany Lions' other two wins came against NCAA tournament-bound opponents, Michigan State and Indiana.) Bingo. Meet the Big Ten in 2008.

What's in store for 2009

The provisional assumption with Penn State in 2009 should be that opponents will score a lot of points, for the Nittany Lions' struggles on defense have proven to be persistent. In each of the past three seasons, opposing Big Ten offenses have made at least 55 percent of their twos and scored at least 1.12 points per possession. Although there was improvement on this front last year, the improvement needs to be seen in context. The baseline for the change was a 2007 team that played possibly the most ineffective defense of the decade in the Big Ten (i.e., even less effective than the defense played by Northwestern last year). And the revamped 2008 defense brought the Nittany Lions only up to a level where they were 10th in the conference, still way below the Big Ten average or, for that matter, the league's ninth-best defense at Michigan.

MEET THE NITTANY LIONS

Jamelle Cornley (6-5, 240, Sr.). Cornley's been a hard worker throughout his career, but he was dealt (or, I guess, dealt himself) a tough gig, being the 6-5 interior player for Penn State. Last year he played virtually the entire year with a bruised left knee before undergoing arthroscopic surgery with two games left in the regular season. He's Ed DeChellis's best returning defensive rebounder, and he makes a credible 52 percent of his twos.

Talor Battle (5-11, 160, So.). As a freshman Battle functioned as a combo guard in a point guard's body, sharing assists pretty evenly with Stanley Pringle and looking for his own shot with a confidence that, alas, was not matched by accuracy. Granted, Michigan will be forgiven for thinking Battle is in fact Kobe Bryant, after the freshman made 7-of-9 threes and scored 28 points (with 13 rebounds!) against the Wolverines on March 1. Speaking of 28, however, that was actually his three-point percentage for the season. And with the line moving out a foot this year, DeChellis may want to draw the young man aside for a frank and candid discussion of discretion, valor, and the better parts thereof.

Stanley Pringle (6-1, 180, Sr.). Ordinarily Pringle would merit mention here only as being PSU's best perimeter shooter last year, one who hit 41 percent of his threes, and as being its worst interior shooter, one who hit only 34 percent of his twos. But as it happens, few players in college basketball this season will elicit as much attention from opposing teams' student sections as Pringle, who was charged with public lewdness and disorderly conduct after a March 27 incident at the Penn State library in which he allegedly was not master of his domain.

Danny Morrissey (6-3, 190, Sr.). Morrissey had a sublime year as a three-point specialist in 2007, but for whatever reason his shooting fell off a bit last year.

David Jackson (6-6, 200, So.). Jackson provides DeChellis with screens on offense and some badly needed length on defense; he never shoots.

Andrew Jones III (6-9, 240, So.). A lot like Jackson, only Jones additionally has proven to be an outstanding offensive rebounder.

Jeff Brooks (6-8, 190, So.). Despite his slender physique, Brooks has given the best indications to date of any of the young Lions that he might be able to help out Cornley on the defensive glass.

Andrew Ott (6-10, 230, So.). Ott is a transfer from Villanova and will become eligible during the second semester. He played all of 16 minutes for the Wildcats last year before deciding a change was needed.

Chris Babb (6-5, 215, Fr.). A shooting guard who's used to having the offense go through him, Babb topped 40 points eight times in his high school career.

Prospectus says

DeChellis must wish for one year in which his team is healthy. My fear, however, is that even if he gets his wish, he might not like what he sees on defense. Not that the offense runs itself, mind you. For a team that shot a fair number of threes last year, Penn State turned the ball over pretty regularly. Still, the primary worry in State College this year should be the same as it's been for a while now: defense.

PURDUE

2008: 25-9 (15-3 Big Ten)
Lost to Xavier 85-78, NCAA Second Round
In-conference offense: 1.05 points per possession (4th)
In-conference defense: 0.94 points allowed per possession (2nd)

What Purdue did well: *Give Wisconsin fits.*

Last year, the Big Ten champion Badgers were 0-2 against Purdue and 16-0 against the rest of the conference. Wisconsin had two shots at the Boilermakers and even had the psychological advantage of hosting the second game (payback, etc.). It didn't matter. The Badgers just weren't the same team when they played Purdue.

One factor that enabled the Boilermakers to succeed where every other Big Ten team failed was clearly their ability to get under Wisconsin's ball-handling skin, a feat generally regarded as impossible with regard to a Bo Ryan team. Not for Purdue. Against the rest of the Big Ten Wisconsin coughed the ball up on just 18 percent of their trips, but in two games against Matt Painter's team they gave the ball away 24 percent of the time.

Creating opponent turnovers is a collective endeavor in West Lafayette, but the Boilermakers do have a ringleader in Chris Kramer, who's posted one of the highest steal rates in the nation in each of his first two seasons. Kramer plainly lives for steals the way most guards live for threes. Opposing offenses need to account for his whereabouts at all times. Certainly Wisconsin will try to this year.

What we learned in 2008: *Two-point shots are optional.*

Going into last season Purdue had lost Carl Landry, a preternaturally efficient scorer who was something of a two-point-making (and foul-drawing) machine. So a year ago at this time, we sage writer types were all saying that Landry was going to be a huge loss for Painter.

Well, guess what? Landry *was* a huge loss. Purdue's two-point percentage didn't just dip, it plunged into a dark and hitherto unexplored sub-Michigan abyss in Landry's absence.

Life without Landry: Purdue offense, 2007 versus 2008
Conference games only
PPP: points per possession

	2007	2008
2FG pct.	50.3	43.7
PPP	1.01	1.05
Record	9-7	15-3

This was easily the worst two-point shooting in the conference last year, recorded by a team that actually improved on offense, went 15-3, and enabled Painter to win Big Ten coach of the year honors in a walk. What happened?

Two things: much better ball-handling and, you guessed it, threes. Duke and South Florida were the only major-conference teams who slashed their in-conference turnover percentages more dramatically than did Purdue last year. (Keaton Grant had a particularly vivid tale to tell here: turnovers a-go-go one year, closed spigot the next.) And Painter would have danced a jig if you'd told him a year ago that his young team would drain 40 percent of its threes in Big Ten play.

I've never really understood the practice of bringing in college coaches, be they basketball or football, to talk to your company about "leadership" or "motivation." As one who has spoken to some of these coaches, I can personally attest that they do indeed put their pants on one leg at a time like the rest of us. Nevertheless, if you really feel you must bring in one such coach, I nominate Painter. He replaced the sun around which his entire offense orbited (a player who, we now know, was NBA ready) with a couple of supporting players, offensively speaking, and a passel of freshmen—highly rated freshmen, to be sure, but not one-and-dones. And in what was supposed to be a "rebuilding" or at least "transition" year, it would appear that Painter decided simply to control what he could control, more or less: shot selection and turnovers. His team shot a lot more threes and committed a lot fewer turnovers. It worked.

Suggested presentation title: "Putting Change to Work, the Matt Painter Way."

What's in store for 2009

Scott Martin transferred to Notre Dame, but everyone else is back: all five starters from a team that outscored Big Ten opponents by 0.11 points per trip in 2008. Historically speaking, having five starters return who outperformed teams the previous year by such a significant margin is a recipe for very happy fans. Not that the Boilermakers are foreordained, mind you. I don't expect Purdue's three-point shooting, for example, to be as good as it was last year, but then again I don't expect their two-point shooting to be as bad.

MEET THE BOILERMAKERS

Robbie Hummel (6-8, 210, So.). Hummel had a surprising, outstanding, and misleading freshman year. Misleading because his season totals would lead you to believe he was merely a commendably efficient role player. Those who saw this team in action, however, know better. By late in the year, Hummel was actually a decisively efficient star. In Purdue's consensus-sealing five-point win at Wisconsin on February 9, for example, Hummel scored 21 points on 8-of-12 shooting. Last year he functioned as the hoops equivalent of a decathlete: defensive rebounding, assists, trips to the line, threes, twos—whatever it took. If Hummel continues to develop along his present trend lines, we will officially have our next paradigmatic cognitive challenge in the field of player evaluation: a force of college basketball nature who still looks like the kid who asks if you want paper or plastic.

E'Twaun Moore (6-3, 180, So.). In an unusually balanced offense, Moore took a few more shots than did any of his teammates last year and had a magnificent season from the perimeter, nailing 43 percent of his threes. His work inside the arc was less rewarding, however. And, strangely for a player who attempted more than 200 twos, Moore for some reason is never fouled.

Chris Kramer (6-3, 210, Jr.). Kramer's felonious streak is alluded to above. In addition, he's the reign-ing Big Ten defensive player of the year and something of a competitor, certainly not one of those laconic, Internet-surfing young people I hear decried nowadays. When Illinois' Demetri McCamey buried a three in Kramer's face to send their Big Ten tournament quarterfinal to overtime (where Purdue would lose), I thought Kramer was going to implode before my eyes. On offense he's a pass-first point guard—assists were split three ways between Kramer, Moore, and Hummel—who poses no shooting threat from the perimeter. Last year Kramer suffered through a season of miserable (62 percent) foul shooting after a freshman year in which he had at least been acceptable (71 percent) in that area.

Keaton Grant (6-4, 205, Jr.). Purdue inflicted a lot of pain on opposing defenses last year by putting Grant and his 44 percent three-point shooting on the floor alongside Hummel (45 percent) and Moore (43). Grant had knee surgery in mid-April and is reportedly on track for a healthy return in time for the start of the season.

Nemanja Calasan (6-9, 245, Sr.). Calasan shot often but not very accurately during limited minutes in 2008. Moreover, his defensive rebounding was strangely subdued for a player of his size in a Purdue uniform. Painter flew the team to Australia in August with the stated purpose of, among other things, wanting Calasan to improve his work on the boards.

JaJuan Johnson (6-10, 210, So.). Johnson and Calasan effectively split minutes last year, with Calasan customarily starting. If they both play the same way they did last year, it'll be interesting to see if Painter gives the honorary status to Johnson. Calasan has intermittent three-point range and is perhaps a better offensive rebounder. But Johnson makes twos at the same (below-average) rate as Calasan, while exceeding Calasan on the defensive glass and bringing shot blocking to the table.

Marcus Green (6-4, 230, Sr.). In averaging 16 minutes a game last year, Green's most important contributions were probably made on the defensive glass, where he provided a modicum of support for Hummel, Calasan, and Johnson. Indeed, of the four players named here, the lowest defensive rebound percentage was posted by Calasan.

Lewis Jackson (5-9, 175, Fr.). There aren't many players under six feet tall who make it to Division I by being slow, granted, but Jackson arrives in West Lafayette labeled as really super-extra fast. He should provide a nice change-up when Kramer needs some rest.

Prospectus says

A TV analyst doing advance work for a Purdue game last year approached Painter at the shoot-around with a sheet of stats provided by yours truly—stats that suggested Purdue was on track to be better than people expected from a team that had just lost to Wofford. With a wave of his hand, Painter dismissed the unsolicited minutiae. "I just want to know if my guys are playing hard," he said. Painter doesn't do tempo-free stats, but tempo-free stats love his team. Both halves of that statement will be true again this year.

WISCONSIN

2008: 31-5 (16-2 Big Ten)
Lost to Davidson 73-56, NCAA Sweet 16
In-conference offense: 1.09 points per possession (1st)
In-conference defense: 0.91 points allowed per possession (1st)

What Wisconsin did well: *Defy expectations.*

A year ago, Wisconsin was coming off the best season in the program's history. The Badgers were ranked number one in the country for the first time ever in February 2007, on their way to a 30-6 season. After a disappointing second-round loss to UNLV, Wisconsin bid farewell to Alando Tucker and Kammron Taylor, the two players who, along with Brian Butch, took almost all the shots in the offense. (Truly. Beyond the Tucker-Taylor-Butch triumvirate, no other Badger that year took more than 18 percent of the team's shots during his minutes on the floor.) In the wake of these departures, it was widely expected that Bo Ryan's team would take a step back.

What in fact took place last year, however, was the exact opposite. Wisconsin found a way to improve on the performance it had shown during its best year ever. The Badgers in 2008 were actually better, on both sides of the ball.

Wisconsin, 2007 versus 2008
Conference games only
PPP: points per possession

Opp. PPP: opponent points per possession
EM: efficiency margin (PPP – Opp. PPP)

	2007	2008
PPP	1.07	1.09
Opp. PPP	0.93	0.91
EM	+0.14	+0.18
Conf. record	13-5	16-2

How did Wisconsin replace Tucker and Taylor and have an even better year?

What we learned in 2008: *Threes are a many-splendored thing.*

The Badgers' offense was even higher-scoring last year than it was in 2007 for one reason and only one reason: threes. Ryan's team was actually *worse* in every other offensive category après-Alando, but the Badgers' performance on their threes was so much better that it lifted the entire offense.

All because of threes: Wisconsin offense, 2007 versus 2008
Conference games only
TO pct.: turnover percentage
Off. reb. pct.: offensive rebound percentage
PPP: points per possession
FTM/FGA: free-throws made per field-goals
    attempted

	2007	2008
3FG pct.	34.1	38.6
2FG pct.	49.4	48.3
TO pct.	17.5	18.7
Off. reb. pct.	33.3	32.5
FTM/FGA (pct.)	28.3	25.6
PPP	1.07	1.09

If you're wondering, Wisconsin devoted the same proportion of its field-goal attempts to threes each season, about 33 percent of its shots. Only Michigan State placed a smaller wager on threes in-conference. Yet even though the Badgers shot threes so infrequently, an improvement in accuracy of less than 5 percent was enough by itself to offset small declines in every other area of performance.

In other words, last year in Madison turnovers were up. Two-point shooting, offensive rebounds, and free-throw proficiency were all down. Still, the offense got better. Threes are a powerful thing.

I said earlier that Wisconsin was better in 2008 on both offense *and* defense. In fact, the improvement was about equal on both sides of the ball. It's just that on defense the improvement was more evenly distributed across activities, namely, better two-point and three-point defense.

What's in store for 2009

Last year the challenge was to replace the shots taken by Tucker and Taylor. This year the task at hand is to replace the defense of Michael Flowers and the defensive rebounding of Brian Butch. Yes, both of those players also brought good things to the table on offense. Flowers made 41 percent of his threes last year, and Butch was far and away the largest single presence within the offense—when he was on the floor (he averaged less than 25 minutes a game). Still, both seniors were particularly valuable on defense. Flowers was invariably assigned to guard the opponent's best perimeter scorer. Butch was the top defensive rebounder on a team renowned for its work on the defensive glass. I think Wisconsin's defense has to slip a little this year for reasons of sheer gravitational pull toward normalcy. Still, if Ryan can fill these two defensive vacancies adequately, the Badgers' defense won't slip very far.

MEET THE BADGERS

Marcus Landry (6-7, 220, Sr.). The realignment that took place in the Wisconsin offense when Alando Tucker departed was a sight to see. No single player took over all of Tucker's possessions and shots, of course. It was a team effort. Among those assuming a larger role in the offense was Landry, who accomplished exactly what every coach hopes his player will accomplish in such a situation: Landry became a little more efficient even as he took more shots. As a case in point, over the course of his first two seasons Landry made just 61 percent of his free throws. Last year, conversely, he shot 71 percent from the line. Landry won't be sending an assist your way anytime soon, but he's fair on the defensive glass, hauling in what little was left last year after Butch and Joe Krabbenhoft had done their work.

Trevon Hughes (6-0, 195, Jr.). Speaking of replacing Tucker's shots, Hughes was only too happy to do his bit. He stepped right in and started firing away.

The results were mixed: Hughes started with a bang last November, and it was hard not to be struck with the assurance and confidence being displayed by a player who had logged a total of 240 minutes before last year. The troubling thing is that the longer the year went on, the worse his shooting totals became, until he finished the season having made just 31 percent of his threes. A sidenote: Since Hughes is fouled quite often, if he could pull a Landry, as it were, and improve on his 69 percent foul shooting, this would be a nice boost for the offense.

Joe Krabbenhoft (6-7, 220, Sr.). Krabbenhoft is pegged as simply a blue-collar type who gets defensive rebounds. Well, he *is* a blue-collar type who gets defensive rebounds. Still, I'd like to see him shoot more. (Keep in mind that the last time I said this about a player was when I opined in that direction with regard to Mario Chalmers on the eve of the Final Four. And look what happened!) I'm not asking for an Alando-in-2007-level barrage, mind you, just a normal 20 percent share of the shots. Krabbenhoft's 53 percent two-point shooting last year tells me he could do good things with those added opportunities. As long as those opportunities are inside the arc.

Jason Bohannon (6-2, 200, Jr.). Speaking of needing to shoot more, Bohannon made 39 percent of his threes last year but accounted for just 16 percent of his team's shots during his minutes. With Flowers no longer in the lineup, Bohannon should and, I trust, will be encouraged to fire away, relatively speaking.

Jon Leuer (6-10, 210, So.). Leuer saw some extended minutes at the beginning of the season last year, but by the time Big Ten play rolled around Ryan was using him pretty strictly as a bridge to the next TV timeout for winded bigs, be they Butch, Krabbenhoft, or whoever. From these glimpses, one would think Leuer has good outside range, but of course you can't really tell until he's put in and left in.

Tim Jarmusz (6-6, 200, So.). He played even less than Leuer did last year, but Jarmusz is touted as a versatile scorer in the making.

Other players to emerge later. Ryan tends to keep his depth seated comfortably on the bench, with the result that when a new season dawns you're seeing "new" players get serious minutes suddenly and for the first time. (Three years ago at this time, I was wondering what I'd see not only from freshmen like Landry and Krabbenhoft but also from sophomores like Butch and Greg Stiemsma.) Obviously, there are more minutes available beyond the six players described above. Candidates for those minutes will include **Jared Berggren (6-10, 235, Fr.)**, **J. P. Gavinski (6-11, 255, So.)**, and **Keaton Nankivil (6-8, 245, So.)**.

Prospectus says

Wisconsin has never missed an NCAA tournament since Bo Ryan arrived in Madison. The coach's ability to replace graduating players and keep his team at or near the top of the Big Ten season after season has rightly become legendary. Last year merely cemented that legend. Nevertheless, there are, of course, variations from year to year, even for the Badgers. Take 2006. Wisconsin went 19-12 that year. Expect this year's Badgers to be somewhere in between 2006 and 2008. I know, of course, that they'll take care of the ball and the defensive glass. I know they won't foul. I don't know, however, if they'll be able to match last year's very good three-point shooting. And to allow conference opponents just 0.91 points per trip two seasons running would, anywhere outside Lawrence, Kansas, be virtually unprecedented in our admittedly thin tempo-free annals. So Wisconsin slipping down a peg this year wouldn't be a shock. Then again, slipping down a peg from the empyrean heights of 2008 still leaves the Badgers with a sweet view, one far above most of the Big Ten.

The Big 12
National Champions and a Regional Imbalance

JOHN GASAWAY

For the first time in its short history, the Big 12 has a reigning national champion in its midst. Kansas had been knocking on that particular door with increasing urgency for the past several seasons. This was the April when the door finally swung open, with a little help from Mario Chalmers and, not least, the Memphis Tigers over the final two minutes of regulation in the national championship game.

The Jayhawks won it all with a mix of speed and power that the rest of the Big 12 has come to know well. Indeed, the only three losses suffered by Kansas all year were on the road in conference play. Once KU was loosed on the rest of Division I, however, the team wasn't to be denied until Bill Self and his players were cutting down the nets in San Antonio. It was a proud moment for a conference that's had no shortage of outstanding teams of late, most notably Texas in 2006, Texas A&M in 2007, and Kansas three years running.

And yet ...

The pride is rather unevenly distributed in the Big 12 these days. Technically, of course, the conference doesn't recognize North and South divisions in basketball as it does in football. (That is, unlike the SEC, the Big 12 doesn't seed its conference basketball tournament according to divisional standings. The Big 12 does, however, schedule its conference games by division.) But if the Big 12 did acknowledge divisional realities, it would have to face the fact that the North was more or less annihilated in its head-to-head competition with the South last year, going just 13-23.

Keep in mind that both the eventual national champions and Michael Beasley were residing in the North, yet the division won just 36 percent of its games against the South. Ordinarily, you'd class that as an outcome so lopsided that it won't happen again anytime soon. But the stark imbalance between regions is likely to continue this season.

Of the six teams in the North, a case could be made that five are at least at risk of taking a step back this year, the potential exception being Missouri. Indeed, each of those five teams comes into the year having lost arguably the best player: Kansas State lost Beasley, Nebraska lost Aleks Maric, Colorado lost Richard Roby, and Iowa State lost Wesley Johnson. Then there's Kansas, which lost six of the eight players who saw minutes in the national championship game, including the entire starting five.

The Jayhawks will reload, of course. Sherron Collins and Cole Aldrich return, and the incoming class of recruits is rated as one of the best in the nation. But on paper, at least, the relative desolation in the North this year is astonishing. The most decorated returning player in the North is Missouri's De-Marre Carroll, an honorable mention All–Big 12 selection last year.

This desolation is a direct consequence of the exceedingly high player turnover and recurrent programmatic turmoil seen in the past few years at places like Iowa State, Colorado, Missouri, and Nebraska. And so, even as the strength of Kansas has waxed, that of the rest of the North has waned: The

Jayhawks are 27-3 against their North brethren over the past three seasons. It's been no contest.

Changing this imbalance will require a quality that's been elusive in the North of late: stability. Keeping the same coaches together with the same players for, dare we say it, an entire calendar year is the kind of outside-the-box thinking these teams sorely need. Continuity can work wonders. Look at Baylor.

The continued renaissance of the Bears should give hope to struggling teams everywhere, be they Oregon State or Northwestern, Rutgers or Colorado, St. John's or Iowa State. For, speaking literally, there can be no hole as deep as the one Baylor just climbed out of. Five short years ago this program was a smoldering ruin, incinerated in a flash by one of the most toxic scandals in the history of collegiate sports. And yet, here is Scott Drew's team today, coming off a trip to the NCAA tournament and poised to do as well if not better in 2009.

With Baylor's resurgence, the quality of Big 12 hoops in the state of Texas is as good as it's been in a long while. Start with Texas, a team that will do its level best this year to replace All-American point guard D. J. Augustin. Then again, replacing All-Americans is rapidly becoming old hat for Rick Barnes, who in the past three seasons alone has had to replace not only Augustin but also LaMarcus Aldridge, P. J. Tucker, Daniel Gibson, and some guy named Kevin Durant. Don't weep for the 2009 Longhorns just yet.

Nearby at Texas A&M, second-year coach Mark Turgeon will try to equal or improve on last year's results: 8-8 in the Big 12 and a 9-seed in the NCAA tournament. Those might sound like relatively humble goals, but taking Final Four–bound UCLA to the 39th minute of a second-round game is a nice "floor" for a program that went 0-16 in the Big 12 as recently as 2004.

The question mark in the Lone Star State is Texas Tech, where Bob Knight fairly stunned the college basketball world with his sudden retirement on February 4. New coach Pat Knight has ten games under his belt and has already shown a willingness to chart his own stylistic path, one that's heavily influenced by, yet not identical to, his father's. Still, the younger Knight must be at least a little chastened by what transpired the last time a son tried to take over for his coaching-legend father in the Big 12 South.

When Sean Sutton took the reins from his father, Eddie, at Oklahoma State in February 2006, it looked as though the program would stay in the family, so

to speak, for at least the foreseeable future. It didn't turn out that way, however. Sutton was forced out on April 1 after two full seasons as head coach. Having swung and missed on OSU alum Bill Self, the Cowboys turned to UMass coach Travis Ford, who joins the Big 12 as the conference's only true rookie coach this season. He'll find that in sophomore James Anderson, he has a pretty fair foundation for his new program.

Meanwhile, at Oklahoma, the foundation is in place: In March, the Sooners won an NCAA tournament game for the first time in three years. The objective now is to reach the top of the Big 12 standings. Blake Griffin's announcement that he would return to Norman for his sophomore season was good news for the conference and tremendous news for Jeff Capel. Griffin, North Carolina's Ty Lawson, and Arizona's Chase Budinger are perhaps the only three players in college basketball this year who can legitimately claim that they would have been drafted in the first round this past summer had they chosen to take that leap. With Griffin, a solid cast of veterans, and a much-lauded class of recruits, Capel may indeed have the ammunition he needs to contend for a Big 12 title. That contest would figure to be waged between Oklahoma, Texas, and possibly Kansas.

The reigning national champs notwithstanding, the Big 12 is likely to continue to feature the most profound North-South imbalance since Appomattox. (Note to today's young history-challenged readers. At Appomattox, the imbalance went the other way.) This tale of two regions has yet to reach the final chapter. It's the best and worst of times in Big 12 country, until further notice.

	2008 Record	Returning Minutes (%)	2009 Prediction
Texas	13-3	81	13-3
Oklahoma	9-7	70	12-4
Kansas	13-3	15	11-5
Baylor	9-7	83	11-5
Oklahoma St.	7-9	75	8-8
Texas A&M	8-8	59	8-8
Kansas St.	10-6	37	8-8
Missouri	6-10	50	7-9
Texas Tech	7-9	65	7-9
Iowa St.	4-12	55	5-11
Nebraska	7-9	73	4-12
Colorado	3-13	43	2-14

BAYLOR

2008: 21-11 (9-7 Big 12)
Lost to Purdue 90-79, NCAA First Round
In-conference offense: 1.08 points per possession (4th)
In-conference defense: 1.07 points allowed per possession (9th)

What Baylor did well: *Score.*

In a conference blessed with the likes of Kansas, Texas, and even Michael Beasley–era Kansas State, it was hard for a team to stand out offensively in 2008. But while no one may have been singing the praises of the high-scoring Baylor Bears, the points were indeed abundant in Waco last year. Scott Drew's team actually improved on both sides of the ball, but the change from "awful" on defense in 2007 to "below average" in 2008 was less impressive than the transformation from "OK" to "very good" on offense. Most importantly, the two improvements together were enough to secure Baylor's first NCAA bid in 20 years. (Yes, 20 years.)

Last year the Bears' three-point shooting became markedly less frequent but notably more accurate. Drew's team also picked up the pace, averaging about 72 possessions per 40 minutes in-conference. Last and most crucial, Baylor took much better care of the ball, committing a turnover on just 17 percent of its trips in Big 12 play. Plenty of threes and very few turnovers netted the Bears a robust 1.08 points per possession against conference foes.

What we learned in 2008: *Opponent turnovers are outside a team's control, only up to a point.*

The Bears' games in 2008 were remarkably turnover free, both for the Bears and for their opponents. Possessions in BU's Big 12 games ended in turnovers just 17 percent of the time for both teams. Among major-conference teams last year, only Texas and Cal played conference games that featured a lower rate of turnovers. In short, Drew's team took excellent care of the ball, and this ability powered a very good offense. But the inability to take the ball away from opponents also constituted this team's primary defensive weakness.

Some defenses can afford to do without opponents' turnovers. (See, for example, Stanford in 2008 or Connecticut in 2006.) Such is not the case, however, with Baylor. A normal number of turnovers from opponents would help a defense that really needs some help. Note, for example, that Drew's group had one of the worst defenses of any team that reached the NCAA tournament last year, allowing conference opponents to score 1.07 points per trip.

What's in store for 2009

Baylor has deployed a veritable fleet of combo guards for a few years now, and last year's growth on offense mostly reflected across-the-board improvement, especially in holding on to the ball. (Truth be known, Tweety Carter was already reliable with the ball; pretty much everyone else, though, cut down on turnovers.) Particularly helpful in this respect was the arrival of freshman LaceDarius Dunn, who stepped in right away and seamlessly blended frequent (and accurate) shooting with a very un-freshman-like lack of turnovers. This year, with the core of the team returning, Drew can probably count on having a high-scoring offense again.

Then again the defense is still worrisome. Bear in mind (har!) that Baylor actually started strong on defense in the Big 12 last year. Over their last 12 conference games, however, the Bears yielded a frightening 1.12 points per possession. There are tremendous opportunities to be had in Waco, then, from even a modest improvement on D. (Less fouling would help. In Big 12 play, only Missouri and Oklahoma State sent opponents to the line at a higher rate than did the Bears.)

MEET THE BEARS

Curtis Jerrells (6-1, 205, Sr.). In 2008 Jerrells logged more minutes and hoisted more shots than did any other Baylor player. He actually suffered through a relatively off year in terms of shooting, hitting just 33 percent of his threes. Still, Jerrells took excellent care of the ball and found the open man often enough to post the team's highest assist rate. For two years running now, Jerrells can be counted on to make some threes, dish some assists, and hit about half his twos. A solid performer.

LaceDarius Dunn (6-4, 200, So.). The coming year lines up very nicely as the proverbial breakout year for Dunn. His playing time was limited his freshman year by a knee "tweak" suffered at the end of November and, not least, by the sheer number of experienced teammates in the backcourt. Good health and the departure of Aaron Bruce, however, should provide more minutes for Dunn, a pure shooter who hit 42 percent of his threes while simultaneously keeping defenses honest with his ability to put the ball on the floor. His defense is a work in progress, but he was far and away the Bears' most efficient option on offense last year. Even more impressive, he was efficient while taking a lot of shots and using a lot of possessions during his minutes on the floor. (He's even a fair defensive rebounder.) Dunn will be heard from.

Henry Dugat (6-0, 170, Sr.). Though he appears slim by Big 12 standards, Dugat's been a steady bookend alongside fellow senior Jerrells throughout their careers in Waco. Dugat is a career 39 percent three-point shooter and is the most likely Bear to record a steal.

Kevin Rogers (6-9, 240, Sr.). Remarkable consistency, thy name is Rogers. For two years in a row, the young man from Dallas has provided Drew with decent defensive rebounding while hitting a little more than half his twos. Indeed, Rogers's skill set (rebounding on both ends of the floor) is unique on this team.

Tweety Carter (5-10, 180, Jr.). If Drew's pack of combo guards contains one player with at least a point-guard emphasis, it's Carter, who's less likely than Jerrells, Dunn, or Dugat to put up a shot. Carter is not only Drew's best defender, but also a capable distributor who hit 40 percent of his threes last year.

Mamadou Diene (7-0, 250, Sr.). A pure shot-blocking specialist who never touches the ball on offense and is often in foul trouble. (Last January, Diene fouled out of *four consecutive games*.) Diene and seven-foot junior **Josh Lomers** comprise Baylor's experienced frontcourt depth.

Anthony Jones (6-10, 190, Fr.). Very highly touted (if slender) recruit from Houston, said to have good three-point range. Following on the heels of Dunn, the arrival of Jones marks the second consecutive year that Baylor's been able to land a top-level recruit.

Prospectus says
There will be the potential to hear a lot about Baylor this year. Rightfully so, given the off-court depths—depths that fairly beggar belief—that this program plumbed in 2003. It's been an incredible comeback, and the Bears are indeed vastly improved. Just remember this, though, when praising Baylor this season: There is likely to be a ceiling on how good this team can really be. The ceiling is defense. Even as the offense has steadily improved with this group of players over each of the past three seasons, the defense has been below average at its best.

In short, Baylor will score a lot of points and so will their opponents. In fact, this team might look a little like 2008-edition Notre Dame (well, minus Luke Harangody). The Irish, like Baylor last year, averaged about 72 possessions per 40 minutes and went as far as their offense could take them. Sounds about right for the ascendant Bears.

COLORADO

2008: 12-20 (3-13 Big 12)
Lost to Oklahoma 54-49, Big 12 Tournament Quarterfinal
In-conference offense: 0.97 points per possession (11th)
In-conference defense: 1.10 points allowed per possession (11th)

What Colorado did well: *Decelerate.*
Jeff Bzdelik enters his second year at Colorado having already accomplished his first order of business in Boulder. Bringing with him a template for offense that served him well at Air Force (namely, a really slow pace, plenty of threes, and very few turnovers), Bzdelik fairly slammed on the brakes in his first year at CU:

Biggest slowdowns from 2007 to 2008
Possessions per 40 minutes.
Conference games only: ACC, Big East, Big Ten, Big 12, Pac-10, and SEC

	2007	2008	%change
1. Colorado	72.6	61.4	-15.4
2. Iowa	63.8	59.2	-7.2
3. Arizona	67.0	63.5	-5.2

Bzdelik doesn't have his entire system installed after just one year, of course, but setting a more deliberate tempo was a start.

What we learned in 2008: *Turnarounds take time.*
There was modest—repeat, *modest*—improvement in Boulder last season, but it was papered over by

the Buffs' second consecutive 3-13 record in the Big 12. Still, on a possession-by-possession basis, CU actually played better last year than it did in 2007: It scored a few more points and allowed a few less.

This slight improvement was achieved despite a drastic falloff in defensive rebounding. (The following will sound odd, but it's backed by the facts: Colorado's defensive boards nosedived last year in the absence of a 6-3 guard, Dominique Coleman, who in 2007 personally hauled in one in every five opponent misses during his minutes.) In fact, Colorado was actually respectable in 2008 in terms of field-goal defense—Kansas State, to take one tournament-worthy example, was worse against the Big 12—but it didn't matter because the Buffs were simply annihilated on their defensive glass. Bzdelik's team couldn't end opponents' possessions. Only Missouri's defense was worse (barely) than the Buffs' in-conference.

What's in store for 2009

This year Bzdelik will turn the page in terms of personnel. Richard Roby, Marcus Hall, and Marcus King-Stockton have all wrapped up their careers. Additionally, starter Xavier Silas and seldom-glimpsed reserve Caleb Patterson both elected to transfer after last year.

The departures are balanced by a raft of freshmen who are set to arrive this year. Bzdelik has had high praise for the freshmen, saying that they're a good fit for his system and that as many as three first-year players may be starters. If so, continued improvement should be the mission along the Front Range in 2009.

MEET THE BUFFS

Cory Higgins (6-5, 175, So.). Last year as a freshman Higgins was a serviceable pass-first role player alongside Roby and Hall. (In the wake of Xavier Silas's season-ending injury in February, the Roby-Hall-Higgins threesome finished the year as the nucleus of the team: Each of the three played far more minutes than did any of the other Buffs.) This year, Higgins will be asked to do more, whether it's shooting, running the offense, or both. Fun fact: Higgins's father, Rod Higgins, is general manager of the Charlotte Bobcats.

Jermyl Jackson-Wilson (6-6, 220, Sr.). Jackson-Wilson's struggles with foul trouble limited his minutes last year. After transferring from Ohio State in 2005, he's labored in the Big 12 trenches as an undersized big man and has helped his team most with his offensive rebounding.

Casey Crawford (6-9, 230, So.). A transfer from Wake Forest, Crawford sat out last year and is projected as a starter this season. His most vital contribution could be some reliable defensive rebounding.

Levi Knutson (6-4, 190, So.). Like Higgins, Knutson was reluctant to shoot last year as a freshman playing alongside the likes of Roby and Hall. Unlike Higgins, however, Knutson might have some potential as a perimeter shooter. In order to fulfill that potential, he may have to battle some incoming freshmen for minutes.

Trey Eckloff (6-9, 220, Fr.). Forward from Englewood, Colorado. Get ready to hear this description a lot: Eckloff is billed as a versatile player who can handle the ball, pass, and shoot out on the perimeter. Just the way Bzdelik likes 'em.

Austin Dufault (6-8, 210, Fr.). See Eckloff description, above, only Dufault's hometown has a cooler name: Killdeer, North Dakota.

Nate Tomlinson (6-2, 180, Fr.). Freshman point guard and native Australian.

Toby Veal (6-7, 210, Fr.). A power forward from Savannah, Veal's been praised by Bzdelik for his rebounding and work around the rim.

Prospectus says

The Big 12 has seen—and is seeing—a lot of rebuilding projects of late. Recently arrived coaches at Nebraska, Iowa State, Missouri, and, yes, Colorado are all doing their level best to bring their teams up to a level where they could at least compete with Kansas. None of the above has quite reached that point, of course, but Bzdelik's record of superefficient offense at Air Force suggests that CU bears watching. If this freshman class pans out and the Buffs come up with some defensive boards, Colorado will be on its way to turning the corner.

2008: 14-18 (4-12 Big 12)
Lost to Texas A&M 60-47, Big 12 Tournament First Round
In-conference offense: 0.92 points per possession (12th)
In-conference defense: 1.02 points allowed per possession (5th)

	2007	*2008*
PPP	0.91	0.92
Opp. PPP	1.01	1.02
EM	-0.10	-0.10
Conf. record	6-10	4-14

What Iowa State did well: *Go through a lot of those "Hi! My Name Is . . ." name tags.*

Iowa State's uneven performance on the court the past few years has reflected an eerily pervasive un-evenness off the court. Take it from head coach Greg McDermott: "We've had a strange amount of re-tention problems in the couple years I've been here."

Strange indeed. Mike Taylor, Corey McIntosh, Dodie Dunson, Cory Johnson, Clayton Vette, Marcus Brister, and, most devastating of all, Wesley Johnson—all left Ames before their eligibility was up. Tay-lor was sent packing at McDermott's direction, it's true. But the sheer volume of departures, voluntary or otherwise, has to have set back McDermott's timetable for rebuilding.

This is, after all, year three: In a "normal" setting, McDermott would be benefiting from the growth, experience, and cohesion of the first players he re-cruited. (Granted, this might indeed happen this year with Craig Brackins.) Instead, the coach is still scrambling to put together a roster that can simply win as many games as they lose in the Big 12.

What we learned in 2008: *Tremendous change can result in no change at all.*

Last year most of the shots in the Iowa State offense were taken by Jiri Hubalek, Wes Johnson, and Craig Brackins. The team leaders in minutes were Rahshon Clark, Bryan Petersen, and Brackins. In 2007, by con-trast, the offense revolved to a striking degree around Mike Taylor. That season's minutes went to Taylor, Johnson, Clark, Corey McIntosh, and Dodie Dunson.

Even with the revolving-door nature of Iowa State's roster the past two seasons, the 2008 and 2007 teams looked remarkably similar on paper.

Doing a 360, not a 180: Iowa State, 2007 vs. 2008
Conference games only
PPP: points per possession
Opp. PPP: opponent points per possession
EM: efficiency margin (PPP – Opp. PPP)

In both years this team's debilitating and chronic weakness was an inability to score points, due to an debilitating and chronic inability to make shots, whether from outside or in close.

This was far and away the worst offense in the Big 12 last year, much worse than Colorado or Texas Tech. Johnson played the entire year with an injured foot, which certainly didn't help matters. Still, a healthy Johnson alone wouldn't have transformed this team into a scoring juggernaut. More to the point, the Cyclones will have the opportunity this year to show what they can do without Johnson, who surprised both his coach and his teammates in May by announcing his decision to transfer. He sub-sequently chose Syracuse as his destination and will be eligible in 2009-2010.

What's in store for 2009
McDermott was hired at Iowa State on the strength of his 2006 team at Northern Iowa. Presumably, if McDermott had his druthers, he'd have the Cy-clones playing like the Panthers played that year: tough defense, no turnovers on offense, and an al-most total surrender on the offensive glass in ex-change for outstanding transition D.

The Cyclones already exhibit the weak offensive rebounding. By the same token, they don't force their opponents into many turnovers. These features of the team represent, for the most part, stylistic choices made by McDermott. Until the features are balanced, however, by the excellent field-goal de-fense, strong defensive rebounding, and, not least, normal shooting that Northern Iowa displayed for its coach in 2006, Iowa State will continue to struggle.

MEET THE CYCLONES

Craig Brackins (6-10, 230, So.). A product of Palmdale, California, Brackins arrived at Iowa State last year and was hailed as the highest-ranked re-cruit to land in Ames in many years. Although he generally struggled on offense as a freshman, such was a common Cyclone affliction in 2008. Besides, Brackins offers at least two promising signs for the near future: He doesn't turn the ball over and he's a serviceable free-throw shooter for someone listed at 6-10. This year he'll have every opportunity to deliver on his promise: He should get a lot of shots with this roster. Note also that Brackins—or someone—will need to carry the load on the defensive glass now that Hubalek is gone.

Bryan Petersen (6-1, 180, Sr.). When Petersen pulled the trigger last year, he was respectable, hitting 39 percent of his threes. But, as it happens, he never pulled the trigger, receding into the background while Johnson, Brackins, and Hubalek took all the shots. (This is a player who attempted 33 free throws the entire year.) Petersen arrived last year as a junior-college transfer and, like Brackins, started all 32 games.

Diante Garrett (6-4, 180, So.). During Garrett's freshman year, his ability to create assists was unsurpassed by any of his teammates. Unfortunately, his ability to commit turnovers was, if anything, equally prodigious. Garrett also struggled with his shot. His improvement would be a huge boost to this team.

Lucca Staiger (6-5, 220, So.). A native of Germany who played high school ball in Decatur, Illinois, Staiger joined the Cyclones last year but was ruled ineligible for one season by the NCAA. (Two teammates on Staiger's club team in Europe were ruled to have received compensation in exchange for playing.) This year McDermott is hoping the young 2-guard can knock down some threes. It's been a while since anyone in an Iowa State uniform has done so consistently.

Jamie Vanderbeken (6-11, 240, Jr.). Junior-college transfer, billed as a big man who can hit his threes.

Dominique Buckley (6-2, 190, Fr.). A product of Detroit, Buckley arrives touted as a pass-first point guard and vocal leader who's ready to compete for minutes.

L. A. Pomlee (6-8, 230, Fr.). This power forward from Davenport, Iowa, was a late addition to the incoming class. McDermott has praised Pomlee for his defense and rebounding in particular.

Prospectus says

Iowa State has been limited by its guard play since McDermott arrived in Ames. Last year Cyclone opponents sagged in the paint and dared ISU to make a three. The strategy worked: Against Big 12 opponents, Iowa State shot threes more frequently than did any other team except Oklahoma State, in spite of the fact that the Cyclones were the worst three-point shooting team in the conference. Until Iowa State can make some of those threes, points will be scarce.

KANSAS

2008: 37-3 (13-3 Big 12)
Beat Memphis 75-68 (OT), National Championship Game
In-conference offense: 1.16 points per possession (1st)
In-conference defense: 0.92 points allowed per possession (1st)

What Kansas did well: *Close the deal.*

Coaches like to preach that championships are the result of effort, but the truth is that in late March and early April there's always more than one really talented team expending a good deal of effort. Championships are, additionally, the product of those capricious and aleatory moments scripted by no coach.

Kansas and Bill Self, at last, benefited from such moments in 2008. You don't come back from nine down with a little more than two minutes left in regulation and beat Memphis in overtime without some good fortune. After four years of tournament frustration in the Self era, the ball finally bounced the Jayhawks' way, in the form of three missed free throws by Chris Douglas-Roberts in the final 75 seconds, and, of course, the game-tying three by Mario Chalmers with two seconds left in regulation.

The national championship game was branded a Memphis collapse by some, and clearly, the Tigers didn't play their best basketball in the game's decisive moments. Nevertheless, an incredible number of things had to go right for Kansas for this particular collapse to occur. The memory of Chalmers's three (which was indeed something of a feat: Chalmers, a right-handed player, was moving to his left and he had Derrick Rose all over him) has obscured all that led up to it. Just in the last two minutes, Darrell Arthur made two very tough shots, while Sherron Collins stole an inbounds pass and nailed a three. The Jayhawks needed all the above even before Chalmers's three. If it was indeed a Memphis collapse, it was also a simultaneous Kansas triumph, one that had to be sweet indeed for a coach making his first trip to the Final Four.

What we learned in 2008: *Sometimes you just have to keep doing what you're doing.*

In terms of Big 12 dominance, national champion Kansas in 2008 was virtually indistinguishable from Elite Eight Kansas in 2007. Both teams outscored their conference opponents by almost a quarter of a point per possession, a fearsome level of superiority seldom seen outside the Memphis-dominated Conference USA.

The largest difference between last year's national championship team and the KU squad that lost in the regional finals to UCLA the previous year was a point in the earlier team's favor: The 2007 Jayhawks forced opponents into many more turnovers than did the 2008 Jayhawks. Nevertheless, last year's defense was one of the best in the nation, a status that fans in Lawrence have become accustomed to.

For the past three seasons, Kansas and UCLA have furnished the twin exemplars of a true talent-defense fusion that by old-school lights shouldn't be possible in the 21st century. Observers lamenting that "nowadays," the most talented players don't play defense obviously haven't been watching the Jayhawks under Bill Self or the Bruins under Ben Howland.

Defense Year In and Year Out: Kansas and UCLA, 2006-2008

Conference games only: opponent points per possession

	2006	*2007*	*2008*
Kansas	0.88	0.89	0.92
UCLA	0.93	0.95	0.96

What's in store for 2009

Like Florida last year, Kansas has said good-bye to the core of its national championship team. Only Sherron Collins and Cole Aldrich return. And like the Gators last year, KU's incoming class of recruits is rated as one of the two or three strongest in the nation.

(By the way, there's something about geography-specific recruiting with Self. In his short time at Illinois, he not only worked Chicago—work that carried over to KU, netting him both Julian Wright and Collins—but also installed a talent pipeline reaching to Texas, a connection that brought in Deron Williams. Now, as shown below, Self has apparently set about recruiting the state of New Jersey. Exhaustively.)

MEET THE JAYHAWKS

Sherron Collins (5-11, 205, Jr.). Any game, like the 2008 national championship game, that leads to a climactic shot, like Mario Chalmers's three that sent the game to overtime, harbors within itself several key plays that are quickly forgotten simply because they weren't the *last* key play. One such play was surely Collins's steal and ensuing three with 1:46 left in regulation. For two years Collins, while seeing significant minutes, nevertheless played behind Russell Robinson, as Bill Self opted to go with experience and defense over speed and offense at the point-guard position. Now the job belongs to Collins.

Cole Aldrich (6-11, 240, So.). Last seen giving Tyler Hansbrough everything he could handle during 17 memorable minutes in the national semifinals, Aldrich will vault from seldom-glimpsed freshman to key veteran this season. Having given signs of being both an outstanding defensive rebounder and an excellent shot-blocker, he'll probably be the foundation of KU's defense in 2009.

Markieff (6-10, 230, Fr.) and Marcus (6-8, 220, Fr.) Morris. Twin power forwards from Pennsauken, New Jersey. Billed by Self as the jewels of a loaded recruiting class, the Morris twins will be needed from day one, now that Arthur, Darnell Jackson, and Sasha Kaun have all departed. Note, however, that the academic eligibility of both players is still in question as this book goes to press.

Travis Releford (6-5, 175, Fr.). A shooting guard from Kansas City. Self thinks Releford is "already a college defender"—high praise from a coach who's seen some great defense played by his teams of late.

Tyshawn Taylor (6-2, 170, Fr.). A shooting guard from Jersey City, Taylor originally committed to Marquette but was granted a release when Tom Crean took the Indiana job.

Quintrell Thomas (6-8, 235, Fr.). Power forward from Elizabeth, New Jersey.

Tyrone Appleton (6-3, 200, Jr.). Shooting guard and junior-college transfer.

Mario Little (6-4, 185, Jr.). Still another new arrival from the junior-college ranks, also a shooting guard.

Prospectus says

Look fast. This could be the first and last time in recent memory when the Kansas defense is less than dominant. Still, this team has the talent to finish near the top of the Big 12, even if that talent is precociously young.

KANSAS STATE

2008: 21-12 (10-6 Big 12)
Lost to Wisconsin 72-55, NCAA Second Round
In-conference offense: 1.11 points per possession (2nd)
In-conference defense: 1.01 points allowed per possession (3rd)

What Kansas State did well: *January.*

You could make a case that no team that didn't get to the Final Four last year had a better month than the one that Michael Beasley–led Kansas State had in January.

A marathon, not a sprint: Kansas State, 2008

Conference games only
PPP: points per possession
Opp. PPP: opponent points per possession
EM: efficiency margin (PPP – Opp. PPP)

	PPP	Opp. PPP	EM	Record
January	1.17	0.95	+0.22	5-0
February and March	1.08	1.03	+0.05	5-6
Overall	1.11	1.00	+0.11	10-6

Granted, the day-and-night effect here was partly an artifact of the schedule. Still, if you'd told anyone before the season started that Kansas State would open Big 12 play, performing virtually as well as eventual national champion Kansas on a possession-by-possession basis (and that this would include a nine-point win at home over the Jayhawks), the person would have been rightly skeptical.

Given that this team, of course, revolved around Michael Beasley the entire season, one might well ask why January was so different from what followed. Basically K-State stopped making their threes, and opponents started making their twos. The Wildcats' three-point shooting in-conference was virtually identical to the Big 12 average, but that's a little misleading: This particular "average" performance was in fact the result of five games of insane outside shooting (43 percent) followed by 11 games of horrific outside shooting (31 percent).

The poor outside shooting reflected a larger reality: K-State's luck simply ran out after February 1. In their last 11 conference games, the Wildcats outscored their opponents by a slight but still significant margin on each possession, yet had only a 5-6 finish to show for their efforts. Nevertheless, the season as a whole qualified as a success for the program, of course, given that the Wildcats won an NCAA tournament game for the first time in 20 years.

What we learned in 2008: *Sometimes, the hype about a freshman is actually justified.*

Michael Beasley didn't exactly lack for coverage last year, of course, but his performance was even better than people realized. In fact, it's an open question whether he had the best individual season we've seen in recent times. Problem is, he had that season in Manhattan, Kansas, of all places, and he's perceived, for better or worse, as a bit too nonchalant. Basketball writers looking to pen valentines would generally prefer that their subjects be either feisty floor-generals or, failing that, aw-shucks strong, silent types. Beasley, goodness knows, is neither feisty nor aw-shucks.

Then again, those rims at either end of the court don't care about your image in the media. On offense, Beasley may have been the single most effective player in the country last year. That's remarkable when you consider the load he carried for a team that didn't have a lot of weapons with which to distract opposing defenses. (Bill Walker, of course, came out of high school ranked as one of the best players in the nation and was promising enough to be drafted in the second round this summer. But looking at just last year, Walker missed a ton of threes, and by February, opponents were simply giving him all the space he wanted outside the arc.)

Beasley not only made his shots, he was ferocious on the offensive glass. Even more impressive, he functioned as the best defensive rebounder in the country last year among major-conference players. Although part of that was middling defensive rebounding from his teammates, the fact remains that when Beasley was on the court he excelled at ending opponents' possessions.

In the run-up to the draft Beasley was widely said to have "character issues," particularly when he was being compared to Derrick Rose. I can't vouch for Beasley's doings 24/7, of course, but I do wonder if this was simply a clumsily worded euphemism for "we wish his personality were different." In any case, Beasley's performance as a college player was startling: He outperformed the hype. He arguably did more to make opponents lose than any other single player in college basketball last year.

What's in store for 2009

Many observers were surprised with how well Texas played in Kevin Durant's absence last year. Will that be the case with a Beasley-less Kansas State this year? Well, no. The Wildcats won't be as good as the Longhorns were last year. Still, Martin has enough depth to win some games in what should be a relatively forgiving Big 12.

MEET THE WILDCATS

Jacob Pullen (6-1, 185, So.). Chicago product Pullen showed some promise during his freshman year as a scoring point guard, taking the few shots that Beasley and Walker chose not to take while simultaneously displaying reasonably good ball handling and the team's highest assist rate. He's not what you'd call a perimeter threat (he shot 30 percent on his threes and 69 percent from the line), but Pullen is respectable from inside the arc. He's also his team's best bet to record a steal. Pullen provides a solid foundation for Martin's team.

Dominique Sutton (6-5, 220, So.). In more than a few recent seasons at K-State, Sutton would have been the most highly touted new arrival in his class. Last year was not such a season, of course, but Sutton will have every opportunity to show what he

has this year. Last season, the wing was academically ineligible until late December and saw only limited action thereafter.

Jamar Samuels (6-8, 200, Fr.). Became eligible in the middle of the season last year but sat out.

Ron Anderson (6-8, 245, So.). Anderson saw limited action last year as a freshman and was an offensive rebounding beast: nothing more and nothing less. Sutton, Samuels, and Anderson all played AAU ball with Beasley.

Darren Kent (6-10, 210, Sr.). One of the few remaining players from the Jim Wooldridge era, Kent will face stiff competition for frontcourt minutes.

Fred Brown (6-3, 185, So.). Brown struggled to get on the floor last year as a freshman shooting guard.

Denis Clemente (6-0, 180, Jr.). A transfer from Miami, Clemente sat out last season. As a sophomore in 2007, he started 15 games as point guard for the Hurricanes and showed a good deal of quickness.

Buchi Awaji (6-3, 175, Jr.). This junior-college transfer and shooting guard takes the ball to the rim and made 40 percent of his threes last year.

Abdul Herrera (6-11, 245, Jr.). Another junior-college transfer, Herrera was a redshirt freshman at Cincinnati in 2005-2006, when Martin was on the staff there.

Jordan Henriquez (6-11, 220, Fr.). A product of Port Chester, New York, who signed in late May, Henriquez blocked 14 shots in *one game*. He's nevertheless being billed as a project who needs to bulk up.

Prospectus says

Kansas State post-Beasley is a riddle, wrapped in a mystery, inside an enigma. Frank Martin is in just his second year as a Division I head coach and, more importantly, his first year without Beasley. Last year the Wildcats played a little like a nascent Great Plains North Carolina, setting a fast pace and going to the offensive glass in waves. (Key differences: K-State shot more threes and way fewer free throws than the Heels did.) But we can't be sure how much of that was Beasley and how much was Martin—we don't yet know the coach's stylistic proclivities. We should discover them this season, however, for this year's Wildcats are a blank slate. Pullen, a sophomore point guard, is the only player on the team who's attempted more than 250 shots in Division I. The team that Martin puts on the floor this year, along with the recruits he lands for next season, will define the stamp that he puts on this program. Last year was about Michael Beasley. This year is about Frank Martin.

MISSOURI

2008: 16-16 (6-10 Big 12)
Lost to Nebraska 61-56, Big 12 Tournament First Round
In-conference offense: 1.04 points per possession (5th)
In-conference defense: 1.10 points allowed per possession (12th)

What Missouri did well: *Put the words "altercation outside a Columbia nightspot" into the zeitgeist.*
The off-court worries for coach Mike Anderson actually started back in the summer of 2007, when DeMarre Carroll suffered a gunshot wound (which, fortunately, turned out to be minor) outside a Columbia nightclub. Just two days later, Kalen Grimes was involved in a late-night incident in St. Louis and charged with second-degree felony assault. He was subsequently dismissed from the team by Anderson.

Worse was yet to come. On January 28, it was reported that point guard Stefhon Hannah, the Tigers' leading scorer, had suffered a broken jaw in yet another late-night altercation. Teammates Leo Lyons, Jason Horton, Darryl Butterfield, and Marshall Brown were also at the scene. All five players were suspended by Anderson. Lyons, Horton, Butterfield, and Brown soon returned to the team. Hannah never did.

Anderson was brought to Columbia in 2006 to run a tight ship after the turmoil and controversy of the Quin Snyder years. He has found doing so to be more of a challenge than he expected.

What we learned in 2008: *Year two of a rebuilding process can be worse than year one.*
Struggling to overcome its personnel losses, Missouri took a significant step back last year. Along with Colorado, the Tigers had the worst defense in the Big 12 in 2008, allowing conference opponents to score 1.10 points per trip. This was a clear fall-off from Anderson's first season in 2007.

What changed? Not the defensive rebounding, which was virtually identical (and quite poor) both years. No, the difference was simply that too many opponent possessions ended with a made two, and not enough ended with a turnover.

**From below-average to worse:
Missouri defense, 2007 vs. 2008**
Conference games only

	2007	2008
Defensive rebound pct.	62.8	62.1
Opp. 2FG pct	46.7	50.0
Opp. turnover pct	22.9	19.5
Opp. points per possession	1.04	1.10
Record	7-9	6-10

True, these stats are a little misleading. Defensive rebounding (along with frequent fouling) has been a constant across the past two years in Columbia, but in this one instance, Anderson would like to see less stability and more change—for the better. Bad defensive rebounding (the worst in the Big 12) was actually Missouri's most prominent feature in 2008 on either side of the ball. It was a deficiency the Tigers covered up surprisingly well in 2007. Not so in 2008.

(A word on luck: Close readers of Ken's Web site will note that statistically speaking, Missouri was one of the unluckiest teams in the country last year. In the season's first five weeks, the Tigers lost games to Michigan State, Arkansas, and Illinois, each by three points or less. Meanwhile, Mizzou was also whomping on the likes of Fordham, Southern, and McNeese State, winning those three games by an average of 35 points—thus, the appearance of statistical bad luck. Once the new year came around and the Tigers started playing Big 12 opponents, however, their luck was no worse than average. If your conference opponents outscore you by 0.06 points per trip, you should indeed go 6-10 or thereabouts.)

What's in store for 2009
A Big 12 coach is entering his third season. Over the course of his first two years, he's seen lots of player turnover and more *L*s than *W*s in-conference. Now he hopes to turn the page and put his stamp on the program. Greg McDermott at Iowa State? Doc Sadler at Nebraska? Mike Anderson at Missouri? Yes!

MEET THE TIGERS

Leo Lyons (6-9, 240, Sr.). On February 26 against Oklahoma State, Lyons had one of the best games any Missouri player has had since the Norm Stewart days: 27 points on 12-of-13 shooting and 18 rebounds. Lyons's late-season performances weren't always so stellar—he ended the season hitting just two of 12 shots against Nebraska in the Big 12 tournament—but it's fair to say big things are now expected from the senior. Last year he made 61 percent of his twos and was a fair defensive rebounder, but he struggled at times to stay out of foul trouble. (A little surprising, because he's not really a shot blocker.) More minutes for Lyons would be good news for the Tigers' offense. In fact, if he can simply maintain his current level of offense, increase his minutes, and improve his defensive rebounding even a little, Lyons can have a big impact on this team's performance.

DeMarre Carroll (6-8, 225, Sr.). A transfer from Vanderbilt and the coach's nephew, Carroll provided Anderson with excellent offensive rebounding last year while making 56 percent of his twos. His lack of strength on the defensive glass wouldn't be too much of an issue on many teams, not for a player like Carroll who contributes in other areas. In Missouri's case, however, those boards are badly needed, and they need to come from someone. If one source turns out to be his own nephew, Anderson would be delighted. Note, however, that last year Carroll was as foul prone as Lyons.

Matt Lawrence (6-7, 205, Sr.). Lawrence was the Haing S. Ngor of college basketball two seasons ago, exemplifying specialized excellence in a supporting role. Indeed, he was one of the most efficient players on offense in the entire nation. Of course he was efficient: He never touched the ball unless he was shooting a three, and he hit 44 percent of his shots from beyond the arc that year. That figure fell all the way down to 35 percent last year, however. Lawrence isn't as central to the offense as Lyons or Carroll, mind you, but a return to 2007-level shooting from the perimeter would be most welcome in Columbia. Really, it's why he's on the floor. One ray of hope for Mizzou fans: Lawrence finished strong last year, hitting 43 percent from outside during the last month of the season.

Keith Ramsey (6-9, 210, Jr.). Power forward and junior-college transfer, likely to appear should Lyons and/or Carroll get into foul trouble. Then again, if Ramsey can alter some shots while rebounding one in every five opponent misses, he could push for a starting slot.

J. T. Tiller (6-3, 185, Jr.). Tiller started 12 games last year, but averaged less than 20 minutes a game. He might be in line for more playing time this year, however, since Keon Lawrence announced his intention to transfer out of the program in June. Last year Tiller struggled mightily on the rare occasions when he attempted a three.

Kim English (6-6, 200, Fr.). Wing from Baltimore, the most highly rated recruit of the still-young Anderson era.

Miguel Paul (6-1, 170, Fr.). Point guard from Lakeland, Florida. "With time, he can become a very good defensive player," says Anderson. Point taken.

Marcus Denmon (6-2, 185, Fr.). A shooting guard from Kansas City, Denmon averaged more than 28 points a game as a high school senior.

Justin Safford (6-8, 225, So.). Safford was a prime recipient of the playing time freed up by Anderson's mass suspensions in late January. He committed a fair number of fouls during those minutes but, hey, he was a freshman.

Zaire Taylor (6-4, 185, Jr.). Transfer from Delaware, sat out last year and has two years of eligibility left. Though he played limited minutes, Taylor nevertheless posted a high steal rate for the Blue Hens in 2007, something that Anderson would love to see from someone in a Missouri uniform this year.

Prospectus says

Missouri's newcomers are earning some positive advance notice. Keep in mind, though, that the most significant event to set this year apart from last year could well be to find some interior defense, in the sense of both defending the rim and getting some defensive boards. If that happens, the disappointments of 2008 can be quickly forgotten.

2008: 20-13 (7-9 Big 12)
Lost to Mississippi 85-75 (OT), NIT Second Round
In-conference offense: 0.98 points per possession (9th)
In-conference defense: 1.02 points allowed per possession (6th)

What Nebraska did well: *Rally.*

Last January 26, the Cornhuskers stood at 0-4 in the Big 12, having just lost on the road to Kansas by 35 points. They had already lost at home to Baylor and on the road to Colorado, and it didn't take too much imagination at that point to envision Doc Sadler's team dropping down a notch or two from the 6-10 record it posted in 2007.

But the Huskers' luck was about to turn. Their next game was at Missouri, and as chance would have it, Tigers coach Mike Anderson had just suspended five of his players, including three starters. Nebraska managed to win that game by four. It was the beginning of a 7-5 stretch to close out the conference season. Most memorable was Nebraska's six-point win on the road against Texas A&M, a slow game in which the Huskers nevertheless played their most efficient offense of the Big 12 campaign. They even made Texas sweat, losing by just four in Austin. If improvement over the course of the season is a coach's first responsibility, Sadler did his job last year.

What we learned in 2008: *Mind your p's and q's when enrolling recruits in classes.*

This year Nebraska will be without the services of the player they thought would be their top recruit, 6-5 guard Roburt Sallie. In May, Sadler announced that the once-prized recruit is now barred from playing for Nebraska or any other Big 12 team, after Sallie enrolled as a part-time student in Lincoln for four days in 2006 without having first met NCAA eligibility requirements.

At the time, Sallie was waiting for a ruling on his eligibility from the NCAA clearinghouse. When the clearinghouse ruled him ineligible, Sallie sat out the season and then played at a junior college for one year. For reasons that are still a little unclear, however, Nebraska re-signed Sallie last November to a letter of intent, even though it knew he would need a waiver from the Big 12 to play. That waiver never came: Nebraska's request was officially denied by the conference office in May. Three weeks later, Sallie signed with Memphis.

What's in store for 2009

Obviously, the big question mark for this year's team is the departure of Aleks Maric. Nebraska was 7-9 last year in the Big 12 with the 6-11 Maric, who was both one of the best all-around rebounders in the nation and the efficient focal point of the Husker offense. Indeed, for each of the past three seasons (even before Sadler's arrival), the offense in Lincoln has gone through Maric. How good will they be now that he's gone?

The most likely answer: not very good. Nebraska's main weakness last year was an offense that failed to score a point per trip in the Big 12. Losing your best offensive player doesn't figure to help matters.

Heading into this season, there is of course, talk of going to a faster tempo in the wake of Maric's departure. Duke's dramatic acceleration last year notwithstanding, however, "faster" tempos are often surprisingly similar in appearance to the naked eye. Teams like Rutgers, Arizona State, and Northwestern, for example, all averaged about five more possessions per 40 minutes last year than they had in 2007. Adding another five possessions to each game may not sound like much, but those teams were in fact undergoing three of the biggest accelerations in major-conference hoops last year. Even assuming Nebraska really does speed thing up, then, fans in Lincoln shouldn't expect their Huskers to suddenly look like the Phoenix Suns.

MEET THE CORNHUSKERS

Ade Dagunduro (6-5, 190, Sr.). Arriving last year as a junior-college transfer, Dagunduro had a tough time just staying on the court early in the season, fouling out of three of Nebraska's first 10 games. He apparently worked on his whistle avoidance, though, because he did a better job staying out of foul trouble after New Year's. On offense Dagunduro was fairly efficient from the field and was fouled at a higher rate than anyone except Maric, but that wasn't necessarily good news for the Huskers. He made just 61 percent of his free throws last year.

Ryan Anderson (6-4, 200, Jr.). In each of his first two seasons, Anderson's been a surprisingly strong defensive rebounder for a player listed as a 6-4 guard. (Then again, during those two years, he was often the second-tallest Husker on the court at any given time.) He's no threat to record an assist or draw a foul, certainly, but Anderson's limited role on offense is still a little puzzling, given that he's a 40 percent career three-point shooter on a team that's not exactly lighting up the scoreboard.

Steve Harley (5-11, 170, Sr.). There aren't many players in the major conferences listed at 5-11 who log big minutes without the benefit of recording assists or attempting plenty of threes. Nevertheless, Steve Harley is one such player. He actually made 41 percent of his threes last year, but he attempted less than two per game. Instead, he endeavored to make his living inside the arc and fared about as well as you'd expect a 5-11 player to fare, hitting just 43 percent of his twos.

Cookie Miller (5-7, 165, So.). Harley looks like Aleks Maric next to Miller, who's listed at 5-7. Miller posted an outstanding steal rate last year, one that was second only to that of Mario Chalmers in the Big 12. In fact, the precocious freshman had back-to-back five-steal games against Iowa State and Kansas State in February. He helped his team force its Big 12 opponents into turnovers on almost 22 percent of their possessions, the best such mark in the conference. Miller was also his team's best bet for an assist. On the other hand he coughed up a fair number of turnovers and his minutes were limited after he returned from a shoulder sprain late in the season.

Sek Henry (6-3, 195, Jr.). Henry attempted 73 threes last year, which may have been unduly optimistic for a career 26 percent three-point shooter.

Christopher Niemann (6-11, 230, Fr.). Niemann played on the same German club team as Iowa State's Lucca Steiger and Washington State's Fabian Boeke, both of whom were required by the NCAA to sit out a season because other players on that team were paid. Niemann may have to sit as well—the matter is still pending as this book goes to press.

Chris Balham (6-8, 235, Jr.). Balham really couldn't get minutes under the old Maric-and-four-little-guys paradigm, but he should get a chance now to show what, if anything, he can do.

Alex Chapman (6-9, 225, So.). Chapman had knee surgery and redshirted last season after transferring from Sheridan College in Wyoming. He, Balham, and fellow redshirt Alonzo Edwards (6-7, 225,

Fr.) will all be candidates to fill the minutes freed up by Maric's departure, assuming Niemann is not available.

Paul Velander (6-2, 190, Sr.). A walk-on for his first three seasons, now on scholarship as a senior.

Prospectus says

Nebraska isn't exactly going to overawe anyone with its talent. Then again the Big 12 North doesn't look like murderer's row this season. Sadler has changed his team's style pretty dramatically in each of his first two seasons at the helm, going from a flurry of threes (2007) to an average balance between threes and twos (last year). Obviously more stylistic changes may be in order this year, now that Maric is gone. Still, whatever the style may be in 2009, it figures to be another challenging year for Nebraska basketball.

OKLAHOMA

2008: 23-12 (9-7 Big 12)
Lost to Louisville 78-48, NCAA Second Round
In-conference offense: 1.01 points per possession (8th)
In-conference defense: 1.03 points allowed per possession (8th)

What Oklahoma did well: *Bounce back.*

Just 12 short months after the program's worst season in over 15 years, Oklahoma returned to the NCAA tournament and won a game before getting blown out by Louisville in the second round. Freshman Blake Griffin suffered a sprained medial collateral ligament in mid-January, but was able to lead OU on a late-season 6-2 charge that netted the Sooners a 6-seed in the tournament. Now, with 2008-edition super freshman Willie Warren arriving in Norman, the trajectory of Oklahoma basketball is clearly on the upswing.

What we learned in 2008: *Your luck can change, dramatically.*

For the second consecutive season, I'm obligated to talk about what is somewhat misleadingly called "luck" in my Oklahoma preview. Last year at this time, I pointed out that the Sooners in 2007 were without a doubt the best 6-10 team in the (admittedly brief) history of the Big 12. Their performance that year was vastly superior to their record. I then opined at some length on how Jeff Capel and his players were due for a few good bounces.

Well, guess what? They got those good bounces in 2008. Man, did they get them …

One team, two extremes of luck: Oklahoma, 2007 vs. 2008

Conference games only
PPP: points per possession
Opp. PPP: opponent points per possession
EM: efficiency margin (PPP – Opp. PPP)

	2007	2008
PPP	1.03	1.01
Opp. PPP	1.00	1.03
EM	+0.03	-0.02
Record	6-10	9-7

Yes, you're reading that correctly. Possession for possession, the 2007 team's performance was better, and by a significant margin. But it was last year's team that went to the NCAA tournament and won a game against Saint Joseph's. How did the 2008-edition Sooners get to the tournament after being outscored over 16 games by their conference opponents? By going 5-1 in Big 12 games decided by six points or less.

Was that luck? Not entirely, of course, and anyway, that's a loaded term. The object of this here sport is to win games, and Oklahoma won games, period. It's just that season in, season out, the teams that win their games with some room to spare are the teams that go deep into the NCAA tournament. The teams that go the cardiac-kids route, conversely, get sent home the first weekend.

Sure, there are exceptions to any tendency, no matter how strong, but the exceptions to this particular tendency are rare. West Virginia in 2005 was the last statistically "lucky" team to make any noise in the tournament, coming within a free throw of the Final Four. Since that year, no major-conference team that was outscored during its conference season has made it past the first weekend. Regardless of their regular-season record, regardless of their seed, and regardless of their opponent, such teams have been found out and sent home.

What's in store for 2009

"Blake Griffin and Willie Warren." Get used to hearing that a lot this year, as in "Oklahoma, led by Blake Griffin and Willie Warren," et cetera, et cetera.

Now then. Oklahoma, led by Blake Griffin and Willie Warren, has a chance to be good this year.

MEET THE SOONERS

Blake Griffin (6-10, 245, So.). Based on what we think we know in the preseason, Griffin can legitimately be classed as one of the two or three best players in the country—when he's not on the free-throw line. Indeed, if there were no such thing as free throws, you could make a case that Griffin was the most effective offensive player in the Big 12 last year. Yes, even more effective than Michael Beasley. Though Griffin turned the ball over at a higher rate, he shot as well as Beasley from the field and was a hair better on the offensive glass while dishing assists at a higher rate. Then again, there *is* such a thing as free throws: Griffin was fouled often last year, but shot just 59 percent from the line. His decision to return to Norman instead of going pro has been widely portrayed as an opportunity to "work on his free-throw shooting." I'm an incurable optimist, but the rest of you out there should probably know the odds are against Griffin in this particular endeavor. His free-throw shooting last year was consistently poor, before and after his knee injury. Not to mention *last* year was supposed to be his opportunity to improve here. (He entered his freshman year saying that "free throw shooting and outside shooting are … some things I'm really working on.") Bottom line: Griffin is teed up to have a monster year on his way to being a lottery pick in 2009. In addition to everything else, he just happens to be one of the nation's preeminent all-around rebounders. Even if his free-throw percentage stays exactly where it is, he is, of course, a gigantic benefit to his team. Free-throw shooting is the only chink in his armor. It is likely to remain so.

Willie Warren (6-4, 190, Fr.). You may have already heard of Warren. He was the leading scorer in the McDonald's All-American game, and by some lights he's the highest-rated recruit in the Big 12 this season. (Given the Kansas recruiting class, that's saying something.) Suffice it to say if Warren's the versatile and explosive scoring machine he's reputed to be, that will be huge for Oklahoma. The Sooners had a severe affliction last year. Basically a two-point shot attempted by anyone (and I do mean *anyone*) besides Blake Griffin was disastrous news. The most pronounced characteristic, whether positive or negative, of the Oklahoma offense last year was poor two-point shooting. This despite the fact that most of those twos were taken by Griffin, who made a very good 57 percent of his shots inside the arc. Meaning Griffin's teammates were horrific when shooting twos. Warren can have an impact on this Sooner affliction both in his own shooting and in the opportunities he creates for teammates. I don't foresee Oklahoma's being a lockdown-tough defensive team this year, but with these two players together on the floor, you have to believe the offense will be much improved over last year.

Tony Crocker (6-6, 195, Jr.). Crocker intrigues me. In each of his first two seasons, his shot selections suggested that both he and his coach see him as a true dual-threat wing. In each of those two seasons, however, Crocker's been more of a uni-threat, scoring efficiently only off his twos in 2007 and only off his threes in 2008. If he at last achieves dual-threat reality this year, it'll be very bad news for opposing defenses already fretting about Griffin and Warren.

Austin Johnson (6-3, 165, Sr.). Johnson's a nominal combo guard who last year shot with the infrequency of a pass-first point guard while posting the highest assist rate of any player on this relatively low-assist team.

Taylor Griffin (6-7, 230, Sr.). Griffin started 20 games last year and provided solid defensive rebounding. In matters related to shooting, he is pretty much the polar opposite of his younger brother, Blake. Taylor Griffin is a 77 percent free-throw shooter who struggled from the field in 2008.

Omar Leary (5-10, 165, Sr.). Leary was a late signee in last year's class of newcomers, arriving in Norman as a junior-college transfer. He was billed as a much-needed point guard, but though he started eight games in November and December, he averaged just 17 minutes per contest for the year and his minutes went down as the season progressed.

Ryan Wright (6-9, 230, Jr.). Transfer from UCLA, sat out last year and has two years of eligibility remaining. Wright couldn't get any minutes playing behind Alfred Aboya, Luc Richard Mbah a Moute, and Lorenzo Mata on two of the now annual Final Four teams featured of late in Westwood.

Juan Pattillo (6-7, 220, Jr.). A junior-college transfer who signed with the Sooners in April, Pattillo arrives touted as an athletic and versatile wing.

Ray Willis (6-6, 185, Fr.). Though Willis is a highly rated recruit, he is reportedly in need of bulking up for the rigors of the Big 12.

Prospectus says

The Sooners might be average on defense this year, but if offense is your thing there are good times ahead. If nothing else, OU games should be faster. In 2008, only Colorado averaged fewer possessions per 40 minutes than Oklahoma did in Big 12 games. Capel's been quoted as saying he'll look at pushing the tempo more now that he has a roster with some depth. With a guard like Warren and a 6-10 freak of athletic nature like Blake Griffin, the coach will have every opportunity to do so.

OKLAHOMA STATE

2008: 17-16 (7-9 Big 12)
Lost to Southern Illinois 69-53, NIT First Round
In-conference offense: 1.02 points per possession (6th)
In-conference defense: 1.03 points allowed per possession (7th)

What Oklahoma State did well: *Improve—not that it helped Sean Sutton.*

First the good news. Oklahoma State was the last team to beat eventual national champion Kansas. And among Big 12 teams, only Baylor made a bigger leap from 2007 to 2008 in terms of points scored versus points allowed per possession in-conference.

Improvement in the Big 12, 2007 to 2008

Conference games only
PPP: points per possession
Opp. PPP: opponent points per possession
EM: efficiency margin (PPP – Opp. PPP)
See top of facing page.

Some disclaimers. The 2007 Cowboys team forms a unique and somewhat sketchy baseline from which to measure progress. OSU that year was surprisingly unsuccessful. The Cowboys started 15-1 and were ranked number 10 in the nation before the bottom fell out. They weren't really as good as they looked over those first 16 games, of course, but

	PPP	2007 Opp. PPP	EM	PPP	2008 Opp. PPP	EM	Change in EM
Baylor	1.03	1.14	-0.11	1.08	1.07	+0.01	+0.12
Oklahoma St.	1.00	1.09	-0.09	1.02	1.03	-0.01	+0.08
Kansas St.	1.05	1.02	+0.03	1.11	1.01	+0.10	+0.07
Colorado	0.94	1.12	-0.18	0.97	1.10	-0.13	+0.05

neither were they as bad as they looked going 7-12 to finish the year.

Speaking of unique and sketchy, head coach Sean Sutton was forced out on April 1 by athletic department VP Mike Holder after two full seasons as head coach. Sutton had three years remaining on his contract and received a buyout in excess of $2 million. Meaning Oklahoma State *really* did not want Sutton as its coach any longer. (By the way, the Sutton saga reinforces the extent to which chilling Orwellian circumlocutions have migrated happily and as if by inherent logic from the former Soviet bloc to Division I athletic departments. The news release from OSU was headlined "Sean Sutton and Mike Holder Reach Mutual Agreement About Future of OSU Basketball." If you ever read about my reaching a "mutual agreement" with my employer, promise me you'll come check my air supply.)

Maybe OSU pulled the trigger because it thought it had a shot at getting Bill Self, who played at Oklahoma State in the 1980s. In the event, however, Self stayed put at Kansas and the Cowboys hired Travis Ford away from UMass. Ford said no to Providence before saying yes to OSU.

What we learned in 2008: *A great recruiting class doesn't always translate into success on the court.*

Oklahoma State's recruiting class of 2005 has fairly become the stuff of legend, mostly for the wrong reasons. Not that we "learned" the truth about perfidious player rankings only in 2008, mind you. Merely that the passage of a couple years does allow one to speak with some added where-are-they-now heft with respect to this particular class.

The Cowboys' recruiting haul in 2005 consisted of high-schoolers Gerald Green, Keith Brumbaugh, Byron Eaton, Roderick Flemings, Kenny Cooper, and Terrel Harris, as well as junior college transfer Mario Boggan. The class was rated as high as third in the nation in 2005, even better than a North Carolina class that featured Tyler Hansbrough, Danny Green, and Marcus Ginyard. But the class hasn't panned out as well as Cowboys fans hoped, to say the very least.

Part of that was entirely outside OSU's control. This was the last class before the one-and-done era dawned. Recruits could still jump directly from high school to the NBA draft, and that's precisely what Green did. Though he did win the slam-dunk contest during the 2007 All-Star weekend, Green played very limited minutes over two-plus seasons with Boston and Minnesota before being released by Houston in March 2008. Brumbaugh enrolled briefly at OSU, but offcourt issues quickly derailed him and he never played a game as a Cowboy.

As for the rest, Boggan had an excellent two-year career in Stillwater: He was named first-team All–Big 12 as a senior and is currently playing in Europe. Flemings averaged about 10 minutes a game as a freshman in 2005-2006, transferred to North Texas, left, played a season of junior-college ball, and has most recently signed a letter of intent to play at Hawaii. Cooper showed signs of promise as a sophomore in 2006-2007, but transferred to Louisiana Tech. Eaton and Harris are, rather iconoclastically, still with the team—see below.

And as for the Cowboys as a team, they haven't played in an NCAA tournament game since this class hit campus. Fans, be careful which recruits you wish for. You might get them.

What's in store for 2009

The group that Travis Ford coached at UMass last year was one of the fastest-paced teams in the nation—and none of that was due to turnovers inflating the number of possessions. The Minutemen neither committed nor forced many turnovers. Indeed, UMass functioned as what I have previously referred to as a POT, a perimeter-oriented team. The defining characteristics of a POT are: a lot of attempted threes, very few offensive rebounds, and very few turnovers. The Minutemen filled the bill in each respect.

Does that mean Oklahoma State will be a POT this year? Could be. Ford's new roster certainly isn't bogged down with a lot of size …

MEET THE COWBOYS

James Anderson (6-6, 195, So.). A McDonald's All-American, Anderson arrived in Stillwater last year with the burden of great expectations and did pretty well. Rebounds and assists are not, as yet, in his repertoire, but he made half his twos and 38 percent of his threes while assuming a larger share of the load on offense than any other Cowboy did. Most importantly, Anderson took good care of the ball. It was a promising start, one that should encourage Ford to give Anderson more touches.

Byron Eaton (5-11, 215, Sr.). Eaton cut way down on his turnover rate last year and posted an outstanding steal rate. He appears laudably aware of his own limitations on offense: He's a good free-throw shooter who manages to draw fouls with uncanny frequency. (He posted a higher free-throw rate than Eric Gordon did last year.) His role in the offense is simple: assists and made free throws, with an occasional three. And the fewer attempted twos, the better.

Obi Muonelo (6-5, 215, Jr.). Muonelo shot more threes last year than any other Cowboy except Anderson, but he made only 34 percent of his attempts from behind the arc. He also struggled with turnovers. On the plus side, he was the only OSU regular not named Eaton who recorded a healthy assist rate.

Terrel Harris (6-5, 190, Sr.). Just six days after taking over as coach in April, Ford suspended Harris "indefinitely" for unspecified transgressions. As this book goes to press, Harris's status with the team is still unresolved. As for on-court considerations, there was a time when Harris was a catch-and-shoot specialist from outside the arc. Last year, conversely, he drove the ball more and had decent results, hitting half his twos. That was the only good news from Harris on offense, however, as he also committed a goodly number of turnovers and made just 28 percent of his threes. (Something went horribly wrong with Harris's perimeter shot last year. He entered the season as a career 43 percent three-point shooter.)

Ibrahima Thomas (6-11, 240, So.). Far and away this team's best defensive rebounder (though not much of a shot blocker), Thomas gives OSU its only length. Note also that Thomas averaged about one

attempted three per game and made 32 percent of them.

Prospectus says

OSU loses its best defender, Marcus Dove, but just about everyone else returns from a team that went 7-9 in the Big 12. For two years running, opponents have shot well from the perimeter, a weakness the Cowboys covered up last year by forcing turnovers on 21 percent of their defensive possessions. If they can continue forcing turnovers and if they can make some threes in Ford's revamped offense, OSU's first above-.500 record in-conference since 2005 will be in the offing.

TEXAS

2008: 31-7 (13-3 Big 12)
Lost to Memphis 85-67, NCAA Elite Eight
In-conference offense: 1.09 points per possession (3rd)
In-conference defense: 1.00 points allowed per possession (2nd)

What Texas did well: *Thrive visually and in the standings without Kevin Durant.*

Texas was even better without Kevin Durant in 2008 than it was with him in 2007, right?

Well, yes and no. Going 13-3 in the Big 12 and getting a 2-seed in the NCAA tournament (last year) is better than 12-4 and a 4-seed (2007). Funny thing is, the 2007 team featured one of the best offenses you'll ever see. Last year's offense, conversely, was still very good, but even with D. J. Augustin and A. J. Abrams, it clearly represented a significant drop-off from the good old Durantian days ...

With or without you: Texas, 2007 vs. 2008
Conference games only
PPP: points per possession
Opp. PPP: opponent points per possession
EM: efficiency margin (PPP – Opp. PPP)

	2007	2008
PPP	1.17	1.09
Opp. PPP	1.05	1.00
EM	+0.12	+0.09
Record	12-4	13-3

With Durant, the Longhorns outscored Big 12 opponents by 0.12 points per trip, a larger margin than the one posted by last year's more successful team. It's not so much that the 2007 team was unlucky as that the 2008 team was phenomenal in tight games: Fully half of Texas's conference games were decided by six points or less, and in those games the 'Horns went an incredible 7-1. In addition to winning the close ones, Rick Barnes's team easily beat Tennessee on a neutral floor in November and, perhaps most memorably, won a thrilling game at UCLA. All in all, it has to be classed as a surprisingly strong post-Durant performance by the Longhorns.

What we learned in 2008: *Below-average shooting need not doom your offense.*

As seen above, Texas played markedly better defense last year than it did in 2007. (Looking at the excellent three-point shooting Big 12 opponents enjoyed against the Longhorns two seasons ago, I wondered aloud if this was merely the price to be paid for the offense of Augustin and Abrams, both of whom are at or under six feet. Not so: Opponents couldn't make a three to save their lives last year.) The stronger defense helped the 'Horns, no question, but to me the really interesting thing about this team is how good it was at scoring. The offense was a far cry from the Durant days, maybe, but the Longhorns were still well above the conference average, despite the uncomfortable little fact that they didn't shoot very well.

To illustrate what Texas was able to do on offense last year, I'm going to combine turnovers and offensive boards into one stat. Call it the "barrage index." The idea is simple: The fewer turnovers you commit and the more offensive rebounds you secure, the more shots you'll get. So as turnover percentage decreases and offensive rebound percentage increases, your barrage index will grow larger. Think of it as a platform: A good BI can either amplify the effects of your good shooting or, alternately, ameliorate the negative effects of your bad shooting.

OK, let's look at the barrage index in the real world. There have been 219 seasons of basketball played by 73 teams in the major conferences over the past three years. And of those 219 seasons, none of them has come anywhere close to duplicating what Texas did last year in terms of generating shots from the field. In this respect, the 2008 Longhorns quite literally stand alone.

Getting more shots: Barrage Index, 2006-2008
Conference games only: ACC, Big East, Big Ten,
  Big 12, Pac-10 & SEC
TO pct.: turnover percentage
Off. Reb. Pct.: offensive rebound percentage

	TO Pct.	Off. Reb Pct.	Barrage Index
1. Texas 2008	14.5	37.6	259.3
2. North Carolina 2008	19.4	43.0	221.6
3. Miami 2007	17.2	38.1	221.5
4. Villanova 2006	16.6	36.4	219.3
5. Miami 2006	17.6	38.1	216.5
6. Connecticut 2006	20.4	43.9	215.2
7. Pitt 2008	18.0	38.5	213.9
8. Notre Dame 2006	16.0	34.2	213.8

Keep in mind that those same 219 seasons testify to a general rule: As turnovers decrease, so do offensive rebounds. So what Texas did last year was revolutionary. It still wasn't enough for them to stay on the floor with Memphis in the Elite Eight, of course, but you could make the case that Barnes took this particular team as far as it could possibly go. And then some.

What's in store for 2009
Turnovers will be up. Giving the ball away to conference opponents on less than 15 percent of your possessions, as Texas did last year, is a feat that's exceedingly difficult to repeat. (The 15 percent barrier has been broken just twice in the aforementioned 219 team-seasons of major-conference ball over the past three years. The other team to pull it off was West Virginia in 2006.) The good news, though, is that it's also very likely that Texas will shoot better than it did last year.

MEET THE LONGHORNS

A. J. Abrams (5-11, 155, Sr.). Abrams raised some hackles in Austin when his decision to enter the draft was announced the night before Augustin's own declaration. To some observers at the time, it looked as if Abrams, who stood little chance of being drafted, was trying to show up his teammate. (In Abrams's defense, his decision, if ill timed, was hardly the first overly optimistic self-assessment uttered by a college player. He, of course, later withdrew from the draft. Augustin was taken with the ninth pick by Charlotte.) All appears to have been forgiven, however, and Abrams is returning for his senior year amid much talk that minutes at the point would help the NBA prospects of a 5-11 shooting guard immensely. That'd be an abrupt departure from the recent past: To date, Abrams has left assists entirely to Augustin and helped a very good offense by hitting his abundant threes without ever committing a turnover. (Note also that Texas is, and for two years has been, a low-assist outfit. The team doesn't need assists to score points.)

Damion James (6-7, 230, Jr.). James is an unbelievably good defensive rebounder for a player listed at just 6-7. Indeed, on the defensive glass he's functionally equivalent to lottery-pick-to-be Blake Griffin—no mean feat, that. James's contributions here are all the more vital because his team is not very good at getting defensive boards. One note of caution, however: James launched almost three threes per game last year and made 41 percent of them. That success rate looks very—what's the word?—fortunate, coming as it did from a career 58 percent free-throw shooter.

Justin Mason (6-2, 200, Jr.). Mason can usually be found guarding the opponent's best perimeter player. On offense he has functioned something like an auxiliary point guard in his first two seasons, responsible for pretty much the only assists that weren't recorded by Augustin. Nevertheless, his degree of direct involvement in the Longhorn offense is the smallest of any player listed here. His attempts from the field are scarce, and his free-throw shooting is spotty.

Gary Johnson (6-7, 235, So.). Johnson was diagnosed with a heart condition before he arrived in Austin for his freshman year, but was cleared to play just before the Big 12 season started. Then he suffered a broken nose and consequently played limited minutes. It's still too soon to know what the highly touted Johnson can do for Barnes.

Connor Atchley (6-10, 225, Sr.). Atchley was this team's silent assassin last year. He's not what you'd call athletic, and the bulk of the shots in this offense went to Augustin, Abrams, and James. But when Atchley did pull the trigger, his shots went in. His effi-

ciency on offense was off the charts in 2008. He's also a surprisingly good shot blocker. Texas fans know how valuable Atchley really is to this team.

Dogus Balbay (6-0, 175, Fr.). Balbay was widely expected to get quality minutes last year in support of Augustin, but he suffered a knee injury before the season and sat out the year.

J'Covan Brown (6-2, 175, Fr.). A shooting guard billed as possessing both perimeter range and the ability to drive to the hoop. Brown announced Texas as his choice in November 2007 but didn't actually sign his letter of intent until April 2008.

Prospectus says
The consistency that Barnes has achieved on offense over the past three seasons with three very different groups of personnel is remarkable. And while it's no small thing to lose your All-American point guard, you could make a case that this season in fact represents the highest degree of year-to-year carryover that Texas has seen in a while. The Longhorns were pretty good last year, even without Kevin Durant. They'll be pretty good this year, even without D. J. Augustin.

TEXAS A&M

2008: 25-11 (8-8 Big 12)
Lost to UCLA 51-49, NCAA Second Round
In-conference offense: 1.01 points per possession (7th)
In-conference defense: 1.01 points allowed per possession (4th)

What Texas A&M did well: *Give its new coach some newly gray hair.*
Texas A&M was a tough team to assess going into last season, having lost both its coach, Billy Gillispie, and its All-American point guard, Acie Law. On the plus side, however, the team returned a core of key veterans, most notably Joseph Jones and Josh Carter, and was welcoming one of the most highly rated freshmen in the nation in the person of DeAndre Jordan. How would all the above net out for first-year coach Mark Turgeon?

Very schizophrenically, it turns out. On the one hand, this team did take Final Four–bound UCLA to the next-to-last possession of the game before losing by four in the second round of the NCAA tournament.

On the other hand, the 2008 Texas A&M offense was the most inconsistent unit seen on either side of the ball in major-conference play over the past three seasons. By "inconsistent" I mean the statistical fluctuation in performance from game to game over the course of the conference season. I've previously christened this measure the "Winehouse Factor," in honor of the famously erratic British pop diva.

Historic inconsistency: highest Winehouse Factors, 2006-2008

Conference games only: ACC, Big East, Big Ten, Big 12, Pac-10, and SEC
Winehouse Factor: standard deviation, points per possession or opp. PPP

	Winehouse Factor
1. Texas A&M offense 2008	0.24
2. Michigan St. offense 2007	0.23
3. Michigan St. offense 2008	0.22
4. DePaul offense 2007	0.22
5. USC defense 2008	0.21

The wild swings in performance exhibited by the Aggies' offense from game to game belied what might have looked like an uneventful 8-8 season in the Big 12. Actually, it was a wild ride. At times, the A&M offense looked unstoppable, as seen in home games against Colorado, Texas Tech, and Texas. At other times, the same offense looked comatose, most notably in a 37-point effort at Oklahoma.

Keep in mind that the 2007 team, somehow perceived nationally as merely a tough defensive unit, actually had an outstanding offense, one that scored 1.13 points per trip in the Big 12. Last year the figure dipped all the way down to 1.01, slightly below the conference average. Viewing the conference season as a whole, then, the Aggies' offense zigged and zagged its erratic way down to what could be called a collapse. The shots simply stopped going in: Joseph Jones went from making 57 percent of his twos to hitting just 49 percent from inside the arc. Josh Carter and Dominique Kirk combined to make 46 percent of their threes in 2007. In 2008, that figure was 39 percent—still very good, of course, but a significant dip from the previous year.

True, the defense slipped a bit, too, but the decline in the offense was, in effect, four times the size of the drop-off in D. Fewer points scored marked the primary difference between 2008 and 2007 in College Station.

What we learned in 2008: *Not all freshmen should enter the draft.*

Somehow this was all made to appear quite normal, but it bears repeating one last time: DeAndre Jordan decided to enter the 2008 NBA draft despite the fact that as a freshman he was unable to earn regular minutes on an 8-8 Big 12 team.

Jordan started 21 games and averaged just 20 minutes a game, and little or none of that bench time was because of foul trouble. (He recorded four fouls in a game just once all year.) Yet the seven-footer decided he was NBA ready.

And why not? He'd been hearing the idea for a while. Jordan was widely projected as a 2008 lottery pick *last* year at this time, when I was writing the preview on the 2007-2008 Aggies. Instead, he ended up being selected by the Clippers in the second round with the 35th pick of the draft.

The freshman year that Jordan experienced should have convinced him to stay in College Station. His shots went in, mind you, but he just didn't take very many, even adjusting for his limited minutes. Moreover, his overall offensive rating was astonishingly low for a player who shoots as well as he did from the field. The culprits here were turnovers and sub–50 percent shooting at the free-throw line. (And opponents had done their homework: They took every opportunity to send Jordan there.)

On defense, Jordan was good both on the glass and as a shot blocker. But, to make some comparisons using nearby players who are considerably shorter, Texas's Damion James was a better defensive rebounder, and the Longhorns' Connor Atchley was a better shot blocker.

Jordan may yet develop into a solid pro. There's no gainsaying that he has the physical tools to do so. But the distance he needs to travel to get there shouldn't have been minimized. It's going to be a long way up, even for a 20-year-old with "upside."

What's in store for 2009

I may question the wisdom of Jordan declaring for the draft, but there's no denying that when he was on the floor last year, he was pretty good at ending opponents' possessions after the first shot. Indeed, defensive rebounding was the strength of an A&M

defense that was, in turn, the strength of the team. Repeating that performance on defense should be the watchword in College Station this year.

MEET THE AGGIES

Josh Carter (6-7, 200, Sr.). After having a year for the ages in 2007, when he made exactly half his threes, Carter came down to earth a bit last year, hitting a much more mortal 38 percent from beyond the arc. Even then he was his team's most efficient option on offense. Carter developed his game a bit last season, venturing inside the arc more often and doing pretty well.

Donald Sloan (6-3, 205, Jr.). Sloan gave perimeter shooting a fair chance last year as a sophomore, and it didn't really work out, as he hit just 28 percent of his threes. The good news is he's a career 51 percent two-point shooter, more than adequate for a player listed at 6-3. And with the three-point line moving a foot further out this season, Turgeon should seriously consider declaring the realm outside the arc completely off-limits for Sloan.

Bryan Davis (6-9, 250, Jr.). After giving hints of being an exceptional defensive presence in limited minutes as a freshman, Davis got on the floor as a sophomore last year (in effect he started the 15 games that Jordan didn't start) and showed some fair offense, hitting 53 percent of his twos. What's a little odd, though, is that his defensive rebounding cratered last season. Turgeon will be looking to Davis this year to clean up opponents' misses.

Derrick Roland (6-4, 190, Jr.). See "Donald Sloan," above. More than a third of Roland's attempts last year were threes, but he only made 28 percent of those shots. Yet he's productive inside the arc. I sense a trend here. With the possible exception of one or both of the freshmen, Turgeon could probably adopt a simple rule with the players listed here: No threes unless your name is Carter.

Chinemelu Elonu (6-10, 235, Jr.). Elonu played sparingly last year, but when he got in the game, he ruled the defensive glass, posting a higher defensive rebound percentage than even Jordan.

David Loubeau (6-8, 210, Fr.). Highly rated recruit who can reportedly play either power forward or wing.

Dashan Harris (6-0, 170, Fr.). A point guard praised by Turgeon for his quickness, defense, and leadership.

Prospectus says
A&M loses Jordan, of course, but also Joseph Jones and Dominique Kirk from last year's NCAA tournament team. That leaves a fair-sized hole to fill. This year the two freshmen, both from Florida, come highly touted. If they live up to their billing and if veterans like Carter, Sloan, and Davis can improve on last year, the Aggies could wriggle their way into the tournament again in 2009.

TEXAS TECH

2008: 16-15 (7-9 Big 12)
Lost to Oklahoma State 76-72, Big 12 Tournament First Round
In-conference offense: 0.97 points per possession (10th)
In-conference defense: 1.08 points allowed per possession (10th)

What Texas Tech did well: *End an era.*
When Bob Knight announced that he was stepping down as the Texas Tech coach on February 4, it was arguably the biggest news of the college basketball season. Certainly it was treated that way. Huge upsets at least take place on a schedule that's known in advance, but Knight's announcement came seemingly out of the blue. The effect was measured in the sudden ringing of cell phones and buzzing of incoming text messages all over the country early on a Monday evening. It was news, yes, but what kind of news?

On the most literal level, it can be said that Knight left the Texas Tech program stronger than when he arrived. In seven campaigns with Knight at the helm, the Red Raiders went 53-49 in-conference. In the two seasons before his arrival, conversely, Tech went 6-26 in the Big 12.

Then again, the relative health of the Texas Tech program really hasn't been the criterion of choice in assessing Knight's post-Indiana career. He won national championships in 1976, 1981, and 1987, and retired as the winningest coach in Division I history (a distinction he'll hold for another three years or so if Mike Krzyzewski continues coaching). If his sojourn in Lubbock didn't quite rise to these heights, it at least provided a smooth seven-year glide path from the storm of controversy into the relative calm of retirement (assuming he has indeed retired for good).

On occasion Knight was criticized for clinging to an offensive scheme that appeared to date from the early 1980s—that is, a scheme that predated the introduction of the three-point shot. Then again, Texas Tech devoted a larger share of its shots to threes in Big 12 play last year than North Carolina did in ACC play, and no one thinks of the Tar Heels as particularly archaic.

It turns out the lack of threes was symptomatic, not malignant. Knight's teams didn't just do without threes; they did without threes *and* offensive rebounds, because the Knight catechism defines mortal sin as exposing your team to fast-break points on the other end. In effect, Knight's teams were limited to one shot per possession and that shot was going to be a two. The Raiders did shoot a lot of free throws with this system, but in recent years they didn't have an exceptional post scorer.

There's nothing wrong with such an approach per se; it's just that by the fourth decade in Knight's career the opposing team was invariably going to be availing itself of additional ways to score points. Knight's 2007 team, led by the preternaturally sure-handed Jarrius Jackson, fairly wrung every last point possible out of this scheme simply by refusing to commit turnovers. That year Tech scored 1.05 points per trip in-conference, a hair above the Big 12 average.

What we learned in 2008: *Pat Knight is his own person.*

Rarely do you get the chance to see a direct, real-time comparison between a father and son in the same profession. But when the father quits his job as a basketball coach just before the halfway mark of the conference season and hands the same players to his son, you have the makings of direct-comparison nirvana. Here's what we find …

It's widely expected and reported that Pat Knight will employ a faster tempo than his father did. Was that true last year? Mostly, but the real surprise is how speedy the Raiders were under *both* Knights.

Texas Tech averaged 71 possessions per 40 minutes in the Big 12 under Pat Knight and 69 trips per 40 under Bob. That's a difference of just a couple possessions per game, but I think it's fair to say Pat's going to be a little more up-tempo than his father.

For one thing, Bob Knight's figures from last year are more than a little skewed by the 83-possession track meet that Tech fell into against Missouri just 12 days before the General's retirement. (Maybe that's what pushed him into it.) So, yes, look for the Red Raiders to exceed the conference average for possessions per 40 minutes in 2009.

Texas Tech also shot more threes under Pat Knight than they did under Bob, though there was no resemblance to Butler under either coach. Perhaps the most visible change of all, however, was the new coach's willingness to deploy an occasional zone defense. His openness to this particular change was well founded: Opponents ate Tech alive on the interior last year. So it'd be nice to report that at long last having the zone in the Texas Tech defensive cupboard stopped or at least slowed the bleeding for the new coach's undersized team.

It didn't. Things actually got worse on defense after Bob Knight left. Opponents turned the ball over much less often, but had much greater success shooting twos. That's one really bad combination.

A meager inheritance: Texas Tech defense, 2008
Conference games only
Opp. TO Pct.: opponent turnover percentage
Opp. PPP: opponent points per possession

	Opp. 2FG Pct.	Opp. TO Pct.	Opp. PPP	Record
Bob Knight	49.6	21.5	0.98	3-3
Pat Knight	54.2	17.7	1.14	4-6

To be sure, Bob did his son no statistical favors by quitting before his team had played its road game at Kansas. That turned out to be a rather momentous occasion: The 109-51 beat-down the Jayhawks laid on Tech that night marked the largest margin of victory in the history of the Big 12 conference.

Fair enough; throw out the Kansas game entirely. The Raiders still gave up 1.10 points per trip to non-KU opponents in conference play under Pat Knight. That won't get it done.

What's in store for 2009
Shooting more threes and operating at a quicker pace should help open things up for the Red Raiders inside the arc, where last year they made just 45 percent of their twos. The larger concern, however, is how well opposing teams will shoot twos. Last year they did so very well indeed.

MEET THE RED RAIDERS

John Roberson (5-11, 165, So.). For a freshman point guard playing under Bob Knight, Roberson took a surprisingly large share of the Raiders' shots last year. Indeed, his prominence in the offense was second only to that of the now departed Martin Zeno. Roberson did a pretty fair job of translating those shots into points, but he also had the highest turnover rate of any player who saw regular minutes.

Alan Voskuil (6-3, 175, Sr.). A pure shooter who hit half his threes in 2008. Feed him the ball, Coach.

Mike Singletary (6-5, 225, So.). What's impressive about Singletary is that as a 6-5 freshman playing limited minutes, he went to the line *a lot*, posting a higher free-throw rate than even a wizened old veteran like Zeno. Singletary started 13 games last year and figures to crack the starting lineup for good as a wing this year.

Darko Cohadarevic (6-9, 245, Jr.). Junior-college transfer. Knight would like some scoring out of his frontcourt this year. It could come from Cohadarevic, a power forward who's reputed to be adept at both passing and hitting his outside shots.

Trevor Cook (6-8, 225, Jr.). Cook was mostly silent on the defensive boards and had very real problems turning the ball over last year. If he can get those two things straightened out, he bears watching: At 6-8, he gives hints of being a legitimate inside-outside threat on offense. He is likely to start as a somewhat undersized power forward.

Nick Okorie (6-1, 180, Jr.). Last year Okorie made 38 percent of his threes and was the leading scorer for South Plains College, which won the NJCAA national tournament.

Damir Suljagic (6-8, 245, Sr.). Suljagic wasn't allowed to see the ball on offense last year, but within his sparse minutes, he was this team's best defensive rebounder.

D'Walyn Roberts (6-7, 195, So.). Roberts arrived as a highly rated recruit, but couldn't get on the floor last year as a freshman wing. His potential is still unknown.

Tyree Graham (6-1, 190, Fr.). The academic eligibility of this combo guard is in doubt as this book goes to press.

Prospectus says

This will be a year of consolidation and reformation for Texas Tech. Mark it a success if a greater share of an improved offense comes from threes—even with the new line—and if the defense improves to the point that it allows less than 1.05 points per trip in the Big 12.

The Pac-10

Where Old Dogs Meet New Tricks

KEN POMEROY

In many respects, last season was the Year of the Pac-10. Nine of its members were selected for post-season play. Three of its teams made the Sweet 16. Five of its players were taken in the first 11 picks of the NBA draft including three of the first five. The impressive season that the conference had in 2007 was augmented by incoming freshmen in 2008 when Kevin Love, O. J. Mayo, Jerryd Bayless, and James Harden raised the level of their respective team's play. Throw in the metamorphosis of Russell Westbrook, and the Pac-10 had an infusion of talent unlike any other conference in the land.

But that talent left the league just as quickly as it entered, providing the names for the West Coast–dominated draft that ensued in June. All except Harden, that is. More about him in a moment. The departures have left a void that should make the Pac-10 the most intriguing conference among the Big Six due to the uncertainty associated with the inexperienced players that will have to lead most of the Pac-10's teams. Some of that inexperience will again be in the form of blue-chip freshmen. UCLA's Jrue Holiday and USC's Demar DeRozan were two of the most sought after high school players in the nation.

More newcomers enter the league in the form of coaches, although two of the three Pac-10 coaches that weren't around last season aren't new at all. Lute Olson is back on the sidelines at Arizona after taking a year off to deal with personal issues. Olson coached the Wildcats for 24 years, but found his system had been overhauled by interim coach Kevin

O'Neill. So in a way, this season is like a new start for him at age 74. Immediately upon his return, Olson was confronted with a first in his coaching career—his prized recruit, point guard Brandon Jennings, decided to forego college for a season of pro ball in Europe.

At Cal, 61-year-old Mike Montgomery takes over for Ben Braun. Montgomery coached 18 seasons across the Bay at Stanford before being lured to the NBA in 2004. He took a position in the Stanford athletic department last season, so it's not like he has a lot of catching up to do. However, like Olson, he has to deal with scrambling to fill an unexpected loss. His star on offense, Ryan Anderson, departed for the NBA after his sophomore season.

The third new coach really is unfamiliar to Pac-10 fans. Craig Robinson, the former Brown coach, has taken over at Oregon State. Thus, the old guard of the league now has to play at least four games a year against some variant of the Princeton offense. Although, Robinson is slightly more devoted to Pete Carril's principles than Arizona State's Herb Sendek.

Speaking of Sendek, his team is positioned well for the upcoming season. While every other program except Oregon State must replace an impact player (or even two or three), Arizona State is the only squad that returns at least 80 percent of the minutes played last season. The most used Sun Devil missing from last season's team is shooting guard Christian Polk. Polk's an interesting measuring stick as to where this program is going. In Sendek's first season in 2007, Polk was the most involved Sun

Devil on the offensive end, getting almost 30 minutes a game and jacking up a total of 359 shots. In 2008, Polk played just 13 minutes per game and only appeared in nine of the team's last 21 contests as the freshmen invasion of Tempe took place.

The leader of the rookies at ASU was Harden. Holiday and DeRozan have received their share of hype in recent months, but if either can do what Harden did last season, I'd be surprised. (If Holiday does, expect to see UCLA in the Final Four for a fourth consecutive season.) While Love and Mayo, and to a lesser extent Bayless, received their share of press last season, Harden was putting together a season that in any other year would have been considered remarkable for a freshman. Given the events of the offseason, perhaps it's remarkable that Harden decided to stick around for at least one more year. With a more experienced team around him, Arizona State is well positioned for a high finish in the conference.

While things will be changing, there's good reason to believe that the tippy-top of the Pac-10 will look the same as it has since 2006. Even in losing Russell Westbrook and Kevin Love to the fourth and fifth selections in the NBA draft, respectively, Ben Howland has reloaded UCLA with what many believe is the best class of incoming freshman in the nation. The five newcomers aren't considered the second coming of the Fab Five, but if they had to play against the rest of the Pac-10, they could more than hold their own.

The class is led by Holiday, the best two-guard prospect in the country and it was augmented by 6-9 J'Mison Morgan who came to UCLA after the coaching upheaval at LSU caused him to rethink his commitment there. The rest of the class is filled by 6-9 Drew Gordon, 6-4 Malcolm Lee, and 6-1 Jerime Anderson. If somehow these guys become sophomores together, it's pretty easy to figure out which team will be the hunted in 2010. But no need to get ahead of ourselves, because UCLA getting back to the Final Four while losing so much talent would be a story unto itself. Of course, not all the faces are new there. Playing basketball in April wouldn't be possible without Darren Collison and Josh Shipp who are both back as seniors.

There are some interesting things going on in the murky middle of the league, also, where every team that earned an NCAA berth last season has serious questions heading into the season. Stanford has to replace the Lopez twins. Washington State no longer

has an experienced backcourt with the departures of Derrick Low and Kyle Weaver. Arizona has to figure how to fill in for Bayless and deal with a couple of last-minute surprises in recruiting. USC needs to replace its two freshmen now playing pro ball, Mayo and Davon Jefferson. Finally, Oregon had a couple players drafted itself—seniors Malik Hairston and Maarty Leunen.

If there's one team in addition to Arizona State that's well positioned to take advantage of the changes it's Oregon State. Just kidding! Although, don't fret Beaver fans, your team will win a conference game this season. Probably multiple games. It's very difficult to go winless in a conference season. To do it two years in a row is practically impossible.

No, the second team that could make serious advances up the Pac-10 ladder is Washington, which returns its three most important starters from last season. Like ASU, the Huskies have a player who doesn't seem to get the acclaim he should in 6-7 Jon Brockman. It's not a team that is likely to romp through the NCAA tournament in March, but just getting back to the tournament would be a healthy step forward for a program that has struggled adjusting to life without Brandon Roy.

In 2009, the Pac-10 won't produce the draft picks or tourney bids it did last season. But there's nothing that says it couldn't produce a national champion, an All-American player (or two) and possibly the biggest surprises in any power conference race this season.

	2008 Record	Returning Minutes(%)	2009 Prediction
UCLA	16-2	47	15-3
Arizona St.	9-9	93	11-7
Arizona	8-10	53	10-8
USC	11-7	68	10-8
Washington	7-11	69	10-8
Washington St.	11-7	52	9-9
Stanford	13-5	55	10-8
Oregon	9-9	49	7-11
California	6-12	60	7-11
Oregon St.	0-18	77	3-15

ARIZONA

2008: 19-15 (8-10 Pac-10)
Lost to West Virginia 75-65, NCAA first round
In-conference offense: 1.08 points per possession (4th)
In-conference defense: 1.06 points allowed per possession (7th)

What Arizona did well: *Make the offseason more exciting than the games.*

Few basketball programs could match the news that Arizona made over the summer. First, there was the coaching drama involving Lute Olson and Kevin O'Neill. As a quick refresher, Olson took a leave of absence last season and O'Neill, who was hired as an assistant prior to the season, took over head coaching duties. Last December, athletic director Jim Livengood announced that O'Neill would be Olson's permanent successor whenever Olson decided to retire, adding a degree of stability to a situation that appeared to be in flux. However, postseason reports were that O'Neill wasn't exactly a player's coach, and when Olson took control of the program back in April, he decided to let O'Neill go.

Following that up, Arizona lost its two most heralded recruits. Brandon Jennings, widely regarded as the country's best prep point guard, elected to play for Pallacanestro Virtus Roma instead of becoming eligible at Arizona. Emmanuel Negedu, one of the better power forward prospects in the country, backed out of his commitment in May, citing the tumultuous recent past of the program. In addition, Jerryd Bayless kept his name in the NBA draft after his freshman season. And somewhere in between, there was one day in April where both Olson and his ex-wife separately aired some of the details of their divorce on a Tucson radio station. Basically, the offseason in Tucson was a lot more interesting than the actual game-playing, which for the second consecutive season resulted in a mediocre seed in the NCAA tournament and lackluster effort in a first-round loss.

What we learned in 2008: *Players like nice coaches and a fast pace.*

Arizona players publicly expressing displeasure with Kevin O'Neill after his departure cited two things: his demeanor and the changes he made to the Wildcats' system. I'm not Dr. Phil, so I can't address whether being nice or confrontational is the best way to motivate young men. The style issue is inter-

esting because last season, Arizona's performance was eerily similar to Olson's last season in charge.

Not just the postseason failure, but the promising start in November and December that turned to disappointment in Pac-10 play. And, yes, the style was different in those two seasons. O'Neill preferred a controlled half-court game on both ends of the floor. It's not as much fun to watch or play as Olson's more fluid style, but plenty of coaches have won using a game plan similar to O'Neill's and others have won using Olson's philosophy. Winning begets happiness a lot more often than happiness begets winning. The timing is what was wrong in this case. If you're going to change the style of a legend, especially if you have an "interim" title, you better win.

What's in store for 2009

It's safe to assume that there will be more running and crashing of the offensive boards at Arizona this season. The main reason that O'Neill was hired as an assistant was to improve Arizona's defense, which has been a consistent liability on Olson's less successful teams. The offense, however, has been consistently excellent. It was last season too, even though the points came slightly less frequently due to a slower pace. Even with the loss of Bayless, it seems that this season should be predictable without O'Neill's influence—a lot more points both scored and allowed, and unless there's a significant defensive improvement, a lot of close games.

MEET THE WILDCATS

Chase Budinger (6-7, 203, Jr.). So much of Arizona's offense went through either Budinger or Bayless last season. Budinger did not flourish in the expanded role nor the more structured offense as his two-point percentage dropped from 56 to 49 between his freshman and sophomore seasons. There are still questions about Budinger's defense, although he did improve his defensive rebounding slightly last season. (His offensive rebounding went in the tank, but that can be explained by O'Neill's increased emphasis on preventing opponents' transition opportunities.)

Jordan Hill (6-10, 226, Jr.). Hill showed that he was an exceptional rebounder and an efficient scorer in a reserve role as a freshman in 2007. And that didn't change once he moved into the starting lineup as a sophomore. What did change was Hill's role in the offense, which became more prominent. A 62 percent field goal percentage indicates that he'll be able to compensate for some of Bayless's lost offense.

Nic Wise (5-10, 178, Jr.). Wise will pick up the point-guard duties for Lute Olson that he shared with Bayless last season. He hit a whopping 48 percent of his threes, but it was only in 77 attempts, so don't get too carried away with him being the second coming of Steve Kerr or Salim Stoudamire. But Wise should be a better than average Pac-10 point guard.

Jamelle Horne (6-6, 204, So.). A lot will be expected from Horne, who wasn't much of a factor for the Wildcats as a freshman. There will be many more opportunities for him to get involved since Budinger, Hill, and Wise are the only returning reliable scorers.

Fendi Onobun (6-6, 235, Sr.). Onobun labored through the season with Tiger Woods–like perseverance, dealing with leg pain that after the season was determined to be a stress fracture. He was an effective offensive rebounder even though he wasn't completely healthy.

Zane Johnson (6-5, 199, So.). Johnson played just 74 minutes last season, but given the lack of bodies Olson has at his disposal, if Johnson can provide some value as a three-point shooter (and that's about all he does on offense) he could see some regular time.

Jeff Withey (6-11, 240, Fr.). Withey became the top player in the Wildcats' recruiting class with the defections of Jennings and Negedu. It's possible he could start as part of a big lineup or spell Hill for a few minutes a game.

Alex Jacobson (6-11, 243, Fr.). Jacobson is one of those big men who isn't quite ready for the college game after finishing high school. He redshirted last season, but is expected to get some time at center this season.

Brendon Lavender (6-4, 180, Fr.). There's not much guard depth on this team, so freshmen figure to see some action in the backcourt. Lavender's an option along with **Kyle Fogg (6-3, 180, Fr.).**

Prospectus says

The loss of Jennings, Negedu, and Bayless hurts a lot. The Wildcats will be relying on Budinger and Hill extensively in 2009. A breakout year for Horne would help things, and with his athleticism, a lot of folks are holding out hope. However, his freshman season didn't give many hints of that happening. Because of the template that has developed over the past three seasons, it's easy to imagine another year where the last couple of weeks are being played to avoid an appearance in the 8/9 game of the NCAA tournament.

ARIZONA STATE

2008: 21-13 (9-9 Pac-10)
Lost to Florida 70-57, NIT quarterfinals
In-conference offense: 1.00 points per possession (9th)
In-conference defense: 1.03 points allowed per possession (5th)

What Arizona State did well: *Upgrade the offense.*
In 2007, Herb Sendek's offense provided a double whammy of dullness: slow and inefficient. Sun Devil fans knew what they were getting when Sendek came on board. Slow was part of the contract. But if Sendek is going to get fans to pack Wells Fargo Arena on a regular basis, his teams are going to have to finish possessions with a score more often than they did in 2007. To that end, ASU made progress in 2008. It wasn't completely obvious, because in terms of ranking within the conference the Sun Devils only moved from last in the league to ninth. But their improvement in absolute terms is a bit more impressive, rising from an inhumane 0.93 points per possession to a more tolerable 1.00. It's still below average and has to improve more for this team to compete for a high tournament seed, but it's a start.

It happened by getting an incredible boost in efficiency inside the arc. In 2007, the Sun Devils were last in the Pac-10 at 46.0 percent on two-point attempts, but improved to 52.1 percent and third last season. What's more, there was also a dramatic increase in production at the free-throw line. ASU made 27 free throws for every 100 field goal attempts in 2007 conference play. Last season, that figure jumped to 41, improving the team from ninth to second in the league in that category. In 2008, Sendek's offense showed signs of becoming what was expected when he was hired—an offense dependent on three-point shooting but able to get production inside the arc as well.

What we learned in 2008: *James Harden can draw contact.*

On a personal level, a big reason the offense improved was the influence of James Harden. The 6-5 freshman became the focal point for scoring almost from day one. (To be precise it was day two. Harden struggled in the season opener against Illinois, going two-for-nine from the field.) Harden got to the free-throw line a staggering 224 times in 34 games. As the season progressed, he became notorious for taking advantage of the way the modern game is officiated. When there's contact between two players in the air, the foul goes against the defender. Harden became a master of seeking, or perhaps creating, contact and earning trips to the free-throw line. His ability to create offense off penetration opened up more options for the ASU offense to succeed.

What's in store for 2009

The top-eight players in terms of minutes return this season. And only Jeff Pendergraph is scheduled to leave in the 2009 offseason. So Arizona State should be a team on the upswing. But keeping Harden in 2010 might be difficult. In that light, there may be more of a sense of urgency in Tempe than one might think. There's still a way to go from the performance of last season to getting near the top of the Pac-10. For one thing, it's difficult to expect to get much more out of Harden. He was already one of the most efficient go-to-guys in the land last season. Improvement is going to have to come from the rest of the team. Guys like Ty Abbott, Jeff Pendergraph and Derek Glasser, and Jamelle McMillan.

MEET THE SUN DEVILS

James Harden (6-4, 218, So.). In addition to being one of the most productive offensive players in the nation, Harden has an impact on the defensive end also. He even blocked 19 shots. He also contributes on the defensive boards better than average for his position and has a nice assist rate. Because he plays for a slow-paced team, Harden probably won't rack up the counting stats in enough quantities to be considered for All-American honors. But that doesn't mean you shouldn't. There aren't many players in the nation capable of having an impact on a game like him.

Jeff Pendergraph (6-9, 230, Sr.). Even with Harden dominating the offense, Pendergraph actually saw his usage increase last season and he was more efficient even with the increased burden. He's by far the best rebounder on a rebounding-challenged team. He's pretty much the only guy that will even try for an offensive rebound.

Ty Abbott (6-3, 200, So.). Abbott was the "other" freshman starter last season, getting a bunch of minutes as a two-guard. Three-quarters of his shots come from three-point range and he made 35 percent of them, so he's a threat that should be respected from there.

Derek Glasser (6-1, 180, Jr.). Glasser split starting duties at point guard with Jamelle McMillan and was a close second to Stanford's Mitch Johnson in assist rate in the Pac-10, helping on 30 percent of his teammates' made field goals.

Jerren Shipp (6-3, 214, So.). Shipp is less of an offensive threat than his older brothers. In fact, he became more timid last season. He's one of three starters more likely to take a three than a two.

Jamelle McMillan (6-1, 165, So.). McMillan got a few starts at point guard, but generally he was less effective than Glasser primarily due to a turnover problem.

Rihards Kuksiks (6-6, 205, So.). The Latvian is another three-point shooting option off the bench, making 37 percent of his attempts as a freshman.

Eric Boateng (6-10, 245, Jr.). Boateng is Pendergraph's replacement, and in terms of field goal percentage and usage, the two are identical. But there are two big differences between them. Boateng is more turnover prone (4.3 per 40 minutes compared to 2.8 for Pendergraph) and can't make a free throw (19-for-52 last season).

Taylor Rohde (6-8, 225, Fr.). As a perimeter-oriented big man, Rohde should fit well into Sendek's offense.

Kraidon Woods (6-8, 192, So.). Woods only played 54 minutes last season, but assuming he's added some bulk, will get more time in 2009.

Johnny Coy (6-7, 200, Fr.). Coy rejected overtures from the Philadelphia Phillies after being selected in baseball's draft over the summer. He'll play two sports at ASU.

Prospectus says

Somebody has to get wins in the Pac-10. In a way, that's a backhanded compliment to the Sun Devils, but it's also necessary to explain how a team that was outscored by 25 points in conference play and lost in the first round of the conference tourney could reasonably become the second-best team in the league.

If Arizona State is to do something special this season, then there needs to be similar improvement this season to what was witnessed in 2008. (By the way, the baseline for "something special" in Tempe is just getting to the NCAA tournament, which they've done only three times in the 64-team era. I'm thinking more along the lines of Sweet 16 in this case, though.) Kids 18 to 22 years old do tend to improve with age, of course. But the improvement last season was partially due to an upgrade in talent. The improvement this season will have to come from within because the top seven or eight in Sendek's rotation will be identical to last season.

CALIFORNIA

2008: 17-16 (6-12 Pac-10)
Lost to Ohio State 73-56, NIT second round
In-conference offense: 1.08 points per possession (3rd)
In-conference defense: 1.14 points allowed per possession (9th)

What Cal did well: *Produce NBA talent.*

Well, we don't know for sure that Cal produced NBA talent last season, but they did have two players selected in the draft—forward Ryan Anderson was selected 21st and center Devon Hardin was taken 50th. That's noteworthy because it can't be often that a second-to-last place team in a conference has two players taken in the draft. The other eight teams that had multiple players selected all made the NCAA tournament, yet Cal wasn't considered for an at-large berth. Not many near-cellar-dwellers have

a couple of names called on draft night, but not many finish six games ahead of the last place team, either.

What we learned in 2008: *Mike Montgomery's third college head-coaching job will be his easiest one yet.*

With Mike Montgomery taking over the coaching duties from Ben Braun this season, it's natural to wonder whether he'll duplicate the success he had at Stanford. This seems as good a time as any to take a look at the aggregated Pac-10 standings over the past 30 seasons.

Conference records since 1979

UCLA	376-164	.696
Arizona	365-175	.676
Stanford	300-240	.556
Cal	248-292	.459
Washington	248-292	.459
USC	247-293	.457
Oregon St.	245-295	.454
Arizona St.	238-302	.441
Oregon	230-310	.426
Washington St.	203-337	.376

One can get a good idea of the long-term conference hierarchy through this exercise. UCLA and Arizona have dominated the Pac-10 over the last three decades. So much so that seven teams have a losing record over this time. Stanford is a clear third, due in large part to the work that Montgomery did in Palo Alto as its head coach for 18 seasons. Then there are six teams that have more or less been on even footing. Finally, there's Washington State. Tony Bennett's ability to win there has been astounding.

What this chart fails to illustrate is that when Montgomery took over at Stanford in 1986, the Cardinal was the Washington State of the league. (Kids, this was back in the day when Oregon State was regularly competing for Pac-10 titles.) Say what you want about Cal, but they haven't been a pushover in recent seasons. The last two seasons were difficult to watch at times, but Ben Braun has put some good teams on the floor. There's no need to build a program from the ground up here. Montgomery should be able to produce a consistent winner soon.

What's in store for 2009

Cal basketball might not need an overhaul, but 2009 will be a transition season in terms of personnel. Anderson and Hardin leave gaping holes in terms of offensive production and rebounding. Patrick Christopher and Jamal Boykin will provide two solid options, but quality depth is lacking on this team. That will change once Montgomery gets one or two full recruiting cycles under his belt.

MEET THE BEARS

Patrick Christopher (6-5, 215, Jr.). Christopher wasn't the most famous Bear last season, but he did get the most minutes. He's a wing who derives fairly efficient scoring from not committing many turnovers and posting an effective field goal percentage of 51.

Jamal Boykin (6-8, 235, Jr.). Because he transferred from Duke early in the 2007 season, Boykin was able to play for Cal last season after the fall semester ended. He flourished in a reserve role, putting up the kinds of tempo-free stats that indicate he'll need no adjustment as a starter. He has great range for a big man, but he could stand to get to the free-throw line more often. He also showed that he's one of the better offensive rebounders in the conference. His board-work on the defensive glass was less than ordinary, but with Anderson and Hardin so proficient in that area, it's difficult to say how much of that is real.

Theo Robertson (6-6, 225, Jr.). Robertson sat out last season with a hip injury. While he's not a voluminous shooter, he's a small forward with some range. He's known more for his defense, though. The big question is whether he'll be the same player he was before hip surgery.

Jerome Randle (5-10, 165, Jr.). Randle made some strides in some areas in his first season as a starter. Most notably, he made 40 percent of his threes. He was less of an offensive factor than he was as a sophomore, but without Anderson around he figures to be more involved again. It will be interesting to see how he adjusts to a situation where he can't choose his spots as often.

D. J. Seeley (6-4, 190, Fr.). Seeley's the most likely true freshman to get significant minutes this season. It wouldn't be a shock if he earns the starting job at the two-guard.

Harper Kamp (6-8, 245, So.). Kamp started his career as a Bear impressively. Basically, he didn't miss shots and he got to the free-throw line frequently. However, he found the going much more difficult in Pac-10 play. In calendar year 2007, Kamp made 25 of his 35 field goal attempts and went to the line 23 times. After New Year's, he shot 28-for-73 and took 25 free-throw attempts.

Nikola Knezevic (6-2, 185, Jr.). Knezevic is another option at either guard position but in 2008 he didn't shoot very much. He prefers to hang out on the perimeter but went just four-for-24 on threes in conference play when his minutes became scarce.

Omondi Amoke (6-6, 225, Fr.). Amoke was a highly rated prospect who had to miss last season due to a calf injury.

Jordan Wilkes (7-0, 235, Jr.). Wilkes has battled injuries at the college level and is on the soft side for a seven-footer. He's only averaged about seven minutes per game in his two healthy seasons at Berkeley. Montgomery actually has another seven-footer on the roster, **Max Zhang (7-2, 220, Fr.)**, but he's very raw. There's also **Taylor Harrison (6-10, 245, So.)** who redshirted last season after undergoing knee surgery. Harrison saw a few minutes in every game in 2007 and his main skill is rebounding. If Montgomery wants to go big, he has options, but none of them will score many points.

Prospectus says

Montgomery doesn't have his players in place yet, but he can at least begin to implement his philosophy. This should have some impact defensively where Cal, to put it bluntly, was miserable last season. The offense will suffer, probably immensely, without Anderson. But the defense has so much room for improvement that it wouldn't shock me if the Bears duplicated their six conference wins of 2008 or even did one better in a weaker Pac-10.

OREGON

2008: 18-14 (9-9 Pac-10)
Lost to Mississippi State 76-69, NCAA first round
In-conference offense: 1.11 points per possession (2nd)
In-conference defense: 1.10 points allowed per possession (8th)

What Oregon did well: *Make it to the tournament without playing defense.*

It's junk-stat time, ladies and gentlemen. I'd like to introduce a little something called "Offensive Dependence." It's a simple measure that tries to identify which teams are most dependent on scoring points for victory. It does this by crediting the deviation of offensive efficiency above average and defensive efficiency below average. Higher scores then denote which teams had both.

National Leaders, Offensive Dependence

(adjusted figures used for efficiency)

Team	Offensive Dependence	Off. Eff./ Rank	Def. Eff./ Rank
Oregon	16.2	120.2/6	99.6/131
Utah St.	16.1	113.1/44	106.6/240
IUPUI	14.9	114.9/34	103.6/195
California	14.6	117.6/16	100.7/152
UMBC	14.4	110.0/68	108.1/265

Oregon led the nation in his category by virtue of an offense that was capable of scoring frequently enough to win a national title and a defense that was bad enough to prevent the Quack Attack from separating from its opponents. Note that you'll never see any national title contenders at the top of this stat or its more boring brother, Defensive Dependence (in which Savannah State took the crown last season) because the great teams don't rely on either side of the ball very heavily. They have balance, something that Oregon hasn't acquired in a while.

What we learned in 2008: *Aaron Brooks was not missed for the reasons we thought he would be.*

Even in retrospect, it seems like the loss of Aaron Brooks to the NBA should have had a negative impact on Oregon's offense. Brooks was replaced by freshman Kamyron Brown at point guard and Brown was simply overwhelmed through most of the Pac-10 season. In turn, shooting guard Tajuan Porter found himself getting fewer open looks for his jump shot, resulting in a marked decrease in offensive productivity from the backcourt.

But overall, Oregon's offense was nearly the same in 2008 as it was with Brooks in the lineup the season before. The defense is what crumbled. It's hard to say if Brooks was truly an impact player on the

defensive. The meek defensive stats available don't hint at it (translation: He didn't have a high steal rate). However, in the one Pac-10 game he missed in 2007, Oregon gave up a whopping 1.25 points per possession to a Washington team that wasn't an offensive juggernaut.

What's in store for 2009

There's a lot to be replaced from last season. Do-it-all wing Malik Hairston and Maarty Leunen, one of the best defensive rebounders in the game, both ended productive four-year careers at Oregon. Leunen actually became a scary-efficient scorer in his senior year, making 49 percent of his threes, 61 percent of his twos, and 79 percent of his free throws.

To top it off, Bryce Taylor, who split his time at the two and the three, also was a senior. All three started every game they appeared in last season. The roster is now stocked with a lot of freshmen (six, actually) and inexperienced players that have struggled in their young careers. Expect there to be a lot of learning opportunities in Eugene this season.

MEET THE DUCKS

Tajuan Porter (5-6, 150, Jr.). Porter is your stereotypical power-conference player under six feet. He's not very effective inside the arc and he rarely shoots free throws. Since Porter plays the two-guard, his offensive damage is going to be done behind the three-point line. To that extent, it appeared that he was hurt by the loss of Aaron Brooks at the point last season. Porter's three-point percentage dropped from 44 to 36.

Joevan Catron (6-6, 235, Jr.). Catron will pick up some of the rebounding slack incurred by Leunen's vacancy. He'll do most of his work around the rim, but he has decent touch when pushed away from the hoop. A lot of the offense should go through Catron this season.

Michael Dunigan (6-10, 235, Fr.). Dunigan comes from Farragut Career Academy in Chicago, the same institution that counts as alums one of the world's best hoopsters, Kevin Garnett, and one of the worst, Pat Sajak. Dunigan may not become Garnett, but he is highly touted and is expected to start at center.

Kamyron Brown (6-2, 170, So.). Brown will run the point for Ernie Kent. He looked much like a freshman in that position last season, struggling with turnovers and shooting percentage, although he rarely shot. He may not have that luxury this season.

Ben Voogd (6-2, 175, Jr.). There's a lot of competition for shooting-guard minutes behind Porter and the LSU transfer should get his opportunities off the bench. A couple of freshmen are also in the mix: **Teondre Williams (6-4, 180, Fr.)** and **Matthew Humphrey (6-5, 175, Fr.).**

LeKendric Longmire (6-5, 200, So.). The long-armed wing was one of three Ducks that shot worse than 40 percent from the free-throw line. Fortunately, none of the trio took very many attempts. Longmire has more athleticism than most Pac-10 players, but he could use it more effectively.

Churchill Odia (6-6, 210, Sr.). Odia was one of the most timid shooters in the country last season. When he does fire, it's going to be a three and he's made a third of those attempts in his three seasons of Division I ball.

Frantz Dorsainvil (6-8, 260, Sr.). Dorsainvil demonstrates the vagaries of junior college recruiting. He was expected to give Oregon a lift in the middle last season, but was glued to the bench after Catron came back from a foot injury in January.

Drew Wiley (6-6, 185, Fr.). In addition to Dunigan, Williams, and Humphrey, three other freshmen arrived in Eugene this season. Wiley might challenge Longmire for time at the wing. **Josh Crittle (6-8, 225, Fr.)** and **Garrett Sim (6-1, 175, Fr.)** may find the court as well.

Prospectus says

Saying a team is rebuilding is a cliché, but if it applies somewhere this season it's the 2009 edition of the Ducks. Porter and Catron are the only proven commodities. Dunigan has the potential to produce right away, although his offense may need some work. Given the youth, the results this season will probably be better served in the context of projecting toward the future. Kent received a contract extension through the 2013 season this summer, and in his ten seasons at Oregon, he's had six players

drafted. If he has another two go to the NBA out of this freshman class, then he should be around a while longer, regardless of Oregon's record this season.

OREGON STATE

2008: 6-25 (0-18 Pac-10)
Lost to Arizona 87-56, Pac-10 first round
In-conference offense: 0.87 points per possession (10th)
In-conference defense: 1.17 points allowed per possession (10th)

What Oregon State did well: *Take care of the ball.*

Despite the fact that Oregon State was one of the worst power conference teams in recent memory, they did practice exceedingly good ball control. On the season, they ranked 44th in the nation by committing turnovers on just 18.6 percent of their offensive possessions. In Pac-10 play, that number dropped to 17.9 percent, good for fourth in the league. It is not an exaggeration to say that the Beavers' ball security was at a level envied by many NCAA tournament teams.

What we learned in 2008: *If you can't make shots, turnover percentage is irrelevant.*

Indeed, one has to wonder if Pac-10 opponents simply didn't bother to try to pressure the OSU offense because it made no sense to do so. Oregon State ranked in the bottom ten nationally in three-point accuracy, two-point accuracy, and the ability to get to the free-throw line. To the defense, the value of an Oregon State turnover was about as low as you'll see in the college game.

What's in store for 2009

After going 0-18 in the Pac-10, Oregon State did what programs at Northwestern, Air Force, Richmond, and Denver have done in recent years when facing the prospect of being unable to compete for their conference championship—they decided to turn to a disciple of the Princeton offense.

The Beavers hired Craig Robinson to take over head coaching duties in the offseason. Robinson played for Pete Carril at Princeton and coached under Bill Carmody at Northwestern, so the Princeton offense is in his blood. As head coach at Brown for the past two seasons, Robinson's system more closely resembled the Princeton offshoot run by John Thompson III than the core model developed by Carril. Robinson is equally interested in recruiting great athletes as he is excellent shooters. His Brown teams had the notable Princeton traits of being supremely accurate from three-point range while ignoring offensive boards and forcing the opponent to play a half-court game itself.

The unique trait of Robinson's system is the ability of his teams to get to the free-throw line. Last season, Brown shot 35 free throws for every 100 field goals attempted, which was the third-best rate in the country. In 2007, Brown led the nation in that measure. The Bears took a lot of three-pointers and played at a slow pace, but the Robinson system is not as extreme in either area as some of the other Princeton variants in existence.

MEET THE BEAVERS

Lathen Wallace (6-3, 200, So.). If there's someone that Robinson can "plug and play" into his system in 2008–2009, it's Wallace. As a freshman, he demonstrated an insatiable desire to launch shots. After being a practice player under Jay John, Wallace was given a bigger role under interim coach Kevin Mouton, and thus most of his stats were accumulated against the best competition on the Beavers' schedule. Those numbers read nicely—he made 38 percent of his threes and took 31 percent of OSU's shots. Over the last four games of the season, Wallace averaged 26 minutes and an efficient 18 points. In a system that should give him a higher quality of shots, Wallace figures to flourish.

Seth Tarver (6-5, 205, Jr.). Tarver's season went the opposite way of Wallace's. He fell out of favor with the interim coach and saw his playing time steadily drop during conference play. He made just 23 percent of his threes against Pac-10 teams so it's not like Mouton had much choice. Given the other options that Robinson has right now, Tarver will get every opportunity to earn back significant minutes.

Daniel Deane (6-8, 245, Jr.). Deane played one season for Utah before parting with the Utes after Ray Giacoletti was fired. He fits the mold of being an inefficient scorer. He should be the best defensive rebounder on the team, also.

Josh Tarver (6-3, 185, Jr.). Josh Tarver's game is similar to his brother's, with a less reliable jump shot. Josh may end up as the starting point guard.

Roeland Schaftenaar (6-11, 240, Jr.). A big man with range can have a prominent place in the Princeton system. Schaftenaar is known to launch a three-ball from time to time but he's a reluctant shooter for good reason—he made just 29 percent of his three-point attempts during his first two seasons in Corvallis. His primary task will be to set screens, but a small improvement in his touch could make him useful as a fourth or fifth shooting option.

Rickey Claitt (6-2, 175, Sr.). Claitt will share point guard duties with Josh Tarver, but he's more of a pure point. He made just three of 29 three-pointers last season, the worst percentage among Division I players with at least 25 attempts. On the positive side, he took a mere 8.3 percent of the Beavers' shots while he played.

Calvin Haynes (6-2, 185, So.). Haynes is another combo guard and posted a sub-40 percent eFG while being one of the Beavers' most frequent shooters.

Omari Johnson (6-7, 205, So.). Johnson brings Pac-10 athleticism to the table and is an above average rebounder for his size.

Calvin Hampton (6-10, 250, Jr.). Hampton is a decent enough defensive rebounder whose offensive game still needs a lot of work.

Prospectus says

After going winless in conference play and only twice coming within single digits of a Pac-10 victory, a reasonable goal in 2009 is to win a couple of conference games and be competitive more often in losses. Should the Beavers find themselves somewhere other than tenth place by the end of season, Robinson would be deserving of conference coach of the year consideration.

Wallace's strong finish should encourage Beavers' fans. The bigger issue is how well Robinson can run a program and fill a roster with Pac-10-level players. Given that he had no scholarships to offer when he was hired (although a couple came open over the summer, Robinson didn't use them), this question won't be answered for at least a couple more seasons.

STANFORD

2008: 28-8 (13-5 Pac-10)
Lost to Texas 82-62, NCAA Sweet 16
In-conference offense: 1.06 points per possession (6th)
In-conference defense: 0.97 points allowed per possession
(2nd)

What Stanford did well: *Play excellent defense without forcing turnovers.*

No doubt turnovers are usually important to a defense's success, but last season Stanford demonstrated that a team can dominate defensively without forcing turnovers. In all fairness, Trent Johnson wasn't the first to prove this—UConn's Jim Calhoun has done this on multiple occasions. Johnson's and Calhoun's systems have a lot in common. They utilize their team's strength, namely a size advantage up front that leads to a miserable two-point percentage for opponents.

Both coaches make it a priority for their defense to funnel the action toward their big men, which leads to missed shots, and outstanding rebounding leads to few second attempts for the opposition. In short, that's how Stanford could finish eighth in conference play in turnover percentage (only ahead of defensive lightweights Oregon and Cal) and finish second in the conference in defensive efficiency.

What we learned in 2008: *Employees of the Stanford athletic department have very long job titles.*

When Johnny Dawkins was introduced as Stanford's head coach in late April, he wasn't merely becoming Coach Dawkins. He became the Anne and Tony Joseph Director of Men's Basketball. In the process he was hired by Jaquish & Kenninger Director of Athletics Bob Bowlsby. As Dawkins embarks on his new job, he'll need all of the donations to the athletic department that he can get to keep Stanford in the national discussion. If that means selling his job title, so be it.

What's in store for 2009

We don't know much about Dawkins's coaching philosophy, considering he's never run a program. But we do know that he's spent ten seasons serving on Mike Krzyzewski's staff at Duke, and four more seasons playing under Coach K. Dawkins has spent zero years coaching or playing at the collegiate level under anyone else. Indeed, initial indications are that Dawkins won't stray too far from the core principles used for years at Duke. Aggressive man-to-man defense and a motion offense dependent on dribble penetration should be the new norm in Palo Alto.

MEET THE CARDINALS

Anthony Goods (6-3, 205, Sr.). A new coach with a new system brings about a certain set of challenges. The bigger adjustment in 2009 will be adapting to life without one or both of the seven-foot Lopez twins on the court, and no player is more affected by that than Goods. Over his last two seasons, he's lurked on the fringes of being an efficient offensive player.

On the positive side of the ledger, he's made about 35 percent of his three-point attempts during that time and about 60 percent of his shots come from there. He also commits very few turnovers, and though he doesn't get to the line that often, he made 75 percent of his free-throw attempts last season. However, he's consistently been a sub-40 percent shooter inside the arc. He figures to be one of the top-two sources for offense this season, and assuming he gets fewer open looks from beyond the arc, he'll do well to maintain his output from last season.

Lawrence Hill (6-8, 215, Sr.). Hill's game took a bit of a step backward last season, although his outstanding sophomore season was a hard act to follow. The primary culprit was a reduction in two-point accuracy from 56 to 43 percent.

Mitch Johnson (6-1, 190, Sr.). Johnson has been the point guard the past two seasons and as one might expect, his role didn't extend much beyond getting the ball to the big men (or, occasionally, Goods). He'll be expected to do more this season. A footnote to his play is that he's one of the better rebounding point guards in the country.

Landry Fields (6-7, 200, Jr.). Fields will get time at the shooting guard spot though he's struggled some with his shot in his first two seasons.

Kenny Brown (6-1, 200, Sr.). Brown is another shooting guard and he played sparingly under Johnson. Most of his shots are three-pointers and he's made 35 percent of them in his three seasons at Stanford.

Jeremy Green (6-4, 190, Fr.). Green is a shooting guard from Austin, Texas. Between graduation and early entries (and the release of 6-10 Miles Plumlee from his commitment), the Cardinal will be a guard-heavy team in 2009. The competition for minutes at the two and three spots will be fierce.

Jarrett Mann (6-4, 180, Fr.). Mann was a heavily recruited wing that stuck with Stanford through the coaching change.

Drew Shiller (6-0, 185, Jr.). Shiller was exclusively a three-point threat in his sophomore season (43 of his 51 attempts were from long range) after having some balance to his game as a freshman.

Josh Owens (6-8, 215, So.). He was relegated to mop-up duty in 2008 but this team is in need of frontline players, so Owens will have the chance to gobble up some minutes.

Will Paul (6-9, 200, So.). If Paul can stay healthy, he'll get some time in the middle for Dawkins. He redshirted last season and was basically a human victory cigar as a freshman in 2007, picking up minutes only at the end of lopsided games.

Prospectus says

The Coach K coaching tree is again in bloom, and Johnny Dawkins may be more devoted to his mentor's principles than any other Kryzyzewski disciple. Dawkins should be very familiar with what he has to work with this season, because the strengths and limitations of 2009 Stanford and 2008 Duke are nearly identical.

This team is severely lacking in size, and every player with Division I experience is perimeter oriented. Don't be surprised if this team hoists over 40 percent of its shots from three-point range, a figure reserved for about a sixth of Division I teams last season. The six returning players that saw meaningful minutes last season took 49 percent of their combined shots from long distance.

The difference between the two teams is the expectations associated with them. Even though Stanford was a three-seed and a Sweet 16 participant last season, the core on both offense and defense is gone. With all of the changes on the floor and on the bench, Dawkins will have been one of the most successful first-year coaches this season by merely getting Stanford into some sort of bubble talk by season's end.

UCLA

2008: 35-4 (16-2 Pac-10)
Lost to Memphis 78-63, NCAA Final Four
In-conference offense: 1.14 points per possession (1st)
In-conference defense: 0.96 points allowed per possession (1st)

What UCLA did well: *Put an offense on the floor capable of winning a national championship.*

On the surface, UCLA's ultimate fate of losing in the national semifinals looked exactly like the previous two seasons, which ended in the same way. A closer look reveals something much different—UCLA had an offense that was among the best in the land. The stifling defense was still in place, but UCLA could also score as consistently as any national power. They were one of nine teams to lead their conference in both offensive and defensive efficiency during conference play, and they finished with the seventh-best adjusted offensive efficiency in Division I. That was easily the best mark since Ben Howland arrived in Westwood.

The Bruins didn't just put up points on the weak and defenseless, they scored 81 in 64 possessions against Washington State, 76 in 62 possessions against Stanford, 84 in 62 possessions against Arizona State, and 76 in 58 possessions versus Xavier. Even though UCLA's past three seasons have ended two wins short of a national title, last season's team looked much more like a champion than the previous two.

What we learned in 2008: *UCLA will be a basketball power as long as Ben Howland is around.*

Not only did UCLA make its third consecutive Final Four appearance, but they had two underclassmen taken in the first five picks of the 2008 NBA draft. They lost another underclassman to the second round of the draft. Consider that before the start of the 2007–2008 season, it wasn't inconceivable that Kevin Love, Russell Westbrook, and Luc Richard Mbah a Moute would all be playing for UCLA again in 2009.

Even with the not-so-expected departures, there's enough talent left over in addition to what most consider to be the nation's best freshman class to keep UCLA near the top of the national polls this season. The Bruins will be two scholarships short of a full load but that's irrelevant. They will still have some talented players who could be getting a lot more minutes elsewhere, and others who will be moving on to the NBA before their eligibility expires. But the ultimate sign that UCLA is as healthy as any program in the land is that the Bruins appear to be immune to sudden personnel changes.

What's in store for 2009

Even though they lose three starters, UCLA will have something that the previous three Final Four teams out of Westwood didn't: two senior starters. While the freshman class grabs headlines, the Bruins wouldn't be considered one of the nation's top teams again were it not for the leadership of Darren Collison and Josh Shipp.

Collison actually had the lowest usage of his college years in 2008, but it was also his most efficient season. That was helped by making an astounding 52.5 percent of his three-point attempts. Granted, he only took about three per game, but that's all that was needed in UCLA's uberefficient offense. Shipp isn't the two-way star that Collison is, but if the freshmen live up to the hype, he'll continue to blend in well as a third or fourth option on offense.

MEET THE BRUINS

Jrue Holiday (6-3, 200, Fr.). As one of the most talented freshmen entering the college game this season, Holiday has the potential to be one and done. Whether that plays out or not, his arrival makes the loss of Russell Westbrook much less painful.

Darren Collison (6-1, 165, Sr.). After playing tentatively while nursing a knee injury in November and December, Collison hit his stride during conference play. He led the nation in three-point percentage among players that took at least 80 shots.

Josh Shipp (6-5, 220, Sr.). Shipp's game changed noticeably last season. In his first two seasons, 38 percent of his shots were three-pointers. Last sea-

son, that figure jumped to 56 percent. As one would expect, he got to the free-throw line less often as a result. He was significantly less involved in the Bruins offense than he was in years past.

J'Mison Morgan (6-10, 275, Fr.). Morgan was headed to LSU before John Brady was fired. UCLA obviously needs a center, and Morgan has the talent to start upon arrival.

Drew Gordon (6-8, 235, Fr.). With Luc Richard Mbah a Moute trying to make an NBA roster, Gordon will have the opportunity to get big minutes at the power forward spot. Given his reputation, he should be able to match or exceed what Mbah a Moute did on the offensive end. Mbah a Moute never developed any shooting touch, and there's some indication that Gordon already has more to work with in that area.

Alfred Aboya (6-8, 235, Jr.). As mentioned above, the Bruins will start two seniors, but there's an outside chance of it being three with Aboya. Based on the arrival of Morgan and Gordon, it appears he'll be the first player off the bench for Ben Howland. Aboya is quiet on the offense and his rebounding numbers dipped last season, although that could be attributed to Kevin Love grabbing every board in sight.

Malcolm Lee (6-4, 170, Fr.) / Jerime Anderson (6-2, 170, Fr.). Collison's decision to stay in school means that the two backcourt prospects of the freshman class will be fighting for playing time behind both Collison and Holiday. They also could hope that Ben Howland occasionally puts three guards on the floor.

James Keefe (6-8, 220, So.). Keefe adds some depth up front and while his offensive ability is limited, he has proven to be an effective offensive rebounder and an occasional shot-blocking threat.

Michael Roll (6-5, 200, Jr.). Roll was a solid perimeter shooter off the bench in his first two seasons. He played just six games last season due to a left foot injury.

Prospectus says

There are bound to be some growing pains as Howland figures out the rotation during the nonconference schedule. The defense should be excellent, but replacing Love is impossible. He was an outstanding scorer, rebounder, and passer, and an underrated shot-blocker (seventh-best block rate in the Pac-10 last season).

The difference between the 2008 UCLA offense and those of seasons past was Love. If somehow the Bruins manage to maintain the offensive quality of last season, they'll clearly be the second-best team in the country. Realistically, it's more likely that the offense sputters more often and the team loses more than two conference games. A one-seed still seems like a reasonable forecast, but this team won't be as dominant as last season.

USC

2008: 21-12 (11-7 Pac-10)
Lost to Kansas State 80-67, NCAA first round
In-conference offense: 1.06 points per possession (7th)
In-conference defense: 1.01 points allowed per possession (3rd)

What USC did well: *Have success without any help from the bench.*

I suppose it's a mild exaggeration to say USC had *no* bench last season. Angelo Johnson did get 23 minutes a game contributing at the point-guard spot. But basically this was a six-man team. Those six players took 94 percent of USC shots. Among teams that received a bid to the NCAA tournament, only UMBC had more dependence on its top-six players.

Getting contributions from the bench is often not a big deal. Let's face it, in the big games a coach is going to want his best players on the floor as much as possible. And unless that team is playing an uptempo style—which Tim Floyd doesn't—having a deep bench is just an insurance policy against foul trouble or injuries.

For the most part, injuries weren't an issue with the Super Six. But Daniel Hackett missed three games in February, including a contest against UCLA that produced an interesting box score. Four USC starters played 40 minutes, and Davon Jefferson may have joined them as a fifth had he not picked up two fouls in the first half, which led coach Tim Floyd to sit Jefferson for the final eight minutes before halftime. That game also featured O. J. Mayo's worst college performance. He had four points and ten

turnovers and went the distance despite having injured his groin in practice earlier in the week.

So for at least one game the depth issues caught up with USC. But for the most part, Floyd got away with a strict six-man rotation without many difficulties.

What we learned in 2008: *No price is too high to get a top prospect.*

Tim Floyd is one of a number of coaches that has no problem giving a scholarship to a player that is expected to spend only one year in school before declaring for the NBA draft. He was willing to accept O. J. Mayo's arrival despite the potential for NCAA trouble that would naturally develop when amateurism and professionalism collided.

However, Floyd raised the stakes as he recruited another likely one-and-done player, 6-6 Demar DeRozan of Compton, California. He spent not one, but two scholarships to lure DeRozan to USC for the 2009 season. DeRozan, of course, is only using one scholarship on his own, but Floyd also gave a scholarship to one Percy Miller, better known as rapper Lil' Romeo. Miller and DeRozan are longtime pals and AAU teammates, but Miller is not expected to get much playing time at USC.

What's in store for 2009

While some might have seen Mayo's season at USC as less than stellar, only three power conference players were more involved in their teams' offenses: Michael Beasley, Luke Harangody, and Sean Singletary. The challenge this season is replacing Mayo's possessions, and those of lesser known one-and-done player Davon Jefferson, in an efficient way. The good news is that USC was about as efficient on possessions used by Mayo as they were on possessions used by everyone else. The problem is that the "everyone else" category includes a collection of players who individually were not taking a lot of shots and were operating in an environment where opposing defenses were focused on Mayo.

If DeRozan does what Mayo did, then problem solved. (Or nearly so. Jefferson's contributions should not be forgotten, either.) Recently, teams with elite offenses that lose ultrahigh-usage players seem to fare just fine. The most obvious examples from last season were Wisconsin (Alando Tucker) and Texas (Kevin Durant). Each team's offense was about as effective without the star player in question as it was the season before.

MEET THE TROJANS

Demar DeRozan (6-5, 195, Fr.). The consensus among scouts right now is that DeRozan is the most NBA-ready of any college freshman. He will do the job that Mayo did last season, and while it's a bit much to think he'll take on the offensive load that Mayo did, the Trojans return a bunch of guys who are not used to shooting much, so expect DeRozan to have one of the highest usage rates of any freshman.

Taj Gibson (6-9, 225, Jr.). Gibson's most valuable asset last season was his shot-blocking where he was second to Robin Lopez in the Pac-10 in block rate. In 2008, he shot less frequently than he did in his freshman season, but expect him to get more involved if only because somebody has to get more involved, and he has the skills to do it.

Daniel Hackett (6-5, 205, Jr.). Hackett will once again get a lot of minutes as USC's starting point-guard. He doesn't have much range, but he also doesn't shoot much. He's most effective driving to the basket.

Dwight Lewis (6-5, 215, Jr.). It's not really clear what Lewis's role will be since he basically played the two-guard most of last season.

Kasey Cunningham (6-7, 225, So.). Cunningham's redshirt freshman season was cut short after nine games when he tore the ACL in his left knee. He took a redshirt in 2007 while recovering from the same injury. While it might seem like Cunningham is a long shot to contribute, he could be following Leon Powe's path to Pac-10 greatness. Powe endured similar knee problems in high school and at Cal before dominating the Pac-10. Cunningham doesn't have the pedigree Powe did out of high school, but he was pursued by several big-time programs.

Leonard Washington (6-6, 230, Fr.). Washington was a late find for Tim Floyd over the summer and figures to see time at the wing.

Angelo Johnson (5-11, 180, So.). Johnson was the backup point guard last season, but his offensive role was extremely limited. He did knock down 40 percent of his three-point attempts.

Donte Smith (5-11, 170, Fr.). Smith is a late juco import who will get minutes at the point.

Keith Wilkinson (6-10, 225, Sr.). Another big man, Wilkinson's influence was exclusively on the defensive end when he saw action last season.

RouSean Cromwell (6-11, 225, Sr.). Cromwell deserves mention simply because he played 166 minutes last season and took exactly eight shots from the field. He took just 3.8 percent of his team's shots while he was on the floor, making him the third-most infrequent shooter in the nation.

Prospectus says

Floyd's proven that he can bring elite talent to USC. He's also proven he can put the kind of defense on the floor that can win championships, either of the conference or NCAA variety. What's yet to be done is finding the supporting players to build an offense that can score consistently. It doesn't appear that this team will be much different. A lot rests on DeRozan. If he can carry the offense as well as Mayo did, then the Trojans could be headed for another midrange seed in March.

WASHINGTON

2008: 16-17 (7-11 Pac-10)
Lost to Valparaiso 72-71, CBI first round
In-conference offense: 1.01 points per possession (8th)
In-conference defense: 1.04 points allowed per possession (6th)

What Washington did well: *Frustrate its fans.*

At their best, the Huskies looked like a tournament team (examples: winning at Arizona State, taking Stanford and Washington State to the wire on the road at the end of the season). At their worst, the Huskies looked like a team that had no business in any postseason tournament (examples: home loss to Cal, CBI loss to Valpo at home). The maddening part was that there was no pattern to Washington's play. Just when you could give up on them, they showed promise. When it looked like they were developing momentum, their season ended with a shocking loss. Outside of a couple incidents in November, there weren't any injuries to speak of. It was a puzzling year in Seattle.

What we learned in 2008: *If Jon Brockman had some shooting touch, he might be playing for pay this season.*

The list of rebounders better than Jon Brockman last season is a short one. I'll give you Kevin Love and Michael Beasley. Nebraska's Aleks Maric deserves mention. And perhaps DeJuan Blair of Pitt. That's it.

The thing is, Brockman (like Blair, but unlike the others) is just 6-7. He also has a solid offensive game that expanded in role last season, in part filling the void left by Spencer Hawes. Brockman shot 54 percent from the field and is very sure-handed, but what holds him back is a lack of range. He isn't a scoring threat beyond ten feet.

In addition, his free-throw shooting plummeted last season, falling to 52 percent after making an acceptable 66 percent his sophomore season. And Brockman gets to the line a lot. That drop in accuracy alone cost him 25 points last season. His loss of touch from the line mirrored his team's. Washington went from 78th in the nation in free-throw percentage (against Division I teams only) to dead last in 2008, shooting a miserable 58.6 percent.

What's in store for 2009

The Huskies return their top-three players in terms of both minutes and offensive contribution. In the Pac-10, that means Washington has above-average continuity. They lose seniors Tim Morris and Ryan Appleby, but they were the last two offensive options among the starters. Also gone is reserve guard Joel Smith, who graduated after his junior season and elected to part ways with the program despite one remaining season of eligibility.

It was thought last season that Lorenzo Romar's team would crank the pace back up to the level of the Brandon Roy teams that preferred to play at around 73 possessions per game. But even without Spencer Hawes requiring more half-court sets, last season's pace was nearly identical to 2007 at around 70 possessions per game. Maybe it's still a personnel thing, but this may be a permanent change in the way a Romar offense works.

MEET THE HUSKIES

Jon Brockman (6-7, 255, Sr.). I've gushed about Brockman enough already. His free-throw shooting will improve this season. At least it better or he'll end up getting sent to the line even more often. Brockman did end up missing the Huskies' Pac-10 tournament loss to Cal last season after rolling an ankle late in the regular-season finale. He had surgery after the season and spent two months rehabbing.

Quincy Pondexter (6-6, 210, Jr.). Pondexter's biggest area of improvement last season was in offensive rebounding, which was a good sign in a program that consistently hammers opponents with second-chance points year after year. The rest of Pondexter's game didn't change much from his freshman season. He is still struggling to find an identity on this team.

Justin Dentmon (5-11, 185, Sr.). Dentmon lost his starting job to Morris early last season. The funny thing is that statistically, Dentmon was Morris's superior on offense by a comfortable margin. Romar won't have much choice this season it would seem. Dentmon seems to be adding to his game each season he plays.

Venoy Overton (5-11, 180, So.). Overton started 26 games at point guard last season but really struggled with both shooting (38 percent eFG) and turnovers. He was third in the conference in steal rate, but Romar questioned his defense at times last season.

Matthew Bryan-Amaning (6-9, 235, So.). There were high hopes that Bryan-Amaning would be an impact freshman, but he shot 41 percent from the field and found playing time difficult to come by. He should get more opportunities this season. Bryan-Amaning managed to score 41 against the Czech Republic in the under-20 European Championship tournament over the summer.

Artem Wallace (6-8, 250, Sr.). Wallace has the potential to be a nice role player. He meets the minimum UW criteria for a frontline player since he's a very good offensive rebounder. However, it's difficult to play him much because in his three seasons he's made 31 of his 101 free-throw attempts. He did turn in a solid 11-point, nine-rebound game in 33 minutes against Cal when Brockman sat due to injury.

Joe Wolfinger (7-0, 255, Jr.). Wolfinger prefers the perimeter. He's the rare seven-footer that shot more threes than twos last season and he actually made 40 percent of the long-range attempts. Amazingly, he took 93 shots from the field and just nine from the free-throw line, an indicator that he's averse to contact.

Elston Turner, Jr. (6-4, 185, Fr.). Both Turner and Scott Suggs (6-6, 190, Fr.) should get some minutes off the bench at shooting guard. Given that an Overton-Dentmon starting tandem is on the small side, Romar won't mind being able to produce a height advantage with a substitute.

Darnell Gant (6-8, 210, Fr.). Gant redshirted last season to add some strength and figures to find himself in Romar's rotation this season.

Prospectus says

Between Brockman, Pondexter, and Dentmon, there's enough experience and ability to get back to the NCAA tournament. Even without much of a talent upgrade, the Huskies are a decent candidate to surprise people. Their Pac-10 record was a game worse than it should have been based on point differential, and they had a historically bad season from the free-throw line. Depth might be an issue this season, but UW has more proven commodities than most of its conference brethren. The combination of circumstances both inside and outside the program should allow this team to get back to the top half of the league in 2009.

WASHINGTON STATE

2008: 16-17 (7-11 Pac-10)
Lost to North Carolina 68-47, NCAA Sweet 16
In-conference offense: 1.09 points per possession (3rd)
In-conference defense: 1.01 points allowed per possession (4th)

What Washington State did well:
Retain Tony Bennett.

It's a story that plays out a few times every spring in college basketball: a coach has success at a school, loses talented players that contributed to the success, then gets pursued by schools with a bigger budget, more tradition, and more resources. Tony Bennett was involved in such a story with Indiana University playing the role of school that always gets its way in these scenarios. The Hoosiers were able to pluck Kelvin Sampson from Oklahoma when

they last had a vacancy, and settled on Marquette's Tom Crean this time around. But Crean wasn't their first choice; it was Bennett. And Bennett elected to stay at Washington State.

What we learned in 2008: *When you don't commit turnovers, it pays to be patient.*

The 2008 edition of Washington State was much like the 2007 version. However, last season's edition was a little bit better owing to improved offensive efficiency. Statistically, the Wazzu offense didn't look much different—the Cougars featured unyielding ball control, shot well, and ignored the offensive glass. The subtle change to the way the offense operated was in that they played slower. The Cougars' average pace of 59.6 possessions per 40 minutes was the slowest of any season that a Bennett has been at the helm in Pullman. Only six teams in Division I played slower last season.

When you don't get offensive rebounds, shot selection is especially important because there are so few opportunities for a second shot. When you don't commit turnovers, the chances of getting a good first shot increase. The Cougars fused those two concepts together last season, creating an offense that had a higher effective shooting percentage on the strength of better shooting inside the arc. In fact, their offense was more dangerous as the pace got slower last season. Even though Washington State's pace was excruciatingly sluggish, enough points were being scored to prevent casual observers from noticing the difference from previous seasons.

What's in store for 2009

Bennett's third season in Pullman has a lot of parallels to John Beilein's fifth at West Virginia. First, he's coming off of consecutive successful seasons despite not having any obvious NBA prospects on the roster. Second, he's losing the best players from those teams. Third, it seems like at least one rebuilding year is inevitable. Beilein's 2007 team held its own against Big East competition despite not having Mike Gansey and Kevin Pittsnogle (among others) from his NCAA tournament teams. The Mountaineers would fail to get an at-large bid, but did win the NIT that season.

Bennett's teams have played great defense, but the difference between his and his father's teams at Wazzu has been an offense that repeatedly finds ways to score. The tandem of Derrick Low and Kyle Weaver led the offensive attack and both will get paid to play somewhere else this season. Given that the defense has been great for four seasons now, it would seem that the offense will be the part that struggles this season. Finding a couple of players that can take care of the ball like Low and Weaver will be crucial to the team's success.

MEET THE COUGARS

Aron Baynes (6-10, 270, Sr.). For what it's worth, Baynes has good range considering he hoisted just one three-point shot last season. It might not be worth much because he is pretty effective in the post as well. Bennett will be relying on him rather heavily to prevent a big drop-off in the team's offense.

Taylor Rochestie (6-1, 186, Sr.). Rochestie actually led the Cougars in minutes last season. He was the third-most dangerous guard on the floor most of the time, but he wasn't a third wheel due to a 43 percent mark on three-pointers. With the lack of experience around him, he may lead the conference in minutes this season. Will his game change without Low and Weaver to distract defenses?

Daven Harmeling (6-7, 225, Sr.). Harmeling should inherit the starting role at the small forward spot, although redshirt freshman **Abe Lodwick (6-7, 196, Fr.)** is expected to pick up some minutes also. Despite his size, Harmeling's value is basically as a perimeter shooter.

Buttressing that point is that his offensive rebounding rate was the lowest of the 368 collegians listed at 6-7 last season. To his credit, he never commits turnovers, either. Put four guys around him that are difficult to guard, and he can be an asset to the offense.

Caleb Forrest (6-8, 228, Sr.). Forrest will need to do his best Robbie Cowgill impression this season.

He seems to be more than capable as his rate stats are nearly identical to Cowgill's senior-season numbers from 2008. The only noticeable difference is in turnovers where Cowgill's rate was microscopic while Forrest's was merely excellent. Forrest is two inches shorter, but he's the stronger of the two players.

Nikola Koprivica (6-6, 211, Jr.). The 20-year-old Serbian struggled to find playing time last season, but that shouldn't be a problem in 2009. The problem for Koprivica is that he's a career 12-for-58 from three-point range and that's a significant part of his game.

New Faces. There are a bunch of new players on Bennett's roster. So many, that Taylor Rochestie volunteered to give up his scholarship so that Bennett could have one more to use. Most notable among them is **Fabian Boeke (6-11, 230, So.)** who was declared ineligible by the NCAA last season and is more of a perimeter-oriented big. The most heralded true freshman is **Klay** (son of former NBA'er Mychal) **Thompson (6-6, 187, Fr.)** who should get serious minutes at the wing and has enough athleticism to mitigate the void left by Weaver.

Prospectus says

Tony Bennett enjoyed the luxury of having one of the most experienced teams in college hoops last season as three seniors and four juniors filled out his rotation. Yes, he'll have four senior starters this season, but only Baynes among them has the proven ability to carry a major chunk of the offensive load.

In particular, losing Weaver is going to be difficult to compensate for because he was an impact defender in addition to being the Cougars' best offensive player. There has to be an adjustment with the kind of personnel losses experienced by this program. Anything on the positive side of .500 in conference play should cement Bennett's status as one of the game's best coaches.

The SEC

The Year of the Freshman Continues

KEN POMEROY

It felt like a down year for the SEC in 2008. Sure, thanks to 4-12 Georgia's winning the SEC tournament, the conference sent six teams to the NCAAs. But none of them could make it past the round of 16, and collectively, they went 4-6 in tournament play. Tennessee was thought to be capable of representing the league as a national title contender, but struggled late in the regular season before suffering a loss in the SEC semifinals and a lopsided defeat to Louisville in the Sweet 16. In addition, it was a transition year for two of the conference's flagship programs—Florida and Kentucky—which contributed to the feeling of a down season. Both Ole Miss and Vanderbilt made it to January undefeated, but neither was able to win an NCAA tournament game. (The Rebels didn't even get there.)

This sounds like a lot of doom and gloom, so it's only fair to see how the SEC's season matched up against previous power conference meltdowns. The ACC and Big Ten have long had an organized series to test the relative strengths of their conferences, and the Big 12 and Pac-10 started a similar version last season. The SEC and Big East will be hooking up this season, but we don't need these artificial matchups to determine conference superiority. In my own mind, I've been organizing a conference challenge on a grander scale.

It's called Ken Pomeroy's Power Conference Showdown. The name is a little self-indulgent, yes, but bear with me. There are no corporate sponsors. Nor is there any "organizing" of this event, per se. I just calculate the record for one conference when one of its members plays a team from another power conference. Here's how last season's standings looked when sorted by the average scoring margin for each conference in Showdown games.

	W-L	Scoring Margin
ACC	34-25	3.4
Big 12	31-26	1.3
Big East	28-29	0.2
Big Ten	22-26	-1.1
Pac-10	18-21	-1.7
SEC	22-28	-3.4

The SEC held up the rear in this event, but its performance doesn't really come close to challenging the worst efforts of this decade. That belongs to either the 2004 Big Ten (17-34, -5.7) or the 2001 Big East (14-29, -5.6). Both conferences deserve special mention for their futility in road games, with the Big Ten going 2-17 and the Big East posting a 3-14 record. By comparison, the SEC only played 10 true road games against power conference foes, so its SOS was a little easier. Regardless, none of these conferences was a postseason maven. The Big Ten sent just three of its 11 teams to the NCAA tournament, racking up three wins. The Big East sent five of its 14 teams to the dance, winning a total of five games. Neither conference had a survivor past the Sweet 16. The SEC's performance in 2007-2008 wasn't uncharted territory for a power conference.

169

Last year may have been a year of transition for the conference, but it was part of what will be at least a two-year process. As in any league, many of the SEC's best players exhausted their eligibility. But the SEC was also hit with the early defections of some of its top talent. LSU's Anthony Randolph and Florida's Marreese Speights put their names in the NBA draft and were picked in the first round. Alabama's Richard Hendrix did the same and was picked late in the second round. Most curious is the case of Mississippi State's Jamont Gordon, who also declared early.

Gordon went through the entire draft process, didn't get picked, and didn't officially sign with an agent. At this point, he could have followed the Randolph Morris plan—return to school, serve an NCAA suspension, and finish the season in Starkville. Then as NBA rules allow, he could have signed as a free agent and possibly played a few NBA games before its season ended. Gordon chose to play for pay despite having to go the free-agent route to get to the NBA, and so he too will not be back. Finally, Georgia's second leading scorer, Billy Humphrey, was thrown off the team by head coach Dennis Felton, and Bruce Pearl dismissed potential starters Ramar Smith and Duke Crews from Tennessee.

The result is even more roster turnover this season than last. Every school but South Carolina brings in at least four new faces, and the Gamecocks are adding a new coach, so there will certainly be some adjustments going on in Columbia as well. The good thing is that many of those recruiting classes are highly rated, especially those at Tennessee, Florida, and Alabama. In particular, Alabama power forward JaMychal Green and Tennessee swingman Scotty Hopson are expected to go right from freshman orientation to double-figure scorer. There will undoubtedly be a handful of other freshmen or junior-college transfers who achieve similar status around the conference.

It's not as though the cupboard is bare for returning talent. Guys like Tyler Smith at Tennessee, Patrick Patterson at Kentucky, A. J. Ogilvy at Vanderbilt, Nick Calathes at Florida, Marcus Thornton at LSU, Jarvis Varnado at Mississippi State, and Chris Warren at Ole Miss should make up a formidable preseason all-conference team.

A season forecast is a bit dicey with this conference, simply because with so many first-time contributors, somebody will no doubt surprise. Florida may have been prepared to take back the title of best team in the conference had Speights stayed. (By the way, count me as shocked that neither the SEC media nor the coaches could find room for Speights on one of the all-SEC teams for last season. Both groups agreed that Speights was not one of the best 15 players in the conference. Sure, he appeared to take a possession off occasionally on defense, but he was simply the most dominant offensive player in the league, not to mention its best rebounder.)

With Speights gone, the mantle of best team in the SEC should remain with Tennessee. The combo of Smith and small forward J. P. Prince is as good as any duo in the league. Like every team in the league (except South Carolina), the Vols' ceiling will be defined by how well a couple of newcomers play. With the lack of experience, the SEC may be in the same boat as it was in last season, with no team capable of getting past the Sweet 16 without a favorable draw. But this provides an opportunity for the teams whose fans do not sing along to "Rocky Top." Without a second (or technically, a first) juggernaut in the conference, there's room for a surprising team or two to be chasing an at-large bid in March.

	2008 Record	Returning Minutes (%)	2009 Prediction
East			
Tennessee	14-2	54	13-3
Florida	8-8	82	12-4
Kentucky	12-4	51	10-6
Vanderbilt	10-6	43	7-9
South Carolina	5-11	87	6-10
Georgia	4-12	56	5-11
West			
Mississippi	7-9	60	10-6
Alabama	5-11	57	9-7
Miss. St.	12-4	53	7-9
LSU	6-10	83	7-9
Arkansas	9-7	19	6-10
Auburn	4-12	66	4-12

One encouraging sign is the two new head coaches hired into vacancies created by midseason resignations last year. LSU was able to snag former Stanford head coach Trent Johnson. In three of his four seasons at Stanford, Johnson led the Cardinal team to the NCAA tournament and was coming off a Sweet 16 appearance as a two-seed. It says a lot that he was willing to leave that situation for a program that had won just 13 games last season. There are better times ahead for the Tigers. Perhaps not immediately, but given Johnson's history at Stanford and Nevada, it would be surprising if he could not win with the resources available in Baton Rouge.

Over at South Carolina, where Dave Odom announced his retirement last January, they hired former Western Kentucky head coach Darrin Horn. Like Johnson, Horn led the Hilltoppers to a Sweet 16 appearance last season. Winning in Columbia is not the fairest measure of a coach, but with Horn, the Gamecocks got someone with a track record of success as a head coach.

All in all, the SEC is in a state of flux, but it's part of a cycle. For two seasons, the conference had the best team in the nation. Now the SEC is struggling to develop a team that has those aspirations. Surely it will happen, and the new faces on the scene this season may be a part of that resurgence.

ALABAMA

2008: 17-16 (5-11 SEC)
Lost to Mississippi State 69-67 (OT), SEC Quarterfinal
In-conference offense: 1.04 points per possession (8th)
In-conference defense: 1.07 points allowed per possession (8th)

What Alabama did well: *Get offensive rebounds from its frontline.*

Not a lot went right for the Tide in 2008, but one positive was the second-chance opportunities provided by its starting front line. While other SEC teams were better on the offensive boards ('Bama was fourth in offensive rebounding percentage during league play), no other team had three starters with rates as high. For a team that didn't shoot particularly well or make many free throws, the work of Richard Hendrix, Alonzo Gee, and Demetrius Jemison after the first shot went up made the offense passable. The trio ranked third, eighth, and 13th, respectively, in the SEC in offensive rebounding rate, combining to grab almost a third of their team's missed shots. Only Florida had as many as two players in the top 15.

What we learned in 2008: *Sharing the basketball is an insignificant contributor to an offense's success.*

At least it is for Mark Gottfried's offense. Last season, 56 percent of Alabama's field goals were assisted, which was easily the highest mark of the 10 teams Gottfried has coached in Tuscaloosa. However, last season's offense was the least effective since the 2003 team. The success of a Gottfried offense is based on scoring off the dribble, so expect the Tide's assist rate to return to its customary place in the bottom third of the nation this season with Ronald Steele returning to the point guard position. Steele's strength has been his slashing and scoring ability and not his passing. Whether the offense can improve in the process is another story. With Hendrix gone, that will be difficult.

What's in store for 2009

Is there any team in the country with more uncertainty surrounding its 2009 projection than Alabama? The Tide welcomes one of the most heralded recruits in the land in 6-8 JaMychal Green. With Hendrix going pro, Green will be expected to play big-time minutes. Whether he delivers like an all-conference hopeful or someone who needs a year to adjust to the college level is up in the air. Additional good news from the offseason is that Steele is coming back, but there's reason to temper the optimism on this front as well. If Steele can perform at the level he did three years ago, in his sophomore season, then he'll be a welcomed addition. But if he plays like he did during his injury-plagued junior season in 2007, then he'll add very little to what returning point guards Brandon Hollinger or Mikhail Torrance could produce. Beyond that, Alabama will need one of its younger returning players to contribute much more than he did last season. Gottfried had a young bench and didn't use it very much last season.

MEET THE CRIMSON TIDE

Alonzo Gee (6-6, 219, Sr.). Gee does just about everything well. He's not a terrific shooter, but he has such a low turnover rate and is a decent enough offensive rebounder that he's an efficient offensive player despite the shooting mediocrity. A team of five Gee clones might be successful in the SEC. He's versatile enough to make it work.

JaMychal Green (6-8, 225, Fr.). Green was known as an excellent rebounder and shot blocker as a high-schooler. He apparently doesn't have much range, but that didn't stop Blake Griffin, who has similar measurements, from being an offensive force as a freshman last season.

Ronald Steele (6-1, 191, Sr.). As mentioned above, Steele is a bit of a mystery man. In his freshman and junior seasons, he was a pass-only point guard. In his sophomore season, he relied on his dynamic scoring ability. Given that Gee is the only proven commodity in terms of creating shots, the Tide needs Steele to be the slashing point guard he was before his knee went bad.

Brandon Hollinger (5-11, 167, Sr.). Hollinger can play either guard position and was a good perimeter shooter (43 percent on threes) in his freshman season, although he shot only rarely.

Demetrius Jemison (6-7, 234, Jr.). Jemison struggled as the fourth option on offense last season. His value in his first two seasons was as a solid rebounder.

Tony Mitchell (6-6, 185, Fr.). Gem number two in Gottfried's recruiting class, Mitchell will be asked to fill the hole left by departing senior Mykal Riley. Riley's contribution to the 2008 team shouldn't be taken for granted, either. While he struggled with his midrange game, he was one of the best long-range threats in the country, taking seven three-pointers a game and making 43 percent of them.

Senario Hillman (6-1, 188, So.). Hillman's a two-guard who shot 15 percent from three-point range and 56 percent inside the arc. It's a mix that made him an acceptable scenario offensively. Another interesting aspect to Hillman is that he had a low turnover rate despite relying on shots in traffic for his points and being a decent assist man from his position. His 50 percent accuracy at the free-throw line suggests he'll continue to struggle with a more distant three-point shot.

Mikhail Torrance (6-5, 196, Jr.). Torrance will be competing for reserve point guard minutes with Hollinger and incoming juco transfer **Anthony Brock (5-9, 170, Jr.).** Torrance's assist rate would have led the SEC had he met the minutes-played requirement. His turnover rate is on the excessive side, but it at least improved, compared with his freshman season.

Yamene Coleman (6-9, 236, Jr.). Coleman could use a little polish on his offensive game. He does have some value on defense, though.

Andrew Steele (6-3, 195, Fr.). Ronald's younger brother, Andrew projects to be a shooting guard and possibly a year away from serious minutes.

Prospectus says

If Steele and Green meet expectations, then the Crimson Tide has a fighting chance to break the .500 mark and get a double-digit seed to the dance. Those chances increase if Jemison or Mitchell becomes a consistent weapon offensively. Let's face it, much as it was in 2006, the SEC West is up for grabs and there are wins to be had on that side of the conference. However much promise there is, much of the optimism depends on the performance of the freshmen. If they don't come through, it could be another lackluster season.

ARKANSAS

2008: 23-12 (9-7 SEC)
Lost to North Carolina 108-77, NCAA Second Round
In-conference offense: 1.05 points per possession (7th)
In-conference defense: 1.00 points allowed per possession (3rd)

What Arkansas did well: *Make good on a new coach's prediction of playing fast-paced ball.*

During his introductory press conference, just about every new coach proclaims that up-tempo, aggressive basketball is in the future for his new program. For most coaches, the oncourt record never justifies this claim. And indeed, when John Pelphrey made similar introductory statements as Arkansas' new head coach in April 2007, there should have been reason for skepticism—his South Alabama teams usually played at a slower-than-average pace, despite Pelphrey's liberal use of a pressing defense. But Pelphrey made good on his preseason statements in 2008. Arkansas' average tempo was the third fastest in the SEC during conference games last season.

What we learned in 2008: *It's a luxury to take over a program with an experienced roster.*

Only three new coaches in the nation last season had more experience at their disposal than John Pelphrey had. (And only one, Joe Pasternack at New Orleans, acquired his veteran roster without being promoted from an assistant coach position at the same school.) Arkansas started four seniors and a sophomore during the 2007-2008 season. It's not terribly unusual for a new coach to inherit all five starters from the previous season, but rarely does such a lucky new coach follow one who was fired the season before. For that reason, 2009 should be viewed as the true beginning of the Pelphrey era. Had Stan Heath led the Razorbacks to a nine-seed in the NCAA tournament (three spots better than in 2007), he probably would have been viewed as merely meeting expectations.

Pelphrey deserves a little extra credit for last season's success since he brought in a significantly different philosophy on both ends of the floor and made it work with players exclusively programmed by Heath before last season. But this season the hard core program-building begins. All five players that started in the Razorbacks' NCAA tournament games are gone, and by the time the SEC tournament tips off, only Stefan Welsh will have played more minutes under Heath than Perphrey. Would-be-junior Patrick Beverley was the most serious of those losses. The Hogs' third-leading scorer was kicked off the team in August for academic reasons.

What's in store for 2009

It's always difficult to make projections about a team that loses seven of its top nine players, but one thing to watch from Arkansas this season is where its offense comes from. Pelphrey's five-year run at South Alabama featured guard-dominated teams that launched a lot of three-pointers, true to the philosophy of Rick Pitino, for whom Pelphrey played his college ball at Kentucky. Pelphrey inherited a couple of skilled big men at Arkansas, namely, Darian Townes and Charles Thomas, and as a team, the Hogs took only about 30 percent of their shots from three-point range, the lowest mark in the conference. With both those men gone and an incoming class heavy on guards, expect to see more long-distance shots this season, despite that fact that the three-point line is being moved back.

MEET THE RAZORBACKS

Michael Washington (6-10, 224, Jr.). Though he might not duplicate what Darian Townes did in the middle of last season, Washington showed signs that he's capable of becoming one of the better all-around centers in the conference, looking at his role off the bench in 2008. Offensively, his finishing ability is not on Townes's level. Washington is more perimeter-oriented than the typical 6-10 player—about one in five of his shots came from three-point range last season. On the other hand, his rebound rates on both ends of the floor and his blocked-shot rate were better than Townes's, although Washington probably faced weaker competition in his limited minutes on the floor.

Stefan Welsh (6-2, 185, Jr.). Welsh will start at the two-guard and generally settles for the three-pointer on offense. He made about a third of his attempts last season. He had the most trouble of anyone adjusting to Pelphrey's offense as his turnover rate exploded.

Jason Henry (6-6, 195, Fr.). Henry was a late signing for Pelphrey, and with Beverley gone, he'll have all the opportunities he wants to showcase his scoring ability.

Rotnei Clarke (6-0, 170, Fr.). Clarke is going to get a lot of minutes at the point guard spot. He's the favorite to take over the starting job usually held by Gary Ervin for the past two seasons.

Courtney Fortson (5-10, 175, Fr.). Like Clarke, Fortson is a highly touted freshman point guard, which means that nearly all of Arkansas' minutes at that position will be handled by rookies this season.

Michael Sanchez (6-8, 231, So.). Sanchez took a redshirt last season, but will battle for a starting role on the front line. He picked up some game experience in the offseason on a team that toured China and included LSU's Garrett Temple and Alabama's Demetrius Jemison.

Marcus Britt (6-2, 191, So.). Britt's offense is limited, but his defense may earn him significant playing time this season.

Andre Clark (6-9, 205, Fr.). Clark enrolled for the spring semester last season, but was redshirted. He's expected to bring a shot-blocking presence to the defense. Fellow freshman **Brandon Moore (6-9, 185)** will see a few minutes at the power forward spot as well.

Montrell McDonald (6-6, 200, Jr.). McDonald has a season of Division I experience at George Washington, where he struggled as a freshman. He has since played a season of juco ball, where he posted an effective field-goal percentage of around 60 and a free-throw rate of around 50 percent. Those numbers bode well for his earning some minutes as a shooting guard/small forward in the SEC.

Prospectus says

It doesn't take a crazy imagination to see Washington being a better-than-average SEC center. There are a lot of newcomers to work into the mix, though, and it would be a bit extreme to think that this team would get anywhere near a tournament berth because of that. Considering that every member of this roster will be eligible to return for the 2010 season, it will be more easy to accept losses as this team develops and prepares to make a more serious run towards the top of the conference in another season. This year will be a much greater challenge for Pelphrey than 2008 was.

AUBURN

2008: 14-16 (4-12 SEC)
Lost to Vanderbilt 93-82, SEC First Round
In-conference offense: 1.06 points per possession (3rd)
In-conference defense: 1.15 points allowed per possession (12th)

What Auburn did well: *Get respectable offense from an undersized lineup with no bench.*

Any analysis of Auburn's 2008 season has to be made with the understanding that Jeff Lebo's team looked much different from what he was expecting in the summer of 2007. Both Korvotney Barber and Josh Dollard were supposed to play the entire season as starters. Barber made it through 10 games before breaking a bone in his nonshooting hand, which sidelined him for the remainder of the season. Dollard was given a medical redshirt for reasons that were never detailed by Auburn. Those were the major alterations to the roster, but for completeness, it's worth mentioning that reserve guard Archie Miaway missed the entire season for academic reasons, and 7-1 center Sylla Boubacar missed all but three games with a broken foot.

The Tigers basically limped through the SEC por-

tion of the schedule with seven available scholarship players. Lebo's starting lineup for most of that time—the "iron five"—had only one player taller than 6-5. For these reasons, the Tigers deserve recognition for putting together the third-best offense in the conference during league play. Granted, it was a distant third behind Tennessee and Florida, and the defense was last in the SEC by a significant margin, but considering the cards Lebo was dealt, the season could have turned into an Oregon State–like disaster. Because the team could score, it didn't.

What we learned in 2008: *Quan Prowell's season deserves mention by somebody somewhere.*

What Quan Prowell did at Auburn last season was borderline amazing. At 6-9, he wasn't just Auburn's center; he was their entire front line. (I'm not exaggerating. Jeff Lebo said essentially the same thing after Auburn's loss to Vanderbilt in the SEC tournament in which Prowell fouled out with just under 12 minutes remaining: "When Quan goes out, our whole front line is gone.") The thing is, had Dollard and Barber played a full season, Prowell would have gotten most of his minutes at the small forward.

As it was, Prowell had to defend centers and play against them offensively. Yet, his efficiency went up simultaneously with an increase in usage. Prowell made 62 percent of his twos and 41 percent of his threes to go from being an ordinary role player in his junior season to one of the most versatile little big men in the country as a senior. Nationwide, there were only eight players who made at least 40 percent of their threes and 60 percent of their twos. Prowell will vanish into the mysterious world of overseas hoops, but let it be known that in different circumstances, in a different time, he could have been a hero to us all.

What's in store for 2009

Lebo has to deal with a couple of planned absences this season in the form of Frank Tolbert and Quan Prowell using up their eligibility. In addition, Dollard was dismissed from the team for an unspecified violation of team rules, and Sylla and reserve forward Matt Heramb elected to transfer. If Auburn wants to think about a .500 record in conference, the defense has to improve. It almost surely will, because the Tigers tested the limits of how poor a power-conference defense can be in 2008. The question is how much improvement will occur.

Getting Barber in the starting lineup everyday will help, as he is a very good defensive rebounder and an excellent shot-blocker. Having Dollard return would have been even better. In 2007 when both players started throughout the season, the defense was actually slightly stronger than the offense. Now, one has to wonder exactly how much better the defense can be.

MEET THE TIGERS

Korvotney Barber (6-7, 225, Sr.). Barber played one more game than allowed for a medical redshirt, so barring a successful appeal, this will be his last season. If so, appreciate his uniqueness now. The dude is a career 43 percent free-throw shooter who's nevertheless made 62 percent of his field-goal attempts. There's a perfectly logical explanation for this—about three-quarters of his shots are layups or dunks, and he has little range beyond that. His offensive rebounding was missed last season.

Rasheem Barrett (6-5, 220, Sr.). Barrett surprised in 2008 in that his effective field-goal percentage jumped from 44 to 51, which included a slight bump upward in usage, also. It will be interesting to see what he does with more help up front this season.

Quantez Robertson (6-3, 193, Sr.). Robertson's specialty is just being there. Over his career, he's played 51 games against SEC opponents and put in at least 30 minutes in all but three of those contests. He's a steady point guard who doesn't shoot much or commit a lot of turnovers.

DeWayne Reed (6-1, 175, Jr.). Reed is a combo guard who found himself in the starting lineup last season but struggled to produce.

Frankie Sullivan (6-2, 170, Fr.). Sullivan can play the point and scored 51 in the Alabama 2A championship game last season.

Lucas Hargrove (6-6, 188, Jr.). The injuries and suspensions gave Hargrove an opportunity for playing time that he otherwise wouldn't have received. The high point of his season was a 28-point effort against Alabama in late February. His rate numbers indicate he could handle more playing time.

Archie Miaway (6-4, 203, Sr.). Miaway is purely a

three-point shooter on offense. He made 33 percent of those shots when he last played in 2007.

Brendon Knox (6-10, 220, Jr.). It's a decade-long tradition at Auburn to heavily recruit the junior-college ranks. Knox is one of four juco signees for Lebo and the most likely to have an impact this season. **Tay Waller (6-2, 180, Jr.)** could also provide some useful minutes as a long-range specialist.

Kenny Gabriel (6-8, 190, Fr.). Gabriel needs to add weight before he can expect big minutes against SEC power forwards.

Prospectus says
Jeff Lebo is in a rare spot. He enters his fifth season with a record of 19-45 in SEC play. Not many coaches get a fifth year under those circumstances, so you can understand why he loaded up on the junior-college kids. He needs a postseason appearance of some sort to justify his boss's patience. The good news is that the Tigers could be starting three seniors, which would give them one of the most experienced lineups in the league. Replacing Prowell and Dollard will prove difficult, though getting to 8-8 seemed like a reasonable expectation with a fully stocked team last season, but with more personnel losses it's less realistic in 2009. Going .500 in the conference would have to be considered a momentum builder, given Auburn's recent history.

FLORIDA

2008: 24-12 (8-8 SEC)
Lost to Massachusetts 78-66, NIT Semifinal
In-conference offense: 1.11 points per possession (2nd)
In-conference defense: 1.10 points allowed per possession (10th)

What Florida did well: *Get a lot of mileage out of little experience.*
Only one team in the land (The Citadel) had less experience than Florida had last season. So naturally, there was some uncertainty as to what the Gators could accomplish in 2008. Overall, the fans had to be pleased that at the beginning of March, Florida had a chance to play itself into an at-large bid. Four consecutive losses before Selection Sunday sealed its fate, but with Billy Donovan playing Walter Hodge and a bunch of new guys, a deep NIT run

wasn't the worst-case scenario envisioned before the season started.

What we learned in 2008: *Billy Donovan believes offense wins championships.*

Aspiring basketball coaches would be well advised to turn to Billy Donovan for guidance on scoring points in the modern game. Even with a bunch of kids who either were fresh out of high school or had spent their college years on the bench, Florida again put together an offense that opponents had great difficulty defending against.

No, it wasn't at the level of the Noah/Horford teams, but those were historically effective offensive squads. Last season's offense was the second best in the SEC and finished 12th nationally in adjusted offensive efficiency. In the five years we've been computing the data, Florida has never finished outside the top 15. Last season, the Gators' main problem was that their three-point accuracy tumbled from an astounding 40.9 percent in 2007 to 36.3. They did, however, excel in the other areas in which they normally excel—two-point shooting, offensive rebounding, and turnovers. That was good enough to score a point per possession in 13 of 16 conference games.

Mark Few's flex offense and John Calipari's dribble-drive motion have become nationally recognized systems copied by others in the coaching profession. It's time Donovan's spread pick-and-roll reaches that status as well.

What's in store for 2009

There was a lot more continuity this summer than in 2007, when Donovan had to make up his mind about moving to the NBA and then had to deal with an entirely new starting lineup. But that's not to say there's an abundance of stability in Gainesville heading into this season. Hopes for 2009 suffered a blow when center Marreese Speights opted to play for money this season. Speights has a lot of potential to realize, but he was also incredibly productive in his only season as a starter. His departure cannot be fixed with a mere Band-Aid.

Additionally, there are five freshmen to assimilate into the mix, which includes five rising sophomores, and all the new Gators will be expecting playing time. No other program in the country will have the quantity of young talent that Florida does this season. But without Speights dominating in the post, even the players who have a history in Gainesville will have to find a new identity to make this season a success.

MEET THE GATORS

Nick Calathes (6-6, 185, So.). Calathes put together as impressive a season as one can while failing to reach 50 in effective field-goal percentage. Though he did log some minutes as a point guard, most of his minutes came elsewhere—and he produced the highest assist rate in the SEC by assisting on a third of his teammates' made baskets. In fact, no other player in Division I listed at 6-6 or taller had a rate that high. While his shooting from the field was mediocre, he did manage to get to the free-throw line 199 times and make 72 percent of those attempts, which offset the effect of his missed shots from the field. Throw in his low turnovers, and there's a lot to build on for his sophomore season.

Walter Hodge (6-0, 170, Sr.). The lone holdover who got significant minutes on the national title teams, Hodge adjusted well to his new surrounding cast. He's an efficient scorer who performs well despite having almost no midrange game. He either shoots threes (he's a career 40 percent shooter) or attacks the hoop.

Jai Lucas (5-11, 150, So.). Lucas arrived in Gainesville with the reputation of an impact playmaker, but didn't exactly distinguish himself in his rookie year. He committed few turnovers, but he also had one of the lowest assist rates for any point guard in the country. Considering how well the Florida offense performed in 2008, Lucas deserved some credit for letting that happen. He is capable of hitting the occasional three-pointer when necessary, but at 5-11, he understandably had lots of trouble finishing in the paint. Without Speights around, he'll have to get more involved offensively this season.

Chandler Parsons (6-9, 200, So.). A younger and more skilled version of fellow Gator Dan Werner, Parsons takes about half his shots from beyond the arc, but needs to be more selective (or, I suppose, more accurate).

The next wave of freshmen. Five more freshmen will suit up for Florida this season, and all five will get some playing time. **Eloy Vargas (6-10, 215)** and **Kenneth Kadji (6-10, 240)** both possess serious size, so Donovan will have options to fill the void of Speights, even if it's crazy to expect another human being to produce like Speights. **Erving Walker (5-6, 160)** will be the smallest player on any power conference team's roster and will try to find time at the point after what Lucas, Hodge, and Calathes give the team. Also coming on board are **Rayford Shipman (6-5, 195)** and **Allan Chaney (6-8, 220),** who will battle for time at one of the forward positions.

Dan Werner (6-7, 235, Jr.). Despite his size, Werner relies heavily on his perimeter shooting offensively. This suffered in SEC play, where he went 21-of-75 (28 percent) on threes. Werner is a solid rebounder, so it's not as if he spends all this time avoiding contact.

Adam Allen (6-8, 225, So.). Ditto Werner's description here with respect to shot selection, however Allen made 42 percent of his 76 three-point attempts.

Alex Tyus (6-8, 203, So.). Tyus is more of a true power forward, but had trouble finding playing time last season.

Prospectus says

Had Speights returned, Florida fans would have been within their rights to contemplate challenging for an SEC title again. Without him, there's going to be some early growing pains as Donovan finds a combination he can be comfortable with during conference play. The nucleus of Calathes, Hodge, Lucas, and Parsons along with the freshmen big men will have Florida competing for an at-large berth. Given the long-term consistency of the offense, a seed in the four-to-six range isn't an unrealistic goal.

GEORGIA

2008: 17-17 (4-12 SEC)
Lost to Xavier 73-61, NCAA First Round
In-conference offense: 0.97 points per possession (12th)
In-conference defense: 1.03 points allowed per possession (6th)

What Georgia did well: *Provide inspiration for any team that thinks its season is over.*
Georgia provided the most improbable tournament feat of 2008 when it won the SEC tournament. Before the SEC tournament began, the chances of Georgia's winning four straight were an estimated 0.31 percent (or about one in 300), according to Bill James's log5 method and winning percentages de-

rived from adjusted offensive and defensive efficiencies. But we don't need to use complicated methods to determine that what Georgia did was unlikely. It went 4-12 during the SEC regular season. Based on its .250 winning percentage, we can crudely assume that Georgia had a 25 percent chance to win a game on a neutral floor against an SEC opponent.

The likelihood that a team with a 25 percent success rate will win four times in a row is 0.39 percent, so it seems reasonable to say that the Bulldogs' accomplishment was highly unusual. Of course, this figure didn't anticipate that a tornado would strike the Georgia Dome during the quarterfinal round—a meteorological event that forced Georgia to win two games in one day in order to reach the championship game.

Only one team has made the NCAA tournament field with a worse conference record. That was the 1997 Fairfield team, which went 2-12 to finish dead last in the MAAC and then proceeded to win three consecutive games in Buffalo to advance to the NCAA tournament, where Fairfield gave a one-seed, North Carolina, a tense battle for 37 minutes. The Stags' 0.143 conference winning percentage suggests their chances of winning three straight games against MAAC competition was 0.29 percent.

A deeper look shows that 1997 Fairfield has an edge on 2008 Georgia in the underdog department. The Stags were outscored by an average of 9.6 points in conference play, whereas Georgia was outscored by a mere 4.3 points per game. Amazingly, Fairfield won the MAAC tourney relatively comfortably—outscoring opponents by a total of 25 points in three games. Meanwhile, Georgia won its four games by a total of 19 points, including two in overtime. But Georgia has the trump card of winning two games in a single day—something no team has ever done on its way to earning an NCAA tournament bid—and that could be an equalizer.

This is not likely to be an argument that you'll overhear in a bar anytime soon. But the tale of Fairfield in 1997 and Georgia in 2008 can provide inspiration for myriad teams that think experiencing March Madness is a lost cause because they've piled up a bunch of regular-season losses.

What we learned in 2008: *The fortunes of a college basketball coach can change in 48 hours.*
Say what you will about the job security for a coach of a big-time basketball program, but in what other line of work can your employers do a 180 on your future after two days of work? Dennis Felton wasn't

exactly getting an endorsement from athletic director Damon Evans on the eve of the SEC tournament, but after Georgia's miracle run, there was little doubt the coach would remain in Athens for this season.

What's in store for 2009

The immediate challenge for Dennis Felton is replacing Sundiata Gaines and Billy Humphrey. Gaines was a four-year starter at point guard, leading Georgia in minutes in each of his four seasons. He was the team's most frequent shooter last season and got to the free-throw line 180 times on a team that struggled in that department. He was also more than an adequate defender, especially considering all the work he had to do offensively.

Humphrey was arrested for a DUI in June and dismissed from the team shortly thereafter. He was about a 40 percent three-point shooter for his career and received starter's minutes in each of his first three seasons. Georgia's offense was the least efficient in the conference during regular season play, and the team was a distant last, so it's hard to imagine the offense getting worse. But at the same time, Felton has lost his two most effective scorers, so scoring is expected to be a challenge again.

MEET THE BULLDOGS

Terrance Woodbury (6-7, 210, Sr.). Because Woodbury plays shorter than his height, preferring to settle for shots on the perimeter, he doesn't get to the line often or rebound particularly well. He's the most likely candidate to inherit the shots that Sundiata Gaines leaves behind, so if Georgia's offense is to improve to respectability this season, he'll have to do better than the 47.5 effective field-goal percentage he posted last season.

Jeremy Price (6-8, 270, So.). Price was expected to give Dennis Felton some minutes as a freshman, and he did just that. He wasn't the most effective scorer, but he did enough as a freshman to warrant optimism for a productive future in Athens. It wouldn't be a shocker if he led the team in scoring this season.

Howard "Trey" Thompkins (6-9, 230, Fr.). Thompkins is the most likely impact player in a recruiting class of five. He'll give the Dawgs some

frontline size, which is needed after the departure of 6-10 senior Dave Bliss.

Albert Jackson (6-10, 250, Jr.). Jackson is raw on the offensive end, making just 44 percent of his shots last season. But given the lack of depth up front, he should see his minutes increase this season.

Zac Swansey (6-1, 175, So.). Swansey is expected to take over the starting point guard role, but he'll play a less prominent role in the offense than Gaines if what Swansey did last season is any indication.

Chris Barnes (6-7, 250, So.). Barnes missed 13 games, mostly because of a knee injury. (Although he did miss one game when he developed an eye infection after forgetting to remove his contacts before sleeping one night.) When he did play, he showed that he could be a competent scorer, rebounder, and shot blocker.

Troy Brewer (6-5, 170, So.). Brewer is strictly a three-point shooter who made 30 percent of those shots in his freshman season.

Travis Leslie (6-4, 185, Fr.). Leslie's a small forward/shooting guard who should get some time with Humphrey no longer available.

Corey Butler (6-3, 195, Sr.). Butler gets occasional use as a shooting guard that can also help on the offensive boards.

Ricky McPhee (6-1, 185, Jr.). McPhee is a transfer from Gardner Webb, where he showed the ability to get shots off but not make many. Still, the ability to create shots is a skill that is needed on this squad. Unfortunately, he only went to the line 21 times in 2006, which suggests that he's another Georgia guard averse to the paint.

Prospectus says

With the departure of Gaines, it's hard to imagine Georgia being more difficult to defend this season. Just about every player Felton puts on the floor this season isn't much of a threat to put the ball on the floor. The good news is that the team is young. The defense had its moments last season, and its improvement could allow this team to get more than four wins in conference play, thereby giving Georgia fans hopes that 2010 or 2011 could be a break-through season as the team gets more experience.

KENTUCKY

2008: 18-13 (12-4 SEC)
Lost to Marquette 74-66, NCAA First Round
In-conference offense: 1.03 points per possession (9th)
In-conference defense: 1.02 points allowed per possession (4th)

What Kentucky did well: *Buy into the style of its new coach.*

Not that UK did it especially well, but the team didn't take long to put Tubby-ball in the rearview mirror and openly embrace what Billy Gillispie likes to do. The team relied on the three-pointer a lot less, both fouled and got fouled a lot more, and defended the three-point line better than in previous seasons. Let's not kid ourselves, though. The 2008 Wildcats were a modest downgrade from Tubby Smith's last team. A couple of injuries didn't help matters any. Shooting guard Jodie Meeks tried to play through a sports hernia until finally shutting it down in mid-February, and center Patrick Patterson missed the last five games of the season with a broken ankle.

Of course, they weren't the only guys who dealt with injuries. In addition to Patterson and Meeks, Ramel Bradley, Joe Crawford, Derrick Jasper, and Ramon Harris missed at least one game to injury. Some observers might have labeled Gillispie's inaugural season in Lexington a disappointment. But considering the rash of injuries and the requirement that his players learn a new style of play, Kentucky did well to find itself in the NCAA tournament at the end of the season.

What we learned in 2008: *Randolph Morris was a better college player than he was given credit for.*

Twenty years from now, no Kentucky fans will be bragging to their kids that they got to see Randolph Morris play. But the single biggest reason for Kentucky's decline last season wasn't the injuries but the inability to replace Morris. Patrick Patterson may eventually surpass what Morris brought to the table in the 2007 season—the freshman production for each was remarkably similar.

Because Morris didn't have the reputation of hustling or being a hard worker, he wasn't a fan fa-

vorite. Obviously, declaring for the draft in 2006, when he had good reason to believe he wouldn't be a first-round pick, didn't score any points with the Cats' faithful, either. But it's important to remember that Morris was the best thing this team had on both ends of the floor in 2007. Even though his NBA career may be brief, his production at Kentucky was extremely difficult to replace.

What's in store for 2009

Kentucky won 12 games in the SEC last season, when its season-long production suggested that it was an 8-8 team. The Wildcats outscored their opponents by a mere 10 points over the 16-game schedule, yet ended up eight games over .500. Across Division I, only Wagner had a bigger positive departure from expected performance. A 41-point loss to Vanderbilt skewed Kentucky's total a bit, but the other 15 games were decided by single-digits at the end of regulation. So while the Wildcats may improve, they also may have a worse conference record to show for it unless their good fortune in close games continues.

And history says it won't. The table lists the nine teams that exceeded their expected record the most in this decade, and what they did the following season. ("Luck" denotes the difference between actual winning percentage and expected winning percentage, based on points scored and allowed during the conference season.)

	Lucky Season		Next Season	
	W-L	Luck	W-L	Luck
2006 UMKC	11-5	+.261	6-8	-.079
2001 UC Irvine	15-1	+.253	13-5	-.017
2000 James Madison	12-4	+.248	6-10	+.008
2006 Western Michigan	10-8	+.221	9-7	-.051
2006 Northern Arizona	12-2	+.215	11-5	+.028
2005 Davidson	16-0	+.215	10-5	-.134
2005 Ark.-Little Rock	10-4	+.214	5-9	-.061
2006 BYU	12-4	+.208	13-3	+.025
2001 Central Michigan	14-4	+.205	5-13	-.040
Average		+.227		-.036

I'm calling the difference between actual record and expected record "luck" because there's no skill in the ability to duplicate success in that category. And that's what this chart demonstrates. Teams that have been extremely lucky one season have gotten what they deserve the next. But they're not special—most teams get what they deserve every season.

MEET THE WILDCATS

Patrick Patterson (6-8, 232, So.). In a normal season, Patterson would have been recognized as one of the better freshmen in the country. But with all the hype over the potential one-and-done players and the lack of Kentucky's appearance in the top 25 during the season, Patterson's consistent production largely went unnoticed. He was no Richard Hendrix or Marreese Speights, but there was no SEC big man other than those two who produced like the Kentucky freshman did. Patterson underwent ankle surgery shortly after the season ended and spent most of the summer recovering from that.

Jodie Meeks (6-4, 207, Jr.). Speaking of offseason surgeries, Meeks underwent a procedure to repair the aforementioned sports hernia. With the loss of Bradley and Crawford, Gillispie desperately needs someone to take some of the vacated offensive load. Even while being less than 100 percent when he did play last season, Meeks demonstrated that he can take plenty of shots and score somewhat efficiently while doing so.

Perry Stevenson (6-9, 201, Jr.). Stevenson was the rock of the team last season as one of only two players who appeared in all 31 games. He's strictly a role player but a very good one. Surround him with versatile offensive players, and Stevenson becomes a very good complement. He's an effective shot blocker as well.

Darius Miller (6-7, 225, Fr.). Miller is a wing who grew up about a two-hour drive from Lexington. He'll be expected to contribute immediately.

Ramon Harris (6-6, 213, Jr.). The latest player to emerge from Anchorage, Harris probably benefited the most from Meeks's injury in terms of playing time. He's a timid shooter, but, like Stevenson, makes a high percentage of his shots.

DeAndre Liggins (6-6, 200, Fr.). Liggins's eligibility is still in doubt as this book goes to press. He appears to bring a similar skill set than the recently transferred Derrick Jasper brought to the team, but perhaps with more offensive game. Despite the freshman's impressive size, he's capable of being a point guard.

Michael Porter (6-2, 190, Jr.). Porter is the other option at the point for Gillispie. His enormous turnover rate last season indicates that Liggins, if eligible, will have the opportunity to start out of the box.

Josh Harrellson (6-11, 270, Jr.). Harrelson is a juco product who is expected to be Stevenson's understudy in the middle.

Kevin Galloway (6-6, 205, Jr.). Galloway comes to UK via the College of Southern Idaho, but he also has 13 games' worth of Division I experience at USC.

A. J. Stewart (6-8, 207, So.). Stewart saw spot duty in 22 games last season, but demonstrated that he was an above-average defensive rebounder.

Prospectus says

It won't be easy to replace Bradley and Crawford, but Patterson and Meeks are a decent enough duo to start with. With a little help from the new faces and a better understanding of what Gillispie wants to do, this team should post a winning record. Kentucky's SEC record won't be a good gauge of whether this team is better than last season's. The nonconference slate will be, however, considering that UK lost every decent challenge it faced before conference play last season. It's a realistic scenario for this team to be two games worse in the SEC than it was last season, but two or three seed lines better when the NCAA tournament draw is announced.

LSU

2008: 13-18 (6-10 SEC)
Lost to South Carolina 77-73, SEC First Round
In-conference offense: 1.01 points per possession (11th)
In-conference defense: 1.06 points allowed per possession (7th)

What LSU did well: *Finish strong.*

With a record of 13-18 and 6-10 in SEC play to go along with a midseason coaching change, the 2007-

2008 LSU season may look like a disaster superficially. But considering that the team was 8-13 and 1-6 (and quite deserving of that record) when Brady was let go on February 8, a midseason U-turn didn't appear likely. Nevertheless, the Tigers went 5-5 from that point on, with their most impressive win coming at Florida on February 13, a game that essentially put the Gators' NCAA hopes on life support.

No single attribute was responsible for the improvement after interim coach Butch Pierre took over. LSU was better in most aspects of the game. Not great, mind you, but better. In the seven conference games under Brady, LSU was outscored by a total of 72 points. In the 10 games under Pierre, the Tigers *outscored* the competition by seven points. It may be overstating things to say that the players had quit under Brady, but perhaps they had lost their way a bit. There was much hand-wringing when Brady was fired. After all, it had just been a season and a half since he took LSU to the Final Four, the culmination of a nine-season effort to resurrect an LSU basketball program that was hit hard by NCAA sanctions after the Lester Earl scandal.

In retrospect, athletic director Skip Bertman had little choice. The team was imploding, the fans were disinterested, and it didn't hurt to try to salvage the rest of the season in an effort to prove to a prospective new coach that the cupboard wasn't entirely bare. Bertman's move did exactly that.

What we learned in 2008: *Size isn't everything.*
Not that this is a shocker, but merely putting tall athletic players on the floor does not automatically make for an effective basketball team. Despite having one of the more impressive shot-blocking duos in the nation in Anthony Randolph and Chris Johnson, LSU's defense was less than ordinary for a power-conference team. Its offense was even worse. The common weakness on both ends of the floor was an inability to rebound.

What's in store for 2009
Trent Johnson was lured from Stanford to take over the reins in Baton Rouge. Stylistically, Johnson's philosophy is similar to Brady's. He has a history of building teams around size and using that size as the cornerstone to create a solid defense that, oddly, doesn't try to force many turnovers. He insists on forcing opponents to take difficult two-point shots without sending them to the free-throw line.

MEET THE TIGERS

Marcus Thornton (6-4, 198, Sr.). Thornton didn't quite get the attention he deserved during his junior season, because his team had nothing to play for by the end of January and Anthony Randolph occupied the eyes of anyone assessing the pro potential of amateur athletes. Thornton got lots of minutes and took lots of shots in his first season of Division I ball. He was second in the conference in scoring average and was slightly more efficient that the average SEC starter. No doubt his scoring numbers also benefitted from the fact that just three of his teammates were willing to shoot. If Trent Johnson's offense is performing well, expect Thornton to be taking fewer shots in 2009 but making a higher percentage.

Tasmin Mitchell (6-7, 230, Jr.). Before we get too carried away wondering how LSU could disintegrate from Final Four team to SEC bottom feeder so quickly, consider that Mitchell was expected to carry a chunk of the offensive load last season, but only logged 66 minutes in three games before injuring an ankle that kept him out the rest of the season. Mitchell is a versatile wing who's an effective scorer, rebounder, and defender.

Chris Johnson (6-11, 205, Sr.). Johnson's importance on the team increased in May, when blue-chip center J'Mison Morgan asked out of his commitment to LSU. Johnson is no slouch, though. He's only a so-so rebounder, considering his size, but he can score in a variety of ways and was third, behind Jarvis Varnado and Steven Hill, in the SEC in block percentage. He can defend centers, but offensively he's more comfortable farther away from the basket.

Terry Martin (6-6, 207, Sr.). In his first full season as a Tiger, Martin hit just 30.5 percent of his three-point attempts. This is a problem because Martin is foremost a spot-up shooter. In SEC play, he was just 14-of-58 (24.1 percent), suggesting that the quality of the defense has a lot to do with his ability to convert. Martin's three-point accuracy should be a good barometer of LSU's offense in 2009. If his teammates are skilled enough to earn the defense's respect, he should get better shots.

Garrett Temple (6-6, 195, Sr.). Temple has had a reputation as a defensive specialist since he was a freshman shutting down J. J. Redick in the NCAA tournament. He was actually a less frequent shooter last season than in his freshman or sophomore seasons. Temple took just one in 10 of his team's shots while on the floor, the second-lowest rate among SEC starters.

Storm Warren (6-8, 215, Fr.). One of two freshmen who should see significant minutes this season, Warren figures to get some run as a power forward with shot-blocking abilities.

Delwan Graham (6-5, 210, Fr.). Graham is the other freshman and will get some time at the small forward.

Garrett Green (6-10, 218, So.). In Trent Johnson's desperate search for big bodies, Green will undoubtedly get a chance to produce a Chris Johnson–like leap from his freshman to sophomore season. The most startling thing about Green's statistical résumé is that he played 241 minutes last season and shot just seven free throws.

Alex Farrer (6-5, 200, So.). Judge Alex was part of an LSU bench that was rarely a factor offensively. Farrer joins **Bo Spencer (6-1, 180, So.)** and **Quintin Thornton (6-8, 225, Sr.)** as scholarship-earning returnees from that group. Considering how rarely the trio shot, it's not likely that any of the three will emerge as a significant contributor in 2009.

Prospectus says

There's a case that every team in the SEC West will gravitate to the .500 mark (or maybe slightly under it), and LSU is no different. Even with the departure of the talented Randolph, the two potential impact freshmen plus the return of Mitchell give the Tigers a shot at finishing in the middle of the SEC in Trent Johnson's first season. The offense will continue to sputter for the most part, but Johnson has the talent in place to put a solid defense on the court. Divisional titles are worth something only in the eye of desperate banner makers, but in LSU's case, it would be progress. Honors more substantial will have to wait until Johnson has a full year or two of recruiting under his belt.

MISSISSIPPI

2008: 24-11 (7-9 SEC)
Lost to Ohio State 81-69, NIT Semifinals
In-conference offense: 1.06 points per possession (4th)
In-conference defense: 1.08 points allowed per possession (9th)

What Ole Miss did well: *Push the tempo.*
After inheriting a slower-than-average team from previous Rebel coach Rod Barnes, Andy Kennedy completed the transformation to an up-tempo product in his second season.

Ole Miss Possessions per 40 minutes
All games (Division I rank)

2004	64.7	(236)
2005	63.7	(288)
2006	66.0	(207)
2007	68.5	(100)
2008	71.2	(42)

The increase in pace was coincident with an increase in offensive efficiency, which was the main shortcoming of the Barnes era. Most importantly, Kennedy has elevated the Rebels' overall play since he took over. It's not to the level of grabbing an NCAA tournament bid yet, but clearly his system is in place. Now it's time to find the talent so that Ole Miss's name gets called on Selection Sunday.

What we learned in 2008: *There's quite possibly an undervaluing of short players in today's recruiting market.*
The single biggest reason for Ole Miss's sudden improvement last season was Chris Warren. At 5-11, Warren was not a highly desired prep player. The only other power-conference school with serious interest was NC State. Nevertheless, Warren became one of the more dynamic point guards in the country upon his arrival. He can hit threes, but can also create off penetration and in transition. He was a great fit for Andy Kennedy's aggressive offense. The emergence of Warren shows that programs in Ole Miss's situation, with a long history of struggling in their league, might do better to take a flyer on short guys rather than bigs.

It wasn't just Warren who could jump in and contribute as a freshman. Other sub-six-footers include St. Mary's Patrick Mills, Penn State's Talor Battle, Nebraska's Cookie Miller, Virginia Tech's Hank Thorns, Michigan's Kelvin Grady, Texas Tech's John Roberson, and UAB's Aaron Johnson. (Florida's Jai Lucas and Syracuse's Jonny Flynn are on that list also, but their immediate impact was expected.) Overall, 46 freshmen shorter than 6-0 appeared in at least 40 percent of their team's minutes, while just 14 freshmen 6-10 or taller found similar playing time. (The population of players shorter than six feet and those 6-10 or taller is roughly equivalent.) I don't know if undersized players are undervalued, but it's clear that they're more likely to make an immediate impact.

What's in store for 2009

Warren and small forward Eniel Polynice make up one of the most exciting tandems in the SEC. If Ole Miss can continue to get out and run, it will continue to put points on the board. But there is a question as to whether the Rebels will be able to run as often as they did last season. Gone from last season's squad are Kenny Williams and Dwayne Curtis, two of the better defensive rebounders in the conference. As the two guys responsible for getting the ball into Warren's hands to start the offensive push, they were very effective. Kennedy will be relying heavily on a freshman and a junior-college transfer to provide rebounding this season.

MEET THE REBELS

Chris Warren (5-11, 170, So.). The other benefit of snagging an undervalued short player off the recruiting trail is that he should stick around for a while, because the NBA front offices value size even more than college recruiters do. The only freshmen who had a higher usage in the SEC last season were Anthony Randolph and A. J. Ogilvy. Randolph is gone to the NBA, and Ogilvy may not make it to his senior season, either.

Eniel Polynice (6-5, 200, Jr.). Polynice struggled as a freshman, but the move to the starting lineup playing alongside Warren helped vault his game to a respectable SEC level as a sophomore. He does a little bit of everything, but an overlooked measure of his performance was a high assist rate. It was ninth-best in the conference and first among non-point-guards.

David Huertas (6-5, 195, Jr.). Huertas brings national-title experience to the team, having played his freshman season at Florida in 2006. Kennedy asks him to shoot lots of threes, and he delivers, making 36 percent of his 208 attempts last season.

Zach Graham (6-5, 220, Jr.). Graham is a little bulkier than Polynice, but was quite similar statistically last season while coming off the bench.

Trevor Gaskins (6-2, 205, So.). Gaskins is another three-point threat. He took about two-thirds of his shots from long range and made 39 percent of them in 2008.

DeAundre Cranston (6-9, 245, Jr.). Cranston comes from Daytona State College and averaged over 10 rebounds a game there last season.

Murphy Holloway (6-7, 215, Fr.). Holloway is the most promising freshman on the roster. He'll bring some athleticism to the forward spot when he plays.

Terrance Henry (6-9, 190, Fr.). Like Holloway, Henry attracted the attention of programs with more tradition than Ole Miss.

Terrico White (6-5, 195, Fr.). White is a possibility in the backcourt.

Malcolm White (6-9, 225, Fr.). Malcolm White played sparingly toward the end of the season. He can hit the offensive boards, but his most unusual stat was playing 173 minutes without recording an assist. That's the most among power-conference players, but pales in comparison to Florida Gulf Coast's Mbainai Narmbaye, who played 441 minutes last season with zero helpers.

Prospectus says

When Ole Miss reeled off 13 consecutive wins to start last season, it appeared that 2008 might be a breakthrough season. Alas, the Rebels' perfect start was very similar to conference mate Vanderbilt. Mississippi had only one true road game, and while the win in Puerto Rico against Clemson was nice, the rest of the schedule didn't feature the quality opponents that would have made Ole Miss's future at the top of the SEC more convincing. Indeed, the final record of 24-11 suggests a breakthrough, but the Rebels' 13-13 record once conference play started suggests otherwise. Getting Ole Miss into at-large consideration remains the long-term goal the Rebels were seeking when they elected to change coaches two seasons ago.

The team will have no seniors and just three juniors on scholarship this season. With the roster continuity expected over the next season or two in Oxford, an improvement on seven wins in conference play will be a good sign of the health of the program in 2009 and 2010. It will mean that the incoming freshmen and rising sophomores who came off the bench last season will have made positive contributions.

MISSISSIPPI STATE

2008: 23-11 (12-4 SEC)
Lost to Memphis 77-74, NCAA Second Round
In-conference offense: 1.05 points per possession (6th)
In-conference defense: 0.96 points allowed per possession (1st)

What Mississippi State did well: *Defend the paint.*
The Bulldogs held opponents to just under 40 percent shooting inside the arc, the best figure in the country. The statistic didn't suffer much in conference play, either. Over time, two-point defense has proven to be a good foundation for a good overall defense and an elite team in general. Of the 50 teams finishing in the top 10 of two-point field-goal percentage defense since 2004, 23 have nabbed a top-four seed. Only 11 teams that were ranked in the top 10 of three-point defense have done so.

So one important building block was in place for the Bulldogs to have an excellent season. That excellent season, however, didn't materialize. It was successful, yes. MSU won the SEC West and grabbed an eight-seed in the tourney where they proceeded to win a first round game and perform well in a tight loss to eventual national runner-up Memphis. But other things prevented this team from being the best in the SEC and getting a two-seed like East division champ Tennessee. The most obvious thing was that in 16 SEC games, opponents took 177 more shots than MSU took.

Mississippi State did take 93 more free throws, but that doesn't make up for the enormous shooting imbalance. The Bulldogs rarely forced turnovers and didn't hit the defensive boards particularly well, either. There's a lot of room for error when you can shut down an opponent's interior game, and Mississippi State used just about all of it.

What we learned in 2008: *Charles Rhodes will not be easily replaced.*
Considering Rhodes played a total of 104 minutes his freshman season, he put together a mighty fine college career from his sophomore season onward. Rhodes immediately prospered upon moving into the starting lineup after Lawrence Roberts and Marcus Campbell left Starkville. For the past three seasons, Rhodes was a reliable scorer as the team's number two option behind Jamont Gordon and was a passable rebounder despite being a 6-8 center.

What's in store for 2009
The offseason was not kind to head coach Rick Stansbury. First, starting two-guard Ben Hansbrough broke the news that he would be happiest playing his final two seasons at Notre Dame. Then, point guard Jamont Gordon decided that he would rather keep his name in the NBA draft, despite having no guarantee that he would even be selected. Both decisions hurt, but Gordon's was by far the most damaging. Having started every Bulldog game for the past three seasons, he dominated the offense at point guard. He led the SEC in usage last season and finished second in each of his first two seasons. He wasn't always the most efficient player, but he took the pressure off his teammates.

The offseason news means Stansbury is down three starters from last season's team. He brings back center Jarvis Varnado, the conference's most intimidating defensive player and hence a big reason why MSU's defense was often dominant, despite forcing few turnovers. Therefore, the defense should remain good enough to keep the team in games. But unless there's another Charles Rhodes story in the making, it's hard to figure out where points will come from. Expect a lot more games in the 60s this season.

MEET THE BULLDOGS

Jarvis Varnado (6-9, 210, Jr.). Varnado staked his claim to being the country's best shot blocker last season by swatting about one in six two-point attempts by his opponents. He has room to improve in other areas, though. Varnado could stand to grab a few more rebounds, and adding a little more bulk should help with this, since the athleticism is there.

His offense is limited to within an arm's reach of the rim. In fact, perhaps no other player in the country takes such a high percentage of his shots inside five feet.

Barry Stewart (6-2, 170, Jr.). After being strictly a three-point shooter his freshman season, Stewart's shot selection became more diverse as a sophomore. His move toward more penetration was a struggle, though—his midrange game was lacking last season.

Phil Turner (6-3, 170, So.). Turner was the biggest minutes-getter off the bench last season. He struggled offensively from the shooting guard spot.

Ravern Johnson (6-7, 175, So.). There are a host of guys who played sparingly last season and who will have to contribute in a meaningful way this season. Johnson averaged about six minutes a game, but he wasn't timid when he did play.

Brian Johnson (6-9, 245, Sr.). Johnson transferred in from Louisville last season and his single greatest problem was handling the basketball. If he limits his turnovers, he can be an effective role player.

Elgin Bailey (6-8, 265, So.). Amazingly, only four times last season was Bailey referred to as "Elgin Baylor" by an announcer. In his cameos, Bailey showed he can grab offensive boards at an impressive rate and get to the line a decent amount.

Dee Bost (6-2, 175, Fr.). Bost had more riding on Gordon's decision than anybody else did. He ran the point for Hargrave Military Academy as the prep school won the national championship. Without a true point guard on the roster, Bost should see a lot of action.

Riley Benock (6-4, 180, So.). The closest thing to a replacement for Ben Hansbrough that Rick Stansbury has, Benock took 33 of his 37 field-goal attempts from three-point range last season, making 42 percent of them.

Jacquiese Holcombe (6-6, 205, Jr.). Holcombe averaged 13.1 points on a true shooting percentage of 58.3 and averaged 7.2 rebounds per game last season at Georgia Perimeter College. Someday, people will be able to use this information to make a decent estimate at how a player will perform at the highest level of college hoops. For now, I just have to eyeball it and say Holcombe will get about 10 minutes a game on this team.

Romero Osby (6-7, 200, Fr.). Another freshman who joins the gaggle of players in the 6-8 to 6-9 range.

Kodi Augustus (6-8, 220, Fr.). Augustus redshirted last season and is a big man with more of a perimeter game.

Prospectus says

The natural analogy for this team is the 2006 team that was young and inexperienced. It followed the 2005 squad that had Roberts and Winsome Frazier, both seniors who led the team to a respectable showing against a one-seed (Duke) in the second round of the NCAA tournament. With Gordon as a freshman and Rhodes as a sophomore, that edition of the Bulldogs went 5-11 in SEC play. There's probably going to be a freshman point guard on this team, too. The influence of Varnado may allow this team to be better than the 2006 team by a game or two.

SOUTH CAROLINA

2008: 14-18 (5-11 SEC)
Lost to Tennessee 89-87, SEC Semifinal
In-conference offense: 1.02 points per possession (10th)
In-conference defense: 1.10 points allowed per possession (11th)

What South Carolina did well: *Take care of the ball.*

Maybe it's not surprising that a team whose guards handled the basketball as much as South Carolina's did should have had such a low turnover rate. But the ability to take care of the ball extended beyond the Gamecock's high-usage, high-minutes backcourt of Devan Downey and Zam Fredrick. No doubt it didn't hurt that those two guys were in charge of the offense's fate on nearly half of its possessions during the season. But it also didn't hurt that three other players in Dave Odom's rotation took more threes than twos, rarely registered an assist, and hence limited risking a turnover more than the typical player would. Still, even the two players who plied their craft in the paint—Mike Holmes and Sam

Muldrow—were amazingly adept at making plays without coughing up the ball.

What we learned in 2008: *It's difficult to win at South Carolina.*

This wasn't learned last season. It's been learned over and over ever since USC joined the Metro Conference in 1983. The past 25 seasons have resulted in just three with a winning record in conference play and zero NCAA tournament wins. The last four coaches to come to Columbia have ended their head-coaching careers there. Even though the Colonial Arena is a shiny and fairly new facility and South Carolina has all the perks that an SEC school gets, former Western Kentucky head coach Darrin Horn took a risk by accepting the job to replace Dave Odom.

If he can lead the program to repeated NCAA tournament appearances, he'll be able to have just about any job in the nation. Based on the last quarter-century of Gamecock basketball, Horn will either become a career assistant, go into the TV business, retire, or become the coach of Northwestern. This is truly one of the most difficult jobs in the college game.

What's in store for 2009

As one would expect with a new coach, there will be some changes this season. Before I talk about upcoming changes, I need to acknowledge the shift that took place last season. After years of having teams that were significantly slower than the typical Division I team, the dynamic backcourt duo who transferred in sped up the Gamecocks' pace to the point that it was actually slightly faster than the of the average college team.

In his first season, Horn will have to rely entirely on players recruited by Odom. Yes, this means a few more spot-up shooters than Horn would like and in general less athleticism than he needs to implement the aggressive defense he deployed at WKU. One thing Carolina fans might expect is that Horn will fix the offense before the defense. Here's how WKU's offensive efficiency (OE) and defensive efficiency (DE) ranked in the Sun Belt over the past five seasons (conference games only).

	OE	DE
2004	2	6
2005	1	10
2006	2	5
2007	1	8
2008	2	1

Horn finally put together the complete team in 2008, but before then, both teams scored lots of points in a typical WKU game. This is because Horn's teams play at a faster-than-average pace in addition to having an offensive focus. If nothing else, Gamecock contests should be more exciting going forward.

MEET THE GAMECOCKS

Devan Downey (5-9, 175, Jr.). Downey's numbers improved on his freshman season at Cincinnati. He used more possessions and became a more efficient scorer while maintaining a high assist rate and committing few turnovers, considering how often he has the ball in his hands. Like most short point guards, he struggles to finish in the paint. Nor does he get to the line much, considering he took over 500 shots from the field.

So overall, his efficiency wouldn't justify his usage on an offensively potent team. But given that Downey's supporting cast won't be changing this season, he's likely to continue to be the most offensively involved Gamecock. He was one of the few players in the country to force a steal on more than one in every 20 possessions, but despite that, he doesn't have a great reputation as a defender.

Zam Fredrick (6-0, 203, Sr.). Just about everything said about Downey could be applied to Fredrick as well. The biggest difference between the two offensively is a lower assist rate and an even lower free-throw rate for Fredrick, who ranked 43rd in that category among the 49 players who got starters' minutes in the SEC last season. Just about every possession went through Downey and Fredrick last year, much as every Western Kentucky possession went through Courtney Lee and Tyrone Brazelton. Expect more of the Downey and Fredrick Show under Horn this season.

Mike Holmes (6-7, 230, So.). The closest thing Odom had to a true center in a starting line-up in which everybody was 6-7 or shorter, Holmes didn't disappoint, considering the height limitation. Only three players in the country committed fewer turnovers per possession used, and each took more threes than twos. Holmes took merely a single three-point shot last season. In fact, against top-25 opponents, nearly half of his shots were inside five feet. Granted, many of those were on put-backs as a result of his excellent offensive rebounding.

Dominique Archie (6-7, 200, Jr.). As the fourth offensive option, Archie has posted effective field-goal percentages of 58 and 54 in his first two seasons. Considering that Carolina's effective field-goal rates have been around 50 percent as a team during that time, Archie is a candidate to take a few more shots to possibly remove a little pressure from Downey and Fredrick.

Brandis Raley-Ross (6-2, 193, So.). Raley-Ross is a sniper who got the attention of stat-heads everywhere by making 30 of his first 46 three-point attempts last season. That, after shooting 31 percent from there as a freshman. True, once SEC play started, he went just 7-of-26. There's more to the story, though. Raley Ross sprained a knee before conference play began, so his struggles were as much due to competition as to health (that and a regression to reality).

Evaldas Baniulis (6-7, 210, Jr.). Baniulis is tall enough to play inside, but took about 80 percent of his shots from beyond the arc last season.

Sam Muldrow (6-9, 216, So.). Muldrow is raw on the offensive end, but he'll be one of the better shot blockers in the conference.

Somebody else. The seven players listed above are the only returning scholarship players who saw meaningful action last season. If Horn is going to play his style, a couple of the four other players on scholarship will have to jump into the pool. **Mitchell Carter (6-10, 260, Jr.)** and **Austin Steed (6-8, 215, So.)** are two of the scholarship holdovers from last season. Horn also gave scholarships to a couple of walk-ons, but that appears to be a temporary arrangement until he restocks the roster with recruits for the 2010 season.

Prospectus says

With Downey and Fredrick, the Gamecocks won't be a doormat, but with the same personnel from a year ago, it's hard to imagine this team becoming a factor in the at-large discussion. If everyone stays healthy, a bid in one of the lesser postseason tournaments is a reasonable, if lofty, goal. And hey, SEC fans, you should circle that South Carolina/Ole Miss game on your calendar. It might be the fastest-paced conference game of the season.

TENNESSEE

2008: 31-5 (14-2 SEC)
Lost to Louisville, 79-60, NCAA Regional Semifinal
In-conference offense: 1.12 points per possession (1st)
In-conference defense: 0.98 points allowed per possession (2nd)

What Tennessee did well: *Keep opponents from scoring.*
The effectiveness of the Tennessee defense can't be measured purely by points allowed per possession. Bruce Pearl's strategy of frequent pressing, when effective, provides his offense with an environment in which it can be more effective. Opposing defenses are frequently not organized after a change of possession, and when things are going really well for the offense, dunks and other high percentage shots ensue. So we should expect that when things are clicking in Knoxville, the team would be more efficient on offense than on defense. Pearl is willing to allow a few easy baskets if it means his defense will create (a few plus one) easy baskets for his team.

In a nutshell, that's how the Vols behaved in Pearl's first two seasons. Statistically, Pearl's style created a substantial offensive improvement over the Buzz Peterson era and modest improvement on the defensive end. But in 2008, the defense was finally able to stand on its own merits, finishing second in the SEC in efficiency. The offense was still statistically better, but only marginally, so for the first time in Pearl's three seasons in Knoxville, there's a strong case that the defense is what carried this team to success.

What we learned in 2008: *Context matters when it comes to a player's stats.*
Take the case of Tyler Smith. The Tennessee forward played his freshman season at Iowa and made an immediate impact in helping keep the Hawkeyes' of-

fense afloat as the program dealt with massive roster turnover from the previous season. Smith was like a lot of other college players who show potential in their rookie season. He had no problem creating shots, but struggled to make them. His production paled in comparison to Adam Haluska, who both took and made shots in impressive quantities. Move ahead to Smith's sophomore season, in which he still took a lot of shots, though not as many as at Iowa, and he made a lot more. His two-point percentage rose from 48 to 56, and he was a much more efficient player. Even though his scoring average dropped by about a point per game, he was a more effective scorer (and rebounder). Who knows if Tyler Smith became a better player, though.

At Iowa, nobody but Haluska could create shots, so Smith had to do this, even if it meant taking a few that he couldn't make. Not to mention that Smith's dad was diagnosed with cancer and passed away just before last season, which may have impacted his game. At Tennessee, the supporting cast was much stronger, and more of Smith's shots were taken closer to the basket. Smith may never shoot as frequently as he did at Iowa, but that's a good thing both for his game and for the health of Tennessee's offense.

What's in store for 2009

By far the biggest challenge for Bruce Pearl is replacing Chris Lofton. For all the angst over Lofton's shooting during his senior season, he was still one of the most productive shooting guards in major college basketball. (As the most productive two-guard in the nation in 2007, he set a tough standard for his senior year.) Between the loss of Lofton, JaJuan Smith, and Jordan Howell, a lot of three-point production has left this team. Tennessee has launched as many three-pointers as just about any power conference team has launched over the past three seasons. The introduction of freshman Scotty Hopson will help fill that void, but this team may be fundamentally different from past Pearl-led Volunteer teams.

MEET THE VOLUNTEERS

Tyler Smith (6-7, 215, Jr.). Besides the talents mentioned above, Smith is also one of the better passing big men around, assisting on over a fifth of his teammates' made shots.

J. P. Prince (6-7, 205, Jr.). The J. P. Prince story is similar to Smith's, except that Prince's experience at a different school (Arizona) went much worse. After a dreadful freshman season, Prince underwent a wisdom-tooth procedure that resulted in a severe infection that kept him on the bench to start the 2007 season. Considering all this (and his ineligibility for play against a weaker schedule in the fall semester, because of transfer rules), Prince's numbers at Tennessee in 2008 were incredibly impressive.

Wayne Chism (6-9, 242, Jr.). Chism does a bunch of things well, though perhaps nothing great. Offensively, his shot selection may be questionable in the half-court game, but he makes up for it with an absurdly low turnover rate, considering his role. Defensively, he's an excellent shot blocker and rebounder.

Bobby Maze (6-2, 185, Jr.). Perhaps the most criticized ingredient on any top team last season was the point guard at Tennessee. Maze played a season as a backup at Oklahoma before spending his transfer season at highly regarded Hutchinson Community College last season. Essentially, though, he appears to be quite similar to Ramar Smith, who ran the point last season. Maze is not the most productive offensive player, because of a lack of perimeter game (though perhaps more than he demonstrated at OU) and an inability to get to the free-throw line. On the plus side, he's capable of setting up his teammates and had a respectable turnover rate his freshman year.

Scotty Hopson (6-7, 185, Fr.). The most prized of Pearl's incoming class, Hopson will add size to the backcourt and has the reputation of being a great shooter.

Emmanuel Negedu (6-7, 230, Fr.). Another freshman who fits the Tennessee mold of undersized big men: He's athletic and long, and it will be a bonus if he can grab offensive rebounds. After the dismissal of Duke Crews in the offseason, Tennessee needs some help in that area.

Brian Williams (6-10, 267, So.). Williams is a raw offensive player whose best asset is his rebounding. When he's on the floor, UT's front line goes from smallish to regular-sized. The same can be said of **Philip Jurick (6-10, 250, Fr.)** if he contributes this season.

Ryan Childress (6-9, 235, Sr.). Childress got few minutes last season and may not get much more this season. But he adds depth and is capable of contributing offensively when he's on the floor.

Josh Tabb (6-4, 196, Jr.). Tabb is a three-point specialist who will get more time with Lofton's departure.

Daniel West (6-1, 165, Fr.). West provides another option at the point.

Prospectus says

With what Tennessee did last season and the state of the rest of the SEC, it's hard to imagine this team not being the class of the league again. The concern is whether it can make the jump to the nation's elite. Without Lofton, it's possible the team will continue the trend of being more dependent on its defense to win games. The thing is, its defense could be that good. Don't be surprised if the Vols can duplicate the two-seed they received last March.

VANDERBILT

2008: 26-8 (10-6 SEC)
Lost to Siena, 83-62, NCAA First Round
In-conference offense: 1.06 points per possession (5th)
In-conference defense: 1.03 points allowed per possession (5th)

What Vanderbilt did well: *Adapt to having a post man being the go-to player.*

Since head coach Kevin Stallings arrived in Nashville for the 1999-2000 season, Vanderbilt has relied heavily on three-point shooting. Even when big men were the Commodores' most valuable offensive weapon, guys like Matt Freije and Dan Langhi relied on perimeter shooting for a large chunk of their success. So last season was unusual as A. J. Ogilvy emerged early in the season as Vanderbilt's top scoring option. The 6-11 Aussie was a true center who plied his craft exclusively in and around the paint.

Overall, though, the behavior of the Vandy offense wasn't much different from what it had been in previous seasons. The players shot the ball well, didn't commit turnovers, and took a lot of threes. The most striking difference was that they got to the free-throw line more often. In short, Ogilvy's main influ-ence was that the Commodores were a more balanced team on offense.

What we learned in 2008: *It matters who you play.*

The Commodores' 16-0 start vaulted them as high as number 13 in the national polls. It was the best start in school history and certainly a reason for fans to get excited. But in terms of projecting them as a true top-15 team going forward, the perfect start showed enough imperfections to cast doubt. At their best, of course, they *were* a top-15 team, as an easy win against Georgia Tech proved. The problem was that at their worst, they were still getting wins while not playing very well. Close home wins over lower-level teams like Tennessee State and Tennessee Martin were indicative of a team that couldn't hang with the nation's elite, but since they were wins, few critics surfaced.

After the perfect start, Vandy would lose four of its next five, and suddenly, people were wondering what happened to the team. All four of those games were on the road and to teams at least comparable to the best team Vanderbilt had played in its non-conference slate. Why was it a surprise that Vandy would struggle during that stretch? Looking back on the entire season, it doesn't appear that the Commodores were a different team at the end of calendar 2007 than they were at the beginning of 2008. They simply played a higher level of competition in 2008 and played half those games away from home.

What's in store for 2009

The key losses from this team are Shan Foster, one of the best shooters in the nation last season, and combo guard Alex Gordon, who also became a reliable scorer. Somewhat less distressing is the transfer of Keegan Bell to Chattanooga, although Bell stood to get some increased responsibilities in the backcourt this season.

To compensate, Stallings brings in a recruiting class that is hailed by recruiting wonks as somewhere between the second- and fifth-best in the SEC. Substantively, little will change. Ogilvy remains in the middle and will be surrounded by guys who have range. As a team, the Commodores don't figure to shoot as well as they did last season, since so many more shots will be taken by freshmen, but in terms of style, there will be little difference between 2009 and 2008.

MEET THE COMMODORES

Andrew Ogilvy (6-11, 250, So.). Whether you call him Andrew or A. J., Ogilvy's season mirrored Vandy's as a team. He was much more productive before the conference season started.

	Pts/40 min	FG%	Reb/40 min
Through Jan. 5	30.1	65.8	11.5
After Jan. 5	22.6	53.2	9.3

His main weakness is that his offense drops off quickly outside six or seven feet. As interior defenses improved over the season, they were able to at least limit the damage Ogilvy did.

Jermaine Beal (6-3, 210, Jr.). Beal stepped up his game in his sophomore season as he moved into the starting point guard role. As a shooter, he went from very timid and inaccurate to less timid and occasionally accurate. Perhaps more importantly, his assist rate mushroomed and his turnover rate nosedived. With Shan Foster and Alex Gordon around last season, Vandy didn't need him to score, but the team will this season.

Andre Walker (6-8, 214, So.). After Ogilvy and Beal, it's totally up in the air where the rest of the team's shots will come from. Walker is as good a bet as any. He played only about 12 minutes per game last season, but averaged 21.5 mpg over the Commodores in the last four games.

Darshawn McClellan (6-7, 220, So.). McClellan was sixth on the team in minutes played, but just 10th in field-goal attempts. He rebounds well but struggles to score.

Jeff Taylor (6-7, 190, Fr.). Stallings will get a lot of minutes from freshmen next season, and if Vandy is to succeed, its highly regarded recruits will need to produce. Taylor has a reputation as a scorer; if this translates to the Division I level, he'll be a starter before too long.

Lance Goulbourne (6-8, 190, Fr.). Goulbourne will bring some depth to the wing position and should get significant minutes immediately.

Brad Tinsley (6-3, 190, Fr.). Tinsley is a point guard who was somewhat of a late bloomer in recruiting circles.

Festus Ezeli (6-11, 245, Fr.). Ezeli is long on raw athleticism and short on basketball skill, since he's only played organized ball for three years. The Nigerian took a redshirt last season, but did get the attention of a few hoops powers before settling on Vandy during the recruiting process, so he may give Stallings some productive minutes on the defensive end.

Steve Tchiengang (6-9, 230, Fr.). Yet another freshman, Tchiengang should see minutes as a power forward who's more perimeter oriented on offense.

George Drake (6-4, 210, Jr.). Drake saw spot duty last season and wasn't afraid to shoot it, but his effective field-goal percentage was right around 32, so that part of his game needs some work if he's to earn more time.

Prospectus says

The equation this season is Ogilvy plus a lot of inexperience. So it seems reasonable that the team will take a step back this season. Battling for wins in the East will be difficult. It's possible that Vandy will extend its five-year run of playing in the postseason, though, since Ogilvy will take some of an opposing defense's attention away from the newcomers. The infusion of freshman talent, however, means that the future of this team is bright.

Overviews

The Atlantic 10

On a Scale of 1 to 10, It's a 14

KEN POMEROY

It was vintage Atlantic 10 basketball last season as the conference produced a team that could compete with the national big boys, reminiscent of 2004 Saint Joseph's, 1995 and 1996 UMass, and 1987 and 1988 Temple. Xavier emerged in nonconference play as the conference's team to beat and proceeded to rip through the league schedule with just two losses. They may have been the league's first Final Four team since the Marcus Camby–led Minutemen in 1996, had last season not been a special year where all roads to San Antonio were blocked by superpower one-seeds. Thus, the Musketeers were felled by UCLA in the regional finals.

The success of the conference ran deeper than just Xavier. Saint Joseph's was the first A-10 team to not win at least a share of the regular season title and get an at-large bid since 2004. By virtue of winning the conference tournament in Atlantic City, Temple was the third conference team to participate in the NCAA tournament. Overall, the Atlantic 10 could make a reasonable case that it was the strongest conference outside of the six perennial power conferences.

When there are 14 teams in a conference, though, a few are bound to career in directions you didn't expect. Duquesne and Fordham appeared to be primed for their best seasons in years, but neither could produce that. At Saint Louis, Rick Majerus seemed like he was inheriting enough spare parts to put a decent product on the floor, but the Billikens struggled. At times, mightily.

For 2009, it looks like the traditional powers will once again occupy the top spots in the league. An important exception could be Charlotte who returns more playing time from last season than any other conference team. The 49ers came to the A-10 from Conference USA in 2006 and were expected to regularly contend for conference titles. It hasn't happened yet and they have just two NIT appearances to show for their tenure in the league, but that might change this season.

Other challengers for the league title and hence an at-large bid are the usual suspects. Xavier, UMass,

	2008 Record	Returning Minutes (%)	2009 Prediction
Xavier	14-2	57	13-3
Charlotte	9-7	83	11-5
UMass	10-6	57	11-5
St. Joseph's	9-7	62	10-6
Temple	11-5	69	9-7
La Salle	8-8	78	9-7
Dayton	8-8	56	9-7
Rhode Island	7-9	63	8-8
G. Washington	5-11	76	7-9
Richmond	9-7	69	7-9
Duquesne	7-9	44	6-10
St. Louis	7-9	53	5-11
Fordham	6-10	31	5-11
St. Bonaventure	2-14	34	2-14

and Saint Joe's each have to replace a critical piece or more from last season's roster, but each program has enough depth to make good things happen this season. One thing that should be different this season is the lack of a banner team getting a lofty seed on Selection Sunday. That, however, may be a good thing for the overall haul of bids that the league will receive. With no juggernaut to inflict double-digit losses on the rest of the league, a three-bid A-10 may happen again.

CHARLOTTE

2008: 20-14 (9-7 A-10)
Lost to Nebraska 67-48, NIT first round
In-conference offense: 1.04 points per possession (9th)
In-conference defense: 1.01 points allowed per possession (2nd)

Charlotte provided a mixed bag of results last season. The optimist saw nonconference wins against Clemson, Davidson, Southern Illinois, and Wake Forest. The pessimist saw that all but the Clemson win was at home and the 49ers incurred losses to lowly Monmouth and Hofstra. Still, Charlotte entered the A-10 tournament with some momentum having won four of its last five regular-season contests. That came to a halt in the tourney semifinals against Temple where Charlotte managed just 45 points in 64 possessions.

That exemplified Charlotte's performance throughout the season. Temple only scored 60 in that game, so the Niners' defense did its job. But Charlotte suffered from long stretches where they couldn't score. That's also how losses to Hofstra and Monmouth occurred. This season, everyone of note returns except for the diminutive Leemire Goldwire, who happened to be Charlotte's lone reliable source of offense. If one or two of the returnees have elevated their scoring ability in the offseason (I'm eyeing 6-7 senior **Lamont Mack**), Charlotte could be challenging the top of the A-10.

DAYTON

2008: 23-11 (8-8 A-10)
Lost to Ohio State 74-63, NIT quarterfinal
In-conference offense: 1.09 points per possession (5th)
In-conference defense: 1.08 points allowed per possession (10th)

Dayton fans are still wondering how their season might have gone had 6-8 freshman **Chris Wright** not broken his ankle in early January. The Flyers roared to a 14-1 start only to see everything go wrong without Wright. If he stays healthy, he'll end up as an all-A-10 selection. He may actually be the best player in the conference. He's a very effective scorer and one of the best rebounders in the country. He'll block shots and he gets to the free-throw line, where he made 80 percent of his tries last season. Unfortunately for Dayton, point guard Brian Roberts was a senior last season and he'll be very difficult to replace.

DUQUESNE

2008: 17-13 (7-9 A-10)
Lost to La Salle 82-79, A-10 first round
In-conference offense: 1.06 points per possession (8th)
In-conference defense: 1.04 points allowed per possession (5th)

Shot-blocker extraordinaire Shawn James left Duquesne a year early to begin a pro career at age 25. Junior point guard Kojo Mensah followed James out the door. What's left on the roster for head coach Ron Everhart is defensive specialist **Damian Saunders,** who showed last season he is capable of erasing his teammates' mistakes on that end of the floor. He might not be the intimidator James was, but he's a force that opposing offenses will have to respect. The Dukes also bring in one of the best freshmen in the A-10 in 6-4 **Melquan Bolding**.

FORDHAM

2008: 12-17 (6-10 A-10)
Lost to Saint Joseph's 80-60, A-10 first round
In-conference offense: 0.99 points per possession (12th)
In-conference defense: 1.05 points allowed per possession (8th)

There's no sugarcoating it: The 2008 Rams' season has to be classified as a disappointment. With four seniors among Dereck Whittenburg's top-five minutes-earners, Fordham saw its conference win total decrease by four from the 2007 season. There's a lot of new blood on this season's roster, but a couple of returnees will lead the way—6-2 shooting guard **Brenton Butler** and 6-5 wing **Mike Moore**. Whittenburg's point guard will be 6-1 freshman **Jio Fontan**, who's a local product and the most highly regarded of a five-man incoming class.

GEORGE WASHINGTON

2008: 9-17 (5-11 A-10)
Did not qualify for A-10 tournament
In-conference offense: 0.99 points per possession (13th)
In-conference defense: 1.07 points allowed per possession (9th)

By virtue of not qualifying for the Atlantic 10 tournament, GW was one of the few college teams to play just 26 games last season. It would be surprising if the Colonials were in that situation again. They return an experienced core of players led by a front line of **Rob Diggs**, **Wynton Witherspoon**, and **Damian Hollis**. Their strength is on the defensive end where Karl Hobbs is a proponent of aggressively defending the paint. The offense has question marks, but Diggs occasionally provided in that area, too. He scored 29 of his team's 57 points in a February win over Dayton.

LA SALLE

2008: 15-17 (8-8 A-10)
Lost to Temple 84-75, A-10 quarterfinals
In-conference offense: 1.09 points per possession (6th)
In-conference defense: 1.11 points allowed per possession (12th)

La Salle struggled defensively, but it may remedy that with the presence of **Vernon Goodridge** this season. Goodridge transferred from Mississippi State where, with Jarvis Varnado, he was part of the most impressive shot-blocking tandem in the nation in 2007. He blocked 11 percent of opponents' two-pointers, a rate that would have been second only to Duquesne's Shawn James in the A-10 last season. If he has the influence on the Explorers' defense that James had with the Dukes, things could get interesting on the north side of Philadelphia.

MASSACHUSETTS

2008: 25-11 (10-6 A-10)
Lost to Ohio State 92-85, NIT finals
In-conference offense: 1.07 points per possession (7th)
In-conference defense: 1.01 points allowed per possession (3rd)

Former Memphis assistant coach and UMass alum Derek Kellogg takes over for Travis Ford this season. The Minutemen should continue to play up-tempo, but there almost has to be a decrease from the freakishly fast pace of 75 possessions per game that UMass played at under Ford last season. Kellogg will have to find a way to replace Gary Forbes, who was not the most efficient UMass player but was the most involved. Look for the skilled backcourt of **Chris Lowe** and **Ricky Harris** to pick up the slack.

On a sad note for stat-heads, reserve center Papa Lo transferred to Bryant in the offseason. Lo was a fan favorite at the Mullins Center and Ford was a master at substituting him on defensive possessions. In just 89 minutes of playing time on the season, Lo took but seven shots and blocked 25 of them. (For reference, consider that in 1,286 minutes last season, Tyler Hansbrough blocked 13 shots.)

RHODE ISLAND

2008: 21-12 (7-9 A-10)
Lost to Creighton 74-73, NIT first round
In-conference offense: 1.12 points per possession (4th)
In-conference defense: 1.12 points allowed per possession (13th)

Like UMass, Rhode Island was known for its free-wheeling style of play last season. Unlike the Minutemen, the Rams' style didn't include defense. Gone are point guard Parfait Bitee and forward Will Daniels. Bitee shot 51 percent from three-point range last season and Daniels shot 55 percent eFG while using a lofty 29 percent of his team's possessions. The new names to keep an eye on are 6-4 guard **Keith Cothran** and 6-6 forward **Lamonte Ulmer**.

RICHMOND

2008: 16-15 (9-7 A-10)
Lost to Virginia 66-64, CBI first round
In-conference offense: 1.03 points per possession (11th)

In-conference defense: 1.05 points allowed per possession (7th)

The Spiders got devastating news in July when 6-9 center **Dan Geriot** injured his knee in a summer-league game necessitating season-ending (or season-preventing) surgery. Geriot had found a nice home in the Princeton offense that has otherwise sputtered under Chris Mooney. The Spiders went 9-7 despite being outscored by 22 points in A-10 play, so they'll probably need a fundamental improvement across the board to post another winning season. Geriot's injury puts more pressure on the backcourt of sophomore **Kevin Anderson** and junior **David Gonzalvez**.

SAINT BONAVENTURE

2008: 8-22 (2-14 A-10)
Did not qualify for A-10 tournament
In-conference offense: 1.04 points per possession (10th)
In-conference defense: 1.18 points allowed per possession (14th)

The Bonnies still haven't recovered from the recruiting scandal of 2003. They'll try again this season as coach Mike Schmidt overhauls the roster. Saint Bonaventure only held two conference opponents below a point per possession—Saint Louis and Duquesne. On the positive side, they were able to score more than 20 points in every game they played, unlike another team in the league.

SAINT JOSEPH'S

2008: 21-13 (9-7 A-10)
Lost to Oklahoma 72-64, NCAA first round
In-conference offense: 1.12 points per possession (2nd)
In-conference defense: 1.08 points allowed per possession (11th)

Last season, Phil Martelli relied heavily on his starters. Only Texas and Niagara got fewer minutes from their bench than the Hawks. Two starters from last season are gone, 6-10 point forward Pat Calathes and 6-8 forward Rob Ferguson, which means the focus of opposing game plans will be 6-9 **Ahmad Nivins**. Nivins is one dimensional, but that dimen-

sion is taking the ball and putting it in the hoop. He made 65 percent of his field goal attempts and got to the free-throw line nearly 200 times, making 74 percent of those.

Saint Joe's Achilles was opponents' three-point shooting. The Hawks' opposition was given plenty of chances to shoot from long range (as has always been the case under Martelli) and they made 37 percent of their attempts.

SAINT LOUIS

2008: 16-15 (7-9 A-10)
Lost to Dayton 63-62 (OT), A-10 first round
In-conference offense: 0.96 points per possession (14th)
In-conference defense: 1.04 points allowed per possession (6th)

The Billikens' 2008 campaign was a forgettable one, except for the fact that they established a shot-clock era record for futility in a 49-20 loss to George Washington on January 10. It doesn't seem possible that a team could actually go a whole game and not get 20 points, thus history may forever have a record of something that was done by SLU last season. Rick Majerus is starting to turn over the roster and fill it with the players he wants. In this class he has the size he craves with 7-0 **Brett Thompson** and 6-11 **Willie Reed**. However, it appears that two hold-overs from the Brad Soderberg era, senior guards **Tommie Liddell** and **Kevin Lisch**, will be the best offensive options.

TEMPLE

2008: 21-13 (11-5 A-10)
Lost to Michigan State 72-61, NCAA first round
In-conference offense: 1.12 points per possession (3rd)
In-conference defense: 1.04 points allowed per possession (4th)

Give Fran Dunphy credit for getting the Temple defense into a state that allowed the team to win the A-10 tournament, thereby earning an automatic bid. The Owls will be heavily dependent on 6-5 wing **Dionte Christmas** this season. With the loss of Mark Tyndale, the Temple roster is left with a bunch of role players offensively, so the defense will need to remain solid for this team to succeed. Most likely to break out of the shadows is 6-9 sophomore **Lavoy Allen**.

XAVIER

2008: 30-7 (14-2 A-10)
Lost to UCLA 76-57, NCAA Elite 8
In-conference offense: 1.13 points per possession (1st)
In-conference defense: 0.98 points allowed per possession (1st)

Xavier lost Stanley Burrell, Drew Lavender, and Josh Duncan from last season's team, and those players were very important in the Musketeers' run to a three-seed and the Elite Eight. However, Xavier was so far ahead of the Atlantic 10 that even a step back leaves them in position to compete for a conference crown. One thing the Muskies won't have trouble doing this season is grabbing rebounds.

With 6-7 **Derrick Brown**, 6-6 **C. J. Anderson**, and 6-9 **Jason Love**, the X-Men retain three of the best rebounders in the league. Brown may get the preseason accolades, but Love is also one to watch. He was nominally a starter but played just 18 minutes per game. With Duncan gone, Love will get more playing time and his impact should be felt in both the rebounding and scoring categories. He made 56 percent of his shots from the field last season.

The biggest problem will be replacing the backcourt duo of Lavender and Burrell, who together missed only two starts the last two seasons. **Dante Jackson** played sparingly last season but will have to fill some of the void, and there are also four true freshmen that are candidates, most notably **Mark Lyons** and **Terrell Holloway**. At press time, Coach Sean Miller was still hoping that Indiana transfer **Jordan Crawford** could be granted immediate eligibility by the NCAA.

Conference USA

Second to One

JOHN GASAWAY

Memphis turned out to be the second-best team in the nation last year, which perhaps was appropriate. The Tigers hail from Conference USA, where in a way there were 11 second-place teams in 2008.

Not literally, of course. UAB would be appalled to be thrown into the same category as Rice. Nevertheless, in terms of that all-important conference barometer known as the NCAA tournament, Conference USA was a one-bid league last year for the second consecutive season. When it came to the biggest spotlight the sport has to offer, there was Memphis and then there was everyone else. The national perception of C-USA and, more important, the conference's correct appraisal of itself will move off that particular dime only when a different team from the league makes the tournament or, better still, the second weekend.

That probably won't take too long. If there's a theme to these previews it's improvement. Eight of the conference's 12 teams bettered their RPI last year over 2007. UAB made notably large strides. And up-and-comers like Southern Miss, Tulsa, and Marshall are all headed in the right direction. I don't foresee Memphis getting dragged into a dogfight for the conference title this season, but I do expect that the Tigers will gradually acquire less comfort and more butterflies on the road in conference play. It's only natural.

One more thing before we get to the predictions. *Man* they foul a lot in this league. Note to the conference office:

Let's get on this. Issue the edict to your coaches or to your refs as you see fit, but issue it. Shooting two free throws for every five shots from the field is far too choppy for the eye. Networks don't ante up big dollars for the rights to free-throw contests, capiche?

Now then, I'm going to crawl out on a limb and say that Memphis will win the regular season title. As for my forecast that the Tigers will actually drop a game this year, allow me to say hello and welcome to any newcomers. Every year I predict that John Calipari's team will go 15-1, and every year they go 16-0. It's tradition. Please note, however, that UAB came within a whisker of making my prediction come true last year in Birmingham.

	2008 Record	Returning Minutes (%)	2009 Prediction
Memphis	16-0	52	15-1
Tulsa	8-8	60	12-4
Southern Miss	9-7	87	11-5
UAB	12-4	75	11-5
Marshall	8-8	55	10-6
UTEP	8-8	65	9-7
Houston	11-5	39	7-9
UCF	9-7	55	6-10
Tulane	6-10	62	6-10
E. Carolina	5-11	41	4-12
SMU	4-12	58	4-12
Rice	0-16	55	1-15

EAST CAROLINA

2008: 11-19 (5-11 C-USA)
Lost to Tulsa 66-49, C-USA Tournament First Round

In-conference offense: 1.00 points per possession (9th)
In-conference defense: 1.14 points allowed per possession (12th)

In coach Mack McCarthy's first season at the helm, East Carolina's offense improved so much it really should be featured at church revivals. **Sam Hinnant**, Darrell Jenkins, and Corey Farmer all helped the metamorphosis along by shooting 40 percent or better on their threes. Jenkins and Farmer are gone, but Hinnant returns along with **James Legan**, who packed a lot of shots and a fair number of makes into just 15 minutes per game last year. For all the good news on offense, however, there was bad news on the other side of the ball, where the defense was simultaneously deteriorating to the point where it was the worst in C-USA. Indeed, the Pirates presented an odd spectacle wherein one of the best defensive rebounders in the country played for one of the nation's worst defensive rebounding teams. That player was Gabe Blair, who has since transferred to Wichita State where he'll fortify an already strong defensive rebounding team. Blair's frontcourt mate John Fields, an excellent shot-blocker and the only Pirate who made twos last year, also chose to leave (UNC-Wilmington). Maybe 6-8 freshman **Darius Morrow**, who originally committed to South Carolina, can pick up some of the slack here for ECU. Still, the departures of Blair and Fields clearly jeopardize what was a budding good-news story in Greenville. Even with a leaky defense, last year's five-win season matched East Carolina's best showing ever in C-USA. It will be a challenge for McCarthy and the Pirates to equal that mark this year.

HOUSTON

2008: 24-10 (11-5 C-USA)
Lost to Tulsa 73-69, CBI Semifinal
In-conference offense: 1.09 points per possession (4th)
In-conference defense: 1.00 points allowed per possession (3rd)

No player in C-USA posted a higher percentage of possessions used last year than Houston's Robert "Fluff" McKiver. He was the alpha and omega of this offense—see for example his 52-point effort against Southern Miss last February. Now McKiver's gone, along with three other starters, and this year looks decidedly more youthful for 63-year-old coach Tom Penders. His most seasoned returnee is junior **Kelvin Lewis**, a 6-4 guard who was exceptionally efficient operating in the long shadow cast by McKiver. If Lewis can come close to that level of efficiency while stepping out into the sunlight and taking on some more possessions, that'll be huge for this inexperienced team. Lewis will be joined by transfer **Aubrey Coleman**, who comes highly touted from Southwest Mississippi College. The new breed in Hofheinz Pavilion will try to carry on an illustrious bit of recent Cougar lore: Houston in the Penders era has excelled on offense mostly by taking care of the ball while, incidentally, shooting vast numbers of threes at a very fast pace (72 possessions per 40 minutes in-conference in 2008). Last year the Cougars committed a turnover on just 16 percent of their trips in C-USA play. If this year's new-look Houston can honor that tradition, they'll surprise some people.

MARSHALL

2008: 16-14 (8-8 C-USA)
Lost to Tulane 48-47, C-USA Tournament First Round
In-conference offense: 1.02 points per possession (8th)
In-conference defense: 1.04 points allowed per possession (9th)

Donnie Jones enters his second season as coach of the Herd with reason for optimism. His team's offense was much improved in 2008, thanks to more accurate shooting. Even better, Marshall's most effective players on offense are back this year, in the form of 6-6 senior **Markel Humphrey**, 6-6 sophomore **Tirrell Baines**, and 6-8 junior **Tyler Wilkerson**. They'll be joined by no fewer than three major-conference transfers who will become eligible this year: 6-3 guard **Brandon Powell**, who arrives at Marshall by way of Florida; 6-7 forward **Octavius Spann**, who decided to leave Georgetown after seeing just 37 minutes of game time during the Hoyas' Final Four season in 2006–2007; and 6-3 guard **Chris Lutz**, who started 34 games over two seasons at Purdue at the dawn of the Matt Painter era. Also available will be point guard **Damier Pitts**, perhaps the highest-rated freshman in the non-Memphis C-USA. Mind you, Marshall's defense is a work in progress. (And don't be fooled by the low-sounding point totals for opponents. The Herd was easily the conference's slowest-paced team last year.) But

Jones has his team on a nice trajectory: The Marshall offense improved as the season progressed in 2008, with the Herd scoring a sterling 1.12 points per trip over the second half of their C-USA schedule. That alone should be grounds for optimism in Huntington. And if for some unforeseen reason the defense shows up too, look out.

MEMPHIS

2008: 38-2 (16-0 C-USA)
Lost to Kansas 75-68 (OT), National Championship Game
In-conference offense: 1.13 points per possession (1st)
In-conference defense: 0.84 points allowed per possession (1st)

Memphis came up a couple minutes short of a national championship, of course, but the Tigers were at least in a position that teams like North Carolina, UCLA, Texas, Georgetown, Duke, and Tennessee were unable to reach themselves: Monday night in April. Not to mention John Calipari's program has made the Elite Eight in each of the past three seasons. They haven't lost a conference game since March 2, 2006. They return **Robert Dozier** and **Antonio Anderson** and welcome **Tyreke Evans** to the fold. The Tigers might be less formidable this season but they're still the Tigers.

I have a theory that if Calipari looked more like Ben Howland or Bo Ryan—more like the scary neighbor and less like the cool uncle—then maybe the Memphis coach would get the acclaim he deserves for presiding over a defensive dynasty. Last year Memphis held their conference opponents to less than 0.85 points per trip. Yes, that was against C-USA competition. Know what? The Tigers played offense against the same C-USA competition and, while of course it was the best such offense in the conference, the performance on that side of the ball was several orders of magnitude beneath what the defense was doing. As long as their coach continues to use product in his hair and smile on occasion, this team will be willfully misunderstood.

A hallmark of that Calipari defense is long and active players on the perimeter who take away your will to try, much less ability to make, threes. The return of Anderson should help this hallmark live on. Anderson will be joined out top by 6-6 newcomer Evans, one of the nation's highest-rated freshmen.

Other new faces will include 6-7 freshman wing **Wesley Witherspoon** and 6-5 guard **Roburt Sallie**, who would be at Nebraska right now if not for an odd enrollment snafu. The new blood will team with returnees like 6-2 junior **Willie Kemp** and 6-5 three-point specialist **Doneal Mack**, who as this book goes to press says he *will* return as a Tiger. Then again he's given different signals on this subject over the summer, so stay tuned.

In the paint, Dozier's a good shot-blocker who'll have the opportunity to show what he can do on the glass without Joey Dorsey fighting him for credit on every rebound. (Actually if things had gone differently on that Monday night in April, you could plausibly have credited Dozier as the hero. As implausible as this might sound for a Memphis player at the end of that game, Dozier went two-of-two at the line and grabbed two offensive boards in the final three minutes.) Also returning is 6-10 junior **Shawn Taggart**, to this point a role player on offense but one who's done pretty well.

In Derrick Rose and Chris Douglas-Roberts, Memphis lost their only two players who combined efficiency with heavy usage on offense. And even the Tigers aren't immune to the implications there: The departures at least raise a question mark for the relative performance of the offense this year. The defensive dynasty will need to continue if the Tigers want to extend their 42-game C-USA winning streak.

RICE

2008: 3-27 (0-16 C-USA)
Lost to Tulsa 66-49, C-USA Tournament First Round
In-conference offense: 0.83 points per possession (12th)
In-conference defense: 1.04 points allowed per possession (7th)

Rice is in a place no stats can reach. Actually, that was part of the problem last year. The Owls weren't in a "place" at all. They were in three different places for their home games. While their true home venue, Autry Court, was being renovated, Rice played home games at Reliant Arena and the Toyota Center in Houston, and at the Merrill Center in Katy. Then the injuries came: Chris Hagan, **Cory Pflieger**, Jasen Williams, and Paulius Packevicius, in that order, were all lost for the year, never to return. For a coach to be dismissed under these circumstances, when the arena that he lobbied for years to renovate is about to reopen, may strike you as a bit harsh. Well, you should have made your voice heard in Houston last March. Willis Wilson is gone and into his place steps former Cal coach Ben Braun. The rebuild starts now.

SMU

2008: 10-20 (4-12 C-USA)
Lost to UTEP 71-49, C-USA Tournament First Round
In-conference offense: 0.93 points per possession (11th)
In-conference defense: 1.09 points allowed per possession (11th)

Last year Matt Doherty did some experimenting with his young team, starting no fewer than ten different players at various points in the season. If there was a constant it was point guard Jon Killen, the only Mustang to start all 30 games. Killen is gone (his 40 percent three-point shooting will be missed), along with backcourt mate Derrick Roberts, but pretty much everyone else is back. **Papa Dia**, a 6-9 sophomore, has already shown his value on the defensive glass but is a work in progress on offense. Frontcourt mate **Bamba Fall**, conversely, made 57 percent of his twos last year and at 7-1 is also a very good shot-blocker. There's a nucleus here—sophomores **Ryan Harp**, **Alex Malone**, and **Mike Walker** combined for 38 starts last year—but the nucleus tended to miss a fair number of shots and, with the exception of Malone, commit a goodly number of turnovers as freshmen. Those numbers should improve this year, but there's a lot of ground to cover between where SMU is now and where they want to be.

SOUTHERN MISS

2008: 19-14 (9-7 C-USA)
Lost to Memphis 69-53, C-USA Tournament Semifinals
In-conference offense: 1.07 points per possession (5th)
In-conference defense: 1.05 points allowed per possession (10th)

The top six scorers from last year's 9-7 team return to Hattiesburg this season, giving Larry Eustachy the blessing and the curse of raised expectations. Southern Miss scores its points largely without threes, by crashing the offensive glass and making a lot of trips to the line. And when you have one of those new-fangled scoring point guards, the offense is pretty much going to go through that player. **Jeremy Wise** is certainly no exception. Last year Wise both took the bulk of this offense's shots and recorded many of its assists, if you can grasp that paradox. More accuracy from the 6-2 junior would be a help, but the real opportunities for improvement here are on defense. Last year, C-USA opponents made more than half their twos and never turned the ball over against the undersized Eagles defense. Perhaps this year seven-footer **Gustavo Lino**, who sat out last season with a torn anterior cruciate ligament, can be of some help here. If not, Southern Miss, a very good defensive rebounding team, will need every defensive board they can lay their hands on. Lastly, a special *Basketball Prospectus* shout-out goes to 6-6 junior **Sai'Quon Stone**, who last year attempted more free throws than shots from the field. (I tell you, only in C-USA.) Bear in mind this was a feat accomplished by just three players in all of Division I who saw nontoken playing time in 2008, yet Stone was actually pulling it off *for the second consecutive year.* You, sir, are a credit to outliers.

TULANE

2008: 17-15 (6-10 C-USA)
Lost to Memphis 75-56, C-USA Tournament Quarterfinals
In-conference offense: 0.97 points per possession (10th)
In-conference defense: 1.04 points allowed per possession (8th)

The Green Wave hit an undertow last year, retreating from 9-7 in 2007 to 6-10 in 2008. Few teams in Division I that defend the interior this well (C-USA opponents made just 45 percent of their twos last year) have so little to show for it on their defensive bottom line. Indeed, in 2008 performance on both sides of the ball suffered, as Dave Dickerson's team struggled to get rebounds on either end of the floor. Not to mention that for the second consecutive year Tulane played uphill, as it were, as they coughed the ball up 22 percent of the time in C-USA play while taking the rock away from opponents on just 19 percent of their trips. Dickerson loses David Gomez, who was the focal point of the offense last year, but

Robinson Louisme, Kevin Sims, and Daniel Puckett return. The 6-7 Louisme has shown some serious flashes—he made 60 percent of his twos and was his team's best defensive rebounder last year—but he's foul-prone. (At his advanced age, the 24-year-old Louisme should have learned how to stay on the floor by now.) Sims, a 5-10 point guard, is the best three-point threat (36 percent) on a team that rarely shoots threes. Also available will be David Booker, a 6-7 transfer from Charlotte. Call this year a success if Dickerson can get the Wave moving in the right direction again, in the neighborhood of .500 in C-USA.

TULSA

2008: 25-14 (8-8 C-USA)
Beat Bradley 70-64, CBI Championship Game
In-conference offense: 1.03 points per possession (6th)
In-conference defense: 0.98 points allowed per possession (2nd)

It's actually not that unusual for a team to improve while their record gets worse. That's exactly what happened with Tulsa last year, as they went 8-8 in C-USA a year after posting a 9-7 mark. Wins are the object of this game, no question, but I'm here to tell you Doug Wojcik's team was better last year, outscoring conference opponents by 0.05 points per trip. This is a consistently strong defensive team but the difference last year was much better offense. Give most of the credit there to Ben Uzoh, who had an outstanding season. For much of the year, after the addition of Ray Reese to the starting lineup, the 6-2 Uzoh was playing as a shooting guard. But in his impact on opposing defenses Uzoh was more like a true double-threat wing, hitting a credible 35 percent of his threes and a phenomenal 57 percent of his twos. Also back this season is seven-footer Jerome Jordan, who posted a better block percentage than Hasheem Thabeet last year, while also acquitting himself well on both the offensive and defensive glass. Continued development from Jordan could land this junior at the proverbial next level. Speaking of the next level, Tulsa's almost a textbook case of a team that takes a big step and

surprises people: the strong defense; the deceivingly mediocre record the previous season; and the seemingly significant loss of three seniors who, as it happens, were relatively low-usage players on offense. Reality doesn't always follow the textbook but I seriously doubt that Wojcik's team will have to content itself with defending their College Basketball Invitational championship.

UAB

2008: 23-11 (12-4 C-USA)
Lost to Virginia Tech 75-49, NIT Second Round
In-conference offense: 1.10 points per possession (3rd)
In-conference defense: 1.03 points allowed per possession (4th)

UAB has been getting smaller for months now. It's like a science-fiction movie where any Blazer over 6-6 is zapped. It started last December when 6-9 sophomore Walter Sharpe was ruled academically ineligible after just 12 games, whereupon he submitted his name for the 2008 NBA draft and was taken near the top of the second round. Last season was also the final go-round for 6-9 senior Frank Holmes. Then when the season ended, 6-7 junior Reggie Huffman announced his intention to go pro and subsequently signed a contract to play in Austria. In July seven-footer Zisis Sarikopoulos decided to transfer to Ohio State. Finally, in August, 6-10 soon-to-be-junior Jeremy Mayfield also announced that he would transfer. The exodus of big men reportedly has Mike Davis looking at tapes of Villanova in 2006. That's right, the Blazers coach is talking about going four-guard. He has the personnel to do it. Last year the offense went through 6-5 wing Robert Vaden and he hit 40 percent of his unbelievably numerous threes. (He averaged more than ten attempts per game.) This year Davis will also be welcoming back 6-2 point guard Paul Delaney, who missed almost all of last year with a knee injury. Channing Toney provided an additional (39 percent) three-point threat last year. And 6-6 freshman Terrence Roderick appears on track to play, after being declared ineligible last year. There, I count four guards. They figure to score many points—and allow about as many.

UCF

2008: 16-15 (9-7 C-USA)
Lost to Southern Miss 68-62, C-USA Tournament Quarterfinals
In-conference offense: 1.10 points per possession (2nd)
In-conference defense: 1.04 points allowed per possession
   (6th)

UCF fell to 9-7 in C-USA play last year after going 11-5 in 2007, despite the fact that in both years the Knights outscored their conference opponents by 0.06 points per trip. Kirk Speraw's team had the best non-Memphis offense in the conference and, more specifically, the best shooting offense period. Speraw even had the marketing savvy to speed up the tempo, adding another four possessions per 40 minutes above the pace shown by the Knights in 2007. If you like efficient offense—sometimes for the opponent too—it was fun to watch. **Jermaine Taylor** combined a starring role in the offense with accuracy in shooting in a way that no player in the league besides Chris Douglas-Roberts and Tulsa's Ben Uzoh could match. But while the 6-4 Taylor returns for his senior season (as does 6-9 starter **Kenrick Zondervan**), the Knights' two superefficient role players from last year, Dave Noel and Mike O'-Donnell, are gone. Speraw has good things to say about redshirt freshman **Chris Baez**, a 6-5 guard, but with a younger team it'll be tough for the Knights to continue their high level of play on offense. Any improvement in the defense will therefore be most welcome. Keep an eye on somewhat foul-prone 6-7 junior **Tony Davis**, the Knights' best defensive rebounder.

UTEP

2008: 19-14 (8-8 C-USA)
Lost to Utah 81-69, CBI First Round
In-conference offense: 1.02 points per possession (7th)
In-conference defense: 1.03 points allowed per possession
   (5th)

What Robert "Fluff" McKiver was to Houston and Robert Vaden was to UAB last year, **Stefon Jackson** was to UTEP. The offense went through him. Oh, how it went through him. Combine Jackson's shots from the field—both twos and threes—with his free-throw attempts, and you'll find that on no fewer than 865 occasions last season Jackson was flinging the ball at the hoop in one way or another. The results were pretty good, not because Jackson was terribly accurate, but because for someone who had the ball in his hands so often he was incredibly adept at not committing turnovers. Nevertheless, it would be best for Tony Barbee's Miners if they got Jackson some help on offense in this, his senior year. Maybe it will come from 6-0 sophomore **Randy Culpepper**, who was not shy about shooting in his own right last year. Also note that **Claude Britten** is a 6-11 sophomore who couldn't get on the floor as a freshman but reportedly has made great strides in the offseason. UTEP is probably a little overvalued in the market of perception right now. They improved their record by two games last year even as their per-possession performance fell off by a hair. But if this offense can evolve past the watch-Stefon stage and develop a second scoring threat, the perception may turn out to be correct after all.

Missouri Valley Conference

Pardon Our Dust

JOHN GASAWAY

With the amount of program-building and rebuilding currently taking place in the Missouri Valley, the conference office should distribute some of those "Excuse the Inconvenience" signs you see at construction sites. Sure such work can be messy. But that it's necessary in this case few will dispute. After all, the Valley had the dreaded "one-bid league" label hung around its neck last year. For the first time since 1998 the Valley had just one team in the NCAA tournament. True, that one team was a fantastic story.

I am writing about Drake's 2008 season almost five months after it ended and I'm still amazed by what I saw from this team, one that went 15-3 in the Valley and earned a five-seed in the NCAA tournament. This from a program that *in each of the previous five seasons* had won no more than seven games in conference play. The Bulldogs burst out of their sub-.500 rut with a superb display of offense. In fact Drake was so good they helped ensure that the Valley received just one bid.

By the end of February it should have been clear that the second best team in the conference was yet another surprise: Illinois State. So it was bad news for the conference as a whole when Drake not only beat the Redbirds in the Missouri Valley Conference tournament title game, but took the further step of virtually disemboweling them in a 79-49 ambush helpfully broadcast on national television by CBS. If the conference office had known their title game was going to turn out like this, they would have signed a deal with ESPNU instead, just to be sure no one saw what happened. Going 13-5 in the Valley, as did Illinois State, would get you an at-large any year you like in the 21st century—except in 2008. Not after a display like that.

So off Drake went, the conference's lone entrant in the NCAA tournament. As you may remember, the Bulldogs were sent home in rather ESPY-ready fashion by Western Kentucky's Ty Rogers after just 45 minutes of tournament play. Mark the conference down as 0-1 in 2008. Truly this is strange territory for the Valley, which had won six tournament games over the previous two tournaments.

The strange territory may continue for one more season. This year the Valley is young. Nine of the 15 players who won all-conference recognition (first and second teams and honorable mention) are gone. The turnover at the top reflects turnover throughout the player ranks: The average Missouri Valley team this year is returning 59 percent of its minutes. Compared to, say, your typical ACC team (73 percent) or Big East team (71 percent), that is not a lot of returning experience.

Not only are the players young, so are their programs. Last year half the coaches in the league were rookies: Keno Davis at Drake, Marty Simmons at Evansville, Tim Jankovich at Illinois State, Kevin McKenna at Indiana State, and Gregg Marshall at Wichita State. This year may seem relatively stable by comparison, the only newcomers being Mark Phelps at Drake (Davis having capped off the Bulldogs' extraordinary year by accepting the position at Providence) and Cuonzo Martin at Missouri State. Nevertheless, it means that six of ten teams are either in just their first or second season under their current coach.

So you'll have to be patient with the Valley. Things are a little disorganized right now—Drake is somehow getting into the NCAA tournament, Southern Illinois is somehow not—while the conference upgrades. But like all upgrades, things should be even better than before when it's done.

	2008 Record	Returning Minutes (%)	2009 Prediction
Creighton	10-8	70	13-5
Drake	15-3	53	12-6
Southern Illinois	11-7	56	11-7
Bradley	9-9	49	10-8
Northern Iowa	9-9	62	9-9
Illinois St.	13-5	49	9-9
Indiana St.	8-10	57	7-11
Missouri St.	8-10	58	7-11
Wichita St.	4-14	56	6-12
Evansville	3-15	83	6-12

BRADLEY

2008: 21-17 (9-9 MVC)
Lost to Tulsa 70-64, CBI Championship Game
In-conference offense: 1.06 points per possession (3rd)
In-conference defense: 1.05 points allowed per possession (8th)

In each of the past two seasons, the Braves have hovered at or around .500 in the Valley by shooting a ton of threes and allowing opponents to make a lot of twos. That was the formula again last year, though there was actually more defense being played by both sides than seen in Bradley games in 2007. Indeed the Braves' defense improved noticeably in conference play last year—unfortunately their offense declined by precisely the same amount. In both seasons Jim Les's team outscored their opponents by the barest of margins, 0.01 points, per possession. Do that and you'll win some and lose some, in roughly equal measures. Don't be surprised to see year three of this dynamic acted out in 2009. The Braves said good-bye to offensive mainstays Daniel Ruffin and Jeremy Crouch, but re-

turnees like 6-5 wing **Andrew Warren** and 6-0 point guard **Sam Maniscalco**, as well as new arrivals like former Iowa State guard **Dodie Dunson**, will likely be happy to have the freed-up shots. As for the interior, you will of course hear this year that Bradley is a poor rebounding team. Maybe they will be now that Matt Salley is gone (**Theron Wilson** will have to pick up that slack), but they weren't last year. The Braves don't do offensive boards because they shoot threes—their personnel is out on the arc. Their defensive rebounding, however, was right at the Valley average last year, as they pulled down 69 percent of their conference opponents' misses. No, the problem for Bradley's defense wasn't the shots that opponents missed, it was the ones they made, to the tune of 51 percent two-point shooting. That level of success inside the arc for opponents is likely to continue. The Braves will again have to score a lot of points to stay around .500.

CREIGHTON

2008: 22-11 (10-8 MVC)
Lost to Florida 82-54, NIT Second Round
In-conference offense: 1.04 points per possession (5th)
In-conference defense: 1.02 points allowed per possession (3rd)

Creighton might be on to something with this **P'Allen Stinnett** guy. In effect, Dana Altman dropped a huge sack of post–Nathan Funk possessions and shots in the 6-3 freshman's lap last year and Stinnett did pretty well, especially when you consider he shot just 32 percent on his threes. He's a 79-percent free-throw shooter, however, suggesting he may yet find the range from the perimeter. And the sophomore's already an efficient scorer inside the arc. Delivering the ball to Stinnett will fall to the two-headed point-guard unit, comprised of 6-1 senior **Josh Dotzler** and 5-11 junior **Cavel Witter**. Dotzler starts and last year posted one of the highest steal rates in the nation. Witter, by contrast, is not shy about looking for his shot. Speaking of which, meet Witter's fellow nonstarter, **Booker Woodfox**, a 6-1 senior who shot more frequently during his scarce minutes last year than even Stinnett. As indeed he should have, since he was in the process of making 42 percent of his threes. He is Altman's most effective returning player on offense and I trust this year he'll not only start but, more important, get more than 17 minutes a game. Down low, 6-9 sophomore **Kenny Lawson** and 6-8 junior **Chad Millard** will try to reverse a dip in defensive rebounding that was the main reason the Jays gave up 1.02 points per trip in-conference last year, as opposed to 0.99 in 2007. Replacing Dane Watts won't be easy—he was accurate on both twos and threes and very good on the defensive glass—but Creighton looks like the favorite for the Missouri Valley Conference title, thanks to a maturing Stinnett and a more visible Woodfox.

DRAKE

2008: 28-5 (15-3 MVC)
Lost to Western Kentucky 101-99 (OT), NCAA Tournament First
  Round
In-conference offense: 1.14 points per possession (1st)
In-conference defense: 1.03 points allowed per possession
  (5th)

What Drake did last year was astonishing. Indeed, one could ask if their performance didn't vitiate the animating principle behind this entire previewing exercise, the idea that you can look at what a team did last year, identify which players departed, look at the ones that are coming in, and make a reasonable assessment of this year's likely outcome. Well, let's see: Entering last year the Bulldogs were coming off a 6-12 year in the Valley. They'd lost their three top players in terms of minutes, a group that included their efficient-scoring star player (Ajay Calvin) and their assist-hoarding point guard (Al Stewart). No returning player last year had averaged more than 22 minutes a game in 2007. You know the rest. Drake went 15-3 and won the Valley by two games, entered the NCAA tournament as a five-seed, and if Western Kentucky's Ty Rogers doesn't hit an incredible shot to beat the buzzer, who knows what else that team could have done. As it was, the season was enough, of course, to install Keno Davis as the new coach at Providence. So now that the Bulldogs have lost three starters from last year, I should predict that they'll beat North Carolina in the national championship game and this time next year Mark Phelps will be coaching the Lakers. I'm not prepared to go that far but first-year coach Phelps should still have a pretty good team. For one thing he has 6-1 junior **Josh Young**, who made half his

twos and 43 percent of his threes last year. Even Young takes a backseat to **Jonathan Cox** in three-point accuracy, though. The 6-8 senior might combine perimeter range (44 percent last year) with defensive rebounding as well as any player in Division I. That's your nucleus right there—how this team fares will be determined by how much help that duo gets from players like 6-5 senior **John Michael Hall**, 6-0 senior **Jacob Baryenbruch**, and 6-8 senior **Brent Heemskerk**. Watch if Phelps keeps the Davis style—heavy on attempted threes and made twos at a slow pace with zero turnovers—or if he tries something new. Either way, we learned last year that you underestimate Drake at your peril.

EVANSVILLE

2008: 9-21 (3-15 MVC)
Lost to Missouri State 69-46, MVC Tournament First Round
In-conference offense: 0.92 points per possession (10th)
In-conference defense: 1.06 points allowed per possession
  (9th)

Like a new administration in its first hundred days, first-year coach Marty Simmons changed the Aces' style on offense dramatically last year, slashing the number of threes that his team attempted. Unfortunately for Simmons, his arrival coincided with the departure of Matt Webster, who had carried the load on an offense that scored 1.05 points per possession in the Valley in 2007. Webster wasn't necessarily a model of efficiency, it's just that what followed happened to be much less efficient: Evansville's offense collapsed last year, registering a meager 0.92 points per trip in-conference. This year Simmons has all five starters returning. It's the last go-round for seniors **Shy Ely**, **Jason Holsinger**, and **Nate Garner**. The first order of business is to make some twos. Once in a great while a player will paradoxically shoot a better percentage on his threes than on his twos—UCLA's Darren Collison and Duke's Greg Paulus are perhaps the two most prominent examples. In addition to having two such rarities on their own roster last year (Holsinger and 6-2 junior **Darin Granger**), Evansville actually came amazingly close to doing that *as a team*, hitting 38 percent of their infrequent threes but just 41 percent of their numerous twos in conference play. Five returning starters will improve that second number.

ILLINOIS STATE

2008: 25-10 (13-5 MVC)
Lost to Dayton 55-48, NIT Second Round
In-conference offense: 1.06 points per possession (2nd)
In-conference defense: 0.99 points allowed per possession (2nd)

Apparently Tim Jankovich was taking really good notes when he was an assistant under Bill Self at Kansas and the Jayhawks were playing some of the best defense to be found anywhere in the nation. As a first-year head coach at Illinois State last season, Jankovich presided over nothing less than a defensive renaissance, one that keyed a turnaround from 6-12 in the Valley in 2007 to 13-5 in 2008. Now the bad news: Jankovich lost three starters from that team and his frontcourt is ailing, with 6-8 senior **Brandon Sampay** and 6-6 junior college transfer **Bobby Hill** both having undergone surgery this summer. Neither player is expected to be available until midseason at the earliest. And though 6-8 junior **Dinma Odiakosa** has successfully stayed away from operating rooms this offseason, he'll need help. Meaning unexpectedly heavy minutes will unavoidably be played by freshmen. It will be up to 6-3 junior wing **Osiris Eldridge** to carry a heavy load on offense. That won't be anything new for the mohawk-sporting Eldridge, who took the lion's share of this offense's shots last year and fared pretty well. He'll team with 6-2 senior **Emmanuel Holloway**, who averaged 19 minutes a game last year. Suffice it to say there are question marks in the near term in Normal. But Jankovich has already shown that when he's outfitted with a roster of healthy players, he can win in the Valley.

INDIANA STATE

2008: 15-16 (8-10 MVC)
Lost to Drake 68-46, MVC Tournament Quarterfinals
In-conference offense: 1.02 points per possession (8th)
In-conference defense: 1.05 points allowed per possession (7th)

The Sycamores are growing before our eyes, going 8-10 in the Valley a year after they posted a 5-13 mark. Granted, Drake and Illinois State were redefining the term "turnaround" in 2008, but Kevin McKenna clearly has his team headed in the right direction. The difference last year was much better of-

fense, despite the fact that nominal star player **Marico Stinson** was having a tough time getting the ball in the basket: The 6-3 Stinson made 35 percent of his threes but just 39 percent of his twos. Nevertheless, teammates like 6-8 **Jay Tunnell** made up for it in their own more subdued fashion, as the offense improved from scoring just 0.94 points per trip in-conference in 2007 to a much more pleasing 1.02 last year. Stinson, Tunnell (who is foul-prone), and 6-0 **Harry Marshall** return as starters this season. Also back is 6-8 sophomore **Isiah Martin**, who posted one of the best block percentages in the nation as a freshman coming off the bench. More minutes for Martin should help improve what was a leaky interior defense in 2008. Note however that the Sycamores lost last year's starter at point guard, Gabe Moore. If the offense is going to continue to improve, McKenna needs to find a replacement who can take excellent care of the ball for a team that doesn't figure to lead the league in shooting.

MISSOURI STATE

2008: 17-16 (8-10 MVC)
Lost to Illinois State 63-58, C-USA Tournament Quarterfinals
In-conference offense: 1.04 points per possession (4th)
In-conference defense: 1.03 points allowed per possession (4th)

First-year coach Cuonzo Martin has taken up residence in the brand new JQH Arena and found that he's working with a slate that, if not blank, at least has plenty of room for new writing. A lot of the shots in this offense last year were taken by two seniors, Dale Lamberth and Deven Mitchell. In their absence Martin will be looking for offense. It could come from 6-4 senior **Chris Cooks**, who last year showed admirable zeal in taking the ball to the rim but also struggled with turnovers. (Cooks, though this may give Martin some pause, is also this team's best returning defensive rebounder.) Another possibility is 6-0 junior **Justin Fuehrmeyer**, who made 36 percent of his threes while leaving the bulk of the shots to Lamberth and Mitchell. Also returning is 6-1 senior **Spencer Laurie**. No, you're not mistaken, Laurie was in fact a senior *last* year, but he was granted an additional year of eligibility by the NCAA in July on account of an injury-shortened sophomore year, during which he played a total of 74 minutes for Quin Snyder–era Missouri. Laurie will be joined this year by his brother, 6-2 senior **Shane Laurie**. There's enough experience here for Martin to put a credible Valley team on the floor in his first season. Past "credible," however, the main challenge will likely be on offense. The now departed Lamberth wasn't a big name nationally, goodness knows. He came late to the featured role on offense and, anyway, with the drama surrounding former coach Barry Hinson's status last year, few people were paying much attention to what was happening on the court. But those who were watching the games saw that Lamberth had an outstanding year on offense. His possessions will now go to other players and it is a near certainty that those possessions will not be translated into as many points. Call Martin's first season a success if this team again scores more points than they allow in conference play.

NORTHERN IOWA

2008: 18-14 (9-9 MVC)
Lost to Illinois State 56-42, MVC Tournament Semifinals
In-conference offense: 1.02 points per possession (7th)
In-conference defense: 1.04 points allowed per possession (6th)

Last year no player in Division I rebounded a higher percentage of opponents' misses during his minutes on the floor than Northern Iowa senior Eric Coleman, who personally hauled in an absolutely absurd 35 percent of the other team's missed shots. At the same time he was a good though not great shotblocker. Coleman had a reputation for being inconsistent and maybe he did give his coach a few gray hairs. But in effect he was a one-man defense who also led his team in both points and, incredibly, assists—to say his absence leaves a hole is putting it mildly. Ben Jacobson will try to fill that hole with, really, the entire team. Let's linger in the paint and start with 7-1 junior **Jordan Eglseder**. He's been used in short stretches to date and his effect on the boards on both ends of the court is profound, plus he's a better shot-blocker than Coleman. Eglseder is not your typical "project" big man: When he's in the game the Panther offense goes through him—even more than it went through Coleman—and he does fine, taking care of the ball and hitting his shots. The only question is whether he can do it for more than 17 minutes a game. **Adam Koch**, conversely, has shown he can acquit himself well on the defensive glass while logging 27 minutes per contest. The 6-8

junior is additionally fouled with astonishing frequency and he shoots 78 percent from the line. Another returning starter is 6-3 senior **Travis Brown**, who made 36 percent of his threes last year. And 6-6 sophomore **Kerwin Dunham** made 17 starts as a freshman. Durham and Brown will likely be making room in the backcourt for the return of 6-2 sophomore **Kwadzo Ahelegbe**, a point guard who missed all of last season with a shoulder injury. If these returnees, particularly Eglseder, can develop and mesh, the Panthers could repeat last year's .500 record in the Valley.

SOUTHERN ILLINOIS

2008: 18-15 (11-7 MVC)
Lost to Arizona State 65-51, NIT Second Round
In-conference offense: 1.02 points per possession (6th)
In-conference defense: 0.96 points allowed per possession (1st)

Southern Illinois missed the NCAA tournament for the first time in seven years in 2008 because they couldn't score enough points. The Saluki defense was yet again excellent last year, but Chris Lowery's team simply couldn't get enough twos to go down. It seems plain in hindsight that Jamaal Tatum's departure after the 2007 season hurt this offense severely—words that would have baffled me completely two years ago. For you see, in 2006 this same Tatum had the inefficient season to end all absurdly inefficient seasons on offense. That year Tatum shot often and shot horribly, yet was gravely contended to be "vital" to the offense because, after all, he was SIU's "leading scorer." Seasons like the one Tatum had move fans to have heartfelt and life-changing tempo-free conversions every day. So how is it that Tatum actually *did* turn out to be vital? For one thing he improved greatly as a senior in 2007. Still, even then Tatum was no master inside the arc: He made 46 percent of his twos that year. What he did do, though, was absorb a tremendous amount of attention and effort from opposing defenses. There was no one to do that last year. The attention and effort rained down with a vengeance on Randal Falker and Matt Shaw and, not coincidentally, their two-point percentages dipped. Now *they're* gone, along with Tyrone Green. So while it's expected that this year SIU will continue to make life miserable for opposing offenses—it's just in the water in Carbondale, right?—it's much tougher to know what we'll see from this offense, probably even for Lowery. He does have 6-1 senior point guard **Bryan Mullins**, who cornered the market on Saluki assists last year while hitting 41 percent of his threes and, not least, winning the Valley's defensive player of the year award. Mullins will be joined by 6-3 junior **Josh Bone** and 6-3 senior **Wesley Clemmons.** Note as well that Lowery has brought in the top recruiting class in the conference, one headlined by the Valley's highest-rated recruit, 6-8 freshman **Anthony Booker**. The new post-Tatum, post-Falker generation of Saluki is finally here. In March 2007 few thought Lowery would choose to stay and see this day, but he has. Let's see what he does with it.

WICHITA STATE

2008: 11-20 (4-14 MVC)
Lost to Indiana State 71-67, MVC Tournament First Round
In-conference offense: 0.99 points per possession (9th)
In-conference defense: 1.07 points allowed per possession (10th)

The Shockers were wiped out by injuries last year and were unable to compete for first-year coach Gregg Marshall. The stats left behind are tellingly ugly but, in terms of team performance, they hold little value for telling us what happens now. Indeed, if the hoops gods had not smiled, at last, on Marshall and given him a late-season home date against last-place Evansville, this team would have gone to its rest without having once savored the sweet taste of victory over its last 26 days. Marshall proved at Winthrop that he can build a program, and this year he's already brought in a recruiting class that is perhaps second only to that of Southern Illinois in the conference. This year, however, keep your eye on two non-freshmen: **Ramon Clemente** and **J. T. Durley**. Clemente is a 6-6 senior who dominates the defensive glass like he's 6-10. And Durley's a 6-7 sophomore who suffered a broken foot over the summer. If he can return healthy, hold on to the ball, and if Marshall persuades him to just give up on the threes already, Durley might develop into a force to be reckoned with.

The Mountain West

Where Have All the Athletes Gone?

KEN POMEROY

The vital signs were good for the Mountain West Conference in 2008. After an offseason of higher than average personnel losses, the conference managed to send a second team to the NCAA tournament for the seventh consecutive season. Considering that the league's rosters are more stable this season, it would be surprising if that streak failed to continue.

Below the surface, however, the Mountain West Conference is starting to take on the appearance of the Ivy League, only with players that are taller, bulkier, and did worse on the SATs. In the two statistics that tend to gauge athleticism, offensive rebounding and blocked shots, the MWC is among the least active conferences in the nation. Only 28 percent of rebounds were grabbed by the offense in MWC games last season, the lowest rate among the 31 Division I conferences. Utah's Luke Nevill led the conference by swatting 6.6 percent of opponents' two-point shots. That was the lowest mark for a league leader of any conference. Finally, the MWC was also the sixth-slowest conference in terms of pace.

It hasn't exactly been a quick transformation to this state. In recent seasons, the conference has produced Joel Anthony and Justin Williams, two of the better shot-blockers in the nation, but the MWC has never been known for that. And contested rebounds haven't been common for a while, although, last season's mark in that category was the lowest recorded by any conference in the past five seasons. One has to wonder if playing over half the season in such a passive environment is poor preparation for the NCAA tournament. In its nine-year history, the MWC has sent just two teams to the Sweet 16 and has a record of 8-20 in the Big Dance.

At the local level, it appears the MWC is on the cusp of dividing into the haves and have-nots. In one corner is a group containing BYU, New Mexico, San Diego State, UNLV, and Utah. Those are the programs that will be competing for conference titles over the next two to three years. For this season, it appears once again that the most talent lies in Provo and Las Vegas. In 2007 and 2008, BYU has won the regular-season title with UNLV finishing second. In both years, UNLV won the conference tournament. It isn't Red Sox versus Yankees, but Cougars versus Rebels is establishing itself as the most relevant rivalry in the Mountain West.

	2008 Record	Returning Minutes (%)	2009 Prediction
BYU	14-2	53	13-3
UNLV	12-4	63	13-3
Utah	7-9	84	10-6
San Diego St.	9-7	87	10-6
New Mexico	11-5	53	9-7
TCU	6-10	65	6-10
Wyoming	5-11	52	5-11
Air Force	8-8	56	4-12
Colorado St.	0-16	83	2-14

AIR FORCE

2008: 16-14 (8-8 MWC)
Lost to San Diego State 53-49, MWC quarterfinals
In-conference offense: 0.95 points per possession (7th)
In-conference defense: 1.00 points allowed per possession (5th)

Air Force managed to attain a .500 conference record despite being outscored by 43 points over its 16 games. The Falcons appear to be in the midst of a rather sudden return to the depths of their conference, a standard location for the Falcons program, which was adjusted by their unlikely ascension in the middle part of this decade. The vaunted offense that rose to fame under Joe Scott, and continued under Chris Mooney and Jeff Bzdelik, fell off the table in the first season under Jeff Reynolds.

Tim Anderson was far and away the team's best player and he was a senior. This season's squad should be led by 6-6 senior **Andrew Henke** who made 42 percent of his threes last season. On an unrelated note, one of the more underrated streaks in America is that the Falcons have lost 16 consecutive conference tournament games. It's especially perplexing considering they haven't had a losing conference record since 2003.

BYU

2008: 27-8 (14-2 MWC)
Lost to Texas A&M 67-62, NCAA first round
In-conference offense: 1.03 points per possession (4th)
In-conference defense: 0.90 points allowed per possession (1st)

After BYU lost four seniors from its top six minutes-earners in 2007, it was expected somebody would emerge from the shadows to become a big-time scorer. That player seemed most likely to be shooting guard **Jonathan Tavernari**. It turned out to be forward **Lee Cummard**.

No major media organization gives out a national Most Improved Player award. If one did, I suspect West Virginia's Joe Alexander or UCLA's Russell Westbrook would have gotten a lot of consideration. The difference between those guys and Cummard is that Cummard hardly ever launched a shot the season before. He went from being the last offensive option to the first. In doing so he made 47 percent of his

threes, 62 percent of his twos, and 86 percent of his free throws. He also led the Cougars in assist rate, blocked a few shots, and forced a few steals. He's the best player in the Mountain West Conference as the season begins.

BYU last lost a Mountain West Conference home game on March 5, 2005. Since then they've reeled off 24 consecutive conference wins in the Marriott Center, part of a 47-game home winning streak overall, the longest in the country heading into the season. If a team is going to unseat BYU at the top of the league, it will help if they conquer Provo. That goes especially for UNLV, who over the last two seasons have beat the Cougars by a combined 37 points at the Thomas and Mack, but lost to them by 53 at the Marriott Center.

COLORADO STATE

2008: 7-25 (0-16 MWC)
Lost to BYU 89-62, MWC quarterfinals
In-conference offense: 0.93 points per possession (8th)
In-conference defense: 1.16 points allowed per possession (9th)

Of the three teams in the nation that failed to win a conference game, Colorado State was the least deserving of that outcome. Four of the Rams' losses came by three points or less. And to say they didn't win a conference game requires the qualifier "regular-season," because they were able to win the 8/9 game in the Mountain West Conference tournament, which ended a 21-game losing streak against Division I teams. For the second consecutive season, head coach Tim Miles has brought in a bevy of new players, all of whom are under-the-radar types, meaning they'll need time to develop. The most notable of the newcomers are 6-10 Purdue transfer **Dan Vandervieren** and 6-5 **Harvey Perry**, who started his career at Washington. Senior guard **Marcus Walker** will continue to be Miles's best offensive weapon.

NEW MEXICO

2008: 24-9 (11-5 MWC)
Lost to California 68-66, NIT first round

In-conference offense: 1.10 points per possession (1st)
In-conference defense: 0.95 points allowed per possession
(2nd)

No surprise, the biggest influence that Steve Alford had in Albuquerque was taking a poor defense by Mountain West Conference standards and making it one of the better units in the country. The shocker was that the Lobos offense also got better under Alford's watch. That bodes well for the long-term prospects of basketball at the Pit. In the short term, however, he has to deal with the departure of J. R. Giddens who filled up a stat sheet just about every way possible and was taken with the 30th pick in the NBA draft. However, he's the only starter that Alford loses, and highly regarded freshman **Philip McDonald** will get an opportunity in Giddens's absence. With his shooting ability, he should fit well on a team that made 42 percent of its threes last season, the second-best figure in the country.

SAN DIEGO STATE

2008: 20-13 (9-7 MWC)
Lost to Florida 73-49, NIT first round
In-conference offense: 1.02 points per possession (5th)
In-conference defense: 0.96 points allowed per possession
(4th)

All five starters return for Steve Fisher's team, which has been at a loss for scoring since Marcus Slaughter left for the pro game after the 2006 season. This team could use a better distribution of its offensive possessions. **Lorrenzo Wade** was the first choice on offense last season but shot just 48 percent in eFG terms. Along with Cummard, he's one of the better passing forwards in the nation. **Richie Williams**, the expected starter at point guard, is rather prominently featured in the O as well, but his eFG percentage was in the low 40s last season.

Once again, the Aztecs will have a lineup that's on the small side, which results in a team that struggles to get second shots. Although, admirably, they are tremendous at preventing opponents from doing the same.

TCU

2008: 14-16 (6-10 MWC)
Lost to UNLV 89-88, MWC quarterfinals
In-conference offense: 0.92 points per possession (9th)
In-conference defense: 1.01 points allowed per possession (7th)

The lone coaching change in the Mountain West occurred at TCU where Neil Dougherty is out after six years of struggling to recruit to a university that is 600 miles from its nearest conference neighbor. He compiled a 30-66 conference record after coming to Fort Worth as one of the more highly regarded assistant coaches in the country, due to his association with Kansas and Roy Williams. The Horned Frogs hired Jim Christian away from Kent State to replace Dougherty. Christian's track record as a head coach indicates that he values defense more than offense. However, his biggest project will be dealing with a team that missed shots with frightening regularity last season. Fortunately, there are three other programs in the conference that need a lot of help as well, thus not all the team's lessons will have to be losses.

UNLV

2008: 27-8 (12-4 MWC)
Lost to Kansas 75-56, NCAA second round
In-conference offense: 1.04 points per possession (3rd)
In-conference defense: 0.96 points allowed per possession (3rd)

The Rebels still apply the "Runnin'" modifier to their nickname, but in Lon Kruger's four seasons as head coach of UNLV he has methodically transformed the offense into one that values ball control, three-point shooting, and isn't afraid to take time off the shot clock.

UNLV offense over the last four seasons with national rank

3PA%: percentage of FGAs that are three point shots

Season	Pace/Rank	TO%/Rank	3PA%/Rank
2005	69.9/61	20.5/113	32.8/166
2006	67.7/126	21.4/175	30.4/229
2007	65.9/200	16.1/3	36.4/116
2008	65.2/235	16.1/7	39.6/59

The shooting part of the transformation is due to the strength of the team being in its backcourt. In 2007, it was **Wink Adams** and Kevin Kruger handling those duties. Last season, it was Adams and Curtis Terry. In 2009, it will be Adams and somebody else, as Terry was a senior. This year Coach Kruger has no choice but to play a nonsenior at point guard. It appears that role will initially go to Memphis transfer **Tre'Von Willis**, and it will be difficult for him to lose the job. The only other true point on the roster is true freshman **Oscar Bellfield**.

Last season the Rebels had one of the smaller frontlines in major college ball but that could change. **Beas Hamga**, a seven-footer from Cameroon, is now eligible to take the floor after sitting out his first season on campus because of an NCAA ruling regarding his precollege classwork in Africa. On a team that didn't start a player over 6-7 last season, Hamga will be a welcome addition, even though his scoring ability may be limited.

In addition to Adams, Willis, and Hamga, two other seniors will fill out the top of Kruger's rotation. **Joe Darger**, at 6-7, and 6-6 **Rene Rougeau** started together nearly the entire season and did well considering their height limitation. But better Mountain West Conference opponents routinely took advantage of mismatches in the paint, to the point where UNLV's in-conference two-point percentage allowed ranked third-to-last in the league. Thus, Kruger is hoping that Hamga will provide a boost to the defense. Hamga's impact is the single biggest unknown in trying to forecast a conference championship for the Ploddin' Rebels.

UTAH

2008: 18-15 (7-9 MWC)
Lost to Tulsa 69-60, CBI second round
In-conference offense: 1.05 points per possession (2nd)
In-conference defense: 1.00 points allowed per possession (6th)

Utah made the transition to a new coach somewhat smoothly last season. There was hardly any change in the offensive character of the team under Jim Boylen, although the ball did go to 7-2 center **Luke Nevill** more often. However there was a major improvement on defense where the Utes were the worst team in the Mountain West Conference in 2007. Their improvement to sixth in the league is a little more impressive when one considers that they allowed 1.17 points per possession in conference games in Ray Giacoletti's last season, the fourth-worst figure in the country.

For the second consecutive season, Utah's on-court performance was quite a bit better than its record indicated. Utah outscored conference foes by 40 points, which normally would equate to a 9-7 record. Eventually, the Utes will get what they deserve. If that happens this season, it would mean a top-four finish in the Mountain West Conference. Of course, it's possible they could actually get better than they deserve for once. Utah only loses point guard Johnnie Bryant from Boylen's six-man rotation and they add some insurance at center. Seven-footer **Jason Washburn** might be the most promising true freshman in the conference.

WYOMING

2008: 12-18 (5-11 MWC)
Lost to Colorado State 68-63, MWC first round
In-conference offense: 0.96 points per possession (6th)
In-conference defense: 1.06 points allowed per possession (8th)

Heath Schroyer promised to bring a speedier attack to Laramie and to some extent he achieved that. The Cowboys actually led the Mountain West Conference in tempo during conference play. But their games averaged a pedestrian 68 possessions per game, which is a testament to the glacial pace that most conference teams preferred to play at. Schroyer will be depending on point guard **Brandon Ewing** again this season. Ewing led the conference in minutes played in 2008, after finishing third and second in his freshman and sophomore seasons, respectively. Ewing's backcourt mate for three seasons and fellow minutes-eater, Brad Jones, is gone. Wichita State transfer **Sean Ogirri** will replace him in the starting lineup and may even be an upgrade.

At a Glance

The Rest of Division I

Or
"Why You Should Be Reading Kyle Whelliston"

KEN POMEROY AND JOHN GASAWAY

To this point we've covered 118 teams. If this were football we'd be making a few last pithy remarks as we exit stage left. Alas, this is basketball. There are over 220 programs remaining in this here galaxy. Fact is, the goal for the overwhelming majority of these remaining teams is to win their conference's automatic bid and play in the NCAA tournament.

However, there are a few teams who will aspire to do more this season.

The two most realistic candidates to win more than one game in the dance are familiar to anyone who's filled out a bracket in recent years: **Gonzaga** and **Davidson**. Gonzaga will have one of the best players in the nation this season in 6-10 sophomore **Austin Daye**. Heck, Daye was one of the best players in the nation *last* season but only played 19 minutes per game. Mark Few, like many others in the coaching fraternity, was reluctant to give his freshman minutes in the face of statistical production.

There are areas where Daye can improve. While he's one of the best defensive rebounders in the nation, he's one of the worst for his size on the offensive end. Even though he posted the second-best shot-blocking rate in the West Coast Conference last season, he is still criticized for allegedly lacking the desire to guard someone. However, considering the Zags generally put four other guys on the floor that have trouble staying in front of their man, Daye's shot-blocking prowess should come in handy. To go

with Daye, Gonzaga returns four starters from a team that went 25-8 and earned a seven-seed in the NCAA tournament.

The Bulldogs' hopes of a fifth Sweet 16 appearance in the last ten seasons were crushed by a first-round loss to Davidson. Davidson's 2008 season was reminiscent of Gonzaga's breakthrough season in 1999. There were a few early-season losses to high-profile opponents. A relatively easy ride through the conference schedule with plenty of dominating wins. Both teams found themselves getting 10-seeds. Both found themselves in the Elite Eight. Even though 10 years have passed, the selection committee may still be punishing teams too harshly for road losses to quality teams and not rewarding them enough for consistently putting away midlevel competition.

The Wildcats return three starters from a year ago including pure-shooting superhero **Stephen Curry**. Curry was as dangerous a three-point threat as there was in college basketball last season. He made 44 percent of his attempts while taking a little more than 10 three-pointers a game. Opponents knew he would shoot a lot and that he was accurate. Yet they could do little to stop him.

The problem for Davidson is that one of its seniors last season was point guard Jason Richards, who was easily the second-most important cog in the Wildcats' machine. The closest thing that Davidson had to a backup point guard in 2008 was Curry himself. Davidson did manage to snag a skilled big man on the recruiting trail in 6-10 **Frank Ben-Eze**, who was eyed by a few power-conference programs. And for those of you looking for more Curry in your hoops diet, Stephen's little brother **Seth Curry** will be playing at **Liberty** this season.

Besides Gonzaga and Davidson, there may not be another at-large quality team from outside the top-ten conferences. **Butler** has been a fixture in the rankings over the past two seasons, but five of their top six players were seniors last season. The lone returning starter, though, is **Matt Howard**. As a freshman last season, Howard was one of the most efficient little big men in the nation. At 6-7, he routinely played in the post and was an effective scoring complement to the four sharpshooters surrounding him. However, this season it's possible that Butler will be overtaken in the Horizon League by **Cleveland State**. The Vikings return three starters including 6-4 **J'Nathan Bullock**, a slashing wing that's awarded free throws in droves and regularly outrebounds taller players. Fans of apostrophes should also keep an eye on fellow starter 6-4 sophomore **D'Aundray Brown**.

Out west, there's still some buzz about **Saint Mary's**. The Gaels of Moraga, California, bring back **Patrick Mills**, **Diamon Simpson**, and **Omar Samhan** from an NCAA tournament team that won 25 games. Mills spent the summer honing his point-guard skills while representing Australia in Beijing during the Summer Olympics. Samhan and Simpson anchor a frontline that produced one of the better defenses in the country.

The Western Athletic Conference would typically produce one or two teams capable of making noise in March, and normally we would devote a section to previewing their teams. But last season, the conference suffered a sharp decline in its level of play with at-large talk pretty much ending before the conference season even started. That probably won't change this season, but Mark Fox and **Nevada** managed to put together one of the better recruiting classes in the nation. It's headlined by 6-8 power forward **Luke Babbitt** who had interest from a number of elite programs. Babbitt elected to stay home in Reno and will have an impact on the Western Athletic Conference immediately. Also headed to Nevada is 6-6 **Joey Shaw**, who showed promise as an athletic wing while playing for Indiana two seasons ago.

Any overview of Division I isn't complete without mentioning **Lester Hudson** of **Tennessee-Martin**. The Skyhawks guard put together a season strikingly similar to Stephen Curry's. He made 39 percent of his 320 three-point attempts but was capable of scoring in a variety of other ways. He played some point guard but he's also an exceptional rebounder, considering he's listed at 6-3. (Hudson actually had a quadruple-double last season. Granted, it was against Central Baptist, which is not a Division I program and is part of something called the National Christian College Athletic Association. But, still, it's a unique accomplishment.) Like Curry, he saved his best for UTM's best competition. Hudson scored 35 against Memphis, 25 against UNLV, and 36 against Vanderbilt. Hudson is the early favorite to win the national scoring title this season, which is probably the only way you'll hear his name. However, if Hudson is playing at a gym near you, it would be worth your time to check him out.

And that's your complete primer on the other couple hundred teams in Division I. In this sport even the most passionate fan seeking to know everything about every team is humbled. Division I hoops alone among the major spectator sports holds this quality of inexhaustibility. It's like music. You just *know* there's more good stuff out there, even though you haven't run across it yet. We encourage you to read your Kyle Whelliston, get out there, and find that good stuff. Maybe we'll bump into you.

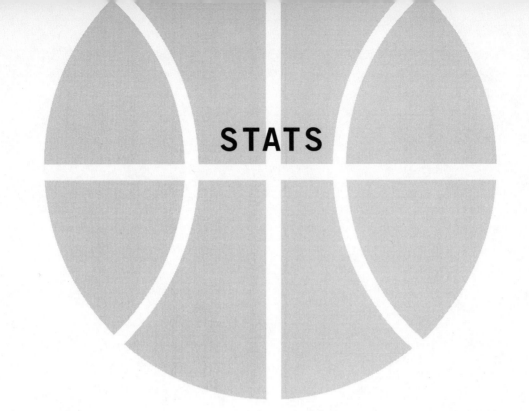

STATS

Statistical Abstract

CONFERENCE-WIDE STATS

The following section contains average stats in various categories for each conference computed from regular season conference action only. These stats are not the conventional kind kept by official scorekeepers, but rather measures that better define a conference's style. Which conference has the most close games? Which conference is the fastest-paced? Those are the kinds of questions you can answer using the data in this section.

Regarding the historical stats, the Summit League includes all data from when it was called the Mid-Continent Conference prior to the 2008 season. The same holds for the Horizon League, which was the Midwestern Collegiate Conference prior to the 2002 season, and the Atlantic Sun Conference, which was the Trans America Athletic Conference prior to 2002.

HOME-COURT RECORDS

Which conference has the most difficult home courts? This decade it's been the Mountain West. While home court is usually an advantage, there have been five times this decade where a conference has collectively had a losing record at home during conference play. Last season's Northeast Conference went 45-54 at home, the worst record of the past nine seasons.

Conference Home-Court Records, 2000-2008

	Conference	W-L	Pct
1	**MWC**	**372-180**	**.674**
2	SEC	581-283	.672
3	MVC	540-270	.667
4	Big Ten	535-268	.666
5	Big 12	573-291	.663
6	MAC	656-346	.655
7	CAA	530-282	.653
8	WAC	459-245	.652
9	Horizon	413-221	.651
10	Big South	375-205	.647
11	ACC	472-264	.641
12	Big Sky	363-205	.639
13	CUSA	581-335	.634
14	Summit	386-232	.625
15	Big East	649-399	.619
16	Sun Belt	496-306	.618
17	SoCon	531-333	.615
18	OVC	499-313	.615
19	Atlantic 10	550-352	.610
20	SWAC	489-320	.604
21	Southland	532-350	.603
22	Atlantic Sun	540-361	.599
23	Patriot	286-192	.598
24	Big West	421-290	.592
25	MAAC	479-331	.591
26	America East	424-296	.589
27	Ivy	296-208	.587
28	Pac 10	75-335	.586
29	NE	555-396	.584
30	MEAC	506-375	.574
31	WCC	280-224	.556
	Total	14844-9008	.622

Conference Home-Court Records, 2008

1	**MAC**	**68-27**	**.716**
2	MVC	62-28	.689
3	Horizon	61-29	.678
	Summit	61-29	.678
5	Big 12	65-31	.677
6	SEC	64-32	.667
7	Big South	37-19	.661
8	CAA	71-37	.657
9	WAC	47-25	.653
	Big Sky	47-25	.653
11	CUSA	62-34	.646
12	SoCon	71-39	.645
13	MWC	46-26	.639
14	Sun Belt	74-43	.632
15	Big East	90-54	.625
16	Big Ten	61-38	.616
17	Atlantic Sun	59-37	.615
18	MEAC	54-34	.614
19	Ivy	34-22	.607
20	ACC	58-38	.604
21	OVC	65-45	.591
22	Southland	56-39	.589
23	WCC	33-23	.589
24	MAAC	53-37	.589
25	Big West	42-30	.583
26	Atlantic 10	64-48	.571
27	SWAC	50-40	.556
28	Patriot	31-25	.554
29	Pac 10	48-42	.533
30	America East	38-34	.528
31	NEC	45-54	.455
	Total	1717-1064	.617

Best Single-Season Home-Court Records Since 2000

1	**2000 MCC**	**44-12**	**.786**
2	2004 MWC	43-13	.768
3	2000 CAA	55-17	.764
4	2001 CAA	42-14	.750
	2007 SEC	72-24	.750

Worst Single-Season Home-Court Records Since 2000

1	**2008 NEC**	**45-54**	**.455**
2	2006 Big West	26-30	.464
3	2001 WCC	27-29	.482
4	2003 WCC	28-28	.500
	2003 Ivy	28-28	.500

PARITY

Which conferences are the most competitive? The Parity Index describes the expected difference between two randomly selected teams' conference win totals in a season. Adjustments are made to account for the varying lengths of different conference schedules. For consistent conference-play mayhem, head to the SWAC. Although last season the Patriot League was the most up for grabs, with seven of its eight teams finishing within two games of .500.

Conference Average Parity Index, 2000-2008

1	**SWAC**	**3.48**
2	Southland	3.72
3	OVC	3.74
4	Southland	3.77
5	MAC	3.79
6	Big Sky	3.83
7	ACC	3.86
8	MVC	3.87
9	NEC	3.90
10	CAA	3.99
11	Horizon	3.99
12	MAAC	4.00
13	Big 12	4.02
14	Sun Belt	4.02
15	Big East	4.03
16	SoCon	4.07
17	Big West	4.09
18	Big South	4.11
19	Atlantic 10	4.21
20	Atlantic Sun	4.28
21	Summit	4.29
22	MEAC	4.31
23	America East	4.31
24	CUSA	4.31
25	Big Ten	4.35
26	WAC	4.35
27	Pac 10	4.41
28	MWC	4.43
29	Patriot	4.60
30	Ivy	4.78
31	WCC	5.01

Conference Average Parity Index, 2008

1	**Patriot**	**2.20**
2	OVC	2.91
3	Big Ten	3.02
4	SWAC	3.12
5	America East	3.16
6	Summit	3.32
7	CAA	3.34
8	Big East	3.58
9	ACC	3.64
10	MAC	3.72
11	MVC	3.79
12	Atlantic 10	3.83
13	Horizon	3.87
14	Big South	4.00
15	Southland	4.03
16	Big Sky	4.04
17	SEC	4.14
18	MAAC	4.27
19	MEAC	4.29
20	Atlantic Sun	4.30
21	Pac 10	4.39
22	WAC	4.50
23	Sun Belt	4.50
24	SoCon	4.57
25	CUSA	4.67
26	NEC	4.82
27	Big West	4.83
28	MWC	4.94
29	Big 12	5.07
30	Ivy	5.39
31	WCC	5.88

Lowest Single-Season Parity Index Since 2000

1	**2003 Ivy**	**6.53**
2	2006 Patriot	6.29
3	2000 Patriot	6.10
4	2001 WCC	6.04
	2002 WCC	6.04

Highest Single-Season Parity Index Since 2000

1	**2004 Big Sky**	**2.04**
2	2008 Patriot	2.20
3	2007 Sun Belt	2.64
4	2004 OVC	2.65
5	2005 SWAC	2.69
	2007 SWAC	2.69

CLOSE GAMES

Close games here are defined as being decided by three points or less or games that went to overtime. Last season, the ACC set a decadal record with over a third of its games falling into the close category. Historically, though, the power conferences tend to produce fewer close games than the rest of Division I.

Conference Close Game Frequency, 2000-2008

*Overtime games not tracked prior to 2003 season

1	**MEAC**	**25.7**	**(226 of 881)**
2	Atlantic Sun	23.8	(214 of 901)
3	WAC	23.3	(164 of 704)
4	Big Sky	23.2	(132 of 568)
5	Sun Belt	23.1	(185 of 802)
6	OVC	22.5	(183 of 812)
7	SWAC	22.4	(181 of 809)
8	ACC	22.3	(164 of 736)
9	Summit	22.2	(137 of 618)
10	CAA	22.2	(180 of 812)
11	MAAC	21.9	(177 of 810)
12	Horizon	21.8	(138 of 634)
13	America East	21.7	(156 of 720)
14	NEC	21.2	(202 of 951)
15	Big East	21.1	(221 of 1048)
16	SEC	21.1	(182 of 864)
17	Big South	20.5	(119 of 580)
18	MVC	20.5	(166 of 810)
19	MAC	20.5	(205 of 1002)
20	Southland	20.4	(180 of 882)
21	Big West	20.4	(145 of 711)
22	SoCon	19.9	(172 of 864)
23	MWC	19.7	(109 of 552)
24	Pac 10	19.6	(159 of 810)
25	Big 12	19.2	(166 of 864)
26	CUSA	18.7	(171 of 916)
27	Patriot	18.6	(89 of 478)
28	Ivy	18.1	(91 of 504)
29	WCC	17.9	(90 of 504)
30	Big Ten	16.9	(136 of 803)
31	Atlantic 10	15.4	(139 of 902)

Conference Close Game Frequency, 2008

1	**ACC**	**36.5**	**(35 of 96)**
2	Big Sky	31.9	(23 of 72)
3	MEAC	28.4	(25 of 88)
4	CAA	27.8	(30 of 108)
	Horizon	27.8	(25 of 90)
	America East	27.8	(20 of 72)
	MVC	27.8	(25 of 90)
8	Southland	26.3	(25 of 95)
9	Atlantic Sun	26.0	(25 of 96)
	SEC	26.0	(25 of 96)
11	OVC	25.5	(28 of 110)
12	NEC	25.3	(25 of 99)
13	Big South	23.2	(13 of 56)
14	Big East	22.9	(33 of 144)
15	Atlantic 10	22.3	(25 of 112)
16	Patriot	21.4	(12 of 56)
17	MWC	20.8	(15 of 72)
18	Summit	20.0	(18 of 90)
19	Big 12	19.8	(19 of 96)
20	MAC	18.9	(18 of 95)
21	CUSA	18.8	(18 of 96)
22	Sun Belt	17.1	(20 of 117)
23	SWAC	16.7	(15 of 90)
	Pac 10	16.7	(15 of 90)
25	MAAC	15.6	(14 of 90)
26	Big Ten	15.2	(15 of 99)
27	Ivy	14.3	(8 of 56)
	WCC	14.3	(8 of 56)
29	SoCon	13.6	(15 of 110)
30	WAC	12.5	(9 of 72)
31	Big West	8.3	(6 of 72)

Highest Close Game Frequency Since 2000

1	**2008 ACC**	**36.5**	**(35 of 96)**
2	2007 MAAC	33.3	(32 of 96)
	2006 Big 12	33.3	(32 of 96)
4	2008 Big Sky	31.9	(23 of 72)
	2000 CAA	31.9	(23 of 72)

Lowest Close Game Frequency Since 2000

1	**2005 Horizon**	**5.6**	**(4 of 72)**
2	2008 Big West	8.3	(6 of 72)
3	2006 Patriot	8.9	(5 of 56)
	2003 Ivy	8.9	(5 of 56)
	2002 WCC	8.9	(5 of 56)

EFFICIENCY

Unlike the previous stats (which I'll refer to as "game" stats), the following tempo-free stats are only available since the 2004 season. The game stats tend to have little correlation from year to year. Tempo-free stats are much more stable, relatively speaking. Some conferences retain distinct characteristics in their style of play.

We start with efficiency, which is the average number of points scored during 100 possessions of conference play. The interpretation of why conferences are different is more complicated than it might seem. Is the consistent offensive explosion of the Summit (née Mid-Con) the result of poor defense, great offense, coaching philosophy, or officiating style? It's probably a mixture of all that and more.

Conference Efficiency, 2004-2008

1	**Summit**	**106.6**
2	OVC	105.6
3	MAAC	104.8
4	ACC	104.8
5	Big Sky	104.7
6	Atlantic 10	104.2
7	Pac 10	103.9
8	MWC	103.8
9	SEC	103.8
10	Big 12	103.7
11	NEC	103.5
12	Big West	103.3
13	Horizon	103.2
14	WCC	103.2
15	Big East	103.2
16	Sun Belt	103.1
17	Atlantic Sun	103.0
18	Big South	102.6
19	Big Ten	102.6
20	WAC	102.6
21	SoCon	102.4
22	MAC	102.4
23	MVC	102.0
24	CAA	102.0
25	Southland	100.8
26	Ivy	100.7
27	CUSA	100.7
28	America East	100.2
29	Patriot	98.1
30	MEAC	97.7
31	SWAC	95.1

Conference Efficiency, 2008

1	**Atlantic 10**	**106.1**
2	WAC	106.0
3	Summit	105.7
4	OVC	105.6
5	Pac 10	105.2
6	ACC	105.0
7	SEC	104.8
8	MAAC	104.6
9	Big South	104.3
10	Big Sky	104.2
11	SoCon	104.0
12	Big West	103.5
13	Big 12	103.4
14	Sun Belt	103.3
15	MVC	103.3
16	NEC	103.0
17	America East	103.0
18	CUSA	102.9
19	Big East	102.7
20	Ivy	102.5
21	Big Ten	101.8
22	Atlantic Sun	101.2
23	CAA	100.7
24	Horizon	100.6
25	MAC	100.3
26	WCC	100.2
27	MWC	100.0
28	Patriot	99.8
29	Southland	99.0
30	SWAC	98.3
31	MEAC	97.7

Highest Conference Efficiency, 2004-2008

1	**2006 Big Sky**	**108.9**
2	2006 Mid-Con	108.6
3	2006 MAAC	108.4
4	2007 A-10	107.9
5	2005 Mid-Con	107.8

Lowest Conference Efficiency, 2004-2008

1	**2005 SWAC**	**91.9**
2	2007 SWAC	93.7
3	2004 SWAC	94.9
4	2005 MEAC	95.4
5	2006 SWAC	96.6

PACE

Pace, synonymous with tempo, is the average number of possessions per 40 minutes of conference action. Historically, a ticket to the typical Southland Conference gets you 12 percent more possessions than one to a Big Ten game. Note that 2007 was a year of extremes in this category, with the five slowest conferences of the time period found in that single season. That year also featured the fastest conference on record, but the Big South's pace was skewed tremendously by the work of VMI. In fact, five of the conference's eight teams preferred to play at a slower than average pace that season.

Conference Pace, 2004-2008

1	**Southland**	**70.0**
2	Atlantic Sun	69.8
3	SWAC	69.6
4	ACC	69.6
5	Big Sky	69.0
6	MAAC	68.6
7	WCC	68.3
8	Big South	68.3
9	SoCon	68.1
10	WAC	67.7
11	NEC	67.6
12	Sun Belt	66.8
13	CUSA	66.6
14	SEC	66.4
15	MEAC	66.3
16	Big West	66.3
17	Big 12	66.3
18	Pac 10	66.2
19	Summit	66.1
20	MAC	66.1
21	Big East	65.6
22	CAA	65.4
23	OVC	65.4
24	Atlantic 10	65.2
25	Patriot	64.5
26	MWC	64.2
27	MVC	64.1
28	America East	64.0
29	Ivy	63.7
30	Horizon	63.1
31	Big Ten	62.5

Conference Pace, 2008

1	**ACC**	**70.8**
2	Atlantic Sun	70.8
3	Southland	69.3
4	WAC	68.8
5	SWAC	68.4
6	MAAC	67.8
7	Big South	67.8
8	NEC	67.6
9	SEC	67.5
10	CUSA	67.4
11	WCC	67.0
12	Big East	66.9
13	Summit	66.7
14	Big Sky	66.7
15	Big 12	66.5
16	Sun Belt	66.4
17	SoCon	66.4
18	OVC	66.3
19	Atlantic 10	66.2
20	Big West	66.0
21	America East	65.3
22	Patriot	65.1
23	MEAC	65.0
24	MAC	65.0
25	Ivy	64.5
26	MWC	64.3
27	Pac 10	64.1
28	CAA	64.1
29	Horizon	62.8
30	MVC	62.6
31	Big Ten	62.3

Fastest Single-Season Conference Pace, 2004-2008

1	**07 Big South**	**74.2**
2	06 SWAC	71.8
3	04 Southland	71.5
4	04 SoCon	71.3
5	06 A-Sun	70.9

Slowest Single-Season Conference Pace, 2004-2008

1	**07 Big Ten**	**61.2**
2	07 Am East	61.5
3	07 Patriot	61.7
4	07 Horizon	61.7
5	07 Ivy	61.8

3-POINT PERCENTAGE

There's not a whole lot of separation among most conferences in this category. The Summit and SWAC stand out, but every other conference is within 2 percent of the D-I average.

Conference 3-Point %, 2004-2008

1	**Summit**	**37.3**
2	Big Sky	36.4
3	WCC	36.3
4	MVC	35.8
5	Big 12	35.7
6	Sun Belt	35.6
7	ACC	35.6
8	OVC	35.6
9	Big West	35.5
10	MAAC	35.5
11	MWC	35.5
12	Pac 10	35.2
13	Patriot	35.2
14	NEC	35.2
15	Ivy	35.2
16	MAC	35.1
17	SEC	34.9
18	Atlantic 10	34.9
19	Horizon	34.9
20	CAA	34.8
21	SoCon	34.8
22	Big Ten	34.6
23	Southland	34.5
24	WAC	34.4
25	Atlantic Sun	34.4
26	America East	34.3
27	Big East	34.2
28	Big South	34.1
29	CUSA	34.0
30	MEAC	33.1
31	SWAC	31.9

Conference 3-Point %, 2008

1	Summit	37.9
2	OVC	37.1
3	America East	37.0
4	MVC	36.7
5	Atlantic 10	36.1
6	MAAC	36.1
7	Big West	36.0
8	Big Sky	35.9
9	WAC	35.9
10	Sun Belt	35.8
11	SoCon	35.6
12	ACC	35.4
13	Pac 10	35.3
14	WCC	35.1
15	Patriot	35.0
16	Horizon	34.9
17	CUSA	34.8
18	Southland	34.8
19	CAA	34.7
20	Big Ten	34.7
21	MWC	34.7
22	Ivy	34.5
23	Big South	34.5
24	Big 12	34.5
25	SEC	34.4
26	NEC	34.3
27	Big East	34.2
28	MAC	34.2
29	Atlantic Sun	33.8
30	SWAC	33.8
31	MEAC	32.5

Best Single-Season Conference 3-Point %, 2004-2008

1	06 Big Sky	39.0
2	06 Mid-Con	38.3
3	04 WCC	38.1
4	08 Summit	37.9
5	05 Mid-Con	37.6

Worst Single-Season Conference 3-Point %, 2004-2008

1	07 SWAC	29.9
2	05 SWAC	30.7
3	04 SWAC	32.2
4	06 MEAC	32.3
5	08 MEAC	32.5

3-POINT ATTEMPT PERCENTAGE

The previous category described three-point accuracy, while this one measures the percentage of field goal attempts taken from beyond the arc. Again, there's not as much contrast historically as one might think. Give credit to the SWAC—their three-point attempts may be futile, but they also don't take many.

Conference 3-Point FGA %, 2004-2008

1	SoCon	36.2
2	Atlantic Sun	36.1
3	Atlantic 10	36.0
4	MVC	35.5
5	Patriot	35.4
6	OVC	35.3
7	SEC	35.2
8	Big Ten	35.0
9	Big West	34.7
10	Big South	34.2
11	America East	34.2
12	CUSA	34.2
13	MAC	34.1
14	MAAC	34.0
15	MWC	34.0
16	Sun Belt	33.9
17	Ivy	33.9
18	NEC	33.7
19	CAA	33.5
20	Big Sky	33.4
21	Summit	33.1
22	Horizon	33.0
23	Big East	32.9
24	Big 12	32.5
25	Southland	32.4
26	MEAC	32.2
27	ACC	31.9
28	WCC	31.9
29	Pac 10	31.2
30	WAC	31.0
31	SWAC	29.2

Conference 3-Point FGA %, 2008

1	Big South	39.6
2	MVC	38.9
3	Big Ten	37.9
4	OVC	37.6
5	Atlantic 10	37.5
6	SoCon	37.5
7	Big West	36.9
8	Patriot	36.6
9	MWC	36.5
10	Big Sky	35.8
11	SEC	35.8
12	Atlantic Sun	35.6
13	MAAC	35.6
14	America East	35.4
15	Horizon	35.3
16	MAC	34.6
17	Sun Belt	34.3
18	CUSA	34.2
19	NEC	34.0
20	Southland	33.4
21	CAA	33.2
22	Big East	33.2
23	WCC	33.1
24	Big 12	32.8
25	Ivy	32.7
26	Pac 10	31.9
27	ACC	31.4
28	MEAC	31.2
29	WAC	30.8
30	Summit	30.8
31	SWAC	29.4

Highest Single-Season Conference 3-Point FGA %, 2004-2008

1	08 Big South	39.6
2	08 MVC	38.9
3	07 MVC	38.3
4	08 Big Ten	37.9
5	07 Patriot	37.7

Lowest Single-Season Conference 3-Point FGA %, 2004-2008

1	06 SWAC	28.1
2	07 SWAC	28.4
3	05 WAC	28.8
4	08 SWAC	29.4
5	06 WCC	29.4

2-POINT PERCENTAGE

A conference's two-point proficiency is loosely related to its three-point shooting. Note the Big East has consistently been one of the poorer shooting teams from either side of the three-point line.

Conference 2-Point %, 2004-2008

1	OVC	50.7
2	Big Sky	50.0
3	NEC	49.7
4	Big South	49.6
5	Summit	49.6
6	Atlantic Sun	49.5
7	MWC	49.5
8	SoCon	49.5
9	Big West	49.4
10	SEC	49.4
11	Pac 10	49.1
12	Ivy	49.0
13	MAC	48.9
14	Big Ten	48.9
15	ACC	48.8
16	WCC	48.7
17	Atlantic 10	48.6
18	WAC	48.5
19	Southland	48.2
20	Sun Belt	48.1
21	MAAC	48.1
22	MVC	48.0
23	Horizon	47.9
24	Big 12	47.8
25	CAA	47.7
26	MEAC	47.7
27	Big East	47.2
28	America East	46.7
29	CUSA	46.2
30	Patriot	45.7
31	SWAC	45.5

Conference 2-Point %, 2008

1	**Big West**	**51.2**
2	WAC	50.6
3	OVC	50.5
4	Big South	50.4
5	Ivy	50.1
6	SoCon	49.8
7	Big Sky	49.8
8	WCC	49.6
9	SEC	49.4
10	NEC	49.2
11	Sun Belt	49.2
12	Atlantic 10	49.1
13	Pac 10	48.9
14	ACC	48.9
15	Atlantic Sun	48.7
16	Summit	48.6
17	Big Ten	48.4
18	MAAC	48.3
19	CUSA	47.8
20	Big 12	47.7
21	MVC	47.6
22	Big East	47.6
23	MAC	47.5
24	CAA	47.5
25	MWC	47.3
26	Southland	47.3
27	Horizon	47.3
28	MEAC	47.0
29	Patriot	46.8
30	America East	46.8
31	SWAC	46.4

Highest Single-Season Conference 2-Point %, 2004-2008

1	**07 Big South**	**52.8**
2	04 OVC	51.7
3	06 A-Sun	51.6
4	05 OVC	51.4
5	08 Big West	51.2

Lowest Single-Season Conference 2-Point %, 2004-2008

1	**07 Patriot**	**44.7**
2	05 SWAC	44.9
3	07 SWAC	44.9
4	05 Patriot	45.2
5	04 SWAC	45.2

FREE THROW PERCENTAGE

Free throw percentage is an underrated predictor of shooting ability while guarded—and this is further substantiated by the conference data shown here. Summit League players make a high percentage of shots while unguarded, and they also have been proficient while guarded, be it from three-point range or two-point range. Ditto for the SWAC, but in the opposite regard.

Conference FT %, 2004-2008

1	**Summit**	**71.4**
2	Ivy	71.3
3	Pac 10	71.2
4	WCC	70.9
5	MWC	70.6
6	MVC	70.5
7	Patriot	70.5
8	MAAC	70.5
9	Big Ten	70.4
10	Big West	70.4
11	ACC	70.3
12	Big Sky	70.3
13	Big 12	70.3
14	MAC	70.0
15	OVC	69.9
16	Horizon	69.9
17	WAC	69.8
18	NEC	69.7
19	Big East	69.5
20	CAA	69.2
21	Sun Belt	69.1
22	Atlantic 10	69.0
23	America East	68.7
24	CUSA	68.7
25	Atlantic Sun	68.7
26	SoCon	68.6
27	SEC	68.4
28	Southland	68.3
29	Big South	67.9
30	MEAC	65.3
31	SWAC	64.8

Conference FT %, 2008

1	**Summit**	**73.2**
2	Ivy	73.0
3	Big West	72.4
4	Patriot	72.0
5	Big Sky	71.4
6	Pac 10	71.3
7	Atlantic 10	70.9
8	MVC	70.8
9	ACC	70.8
10	America East	70.8
11	Big 12	70.7
12	MAC	70.3
13	NEC	70.3
14	Sun Belt	70.1
15	MWC	70.1
16	WAC	69.9
17	CAA	69.6
18	CUSA	69.5
19	Horizon	69.3
20	OVC	69.3
21	Big Ten	69.3
22	MAAC	69.2
23	WCC	69.0
24	Big East	68.6
25	SoCon	68.3
26	Big South	67.9
27	SEC	67.9
28	Southland	67.4
29	SWAC	66.8
30	Atlantic Sun	66.4
31	MEAC	64.2

Highest Single-Season Conference FT %, 2004-2008

1	**08 Summit**	**73.2**
2	08 Ivy	73.0
3	07 Summit	72.8
4	08 Big West	72.4
5	06 Pac 10	72.4

Lowest Single-Season Conference FT %, 2004-2008

1	**05 SWAC**	**63.0**
2	06 SWAC	64.0
3	08 MEAC	64.2
4	05 MEAC	64.6
5	07 SWAC	64.9

OFFENSIVE REBOUNDING PERCENTAGE

Which conference's rebounding battles are the fiercest? The ACC and Big East come out on top when it comes to the percentage of missed shots being rebounded by the offense. Ivy League players are the most passive when it comes to battling for second shot opportunities.

Conference OR %, 2004-2008

1	**ACC**	**35.3**
2	Big East	35.2
3	MEAC	35.0
4	Atlantic Sun	34.7
5	MAAC	34.2
6	Southland	34.0
7	Sun Belt	34.0
8	Atlantic 10	34.0
9	SEC	33.9
10	Big 12	33.8
11	CUSA	33.6
12	Horizon	33.6
13	SWAC	33.5
14	MAC	33.4
15	Big South	33.3
16	OVC	33.2
17	Pac 10	33.2
18	NEC	33.2
19	SoCon	33.1
20	Summit	33.0
21	WCC	33.0
22	WAC	32.9
23	America East	32.8
24	CAA	32.7
25	Big Ten	32.3
26	Big West	32.2
27	Big Sky	31.9
28	Patriot	31.7
29	MWC	31.7
30	MVC	31.4
31	Ivy	30.5

Conference OR %, 2008

1	**MEAC**	**35.4**
2	Atlantic Sun	34.6
3	ACC	34.3
4	MAAC	34.2
5	SEC	34.1
6	Southland	33.8
7	MAC	33.6
8	Big East	33.6
9	Patriot	33.4
10	NEC	33.2
11	CUSA	32.7
12	Sun Belt	32.7
13	SWAC	32.6
14	Summit	32.4
15	America East	32.4
16	WAC	32.2
17	Pac 10	32.2
18	Atlantic 10	32.2
19	SoCon	32.0
20	Big 12	32.0
21	Big Ten	31.8
22	OVC	31.8
23	WCC	31.7
24	CAA	31.5
25	MVC	31.5
26	Big South	31.4
27	Big Sky	30.8
28	Horizon	30.3
29	Big West	30.1
30	Ivy	28.9
31	MWC	28.0

Highest Single-Season Conference OR %, 2004-2008

1	**04 ACC**	**37.0**
2	05 Big East	36.8
3	07 MEAC	36.1
4	04 Big East	36.0
5	06 Horizon	36.0

Lowest Single-Season Conference OR %, 2004-2008

1	**08 MWC**	**28.0**
2	08 Ivy	28.9
3	08 Big West	30.1
4	07 Patriot	30.2
5	05 Big Sky	30.2

TURNOVER PERCENTAGE

There seems to be a trend for the better conferences to commit fewer turnovers. The Big East is one of the more interesting stories to come out of these lists. They don't commit turnovers, but they shoot poorly and grab a lot of offensive boards. You'd think those would be characteristics consistent with a fast-paced league since their teams would be taking quick shots to get those offensive rebounds, thereby creating an artificially low turnover rate. Yet the Big East ranks on the slower side of the D-I spectrum when it comes to pace.

Conference TO %, 2004-2008

1	**Big East**	**19.6**
2	MAAC	19.7
3	WAC	19.7
4	Horizon	19.8
5	Pac 10	19.8
6	Atlantic 10	19.8
7	Big 12	20.0
8	CAA	20.1
9	Summit	20.1
10	Big Ten	20.2
11	MWC	20.3
12	SEC	20.3
13	OVC	20.5
14	Big Sky	20.6
15	CUSA	20.6
16	ACC	20.6
17	Big South	20.6
18	America East	20.7
19	Sun Belt	20.8
20	MVC	20.8
21	Big West	20.8
22	NEC	20.8
23	WCC	21.0
24	SoCon	21.2
25	Atlantic Sun	21.4
26	Ivy	21.7
27	MAC	21.8
28	Southland	22.1
29	SWAC	22.1
30	Patriot	22.2
31	MEAC	23.4

Conference TO %, 2008

1	**Pac 10**	**18.4**
2	Big 12	18.6
3	Big South	18.7
4	SEC	19.1
5	WAC	19.1
6	Atlantic 10	19.2
7	MWC	19.3
8	Big East	19.4
9	Horizon	19.4
10	SoCon	19.9
11	ACC	20.0
12	CUSA	20.1
13	Summit	20.1
14	Ivy	20.2
15	CAA	20.2
16	Big Ten	20.3
17	NEC	20.4
18	OVC	20.5
19	America East	20.5
20	MAAC	20.5
21	Big Sky	20.5
22	MVC	20.6
23	SWAC	20.9
24	Sun Belt	21.0
25	Big West	21.7
26	Atlantic Sun	21.8
27	WCC	22.1
28	MAC	22.2
29	MEAC	22.3
30	Patriot	22.6
31	Southland	22.8

Lowest Single-Season Conference TO%, 2008

1	**07 Horizon**	**18.4**
2	08 Pac 10	18.4
3	08 Big 12	18.6
4	08 Big South	18.7
5	05 MAAC	18.8

Highest Single-Season Conference TO%, 2008

1	**05 MEAC**	**24.4**
2	04 MEAC	23.7
3	06 MEAC	23.4
4	07 MEAC	23.3
5	06 Patriot	23.1

FTA PER 100 POSSESSIONS

Typically when talking in Four Factors lingo, we use free throw attempts per 100 field goal attempts to assess how well a team gets to the line. But since we're not really assessing a conference's effectiveness in terms of scoring or defending, we're using possessions in the denominator here to determine how frequently fouls are called in each conference. In terms of real time elapsed, the Big Ten has to have the shortest games in the nation. Their games have the fewest possessions and their officials call the fewest fouls per possession.

Conference FTA per 100 Possessions, 2004-2008

1	**CUSA**	**32.8**
2	Big Sky	32.6
3	MEAC	32.5
4	SWAC	32.4
5	Southland	32.3
6	MAC	32.1
7	Summit	32.0
8	ACC	31.3
9	Patriot	31.1
10	MAAC	30.9
11	Sun Belt	30.8
12	Big 12	30.5
13	MWC	30.4
14	OVC	30.4
15	MVC	29.9
16	Ivy	29.9
17	CAA	29.8
18	Atlantic 10	29.8
19	WCC	29.8
20	Big South	29.7
21	Big East	29.5
22	America East	29.5
23	Atlantic Sun	29.4
24	Horizon	29.3
25	Pac 10	29.3
26	NEC	28.8
27	Big West	28.8
28	SEC	28.5
29	SoCon	28.2
30	Big Ten	28.1
31	WAC	28.0

Conference FTA per 100 Possessions, 2008

1	**Southland**	**33.4**
2	Summit	33.0
3	CUSA	32.8
4	SWAC	32.6
5	Big Sky	32.2
6	MAC	31.9
7	Sun Belt	31.6
8	MEAC	31.4
9	MAAC	31.4
10	Atlantic Sun	31.3
11	Patriot	31.2
12	MVC	31.2
13	Big 12	31.2
14	Atlantic 10	30.8
15	ACC	30.6
16	Big East	30.2
17	Pac 10	29.9
18	Ivy	29.8
19	OVC	29.8
20	America East	29.7
21	WAC	29.3
22	MWC	29.2
23	Big West	29.0
24	CAA	28.3
25	Big Ten	27.9
26	SEC	27.7
27	NEC	27.6
28	Horizon	27.5
29	WCC	27.3
30	SoCon	26.8
31	Big South	26.2

Highest Single-Season FTA per 100 Possessions, 2004-2008

1	**07 Big Sky**	**34.4**
2	07 CUSA	34.1
3	04 MEAC	34.0
4	04 MAC	33.8
5	04 Mid-Con	33.7

Lowest Single-Season FTA per 100 Possessions, 2004-2008

1	**06 WAC**	**25.9**
2	08 Big South	26.2
3	08 SoCon	26.8
4	06 Big Ten	26.9
5	05 Big West	27.0

INDIVIDUAL STATS BY CONFERENCE

This section contains last season's individual leaders in various tempo-free statistical categories for each conference. The data is based on all games played during the season, conference or otherwise. The following measures are used in this section . . .

Offensive rating The points a player produces per 100 offensive possessions. This measure was developed by Dean Oliver and explained in his book, *Basketball on Paper.* This is heavily dependent on context, especially usage, so we sort the players by the percentage of their team's possessions that they used. Typically, it is easier for a player who takes a lesser share of his team's offensive load to attain a higher offensive rating. Thus, a player who can both be his team's top offensive option and be efficient is valuable.

Turnover percentage The percentage of a player's possessions that results in a turnover. Players are typically measured in terms of points, rebounds, and assists. However, the ability to limit turnovers is normally as important to a team's offensive success as rebounding (and more important than assist totals). This measure, too, is heavily dependent on context.

Usage Usage defines a player's involvement in the offense in terms of the percentage of his team's possessions that he uses.

Assist rate The percentage of his teammates' made baskets that a player assists on.

Block rate The percentage of opponents' shots blocked by a player. Since three-point attempts are rarely blocked, this is estimated by dividing blocks by opponents' two-point attempts and adjusting for playing time.

Rebounding percentage (offensive and defensive) The percentage of available rebounds recorded by a player at either the offensive or defensive end, adjusted for playing time.

Steal rate The percentage of a player's defensive possessions on which he records a steal.

Percentage of minutes played The percentage of possible minutes a player was on the floor for his team during the season.

ACC INDIVIDUAL STATISTICS

Offensive Rating

(Pct. of possessions used in parenthesis)

At least 28% of possessions used

1 Sean Singletary, Virginia	110.3	(30.9)
2 Tyrese Rice, Boston College	109.9	(28.3)

At least 24% of possessions used

1 Tyler Hansbrough, N. Carolina	125.2	(26.8)
2 Terrence Oglesby, Clemson	116.2	(24.3)
3 Jack McClinton, Miami FL	113.7	(25.5)
4 Sean Singletary, Virginia	110.3	(30.9)
5 Tyrese Rice, Boston College	109.9	(28.3)
6 J.J. Hickson, N. Carolina St.	107.3	(26.8)
7 James Johnson, Wake Forest	104.9	(25.9)
8 Jeff Teague, Wake Forest	103.6	(24.1)
9 Greivis Vasquez, Maryland	101.7	(26.8)
10 Matt Causey, Georgia Tech	100.2	(25.3)
11 Jason Rich, Florida St.	99.3	(24.1)
12 Demontez Stitt, Clemson	94.3	(24.1)
13 Jeff Allen, Virginia Tech	92.8	(24.6)

At least 20% of possessions used

1 Tyler Hansbrough, N. Carolina	125.2	(26.8)
2 Ty Lawson, N. Carolina	123.0	(22.8)
3 K.C. Rivers, Clemson	120.4	(20.8)
4 Wayne Ellington, N. Carolina	119.9	(20.9)
5 Danny Green, North Carolina	116.3	(22.6)
6 Terrence Oglesby, Clemson	116.2	(24.3)
7 Jeremis Smith, Georgia Tech	114.2	(20.3)
8 Jack McClinton, Miami FL	113.7	(25.5)
9 Zach Peacock, Georgia Tech	110.7	(22.2)
10 Sean Singletary, Virginia	110.3	(30.9)
11 Tyrese Rice, Boston College	109.9	(28.3)
12 Maurice Miller, Georgia Tech	109.1	(22.0)
13 Gavin Grant, N. Carolina St.	108.6	(23.9)
14 Trevor Booker, Clemson	108.4	(20.9)
15 Kyle Singler, Duke	107.9	(22.1)
16 DeMarcus Nelson, Duke	107.7	(23.3)
17 J.J. Hickson, N. Carolina St.	107.3	(26.8)
18 A.D. Vassallo, Virginia Tech	106.9	(24.0)
19 Toney Douglas, Florida St.	105.1	(23.5)
20 James Johnson, Wake Forest	104.9	(25.9)

ALL PLAYERS

1 Jon Scheyer, Duke	127.6	(17.4)
2 Tyler Hansbrough, N. Carolina	125.2	(26.8)
3 Anthony Morrow, Georgia Tech	123.3	(18.6)

4 Ty Lawson, North Carolina	123.0	(22.8)
5 James Dews, Miami FL	120.9	(16.0)
6 K.C. Rivers, Clemson	120.4	(20.8)
7 Wayne Ellington, N. Carolina	119.9	(20.9)
8 Greg Paulus, Duke	119.7	(18.2)
9 Corey Raji, Boston College	119.0	(18.8)
10 Danny Green, North Carolina	116.3	(22.6)
11 Terrence Oglesby, Clemson	116.2	(24.3)
12 Cliff Hammonds, Clemson	115.5	(16.7)
13 Brian Asbury, Miami FL	115.5	(18.0)
14 Jeremis Smith, Georgia Tech	114.2	(20.3)
15 Jack McClinton, Miami FL	113.7	(25.5)
16 Zach Peacock, Georgia Tech	110.7	(22.2)
17 Adrian Joseph, Virginia	110.5	(19.0)
18 Sean Singletary, Virginia	110.3	(30.9)
19 J.T. Thompson, Virginia Tech	110.1	(16.0)
20 Tyrese Rice, Boston College	109.9	(28.3)

Turnover Rate

(Pct. of possessions used in parenthesis)

At least 28% of possessions used

1 Tyrese Rice, Boston College	18.5	(28.3)
2 Sean Singletary, Virginia	20.6	(30.9)

At least 24% of possessions used

1 Tyler Hansbrough, N. Carolina	12.7	(26.8)
2 Terrence Oglesby, Clemson	15.6	(24.3)
3 Jack McClinton, Miami FL	17.8	(25.5)
4 Tyrese Rice, Boston College	18.5	(28.3)
5 James Johnson, Wake Forest	19.4	(25.9)
6 Jeff Teague, Wake Forest	19.9	(24.1)
7 Jason Rich, Florida St.	20.1	(24.1)
8 Sean Singletary, Virginia	20.6	(30.9)
9 J.J. Hickson, N. Carolina St.	20.9	(26.8)
10 Jeff Allen, Virginia Tech	22.8	(24.6)
11 Greivis Vasquez, Maryland	24.4	(26.8)
12 Demontez Stitt, Clemson	28.4	(24.1)
13 Matt Causey, Georgia Tech	29.2	(25.3)

At least 20% of possessions used

1 K.C. Rivers, Clemson	9.9	(20.8)
2 Tyler Hansbrough, N. Carolina	12.7	(26.8)
3 Wayne Ellington, North Carolina	13.7	(20.9)
4 Terrence Oglesby, Clemson	15.6	(24.3)
5 Deron Washington, Virginia Tech	16.2	(23.0)
6 Zach Peacock, Georgia Tech	16.5	(22.2)
7 Jeremis Smith, Georgia Tech	16.7	(20.3)
8 Dwayne Collins, Miami FL	17.0	(23.0)

9 Gerald Henderson, Duke	17.1	(24.0)
10 A.D. Vassallo, Virginia Tech	17.7	(24.0)
11 Jack McClinton, Miami FL	17.8	(25.5)
12 DeMarcus Nelson, Duke	18.4	(23.3)
13 Tyrese Rice, Boston College	18.5	(28.3)
14 Kyle Singler, Duke	18.7	(22.1)
15 Chas McFarland, Wake Forest	18.7	(21.5)
16 James Johnson, Wake Forest	19.4	(25.9)
17 Toney Douglas, Florida St.	19.5	(23.5)
18 James Gist, Maryland	19.6	(24.0)
19 Gavin Grant, North Carolina St.	19.8	(23.9)
20 Shamari Spears, Boston College	19.8	(20.4)

ALL PLAYERS

1 K.C. Rivers, Clemson	9.9	(20.8)
2 Anthony Morrow, Georgia Tech	10.3	(18.6)
3 James Dews, Miami FL	10.4	(16.0)
4 Jon Scheyer, Duke	11.9	(17.4)
5 Tyler Hansbrough, N. Carolina	12.7	(26.8)
6 Harvey Hale, Wake Forest	13.4	(18.3)
7 Wayne Ellington, North Carolina	13.7	(20.9)
8 Mike Scott, Virginia	14.0	(17.2)
9 Corey Raji, Boston College	14.8	(18.8)
10 Adrian Joseph, Virginia	14.9	(19.0)
11 Terrence Oglesby, Clemson	15.6	(24.3)
12 Anthony King, Miami FL	16.2	(18.4)
13 Deron Washington, Virginia Tech	16.2	(23.0)
14 Zach Peacock, Georgia Tech	16.5	(22.2)
15 Jeremis Smith, Georgia Tech	16.7	(20.3)
16 J.T. Thompson, Virginia Tech	16.9	(16.0)
17 Deon Thompson, North Carolina	17.0	(19.7)
18 Dwayne Collins, Miami FL	17.0	(23.0)
19 Gerald Henderson, Duke	17.1	(24.0)
20 Ralph Mims, Florida St.	17.1	(19.5)

Usage (Pct. of Possessions Used)

1 Sean Singletary, Virginia	30.9
2 Tyrese Rice, Boston College	28.3
3 Greivis Vasquez, Maryland	26.8
4 J.J. Hickson, North Carolina St.	26.8
5 Tyler Hansbrough, North Carolina	26.8
6 James Johnson, Wake Forest	25.9
7 Jack McClinton, Miami FL	25.5
8 Matt Causey, Georgia Tech	25.3
9 Jeff Allen, Virginia Tech	24.6
10 Terrence Oglesby, Clemson	24.3
11 Demontez Stitt, Clemson	24.1
12 Jason Rich, Florida St.	24.1
13 Jeff Teague, Wake Forest	24.0

14 James Gist, Maryland	24.0
15 Gerald Henderson, Duke	24.0
16 A.D. Vassallo, Virginia Tech	24.0
17 Rakim Sanders, Boston College	24.0
18 Gavin Grant, North Carolina St.	23.9
19 Toney Douglas, Florida St.	23.5
20 DeMarcus Nelson, Duke	23.3
21 Bambale Osby, Maryland	23.3
22 James Mays, Clemson	23.2
23 Brandon Costner, N. Carolina St.	23.1
24 Deron Washington, Virginia Tech	23.0
25 Dwayne Collins, Miami FL	23.0

Assist Rate

1 Sean Singletary, Virginia	37.7
2 Matt Causey, Georgia Tech	37.5
3 Greivis Vasquez, Maryland	36.9
4 Ty Lawson, North Carolina	32.9
5 Tyrese Rice, Boston College	29.2
6 Hank Thorns, Virginia Tech	28.4
7 Maurice Miller, Georgia Tech	28.2
8 Ishmael Smith, Wake Forest	27.4
9 Eric Hayes, Maryland	23.9
10 Biko Paris, Boston College	23.1
11 Demontez Stitt, Clemson	22.4
12 Malcolm Delaney, Virginia Tech	22.2
13 Gavin Grant, North Carolina St.	22.1
14 Javier Gonzalez, N. Carolina St.	21.2
15 Lance Hurdle, Miami FL	20.2

Block Rate

1 Tyrelle Blair, Boston College	14.2
2 Chas McFarland, Wake Forest	8.4
3 Bambale Osby, Maryland	7.2
4 Trevor Booker, Clemson	6.9
5 James Gist, Maryland	6.7
6 Jimmy Graham, Miami FL	6.7
7 Gani Lawal, Georgia Tech	6.5
8 Alade Aminu, Georgia Tech	6.3
9 Anthony King, Miami FL	6.3
10 Deon Thompson, North Carolina	5.9
11 James Johnson, Wake Forest	5.1
12 Danny Green, North Carolina	5.1
13 Dwayne Collins, Miami FL	5.0
14 Jeff Allen, Virginia Tech	4.8
15 J.J. Hickson, North Carolina St.	4.8

Offensive Rebounding Percentage

1 Dwayne Collins, Miami FL	14.4
2 Tyler Hansbrough, North Carolina	13.0
3 Alade Aminu, Georgia Tech	12.9
4 James Mays, Clemson	12.8
5 Mike Scott, Virginia	12.7
6 Corey Raji, Boston College	12.0
7 J.J. Hickson, North Carolina St.	11.7
8 Ryan Reid, Florida St.	11.7
9 Chas McFarland, Wake Forest	11.6
10 Shamari Spears, Boston College	11.5
11 Anthony King, Miami FL	11.3
12 James Johnson, Wake Forest	11.1
13 Gani Lawal, Georgia Tech	11.0
14 Jeremis Smith, Georgia Tech	10.7
15 J.T. Thompson, Virginia Tech	10.6

Steal Rate

1 Toney Douglas, Florida St.	4.35
2 Jeff Allen, Virginia Tech	4.34
3 James Mays, Clemson	3.54
4 Jeff Teague, Wake Forest	3.47
5 K.C. Rivers, Clemson	3.46
6 Maurice Miller, Georgia Tech	3.33
7 Ty Lawson, North Carolina	3.32
8 Ralph Mims, Florida St.	3.18
9 Cliff Hammonds, Clemson	3.18
10 Hank Thorns, Virginia Tech	3.17
11 Javier Gonzalez, North Carolina St.	3.15
12 D'Andre Bell, Georgia Tech	2.99
13 Matt Causey, Georgia Tech	2.98
14 Sean Singletary, Virginia	2.98
15 Jeremis Smith, Georgia Tech	2.93

Defensive Rebounding Percentage

1 Jeff Allen, Virginia Tech	22.3
2 J.J. Hickson, North Carolina St.	21.9
3 Dwayne Collins, Miami FL	20.9
4 Uche Echefu, Florida St.	20.7
5 Anthony King, Miami FL	20.7
6 Jeremis Smith, Georgia Tech	20.6
7 Trevor Booker, Clemson	20.5
8 Tyler Hansbrough, North Carolina	19.8
9 James Johnson, Wake Forest	19.5
10 Mike Scott, Virginia	19.3
11 James Gist, Maryland	19.0
12 Jimmy Graham, Miami FL	19.0
13 Adrian Joseph, Virginia	18.6
14 Chas McFarland, Wake Forest	17.7
15 Brandon Costner, North Carolina St.	16.6

Pct. of Possible Minutes Played

1 Greivis Vasquez, Maryland	92.2
2 Tyrese Rice, Boston College	91.5
3 Toney Douglas, Florida St.	86.7
4 A.D. Vassallo, Virginia Tech	84.6
5 Sean Singletary, Virginia	84.0
6 Cliff Hammonds, Clemson	83.6
7 Jason Rich, Florida St.	83.1
8 Deron Washington, Virginia Tech	81.6
9 Tyler Hansbrough, North Carolina	81.4
10 Ishmael Smith, Wake Forest	79.5

AMERICA EAST
INDIVIDUAL STATISTICS

Offensive Rating

(Pct. of possessions used in parenthesis)

At least 28% of possessions used

1 Marqus Blakely, Vermont	108.8	(28.7)
2 Brian Lillis, Albany	101.2	(30.3)
3 Corey Lowe, Boston U.	98.0	(30.4)
4 Warren McLendon, Hartford	92.9	(30.9)
5 Lazar Trifunovic, Binghamton	92.7	(29.1)

At least 24% of possessions used

1 Cavell Johnson, UMBC	110.2	(24.5)
2 Brian Hodges, UMBC	109.7	(24.4)
3 Marqus Blakely, Vermont	108.8	(28.7)
4 Mike Trimboli, Vermont	104.6	(26.3)
5 Brian Lillis, Albany	101.2	(30.3)
6 Ricky Lucas, Stony Brook	100.5	(25.1)
7 John Holland, Boston U.	100.3	(24.7)
8 Richard Forbes, Binghamton	98.7	(24.8)
9 Mike Christensen, New Hamp.	98.2	(25.0)
10 Corey Lowe, Boston U.	98.0	(30.4)
11 Kaimondre Owes, Maine	93.4	(24.2)
12 Warren McLendon, Hartford	92.9	(30.9)
13 Lazar Trifunovic, Binghamton	92.7	(29.1)

At least 20% of possessions used

1 Ray Barbosa, UMBC	112.9	(23.8)
2 Cavell Johnson, UMBC	110.2	(24.5)
3 Jon Iati, Albany	110.0	(20.2)
4 Brian Hodges, UMBC	109.7	(24.4)
5 Mike Gordon, Binghamton	109.1	(20.3)
6 Marqus Blakely, Vermont	108.8	(28.7)
7 Darryl Proctor, UMBC	108.6	(22.6)
8 Joe Zeglinski, Hartford	108.5	(23.1)
9 Mike Trimboli, Vermont	104.6	(26.3)
10 Eric Gilchrese, New Hampshire	104.1	(23.3)
11 Morgan Sabia, Hartford	103.6	(20.9)
12 Tyrece Gibbs, New Hampshire	102.4	(22.7)
13 Mark Socoby, Maine	102.2	(21.0)
14 Brian Lillis, Albany	101.2	(30.3)
15 Carlos Strong, Boston U.	100.8	(22.3)
16 Ricky Lucas, Stony Brook	100.5	(25.1)
17 John Holland, Boston U.	100.3	(24.7)
18 Richard Forbes, Binghamton	98.7	(24.8)
19 Mike Christensen, New Hamp.	98.2	(25.0)
20 Mitchell Beauford, Stony Brook	98.1	(22.6)

ALL PLAYERS

1 Demetrius Young, Stony Brook	124.5	(11.7)
2 Jay Greene, UMBC	122.0	(15.1)
3 Reggie Fuller, Binghamton	117.6	(14.4)
4 Matt Spadafora, UMBC	114.3	(13.0)
5 Ray Barbosa, UMBC	112.9	(23.8)
6 Brent Wilson, Albany	111.2	(16.6)
7 Cavell Johnson, UMBC	110.2	(24.5)
8 Jon Iati, Albany	110.0	(20.2)
9 Brian Hodges, UMBC	109.7	(24.4)
10 Mike Gordon, Binghamton	109.1	(20.3)
11 Marqus Blakely, Vermont	108.8	(28.7)
12 Darryl Proctor, UMBC	108.6	(22.6)
13 Joe Zeglinski, Hartford	108.5	(23.1)
14 Dwayne Jackson, Binghamton	108.1	(19.6)
15 Kyle Cieplicki, Vermont	106.0	(16.0)
16 Jaret Von Rosenberg, Hartford	104.8	(17.4)
17 Mike Trimboli, Vermont	104.6	(26.3)
18 Eric Gilchrese, New Hampshire	104.1	(23.3)
19 Morgan Sabia, Hartford	103.6	(20.9)
20 Jerel Hastings, Albany	102.8	(15.0)

Turnover Rate

(Pct. of possessions used in parenthesis)

At least 28% of possessions used

1 Marqus Blakely, Vermont	14.6	(28.7)
2 Warren McLendon, Hartford	19.0	(30.9)
3 Corey Lowe, Boston U.	19.1	(30.4)
4 Brian Lillis, Albany	20.4	(30.3)
5 Lazar Trifunovic, Binghamton	21.9	(29.1)

At least 24% of possessions used

1 Cavell Johnson, UMBC	10.1	(24.5)
2 Brian Hodges, UMBC	11.3	(24.4)
3 Marqus Blakely, Vermont	14.6	(28.7)
4 John Holland, Boston U.	16.8	(24.7)
5 Warren McLendon, Hartford	19.0	(30.9)
6 Ricky Lucas, Stony Brook	19.0	(25.1)
7 Corey Lowe, Boston U.	19.1	(30.4)
8 Brian Lillis, Albany	20.4	(30.3)
9 Mike Trimboli, Vermont	21.8	(26.3)
10 Lazar Trifunovic, Binghamton	21.9	(29.1)
11 Mike Christensen, New Hampshire	23.2	(25.0)
12 Richard Forbes, Binghamton	23.9	(24.8)
13 Kaimondre Owes, Maine	27.6	(24.2)

1 Cavell Johnson, UMBC	10.1	(24.5)
2 Brian Hodges, UMBC	11.3	(24.4)
3 Ray Barbosa, UMBC	12.9	(23.8)
4 Mitchell Beauford, Stony Brook	13.4	(22.6)
5 Darryl Proctor, UMBC	13.5	(22.6)
6 Carlos Strong, Boston U.	14.1	(22.3)
7 Marqus Blakely, Vermont	14.6	(28.7)
8 Joe Zeglinski, Hartford	14.6	(23.1)
9 Alvin Abreu, New Hampshire	16.5	(22.1)
10 John Holland, Boston U.	16.8	(24.7)
11 Mike Gordon, Binghamton	17.5	(20.3)
12 Morgan Sabia, Hartford	17.8	(20.9)
13 Jon Iati, Albany	17.9	(20.2)
14 Eric Gilchrese, New Hampshire	18.3	(23.3)
15 Colin McIntosh, Vermont	18.5	(21.8)
16 Tyrece Gibbs, New Hampshire	19.0	(22.7)
17 Warren McLendon, Hartford	19.0	(30.9)
18 Ricky Lucas, Stony Brook	19.0	(25.1)
19 Corey Lowe, Boston U.	19.1	(30.4)
20 Brian Lillis, Albany	20.4	(30.3)

ALL PLAYERS

1 Cavell Johnson, UMBC	10.1	(24.5)
2 Brian Hodges, UMBC	11.3	(24.4)
3 Matt Spadafora, UMBC	12.2	(13.0)
4 Ray Barbosa, UMBC	12.9	(23.8)
5 Mitchell Beauford, Stony Brook	13.4	(22.6)
6 Darryl Proctor, UMBC	13.5	(22.6)
7 Carlos Strong, Boston U.	14.1	(22.3)
8 Marqus Blakely, Vermont	14.6	(28.7)
9 Joe Zeglinski, Hartford	14.6	(23.1)
10 Brent Wilson, Albany	15.4	(16.6)
11 Demetrius Young, Stony Brook	16.4	(11.7)
12 Alvin Abreu, New Hampshire	16.5	(22.1)
13 John Holland, Boston U.	16.8	(24.7)
14 Dwayne Jackson, Binghamton	17.4	(19.6)
15 Mike Gordon, Binghamton	17.5	(20.3)
16 Morgan Sabia, Hartford	17.8	(20.9)
17 Jon Iati, Albany	17.9	(20.2)
18 Eric Gilchrese, New Hampshire	18.3	(23.3)
19 Brian Connelly, Albany	18.4	(19.5)
20 Colin McIntosh, Vermont	18.5	(21.8)

Usage (Pct. of Possessions Used)

1 Warren McLendon, Hartford	30.9
2 Corey Lowe, Boston U.	30.4
3 Brian Lillis, Albany	30.3
4 Lazar Trifunovic, Binghamton	29.1
5 Marqus Blakely, Vermont	28.7

6 Mike Trimboli, Vermont	26.3
7 Ricky Lucas, Stony Brook	25.1
8 Mike Christensen, New Hampshire	25.0
9 Richard Forbes, Binghamton	24.8
10 John Holland, Boston U.	24.7
11 Cavell Johnson, UMBC	24.5
12 Brian Hodges, UMBC	24.4
13 Kaimondre Owes, Maine	24.2
14 Ray Barbosa, UMBC	23.8
15 Eric Gilchrese, New Hampshire	23.3
16 Joe Zeglinski, Hartford	23.1
17 Junior Bernal, Maine	22.9
18 Tyrece Gibbs, New Hampshire	22.7
19 Brian Andre, Maine	22.7
20 Darryl Proctor, UMBC	22.6
21 Mitchell Beauford, Stony Brook	22.6
22 Scott Brittain, Boston U.	22.4
23 Carlos Strong, Boston U.	22.3
24 Alvin Abreu, New Hampshire	22.1
25 Colin McIntosh, Vermont	21.8

Assist Rate

1 Jay Greene, UMBC	33.3
2 Corey Lowe, Boston U.	27.5
3 Brian Lillis, Albany	26.9
4 Eddie Castellanos, Stony Brook	26.7
5 Nick Vier, Vermont	26.0
6 Marques Johnson, Boston U.	25.9
7 Mike Trimboli, Vermont	25.6
8 Eric Gilchrese, New Hampshire	24.2
9 Mike Gordon, Binghamton	22.7
10 Jaret Von Rosenberg, Hartford	22.4
11 Junior Bernal, Maine	21.8
12 Tyrece Gibbs, New Hampshire	21.4
13 Michael Turner, Hartford	20.6
14 Mike Christensen, New Hampshire	19.8
15 Josh Martin, Albany	19.7

Block Rate

1 Cavell Johnson, UMBC	9.2
2 Warren McLendon, Hartford	9.0
3 Marqus Blakely, Vermont	8.2
4 Emanuel Neto, Stony Brook	6.9
5 Reggie Fuller, Binghamton	5.8
6 Scott Brittain, Boston U.	4.9
7 Colin McIntosh, Vermont	4.3
8 Brian Andre, Maine	3.2
9 Justin Fry, UMBC	3.1

10 Brian Lillis, Albany	2.8	
11 Morgan Sabia, Hartford	2.5	
12 Philippe Tchekane Bofia, Maine	2.5	
13 Mike Christensen, New Hampshire	2.2	
14 Tyrece Gibbs, New Hampshire	2.0	
15 Dane Diliegro, New Hampshire	2.0	

Offensive Rebounding Percentage

1 Marqus Blakely, Vermont	12.8
2 Brian Andre, Maine	12.8
3 Reggie Fuller, Binghamton	11.0
4 Demetrius Young, Stony Brook	10.1
5 Dane Diliegro, New Hampshire	10.0
6 Cavell Johnson, UMBC	10.0
7 Emanuel Neto, Stony Brook	10.0
8 Scott Brittain, Boston U.	8.3
9 Darryl Proctor, UMBC	8.2
10 Jerel Hastings, Albany	7.9
11 Sean McNally, Maine	7.8
12 Justin Fry, UMBC	7.6
13 John Holland, Boston U.	7.4
14 Colin McIntosh, Vermont	7.3
15 Warren McLendon, Hartford	6.8

Defensive Rebounding Percentage

1 Marqus Blakely, Vermont	23.7
2 Lazar Trifunovic, Binghamton	22.3
3 Dane Diliegro, New Hampshire	20.3
4 Emanuel Neto, Stony Brook	20.3
5 Warren McLendon, Hartford	19.7
6 Scott Brittain, Boston U.	19.2
7 Darryl Proctor, UMBC	19.1
8 Cavell Johnson, UMBC	19.0
9 Mike Christensen, New Hampshire	18.4
10 Brent Wilson, Albany	17.4
11 Demetrius Young, Stony Brook	17.1
12 Reggie Fuller, Binghamton	16.9
13 Sean McNally, Maine	16.9
14 Brian Lillis, Albany	16.7
15 John Holland, Boston U.	16.2

Steal Rate

1 Mike Gordon, Binghamton	3.77
2 Michael Turner, Hartford	3.66
3 Eric Gilchrese, New Hampshire	3.52
4 John Holland, Boston U.	3.51
5 Marqus Blakely, Vermont	3.28
6 Jaret Von Rosenberg, Hartford	3.27
7 Richard Forbes, Binghamton	3.18
8 Junior Bernal, Maine	3.06
9 Darryl Proctor, UMBC	3.06
10 Brian Lillis, Albany	3.03
11 Eddie Castellanos, Stony Brook	3.01
12 Tyler Morris, Boston U.	2.75
13 Mitchell Beauford, Stony Brook	2.65
14 Ricky Lucas, Stony Brook	2.45
15 Reggie Fuller, Binghamton	2.37

Pct. of Possible Minutes Played

1 Jay Greene, UMBC	91.8
2 Mike Trimboli, Vermont	90.4
3 Darryl Proctor, UMBC	89.4
4 Mike Gordon, Binghamton	89.3
5 Tyrece Gibbs, New Hampshire	88.3
6 Mark Socoby, Maine	88.1
7 Joe Zeglinski, Hartford	87.0
8 Ray Barbosa, UMBC	82.7
9 Michael Turner, Hartford	82.5
10 Alvin Abreu, New Hampshire	81.4

ATLANTIC 10
INDIVIDUAL STATISTICS

Offensive Rating

(Pct. of possessions used in parenthesis)

At least 28% of possessions used

1 Will Daniels, Rhode Island	110.3	(28.9)
2 Gary Forbes, Massachusetts	99.8	(29.5)
3 Dan Geriot, Richmond	99.3	(28.5)
4 Kojo Mensah, Duquesne	97.6	(29.6)

At least 24% of possessions used

1 Josh Duncan, Xavier	120.8	(25.1)
2 Brian Roberts, Dayton	117.9	(26.7)
3 Pat Calathes, Saint Joseph's	115.4	(26.7)
4 Bryant Dunston, Fordham	111.1	(25.4)
5 Will Daniels, Rhode Island	110.3	(28.9)
6 Dionte Christmas, Temple	108.8	(27.3)
7 Kevin Lisch, St. Louis	108.2	(24.7)
8 Mark Tyndale, Temple	105.2	(25.7)
9 Rob Diggs, George Washington	104.7	(25.2)
10 Leemire Goldwire, Charlotte	104.5	(27.3)
11 C.J. Anderson, Xavier	103.1	(24.4)
12 Michael Lee, St. Bonaventure	102.7	(25.7)
13 Marcus Stout, Fordham	100.3	(25.6)
14 Gary Forbes, Massachusetts	99.8	(29.5)
15 Dan Geriot, Richmond	99.3	(28.5)
16 Rodney Green, La Salle	98.3	(26.9)
17 Kojo Mensah, Duquesne	97.6	(29.6)
18 Lamont Mack, Charlotte	94.7	(26.1)
19 Jerrell Williams, La Salle	88.6	(27.3)

At least 20% of possessions used

1 Josh Duncan, Xavier	120.8	(25.1)
2 Kieron Achara, Duquesne	118.2	(23.2)
3 Brian Roberts, Dayton	117.9	(26.7)
4 Ahmad Nivins, Saint Joseph's	116.3	(20.2)
5 Pat Calathes, Saint Joseph's	115.4	(26.7)
6 Bryant Dunston, Fordham	111.1	(25.4)
7 Shawn James, Duquesne	110.7	(22.8)
8 Will Daniels, Rhode Island	110.3	(28.9)
9 Ricky Harris, Massachusetts	109.1	(23.4)
10 Dionte Christmas, Temple	108.8	(27.3)
11 Tyler Relph, St. Bonaventure	108.2	(20.4)
12 Kevin Lisch, St. Louis	108.2	(24.7)
13 Dante Milligan, Massachusetts	107.8	(22.2)
14 Kimmani Barrett, La Salle	107.2	(21.1)
15 Tasheed Carr, Saint Joseph's	106.8	(21.7)
16 Mark Tyndale, Temple	105.2	(25.7)
17 Rob Diggs, George Washington	104.7	(25.2)

18 Reggie Jackson, Duquesne	104.6	(23.3)
19 Leemire Goldwire, Charlotte	104.5	(27.3)
20 Wynton Witherspoon, G.W.	104.2	(21.8)

ALL PLAYERS

1 Darnell Harris, La Salle	128.0	(18.3)
2 Jimmy Baron, Rhode Island	126.8	(19.6)
3 B.J. Raymond, Xavier	121.6	(18.2)
4 Chris Clark, Temple	121.6	(15.8)
5 Josh Duncan, Xavier	120.8	(25.1)
6 Rob Ferguson, Saint Joseph's	120.2	(16.6)
7 Parfait Bitee, Rhode Island	119.6	(19.3)
8 Drew Lavender, Xavier	118.9	(19.3)
9 Etienne Brower, Massachusetts	118.5	(17.7)
10 Kieron Achara, Duquesne	118.2	(23.2)
11 Brian Roberts, Dayton	117.9	(26.7)
12 Derrick Brown, Xavier	117.7	(19.7)
13 Aaron Jackson, Duquesne	116.6	(16.6)
14 Ahmad Nivins, Saint Joseph's	116.3	(20.2)
15 Lavoy Allen, Temple	116.1	(15.5)
16 Pat Calathes, Saint Joseph's	115.4	(26.7)
17 Jason Love, Xavier	114.2	(19.2)
18 Noel Wilmore, G. Washington	113.6	(14.5)
19 Marcus Johnson, Dayton	112.0	(18.8)
20 Bryant Dunston, Fordham	111.1	(25.4)

Turnover Rate

(Pct. of possessions used in parenthesis)

At least 28% of possessions used

1 Will Daniels, Rhode Island	16.3	(28.9)
2 Gary Forbes, Massachusetts	16.5	(29.5)
3 Dan Geriot, Richmond	18.7	(28.5)
4 Kojo Mensah, Duquesne	22.9	(29.6)

At least 24% of possessions used

1 Bryant Dunston, Fordham	13.8	(25.4)
2 Leemire Goldwire, Charlotte	15.5	(27.3)
3 Pat Calathes, Saint Joseph's	15.6	(26.7)
4 Kevin Lisch, St. Louis	16.0	(24.7)
5 Rob Diggs, George Washington	16.2	(25.2)
6 Will Daniels, Rhode Island	16.3	(28.9)
7 Gary Forbes, Massachusetts	16.5	(29.5)
8 Dionte Christmas, Temple	16.8	(27.3)
9 Marcus Stout, Fordham	17.0	(25.6)
10 Josh Duncan, Xavier	17.9	(25.1)
11 Michael Lee, St. Bonaventure	18.4	(25.7)
12 Dan Geriot, Richmond	18.7	(28.5)
13 Brian Roberts, Dayton	19.1	(26.7)
14 Lamont Mack, Charlotte	20.0	(26.1)

15 Mark Tyndale, Temple	21.7	(25.7)
16 C.J. Anderson, Xavier	21.7	(24.4)
17 Kojo Mensah, Duquesne	22.9	(29.6)
18 Rodney Green, La Salle	24.9	(26.9)
19 Jerrell Williams, La Salle	25.0	(27.3)

At least 20% of possessions used

1 Bryant Dunston, Fordham	13.8	(25.4)
2 Ricky Harris, Massachusetts	14.0	(23.4)
3 Charles Little, Dayton	14.6	(23.7)
4 Leemire Goldwire, Charlotte	15.5	(27.3)
5 Pat Calathes, Saint Joseph's	15.6	(26.7)
6 Wynton Witherspoon, G.W.	15.7	(21.8)
7 Kevin Lisch, St. Louis	16.0	(24.7)
8 Rob Diggs, George Washington	16.2	(25.2)
9 Will Daniels, Rhode Island	16.3	(28.9)
10 Zarryon Fereti, St. Bonaventure	16.5	(21.7)
11 Gary Forbes, Massachusetts	16.5	(29.5)
12 Dionte Christmas, Temple	16.8	(27.3)
13 Marcus Stout, Fordham	17.0	(25.6)
14 Maureece Rice, G. Washington	17.3	(21.1)
15 Bill Clark, Duquesne	17.4	(21.0)
16 Kieron Achara, Duquesne	17.4	(23.2)
17 Josh Duncan, Xavier	17.9	(25.1)
18 Tommie Liddell, St. Louis	18.2	(23.6)
19 Michael Lee, St. Bonaventure	18.4	(25.7)
20 Kevin Anderson, Richmond	18.6	(21.0)

ALL PLAYERS

1 Darnell Harris, La Salle	10.0	(18.3)
2 Jimmy Baron, Rhode Island	11.5	(19.6)
3 B.J. Raymond, Xavier	12.2	(18.2)
4 Ryan Brooks, Temple	12.6	(16.7)
5 Etienne Brower, Massachusetts	13.4	(17.7)
6 Darrin Govens, Saint Joseph's	13.6	(19.5)
7 Chris Clark, Temple	13.7	(15.8)
8 Bryant Dunston, Fordham	13.8	(25.4)
9 Ricky Harris, Massachusetts	14.0	(23.4)
10 Charles Little, Dayton	14.6	(23.7)
11 Rob Ferguson, Saint Joseph's	14.9	(16.6)
12 Andres Sandoval, Dayton	15.3	(18.0)
13 Lamonte Ulmer, Rhode Island	15.4	(17.4)
14 Leemire Goldwire, Charlotte	15.5	(27.3)
15 Pat Calathes, Saint Joseph's	15.6	(26.7)
16 Lavoy Allen, Temple	15.7	(15.5)
17 Wynton Witherspoon, G.W.	15.7	(21.8)
18 Noel Wilmore, G. Washington	15.9	(14.5)
19 Kevin Lisch, St. Louis	16.0	(24.7)
20 Rob Diggs, George Washington	16.2	(25.2)

Usage (Pct. of Possessions Used)

1 Kojo Mensah, Duquesne	29.6
2 Gary Forbes, Massachusetts	29.5
3 Will Daniels, Rhode Island	28.9
4 Dan Geriot, Richmond	28.5
5 Dionte Christmas, Temple	27.3
6 Leemire Goldwire, Charlotte	27.3
7 Jerrell Williams, La Salle	27.3
8 Rodney Green, La Salle	26.9
9 Pat Calathes, Saint Joseph's	26.7
10 Brian Roberts, Dayton	26.7
11 Lamont Mack, Charlotte	26.1
12 Mark Tyndale, Temple	25.7
13 Michael Lee, St. Bonaventure	25.7
14 Marcus Stout, Fordham	25.6
15 Bryant Dunston, Fordham	25.4
16 Rob Diggs, George Washington	25.2
17 Josh Duncan, Xavier	25.1
18 Kevin Lisch, St. Louis	24.7
19 C.J. Anderson, Xavier	24.4
20 Charles Little, Dayton	23.7
21 Tommie Liddell, St. Louis	23.6
22 Ricky Harris, Massachusetts	23.4
23 Reggie Jackson, Duquesne	23.3
24 Kieron Achara, Duquesne	23.2
25 Shawn James, Duquesne	22.8

Assist Rate

1 Chris Lowe, Massachusetts	33.6
2 Tasheed Carr, Saint Joseph's	33.1
3 Drew Lavender, Xavier	28.2
4 Reggie Jackson, Duquesne	28.1
5 Dijuan Harris, Charlotte	28.0
6 Parfait Bitee, Rhode Island	27.6
7 Tyler Relph, St. Bonaventure	26.1
8 Kojo Mensah, Duquesne	25.7
9 Brian Roberts, Dayton	23.9
10 Mark Tyndale, Temple	23.7
11 Kevin Lisch, St. Louis	23.7
12 Rodney Green, La Salle	22.9
13 Aaron Jackson, Duquesne	22.8
14 Stanley Burrell, Xavier	21.9
15 Maureece Rice, G. Washington	21.7

Block Rate

1	Shawn James, Duquesne	15.9
2	Dante Milligan, Massachusetts	9.4
3	Bryant Dunston, Fordham	8.7
4	Tony Gaffney, Massachusetts	7.7
5	Kieron Achara, Duquesne	7.5
6	Sergio Olmos, Temple	7.4
7	Bryce Husak, St. Louis	6.8
8	Charlie Coley, Charlotte	6.1
9	Lavoy Allen, Temple	6.0
10	Damian Saunders, Duquesne	5.6
11	Jason Love, Xavier	5.2
12	Rob Diggs, George Washington	5.0
13	Kahiem Seawright, Rhode Island	4.5
14	Pat Calathes, Saint Joseph's	4.4
15	Rob Ferguson, Saint Joseph's	4.2

Offensive Rebounding Percentage

1	Jason Love, Xavier	17.4
2	Jerrell Williams, La Salle	13.2
3	Kimmani Barrett, La Salle	12.6
4	Dante Milligan, Massachusetts	12.4
5	D'Lancy Carter, St. Bonaventure	12.3
6	Kahiem Seawright, Rhode Island	11.9
7	Rob Diggs, George Washington	11.5
8	Charles Little, Dayton	11.1
9	Shawn James, Duquesne	10.9
10	Bryant Dunston, Fordham	10.7
11	C.J. Anderson, Xavier	10.7
12	Lamonte Ulmer, Rhode Island	10.4
13	Kurt Huelsman, Dayton	10.0
14	An'Juan Wilderness, Charlotte	9.9
15	Charles Dewhurst, Charlotte	9.7

Defensive Rebounding Percentage

1	Bryant Dunston, Fordham	26.1
2	Jerrell Williams, La Salle	20.9
3	Damian Hollis, George Washington	20.7
4	Bryce Husak, St. Louis	20.6
5	Pat Calathes, Saint Joseph's	20.1

6	Shawn James, Duquesne	19.7
7	Kahiem Seawright, Rhode Island	19.3
8	Jason Love, Xavier	19.2
9	Michael Lee, St. Bonaventure	18.6
10	Dan Geriot, Richmond	18.4
11	Derrick Brown, Xavier	18.4
12	Barry Eberhardt, St. Louis	18.1
13	Mark Tyndale, Temple	18.1
14	Josh Duncan, Xavier	17.8
15	Lamont Mack, Charlotte	17.7

Steal Rate

1	London Warren, Dayton	4.61
2	Keith Cothran, Rhode Island	4.48
3	Leemire Goldwire, Charlotte	3.58
4	Damian Saunders, Duquesne	3.53
5	Ryan Butler, Richmond	3.53
6	Xavier Alexander, G. Washington	3.40
7	Oumar Sylla, Richmond	3.38
8	Kevin Anderson, Richmond	3.16
9	Kojo Mensah, Duquesne	3.13
10	Garrett Williamson, Saint Joseph's	3.00
11	Dijuan Harris, Charlotte	2.94
12	Tony Gaffney, Massachusetts	2.92
13	Tasheed Carr, Saint Joseph's	2.89
14	Aaron Jackson, Duquesne	2.85
15	Andres Sandoval, Dayton	2.84

Pct. of Possible Minutes Played

1	Mark Tyndale, Temple	92.2
2	Dionte Christmas, Temple	91.7
3	Michael Lee, St. Bonaventure	90.7
4	Zarryon Fereti, St. Bonaventure	90.3
5	Kevin Anderson, Richmond	85.3
6	Brian Roberts, Dayton	85.1
7	Tommie Liddell, St. Louis	84.9
8	Kevin Lisch, St. Louis	84.8
9	Gary Forbes, Massachusetts	84.0
10	Marcus Stout, Fordham	83.7

ATLANTIC SUN
INDIVIDUAL STATISTICS

Offensive Rating

(Pct. of possessions used in parenthesis)

At least 28% of possessions used

1 Jonathan Rodriguez, Campbell	106.9	(29.6)
2 Garfield Blair, Stetson	101.8	(28.6)
3 Thomas Sanders, Gardner Webb	100.1	(30.5)
4 Casey Wohlleb, Fla. Gulf Coast	99.5	(29.3)
5 James Florence, Mercer	89.6	(33.2)

At least 24% of possessions used

1 Justin Hare, Belmont	113.1	(24.2)
2 Marcus Allen, Jacksonville	111.0	(24.1)
3 Kevin Tiggs, E. Tennessee St.	107.6	(24.2)
4 Alex Renfroe, Belmont	107.3	(25.0)
5 Jonathan Rodriguez, Campbell	106.9	(29.6)
6 Adnan Hodzic, Lipscomb	106.8	(24.4)
7 Landon Adler, Fla. Gulf Coast	102.6	(28.0)
8 Garfield Blair, Stetson	101.8	(28.6)
9 Ronell Wooten, Kennesaw St.	101.0	(24.6)
10 Lehmon Colbert, Jacksonville	100.9	(24.3)
11 Thomas Sanders, Gardner Webb	100.1	(30.5)
12 Casey Wohlleb, Fla. Gulf Coast	99.5	(29.3)
13 Eddie Ard, Lipscomb	99.2	(25.8)
14 Courtney Pigram, E. Tenn. St.	98.0	(25.5)
15 Luke Payne, USC Upstate	96.4	(26.0)
16 Josh Slater, Lipscomb	94.8	(25.7)
17 Shuan Stegall, Kennesaw St.	93.8	(27.4)
18 James Florence, Mercer	89.6	(33.2)
19 A.J. Smith, Stetson	84.6	(26.8)
20 Tom Hammonds, North Florida	83.8	(24.6)

At least 20% of possessions used

1 Matthew Dotson, Belmont	119.2	(21.6)
2 Shane Dansby, Belmont	116.3	(21.0)
3 Grayson Flittner, Gardner Webb	115.1	(21.0)
4 Justin Hare, Belmont	113.1	(24.2)
5 Shaddean Aaron, Mercer	112.6	(21.4)
6 Ben Smith, Jacksonville	112.2	(23.0)
7 Marcus Allen, Jacksonville	111.0	(24.1)
8 Kevin Tiggs, E. Tennessee St.	107.6	(24.2)
9 Alex Renfroe, Belmont	107.3	(25.0)
10 Jonathan Rodriguez, Campbell	106.9	(29.6)
11 Adnan Hodzic, Lipscomb	106.8	(24.4)
12 Kyle Vejraska, Campbell	105.4	(22.0)
13 Aaron Linn, Gardner Webb	103.3	(21.1)
14 Nate Blank, Gardner Webb	103.0	(20.1)
15 Landon Adler, Fla. Gulf Coast	102.6	(28.0)

16 Brian Pfohl, Mercer	102.1	(20.3)
17 Garfield Blair, Stetson	101.8	(28.6)
18 Ronell Wooten, Kennesaw St.	101.0	(24.6)
19 Lehmon Colbert, Jacksonville	100.9	(24.3)
20 Thomas Sanders, Gardner Webb	100.1	(30.5)

ALL PLAYERS

1 Travis Strong, E. Tenn. St.	119.4	(19.4)
2 Matthew Dotson, Belmont	119.2	(21.6)
3 Shane Dansby, Belmont	116.3	(21.0)
4 Grayson Flittner, Gardner Webb	115.1	(21.0)
5 Kenyona Swader, E. Tenn. St.	113.5	(17.7)
6 Justin Hare, Belmont	113.1	(24.2)
7 Ayron Hardy, Jacksonville	113.1	(14.1)
8 Shaddean Aaron, Mercer	112.6	(21.4)
9 Ben Smith, Jacksonville	112.2	(23.0)
10 Marcus Allen, Jacksonville	111.0	(24.1)
11 Delvin Franklin, Fla. Gulf Cst.	109.8	(16.3)
12 Mark Lohuis, Stetson	108.3	(13.5)
13 Kevin Tiggs, E. Tennessee St.	107.6	(24.2)
14 Jake Wohlfeil, Campbell	107.5	(15.9)
15 Alex Renfroe, Belmont	107.3	(25.0)
16 Jonathan Rodriguez, Campbell	106.9	(29.6)
17 Brandon Brown, Lipscomb	106.9	(17.4)
18 Adnan Hodzic, Lipscomb	106.8	(24.4)
19 Auryn MacMillan, Gardner Webb	106.5	(12.9)
20 Jordan Campbell, Belmont	106.5	(17.0)

Turnover Rate

(Pct. of possessions used in parenthesis)

At least 28% of possessions used

1 Casey Wohlleb, Fla. Gulf Coast	16.7	(29.3)
2 Thomas Sanders, Gardner Webb	19.0	(30.5)
3 James Florence, Mercer	19.1	(33.2)
4 Jonathan Rodriguez, Campbell	19.5	(29.6)
5 Garfield Blair, Stetson	23.0	(28.6)

At least 24% of possessions used

1 Justin Hare, Belmont	16.1	(24.2)
2 Ronell Wooten, Kennesaw St.	16.3	(24.6)
3 Casey Wohlleb, Fla. Gulf Coast	16.7	(29.3)
4 Eddie Ard, Lipscomb	16.7	(25.8)
5 Luke Payne, USC Upstate	17.4	(26.0)
6 Adnan Hodzic, Lipscomb	17.9	(24.4)
7 Marcus Allen, Jacksonville	18.7	(24.1)
8 Thomas Sanders, Gardner Webb	19.0	(30.5)
9 James Florence, Mercer	19.1	(33.2)
10 Courtney Pigram, E. Tenn. St.	19.1	(25.5)
11 Landon Adler, Fla. Gulf Coast	19.2	(28.0)

12 Jonathan Rodriguez, Campbell	19.5	(29.6)
13 Tom Hammonds, North Florida	21.2	(24.6)
14 Garfield Blair, Stetson	23.0	(28.6)
15 Kevin Tiggs, East Tennessee St.	23.7	(24.2)
16 Lehmon Colbert, Jacksonville	23.9	(24.3)
17 Shuan Stegall, Kennesaw St.	24.1	(27.4)
18 Alex Renfroe, Belmont	25.2	(25.0)
19 Josh Slater, Lipscomb	27.5	(25.7)
20 A.J. Smith, Stetson	30.6	(26.8)

At least 20% of possessions used

1 Shane Dansby, Belmont	12.4	(21.0)
2 Matthew Dotson, Belmont	13.9	(21.6)
3 Shaddean Aaron, Mercer	14.0	(21.4)
4 Grayson Flittner, Gardner Webb	16.0	(21.0)
5 Justin Hare, Belmont	16.1	(24.2)
6 Ronell Wooten, Kennesaw St.	16.3	(24.6)
7 Eddie Ard, Lipscomb	16.7	(25.8)
8 Casey Wohlleb, Fla. Gulf Coast	16.7	(29.3)
9 Luke Payne, USC Upstate	17.4	(26.0)
10 Adnan Hodzic, Lipscomb	17.9	(24.4)
11 Marcus Allen, Jacksonville	18.7	(24.1)
12 Stan Januska, North Florida	18.7	(20.3)
13 Nate Blank, Gardner Webb	18.9	(20.1)
14 Thomas Sanders, Gardner Webb	19.0	(30.5)
15 Courtney Pigram, E. Tenn. St.	19.1	(25.5)
16 James Florence, Mercer	19.1	(33.2)
17 Adam Liddell, Fla. Gulf Coast	19.2	(21.3)
18 Landon Adler, Fla. Gulf Coast	19.2	(28.0)
19 Kyle Vejraska, Campbell	19.2	(22.0)
20 Jonathan Rodriguez, Campbell	19.5	(29.6)

ALL PLAYERS

1 Travis Strong, E. Tennessee St.	11.3	(19.4)
2 Shane Dansby, Belmont	12.4	(21.0)
3 Brandon Brown, Lipscomb	12.8	(17.4)
4 Matthew Dotson, Belmont	13.9	(21.6)
5 Shaddean Aaron, Mercer	14.0	(21.4)
6 Mark Lohuis, Stetson	14.9	(13.5)
7 LaKory Daniels, Lipscomb	15.2	(15.5)
8 Grayson Flittner, Gardner Webb	16.0	(21.0)
9 Justin Hare, Belmont	16.1	(24.2)
10 Reggie Bishop, Campbell	16.2	(19.1)
11 Ronell Wooten, Kennesaw St.	16.3	(24.6)
12 Jon-Michael Nickerson, Ken. St.	16.6	(17.2)
13 Eddie Ard, Lipscomb	16.7	(25.8)
14 Casey Wohlleb, Fla. Gulf Coast	16.7	(29.3)
15 Jake Wohlfeil, Campbell	16.8	(15.9)
16 Delvin Franklin, Fla. Gulf Cst	16.9	(16.3)
17 Kenyona Swader, E. Tenn. St.	17.0	(17.7)
18 Mezie Uzochukwu, USC Upstate	17.2	(17.8)

19 Luke Payne, USC Upstate	17.4	(26.0)
20 Sheldon Oliver, Stetson	17.4	(17.7)

Usage (Pct. of Possessions Used)

1 James Florence, Mercer	33.2
2 Thomas Sanders, Gardner Webb	30.5
3 Jonathan Rodriguez, Campbell	29.6
4 Casey Wohlleb, Fla. Gulf Coast	29.3
5 Garfield Blair, Stetson	28.6
6 Landon Adler, Fla. Gulf Coast	28.0
7 Shuan Stegall, Kennesaw St.	27.4
8 A.J. Smith, Stetson	26.8
9 Luke Payne, USC Upstate	26.0
10 Eddie Ard, Lipscomb	25.8
11 Josh Slater, Lipscomb	25.7
12 Courtney Pigram, E. Tenn. St.	25.5
13 Alex Renfroe, Belmont	25.0
14 Ronell Wooten, Kennesaw St.	24.6
15 Tom Hammonds, North Florida	24.6
16 Adnan Hodzic, Lipscomb	24.4
17 Lehmon Colbert, Jacksonville	24.3
18 Justin Hare, Belmont	24.2
19 Kevin Tiggs, E. Tennessee St.	24.2
20 Marcus Allen, Jacksonville	24.1
21 Jeremy Byrd, USC Upstate	23.4
22 Bobby Davis, USC Upstate	23.3
23 Ben Smith, Jacksonville	23.0
24 Cortez Riley, North Florida	22.5
25 Kyle Vejraska, Campbell	22.0

Assist Rate

1 Alex Renfroe, Belmont	32.4
2 Rob Quaintance, Fla. Gulf Coast	31.1
3 Junard Hartley, Campbell	28.7
4 Julius Perkins, Campbell	28.2
5 Jeremy Byrd, USC Upstate	26.0
6 Ben Smith, Jacksonville	25.9
7 Jocolby Davis, E. Tennessee St.	25.1
8 Josh Slater, Lipscomb	24.4
9 Chris Timberlake, North Florida	22.8
10 Shuan Stegall, Kennesaw St.	21.9
11 Mark Hall, Mercer	21.8
12 Luke Payne, USC Upstate	21.8
13 Grayson Flittner, Gardner Webb	21.8
14 Thomas Sanders, Gardner Webb	21.4
15 Cortez Riley, North Florida	21.3

Block Rate

1 James Grimball, North Florida	7.1
2 Auryn MacMillan, Gardner Webb	6.2
3 Calvin Henry, Mercer	5.6
4 Jason Hopkins, Lipscomb	5.3
5 Nick Schneiders, USC Upstate	5.2
6 Sam Dolan, Mercer	4.5
7 Jon-Michael Nickerson, Kenn. St.	4.4
8 Andrew Reed, E. Tennessee St.	4.2
9 Kyle Vejraska, Campbell	4.0
10 DeVon Jones, North Florida	3.8
11 Justin Cecil, North Florida	3.6
12 Ayron Hardy, Jacksonville	3.5
13 Marcus Allen, Jacksonville	3.1
14 Terike Barrowes, Fla. Gulf Coast	2.8
15 Adam Liddell, Fla. Gulf Coast	2.8

Offensive Rebounding Percentage

1 Tanner Jacobs, Kennesaw St.	12.9
2 Jason Hopkins, Lipscomb	12.2
3 Marcus Allen, Jacksonville	11.9
4 Landon Adler, Fla. Gulf Coast	11.8
5 Sheldon Oliver, Stetson	11.7
6 Adnan Hodzic, Lipscomb	11.5
7 James Grimball, North Florida	11.4
8 Nick Schneiders, USC Upstate	10.9
9 Kevin Tiggs, E. Tennessee St.	10.7
10 Thomas Sanders, Gardner Webb	10.6
11 Eric Diaz, Stetson	10.5
12 Terike Barrowes, Fla. Gulf Coast	10.5
13 Jonathan Rodriguez, Campbell	9.9
14 Thomas Pfaff, Lipscomb	9.5
15 Kyle Vejraska, Campbell	9.4

Defensive Rebounding Percentage

1 Landon Adler, Fla. Gulf Coast	26.4
2 Jason Hopkins, Lipscomb	23.2
3 Thomas Sanders, Gardner Webb	23.1
4 Jonathan Rodriguez, Campbell	22.6

5 Kenyona Swader, E. Tennessee St.	21.6
6 Bobby Davis, USC Upstate	21.4
7 Marcus Allen, Jacksonville	20.4
8 James Grimball, North Florida	20.1
9 Nick Schneiders, USC Upstate	19.3
10 Jordan Campbell, Belmont	19.2
11 Brandon Brown, Lipscomb	19.1
12 Calvin Henry, Mercer	17.0
13 Shuan Stegall, Kennesaw St.	17.0
14 Shane Dansby, Belmont	16.8
15 Andrew Reed, E. Tennessee St.	16.6

Steal Rate

1 Jeremy Byrd, USC Upstate	6.45
2 J.D. Pollock, Kennesaw St.	4.92
3 Rob Quaintance, Fla. Gulf Coast	4.05
4 Jordan Campbell, Belmont	3.84
5 Alex Renfroe, Belmont	3.73
6 Kris Thomas, Stetson	3.64
7 Landon Adler, Fla. Gulf Coast	3.43
8 Travis Strong, E. Tennessee St.	3.21
9 Julius Perkins, Campbell	3.14
10 Junard Hartley, Campbell	3.06
11 James Florence, Mercer	2.93
12 Adam Liddell, Fla. Gulf Coast	2.93
13 Michael Lusk, Lipscomb	2.90
14 Shuan Stegall, Kennesaw St.	2.86
15 Aaron Linn, Gardner Webb	2.86

Pct. of Possible Minutes Played

1 Ben Smith, Jacksonville	89.0
2 Rob Quaintance, Fla. Gulf Coast	87.3
3 Jonathan Rodriguez, Campbell	86.9
4 Ronell Wooten, Kennesaw St.	82.0
5 Courtney Pigram, E. Tennessee St.	81.5
6 Luke Payne, USC Upstate	80.8
7 Shaddean Aaron, Mercer	80.7
8 Thomas Sanders, Gardner Webb	80.5
9 Grayson Flittner, Gardner Webb	80.4
10 Tom Hammonds, North Florida	79.2

BIG 12
INDIVIDUAL STATISTICS

Offensive Rating

(Pct. of possessions used in parenthesis)

At least 28% of possessions used

1 Michael Beasley, Kansas St.	119.8	(33.5)
2 Aleks Maric, Nebraska	113.2	(29.4)
3 Blake Griffin, Oklahoma	109.4	(28.7)
4 Richard Roby, Colorado	100.9	(29.1)
5 Longar Longar, Oklahoma	93.5	(28.2)

At least 24% of possessions used

1 Michael Beasley, Kansas St.	119.8	(33.5)
2 LaceDarius Dunn, Baylor	119.3	(25.9)
3 D.J. Augustin, Texas	115.5	(27.9)
4 Aleks Maric, Nebraska	113.2	(29.4)
5 Leo Lyons, Missouri	111.7	(27.3)
6 DeMarre Carroll, Missouri	111.0	(25.0)
7 Curtis Jerrells, Baylor	110.4	(25.3)
8 Blake Griffin, Oklahoma	109.4	(28.7)
9 Bill Walker, Kansas St.	108.5	(27.8)
10 Darrell Arthur, Kansas	108.4	(25.1)
11 Stefhon Hannah, Missouri	107.0	(28.0)
12 Jiri Hubalek, Iowa St.	102.2	(27.6)
13 Martin Zeno, Texas Tech	101.9	(26.1)
14 Richard Roby, Colorado	100.9	(29.1)
15 Ade Dagunduro, Nebraska	99.1	(24.2)
16 Craig Brackins, Iowa St.	96.8	(24.2)
17 Wesley Johnson, Iowa St.	96.1	(27.0)
18 Longar Longar, Oklahoma	93.5	(28.2)
19 Diante Garrett, Iowa St.	79.8	(24.1)

At least 20% of possessions used

1 Darnell Jackson, Kansas	123.3	(20.1)
2 Michael Beasley, Kansas St.	119.8	(33.5)
3 LaceDarius Dunn, Baylor	119.3	(25.9)
4 D.J. Augustin, Texas	115.5	(27.9)
5 Aleks Maric, Nebraska	113.2	(29.4)
6 Brandon Rush, Kansas	112.1	(21.9)
7 Leo Lyons, Missouri	111.7	(27.3)
8 DeMarre Carroll, Missouri	111.0	(25.0)
9 Joseph Jones, Texas A&M	110.4	(23.4)
10 Curtis Jerrells, Baylor	110.4	(25.3)
11 Damion James, Texas	110.0	(23.3)
12 Kevin Rogers, Baylor	109.8	(21.0)
13 Blake Griffin, Oklahoma	109.4	(28.7)
14 Byron Eaton, Oklahoma St.	109.2	(22.3)
15 Bill Walker, Kansas St.	108.5	(27.8)
16 Darrell Arthur, Kansas	108.4	(25.1)

17 Marcus Hall, Colorado	107.5	(22.1)
18 Sherron Collins, Kansas	107.1	(21.3)
19 James Anderson, Oklahoma St.	107.0	(22.1)
20 Stefhon Hannah, Missouri	107.0	(28.0)

ALL PLAYERS

1 Connor Atchley, Texas	127.1	(15.4)
2 Mario Chalmers, Kansas	124.5	(19.7)
3 Darnell Jackson, Kansas	123.3	(20.1)
4 A.J. Abrams, Texas	120.8	(19.8)
5 Josh Carter, Texas A&M	120.7	(19.4)
6 Michael Beasley, Kansas St.	119.8	(33.5)
7 LaceDarius Dunn, Baylor	119.3	(25.9)
8 D.J. Augustin, Texas	115.5	(27.9)
9 Sasha Kaun, Kansas	115.2	(18.5)
10 Alan Voskuil, Texas Tech	114.9	(16.8)
11 Dominique Kirk, Texas A&M	114.6	(15.6)
12 Aleks Maric, Nebraska	113.2	(29.4)
13 Brandon Rush, Kansas	112.1	(21.9)
14 Tweety Carter, Baylor	112.0	(19.0)
15 Leo Lyons, Missouri	111.7	(27.3)
16 DeMarre Carroll, Missouri	111.0	(25.0)
17 Justin Mason, Texas	110.7	(14.0)
18 Joseph Jones, Texas A&M	110.4	(23.4)
19 Curtis Jerrells, Baylor	110.4	(25.3)
20 Damion James, Texas	110.0	(23.3)

Turnover Rate

(Pct. of possessions used in parenthesis)

At least 28% of possessions used

1 Michael Beasley, Kansas St.	15.1	(33.5)
2 Aleks Maric, Nebraska	17.2	(29.4)
3 Blake Griffin, Oklahoma	17.3	(28.7)
4 Richard Roby, Colorado	21.1	(29.1)
5 Longar Longar, Oklahoma	22.2	(28.2)

At least 24% of possessions used

1 DeMarre Carroll, Missouri	13.2	(25.0)
2 LaceDarius Dunn, Baylor	14.6	(25.9)
3 Michael Beasley, Kansas St.	15.1	(33.5)
4 Curtis Jerrells, Baylor	15.1	(25.3)
5 Craig Brackins, Iowa St.	15.3	(24.2)
6 Jiri Hubalek, Iowa St.	15.3	(27.6)
7 Leo Lyons, Missouri	16.0	(27.3)
8 D.J. Augustin, Texas	16.2	(27.9)
9 Aleks Maric, Nebraska	17.2	(29.4)
10 Blake Griffin, Oklahoma	17.3	(28.7)
11 Darrell Arthur, Kansas	17.5	(25.1)
12 Wesley Johnson, Iowa St.	17.6	(27.0)

13 Martin Zeno, Texas Tech	17.9	(26.1)
14 Bill Walker, Kansas St.	19.0	(27.8)
15 Stefhon Hannah, Missouri	20.4	(28.0)
16 Richard Roby, Colorado	21.1	(29.1)
17 Ade Dagunduro, Nebraska	21.4	(24.2)
18 Longar Longar, Oklahoma	22.2	(28.2)
19 Diante Garrett, Iowa St.	27.3	(24.1)

At least 20% of possessions used

1 Damion James, Texas	13.0	(23.3)
2 DeMarre Carroll, Missouri	13.2	(25.0)
3 Joseph Jones, Texas A&M	13.9	(23.4)
4 LaceDarius Dunn, Baylor	14.6	(25.9)
5 Kevin Rogers, Baylor	15.0	(21.0)
6 Michael Beasley, Kansas St.	15.1	(33.5)
7 Curtis Jerrells, Baylor	15.1	(25.3)
8 Darnell Jackson, Kansas	15.2	(20.1)
9 Jiri Hubalek, Iowa St.	15.3	(27.6)
10 Craig Brackins, Iowa St.	15.3	(24.2)
11 Steve Harley, Nebraska	15.7	(20.1)
12 Henry Dugat, Baylor	15.7	(22.4)
13 Leo Lyons, Missouri	16.0	(27.3)
14 D.J. Augustin, Texas	16.2	(27.9)
15 Brandon Rush, Kansas	16.2	(21.9)
16 Marcus Hall, Colorado	17.0	(22.1)
17 James Anderson, Oklahoma St.	17.1	(22.1)
18 Aleks Maric, Nebraska	17.2	(29.4)
19 Blake Griffin, Oklahoma	17.3	(28.7)
20 Darrell Arthur, Kansas	17.5	(25.1)

ALL PLAYERS

1 A.J. Abrams, Texas	7.2	(19.8)
2 Josh Carter, Texas A&M	8.5	(19.4)
3 Matt Lawrence, Missouri	11.3	(15.2)
4 Connor Atchley, Texas	12.8	(15.4)
5 Damion James, Texas	13.0	(23.3)
6 DeMarre Carroll, Missouri	13.2	(25.0)
7 Joseph Jones, Texas A&M	13.9	(23.4)
8 Sasha Kaun, Kansas	14.1	(18.5)
9 David Godbold, Oklahoma	14.5	(16.3)
10 LaceDarius Dunn, Baylor	14.6	(25.9)
11 Kevin Rogers, Baylor	15.0	(21.0)
12 Curtis Jerrells, Baylor	15.1	(25.3)
13 Michael Beasley, Kansas St.	15.1	(33.5)
14 Darnell Jackson, Kansas	15.2	(20.1)
15 Craig Brackins, Iowa St.	15.3	(24.2)
16 Jiri Hubalek, Iowa St.	15.3	(27.6)
17 Henry Dugat, Baylor	15.7	(22.4)
18 Steve Harley, Nebraska	15.7	(20.1)
19 Austin Johnson, Oklahoma	15.9	(15.8)
20 Rahshon Clark, Iowa St.	15.9	(15.1)

Usage (Pct. of Possessions Used)

1 Michael Beasley, Kansas St.	33.5
2 Aleks Maric, Nebraska	29.4
3 Richard Roby, Colorado	29.1
4 Blake Griffin, Oklahoma	28.7
5 Longar Longar, Oklahoma	28.2
6 Stefhon Hannah, Missouri	28.0
7 D.J. Augustin, Texas	27.9
8 Bill Walker, Kansas St.	27.8
9 Jiri Hubalek, Iowa St.	27.6
10 Leo Lyons, Missouri	27.3
11 Wesley Johnson, Iowa St.	27.0
12 Martin Zeno, Texas Tech	26.1
13 LaceDarius Dunn, Baylor	25.9
14 Curtis Jerrells, Baylor	25.3
15 Darrell Arthur, Kansas	25.1
16 DeMarre Carroll, Missouri	25.0
17 Ade Dagunduro, Nebraska	24.2
18 Craig Brackins, Iowa St.	24.2
19 Diante Garrett, Iowa St.	24.1
20 Joseph Jones, Texas A&M	23.4
21 Bryan Davis, Texas A&M	23.4
22 Damion James, Texas	23.3
23 John Roberson, Texas Tech	23.2
24 Obi Muonelo, Oklahoma St.	23.0
25 DeAndre Jordan, Texas A&M	22.6

Assist Rate

1 Stefhon Hannah, Missouri	35.3
2 D.J. Augustin, Texas	30.5
3 Diante Garrett, Iowa St.	27.8
4 Cookie Miller, Nebraska	26.8
5 Marcus Hall, Colorado	25.8
6 Jacob Pullen, Kansas St.	25.1
7 Byron Eaton, Oklahoma St.	24.9
8 Mario Chalmers, Kansas	24.5
9 Curtis Jerrells, Baylor	23.5
10 John Roberson, Texas Tech	22.7
11 Russell Robinson, Kansas	22.5
12 Sherron Collins, Kansas	22.1
13 Donald Sloan, Texas A&M	22.0
14 Dominique Kirk, Texas A&M	21.2
15 Jason Horton, Missouri	21.2

Block Rate

1	Marcus King-Stockton, Colorado	10.8
2	Connor Atchley, Texas	8.5
3	Sasha Kaun, Kansas	8.0
4	Aleks Maric, Nebraska	7.6
5	DeAndre Jordan, Texas A&M	6.5
6	Darrell Arthur, Kansas	6.2
7	Michael Beasley, Kansas St.	5.4
8	Jermyl Jackson-Wilson, Colorado	5.0
9	Damion James, Texas	4.8
10	Bryan Davis, Texas A&M	4.7
11	Longar Longar, Oklahoma	4.4
12	Marcus Dove, Oklahoma St.	3.8
13	Rahshon Clark, Iowa St.	3.8
14	Taylor Griffin, Oklahoma	3.7
15	Craig Brackins, Iowa St.	3.5

Offensive Rebounding Percentage

1	Aleks Maric, Nebraska	16.8
2	Blake Griffin, Oklahoma	13.7
3	Michael Beasley, Kansas St.	13.3
4	DeMarre Carroll, Missouri	12.2
5	DeAndre Jordan, Texas A&M	11.6
6	Darrell Arthur, Kansas	11.6
7	Damion James, Texas	11.3
8	Sasha Kaun, Kansas	11.3
9	Jermyl Jackson-Wilson, Colorado	11.2
10	Joseph Jones, Texas A&M	11.1
11	Jiri Hubalek, Iowa St.	10.5
12	Darnell Jackson, Kansas	10.4
13	Ibrahima Thomas, Oklahoma St.	10.3
14	Kevin Rogers, Baylor	10.0
15	Bill Walker, Kansas St.	9.8

Defensive Rebounding Percentage

1	Michael Beasley, Kansas St.	29.9
2	Aleks Maric, Nebraska	25.4
3	Blake Griffin, Oklahoma	24.7
4	Damion James, Texas	24.6
5	DeAndre Jordan, Texas A&M	22.3

6	Jiri Hubalek, Iowa St.	22.0
7	Kevin Rogers, Baylor	21.9
8	Darnell Jackson, Kansas	20.6
9	Leo Lyons, Missouri	19.0
10	Ibrahima Thomas, Oklahoma St.	18.8
11	Jermyl Jackson-Wilson, Colorado	18.5
12	Taylor Griffin, Oklahoma	17.9
13	Richard Roby, Colorado	17.6
14	Darrell Arthur, Kansas	17.2
15	Ryan Anderson, Nebraska	17.1

Steal Rate

1	Mario Chalmers, Kansas	4.81
2	Cookie Miller, Nebraska	4.51
3	Byron Eaton, Oklahoma St.	4.17
4	Russell Robinson, Kansas	4.16
5	Stefhon Hannah, Missouri	3.75
6	Marcus Dove, Oklahoma St.	3.29
7	Marcus Hall, Colorado	3.07
8	Ryan Anderson, Nebraska	2.97
9	Henry Dugat, Baylor	2.93
10	Terrel Harris, Oklahoma St.	2.92
11	Jason Horton, Missouri	2.91
12	Jacob Pullen, Kansas St.	2.87
13	Aleks Maric, Nebraska	2.82
14	Sherron Collins, Kansas	2.80
15	A.J. Abrams, Texas	2.70

Pct. of Possible Minutes Played

1	Marcus Hall, Colorado	93.2
2	D.J. Augustin, Texas	92.9
3	A.J. Abrams, Texas	87.1
4	Richard Roby, Colorado	86.0
5	Martin Zeno, Texas Tech	85.6
6	Marcus Dove, Oklahoma St.	84.7
7	Alan Voskuil, Texas Tech	84.7
8	Cory Higgins, Colorado	83.3
9	Justin Mason, Texas	81.7
10	Michael Beasley, Kansas St.	78.3

BIG EAST
INDIVIDUAL STATISTICS

Offensive Rating

(Pct. of possessions used in parenthesis)

At least 28% of possessions used

1 Luke Harangody, Notre Dame	110.2	(32.9)
2 Joe Alexander, West Virginia	108.0	(28.4)
3 Dar Tucker, DePaul	107.4	(28.1)
4 Corey Chandler, Rutgers	86.2	(30.6)

At least 24% of possessions used

1 Roy Hibbert, Georgetown	118.8	(26.1)
2 Luke Harangody, Notre Dame	110.2	(32.9)
3 Sam Young, Pittsburgh	110.1	(26.7)
4 Deonta Vaughn, Cincinnati	109.5	(27.3)
5 DeJuan Blair, Pittsburgh	109.2	(24.4)
6 Draelon Burns, DePaul	108.6	(27.1)
7 Joe Alexander, West Virginia	108.0	(28.4)
8 Dar Tucker, DePaul	107.4	(28.1)
9 Scottie Reynolds, Villanova	105.6	(25.1)
10 Dominic James, Marquette	104.7	(24.9)
11 Jerel McNeal, Marquette	104.4	(27.5)
12 Kentrell Gransberry, S. Fla.	101.5	(28.0)
13 Jerome Dyson, Connecticut	100.7	(24.7)
14 Derrick Caracter, Louisville	100.4	(27.3)
15 Weyinmi Efejuku, Providence	97.9	(26.8)
16 Anthony Mason, St. John's	95.3	(26.9)
17 Corey Fisher, Villanova	94.1	(25.5)
18 Corey Chandler, Rutgers	86.2	(30.6)

At least 20% of possessions used

1 David Padgett, Louisville	122.6	(21.9)
2 Roy Hibbert, Georgetown	118.8	(26.1)
3 Randall Hanke, Providence	118.3	(20.1)
4 Will Walker, DePaul	115.2	(21.1)
5 Larry Wright, St. John's	115.1	(20.3)
6 A.J. Price, Connecticut	114.4	(23.9)
7 Jonny Flynn, Syracuse	112.9	(21.7)
8 Rob Kurz, Notre Dame	112.8	(21.0)
9 Da'Sean Butler, West Virginia	111.9	(21.6)
10 Jeremy Hazell, Seton Hall	111.7	(20.4)
11 Dominique Jones, South Florida	111.3	(24.0)
12 Wesley Matthews, Marquette	111.2	(20.1)
13 Luke Harangody, Notre Dame	110.2	(32.9)
14 Sam Young, Pittsburgh	110.1	(26.7)
15 Lazar Hayward, Marquette	109.8	(23.6)
16 Deonta Vaughn, Cincinnati	109.5	(27.3)
17 Levance Fields, Pittsburgh	109.4	(23.3)
18 DeJuan Blair, Pittsburgh	109.2	(24.4)

19 Draelon Burns, DePaul	108.6	(27.1)
20 Joe Alexander, West Virginia	108.0	(28.4)

ALL PLAYERS

1 Ryan Ayers, Notre Dame	123.3	(12.2)
2 Alex Ruoff, West Virginia	122.9	(19.3)
3 David Padgett, Louisville	122.6	(21.9)
4 Jonathan Wallace, Georgetown	121.8	(18.3)
5 John Garcia, Seton Hall	120.0	(16.4)
6 Roy Hibbert, Georgetown	118.8	(26.1)
7 Darris Nichols, West Virginia	118.8	(15.4)
8 Randall Hanke, Providence	118.3	(20.1)
9 Doug Wiggins, Connecticut	117.5	(18.1)
10 Gilbert Brown, Pittsburgh	115.8	(15.4)
11 Jerry Smith, Louisville	115.4	(17.9)
12 Hasheem Thabeet, Connecticut	115.3	(16.1)
13 Will Walker, DePaul	115.2	(21.1)
14 Larry Wright, St. John's	115.1	(20.3)
15 Austin Freeman, Georgetown	115.0	(18.4)
16 Kyle McAlarney, Notre Dame	115.0	(18.4)
17 Dwayne Anderson, Villanova	114.9	(15.3)
18 A.J. Price, Connecticut	114.4	(23.9)
19 Ronald Ramon, Pittsburgh	114.1	(14.6)
20 Andre McGee, Louisville	113.7	(16.5)

Turnover Rate

(Pct. of possessions used in parenthesis)

At least 28% of possessions used

1 Dar Tucker, DePaul	11.4	(28.1)
2 Luke Harangody, Notre Dame	13.5	(32.9)
3 Joe Alexander, West Virginia	14.8	(28.4)
4 Corey Chandler, Rutgers	23.1	(30.6)

At least 24% of possessions used

1 Dar Tucker, DePaul	11.4	(28.1)
2 Draelon Burns, DePaul	12.0	(27.1)
3 Luke Harangody, Notre Dame	13.5	(32.9)
4 Joe Alexander, West Virginia	14.8	(28.4)
5 Kentrell Gransberry, S. Fla.	15.4	(28.0)
6 Roy Hibbert, Georgetown	15.6	(26.1)
7 Sam Young, Pittsburgh	16.5	(26.7)
8 Dominic James, Marquette	16.5	(24.9)
9 DeJuan Blair, Pittsburgh	18.2	(24.4)
10 Jerel McNeal, Marquette	19.5	(27.5)
11 Anthony Mason, St. John's	19.6	(26.9)
12 Corey Fisher, Villanova	20.5	(25.5)
13 Deonta Vaughn, Cincinnati	21.1	(27.3)
14 Scottie Reynolds, Villanova	21.5	(25.1)
15 Derrick Caracter, Louisville	23.0	(27.3)

16 Corey Chandler, Rutgers	23.1	(30.6)
17 Jerome Dyson, Connecticut	23.1	(24.7)
18 Weyinmi Efejuku, Providence	23.3	(26.8)

At least 20% of possessions used

1 Larry Wright, St. John's	9.6	(20.3)
2 Jeremy Hazell, Seton Hall	10.0	(20.4)
3 Will Walker, DePaul	10.6	(21.1)
4 Dar Tucker, DePaul	11.4	(28.1)
5 Draelon Burns, DePaul	12.0	(27.1)
6 Luke Harangody, Notre Dame	13.5	(32.9)
7 John Williamson, Cincinnati	13.5	(23.9)
8 Da'Sean Butler, West Virginia	13.9	(21.6)
9 Joe Alexander, West Virginia	14.8	(28.4)
10 Brian Laing, Seton Hall	15.0	(23.7)
11 Levance Fields, Pittsburgh	15.0	(23.3)
12 Kentrell Gransberry, S. Fla.	15.4	(28.0)
13 Roy Hibbert, Georgetown	15.6	(26.1)
14 Dominique Jones, South Florida	16.0	(24.0)
15 Wesley Matthews, Marquette	16.3	(20.1)
16 Dominic James, Marquette	16.5	(24.9)
17 Sam Young, Pittsburgh	16.5	(26.7)
18 Donte Greene, Syracuse	17.0	(23.2)
19 Randall Hanke, Providence	17.3	(20.1)
20 Lazar Hayward, Marquette	17.4	(23.6)

ALL PLAYERS

1 Larry Wright, St. John's	9.6	(20.3)
2 Jeremy Hazell, Seton Hall	10.0	(20.4)
3 Will Walker, DePaul	10.6	(21.1)
4 Dar Tucker, DePaul	11.4	(28.1)
5 Draelon Burns, DePaul	12.0	(27.1)
6 Ryan Ayers, Notre Dame	12.2	(12.2)
7 Larry Davis, Seton Hall	12.5	(17.2)
8 Darris Nichols, West Virginia	12.7	(15.4)
9 Luke Harangody, Notre Dame	13.5	(32.9)
10 John Williamson, Cincinnati	13.5	(23.9)
11 Dwain Williams, Providence	13.5	(17.2)
12 Da'Sean Butler, West Virginia	13.9	(21.6)
13 John Garcia, Seton Hall	14.3	(16.4)
14 Joe Alexander, West Virginia	14.8	(28.4)
15 Karron Clarke, DePaul	14.8	(16.8)
16 Levance Fields, Pittsburgh	15.0	(23.3)
17 Brian Laing, Seton Hall	15.0	(23.7)
18 David Cubillan, Marquette	15.1	(15.3)
19 Kentrell Gransberry, S. Fla.	15.4	(28.0)
20 Roy Hibbert, Georgetown	15.6	(26.1)

Usage (Pct. of Possessions Used)

1 Luke Harangody, Notre Dame	32.9
2 Corey Chandler, Rutgers	30.6
3 Joe Alexander, West Virginia	28.4
4 Dar Tucker, DePaul	28.1
5 Kentrell Gransberry, S. Fla.	28.0
6 Jerel McNeal, Marquette	27.5
7 Deonta Vaughn, Cincinnati	27.3
8 Derrick Caracter, Louisville	27.3
9 Draelon Burns, DePaul	27.1
10 Anthony Mason, St. John's	26.9
11 Weyinmi Efejuku, Providence	26.8
12 Sam Young, Pittsburgh	26.7
13 Roy Hibbert, Georgetown	26.1
14 Corey Fisher, Villanova	25.5
15 Scottie Reynolds, Villanova	25.1
16 Dominic James, Marquette	24.9
17 Jerome Dyson, Connecticut	24.7
18 DeJuan Blair, Pittsburgh	24.4
19 Dominique Jones, South Florida	24.0
20 A.J. Price, Connecticut	23.9
21 John Williamson, Cincinnati	23.9
22 DaJuan Summers, Georgetown	23.8
23 Brian Laing, Seton Hall	23.7
24 Lazar Hayward, Marquette	23.6
25 Jeff Adrien, Connecticut	23.4

Assist Rate

1 A.J. Price, Connecticut	36.1
2 Levance Fields, Pittsburgh	31.7
3 Deonta Vaughn, Cincinnati	30.9
4 Tory Jackson, Notre Dame	29.7
5 Chris Howard, South Florida	29.4
6 Dominic James, Marquette	28.6
7 Eugene Lawrence, St. John's	27.9
8 Jonny Flynn, Syracuse	26.8
9 Malik Boothe, St. John's	26.1
10 Corey Fisher, Villanova	25.8
11 Cliff Clinkscales, DePaul	25.7
12 Geoff McDermott, Providence	25.7
13 Jamual Warren, Cincinnati	25.1
14 Eugene Harvey, Seton Hall	24.9
15 Jerel McNeal, Marquette	24.9

Block Rate

1 Hasheem Thabeet, Connecticut	12.9
2 Hamady N'Diaye, Rutgers	12.3
3 Roy Hibbert, Georgetown	9.8
4 Wellington Smith, West Virginia	9.2
5 John Garcia, Seton Hall	8.4
6 Earl Clark, Louisville	6.5
7 Ousmane Barro, Marquette	6.4
8 Derrick Caracter, Louisville	5.8
9 Joe Alexander, West Virginia	5.4
10 David Padgett, Louisville	5.3
11 Donte Greene, Syracuse	4.8
12 Randall Hanke, Providence	4.8
13 Rob Kurz, Notre Dame	4.8
14 Arinze Onuaku, Syracuse	4.6
15 DeJuan Blair, Pittsburgh	4.6

Offensive Rebounding Percentage

1 DeJuan Blair, Pittsburgh	16.6
2 John Garcia, Seton Hall	15.1
3 Derrick Caracter, Louisville	14.0
4 Luke Harangody, Notre Dame	13.3
5 Kentrell Gransberry, S. Fla.	12.8
6 Arinze Onuaku, Syracuse	12.1
7 Mac Koshwal, DePaul	12.0
8 Ousmane Barro, Marquette	11.7
9 Tyrell Biggs, Pittsburgh	11.5
10 Roy Hibbert, Georgetown	11.5
11 Byron Joynes, Rutgers	11.1
12 Hasheem Thabeet, Connecticut	10.9
13 John Williamson, Cincinnati	10.8
14 Randall Hanke, Providence	10.7
15 Dante Cunningham, Villanova	10.6

Defensive Rebounding Percentage

1 Kentrell Gransberry, S. Fla.	24.9
2 Luke Harangody, Notre Dame	24.2
3 DeJuan Blair, Pittsburgh	23.2
4 Earl Clark, Louisville	22.7
5 John Garcia, Seton Hall	22.2

6 Lazar Hayward, Marquette	20.8
7 Wesley Green, DePaul	20.6
8 Geoff McDermott, Providence	19.8
9 Ousmane Barro, Marquette	19.7
10 Hamady N'Diaye, Rutgers	18.8
11 Jeff Adrien, Connecticut	18.4
12 Byron Joynes, Rutgers	18.4
13 Mac Koshwal, DePaul	18.0
14 Rob Kurz, Notre Dame	17.8
15 D.J. Kennedy, St. John's	17.8

Steal Rate

1 Corey Chandler, Rutgers	4.24
2 Jeff Xavier, Providence	4.16
3 Jerel McNeal, Marquette	4.16
4 Dwayne Anderson, Villanova	3.99
5 DeJuan Blair, Pittsburgh	3.87
6 Jerome Dyson, Connecticut	3.68
7 Eugene Lawrence, St. John's	3.64
8 Andre McGee, Louisville	3.56
9 Jerry Smith, Louisville	3.54
10 Dominic James, Marquette	3.38
11 Scoop Jardine, Syracuse	3.20
12 Doug Wiggins, Connecticut	3.10
13 Reggie Redding, Villanova	3.09
14 Draelon Burns, DePaul	3.07
15 Tory Jackson, Notre Dame	3.00

Pct. of Possible Minutes Played

1 Brian Laing, Seton Hall	93.9
2 Eugene Harvey, Seton Hall	90.1
3 Paul Harris, Syracuse	90.0
4 Terrence Williams, Louisville	89.5
5 Donte Greene, Syracuse	89.2
6 Kyle McAlarney, Notre Dame	88.9
7 Jonny Flynn, Syracuse	88.5
8 Dominique Jones, South Florida	87.1
9 Geoff McDermott, Providence	86.6
10 Darris Nichols, West Virginia	85.5

BIG SKY
INDIVIDUAL STATISTICS

Offensive Rating

(Pct. of possessions used in parenthesis)

At least 28% of possessions used

1 Kyle Landry, Northern Arizona	120.4	(30.3)
2 Carlos Taylor, Montana St.	108.9	(29.3)
3 Adris DeLeon, E. Washington	94.4	(31.0)
4 Loren Leath, Sacramento St.	86.2	(28.1)

At least 24% of possessions used

1 Kyle Landry, Northern Arizona	120.4	(30.3)
2 Matt Martin, Montana	114.1	(24.5)
3 Carlos Taylor, Montana St.	108.9	(29.3)
4 Jordan Hasquet, Montana	107.3	(24.8)
5 Kellen McCoy, Weber St.	105.5	(26.0)
6 Daviin Davis, Weber St.	97.5	(24.8)
7 Adris DeLeon, E. Washington	94.4	(31.0)
8 Loren Leath, Sacramento St.	86.2	(28.1)

At least 20% of possessions used

1 Kyle Landry, Northern Arizona	120.4	(30.3)
2 Scott Morrison, Portland St.	117.6	(21.3)
3 Jeremiah Dominguez, Port. St.	117.2	(22.5)
4 Andrew Strait, Montana	115.8	(21.1)
5 Matt Martin, Montana	114.1	(24.5)
6 Deonte Huff, Portland St.	112.1	(23.7)
7 Sean Taibi, Northern Colorado	111.7	(21.8)
8 Divaldo Mbunga, Montana St.	110.1	(23.2)
9 Carlos Taylor, Montana St.	108.9	(29.3)
10 Jabril Banks, N. Colorado	108.3	(22.1)
11 Jordan Hasquet, Montana	107.3	(24.8)
12 Arturas Valeika, Weber St.	107.0	(20.2)
13 Kellen McCoy, Weber St.	105.5	(26.0)
14 Josh Wilson, Northern Arizona	105.2	(23.1)
15 Matt Stucki, Idaho St.	102.1	(22.0)
16 Mecklen Davis, Montana St.	102.1	(21.6)
17 Jefferson Mason, N. Colorado	101.1	(23.5)
18 Will Figures, N. Colorado	100.0	(21.3)
19 Dezmon Harris, Weber St.	98.8	(23.5)
20 Daviin Davis, Weber St.	97.5	(24.8)

ALL PLAYERS

1 Demetrius Monroe, Idaho St.	122.3	(13.1)
2 Kyle Landry, Northern Arizona	120.4	(30.3)
3 Scott Morrison, Portland St.	117.6	(21.3)
4 Jeremiah Dominguez, Port. St.	117.2	(22.5)
5 Andrew Strait, Montana	115.8	(21.1)
6 Kellen Williams, E. Washington	115.7	(19.8)

7 Ryan Staudacher, Montana	115.4	(14.0)
8 Matt Martin, Montana	114.1	(24.5)
9 Casey Durham, Montana St.	112.4	(16.2)
10 Deonte Huff, Portland St.	112.1	(23.7)
11 Sean Taibi, Northern Colorado	111.7	(21.8)
12 Branden Johnson, Montana St.	110.3	(19.9)
13 Divaldo Mbunga, Montana St.	110.1	(23.2)
14 Tyrell Mara, Portland St.	109.1	(14.9)
15 Carlos Taylor, Montana St.	108.9	(29.3)
16 Nathan Geiser, N. Arizona	108.3	(17.5)
17 Jabril Banks, N. Colorado	108.3	(22.1)
18 Jordan Hasquet, Montana	107.3	(24.8)
19 Arturas Valeika, Weber St.	107.0	(20.2)
20 Kyle Sharp, Montana	106.8	(17.6)

Turnover Rate

(Pct. of possessions used in parenthesis)

At least 28% of possessions used

1 Kyle Landry, Northern Arizona	11.5	(30.3)
2 Loren Leath, Sacramento St.	15.5	(28.1)
3 Carlos Taylor, Montana St.	16.7	(29.3)
4 Adris DeLeon, E. Washington	19.4	(31.0)

At least 24% of possessions used

1 Kyle Landry, Northern Arizona	11.5	(30.3)
2 Jordan Hasquet, Montana	14.7	(24.8)
3 Matt Martin, Montana	15.1	(24.5)
4 Loren Leath, Sacramento St.	15.5	(28.1)
5 Carlos Taylor, Montana St.	16.7	(29.3)
6 Adris DeLeon, E. Washington	19.4	(31.0)
7 Daviin Davis, Weber St.	21.8	(24.8)
8 Kellen McCoy, Weber St.	22.6	(26.0)

At least 20% of possessions used

1 Kyle Landry, Northern Arizona	11.5	(30.3)
2 Scott Morrison, Portland St.	13.5	(21.3)
3 Jordan Hasquet, Montana	14.7	(24.8)
4 Matt Martin, Montana	15.1	(24.5)
5 Loren Leath, Sacramento St.	15.5	(28.1)
6 Sean Taibi, Northern Colorado	15.7	(21.8)
7 Andrew Strait, Montana	16.6	(21.1)
8 Carlos Taylor, Montana St.	16.7	(29.3)
9 Donnie Carson, Idaho St.	17.6	(21.9)
10 Divaldo Mbunga, Montana St.	17.9	(23.2)
11 Mecklen Davis, Montana St.	19.3	(21.6)
12 Adris DeLeon, E. Washington	19.4	(31.0)
13 Deonte Huff, Portland St.	20.0	(23.7)
14 Jeremiah Dominguez, Port. St.	20.8	(22.5)
15 Jefferson Mason, N. Colorado	20.9	(23.5)

16 Arturas Valeika, Weber St.	21.4	(20.2)
17 Jabril Banks, N. Colorado	21.5	(22.1)
18 Daviin Davis, Weber St.	21.8	(24.8)
19 Matt Stucki, Idaho St.	22.0	(22.0)
20 Steve Panos, Weber St.	22.4	(20.8)

ALL PLAYERS

1 Demetrius Monroe, Idaho St.	8.9	(13.1)
2 Kyle Landry, Northern Arizona	11.5	(30.3)
3 Kellen Williams, E. Washington	13.0	(19.8)
4 Scott Morrison, Portland St.	13.5	(21.3)
5 Adrian Zamora, Montana St.	14.5	(14.2)
6 Jordan Hasquet, Montana	14.7	(24.8)
7 Nathan Geiser, N. Arizona	14.8	(17.5)
8 Matt Martin, Montana	15.1	(24.5)
9 Loren Leath, Sacramento St.	15.5	(28.1)
10 Sean Taibi, Northern Colorado	15.7	(21.8)
11 Ryan Staudacher, Montana	16.1	(14.0)
12 Andrew Strait, Montana	16.6	(21.1)
13 Carlos Taylor, Montana St.	16.7	(29.3)
14 Donnie Carson, Idaho St.	17.6	(21.9)
15 Milan Stanojevic, E. Washington	17.7	(18.1)
16 Branden Johnson, Montana St.	17.9	(19.9)
17 Divaldo Mbunga, Montana St.	17.9	(23.2)
18 Marcus Hinton, E. Washington	18.8	(19.6)
19 Brandon Moore, E. Washington	18.9	(20.0)
20 Brody Van Brocklin, Weber St.	19.0	(11.7)

Usage (Pct. of Possessions Used)

1 Adris DeLeon, E. Washington	31.0
2 Kyle Landry, Northern Arizona	30.3
3 Carlos Taylor, Montana St.	29.3
4 Loren Leath, Sacramento St.	28.1
5 Kellen McCoy, Weber St.	26.0
6 Jordan Hasquet, Montana	24.8
7 Daviin Davis, Weber St.	24.8
8 Matt Martin, Montana	24.5
9 Deonte Huff, Portland St.	23.7
10 Vinnie McGhee, Sacramento St.	23.5
11 Dezmon Harris, Weber St.	23.5
12 Jefferson Mason, N. Colorado	23.5
13 Bobby Howard, Montana St.	23.3
14 Divaldo Mbunga, Montana St.	23.2
15 Josh Wilson, Northern Arizona	23.1
16 Amorrow Morgan, Idaho St.	22.5
17 Jeremiah Dominguez, Port. St.	22.5
18 Jabril Banks, Northern Colorado	22.1
19 Austin Kilpatrick, Idaho St.	22.1
20 Matt Stucki, Idaho St.	22.0
21 Donnie Carson, Idaho St.	21.9

22 Sean Taibi, N. Colorado	21.8
23 Cameron Rundles, Montana	21.6
24 Mecklen Davis, Montana St.	21.6
25 Will Figures, N. Colorado	21.3

Assist Rate

1 Josh Wilson, Northern Arizona	35.1
2 Vinnie McGhee, Sacramento St.	33.1
3 Adris DeLeon, E. Washington	30.5
4 Jeremiah Dominguez, Port. St.	27.4
5 Matt Stucki, Idaho St.	24.9
6 Matt Martin, Montana	24.3
7 Ceylon Elgin-Taylor, Montana	24.3
8 Cameron Rundles, Montana	23.0
9 Kellen McCoy, Weber St.	22.7
10 Amorrow Morgan, Idaho St.	21.9
11 Daviin Davis, Weber St.	21.1
12 Gary Gibson, E. Washington	20.6
13 Juan Pablo Silveira, Weber St.	19.9
14 Thanasi Panagiotakopoulos, UNC	19.3
15 Matt Johnson, Northern Arizona	18.8

Block Rate

1 Scott Morrison, Portland St.	7.8
2 Daviin Davis, Weber St.	7.1
3 Adrian Zamora, Montana St.	6.3
4 Austin Kilpatrick, Idaho St.	5.3
5 Justin Williams, Sacramento St.	5.2
6 Divaldo Mbunga, Montana St.	5.2
7 Arturas Valeika, Weber St.	5.0
8 Kyle Landry, Northern Arizona	4.0
9 Matthew Brunell, E. Washington	3.8
10 Brandon Moore, E. Washington	3.4
11 Kyle Sharp, Montana	3.1
12 Jefferson Mason, N. Colorado	2.6
13 Kyle Coston, Portland St.	2.6
14 Andrew Strait, Montana	2.4
15 Branden Johnson, Montana St.	2.3

Offensive Rebounding Percentage

1 Kyle Landry, Northern Arizona	14.7
2 Arturas Valeika, Weber St.	13.0
3 Divaldo Mbunga, Montana St.	12.0
4 Scott Morrison, Portland St.	11.6
5 Robert Palacios, Northern Colorado	10.9
6 Taylor Montgomery, N. Colorado	10.6

7 Demetrius Monroe, Idaho St.	10.5
8 Kyle Sharp, Montana	10.5
9 Brandon Moore, E. Washington	10.4
10 Kellen Williams, E. Washington	9.8
11 Logan Kinghorn, Idaho St.	9.7
12 Mecklen Davis, Montana St.	9.1
13 Tyrell Mara, Portland St.	8.7
14 Jabril Banks, Northern Colorado	8.6
15 Deonte Huff, Portland St.	8.5

Defensive Rebounding Percentage

1 Arturas Valeika, Weber St.	30.4
2 Kyle Landry, Northern Arizona	24.3
3 Adrian Zamora, Montana St.	21.4
4 Jordan Hasquet, Montana	21.0
5 Brandon Moore, E. Washington	20.8
6 Kyle Sharp, Montana	20.7
7 Andrew Strait, Montana	20.1
8 Kellen Williams, E. Washington	20.0
9 Jefferson Mason, Northern Colorado	19.8
10 Demetrius Monroe, Idaho St.	19.7
11 Scott Morrison, Portland St.	18.5
12 Logan Kinghorn, Idaho St.	17.7
13 Robert Palacios, Northern Colorado	17.0
14 Justin Williams, Sacramento St.	16.0
15 Jabril Banks, Northern Colorado	15.9

Steal Rate

1 Justin Williams, Sacramento St.	4.22
2 Jeremiah Dominguez, Portland St.	3.71
3 Robert Palacios, Northern Colorado	3.66
4 Thanasi Panagiotakopoulos, UNC	3.11
5 Jefferson Mason, Northern Colorado	2.91
6 Loren Leath, Sacramento St.	2.80
7 Gary Gibson, E. Washington	2.77
8 Clark Woods, Sacramento St.	2.74
9 Daviin Davis, Weber St.	2.57
10 Marcus Hinton, E. Washington	2.52
11 Kellen McCoy, Weber St.	2.52
12 Deonte Huff, Portland St.	2.45
13 Casey Durham, Montana St.	2.42
14 Milan Stanojevic, E. Washington	2.37
15 Matt Stucki, Idaho St.	2.30

Pct. of Possible Minutes Played

1 Kellen Williams, E. Washington	88.3
2 Matt Stucki, Idaho St.	84.3
3 Vinnie McGhee, Sacramento St.	84.3
4 Amorrow Morgan, Idaho St.	78.3
5 Ryan Staudacher, Montana	78.2
6 Jordan Hasquet, Montana	77.5
7 Josh Wilson, Northern Arizona	77.3
8 Deonte Huff, Portland St.	75.8
9 Arturas Valeika, Weber St.	74.5
10 Jeremiah Dominguez, Portland St.	74.1

BIG SOUTH
INDIVIDUAL STATISTICS

Offensive Rating

(Pct. of possessions used in parenthesis)

At least 28% of possessions used

1 Arizona Reid, High Point	118.3	(31.8)
2 Reggie Williams, VMI	117.4	(30.9)

At least 24% of possessions used

1 Arizona Reid, High Point	118.3	(31.8)
2 Kenny George, UNC Asheville	117.5	(25.3)
3 Reggie Williams, VMI	117.4	(30.9)
4 Alex McLean, Liberty	111.5	(24.6)
5 Omar Carter, Char. Southern	104.4	(27.6)
6 Travis Holmes, VMI	103.8	(26.3)
7 Mike Jefferson, High Point	103.3	(25.7)
8 Anthony Breeze, C. Carolina	102.9	(24.3)
9 Jamarco Warren, Char. Southern	97.6	(25.2)
10 Martell McDuffy, Radford	94.2	(24.1)
11 Amir Johnson, Radford	89.9	(25.1)

At least 20% of possessions used

1 Arizona Reid, High Point	118.3	(31.8)
2 Kenny George, UNC Asheville	117.5	(25.3)
3 Reggie Williams, VMI	117.4	(30.9)
4 Anthony Smith, Liberty	114.6	(20.5)
5 Bryan Smithson, UNC Asheville	112.6	(22.8)
6 Jack Leasure, Coastal Carolina	112.4	(20.9)
7 Chavis Holmes, VMI	112.2	(23.4)
8 Alex McLean, Liberty	111.5	(24.6)
9 Michael Jenkins, Winthrop	106.5	(23.8)
10 K.J. Garland, UNC Asheville	105.7	(21.3)
11 Shelton Carter, Char. Southern	105.4	(20.3)
12 Kenny Thomas, Radford	104.7	(22.4)
13 Omar Carter, Char. Southern	104.4	(27.6)
14 Travis Holmes, VMI	103.8	(26.3)
15 Mike Jefferson, High Point	103.3	(25.7)
16 Anthony Breeze, C. Carolina	102.9	(24.3)
17 TeeJay Bannister, Liberty	102.8	(24.0)
18 Taj McCullough, Winthrop	101.2	(23.8)
19 Phil Wallace, Coastal Carolina	100.3	(22.9)
20 Vincent James, UNC Asheville	99.9	(23.5)

ALL PLAYERS

1 Chris Moore, Char. Southern	123.4	(18.5)
2 Cruz Daniels, High Point	120.3	(14.2)
3 Arizona Reid, High Point	118.3	(31.8)
4 Kenny George, UNC Asheville	117.5	(25.3)
5 Reggie Williams, VMI	117.4	(30.9)

6 Reid Augst, UNC Asheville	116.7	(16.7)
7 Anthony Smith, Liberty	114.6	(20.5)
8 Chris Gaynor, Winthrop	114.6	(17.0)
9 Eugene Harris, High Point	113.4	(18.1)
10 Bryan Smithson, UNC Asheville	112.6	(22.8)
11 Jack Leasure, Coastal Carolina	112.4	(20.9)
12 Chavis Holmes, VMI	112.2	(23.4)
13 Alex McLean, Liberty	111.5	(24.6)
14 Willie Bell, VMI	110.7	(14.9)
15 Rell Porter, Liberty	108.3	(12.4)
16 Sean Smith, UNC Asheville	108.0	(16.0)
17 Michael Jenkins, Winthrop	106.5	(23.8)
18 K.J. Garland, UNC Asheville	105.7	(21.3)
19 Shelton Carter, Char. Southern	105.4	(20.3)
20 Giedrius Knysas, Char. Southern	105.1	(13.2)

Turnover Rate

(Pct. of possessions used in parenthesis)

At least 28% of possessions used

1 Arizona Reid, High Point	11.3	(31.8)
2 Reggie Williams, VMI	13.5	(30.9)

At least 24% of possessions used

1 Arizona Reid, High Point	11.3	(31.8)
2 Reggie Williams, VMI	13.5	(30.9)
3 Alex McLean, Liberty	14.7	(24.6)
4 Jamarco Warren, Char. Southern	16.4	(25.2)
5 Anthony Breeze, C. Carolina	17.1	(24.3)
6 Omar Carter, Char. Southern	17.3	(27.6)
7 Travis Holmes, VMI	18.2	(26.3)
8 Kenny George, UNC Asheville	19.2	(25.3)
9 Martell McDuffy, Radford	23.4	(24.1)
10 Mike Jefferson, High Point	24.3	(25.7)
11 Amir Johnson, Radford	26.0	(25.1)

At least 20% of possessions used

1 Arizona Reid, High Point	11.3	(31.8)
2 Anthony Smith, Liberty	13.3	(20.5)
3 Reggie Williams, VMI	13.5	(30.9)
4 Chavis Holmes, VMI	14.2	(23.4)
5 Alex McLean, Liberty	14.7	(24.6)
6 Michael Jenkins, Winthrop	15.2	(23.8)
7 Jack Leasure, Coastal Carolina	15.6	(20.9)
8 Jamarco Warren, Char. Southern	16.4	(25.2)
9 Phil Wallace, Coastal Carolina	16.4	(22.9)
10 Taj McCullough, Winthrop	16.9	(23.8)
11 Bryan Smithson, UNC Asheville	17.1	(22.8)
12 Anthony Breeze, C. Carolina	17.1	(24.3)
13 Omar Carter, Char. Southern	17.3	(27.6)

14 Charles Corbin, Winthrop	17.6	(22.0)
15 Travis Holmes, VMI	18.2	(26.3)
16 K.J. Garland, UNC Asheville	19.1	(21.3)
17 Kenny George, UNC Asheville	19.2	(25.3)
18 Vincent James, UNC Asheville	20.9	(23.5)
19 Shelton Carter, Char. Southern	21.5	(20.3)
20 Kenny Thomas, Radford	21.8	(22.4)

ALL PLAYERS

1 Arizona Reid, High Point	11.3	(31.8)
2 Chris Moore, Char. Southern	12.9	(18.5)
3 Anthony Smith, Liberty	13.3	(20.5)
4 Reggie Williams, VMI	13.5	(30.9)
5 Chavis Holmes, VMI	14.2	(23.4)
6 Christian Hunter, VMI	14.6	(14.7)
7 Alex McLean, Liberty	14.7	(24.6)
8 Michael Jenkins, Winthrop	15.2	(23.8)
9 Jack Leasure, Coastal Carolina	15.6	(20.9)
10 Sean Smith, UNC Asheville	16.4	(16.0)
11 Jamarco Warren, Char. Southern	16.4	(25.2)
12 Phil Wallace, Coastal Carolina	16.4	(22.9)
13 Eric Hall, Radford	16.6	(16.2)
14 Reid Augst, UNC Asheville	16.6	(16.7)
15 Taj McCullough, Winthrop	16.9	(23.8)
16 Bryan Smithson, UNC Asheville	17.1	(22.8)
17 Anthony Breeze, C. Carolina	17.1	(24.3)
18 Omar Carter, Char. Southern	17.3	(27.6)
19 Charles Corbin, Winthrop	17.6	(22.0)
20 John Williams, UNC Asheville	17.7	(17.2)

Usage (Pct. of Possessions Used)

1 Arizona Reid, High Point	31.8
2 Reggie Williams, VMI	30.9
3 Omar Carter, Char. Southern	27.6
4 Travis Holmes, VMI	26.3
5 Mike Jefferson, High Point	25.7
6 Kenny George, NC Asheville	25.3
7 Jamarco Warren, Char. Southern	25.2
8 Amir Johnson, Radford	25.1
9 Alex McLean, Liberty	24.6
10 Anthony Breeze, C. Carolina	24.3
11 Martell McDuffy, Radford	24.1
12 TeeJay Bannister, Liberty	24.0
13 Michael Jenkins, Winthrop	23.8
14 Taj McCullough, Winthrop	23.8
15 Vincent James, NC Asheville	23.5
16 Chavis Holmes, VMI	23.4
17 Phil Wallace, Coastal Carolina	22.9
18 Bryan Smithson, NC Asheville	22.8
19 Kenny Thomas, Radford	22.4

20 Charles Corbin, Winthrop	22.0
21 B.J. Jenkins, Liberty	21.3
22 K.J. Garland, NC Asheville	21.3
23 Jack Leasure, Coastal Carolina	20.9
24 Tovi Bailey, Char. Southern	20.7
25 Anthony Smith, Liberty	20.5

Assist Rate

1 TeeJay Bannister, Liberty	45.6
2 Mike Jefferson, High Point	37.2
3 Amir Johnson, Radford	31.9
4 K.J. Garland, NC Asheville	28.6
5 Chris Gaynor, Winthrop	25.8
6 Reggie Williams, VMI	22.3
7 Bryan Smithson, NC Asheville	21.8
8 Logan Johnson, Coastal Carolina	21.1
9 Adam Lonon, VMI	20.8
10 Tovi Bailey, Char. Southern	20.4
11 B.J. Jenkins, Liberty	19.1
12 Chris Moore, Char. Southern	18.8
13 Arizona Reid, High Point	18.3
14 Michael Jenkins, Winthrop	18.3
15 Mario Sisinni, Coastal Carolina	18.1

Block Rate

1 Kenny George, NC Asheville	17.3
2 Cruz Daniels, High Point	14.0
3 Eric Hall, Radford	8.9
4 John Williams, NC Asheville	7.8
5 Mantoris Robinson, Winthrop	4.7
6 Anthony Breeze, Coastal Carolina	4.4
7 Vincent James, NC Asheville	2.6
8 Taj McCullough, Winthrop	2.4
9 Shelton Carter, Char. Southern	2.3
10 Garrett Moles, NC Asheville	2.3
11 Willie Bell, VMI	2.2
12 Travis Holmes, VMI	2.0
13 Reggie Williams, VMI	1.9
14 Rell Porter, Liberty	1.8
15 Michael Jenkins, Winthrop	1.8

Offensive Rebounding Percentage

1 Eric Hall, Radford	13.6
2 Cruz Daniels, High Point	12.7
3 Arizona Reid, High Point	12.4
4 Phil Wallace, Coastal Carolina	12.2

5 Alex McLean, Liberty 11.1
6 Charles Corbin, Winthrop 10.8
7 Anthony Breeze, Coastal Carolina 10.4
8 Reggie Williams, VMI 9.9
9 Giedrius Knysas, Char. Southern 9.8
10 Willie Bell, VMI 9.6
11 John Williams, NC Asheville 9.4
12 Kenny George, NC Asheville 9.0
13 Joey Lynch-Flohr, Radford 8.4
14 Garrett Moles, NC Asheville 7.8
15 Mantoris Robinson, Winthrop 7.8

Defensive Rebounding Percentage

1 Kenny George, NC Asheville 29.8
2 Arizona Reid, High Point 24.3
3 Alex McLean, Liberty 21.9
4 Eric Hall, Radford 19.6
5 Reggie Williams, VMI 18.4
6 Omar Carter, Char. Southern 18.2
7 Taj McCullough, Winthrop 17.7
8 Anthony Breeze, Coastal Carolina 17.1
9 Shelton Carter, Char. Southern 17.0
10 Travis Holmes, VMI 15.9
11 Joey Lynch-Flohr, Radford 15.9
12 Phil Wallace, Coastal Carolina 15.8
13 Cruz Daniels, High Point 15.6
14 John Williams, NC Asheville 15.4
15 David Campbell, High Point 14.8

Steal Rate

1 Chris Gaynor, Winthrop 5.39
2 Adam Lonon, VMI 4.39
3 Travis Holmes, VMI 3.81
4 Chavis Holmes, VMI 3.77
5 Taj McCullough, Winthrop 3.17
6 Reggie Williams, VMI 3.03
7 Willie Bell, VMI 3.01
8 Bryan Smithson, NC Asheville 3.00
9 Arizona Reid, High Point 2.99
10 Amir Johnson, Radford 2.93
11 B.J. Jenkins, Liberty 2.69
12 Vincent James, NC Asheville 2.67
13 Omar Carter, Char. Southern 2.39
14 Martell McDuffy, Radford 2.35
15 Mike Jefferson, High Point 2.29

Pct. of Possible Minutes Played

1 Jack Leasure, Coastal Carolina 92.8
2 K.J. Garland, NC Asheville 91.2
3 Arizona Reid, High Point 88.1
4 Mike Jefferson, High Point 87.6
5 Anthony Smith, Liberty 85.7
6 Eugene Harris, High Point 83.0
7 Chris Gaynor, Winthrop 82.1
8 Amir Johnson, Radford 81.9
9 Alex McLean, Liberty 81.8
10 Michael Jenkins, Winthrop 79.3

BIG TEN
INDIVIDUAL STATISTICS

Offensive Rating

(Pct. of possessions used in parenthesis)

At least 28% of possessions used

1 Eric Gordon, Indiana	110.0	(29.9)
2 Brian Butch, Wisconsin	106.3	(28.2)
3 Manny Harris, Michigan	94.8	(30.5)

At least 24% of possessions used

1 Eric Gordon, Indiana	110.0	(29.9)
2 Raymar Morgan, Michigan St.	109.7	(25.9)
3 Kosta Koufos, Ohio St.	108.8	(26.6)
4 Brian Butch, Wisconsin	106.3	(28.2)
5 Shaun Pruitt, Illinois	104.5	(26.2)
6 Kalin Lucas, Michigan St.	103.4	(25.3)
7 DeShawn Sims, Michigan	95.2	(26.1)
8 Tony Freeman, Iowa	95.1	(26.5)
9 Manny Harris, Michigan	94.8	(30.5)

At least 20% of possessions used

1 D.J. White, Indiana	120.3	(23.5)
2 Drew Neitzel, Michigan St.	119.9	(21.7)
3 Jamar Butler, Ohio St.	115.7	(23.0)
4 Eric Gordon, Indiana	110.0	(29.9)
5 Raymar Morgan, Michigan St.	109.7	(25.9)
6 E'Twaun Moore, Purdue	109.4	(21.6)
7 Kosta Koufos, Ohio St.	108.8	(26.6)
8 Lawrence McKenzie, Minnesota	107.3	(22.9)
9 Craig Moore, Northwestern	107.0	(20.6)
10 Brian Butch, Wisconsin	106.3	(28.2)
11 Marcus Landry, Wisconsin	105.3	(21.6)
12 Jordan Crawford, Indiana	104.5	(22.1)
13 Shaun Pruitt, Illinois	104.5	(26.2)
14 Kevin Coble, Northwestern	103.7	(24.0)
15 Lawrence Westbrook, Minnesota	103.5	(21.6)
16 Kalin Lucas, Michigan St.	103.4	(25.3)
17 Cyrus Tate, Iowa	102.1	(21.5)
18 Dan Coleman, Minnesota	101.6	(23.5)
19 Trevon Hughes, Wisconsin	101.0	(23.2)
20 Calvin Brock, Illinois	100.8	(20.7)

ALL PLAYERS

1 Robbie Hummel, Purdue	126.7	(19.8)
2 Lance Stemler, Indiana	122.9	(10.3)
3 Blake Hoffarber, Minnesota	120.6	(18.2)
4 D.J. White, Indiana	120.3	(23.5)
5 Drew Neitzel, Michigan St.	119.9	(21.7)
6 Jason Bohannon, Wisconsin	119.8	(15.2)
7 Armon Bassett, Indiana	119.8	(17.5)
8 Drew Naymick, Michigan St.	119.8	(9.6)
9 Jamar Butler, Ohio St.	115.7	(23.0)
10 Goran Suton, Michigan St.	113.6	(19.1)
11 Keaton Grant, Purdue	113.1	(18.9)
12 Trent Meacham, Illinois	112.2	(17.8)
13 Othello Hunter, Ohio St.	111.6	(18.8)
14 Joe Krabbenhoft, Wisconsin	110.9	(16.1)
15 Mike Walker, Penn St.	110.7	(16.6)
16 Eric Gordon, Indiana	110.0	(29.9)
17 Danny Morrissey, Penn St.	109.7	(18.1)
18 Raymar Morgan, Michigan St.	109.7	(25.9)
19 E'Twaun Moore, Purdue	109.4	(21.6)
20 Kosta Koufos, Ohio St.	108.8	(26.6)

Turnover Rate

(Pct. of possessions used in parenthesis)

At least 28% of possessions used

1 Brian Butch, Wisconsin	13.1	(28.2)
2 Eric Gordon, Indiana	20.6	(29.9)
3 Manny Harris, Michigan	22.0	(30.5)

At least 24% of possessions used

1 Kosta Koufos, Ohio St.	12.6	(26.6)
2 Brian Butch, Wisconsin	13.1	(28.2)
3 DeShawn Sims, Michigan	15.8	(26.1)
4 Shaun Pruitt, Illinois	19.4	(26.2)
5 Raymar Morgan, Michigan St.	19.8	(25.9)
6 Kalin Lucas, Michigan St.	19.8	(25.3)
7 Eric Gordon, Indiana	20.6	(29.9)
8 Manny Harris, Michigan	22.0	(30.5)
9 Tony Freeman, Iowa	23.2	(26.5)

At least 20% of possessions used

1 Kevin Coble, Northwestern	11.6	(24.0)
2 Kosta Koufos, Ohio St.	12.6	(26.6)
3 Drew Neitzel, Michigan St.	12.8	(21.7)
4 Brian Butch, Wisconsin	13.1	(28.2)
5 D.J. White, Indiana	14.4	(23.5)
6 E'Twaun Moore, Purdue	15.5	(21.6)
7 DeShawn Sims, Michigan	15.8	(26.1)
8 Dan Coleman, Minnesota	16.1	(23.5)
9 Craig Moore, Northwestern	16.7	(20.6)
10 Spencer Tollackson, Minnesota	17.0	(23.8)
11 Justin Johnson, Iowa	17.1	(21.1)
12 Scott Martin, Purdue	17.2	(23.8)
13 Michael Thompson, Northwestern	17.7	(22.1)
14 Marcus Landry, Wisconsin	18.2	(21.6)
15 Brian Randle, Illinois	18.3	(23.4)

16 Trevon Hughes, Wisconsin	19.0	(23.2)	22 Lawrence McKenzie, Minnesota	22.9	
17 Jamelle Cornley, Penn St.	19.3	(23.4)	23 Demetri McCamey, Illinois	22.3	
18 Shaun Pruitt, Illinois	19.4	(26.2)	24 Michael Thompson, Northwestern	22.1	
19 Jamar Butler, Ohio St.	19.7	(23.0)	25 Jordan Crawford, Indiana	22.1	
20 Raymar Morgan, Michigan St.	19.8	(25.9)			

ALL PLAYERS

1 Lance Stemler, Indiana	6.8	(10.3)
2 Mike Walker, Penn St.	10.3	(16.6)
3 JaJuan Johnson, Purdue	11.2	(18.9)
4 Kevin Coble, Northwestern	11.6	(24.0)
5 Kosta Koufos, Ohio St.	12.6	(26.6)
6 Drew Neitzel, Michigan St.	12.8	(21.7)
7 Brian Butch, Wisconsin	13.1	(28.2)
8 Blake Hoffarber, Minnesota	13.1	(18.2)
9 Jason Okrzesik, Northwestern	14.3	(19.6)
10 D.J. White, Indiana	14.4	(23.5)
11 Sterling Williams, Northwestern	14.4	(14.6)
12 Robbie Hummel, Purdue	14.8	(19.8)
13 E'Twaun Moore, Purdue	15.5	(21.6)
14 DeShawn Sims, Michigan	15.8	(26.1)
15 Dan Coleman, Minnesota	16.1	(23.5)
16 Craig Moore, Northwestern	16.7	(20.6)
17 Jason Bohannon, Wisconsin	16.8	(15.2)
18 Anthony Wright, Michigan	16.9	(17.6)
19 Spencer Tollackson, Minnesota	17.0	(23.8)
20 Justin Johnson, Iowa	17.1	(21.1)

Usage (Pct. of Possessions Used)

1 Manny Harris, Michigan	30.5
2 Eric Gordon, Indiana	29.9
3 Brian Butch, Wisconsin	28.2
4 Kosta Koufos, Ohio St.	26.6
5 Tony Freeman, Iowa	26.5
6 Shaun Pruitt, Illinois	26.2
7 DeShawn Sims, Michigan	26.1
8 Raymar Morgan, Michigan St.	25.9
9 Kalin Lucas, Michigan St.	25.3
10 Kevin Coble, Northwestern	24.0
11 Spencer Tollackson, Minnesota	23.8
12 Nemanja Calasan, Purdue	23.8
13 Scott Martin, Purdue	23.8
14 D.J. White, Indiana	23.5
15 Dan Coleman, Minnesota	23.5
16 Brian Randle, Illinois	23.4
17 Jamelle Cornley, Penn St.	23.4
18 Talor Battle, Penn St.	23.2
19 Trevon Hughes, Wisconsin	23.2
20 Jamar Butler, Ohio St.	23.0
21 Jeff Peterson, Iowa	22.9

Assist Rate

1 Jamar Butler, Ohio St.	32.5
2 Travis Walton, Michigan St.	30.3
3 Kalin Lucas, Michigan St.	30.0
4 Jeff Peterson, Iowa	29.8
5 Al Nolen, Minnesota	28.3
6 Michael Thompson, Northwestern	26.6
7 Demetri McCamey, Illinois	26.0
8 Tony Freeman, Iowa	25.6
9 Drew Neitzel, Michigan St.	24.8
10 Kelvin Grady, Michigan	24.1
11 Stanley Pringle, Penn St.	22.8
12 Talor Battle, Penn St.	22.7
13 Lawrence Westbrook, Minnesota	21.3
14 Lawrence McKenzie, Minnesota	20.9
15 Chester Frazier, Illinois	20.8

Block Rate

1 Ekpe Udoh, Michigan	12.3
2 Drew Naymick, Michigan St.	9.1
3 Kurt Looby, Iowa	9.1
4 Kosta Koufos, Ohio St.	7.6
5 Damian Johnson, Minnesota	7.6
6 JaJuan Johnson, Purdue	7.2
7 Othello Hunter, Ohio St.	6.3
8 Dan Coleman, Minnesota	5.7
9 D.J. White, Indiana	5.4
10 Goran Suton, Michigan St.	4.0
11 Brian Butch, Wisconsin	3.7
12 Scott Martin, Purdue	3.6
13 Jeff Ryan, Northwestern	3.1
14 DeShawn Sims, Michigan	3.0
15 Marcus Landry, Wisconsin	2.9

Offensive Rebounding Percentage

1 Shaun Pruitt, Illinois	13.9
2 Goran Suton, Michigan St.	13.5
3 Andrew Jones, Penn St.	13.2
4 Kosta Koufos, Ohio St.	12.1
5 D.J. White, Indiana	11.4
6 Cyrus Tate, Iowa	11.3

7 Othello Hunter, Ohio St.	11.2
8 Kurt Looby, Iowa	10.9
9 Brian Butch, Wisconsin	10.9
10 Robbie Hummel, Purdue	10.5
11 Damian Johnson, Minnesota	10.3
12 Raymar Morgan, Michigan St.	10.0
13 Brian Randle, Illinois	9.7
14 Ekpe Udoh, Michigan	9.3
15 Nemanja Calasan, Purdue	9.3

Defensive Rebounding Percentage

1 D.J. White, Indiana	24.1
2 Goran Suton, Michigan St.	22.6
3 Brian Butch, Wisconsin	21.2
4 Kurt Looby, Iowa	20.7
5 Seth Gorney, Iowa	19.6
6 Jamarcus Ellis, Indiana	19.2
7 Shaun Pruitt, Illinois	18.6
8 Kevin Coble, Northwestern	18.5
9 Cyrus Tate, Iowa	18.3
10 Dan Coleman, Minnesota	17.0
11 Joe Krabbenhoft, Wisconsin	16.8
12 Jamelle Cornley, Penn St.	16.8
13 Brian Randle, Illinois	16.5
14 Robbie Hummel, Purdue	16.1
15 JaJuan Johnson, Purdue	16.0

Steal Rate

1 Al Nolen, Minnesota	5.21
2 Chris Kramer, Purdue	4.72
3 Damian Johnson, Minnesota	4.66
4 Trevon Hughes, Wisconsin	3.75
5 Craig Moore, Northwestern	3.31
6 Michael Flowers, Wisconsin	3.31
7 Evan Turner, Ohio St.	2.87
8 Jamarcus Ellis, Indiana	2.85
9 Sterling Williams, Northwestern	2.80
10 Robbie Hummel, Purdue	2.73
11 Jason Okrzesik, Northwestern	2.69
12 Stanley Pringle, Penn St.	2.68
13 Talor Battle, Penn St.	2.67
14 Scott Martin, Purdue	2.65
15 Manny Harris, Michigan	2.63

Pct. of Possible Minutes Played

1 Jamar Butler, Ohio St.	90.3
2 Justin Johnson, Iowa	88.9
3 Michael Thompson, Northwestern	88.8
4 Craig Moore, Northwestern	88.5
5 Eric Gordon, Indiana	83.1
6 D.J. White, Indiana	82.8
7 Manny Harris, Michigan	82.6
8 David Lighty, Ohio St.	79.8
9 Chester Frazier, Illinois	79.7
10 Michael Flowers, Wisconsin	79.1

CAA INDIVIDUAL STATISTICS

Offensive Rating

Pct. of possessions used in parenthesis)

At least 28% of possessions used

1 Eric Maynor, VCU	111.3	(28.9)
2 T.J. Carter, UNC Wilmington	109.2	(28.1)
3 Antoine Agudio, Hofstra	105.5	(29.4)
4 Folarin Campbell, George Mason	103.1	(28.5)
5 Abdulai Jalloh, James Madison	97.8	(30.3)

At least 24% of possessions used

1 Eric Maynor, VCU	111.3	(28.9)
2 T.J. Carter, UNC Wilmington	109.2	(28.1)
3 Leonard Mendez, Georgia St.	106.8	(24.2)
4 Antoine Agudio, Hofstra	105.5	(29.4)
5 Matt Janning, Northeastern	105.2	(24.4)
6 Frank Elegar, Drexel	104.9	(24.4)
7 Folarin Campbell, George Mason	103.1	(28.5)
8 Charles Jenkins, Hofstra	99.0	(24.7)
9 Abdulai Jalloh, James Madison	97.8	(30.3)
10 Laimis Kisielius, Wm. & Mary	95.2	(25.4)
11 Herb Courtney, Delaware	93.3	(25.2)
12 Marc Egerson, Delaware	92.0	(25.5)

At least 20% of possessions used

1 Will Thomas, George Mason	126.5	(21.4)
2 Jamal Shuler, VCU	112.4	(21.9)
3 Eric Maynor, VCU	111.3	(28.9)
4 T.J. Carter, UNC Wilmington	109.2	(28.1)
5 Vladimir Kuljanin, UNCW	108.9	(22.1)
6 Todd Hendley, UNC Wilmington	108.9	(21.4)
7 Josh Thornton, Towson	107.5	(21.6)
8 Terrance Carter, JMU	107.5	(22.2)
9 Leonard Mendez, Georgia St.	106.8	(24.2)
10 Gerald Lee, Old Dominion	106.3	(23.4)
11 Juwann James, James Madison	106.1	(22.1)
12 Antoine Agudio, Hofstra	105.5	(29.4)
13 Matt Janning, Northeastern	105.2	(24.4)
14 Frank Elegar, Drexel	104.9	(24.4)
15 Danny Sumner, William & Mary	103.7	(22.6)
16 Folarin Campbell, George Mason	103.1	(28.5)
17 John Vaughan, George Mason	103.0	(21.8)
18 Pierre Curtis, James Madison	102.3	(20.1)
19 Junior Hairston, Towson	99.9	(21.9)
20 Nkem Ojougboh, Northeastern	99.5	(20.8)

1 Will Thomas, George Mason	126.5	(21.4)
2 Daniel Fountain, UNCW	116.2	(18.5)
3 Kyle Swanston, James Madison	116.0	(15.0)
4 Louis Birdsong, George Mason	114.4	(15.6)
5 Jamal Shuler, VCU	112.4	(21.9)
6 Jim Ledsome, Delaware	112.1	(11.6)
7 Eric Maynor, VCU	111.3	(28.9)
8 Brian Henderson, Old Dominion	111.3	(19.1)
9 David Schneider, Wm. & Mary	110.5	(19.7)
10 T.J. Carter, UNC Wilmington	109.2	(28.1)
11 Manny Adako, Northeastern	109.1	(18.8)
12 Todd Hendley, UNC Wilmington	108.9	(21.4)
13 Vladimir Kuljanin, UNCW	108.9	(22.1)
14 Jonathan Pease, Towson	108.9	(17.8)
15 Jonathan Adams, Old Dominion	108.1	(17.2)
16 Terrance Carter, JMU	107.5	(22.2)
17 Josh Thornton, Towson	107.5	(21.6)
18 Dre Smith, George Mason	107.2	(17.9)
19 Ben Finney, Old Dominion	106.8	(20.0)
20 Leonard Mendez, Georgia St.	106.8	(24.2)

Turnover Rate

(Pct. of possessions used in parenthesis)

At least 28% of possessions used

1 Antoine Agudio, Hofstra	18.1	(29.4)
2 Eric Maynor, VCU	18.2	(28.9)
3 T.J. Carter, UNC Wilmington	18.3	(28.1)
4 Folarin Campbell, George Mason	20.2	(28.5)
5 Abdulai Jalloh, James Madison	26.8	(30.3)

At least 24% of possessions used

1 Leonard Mendez, Georgia St.	14.9	(24.2)
2 Laimis Kisielius, Wm. & Mary	17.2	(25.4)
3 Antoine Agudio, Hofstra	18.1	(29.4)
4 Herb Courtney, Delaware	18.1	(25.2)
5 Frank Elegar, Drexel	18.1	(24.4)
6 Eric Maynor, VCU	18.2	(28.9)
7 T.J. Carter, UNC Wilmington	18.3	(28.1)
8 Matt Janning, Northeastern	19.4	(24.4)
9 Folarin Campbell, George Mason	20.2	(28.5)
10 Charles Jenkins, Hofstra	22.8	(24.7)
11 Marc Egerson, Delaware	23.6	(25.5)
12 Abdulai Jalloh, James Madison	26.8	(30.3)

At least 20% of possessions used

1 Eugene Spates, Northeastern	10.9	(22.3)
2 Will Thomas, George Mason	12.6	(21.4)

3 Jamal Shuler, VCU	12.9	(21.9)
4 Rocky Coleman, Towson	13.4	(20.4)
5 Leonard Mendez, Georgia St.	14.9	(24.2)
6 Junior Hairston, Towson	15.4	(21.9)
7 Gerald Lee, Old Dominion	16.3	(23.4)
8 John Vaughan, George Mason	16.9	(21.8)
9 Laimis Kisielius, Wm. & Mary	17.2	(25.4)
10 Josh Thornton, Towson	17.5	(21.6)
11 Nkem Ojougboh, Northeastern	17.7	(20.8)
12 Danny Sumner, William & Mary	17.9	(22.6)
13 Frank Elegar, Drexel	18.1	(24.4)
14 Antoine Agudio, Hofstra	18.1	(29.4)
15 Herb Courtney, Delaware	18.1	(25.2)
16 Eric Maynor, VCU	18.2	(28.9)
17 T.J. Carter, UNC Wilmington	18.3	(28.1)
18 Tony Durant, Towson	18.5	(22.1)
19 Alphonso Dawson, Delaware	18.5	(23.6)
20 Terrance Carter, James Madison	18.7	(22.2)

ALL PLAYERS

1 Eugene Spates, Northeastern	10.9	(22.3)
2 Will Thomas, George Mason	12.6	(21.4)
3 Jamal Shuler, VCU	12.9	(21.9)
4 Dre Smith, George Mason	13.1	(17.9)
5 Rocky Coleman, Towson	13.4	(20.4)
6 Daniel Fountain, UNC Wilmington	13.8	(18.5)
7 Brian Henderson, Old Dominion	13.9	(19.1)
8 Kyle Swanston, James Madison	14.1	(15.0)
9 Leonard Mendez, Georgia St.	14.9	(24.2)
10 Ben Finney, Old Dominion	15.1	(20.0)
11 Junior Hairston, Towson	15.4	(21.9)
12 Louis Birdsong, George Mason	15.6	(15.6)
13 Tramayne Hawthorne, Drexel	15.9	(19.5)
14 David Schneider, William & Mary	15.9	(19.7)
15 Larry Sanders, VCU	15.9	(18.1)
16 Jonathan Pease, Towson	15.9	(17.8)
17 Gerald Lee, Old Dominion	16.3	(23.4)
18 John Vaughan, George Mason	16.9	(21.8)
19 Frank Hassell, Old Dominion	16.9	(17.8)
20 Laimis Kisielius, Wm. & Mary	17.2	(25.4)

Usage (Pct. of Possessions Used)

1 Abdulai Jalloh, James Madison	30.3
2 Antoine Agudio, Hofstra	29.4
3 Eric Maynor, VCU	28.9
4 Folarin Campbell, George Mason	28.5
5 T.J. Carter, UNC Wilmington	28.1
6 Marc Egerson, Delaware	25.5
7 Laimis Kisielius, Wm. & Mary	25.4
8 Herb Courtney, Delaware	25.2

9 Charles Jenkins, Hofstra	24.7
10 Matt Janning, Northeastern	24.4
11 Frank Elegar, Drexel	24.4
12 Leonard Mendez, Georgia St.	24.2
13 Alphonso Dawson, Delaware	23.6
14 Edwin Santiago, Delaware	23.5
15 Gerald Lee, Old Dominion	23.4
16 Scott Rodgers, Drexel	23.3
17 Nathaniel Lester, Hofstra	23.1
18 Gerald Colds, Drexel	22.7
19 Danny Sumner, William & Mary	22.6
20 Brandon Johnson, Old Dominion	22.5
21 Eugene Spates, Northeastern	22.3
22 Terrance Carter, James Madison	22.2
23 Juwann James, James Madison	22.1
24 Tony Durant, Towson	22.1
25 Vladimir Kuljanin, UNCW	22.1

Assist Rate

1 Eric Maynor, VCU	39.1
2 Brandon Johnson, Old Dominion	33.1
3 C.C. Williams, Towson	31.5
4 Brian Johnson, Delaware	30.8
5 Pierre Curtis, James Madison	26.5
6 T.J. Carter, UNC Wilmington	26.3
7 Greg Johnson, Hofstra	24.9
8 David Schneider, William & Mary	23.8
9 Tramayne Hawthorne, Drexel	23.1
10 Chaisson Allen, Northeastern	22.1
11 Folarin Campbell, George Mason	21.9
12 D.J. Jones, Georgia St.	21.3
13 Marc Egerson, Delaware	21.1
14 Laimis Kisielius, Wm. & Mary	21.0
15 Abdulai Jalloh, James Madison	20.9

Block Rate

1 Larry Sanders, VCU	19.3
2 Dane Johnson, Hofstra	11.1
3 Frank Hassell, Old Dominion	7.3
4 Frank Elegar, Drexel	6.9
5 Junior Hairston, Towson	6.0
6 Jim Ledsome, Delaware	5.4
7 Louis Birdsong, George Mason	4.6
8 Herb Courtney, Delaware	4.3
9 Michael Anderson, VCU	4.1
10 Justin Billingslea, Georgia St.	4.0
11 Darren Townes, Hofstra	3.6
12 Jonathan Adams, Old Dominion	3.5

13 Nkem Ojougboh, Northeastern   3.4
14 Gerald Lee, Old Dominion   3.3
15 Vladimir Kuljanin, UNC Wilmington   3.0

Offensive Rebounding Percentage

1 Ben Finney, Old Dominion   12.9
2 Vladimir Kuljanin, UNC Wilmington   12.7
3 Louis Birdsong, George Mason   11.6
4 Juwann James, James Madison   11.4
5 Larry Sanders, VCU   11.1
6 Rashad Chase, Georgia St.   10.9
7 Gerald Lee, Old Dominion   9.8
8 Dane Johnson, Hofstra   9.8
9 Frank Hassell, Old Dominion   9.8
10 Terrance Carter, James Madison   9.7
11 Darren Townes, Hofstra   9.5
12 Peter Stein, William & Mary   9.5
13 Nkem Ojougboh, Northeastern   9.5
14 Todd Hendley, UNC Wilmington   9.2
15 Junior Hairston, Towson   9.0

Defensive Rebounding Percentage

1 Rashad Chase, Georgia St.   27.3
2 Will Thomas, George Mason   26.7
3 Larry Sanders, VCU   23.9
4 Vladimir Kuljanin, UNC Wilmington   23.6
5 Frank Elegar, Drexel   23.4
6 Junior Hairston, Towson   23.1
7 Dane Johnson, Hofstra   19.4
8 Marc Egerson, Delaware   18.6
9 Frank Hassell, Old Dominion   18.4
10 Abdulai Jalloh, James Madison   17.8
11 Darren Townes, Hofstra   17.0
12 Jonathan Adams, Old Dominion   16.9
13 Jonathan Pease, Towson   16.6
14 Herb Courtney, Delaware   16.4
15 Terrance Carter, James Madison   16.1

Steal Rate

1 Brandon Johnson, Old Dominion   6.11
2 D.J. Jones, Georgia St.   3.76
3 Chaisson Allen, Northeastern   3.73
4 Joey Rodriguez, VCU   3.71
5 Tramayne Hawthorne, Drexel   3.46
6 Jonathan Pease, Towson   3.42
7 Ben Finney, Old Dominion   3.37
8 Abdulai Jalloh, James Madison   3.24
9 Edwin Santiago, Delaware   3.22
10 Chris Alvarez, Northeastern   3.16
11 David Schneider, William & Mary   3.12
12 Chad Tomko, UNC Wilmington   3.10
13 Juwann James, James Madison   3.00
14 Charles Jenkins, Hofstra   2.85
15 Jamal Shuler, VCU   2.77

Pct. of Possible Minutes Played

1 Brian Johnson, Delaware   92.3
2 Matt Janning, Northeastern   89.9
3 Will Thomas, George Mason   88.1
4 Eric Maynor, VCU   86.8
5 Antoine Agudio, Hofstra   86.6
6 David Schneider, William & Mary   86.0
7 Chaisson Allen, Northeastern   85.4
8 Leonard Mendez, Georgia St.   85.2
9 Scott Rodgers, Drexel   83.2
10 Charles Jenkins, Hofstra   82.3

CONFERENCE USA
INDIVIDUAL STATISTICS

Offensive Rating

(Pct. of possessions used in parenthesis)

At least 28% of possessions used

1 Rob McKiver, Houston	114.9	(30.0)
2 Jermaine Taylor, Central Florida	109.6	(29.4)
3 Stefon Jackson, Texas El Paso	108.4	(30.6)
4 Robert Vaden, UAB	108.4	(28.1)
5 Jeremy Wise, Southern Miss	105.5	(29.7)

At least 24% of possessions used

1 Chris Douglas-Roberts, Memphis	117.5	(26.6)
2 Rob McKiver, Houston	114.9	(30.0)
3 Derrick Rose, Memphis	111.8	(27.2)
4 Jermaine Taylor, Central Florida	109.6	(29.4)
5 David Gomez, Tulane	108.6	(25.2)
6 Stefon Jackson, Texas El Paso	108.4	(30.6)
7 Robert Vaden, UAB	108.4	(28.1)
8 Jeremy Wise, Southern Miss	105.5	(29.7)
9 Randy Culpepper, Texas El Paso	103.1	(24.4)
10 Mark Dorris, Marshall	99.1	(25.7)
11 Lawrence Ghoram, Rice	84.9	(24.6)
12 Papa Dia, Southern Methodist	84.1	(27.5)
13 Alex Malone, Southern Methodist	83.9	(25.5)

At least 20% of possessions used

1 Chris Douglas-Roberts, Memphis	117.5	(26.6)
2 Rob McKiver, Houston	114.9	(30.0)
3 Ben Uzoh, Tulsa	114.4	(24.0)
4 Derrick Rose, Memphis	111.8	(27.2)
5 Tyler Wilkerson, Marshall	111.2	(21.8)
6 Jermaine Taylor, Central Florida	109.6	(29.4)
7 David Gomez, Tulane	108.6	(25.2)
8 Stefon Jackson, Texas El Paso	108.4	(30.6)
9 Robert Vaden, UAB	108.4	(28.1)
10 Tirrell Baines, Marshall	108.4	(22.5)
11 Robinson Louisme, Tulane	108.2	(23.7)
12 Markel Humphrey, Marshall	107.3	(21.5)
13 Courtney Beasley, Southern Miss	106.7	(20.2)
14 Jerome Jordan, Tulsa	106.4	(22.2)
15 Marvin Kilgore, Texas El Paso	106.4	(22.4)
16 Jeremy Wise, Southern Miss	105.5	(29.7)
17 R.L. Horton, Southern Miss	103.9	(20.2)
18 Bamba Fall, Southern Methodist	103.9	(21.7)
19 Lawrence Kinnard, UAB	103.5	(21.0)
20 Randy Culpepper, Texas El Paso	103.1	(24.4)

ALL PLAYERS

1 Kelvin Lewis, Houston	123.0	(17.8)
2 Dion Dowell, Houston	122.3	(16.7)
3 Dave Noel, Central Florida	117.7	(19.6)
4 Chris Douglas-Roberts, Memphis	117.5	(26.6)
5 Shawn Taggart, Memphis	116.0	(16.5)
6 Rob McKiver, Houston	114.9	(30.0)
7 Ben Uzoh, Tulsa	114.4	(24.0)
8 Joey Dorsey, Memphis	113.4	(14.7)
9 Derrick Rose, Memphis	111.8	(27.2)
10 Tyler Wilkerson, Marshall	111.2	(21.8)
11 Antonio Anderson, Memphis	111.2	(16.0)
12 Mike O'Donnell, Central Florida	111.1	(17.6)
13 Sam Hinnant, East Carolina	110.3	(18.1)
14 Reggie Huffman, UAB	109.7	(20.0)
15 Jermaine Taylor, Central Florida	109.6	(29.4)
16 David Gomez, Tulane	108.6	(25.2)
17 Stefon Jackson, Texas El Paso	108.4	(30.6)
18 Robert Vaden, UAB	108.4	(28.1)
19 Tirrell Baines, Marshall	108.4	(22.5)
20 Robinson Louisme, Tulane	108.2	(23.7)

Turnover Rate

(Pct. of possessions used in parenthesis)

At least 28% of possessions used

1 Stefon Jackson, Texas El Paso	11.9	(30.6)
2 Rob McKiver, Houston	13.6	(30.0)
3 Jermaine Taylor, Central Florida	15.2	(29.4)
4 Robert Vaden, UAB	17.2	(28.1)
5 Jeremy Wise, Southern Miss	19.6	(29.7)

At least 24% of possessions used

1 Stefon Jackson, Texas El Paso	11.9	(30.6)
2 Randy Culpepper, Texas El Paso	13.4	(24.4)
3 Rob McKiver, Houston	13.6	(30.0)
4 Jermaine Taylor, Central Florida	15.2	(29.4)
5 Chris Douglas-Roberts, Memphis	15.4	(26.6)
6 David Gomez, Tulane	17.0	(25.2)
7 Robert Vaden, UAB	17.2	(28.1)
8 Derrick Rose, Memphis	19.1	(27.2)
9 Mark Dorris, Marshall	19.3	(25.7)
10 Jeremy Wise, Southern Miss	19.6	(29.7)
11 Alex Malone, Southern Methodist	20.2	(25.5)
12 Papa Dia, Southern Methodist	21.9	(27.5)
13 Lawrence Ghoram, Rice	26.9	(24.6)

At least 20% of possessions used

1 Stefon Jackson, Texas El Paso	11.9	(30.6)
2 Randy Culpepper, Texas El Paso	13.4	(24.4)

3 Rob McKiver, Houston	13.6	(30.0)
4 R.L. Horton, Southern Miss	14.5	(20.2)
5 Jermaine Taylor, Central Florida	15.2	(29.4)
6 Lawrence Kinnard, UAB	15.2	(21.0)
7 Chris Douglas-Roberts, Memphis	15.4	(26.6)
8 Markel Humphrey, Marshall	15.8	(21.5)
9 Courtney Beasley, Southern Miss	16.3	(20.2)
10 Patrick Britton, Rice	16.7	(22.5)
11 John Fields, East Carolina	16.8	(21.3)
12 Robinson Louisme, Tulane	16.8	(23.7)
13 David Gomez, Tulane	17.0	(25.2)
14 Robert Vaden, UAB	17.2	(28.1)
15 Tyler Wilkerson, Marshall	17.8	(21.8)
16 Tirrell Baines, Marshall	17.9	(22.5)
17 Ben Uzoh, Tulsa	18.3	(24.0)
18 Marvin Kilgore, Texas El Paso	18.4	(22.4)
19 Derrick Rose, Memphis	19.1	(27.2)
20 Mark Dorris, Marshall	19.3	(25.7)

ALL PLAYERS

1 Kelvin Lewis, Houston	9.0	(17.8)
2 Stefon Jackson, Texas El Paso	11.9	(30.6)
3 Shawn Taggart, Memphis	11.9	(16.5)
4 Dion Dowell, Houston	12.2	(16.7)
5 Matt Walls, Marshall	13.3	(17.2)
6 Randy Culpepper, Texas El Paso	13.4	(24.4)
7 Rob McKiver, Houston	13.6	(30.0)
8 Sam Hinnant, East Carolina	14.0	(18.1)
9 R.L. Horton, Southern Miss	14.5	(20.2)
10 Reggie Huffman, UAB	15.0	(20.0)
11 Gabe Blair, East Carolina	15.1	(19.7)
12 Lawrence Kinnard, UAB	15.2	(21.0)
13 Jermaine Taylor, Central Florida	15.2	(29.4)
14 Mike O'Donnell, Central Florida	15.3	(17.6)
15 Chris Douglas-Roberts, Memphis	15.4	(26.6)
16 Antonio Anderson, Memphis	15.6	(16.0)
17 Markel Humphrey, Marshall	15.8	(21.5)
18 Courtney Beasley, Southern Miss	16.3	(20.2)
19 Craig Craft, Southern Miss	16.5	(19.9)
20 Joey Dorsey, Memphis	16.5	(14.7)

Usage (Pct. of Possessions Used)

1 Stefon Jackson, Texas El Paso	30.6
2 Rob McKiver, Houston	30.0
3 Jeremy Wise, Southern Miss	29.7
4 Jermaine Taylor, Central Florida	29.4
5 Robert Vaden, UAB	28.1
6 Papa Dia, Southern Methodist	27.5
7 Derrick Rose, Memphis	27.2
8 Chris Douglas-Roberts, Memphis	26.6

9 Mark Dorris, Marshall	25.7
10 Alex Malone, Southern Methodist	25.5
11 David Gomez, Tulane	25.2
12 Lawrence Ghoram, Rice	24.6
13 Randy Culpepper, Texas El Paso	24.4
14 Rodney Foster, Rice	24.0
15 Ben Uzoh, Tulsa	24.0
16 Darryl Merthie, Marshall	23.9
17 Robinson Louisme, Tulane	23.7
18 Paulius Packevicius, Rice	22.8
19 Patrick Britton, Rice	22.5
20 Tirrell Baines, Marshall	22.5
21 Marvin Kilgore, Texas El Paso	22.4
22 Jerome Jordan, Tulsa	22.2
23 Jon Killen, Southern Methodist	22.1
24 Tyler Wilkerson, Marshall	21.8
25 Bamba Fall, Southern Methodist	21.7

Assist Rate

1 Darrell Jenkins, East Carolina	46.3
2 Jon Killen, Southern Methodist	33.9
3 Lanny Smith, Houston	31.8
4 Marvin Kilgore, Texas El Paso	31.5
5 Derrick Rose, Memphis	30.4
6 Aaron Johnson, UAB	30.4
7 Chip Cartwright, Central Florida	30.3
8 Julyan Stone, Texas El Paso	26.3
9 Ed Berrios, UAB	26.2
10 Jeremy Wise, Southern Miss	26.2
11 Rodney Foster, Rice	24.2
12 Darryl Merthie, Marshall	24.2
13 Kevin Sims, Tulane	23.4
14 Brett McDade, Tulsa	20.9
15 P. Altidor-Cespedes, Marshall	19.6

Block Rate

1 Jerome Jordan, Tulsa	14.6
2 Bamba Fall, Southern Methodist	8.7
3 John Fields, East Carolina	8.1
4 Joey Dorsey, Memphis	7.6
5 Robert Dozier, Memphis	7.0
6 Tony Davis, Central Florida	6.8
7 Robinson Louisme, Tulane	6.3
8 David Gomez, Tulane	6.1
9 Donnie Stith, Tulane	5.8
10 Dion Dowell, Houston	5.8
11 Shawn Taggart, Memphis	5.5
12 Tyler Wilkerson, Marshall	5.2

13 Paulius Packevicius, Rice 4.8
14 Tafari Toney, Houston 4.1
15 Gabe Blair, East Carolina 3.7

Offensive Rebounding Percentage

1 Joey Dorsey, Memphis 15.2
2 Reggie Huffman, UAB 13.8
3 Tyler Wilkerson, Marshall 12.9
4 Jerome Jordan, Tulsa 12.9
5 Tafari Toney, Houston 12.2
6 Tirrell Baines, Marshall 11.9
7 Robinson Louisme, Tulane 11.8
8 Suleiman Braimoh, Rice 11.1
9 John Fields, East Carolina 11.0
10 Robert Dozier, Memphis 10.9
11 Shawn Taggart, Memphis 10.9
12 Calvin Walls, Tulsa 10.7
13 Andre Stephens, Southern Miss 10.7
14 Tony Davis, Central Florida 10.4
15 Kenrick Zondervan, Central Florida 10.3

Defensive Rebounding Percentage

1 Paulius Packevicius, Rice 26.5
2 Joey Dorsey, Memphis 25.7
3 Gabe Blair, East Carolina 23.7
4 Reggie Huffman, UAB 22.9
5 Papa Dia, Southern Methodist 21.7
6 Jerome Jordan, Tulsa 21.7
7 Tony Davis, Central Florida 21.0
8 Tyler Wilkerson, Marshall 20.4
9 Lawrence Kinnard, UAB 19.9
10 Robinson Louisme, Tulane 19.5
11 Tafari Toney, Houston 18.7
12 Julyan Stone, Texas El Paso 17.9
13 Calvin Walls, Tulsa 17.9
14 Bamba Fall, Southern Methodist 17.9
15 David Gomez, Tulane 17.2

Steal Rate

1 Julyan Stone, Texas El Paso 3.94
2 Randy Culpepper, Texas El Paso 3.67
3 Mark Dorris, Marshall 3.58
4 Gabe Blair, East Carolina 3.32
5 Chip Cartwright, Central Florida 2.90
6 Mike O'Donnell, Central Florida 2.80
7 Tony Davis, Central Florida 2.67
8 Rob McKiver, Houston 2.65
9 Reggie Huffman, UAB 2.64
10 Rodney Foster, Rice 2.63
11 Aaron Johnson, UAB 2.53
12 Papa Dia, Southern Methodist 2.48
13 Jon Killen, Southern Methodist 2.44
14 Joey Dorsey, Memphis 2.43
15 Robert Dozier, Memphis 2.42

Pct. of Possible Minutes Played

1 Jon Killen, Southern Methodist 87.1
2 Rob McKiver, Houston 87.0
3 Stefon Jackson, Texas El Paso 86.4
4 Kevin Sims, Tulane 86.2
5 Jeremy Wise, Southern Miss 85.6
6 Robert Vaden, UAB 84.8
7 Jermaine Taylor, Central Florida 81.7
8 Dave Noel, Central Florida 80.9
9 Ben Uzoh, Tulsa 78.9
10 Mike O'Donnell, Central Florida 78.3

HORIZON LEAGUE
INDIVIDUAL STATISTICS

Offensive Rating

(Pct. of possessions used in parenthesis)

At least 28% of possessions used

1 Mike Green, Butler	110.8	(29.2)
2 Jon Goode, Detroit	107.1	(30.6)
3 Jarryd Loyd, Valparaiso	97.9	(30.1)
4 Cedric Jackson, Cleveland St.	97.3	(29.2)
5 J.R. Blount, Loyola Chicago	94.7	(29.1)

At lest 24% of possessions used

1 Matt Howard, Butler	123.1	(26.0)
2 Mike Schachtner, UW Green Bay	117.4	(24.6)
3 Josh Mayo, Illinois-Chicago	115.4	(25.7)
4 Mike Green, Butler	110.8	(29.2)
5 Jon Goode, Detroit	107.1	(30.6)
6 J'Nathan Bullock, Cleveland St	104.8	(26.4)
7 Jarryd Loyd, Valparaiso	97.9	(30.1)
8 Joe Davis, Cleveland St.	97.4	(25.5)
9 Cedric Jackson, Cleveland St.	97.3	(29.2)
10 Rahmon Fletcher, UW Green Bay	97.2	(26.6)
11 Byron Davis, Youngstown St.	95.9	(24.4)
12 J.R. Blount, Loyola Chicago	94.7	(29.1)
13 Karl White, Illinois-Chicago	94.1	(24.3)

At least 20% of possessions used

1 Pete Campbell, Butler	127.6	(20.4)
2 Matt Howard, Butler	123.1	(26.0)
3 Mike Schachtner, UW Green Bay	117.4	(24.6)
4 Josh Mayo, Illinois-Chicago	115.4	(25.7)
5 Mike Green, Butler	110.8	(29.2)
6 Brandon McPherson, Valparaiso	110.2	(20.3)
7 Jon Goode, Detroit	107.1	(30.6)
8 Vaughn Duggins, Wright St.	106.5	(23.6)
9 A.J. Graves, Butler	106.3	(22.1)
10 J'Nathan Bullock, Cleveland St.	104.8	(26.4)
11 Jordan Pleiman, Wright St.	104.5	(20.6)
12 Todd Brown, Wright St.	104.3	(22.5)
13 Urule Igbavboa, Valparaiso	102.7	(22.0)
14 Vytas Sulskis, Youngstown St.	100.0	(21.0)
15 Bryan Bouchie, Valparaiso	98.9	(23.0)
16 Jack Liles, Youngstown St.	98.6	(22.6)
17 Jarryd Loyd, Valparaiso	97.9	(30.1)
18 Joe Davis, Cleveland St.	97.4	(25.5)
19 Cedric Jackson, Cleveland St.	97.3	(29.2)
20 Rahmon Fletcher, UW Green Bay	97.2	(26.6)

ALL PLAYERS

1 Pete Campbell, Butler	127.6	(20.4)
2 Ryan Tillema, UW Green Bay	125.9	(19.8)
3 Matt Howard, Butler	123.1	(26.0)
4 Mike Schachtner, UW Green Bay	117.4	(24.6)
5 Marcus Skinner, UW Milwaukee	116.1	(17.3)
6 Josh Mayo, Illinois-Chicago	115.4	(25.7)
7 Drew Streicher, Butler	114.9	(9.7)
8 Zach Everingham, Detroit	114.2	(14.4)
9 Robert Kreps, Illinois-Chicago	113.8	(19.0)
10 Jermaine Dailey, Ill-Chicago	112.9	(13.9)
11 Shawn Huff, Valparaiso	112.1	(19.2)
12 Randy Berry, UW Green Bay	111.7	(15.5)
13 Mike Green, Butler	110.8	(29.2)
14 Brandon McPherson, Valparaiso	110.2	(20.3)
15 Paige Paulsen, UW Milwaukee	109.6	(19.1)
16 Cordero Barkley, UW Green Bay	109.5	(14.4)
17 Jon Goode, Detroit	107.1	(30.6)
18 Ross Forman, Loyola Chicago	106.5	(13.8)
19 Scottie Wilson, Wright St.	106.5	(19.4)
20 Vaughn Duggins, Wright St.	106.5	(23.6)

Turnover Rate

(Pct. of possessions used in parenthesis)

At least 28% of possessions used

1 J.R. Blount, Loyola Chicago	16.9	(29.1)
2 Jon Goode, Detroit	17.8	(30.6)
3 Mike Green, Butler	19.7	(29.2)
4 Jarryd Loyd, Valparaiso	20.4	(30.1)
5 Cedric Jackson, Cleveland St.	25.5	(29.2)

At least 24% of possessions used

1 Mike Schachtner, UW Green Bay	12.0	(24.6)
2 Matt Howard, Butler	14.3	(26.0)
3 Joe Davis, Cleveland St.	16.3	(25.5)
4 J.R. Blount, Loyola Chicago	16.9	(29.1)
5 Jon Goode, Detroit	17.8	(30.6)
6 J'Nathan Bullock, Cleveland St.	18.2	(26.4)
7 Josh Mayo, Illinois-Chicago	18.3	(25.7)
8 Byron Davis, Youngstown St.	19.2	(24.4)
9 Mike Green, Butler	19.7	(29.2)
10 Jarryd Loyd, Valparaiso	20.4	(30.1)
11 Karl White, Illinois-Chicago	21.2	(24.3)
12 Cedric Jackson, Cleveland St.	25.5	(29.2)
13 Rahmon Fletcher, UW Green Bay	28.1	(26.6)

At least 20% of possessions used

1 Pete Campbell, Butler	8.6	(20.4)
2 Mike Schachtner, UW Green Bay	12.0	(24.6)

3 Todd Brown, Wright St.	12.8	(22.5)
4 A.J. Graves, Butler	13.7	(22.1)
5 Matt Howard, Butler	14.3	(26.0)
6 Josh Samarco, Detroit	15.7	(20.9)
7 Bryan Bouchie, Valparaiso	16.1	(23.0)
8 Joe Davis, Cleveland St.	16.3	(25.5)
9 Ricky Franklin, UW Milwaukee	16.8	(20.8)
10 Vaughn Duggins, Wright St.	16.9	(23.6)
11 J.R. Blount, Loyola Chicago	16.9	(29.1)
12 John Barber, Youngstown St.	17.2	(23.9)
13 Brandon McPherson, Valparaiso	17.6	(20.3)
14 Jon Goode, Detroit	17.8	(30.6)
15 Deion James, UW Milwaukee	17.8	(22.0)
16 J'Nathan Bullock, Cleveland St.	18.2	(26.4)
17 Jack Liles, Youngstown St.	18.2	(22.6)
18 Vytas Sulskis, Youngstown St.	18.3	(21.0)
19 Josh Mayo, Illinois-Chicago	18.3	(25.7)
20 Chris Hayes, Detroit	18.5	(22.9)

ALL PLAYERS

1 Pete Campbell, Butler	8.6	(20.4)
2 Scott VanderMeer, Ill.-Chicago	9.0	(19.5)
3 Mike Schachtner, UW Green Bay	12.0	(24.6)
4 Marcus Skinner, UW Milwaukee	12.4	(17.3)
5 Todd Brown, Wright St.	12.8	(22.5)
6 Paige Paulsen, UW Milwaukee	13.1	(19.1)
7 Ryan Tillema, UW Green Bay	13.4	(19.8)
8 A.J. Graves, Butler	13.7	(22.1)
9 Matt Howard, Butler	14.3	(26.0)
10 Robert Bush, Illinois-Chicago	15.2	(18.3)
11 Ross Forman, Loyola Chicago	15.4	(13.8)
12 Josh Samarco, Detroit	15.7	(20.9)
13 Cordero Barkley, UW Green Bay	16.0	(14.4)
14 Eulis Stephens, Detroit	16.1	(20.0)
15 Bryan Bouchie, Valparaiso	16.1	(23.0)
16 Joe Davis, Cleveland St.	16.3	(25.5)
17 Dwight Holmes, Youngstown St.	16.5	(15.9)
18 Jake Diebler, Valparaiso	16.6	(11.0)
19 Ricky Franklin, UW Milwaukee	16.8	(20.8)
20 Vaughn Duggins, Wright St.	16.9	(23.6)

Usage (Pct. of Possessions Used)

1 Jon Goode, Detroit	30.6
2 Jarryd Loyd, Valparaiso	30.1
3 Cedric Jackson, Cleveland St.	29.2
4 Mike Green, Butler	29.2
5 J.R. Blount, Loyola Chicago	29.1
6 Rahmon Fletcher, UW Green Bay	26.6
7 J'Nathan Bullock, Cleveland St.	26.4

8 Matt Howard, Butler	26.0
9 Josh Mayo, Illinois-Chicago	25.7
10 Joe Davis, Cleveland St.	25.5
11 Mike Schachtner, UW Green Bay	24.6
12 Byron Davis, Youngstown St.	24.4
13 Karl White, Illinois-Chicago	24.3
14 John Barber, Youngstown St.	23.9
15 Vaughn Duggins, Wright St.	23.6
16 Bryan Bouchie, Valparaiso	23.0
17 Chris Hayes, Detroit	22.9
18 Jack Liles, Youngstown St.	22.6
19 Todd Brown, Wright St.	22.5
20 A.J. Graves, Butler	22.1

Assist Rate

1 Cedric Jackson, Cleveland St.	34.8
2 Jarryd Loyd, Valparaiso	34.8
3 Mike Green, Butler	34.1
4 Spencer Stewart, Ill.-Chicago	31.2
5 Rahmon Fletcher, UW Green Bay	29.4
6 Will Graham, Wright St.	24.5
7 Zach Everingham, Detroit	23.2
8 Josh Mayo, Illinois-Chicago	22.8
9 Jon Goode, Detroit	22.7
10 Vance Cooksey, Youngstown St.	21.2
11 Deonte Roberts, UW Milwaukee	20.6
12 J.R. Blount, Loyola Chicago	19.9
13 Vaughn Duggins, Wright St.	19.2
14 Ricky Franklin, UW Milwaukee	18.9
15 Brandon McPherson, Valparaiso	18.4

Block Rate

1 Scott VanderMeer, Ill.-Chicago	10.4
2 George Tandy, Cleveland St.	7.6
3 Matt Howard, Butler	5.3
4 Jermaine Dailey, Illinois-Chicago	4.7
5 Michael Harrington, Detroit	4.3
6 Marcus Skinner, UW Milwaukee	4.2
7 Terry Evans, UW Green Bay	4.1
8 Bryan Bouchie, Valparaiso	4.1
9 Jack Liles, Youngstown St.	3.8
10 Randy Berry, UW Green Bay	3.7
11 Dwight Holmes, Youngstown St.	3.7
12 Tracy Robinson, Loyola Chicago	3.2
13 Chris Hayes, Detroit	3.2
14 Kevin Francis, Cleveland St.	3.0
15 Cordero Barkley, UW Green Bay	2.5

Offensive Rebounding Percentage

1 Matt Howard, Butler	13.2
2 Marcus Skinner, UW Milwaukee	12.3
3 Kevin Francis, Cleveland St.	11.5
4 Jordan Pleiman, Wright St.	11.4
5 Jermaine Dailey, Illinois-Chicago	10.5
6 Randy Berry, UW Green Bay	10.1
7 Jeremy Buttell, Illinois-Chicago	10.0
8 Scott VanderMeer, Illinois-Chicago	9.7
9 Michael Harrington, Detroit	9.6
10 Scottie Wilson, Wright St.	9.1
11 George Tandy, Cleveland St.	9.1
12 Jack Liles, Youngstown St.	8.7
13 J'Nathan Bullock, Cleveland St.	8.7
14 Andy Polka, Loyola Chicago	8.0
15 D'Aundray Brown, Cleveland St.	7.8

Defensive Rebounding Percentage

1 Urule Igbavboa, Valparaiso	23.4
2 Jeremy Buttell, Illinois-Chicago	22.5
3 Scott VanderMeer, Illinois-Chicago	22.2
4 Jordan Pleiman, Wright St.	21.2
5 Scottie Wilson, Wright St.	21.1
6 Mike Green, Butler	20.8
7 Marcus Skinner, UW Milwaukee	19.9
8 Chris Hayes, Detroit	19.6
9 John Barber, Youngstown St.	19.4
10 Terry Evans, UW Green Bay	19.3
11 George Tandy, Cleveland St.	18.4
12 Andy Polka, Loyola Chicago	18.4
13 Vytas Sulskis, Youngstown St.	18.0
14 J'Nathan Bullock, Cleveland St.	17.9
15 Matt Howard, Butler	16.6

Steal Rate

1 Cedric Jackson, Cleveland St.	5.00
2 Woody Payne, Detroit	4.56
3 Terry Evans, UW Green Bay	3.72
4 Vance Cooksey, Youngstown St.	3.06
5 A.J. Graves, Butler	2.97
6 Rahmon Fletcher, UW Green Bay	2.88
7 Will Graham, Wright St.	2.83
8 George Tandy, Cleveland St.	2.74
9 Vytas Sulskis, Youngstown St.	2.57
10 Mike Green, Butler	2.53
11 Chris Hayes, Detroit	2.48
12 Zach Everingham, Detroit	2.45
13 Karl White, Illinois-Chicago	2.44
14 Robert Kreps, Illinois-Chicago	2.42
15 Julian Betko, Butler	2.38

Pct. of Possible Minutes Played

1 Byron Davis, Youngstown St.	88.6
2 A.J. Graves, Butler	87.0
3 Vaughn Duggins, Wright St.	85.6
4 Todd Brown, Wright St.	85.6
5 Paige Paulsen, UW Milwaukee	84.9
6 J.R. Blount, Loyola Chicago	84.8
7 Mike Green, Butler	83.2
8 John Barber, Youngstown St.	80.9
9 Josh Mayo, Illinois-Chicago	80.3
10 Andy Polka, Loyola Chicago	79.2

INDEPENDENTS
INDIVIDUAL STATISTICS

Offensive Rating

(Pct. of possessions used in parenthesis)

At least 28% of possessions used

1 David Holston, Chicago St.	112.9	(32.4)
2 Kirk Williams, Longwood	94.5	(28.3)
3 Bryan Ayala, NC Central	82.8	(28.9)

At least 24% of possessions used

1 Ryan Toolson, Utah Valley St.	124.7	(27.1)
2 David Holston, Chicago St.	112.9	(32.4)
3 John Cantrell, Chicago St.	103.9	(24.5)
4 Terence Johns, CS Bakersfield	99.0	(25.8)
5 Al'Lonzo Coleman, Presbyterian	95.5	(25.2)
6 Kirk Williams, Longwood	94.5	(28.3)
7 Joseph Flegler, Savannah St.	92.2	(25.4)
8 Nesho Milosevic, NJIT	84.0	(27.7)
9 Brian Fisher, Winston Salem St.	83.5	(25.6)
10 Bryan Ayala, NC Central	82.8	(28.9)
11 Anthony Jones, Savannah St.	77.5	(26.3)
12 Justin Garris, NJIT	71.9	(25.2)

At least 20% of possessions used

1 Ryan Toolson, Utah Valley St.	124.7	(27.1)
2 Paul Stoll, UT-Pan American	121.1	(22.9)
3 David Holston, Chicago St.	112.9	(32.4)
4 Jordan Brady, Utah Valley St.	110.7	(20.1)
5 Pat Kiscaden, Presbyterian	109.2	(22.3)
6 Darrell Wonge, Winston Salem St.	104.7	(20.1)
7 Nathan Hawkins, UT-Pan American	104.7	(21.2)
8 Zach Trader, UT-Pan American	104.4	(22.8)
9 John Cantrell, Chicago St.	103.9	(24.5)
10 Ryan Bogan, Longwood	101.3	(20.2)
11 Demarcus Hall, CS Bakersfield	101.1	(22.6)
12 Trent Blakley, CS Bakersfield	101.0	(21.4)
13 Bryan Bostic, Presbyterian	99.8	(22.5)
14 Terence Johns, CS Bakersfield	99.0	(25.8)
15 Pierre Miller, Presbyterian	96.9	(20.7)
16 Al'Lonzo Coleman, Presbyterian	95.5	(25.2)
17 Kirk Williams, Longwood	94.5	(28.3)
18 Lazarius Coleman, Savannah St.	94.1	(20.9)
19 Jamal Durham, Winston Salem St.	93.7	(23.0)
20 Brian Burrell, UT-Pan American	92.5	(23.3)

ALL PLAYERS

1 Ryan Toolson, Utah Valley St.	124.7	(27.1)
2 Paul Stoll, UT-Pan American	121.1	(22.9)
3 Dexter Shankle, UT-Pan American	117.3	(11.2)
4 David Holston, Chicago St.	112.9	(32.4)
5 Jordan Brady, Utah Valley St.	110.7	(20.1)
6 Pat Kiscaden, Presbyterian	109.2	(22.3)
7 Darrell Wonge, Winston Salem St	104.7	(20.1)
8 Nathan Hawkins, UT-Pan American	104.7	(21.2)
9 Zach Trader, UT-Pan American	104.4	(22.8)
10 John Cantrell, Chicago St.	103.9	(24.5)
11 Chidozie Chukwumah, Chicago St.	103.4	(15.2)
12 Josh Johnson, Presbyterian	102.5	(17.0)
13 Ryan Bogan, Longwood	101.3	(20.2)
14 Demarcus Hall, CS Bakersfield	101.1	(22.6)
15 Zack Grasmick, CS Bakersfield	101.1	(15.3)
16 Trent Blakley, CS Bakersfield	101.0	(21.4)
17 Bryan Bostic, Presbyterian	99.8	(22.5)
18 Carl Montgomery, Chicago St.	99.3	(18.5)
19 Terence Johns, CS Bakersfield	99.0	(25.8)
20 Lamar Barrett, Longwood	98.5	(19.9)

Turnover Rate

(Pct. of possessions used in parenthesis)

At least 28% of possessions used

1 David Holston, Chicago St.	19.8	(32.4)
2 Kirk Williams, Longwood	21.2	(28.3)
3 Bryan Ayala, NC Central	21.9	(28.9)

At least 24% of possessions used

1 Terence Johns, CS Bakersfield	14.8	(25.8)
2 Ryan Toolson, Utah Valley St.	15.2	(27.1)
3 John Cantrell, Chicago St.	18.2	(24.5)
4 David Holston, Chicago St.	19.8	(32.4)
5 Kirk Williams, Longwood	21.2	(28.3)
6 Al'Lonzo Coleman, Presbyterian	21.2	(25.2)
7 Bryan Ayala, NC Central	21.9	(28.9)
8 Brian Fisher, Winston Salem St.	22.2	(25.6)
9 Nesho Milosevic, NJIT	23.4	(27.7)
10 Joseph Flegler, Savannah St.	25.6	(25.4)
11 Justin Garris, NJIT	26.7	(25.2)
12 Anthony Jones, Savannah St.	27.7	(26.3)

At least 20% of possessions used

1 Nathan Hawkins, UTPA	10.8	(21.2)
2 Trent Blakley, CS Bakersfield	13.3	(21.4)
3 Demarcus Hall, CS Bakersfield	13.6	(22.6)
4 Terence Johns, CS Bakersfield	14.8	(25.8)
5 Ryan Toolson, Utah Valley St.	15.2	(27.1)
6 Jamal Durham, Winston Salem St.	15.5	(23.0)
7 Darrell Wonge, WSSU	16.1	(20.1)
8 Pat Kiscaden, Presbyterian	16.9	(22.3)
9 Zach Trader, UT-Pan American	17.0	(22.8)

10 Brian Burrell, UT-Pan American	17.1	(23.3)
11 John Cantrell, Chicago St.	18.2	(24.5)
12 Jordan Brady, Utah Valley St.	18.3	(20.1)
13 Ryan Bogan, Longwood	19.1	(20.2)
14 David Holston, Chicago St.	19.8	(32.4)
15 Kraig Peters, NJIT	20.2	(22.4)
16 Darius Floyd, Winston Salem St.	20.3	(20.8)
17 Lazarius Coleman, Savannah St.	20.5	(20.9)
18 Al'Lonzo Coleman, Presbyterian	21.2	(25.2)
19 Kirk Williams, Longwood	21.2	(28.3)
20 Bryan Ayala, NC Central	21.9	(28.9)

ALL PLAYERS

1 Nathan Hawkins, UT-Pan American	10.8	(21.2)
2 Trent Blakley, CS Bakersfield	13.3	(21.4)
3 Demarcus Hall, CS Bakersfield	13.6	(22.6)
4 Terence Johns, CS Bakersfield	14.8	(25.8)
5 Ryan Toolson, Utah Valley St.	15.2	(27.1)
6 Jamal Durham, Winston Salem St.	15.5	(23.0)
7 Dexter Shankle, UT-Pan American	15.5	(11.2)
8 Lamar Barrett, Longwood	15.8	(19.9)
9 Darrell Wonge, Winston Salem St.	16.1	(20.1)
10 Cory Brown, CS Bakersfield	16.2	(16.1)
11 Pat Kiscaden, Presbyterian	16.9	(22.3)
12 Zach Trader, UT-Pan American	17.0	(22.8)
13 Brian Burrell, UT-Pan American	17.1	(23.3)
14 Carl Montgomery, Chicago St.	18.0	(18.5)
15 John Cantrell, Chicago St.	18.2	(24.5)
16 Jordan Brady, Utah Valley St.	18.3	(20.1)
17 Tawrence Walton, Chicago St.	18.7	(17.3)
18 Josh Johnson, Presbyterian	19.0	(17.0)
19 Ryan Bogan, Longwood	19.1	(20.2)
20 Richard Troyer, Utah Valley St.	19.4	(19.0)

Usage (Pct. of Possessions Used)

1 David Holston, Chicago St.	32.4
2 Bryan Ayala, NC Central	28.9
3 Kirk Williams, Longwood	28.3
4 Nesho Milosevic, NJIT	27.7
5 Ryan Toolson, Utah Valley St.	27.1
6 Anthony Jones, Savannah St.	26.3
7 Terence Johns, CS Bakersfield	25.8
8 Brian Fisher, Winston Salem St.	25.6
9 Joseph Flegler, Savannah St.	25.4
10 Justin Garris, NJIT	25.2
11 Al'Lonzo Coleman, Presbyterian	25.2
12 John Cantrell, Chicago St.	24.5
13 Charles Futrell, NC Central	23.5
14 Brian Burrell, UT-Pan American	23.3
15 Jamal Durham, Winston Salem St.	23.0

16 Paul Stoll, UT-Pan American	22.9
17 Zach Trader, UT-Pan American	22.8
18 Demarcus Hall, CS Bakersfield	22.6
19 Bryan Bostic, Presbyterian	22.5
20 Kraig Peters, NJIT	22.4
21 Pat Kiscaden, Presbyterian	22.3
22 Jheryl Wilson, NJIT	22.3
23 Donavan Bragg, CS Bakersfield	22.1
24 Trent Blakley, CS Bakersfield	21.4
25 Nathan Hawkins, UT-Pan American	21.2

Assist Rate

1 Paul Stoll, UT-Pan American	42.1
2 David Holston, Chicago St.	34.3
3 Bryan Ayala, NC Central	33.9
4 Pierre Miller, Presbyterian	29.5
5 J'Mell Walters, NC Central	28.6
6 Joseph Flegler, Savannah St.	27.1
7 Isiah Tucker, Winston Salem St.	27.0
8 Donavan Bragg, CS Bakersfield	27.0
9 Ryan Lamb, Presbyterian	25.0
10 Brandon Giles, Longwood	24.9
11 Raye Bailey, Savannah St.	24.1
12 Jheryl Wilson, NJIT	23.2
13 Alex Johnson, CS Bakersfield	22.8
14 Josh Olsen, Utah Valley St.	21.1
15 Mike Wilson, Chicago St.	20.4

Block Rate

1 Chidozie Chukwumah, Chicago St.	11.0
2 Paul Davis, Winston Salem St.	8.8
3 Dan Stonkus, NJIT	7.0
4 Cory Brown, CS Bakersfield	5.3
5 Lazarius Coleman, Savannah St.	3.7
6 Carl Montgomery, Chicago St.	3.5
7 Marius Vaskys, NC Central	2.9
8 Charles Futrell, NC Central	2.5
9 Jamal Durham, Winston Salem St.	2.5
10 Josh Johnson, Presbyterian	2.4
11 Jordan Brady, Utah Valley St.	2.1
12 Demarcus Hall, CS Bakersfield	2.0
13 Al'Lonzo Coleman, Presbyterian	2.0
14 Nesho Milosevic, NJIT	1.9
15 Justin Garris, NJIT	1.9

Offensive Rebounding Percentage

1 Carl Montgomery, Chicago St.	12.2
2 Lazarius Coleman, Savannah St.	11.8
3 Jordan Brady, Utah Valley St.	11.4
4 Paul Davis, Winston Salem St.	10.6
5 Nesho Milosevic, NJIT	10.4
6 Chidozie Chukwumah, Chicago St.	9.6
7 Demarcus Hall, CS Bakersfield	8.8
8 Darrell Wonge, Winston Salem St.	8.6
9 Trent Blakley, CS Bakersfield	8.5
10 Marius Vaskys, NC Central	8.5
11 Tawrence Walton, Chicago St.	8.3
12 Lamar Barrett, Longwood	8.1
13 Nathan Hawkins, UT-Pan American	8.1
14 Cory Brown, CS Bakersfield	7.8
15 Travis Sligh, Presbyterian	7.5

Steal Rate

1 Paul Stoll, UT-Pan American	4.45
2 Al'Lonzo Coleman, Presbyterian	4.42
3 Isiah Tucker, Winston Salem St.	3.71
4 Justin Garris, NJIT	3.50
5 Roy Peake, Winston Salem St.	3.45
6 David Holston, Chicago St.	3.42
7 Josh Olsen, Utah Valley St.	3.32
8 Anthony Jones, Savannah St.	3.26
9 John Cantrell, Chicago St.	3.19
10 Lamar Barrett, Longwood	3.01
11 Patrick Hardy, Savannah St.	2.98
12 Bryan Ayala, NC Central	2.98
13 Brian Fisher, Winston Salem St.	2.96
14 Kirk Williams, Longwood	2.92
15 Raye Bailey, Savannah St.	2.79

Defensive Rebounding Percentage

1 Nesho Milosevic, NJIT	22.4
2 Paul Davis, Winston Salem St.	22.3
3 Jordan Brady, Utah Valley St.	20.8
4 Lazarius Coleman, Savannah St.	18.4
5 Trent Blakley, CS Bakersfield	18.3
6 Chris Linton, Savannah St.	18.3
7 Al'Lonzo Coleman, Presbyterian	17.8
8 Carl Montgomery, Chicago St.	17.7
9 Demarcus Hall, CS Bakersfield	17.5
10 Tawrence Walton, Chicago St.	16.9
11 Bryan Bostic, Presbyterian	16.0
12 Charles Futrell, NC Central	15.9
13 Kirk Williams, Longwood	15.8
14 Zach Trader, UT-Pan American	15.7
15 Brian Burrell, UT-Pan American	15.7

Pct. of Possible Minutes Played

1 Ryan Toolson, Utah Valley St.	92.8
2 Charles Futrell, NC Central	92.8
3 Zach Trader, UT-Pan American	83.9
4 David Holston, Chicago St.	82.8
5 Brian Burrell, UT-Pan American	82.8
6 Paul Stoll, UT-Pan American	82.4
7 Kirk Williams, Longwood	81.4
8 Jordan Brady, Utah Valley St.	78.6
9 Kraig Peters, NJIT	78.4
10 Bryan Ayala, NC Central	78.3

IVY LEAGUE
INDIVIDUAL STATISTICS

Offensive Rating

(Pct. of possessions used in parenthesis)

At least 28% of possessions used

(No players qualified)

At least 24% of possessions used

1 John Baumann, Columbia	111.6	(25.8)
2 Mark McAndrew, Brown	110.4	(26.3)
3 Louis Dale, Cornell	110.2	(28.0)
4 Alex Barnett, Dartmouth	102.9	(25.9)
5 Jeremy Lin, Harvard	96.0	(24.6)
6 Zach Finley, Princeton	87.9	(28.0)

At least 20% of possessions used

1 Damon Huffman, Brown	115.0	(21.5)
2 Evan Harris, Harvard	112.8	(20.1)
3 John Baumann, Columbia	111.6	(25.8)
4 Mark McAndrew, Brown	110.4	(26.3)
5 Louis Dale, Cornell	110.2	(28.0)
6 Ross Morin, Yale	108.8	(21.1)
7 Jeff Foote, Cornell	107.9	(21.4)
8 Alexander Zampier, Yale	107.8	(22.2)
9 Tyler Bernardini, Penn	105.8	(23.2)
10 Brian Grandieri, Penn	104.4	(21.9)
11 DeVon Mosley, Dartmouth	103.0	(21.1)
12 Alex Barnett, Dartmouth	102.9	(25.9)
13 Travis Pinick, Yale	102.1	(22.2)
14 Noah Savage, Princeton	101.4	(22.3)
15 Alex Tyler, Cornell	101.4	(20.3)
16 Matt Kyle, Yale	98.2	(21.2)
17 Jeremy Lin, Harvard	96.0	(24.6)
18 Ben Nwachukwu, Columbia	95.9	(23.7)
19 Lincoln Gunn, Princeton	93.4	(20.2)
20 Niko Scott, Columbia	92.8	(22.9)

ALL PLAYERS

1 Adam Gore, Cornell	124.2	(16.0)
2 Peter Sullivan, Brown	116.1	(16.7)
3 Damon Huffman, Brown	115.0	(21.5)
4 Jason Hartford, Cornell	115.0	(18.8)
5 Ryan Wittman, Cornell	114.6	(19.5)
6 K.J. Matsui, Columbia	113.3	(15.8)
7 Evan Harris, Harvard	112.8	(20.1)
8 John Baumann, Columbia	111.6	(25.8)
9 Pat Magnarelli, Harvard	110.9	(19.1)
10 Mark McAndrew, Brown	110.4	(26.3)
11 Louis Dale, Cornell	110.2	(28.0)

12 Ross Morin, Yale	108.8	(21.1)
13 Jeff Foote, Cornell	107.9	(21.4)
14 Alexander Zampier, Yale	107.8	(22.2)
15 Jack Eggleston, Penn	106.9	(15.6)
16 Tyler Bernardini, Penn	105.8	(23.2)
17 Brett Loscalzo, Columbia	105.8	(12.5)
18 Chris Skrelja, Brown	105.4	(18.9)
19 Caleb Holmes, Yale	105.0	(19.8)
20 Brian Grandieri, Penn	104.4	(21.9)

Turnover Rate

(Pct. of possessions used in parenthesis)

At least 28% of possessions used

(No players qualified)

At least 24% of possessions used

1 Alex Barnett, Dartmouth	13.0	(25.9)
2 John Baumann, Columbia	15.3	(25.8)
3 Mark McAndrew, Brown	19.5	(26.3)
4 Jeremy Lin, Harvard	21.0	(24.6)
5 Louis Dale, Cornell	22.2	(28.0)
6 Zach Finley, Princeton	24.0	(28.0)

At least 20% of possessions used

1 Alex Barnett, Dartmouth	13.0	(25.9)
2 Damon Huffman, Brown	13.3	(21.5)
3 Brian Grandieri, Penn	15.0	(21.9)
4 John Baumann, Columbia	15.3	(25.8)
5 DeVon Mosley, Dartmouth	16.9	(21.1)
6 Alexander Zampier, Yale	17.0	(22.2)
7 Evan Harris, Harvard	17.9	(20.1)
8 Tyler Bernardini, Penn	18.0	(23.2)
9 Jeff Foote, Cornell	18.3	(21.4)
10 Niko Scott, Columbia	18.5	(22.9)
11 Noah Savage, Princeton	19.4	(22.3)
12 Mark McAndrew, Brown	19.5	(26.3)
13 Ross Morin, Yale	19.7	(21.1)
14 Jeremy Lin, Harvard	21.0	(24.6)
15 Alex Tyler, Cornell	21.1	(20.3)
16 Louis Dale, Cornell	22.2	(28.0)
17 Ben Nwachukwu, Columbia	22.6	(23.7)
18 Travis Pinick, Yale	22.7	(22.2)
19 Eric Flato, Yale	22.9	(22.7)
20 Zach Finley, Princeton	24.0	(28.0)

ALL PLAYERS

1 Alex Barnett, Dartmouth	13.0	(25.9)
2 Damon Huffman, Brown	13.3	(21.5)
3 Adam Gore, Cornell	14.3	(16.0)

4 Ryan Wittman, Cornell	14.4	(19.5)
5 Brian Grandieri, Penn	15.0	(21.9)
6 John Baumann, Columbia	15.3	(25.8)
7 Michael Giovacchini, Dartmouth	16.0	(15.4)
8 Jason Hartford, Cornell	16.6	(18.8)
9 Kyle Koncz, Princeton	16.8	(17.2)
10 DeVon Mosley, Dartmouth	16.9	(21.1)
11 Alexander Zampier, Yale	17.0	(22.2)
12 Pat Magnarelli, Harvard	17.7	(19.1)
13 Evan Harris, Harvard	17.9	(20.1)
14 Tyler Bernardini, Penn	18.0	(23.2)
15 Jeff Foote, Cornell	18.3	(21.4)
16 Niko Scott, Columbia	18.5	(22.9)
17 Jack Eggleston, Penn	19.2	(15.6)
18 Dan McGeary, Harvard	19.2	(18.5)
19 Kevin Egee, Penn	19.3	(15.8)
20 Noah Savage, Princeton	19.4	(22.3)

Usage (Pct. of Possessions Used)

1 Louis Dale, Cornell	28.0
2 Zach Finley, Princeton	28.0
3 Mark McAndrew, Brown	26.3
4 Alex Barnett, Dartmouth	25.9
5 John Baumann, Columbia	25.8
6 Jeremy Lin, Harvard	24.6
7 Drew Housman, Harvard	23.8
8 Ben Nwachukwu, Columbia	23.7
9 Tyler Bernardini, Penn	23.2
10 Niko Scott, Columbia	22.9
11 Eric Flato, Yale	22.7
12 Noah Savage, Princeton	22.3
13 Travis Pinick, Yale	22.2
14 Alexander Zampier, Yale	22.2
15 Harrison Gaines, Penn	22.2
16 Brian Grandieri, Penn	21.9
17 Damon Huffman, Brown	21.5
18 Jeff Foote, Cornell	21.4
19 Matt Kyle, Yale	21.2
20 DeVon Mosley, Dartmouth	21.1
21 Ross Morin, Yale	21.1
22 Alex Tyler, Cornell	20.3
23 Lincoln Gunn, Princeton	20.2
24 Evan Harris, Harvard	20.1
25 Caleb Holmes, Yale	19.8

Assist Rate

1 Harrison Gaines, Penn	34.8
2 Louis Dale, Cornell	32.9
3 Jeremy Lin, Harvard	25.7
4 Chris Skrelja, Brown	25.1
5 Lincoln Gunn, Princeton	23.1
6 Alexander Zampier, Yale	23.1
7 Scott Friske, Brown	22.2
8 Brett Loscalzo, Columbia	22.0
9 Niko Scott, Columbia	21.6
10 Kevin Bulger, Columbia	20.5
11 Travis Pinick, Yale	19.7
12 Drew Housman, Harvard	19.4
13 Kevin Steuerer, Princeton	19.1
14 Mack Montgomery, Columbia	17.6
15 Michael Giovacchini, Dartmouth	17.2

Block Rate

1 Matt Mullery, Brown	8.7
2 Matt Kyle, Yale	8.3
3 Jeff Foote, Cornell	6.9
4 Zach Finley, Princeton	4.9
5 Ben Nwachukwu, Columbia	4.3
6 Alex Barnett, Dartmouth	3.9
7 Evan Harris, Harvard	3.7
8 Pat Magnarelli, Harvard	3.2
9 Alex Tyler, Cornell	2.9
10 Kevin Egee, Penn	2.4
11 Travis Pinick, Yale	2.3
12 Scott Friske, Brown	2.1
13 Ross Morin, Yale	2.0
14 Jeremy Lin, Harvard	1.9
15 Jason Hartford, Cornell	1.7

Offensive Rebounding Percentage

1 Travis Pinick, Yale	12.9
2 Jason Hartford, Cornell	11.1
3 Jeff Foote, Cornell	10.9
4 Ben Nwachukwu, Columbia	10.4
5 Andrew Pusar, Harvard	9.4
6 Pat Magnarelli, Harvard	8.8
7 John Baumann, Columbia	8.8
8 Matt Kyle, Yale	8.6
9 Ross Morin, Yale	8.4
10 Zach Finley, Princeton	7.5
11 Evan Harris, Harvard	7.3
12 Alex Tyler, Cornell	7.2

13 Johnathan Ball, Dartmouth   7.1
14 Brian Grandieri, Penn   6.6
15 Chris Skrelja, Brown   6.2

Defensive Rebounding Percentage

1 Jeff Foote, Cornell	23.8
2 Alex Barnett, Dartmouth	21.1
3 Travis Pinick, Yale	21.0
4 Johnathan Ball, Dartmouth	20.3
5 Ross Morin, Yale	19.6
6 Chris Skrelja, Brown	18.8
7 Matt Kyle, Yale	18.7
8 Mack Montgomery, Columbia	18.3
9 Pat Magnarelli, Harvard	18.2
10 Ben Nwachukwu, Columbia	17.7
11 John Baumann, Columbia	17.3
12 Evan Harris, Harvard	16.9
13 Scott Friske, Brown	16.8
14 Zach Finley, Princeton	16.8
15 Kyle Koncz, Princeton	16.3

Steal Rate

1 Alexander Zampier, Yale	5.45
2 Travis Pinick, Yale	4.39
3 Marcus Schroeder, Princeton	3.68
4 Jeremy Lin, Harvard	3.57
5 DeVon Mosley, Dartmouth	3.42
6 Scott Friske, Brown	3.13
7 Johnathan Ball, Dartmouth	2.92
8 Evan Harris, Harvard	2.75
9 Kevin Bulger, Columbia	2.65
10 Drew Housman, Harvard	2.61
11 Mark McAndrew, Brown	2.50
12 Eric Flato, Yale	2.49
13 Louis Dale, Cornell	2.44
14 Adam Gore, Cornell	2.28
15 Nick Holmes, Yale	2.23

Pct. of Possible Minutes Played

1 Damon Huffman, Brown	85.3
2 Chris Skrelja, Brown	85.0
3 Ryan Wittman, Cornell	83.9
4 Mark McAndrew, Brown	82.2
5 Kyle Koncz, Princeton	79.7
6 Alex Barnett, Dartmouth	78.8
7 John Baumann, Columbia	78.5
8 Jeremy Lin, Harvard	77.7
9 Brian Grandieri, Penn	77.5
10 Eric Flato, Yale	76.3

MAAC INDIVIDUAL STATISTICS

Offensive Rating

(Pct. of possessions used in parenthesis)

At least 28% of possessions used

1 Jason Thompson, Rider	110.9	(29.2)
2 Charron Fisher, Niagara	105.8	(35.1)
3 Gerald Brown, Loyola MD	104.4	(30.8)
4 Darrell Lampley, St. Peter's	85.4	(28.7)

At least 24% of possessions used

1 Alex Franklin, Siena	112.3	(24.6)
2 Jason Thompson, Rider	110.9	(29.2)
3 Kenny Hasbrouck, Siena	106.5	(25.0)
4 Charron Fisher, Niagara	105.8	(35.1)
5 Gerald Brown, Loyola MD	104.4	(30.8)
6 Gary Springer, Iona	102.6	(26.7)
7 Jay Gavin, Marist	101.0	(26.2)
8 Todd Sowell, St. Peter's	99.4	(25.0)
9 Greg Nero, Fairfield	98.0	(25.3)
10 Rashad Green, Manhattan	92.9	(24.2)
11 Frank Turner, Canisius	90.2	(27.3)
12 Darrell Lampley, St. Peter's	85.4	(28.7)
13 Elton Frazier, Canisius	80.6	(24.5)

At least 20% of possessions used

1 Ryan Thompson, Rider	117.3	(21.6)
2 Marquis Sullivan, Loyola MD	114.6	(21.8)
3 Edwin Ubiles, Siena	113.9	(22.7)
4 Alex Franklin, Siena	112.3	(24.6)
5 Devon Clarke, Iona	111.1	(21.9)
6 Jason Thompson, Rider	110.9	(29.2)
7 Michael Tuck, Loyola MD	108.1	(20.6)
8 Devon Austin, Manhattan	107.4	(21.0)
9 Kenny Hasbrouck, Siena	106.5	(25.0)
10 Charron Fisher, Niagara	105.8	(35.1)
11 Tyrone Lewis, Niagara	104.8	(22.8)
12 Gerald Brown, Loyola MD	104.4	(30.8)
13 Gary Springer, Iona	102.6	(26.7)
14 Ryan Stilphen, Marist	102.2	(20.8)
15 Antoine Pearson, Manhattan	101.4	(22.3)
16 Jay Gavin, Marist	101.0	(26.2)
17 Darryl Crawford, Manhattan	100.9	(23.8)
18 Anthony Johnson, Fairfield	100.2	(20.4)
19 Greg Logins, Canisius	100.1	(20.5)
20 Todd Sowell, St. Peter's	99.4	(25.0)

ALL PLAYERS

1 Tay Fisher, Siena	127.2	(16.9)
2 Benson Egemonye, Niagara	124.4	(16.1)
3 Brett Harvey, Loyola MD	121.2	(15.7)
4 T. Vazquez-Simmons, Canisius	118.0	(10.9)
5 Ryan Thompson, Rider	117.3	(21.6)
6 Harris Mansell, Rider	117.2	(19.3)
7 Herbie Allen, Fairfield	114.7	(17.0)
8 Marquis Sullivan, Loyola MD	114.6	(21.8)
9 Ben Farmer, Marist	113.9	(14.5)
10 Edwin Ubiles, Siena	113.9	(22.7)
11 Stanley Hodge, Niagara	112.7	(18.9)
12 Alex Franklin, Siena	112.3	(24.6)
13 Devon Clarke, Iona	111.1	(21.9)
14 Jason Thompson, Rider	110.9	(29.2)
15 Spongy Benjamin, Marist	110.0	(18.1)
16 Mike Evanovich, Fairfield	109.4	(19.4)
17 Jonathan Han, Fairfield	109.3	(19.7)
18 Michael Tuck, Loyola MD	108.1	(20.6)
19 Josh Duell, Siena	107.9	(13.2)
20 Devon Austin, Manhattan	107.4	(21.0)

Turnover Rate

(Pct. of possessions used in parenthesis)

At least 28% of possessions used

1 Charron Fisher, Niagara	13.0	(35.1)
2 Jason Thompson, Rider	16.2	(29.2)
3 Gerald Brown, Loyola MD	17.7	(30.8)
4 Darrell Lampley, St. Peter's	23.5	(28.7)

At least 24% of possessions used

1 Kenny Hasbrouck, Siena	12.9	(25.0)
2 Charron Fisher, Niagara	13.0	(35.1)
3 Alex Franklin, Siena	15.4	(24.6)
4 Jason Thompson, Rider	16.2	(29.2)
5 Gerald Brown, Loyola MD	17.7	(30.8)
6 Todd Sowell, St. Peter's	18.8	(25.0)
7 Greg Nero, Fairfield	20.7	(25.3)
8 Jay Gavin, Marist	21.1	(26.2)
9 Gary Springer, Iona	22.2	(26.7)
10 Darrell Lampley, St. Peter's	23.5	(28.7)
11 Elton Frazier, Canisius	23.5	(24.5)
12 Rashad Green, Manhattan	24.5	(24.2)
13 Frank Turner, Canisius	24.6	(27.3)

At least 20% of possessions used

1 Edwin Ubiles, Siena	12.2	(22.7)
2 Chris Smith, Manhattan	12.4	(22.6)
3 Kenny Hasbrouck, Siena	12.9	(25.0)
4 Charron Fisher, Niagara	13.0	(35.1)
5 Devon Austin, Manhattan	13.6	(21.0)
6 Marquis Sullivan, Loyola MD	14.1	(21.8)

7 Darryl Crawford, Manhattan	14.9	(23.8)
8 Alex Franklin, Siena	15.4	(24.6)
9 Tyrone Lewis, Niagara	15.7	(22.8)
10 Jason Thompson, Rider	16.2	(29.2)
11 Gerald Brown, Loyola MD	17.7	(30.8)
12 Anthony Johnson, Fairfield	18.1	(20.4)
13 Wesley Jenkins, St. Peter's	18.6	(22.0)
14 Todd Sowell, St. Peter's	18.8	(25.0)
15 Michael Tuck, Loyola MD	19.1	(20.6)
16 Ryan Thompson, Rider	19.4	(21.6)
17 Greg Nero, Fairfield	20.7	(25.3)
18 Ryan Stilphen, Marist	21.0	(20.8)
19 Jay Gavin, Marist	21.1	(26.2)
20 Yorel Hawkins, Fairfield	21.4	(21.0)

ALL PLAYERS

1 Tay Fisher, Siena	11.3	(16.9)
2 Edwin Ubiles, Siena	12.2	(22.7)
3 Chris Smith, Manhattan	12.4	(22.6)
4 Kenny Hasbrouck, Siena	12.9	(25.0)
5 Charron Fisher, Niagara	13.0	(35.1)
6 Devon Austin, Manhattan	13.6	(21.0)
7 Ben Farmer, Marist	13.9	(14.5)
8 Marquis Sullivan, Loyola MD	14.1	(21.8)
9 Josh Duell, Siena	14.4	(13.2)
10 Darryl Crawford, Manhattan	14.9	(23.8)
11 Harris Mansell, Rider	15.3	(19.3)
12 Alex Franklin, Siena	15.4	(24.6)
13 Benson Egemonye, Niagara	15.6	(16.1)
14 Tyrone Lewis, Niagara	15.7	(22.8)
15 Jason Thompson, Rider	16.2	(29.2)
16 Warren Edney, Fairfield	17.0	(17.2)
17 Brett Harvey, Loyola MD	17.5	(15.7)
18 Gerald Brown, Loyola MD	17.7	(30.8)
19 T. Vazquez-Simmons, Canisius	17.8	(10.9)
20 Anthony Johnson, Fairfield	18.1	(20.4)

Usage (Pct. of Possessions Used)

1 Charron Fisher, Niagara	35.1
2 Gerald Brown, Loyola MD	30.8
3 Jason Thompson, Rider	29.2
4 Darrell Lampley, St. Peter's	28.7
5 Frank Turner, Canisius	27.3
6 Gary Springer, Iona	26.7
7 Jay Gavin, Marist	26.2
8 Greg Nero, Fairfield	25.3
9 Kenny Hasbrouck, Siena	25.0
10 Todd Sowell, St. Peter's	25.0
11 Alex Franklin, Siena	24.6
12 Elton Frazier, Canisius	24.5

13 Rashad Green, Manhattan	24.2
14 Darryl Crawford, Manhattan	23.8
15 Dexter Gray, Iona	23.2
16 Tyrone Lewis, Niagara	22.8
17 Edwin Ubiles, Siena	22.7
18 Chris Smith, Manhattan	22.6
19 Antoine Pearson, Manhattan	22.3
20 Nick Leon, St. Peter's	22.3
21 Wesley Jenkins, St. Peter's	22.0
22 Devon Clarke, Iona	21.9
23 Marquis Sullivan, Loyola MD	21.8
24 Ryan Thompson, Rider	21.6
25 Kyle Camper, Iona	21.5

Assist Rate

1 Jonathan Han, Fairfield	35.6
2 Frank Turner, Canisius	33.3
3 Brian Rudolph, Loyola MD	30.6
4 Ronald Moore, Siena	28.7
5 Kyle Camper, Iona	27.3
6 David Devezin, Marist	25.6
7 Brett Harvey, Loyola MD	25.4
8 Anthony Nelson, Niagara	25.1
9 Justin Robinson, Rider	23.2
10 Nick Leon, St. Peter's	21.8
11 Stanley Hodge, Niagara	19.8
12 De'Shaune Griffin, Iona	19.7
13 Ryan Thompson, Rider	18.9
14 Rashon Dwight, Iona	18.6
15 Herbie Allen, Fairfield	18.4

Block Rate

1 Tomas Vazquez-Simmons, Canisius	11.4
2 Jason Thompson, Rider	8.6
3 Todd Sowell, St. Peter's	7.6
4 Omari Isreal, Loyola MD	6.6
5 Benson Egemonye, Niagara	6.1
6 Anthony Johnson, Fairfield	5.7
7 Gary Springer, Iona	5.5
8 Greg Nero, Fairfield	4.4
9 Dexter Gray, Iona	3.9
10 Devon Clarke, Iona	3.7
11 Andrew Gabriel, Manhattan	3.7
12 Devon Austin, Manhattan	3.1
13 Elton Frazier, Canisius	3.0
14 Edwin Ubiles, Siena	3.0
15 Spongy Benjamin, Marist	3.0

Offensive Rebounding Percentage

1 Gary Springer, Iona	17.0
2 Todd Sowell, St. Peter's	15.4
3 Benson Egemonye, Niagara	14.2
4 Greg Nero, Fairfield	12.8
5 Anthony Johnson, Fairfield	12.1
6 Spongy Benjamin, Marist	11.6
7 Jason Thompson, Rider	11.2
8 Elton Frazier, Canisius	10.7
9 Mike Ringgold, Rider	10.0
10 Andrew Gabriel, Manhattan	9.9
11 Alex Franklin, Siena	9.6
12 Devon Clarke, Iona	9.6
13 Michael Tuck, Loyola MD	9.4
14 Omari Isreal, Loyola MD	9.4
15 Tomas Vazquez-Simmons, Canisius	8.9

Defensive Rebounding Percentage

1 Jason Thompson, Rider	27.8
2 Gary Springer, Iona	24.2
3 Todd Sowell, St. Peter's	21.4
4 Greg Logins, Canisius	20.4
5 Alex Franklin, Siena	20.3
6 Rashad Green, Manhattan	20.0
7 Michael Tuck, Loyola MD	18.7
8 Charron Fisher, Niagara	18.3
9 Anthony Johnson, Fairfield	18.1
10 Spongy Benjamin, Marist	17.6
11 Patrick Bouli, Manhattan	17.1
12 Akeem Gooding, St. Peter's	16.3
13 Ryan Stilphen, Marist	15.5
14 Yorel Hawkins, Fairfield	15.5
15 Omari Isreal, Loyola MD	15.5

Steal Rate

1 Kenny Hasbrouck, Siena	4.07
2 Rashad Green, Manhattan	3.46
3 Patrick Bouli, Manhattan	3.32
4 Tyrone Lewis, Niagara	3.19
5 Alex Franklin, Siena	3.06
6 Gerald Brown, Loyola MD	2.95
7 Wesley Jenkins, St. Peter's	2.84
8 Jonathan Han, Fairfield	2.78
9 Ryan Thompson, Rider	2.75
10 Ronald Moore, Siena	2.68
11 Tay Fisher, Siena	2.66
12 Mike Ringgold, Rider	2.66
13 Devon Clarke, Iona	2.60
14 Justin Robinson, Rider	2.52
15 Charron Fisher, Niagara	2.51

Pct. of Possible Minutes Played

1 Jonathan Han, Fairfield	94.2
2 Charron Fisher, Niagara	93.0
3 Anthony Nelson, Niagara	88.9
4 Tyrone Lewis, Niagara	86.8
5 Jason Thompson, Rider	86.2
6 Frank Turner, Canisius	84.4
7 David Devezin, Marist	84.1
8 Stanley Hodge, Niagara	83.2
9 Edwin Ubiles, Siena	82.2
10 Ryan Thompson, Rider	79.6

MAC INDIVIDUAL STATISTICS

Offensive Rating

(Pct. of possessions used in parenthesis)

At least 28% of possessions used

1 Jeremiah Wood, Akron	102.2	(30.5)
2 Anthony Newell, Ball St.	96.2	(29.9)
3 Al Fisher, Kent St.	93.2	(29.7)
4 Tyrone Kent, Toledo	88.0	(32.0)

At least 24% of possessions used

1 Leon Williams, Ohio	120.5	(26.7)
2 Joe Reitz, Western Michigan	114.5	(26.6)
3 David Kool, Western Michigan	111.1	(25.8)
4 Giordan Watson, C. Michigan	109.7	(26.6)
5 Tim Pollitz, Miami OH	106.4	(27.8)
6 Carlos Medlock, E. Michigan	104.5	(27.6)
7 Justin Dobbins, E. Michigan	102.8	(24.4)
8 Jeremiah Wood, Akron	102.2	(30.5)
9 Anthony Newell, Ball St.	96.2	(29.9)
10 Al Fisher, Kent St.	93.2	(29.7)
11 Nate Miller, Bowling Green	92.7	(26.7)
12 Jake Anderson, N. Illinois	91.3	(25.5)
13 Nate Minnoy, Central Michigan	88.5	(27.7)
14 Tyrone Kent, Toledo	88.0	(32.0)
15 Jonathan Amos, Toledo	87.7	(26.6)
16 Rodney Pierce, Buffalo	82.4	(24.8)

At least 20% of possessions used

1 Leon Williams, Ohio	120.5	(26.7)
2 Nick Dials, Akron	116.5	(20.7)
3 Joe Reitz, Western Michigan	114.5	(26.6)
4 Bubba Walther, Ohio	114.0	(21.8)
5 Michael Bramos, Miami OH	113.3	(23.9)
6 David Kool, Western Michigan	111.1	(25.8)
7 Jerome Tillman, Ohio	110.3	(21.3)
8 Jarred Axon, Eastern Michigan	110.1	(23.7)
9 Haminn Quaintance, Kent St.	110.1	(21.6)
10 Giordan Watson, C. Michigan	109.7	(26.6)
11 Chris Singletary, Kent St.	109.7	(22.9)
12 Peyton Stovall, Ball St.	106.5	(22.1)
13 Tim Pollitz, Miami OH	106.4	(27.8)
14 Chris McKnight, Akron	104.9	(20.7)
15 Carlos Medlock, E. Michigan	104.5	(27.6)
16 Kenny Hayes, Miami OH	103.8	(23.3)
17 Andy Robinson, Buffalo	103.1	(23.9)
18 Justin Dobbins, E. Michigan	102.8	(24.4)
19 Jeremiah Wood, Akron	102.2	(30.5)
20 Shawntes Gary, W. Michigan	100.2	(20.3)

ALL PLAYERS

1 Leon Williams, Ohio	120.5	26.7)
2 Mike Scott, Kent St.	120.1	(18.7)
3 Brian Moten, Bowling Green	118.3	(16.1)
4 Nick Dials, Akron	116.5	(20.7)
5 Nate Linhart, Akron	114.6	(15.7)
6 Joe Reitz, Western Michigan	114.5	(26.6)
7 Bubba Walther, Ohio	114.0	(21.8)
8 Jordan Bitzer, C. Michigan	113.6	(15.1)
9 Michael Bramos, Miami OH	113.3	(23.9)
10 David Kool, Western Michigan	111.1	(25.8)
11 Jerome Tillman, Ohio	110.3	(21.3)
12 Jarred Axon, Eastern Michigan	110.1	(23.7)
13 Haminn Quaintance, Kent St.	110.1	(21.6)
14 Chris Singletary, Kent St.	109.7	(22.9)
15 Giordan Watson, C. Michigan	109.7	(26.6)
16 Tyler Dierkers, Miami OH	109.2	(15.2)
17 Travis Lewis, Eastern Michigan	108.3	(12.3)
18 Cedrick Middleton, Akron	107.7	(19.0)
19 Andrew Hershberger, W. Mich.	107.0	(14.4)
20 Peyton Stovall, Ball St.	106.5	(22.1)

Turnover Rate

(Pct. of possessions used in parenthesis)

At least 28% of possessions used

1 Anthony Newell, Ball St.	10.4	(29.9)
2 Jeremiah Wood, Akron	20.1	(30.5)
3 Tyrone Kent, Toledo	24.8	(32.0)
4 Al Fisher, Kent St.	26.9	(29.7)

At least 24% of possessions used

1 Anthony Newell, Ball St.	10.4	(29.9)
2 Giordan Watson, C. Michigan	17.7	(26.6)
3 Nate Miller, Bowling Green	17.9	(26.7)
4 David Kool, Western Michigan	17.9	(25.8)
5 Leon Williams, Ohio	18.4	(26.7)
6 Tim Pollitz, Miami OH	18.7	(27.8)
7 Joe Reitz, Western Michigan	18.8	(26.6)
8 Justin Dobbins, E. Michigan	19.9	(24.4)
9 Jeremiah Wood, Akron	20.1	(30.5)
10 Carlos Medlock, E. Michigan	24.1	(27.6)
11 Jake Anderson, N. Illinois	24.2	(25.5)
12 Tyrone Kent, Toledo	24.8	(32.0)
13 Nate Minnoy, Central Michigan	25.2	(27.7)
14 Jonathan Amos, Toledo	25.4	(26.6)
15 Rodney Pierce, Buffalo	25.9	(24.8)
16 Al Fisher, Kent St.	26.9	(29.7)

At least 20% of possessions used

1 Anthony Newell, Ball St.	10.4	(29.9)
2 Michael Bramos, Miami OH	10.7	(23.9)
3 Sean Smiley, Buffalo	14.4	(23.8)
4 Jarred Axon, Eastern Michigan	14.4	(23.7)
5 Andy Robinson, Buffalo	15.8	(23.9)
6 Kenny Hayes, Miami OH	16.9	(23.3)
7 Giordan Watson, C. Michigan	17.7	(26.6)
8 Peyton Stovall, Ball St.	17.9	(22.1)
9 Nate Miller, Bowling Green	17.9	(26.7)
10 David Kool, Western Michigan	17.9	(25.8)
11 Rashaun McLemore, Ball St.	18.0	(22.8)
12 Leon Williams, Ohio	18.4	(26.7)
13 Tim Pollitz, Miami OH	18.7	(27.8)
14 Shawntes Gary, Western Michigan	18.8	(20.3)
15 Joe Reitz, Western Michigan	18.8	(26.6)
16 Bubba Walther, Ohio	18.8	(21.8)
17 Bert Whittington, Ohio	19.1	(23.0)
18 Jerome Tillman, Ohio	19.5	(21.3)
19 Jerrah Young, Toledo	19.9	(21.4)
20 Justin Dobbins, E. Michigan	19.9	(24.4)

ALL PLAYERS

1 Anthony Newell, Ball St.	10.4	(29.9)
2 Michael Bramos, Miami OH	10.7	(23.9)
3 Nate Linhart, Akron	14.3	(15.7)
4 Sean Smiley, Buffalo	14.4	(23.8)
5 Mike Scott, Kent St.	14.4	(18.7)
6 Jarred Axon, Eastern Michigan	14.4	(23.7)
7 Brian Moten, Bowling Green	14.8	(16.1)
8 Rodriquez Sherman, Kent St.	15.2	(17.6)
9 Marcus Van, Central Michigan	15.7	(19.1)
10 Andy Robinson, Buffalo	15.8	(23.9)
11 Jordan Bitzer, Central Michigan	16.3	(15.1)
12 Andre Ricks, Western Michigan	16.5	(17.1)
13 Quade Milum, Akron	16.5	(16.7)
14 Cedrick Middleton, Akron	16.7	(19.0)
15 Kenny Hayes, Miami OH	16.9	(23.3)
16 Giordan Watson, C. Michigan	17.7	(26.6)
17 Peyton Stovall, Ball St.	17.9	(22.1)
18 Nate Miller, Bowling Green	17.9	(26.7)
19 David Kool, Western Michigan	17.9	(25.8)
20 Rashaun McLemore, Ball St.	18.0	(22.8)

Usage (Pct. of Possessions Used)

1 Tyrone Kent, Toledo	32.0
2 Jeremiah Wood, Akron	30.5
3 Anthony Newell, Ball St.	29.9
4 Al Fisher, Kent St.	29.7
5 Tim Pollitz, Miami OH	27.8

6 Nate Minnoy, Central Michigan	27.7
7 Carlos Medlock, E. Michigan	27.6
8 Nate Miller, Bowling Green	26.7
9 Leon Williams, Ohio	26.7
10 Jonathan Amos, Toledo	26.6
11 Joe Reitz, Western Michigan	26.6
12 Giordan Watson, C. Michigan	26.6
13 David Kool, Western Michigan	25.8
14 Jake Anderson, N. Illinois	25.5
15 Rodney Pierce, Buffalo	24.8
16 Justin Dobbins, E. Michigan	24.4
17 Andy Robinson, Buffalo	23.9
18 Michael Bramos, Miami OH	23.9
19 Sean Smiley, Buffalo	23.8
20 Jarred Axon, Eastern Michigan	23.7
21 Melvin Goins, Ball St.	23.5
22 Chris Knight, Bowling Green	23.3
23 Kenny Hayes, Miami OH	23.3
24 Jarvis Nichols, N. Illinois	23.2
25 Bert Whittington, Ohio	23.0

Assist Rate

1 Carlos Medlock, E. Michigan	30.9
2 Giordan Watson, C. Michigan	30.1
3 Michael Allen, Ohio	28.7
4 Al Fisher, Kent St.	28.3
5 Bubba Walther, Ohio	27.9
6 Michael Redell, W. Michigan	27.5
7 Nick Dials, Akron	26.9
8 Byron Mulkey, Buffalo	25.3
9 Tyrone Kent, Toledo	23.8
10 Rodney Pierce, Buffalo	23.4
11 Tim Pollitz, Miami OH	22.7
12 Jeremiah Wood, Akron	21.7
13 Joe Jakubowski, Bowling Green	21.2
14 Jake Anderson, N. Illinois	20.1
15 Jonathan Amos, Toledo	19.8

Block Rate

1 Otis Polk, Bowling Green	9.9
2 Haminn Quaintance, Kent St.	8.3
3 Marcus Van, Central Michigan	7.0
4 Marc Larson, Bowling Green	6.7
5 Jerrah Young, Toledo	5.4
6 Michael Bramos, Miami OH	5.2
7 Egan Grafel, Northern Illinois	4.7
8 Chris Knight, Bowling Green	3.8
9 Andrew Hershberger, W. Michigan	3.7

10 Quade Milum, Akron	3.7
11 Max Boudreau, Buffalo	3.6
12 Justin Dobbins, Eastern Michigan	3.5
13 Shaun Logan, Northern Illinois	3.3
14 Leon Williams, Ohio	3.1
15 Shawntes Gary, Western Michigan	2.8

Offensive Rebounding Percentage

1 Leon Williams, Ohio	18.0
2 Marcus Van, Central Michigan	14.8
3 Haminn Quaintance, Kent St.	13.6
4 Jeremiah Wood, Akron	13.3
5 Otis Polk, Bowling Green	13.1
6 Joe Reitz, Western Michigan	12.8
7 Egan Grafel, Northern Illinois	10.3
8 Malik Perry, Ball St.	10.2
9 Chris Knight, Bowling Green	10.0
10 Justin Dobbins, Eastern Michigan	10.0
11 Calvin Betts, Buffalo	9.9
12 Jerrah Young, Toledo	9.9
13 Tyler Dierkers, Miami OH	9.8
14 Max Boudreau, Buffalo	9.3
15 Tim Pollitz, Miami OH	9.1

Defensive Rebounding Percentage

1 Anthony Newell, Ball St.	22.7
2 Marcus Van, Central Michigan	22.4
3 Leon Williams, Ohio	22.0
4 Travis Lewis, Eastern Michigan	21.7
5 Jeremiah Wood, Akron	21.1
6 Jerome Tillman, Ohio	20.8
7 Joe Reitz, Western Michigan	20.6
8 Calvin Betts, Buffalo	20.2
9 Haminn Quaintance, Kent St.	20.1
10 Chris Knight, Bowling Green	18.8
11 Tyler Dierkers, Miami OH	17.6
12 Shawntes Gary, Western Michigan	16.8
13 Tim Pollitz, Miami OH	16.7
14 Andrew Hershberger, W. Michigan	16.4
15 Jonathan Amos, Toledo	16.0

Steal Rate

1 Chris Singletary, Kent St.	5.05
2 Jonathan Amos, Toledo	5.02
3 Haminn Quaintance, Kent St.	4.03
4 Melvin Goins, Ball St.	3.89
5 Andy Robinson, Buffalo	3.71
6 Travis Lewis, Eastern Michigan	3.69
7 Nate Linhart, Akron	3.45
8 Jordan Bitzer, Central Michigan	3.43
9 Cedrick Middleton, Akron	3.24
10 Giordan Watson, Central Michigan	3.24
11 Robbie Harman, Central Michigan	3.11
12 Bubba Walther, Ohio	3.09
13 Tyrone Kent, Toledo	3.01
14 Jeremy Allen, Central Michigan	2.97
15 Bert Whittington, Ohio	2.93

Pct. of Possible Minutes Played

1 Peyton Stovall, Ball St.	88.6
2 Tyrone Kent, Toledo	88.3
3 Tim Pollitz, Miami OH	87.1
4 Nate Miller, Bowling Green	82.5
5 Mike Scott, Kent St.	82.1
6 Giordan Watson, Central Michigan	81.6
7 Carlos Medlock, Eastern Michigan	80.7
8 Ridley Johnson, Toledo	79.5
9 David Kool, Western Michigan	79.4
10 Nick Dials, Akron	79.2

MEAC INDIVIDUAL STATISTICS

Offensive Rating

(Pct. of possessions used in parenthesis)

At least 28% of possessions used

1 Roy Bright, Delaware St.	109.3	(28.3)
2 Jamar Smith, Morgan St.	107.6	(28.5)
3 Rashad West, Hampton	98.7	(30.6)
4 Tony Murphy, Norfolk St.	97.0	(28.2)
5 Ed Tyson, Md.-Eastern Shore	95.5	(30.4)

At least 24% of possessions used

1 Tywain McKee, Coppin St.	111.4	(25.3)
2 Roy Bright, Delaware St.	109.3	(28.3)
3 Jamar Smith, Morgan St.	107.6	(28.5)
4 Michael Deloach, Norfolk St.	104.6	(28.0)
5 John Holmes, Bethune Cookman	103.1	(27.3)
6 Steven Rush, North Carolina A&T	99.1	(25.4)
7 Rashad West, Hampton	98.7	(30.6)
8 Jason Johnson, S. Carolina St.	97.5	(25.1)
9 Tony Murphy, Norfolk St.	97.0	(28.2)
10 Vincent Simpson, Hampton	96.9	(24.5)
11 Ed Tyson, Md.-Eastern Shore	95.5	(30.4)
12 Eugene Myatt, Howard	92.6	(26.0)
13 Randy Hampton, Howard	92.5	(24.3)
14 Jason Wills, North Carolina A&T	92.0	(24.4)
15 Matthew Pilgrim, Hampton	87.5	(24.5)
16 Marc Davis, Md.-Eastern Shore	75.5	(27.9)

At least 20% of possessions used

1 Reggie Holmes, Morgan St.	114.8	(23.6)
2 Donald Johnson, Delaware St.	111.5	(20.2)
3 Tywain McKee, Coppin St.	111.4	(25.3)
4 Roy Bright, Delaware St.	109.3	(28.3)
5 Jamar Smith, Morgan St.	107.6	(28.5)
6 Corey Lyons, Norfolk St.	105.2	(22.1)
7 Leslie Robinson, Florida A&M	105.2	(23.0)
8 Michael Deloach, Norfolk St.	104.6	(28.0)
9 John Holmes, Bethune Cookman	103.1	(27.3)
10 Ed Jones, North Carolina A&T	100.7	(20.4)
11 Marquise Kately, Morgan St.	100.1	(23.8)
12 Lamar Twitty, Florida A&M	99.3	(23.3)
13 Steven Rush, North Carolina A&T	99.1	(25.4)
14 Rashad West, Hampton	98.7	(30.6)
15 Dewayne Pettus, Bethune Cookman	97.9	(23.8)
16 Jason Johnson, S. Carolina St.	97.5	(25.1)
17 Tony Murphy, Norfolk St.	97.0	(28.2)
18 Vincent Simpson, Hampton	96.9	(24.5)
19 Ed Tyson, Md.-Eastern Shore	95.5	(30.4)
20 Antwan Harrison, Coppin St.	94.4	(23.7)

ALL PLAYERS

1 Julius Carter, S. Carolina St.	115.6	(19.7)
2 Reggie Holmes, Morgan St.	114.8	(23.6)
3 Jason Flagler, S. Carolina St.	113.1	(18.1)
4 Donald Johnson, Delaware St.	111.5	(20.2)
5 Tywain McKee, Coppin St.	111.4	(25.3)
6 Brandon Monroe, Norfolk St.	110.6	(12.7)
7 Thomas Coleman, N.C. A&T	110.0	(16.6)
8 Roy Bright, Delaware St.	109.3	(28.3)
9 B.J. Nimocks, UMES	108.7	(13.9)
10 Austin Ewing, N. Carolina A&T	107.6	(19.4)
11 Jamar Smith, Morgan St.	107.6	(28.5)
12 Leslie Robinson, Florida A&M	105.2	(23.0)
13 Corey Lyons, Norfolk St.	105.2	(22.1)
14 Michael Deloach, Norfolk St.	104.6	(28.0)
15 John Holmes, Bethune Cookman	103.1	(27.3)
16 Trevor Welcher, Delaware St.	102.7	(14.1)
17 Boubacar Coly, Morgan St.	101.6	(17.2)
18 Frisco Sandidge, Delaware St.	101.5	(20.0)
19 Joe Dickens, Delaware St.	101.1	(19.9)
20 Adrian Woodard, Hampton	100.8	(15.5)

Turnover Rate

(Pct. of possessions used in parenthesis)

At least 28% of possessions used

1 Roy Bright, Delaware St.	9.2	(28.3)
2 Jamar Smith, Morgan St.	14.2	(28.5)
3 Ed Tyson, Md.-Eastern Shore	16.6	(30.4)
4 Tony Murphy, Norfolk St.	19.4	(28.2)
5 Rashad West, Hampton	20.7	(30.6)

At least 24% of possessions used

1 Roy Bright, Delaware St.	9.2	(28.3)
2 Jamar Smith, Morgan St.	14.2	(28.5)
3 Ed Tyson, Md.-Eastern Shore	16.6	(30.4)
4 Tywain McKee, Coppin St.	17.9	(25.3)
5 Eugene Myatt, Howard	18.0	(26.0)
6 Jason Johnson, S. Carolina St.	18.5	(25.1)
7 Steven Rush, North Carolina A&T	19.3	(25.4)
8 Tony Murphy, Norfolk St.	19.4	(28.2)
9 Michael Deloach, Norfolk St.	19.8	(28.0)
10 John Holmes, Bethune Cookman	20.5	(27.3)
11 Rashad West, Hampton	20.7	(30.6)
12 Vincent Simpson, Hampton	21.3	(24.5)
13 Matthew Pilgrim, Hampton	25.5	(24.5)
14 Randy Hampton, Howard	25.6	(24.3)
15 Jason Wills, North Carolina A&T	25.8	(24.4)
16 Marc Davis, Md.-Eastern Shore	26.4	(27.9)

1 Roy Bright, Delaware St.	9.2	(28.3)
2 Reggie Holmes, Morgan St.	11.5	(23.6)
3 Donald Johnson, Delaware St.	12.4	(20.2)
4 Jamar Smith, Morgan St.	14.2	(28.5)
5 Corey Lyons, Norfolk St.	15.8	(22.1)
6 Lamar Twitty, Florida A&M	16.3	(23.3)
7 Ed Tyson, Md.-Eastern Shore	16.6	(30.4)
8 Leslie Robinson, Florida A&M	16.8	(23.0)
9 Marquise Kately, Morgan St.	17.4	(23.8)
10 Tywain McKee, Coppin St.	17.9	(25.3)
11 Eugene Myatt, Howard	18.0	(26.0)
12 Julian Conyers, Coppin St.	18.0	(20.6)
13 Jason Johnson, S, Carolina St.	18.5	(25.1)
14 Dewayne Pettus, Bethune Cookman	18.9	(23.8)
15 Steven Rush, North Carolina A&T	19.3	(25.4)
16 Tony Murphy, Norfolk St.	19.4	(28.2)
17 Ed Jones, North Carolina A&T	19.6	(20.4)
18 Michael Deloach, Norfolk St.	19.8	(28.0)
19 Dominique Whatley, Beth. Cook.	19.9	(21.7)
20 Akini Akini, Florida A&M	19.9	(23.0)

ALL PLAYERS

1 Roy Bright, Delaware St.	9.2	(28.3)
2 Reggie Holmes, Morgan St.	11.5	(23.6)
3 Donald Johnson, Delaware St.	12.4	(20.2)
4 Joe Dickens, Delaware St.	12.8	(19.9)
5 Jamar Smith, Morgan St.	14.2	(28.5)
6 Julius Carter, S. Carolina St.	15.1	(19.7)
7 Corey Lyons, Norfolk St.	15.8	(22.1)
8 Larry Jackson, Florida A&M	15.8	(17.9)
9 Lamar Twitty, Florida A&M	16.3	(23.3)
10 Jason Flagler, S. Carolina St.	16.4	(18.1)
11 Ed Tyson, Md.-Eastern Shore	16.6	(30.4)
12 Leslie Robinson, Florida A&M	16.8	(23.0)
13 Brandon Monroe, Norfolk St.	16.9	(12.7)
14 Marquise Kately, Morgan St.	17.4	(23.8)
15 Tywain McKee, Coppin St.	17.9	(25.3)
16 Eugene Myatt, Howard	18.0	(26.0)
17 Julian Conyers, Coppin St.	18.0	(20.6)
18 Jason Johnson, S. Carolina St.	18.5	(25.1)
19 Adrian Woodard, Hampton	18.7	(15.5)
20 Dewayne Pettus, Bethune Cookman	18.9	(23.8)

Usage (Pct. of Possessions Used)

1 Rashad West, Hampton	30.6
2 Ed Tyson, Md.-Eastern Shore	30.4
3 Jamar Smith, Morgan St.	28.5
4 Roy Bright, Delaware St.	28.3
5 Tony Murphy, Norfolk St.	28.2

6 Michael Deloach, Norfolk St.	28.0
7 Marc Davis, Md.-Eastern Shore	27.9
8 John Holmes, Bethune Cookman	27.3
9 Eugene Myatt, Howard	26.0
10 Steven Rush, North Carolina A&T	25.4
11 Tywain McKee, Coppin St.	25.3
12 Jason Johnson, S. Carolina St.	25.1
13 Matthew Pilgrim, Hampton	24.5
14 Vincent Simpson, Hampton	24.5
15 Jason Wills, North Carolina A&T	24.4
16 Randy Hampton, Howard	24.3
17 Marquise Kately, Morgan St.	23.8
18 Dewayne Pettus, Bethune Cookman	23.8
19 Antwan Harrison, Coppin St.	23.7
20 Reggie Holmes, Morgan St.	23.6
21 Lamar Twitty, Florida A&M	23.3
22 Jimmy Hudson, Bethune Cookman	23.1
23 Leslie Robinson, Florida A&M	23.0
24 Akini Akini, Florida A&M	23.0
25 Corey Lyons, Norfolk St.	22.1

Assist Rate

1 Michael Deloach, Norfolk St.	26.8
2 Marc Davis, Md.-Eastern Shore	25.8
3 Trevor Welcher, Delaware St.	25.0
4 Jermaine Bolden, Morgan St.	25.0
5 Joe Ballard, Florida A&M	24.5
6 Jordan Brooks, Hampton	24.4
7 Tywain McKee, Coppin St.	24.0
8 Rashad West, Hampton	24.0
9 Jerrell Green, Morgan St.	23.5
10 Byron Taylor, Florida A&M	22.3
11 Jessie Burton, S. Carolina St.	20.0
12 Carrio Bennett, S. Carolina St.	19.8
13 Joey Woods, Bethune Cookman	19.7
14 Vincent Simpson, Hampton	19.1
15 Jason Wills, North Carolina A&T	18.9

Block Rate

1 Thomas Coleman, N. Carolina A&T	10.2
2 Boubacar Coly, Morgan St.	7.8
3 Jason Johnson, South Carolina St.	6.3
4 Matthew Pilgrim, Hampton	6.2
5 Larry Vickers, Norfolk St.	6.2
6 Adam Walker, Howard	4.9
7 Paul Kirkpatrick, Howard	4.8
8 Donte Harrison, Hampton	4.8
9 Ishmawiyl McFadden, UMES	4.2

10 Julius Carter, South Carolina St.   4.2
11 Kandi Mukole, Howard   3.9
12 Akini Akini, Florida A&M   3.8
13 Theo Smalling, Hampton   3.7
14 Robert Pressey, Coppin St.   3.3
15 Michael Freeman, Hampton   3.1

Offensive Rebounding Percentage

1	Jason Johnson, South Carolina St.	13.6
2	Brandon Monroe, Norfolk St.	12.8
3	Donte Harrison, Hampton	11.9
4	Julius Carter, South Carolina St.	11.5
5	Boubacar Coly, Morgan St.	10.9
6	B.J. Nimocks, Md.-Eastern Shore	10.9
7	Frisco Sandidge, Delaware St.	10.3
8	Matthew Pilgrim, Hampton	10.2
9	Akini Akini, Florida A&M	10.0
10	Thomas Coleman, North Carolina A&T	9.9
11	Robert Pressey, Coppin St.	9.8
12	Adrian Woodard, Hampton	9.5
13	Paul Kirkpatrick, Howard	9.4
14	Theo Smalling, Hampton	9.3
15	John Holmes, Bethune Cookman	9.1

Defensive Rebounding Percentage

1	Boubacar Coly, Morgan St.	26.8
2	Robert Pressey, Coppin St.	19.2
3	Jason Johnson, South Carolina St.	18.5
4	Matthew Pilgrim, Hampton	18.4
5	Akini Akini, Florida A&M	18.2
6	Julius Carter, South Carolina St.	18.0
7	Jason Wills, North Carolina A&T	17.6
8	Thomas Coleman, North Carolina A&T	17.6
9	Larry Vickers, Norfolk St.	17.4
10	Brandon Monroe, Norfolk St.	17.2
11	Trahern Chaplin, N. Carolina A&T	16.7
12	Theo Smalling, Hampton	16.6
13	Roy Bright, Delaware St.	16.4
14	John Holmes, Bethune Cookman	16.2
15	Lamar Twitty, Florida A&M	16.1

Steal Rate

1	Michael Deloach, Norfolk St.	4.00
2	Angelo Hernandez, N. Carolina A&T	3.66
3	Matthew Pilgrim, Hampton	3.52
4	Vince Goldsberry, Coppin St.	3.38
5	Jermaine Bolden, Morgan St.	3.36
6	Joe Ballard, Florida A&M	3.24
7	Marc Davis, Md.-Eastern Shore	3.17
8	Vincent Simpson, Hampton	2.91
9	Denzel Jackson, Md.-Eastern Shore	2.87
10	Tony Murphy, Norfolk St.	2.83
11	Reggie Holmes, Morgan St.	2.79
12	Dewayne Pettus, Bethune Cookman	2.75
13	Michael Freeman, Hampton	2.75
14	Mike Miller, Coppin St.	2.69
15	Jordan Brooks, Hampton	2.68

Pct. of Possible Minutes Played

1	Ed Tyson, Md.-Eastern Shore	91.9
2	Tony Murphy, Norfolk St.	87.1
3	Boubacar Coly, Morgan St.	84.6
4	Roy Bright, Delaware St.	84.1
5	Marquise Kately, Morgan St.	80.8
6	Dewayne Pettus, Bethune Cookman	80.4
7	Tywain McKee, Coppin St.	79.9
8	Corey Lyons, Norfolk St.	78.6
9	Rashad West, Hampton	78.1
10	Joe Ballard, Florida A&M	76.8

MVC INDIVIDUAL STATISTICS

Offensive Rating

(Pct. of possessions used in parenthesis)

At least 28% of possessions used

1 Eric Coleman, Northern Iowa	106.0	(32.1)
2 P'Allen Stinnett, Creighton	102.0	(28.5)
3 Cavel Witter, Creighton	101.2	(28.6)

At least 24% of possessions used

1 Booker Woodfox, Creighton	114.1	(25.7)
2 Deven Mitchell, Missouri St.	113.7	(25.0)
3 Randal Falker, S. Illinois	108.3	(26.8)
4 Daniel Ruffin, Bradley	106.9	(25.4)
5 Eric Coleman, Northern Iowa	106.0	(32.1)
6 Osiris Eldridge, Illinois St.	105.3	(27.7)
7 P.J. Couisnard, Wichita St.	103.5	(24.7)
8 P'Allen Stinnett, Creighton	102.0	(28.5)
9 Cavel Witter, Creighton	101.2	(28.6)
10 Shy Ely, Evansville	94.8	(27.4)
11 Chris Cooks, Missouri St.	89.8	(27.1)

At least 20% of possessions used

1 Dale Lamberth, Missouri St.	121.8	(22.2)
2 Josh Young, Drake	120.2	(22.0)
3 Dane Watts, Creighton	116.0	(21.9)
4 Booker Woodfox, Creighton	114.1	(25.7)
5 Adam Emmenecker, Drake	113.8	(20.6)
6 Deven Mitchell, Missouri St.	113.7	(25.0)
7 Andrew Warren, Bradley	113.0	(20.3)
8 Jeremy Crouch, Bradley	110.9	(22.0)
9 Gabriel Moore, Indiana St.	108.8	(22.1)
10 Leonard Houston, Drake	108.6	(23.9)
11 Randal Falker, S. Illinois	108.3	(26.8)
12 Bryan Mullins, S. Illinois	107.7	(20.3)
13 Daniel Ruffin, Bradley	106.9	(25.4)
14 Theron Wilson, Bradley	106.9	(20.9)
15 Eric Coleman, Northern Iowa	106.0	(32.1)
16 Adam Koch, Northern Iowa	105.9	(21.8)
17 Osiris Eldridge, Illinois St.	105.3	(27.7)
18 Harry Marshall, Indiana St.	104.9	(20.3)
19 Matt Braeuer, Wichita St.	104.1	(20.5)
20 P.J. Couisnard, Wichita St.	103.5	(24.7)

ALL PLAYERS

1 Brent Heemskerk, Drake	127.2	(12.7)
2 Jonathan Cox, Drake	122.7	(18.4)
3 Adam Viet, Northern Iowa	122.1	(12.7)
4 Dale Lamberth, Missouri St.	121.8	(22.2)
5 Josh Young, Drake	120.2	(22.0)

6 Klayton Korver, Drake	117.2	(18.3)
7 Dane Watts, Creighton	116.0	(21.9)
8 Booker Woodfox, Creighton	114.1	(25.7)
9 Adam Emmenecker, Drake	113.8	(20.6)
10 Deven Mitchell, Missouri St.	113.7	(25.0)
11 Andrew Warren, Bradley	113.0	(20.3)
12 Jeremy Crouch, Bradley	110.9	(22.0)
13 Sam Maniscalco, Bradley	110.1	(15.7)
14 Jay Tunnell, Indiana St.	110.1	(19.3)
15 Nick Bahe, Creighton	110.1	(14.3)
16 Darin Granger, Evansville	109.4	(17.0)
17 Gabriel Moore, Indiana St.	108.8	(22.1)
18 Leonard Houston, Drake	108.6	(23.9)
19 Randal Falker, S. Illinois	108.3	(26.8)
20 Bryan Mullins, S. Illinois	107.7	(20.3)

Turnover Rate

(Pct. of possessions used in parenthesis)

At least 28% of possessions used

1 Eric Coleman, Northern Iowa	18.8	(32.1)
2 P'Allen Stinnett, Creighton	21.4	(28.5)
3 Cavel Witter, Creighton	26.6	(28.6)

At least 24% of possessions used

1 Booker Woodfox, Creighton	12.2	(25.7)
2 Osiris Eldridge, Illinois St.	15.7	(27.7)
3 P.J. Couisnard, Wichita St.	16.7	(24.7)
4 Eric Coleman, Northern Iowa	18.8	(32.1)
5 Shy Ely, Evansville	19.0	(27.4)
6 Deven Mitchell, Missouri St.	20.1	(25.0)
7 Randal Falker, S. Illinois	20.5	(26.8)
8 P'Allen Stinnett, Creighton	21.4	(28.5)
9 Daniel Ruffin, Bradley	22.6	(25.4)
10 Cavel Witter, Creighton	26.6	(28.6)
11 Chris Cooks, Missouri St.	29.5	(27.1)

At least 20% of possessions used

1 Dale Lamberth, Missouri St.	9.8	(22.2)
2 Booker Woodfox, Creighton	12.2	(25.7)
3 Josh Young, Drake	14.7	(22.0)
4 Andrew Warren, Bradley	14.7	(20.3)
5 Osiris Eldridge, Illinois St.	15.7	(27.7)
6 Leonard Houston, Drake	15.9	(23.9)
7 Theron Wilson, Bradley	16.6	(20.9)
8 P.J. Couisnard, Wichita St.	16.7	(24.7)
9 Jeremy Crouch, Bradley	17.5	(22.0)
10 Marico Stinson, Indiana St.	18.0	(23.9)
11 Harry Marshall, Indiana St.	18.1	(20.3)
12 Dane Watts, Creighton	18.8	(21.9)

13 Eric Coleman, Northern Iowa	18.8	(32.1)		19 Gabriel Moore, Indiana St.	22.1	
14 Shy Ely, Evansville	19.0	(27.4)		20 Jeremy Crouch, Bradley	22.0	
15 Phillip Thomasson, Wichita St.	19.5	(21.5)		21 Josh Young, Drake	22.0	
16 Matt Shaw, S. Illinois	19.8	(23.5)		22 Dane Watts, Creighton	21.9	
17 Matt Braeuer, Wichita St.	19.9	(20.5)		23 Adam Koch, Northern Iowa	21.8	
18 Deven Mitchell, Missouri St.	20.1	(25.0)		24 Phillip Thomasson, Wichita St.	21.5	
19 Randal Falker, S. Illinois	20.5	(26.8)		25 Theron Wilson, Bradley	20.9	
20 P'Allen Stinnett, Creighton	21.4	(28.5)				

ALL PLAYERS

1 Klayton Korver, Drake	8.8	(18.3)
2 Darin Granger, Evansville	9.0	(17.0)
3 Dale Lamberth, Missouri St.	9.8	(22.2)
4 Booker Woodfox, Creighton	12.2	(25.7)
5 Adam Viet, Northern Iowa	13.7	(12.7)
6 Levi Dyer, Illinois St.	13.9	(17.9)
7 Jonathan Cox, Drake	14.5	(18.4)
8 Andrew Warren, Bradley	14.7	(20.3)
9 Josh Young, Drake	14.7	(22.0)
10 Travis Brown, Northern Iowa	15.5	(17.4)
11 Brent Heemskerk, Drake	15.6	(12.7)
12 Osiris Eldridge, Illinois St.	15.7	(27.7)
13 Leonard Houston, Drake	15.9	(23.9)
14 Isiah Martin, Indiana St.	16.0	(15.7)
15 Jay Tunnell, Indiana St.	16.5	(19.3)
16 Theron Wilson, Bradley	16.6	(20.9)
17 P.J. Couisnard, Wichita St.	16.7	(24.7)
18 Emmanuel Holloway, Illinois St.	16.8	(18.5)
19 Jeremy Crouch, Bradley	17.5	(22.0)
20 Marico Stinson, Indiana St.	18.0	(23.9)

Usage (Pct. of Possessions Used)

1 Eric Coleman, Northern Iowa	32.1
2 Cavel Witter, Creighton	28.6
3 P'Allen Stinnett, Creighton	28.5
4 Osiris Eldridge, Illinois St.	27.7
5 Shy Ely, Evansville	27.4
6 Chris Cooks, Missouri St.	27.1
7 Randal Falker, S. Illinois	26.8
8 Booker Woodfox, Creighton	25.7
9 Daniel Ruffin, Bradley	25.4
10 Deven Mitchell, Missouri St.	25.0
11 P.J. Couisnard, Wichita St.	24.7
12 Marico Stinson, Indiana St.	23.9
13 Leonard Houston, Drake	23.9
14 Matt Shaw, Southern Illinois	23.5
15 Jason Holsinger, Evansville	22.3
16 Dale Lamberth, Missouri St.	22.2
17 Anthony Slack, Illinois St.	22.2
18 Gal Mekel, Wichita St.	22.1

Assist Rate

1 Adam Emmenecker, Drake	36.0
2 Daniel Ruffin, Bradley	35.7
3 Bryan Mullins, S. Illinois	33.7
4 Jason Holsinger, Evansville	31.3
5 Gabriel Moore, Indiana St.	31.0
6 Cavel Witter, Creighton	30.3
7 Josh Dotzler, Creighton	30.0
8 Justin Fuehrmeyer, Missouri St.	27.5
9 Gal Mekel, Wichita St.	27.4
10 Boo Richardson, Illinois St.	24.3
11 Eric Coleman, Northern Iowa	24.1
12 Matt Braeuer, Wichita St.	23.7
13 Spencer Laurie, Missouri St.	23.0
14 Dom Johnson, Illinois St.	22.4
15 Kavon Lacey, Evansville	21.5

Block Rate

1 Isiah Martin, Indiana St.	11.8
2 Anthony Slack, Illinois St.	7.3
3 Eric Coleman, Northern Iowa	7.1
4 Randal Falker, Southern Illinois	6.6
5 Brent Heemskerk, Drake	5.9
6 Chad Millard, Creighton	5.3
7 Dane Watts, Creighton	4.2
8 Matt Salley, Bradley	4.2
9 Jonathan Cox, Drake	4.2
10 Dinma Odiakosa, Illinois St.	3.3
11 P.J. Couisnard, Wichita St.	3.2
12 Phillip Thomasson, Wichita St.	2.6
13 Deven Mitchell, Missouri St.	2.4
14 Matt Shaw, Southern Illinois	2.3
15 Levi Dyer, Illinois St.	2.2

Offensive Rebounding Percentage

1 Randal Falker, Southern Illinois	15.2
2 Ramon Clemente, Wichita St.	12.5
3 Dinma Odiakosa, Illinois St.	12.3

4 Matt Salley, Bradley	12.2
5 Anthony Slack, Illinois St.	12.1
6 Adam Arnold, Indiana St.	11.8
7 Dane Watts, Creighton	11.2
8 Nate Garner, Evansville	10.9
9 Brent Heemskerk, Drake	10.8
10 Eric Coleman, Northern Iowa	9.9
11 Jonathan Cox, Drake	9.8
12 Dale Lamberth, Missouri St.	9.4
13 Deven Mitchell, Missouri St.	9.3
14 Jay Tunnell, Indiana St.	9.0
15 Chris Cooks, Missouri St.	8.9

Defensive Rebounding Percentage

1 Eric Coleman, Northern Iowa	35.0
2 Matt Shaw, Southern Illinois	24.6
3 Jonathan Cox, Drake	24.0
4 Ramon Clemente, Wichita St.	23.4
5 Anthony Slack, Illinois St.	23.0
6 Matt Salley, Bradley	22.0
7 Dane Watts, Creighton	19.2
8 Adam Arnold, Indiana St.	19.2
9 Todd McCoy, Indiana St.	18.7
10 Dinma Odiakosa, Illinois St.	18.2
11 Adam Koch, Northern Iowa	18.2
12 Deven Mitchell, Missouri St.	17.8
13 Jay Tunnell, Indiana St.	17.5
14 Randal Falker, Southern Illinois	17.1
15 Shy Ely, Evansville	16.6

Steal Rate

1 Josh Dotzler, Creighton	4.44
2 Bryan Mullins, Southern Illinois	3.95
3 P'Allen Stinnett, Creighton	3.94
4 Gabriel Moore, Indiana St.	3.88
5 Boo Richardson, Illinois St.	3.29
6 Daniel Ruffin, Bradley	3.17
7 Deven Mitchell, Missouri St.	3.10
8 P.J. Couisnard, Wichita St.	3.09
9 Emmanuel Holloway, Illinois St.	3.02
10 Adam Emmenecker, Drake	3.01
11 Andrew Warren, Bradley	2.81
12 Leonard Houston, Drake	2.80
13 Osiris Eldridge, Illinois St.	2.73
14 Josh Young, Drake	2.73
15 Theron Wilson, Bradley	2.62

Pct. of Possible Minutes Played

1 Jeremy Crouch, Bradley	85.6
2 Jared Josten, Northern Iowa	83.2
3 Gabriel Moore, Indiana St.	83.1
4 Adam Emmenecker, Drake	82.2
5 Shy Ely, Evansville	81.1
6 Bryan Mullins, Southern Illinois	80.7
7 Jason Holsinger, Evansville	79.9
8 P.J. Couisnard, Wichita St.	79.4
9 Leonard Houston, Drake	78.3
10 Matt Shaw, Southern Illinois	77.8

MOUNTAIN WEST
INDIVIDUAL STATISTICS

Offensive Rating

(Pct. of possessions used in parenthesis)

At least 28% of possessions used

1 Luke Nevill, Utah	106.7	(29.3)
2 Marcus Walker, Colorado St.	101.9	(28.3)
3 Trent Plaisted, BYU	100.5	(29.9)
4 Lorrenzo Wade, San Diego St.	99.6	(28.2)

At least 24% of possessions used

1 Wink Adams, UNLV	110.9	(26.7)
2 J.R. Giddens, New Mexico	108.5	(27.1)
3 Tim Anderson, Air Force	107.1	(24.2)
4 Luke Nevill, Utah	106.7	(29.3)
5 Brandon Ewing, Wyoming	103.7	(24.3)
6 Marcus Walker, Colorado St.	101.9	(28.3)
7 Trent Plaisted, BYU	100.5	(29.9)
8 Lorrenzo Wade, San Diego St.	99.6	(28.2)
9 Kevin Langford, TCU	95.8	(26.1)

At least 20% of possessions used

1 Lee Cummard, BYU	124.8	(22.1)
2 Johnnie Bryant, Utah	119.9	(22.2)
3 Jamaal Smith, New Mexico	117.3	(21.2)
4 Joe Darger, UNLV	112.9	(20.5)
5 Wink Adams, UNLV	110.9	(26.7)
6 J.R. Giddens, New Mexico	108.5	(27.1)
7 Tim Anderson, Air Force	107.1	(24.2)
8 Luke Nevill, Utah	106.7	(29.3)
9 Henry Salter, TCU	106.2	(23.4)
10 Curtis Terry, UNLV	104.5	(20.9)
11 Brandon Ewing, Wyoming	103.7	(24.3)
12 Dairese Gary, New Mexico	102.7	(21.3)
13 Marcus Walker, Colorado St.	101.9	(28.3)
14 Andrew Henke, Air Force	101.6	(23.8)
15 Daniel Faris, New Mexico	101.6	(22.4)
16 Trent Plaisted, BYU	100.5	(29.9)
17 Ryan Amoroso, San Diego St.	100.2	(21.3)
18 Jonathan Tavernari, BYU	99.9	(23.9)
19 Lorrenzo Wade, San Diego St.	99.6	(28.2)
20 Brent Hackett, TCU	99.0	(23.6)

ALL PLAYERS

1 Chad Toppert, New Mexico	130.3	(16.1)
2 Lee Cummard, BYU	124.8	(22.1)
3 Johnnie Bryant, Utah	119.9	(22.2)
4 Shaun Green, Utah	119.7	(13.3)
5 Roman Martinez, New Mexico	117.5	(16.3)

6 Jamaal Smith, New Mexico	117.3	(21.2)
7 Joe Darger, UNLV	112.9	(20.5)
8 Sam Burgess, BYU	111.4	(15.1)
9 Willis Gardner, Colorado St.	111.4	(18.0)
10 Wink Adams, UNLV	110.9	(26.7)
11 Billy White, San Diego St.	110.8	(15.9)
12 J.R. Giddens, New Mexico	108.5	(27.1)
13 Lawrence Borha, Utah	108.3	(17.2)
14 Darren Prentice, New Mexico	108.1	(19.7)
15 Rene Rougeau, UNLV	108.1	(18.4)
16 Tim Anderson, Air Force	107.1	(24.2)
17 Luke Nevill, Utah	106.7	(29.3)
18 Matt Shaw, UNLV	106.3	(19.8)
19 Henry Salter, TCU	106.2	(23.4)
20 Curtis Terry, UNLV	104.5	(20.9)

Turnover Rate

(Pct. of possessions used in parenthesis)

At least 28% of possessions used

1 Marcus Walker, Colorado St.	14.5	(28.3)
2 Luke Nevill, Utah	16.3	(29.3)
3 Trent Plaisted, BYU	16.7	(29.9)
4 Lorrenzo Wade, San Diego St.	19.1	(28.2)

At least 24% of possessions used

1 Wink Adams, UNLV	12.9	(26.7)
2 Marcus Walker, Colorado St.	14.5	(28.3)
3 Tim Anderson, Air Force	14.6	(24.2)
4 J.R. Giddens, New Mexico	15.2	(27.1)
5 Luke Nevill, Utah	16.3	(29.3)
6 Trent Plaisted, BYU	16.7	(29.9)
7 Lorrenzo Wade, San Diego St.	19.1	(28.2)
8 Kevin Langford, TCU	19.8	(26.1)
9 Brandon Ewing, Wyoming	21.1	(24.3)

At least 20% of possessions used

1 Joe Darger, UNLV	8.8	(20.5)
2 Johnnie Bryant, Utah	12.6	(22.2)
3 Wink Adams, UNLV	12.9	(26.7)
4 Brent Hackett, TCU	13.4	(23.6)
5 Henry Salter, TCU	13.8	(23.4)
6 Daniel Faris, New Mexico	14.4	(22.4)
7 Jonathan Tavernari, BYU	14.5	(23.9)
8 Marcus Walker, Colorado St.	14.5	(28.3)
9 Tim Anderson, Air Force	14.6	(24.2)
10 J.R. Giddens, New Mexico	15.2	(27.1)
11 Ryan Amoroso, San Diego St.	15.4	(21.3)
12 Luke Nevill, Utah	16.3	(29.3)
13 Trent Plaisted, BYU	16.7	(29.9)

14 Lee Cummard, BYU	18.5	(22.1)
15 Lorrenzo Wade, San Diego St.	19.1	(28.2)
16 Jamaal Smith, New Mexico	19.5	(21.2)
17 Kevin Langford, TCU	19.8	(26.1)
18 Andrew Henke, Air Force	20.0	(23.8)
19 Brandon Ewing, Wyoming	21.1	(24.3)
20 Kelvin Davis, San Diego St.	21.5	(21.5)

ALL PLAYERS

1 Joe Darger, UNLV	8.8	(20.5)
2 Chad Toppert, New Mexico	10.7	(16.1)
3 Matt Shaw, UNLV	11.9	(19.8)
4 Johnnie Bryant, Utah	12.6	(22.2)
5 Shaun Green, Utah	12.8	(13.3)
6 Wink Adams, UNLV	12.9	(26.7)
7 Brent Hackett, TCU	13.4	(23.6)
8 Henry Salter, TCU	13.8	(23.4)
9 Daniel Faris, New Mexico	14.4	(22.4)
10 Jonathan Tavernari, BYU	14.5	(23.9)
11 Marcus Walker, Colorado St.	14.5	(28.3)
12 Rene Rougeau, UNLV	14.5	(18.4)
13 Tim Anderson, Air Force	14.6	(24.2)
14 J.R. Giddens, New Mexico	15.2	(27.1)
15 Ryan Amoroso, San Diego St.	15.4	(21.3)
16 Corey Bailey, UNLV	16.0	(15.6)
17 Luke Nevill, Utah	16.3	(29.3)
18 Roman Martinez, New Mexico	16.6	(16.3)
19 Trent Plaisted, BYU	16.7	(29.9)
20 Willis Gardner, Colorado St.	17.0	(18.0)

Usage (Pct. of Possessions Used)

1 Trent Plaisted, BYU	29.9
2 Luke Nevill, Utah	29.3
3 Marcus Walker, Colorado St.	28.3
4 Lorrenzo Wade, San Diego St.	28.2
5 J.R. Giddens, New Mexico	27.1
6 Wink Adams, UNLV	26.7
7 Kevin Langford, TCU	26.1
8 Brandon Ewing, Wyoming	24.3
9 Tim Anderson, Air Force	24.2
10 Jonathan Tavernari, BYU	23.9
11 Andrew Henke, Air Force	23.8
12 Brent Hackett, TCU	23.6
13 Henry Salter, TCU	23.4
14 Tyson Johnson, Wyoming	23.1
15 Daniel Faris, New Mexico	22.4
16 Johnnie Bryant, Utah	22.2
17 Lee Cummard, BYU	22.1
18 Josh Simmons, Colorado St.	22.1
19 Brad Jones, Wyoming	21.9

20 Kelvin Davis, San Diego St.	21.5
21 Richie Williams, San Diego St.	21.4
22 Ryan Amoroso, San Diego St.	21.3
23 Dairese Gary, New Mexico	21.3
24 Jesse Woodard, Colorado St.	21.3
25 Jamaal Smith, New Mexico	21.2

Assist Rate

1 Luka Drca, Utah	32.7
2 Curtis Terry, UNLV	30.3
3 Lorrenzo Wade, San Diego St.	26.0
4 Dairese Gary, New Mexico	25.8
5 Jason Ebie, TCU	25.7
6 Brandon Ewing, Wyoming	24.9
7 Lee Cummard, BYU	24.0
8 Richie Williams, San Diego St.	23.4
9 Darren Prentice, New Mexico	22.5
10 J.R. Giddens, New Mexico	22.5
11 Wink Adams, UNLV	21.9
12 Ben Murdock, BYU	21.8
13 Tim Anderson, Air Force	21.3
14 Brad Jones, Wyoming	20.9
15 Marcus Walker, Colorado St.	20.2

Block Rate

1 Luke Nevill, Utah	6.6
2 Alvarado Parker, TCU	6.5
3 Joseph Taylor, Wyoming	6.1
4 J.R. Giddens, New Mexico	4.9
5 Rene Rougeau, UNLV	4.7
6 Matt Shaw, UNLV	3.9
7 Daniel Faris, New Mexico	3.6
8 Ryan Dermody, Wyoming	3.6
9 Trent Plaisted, BYU	3.5
10 Shaun Green, Utah	3.4
11 Keith Maren, Air Force	3.3
12 Billy White, San Diego St.	3.2
13 Lee Cummard, BYU	3.1
14 Lorrenzo Wade, San Diego St.	2.3
15 Kevin Langford, TCU	2.0

Offensive Rebounding Percentage

1 John Ortiz, TCU	11.1
2 Alvarado Parker, TCU	10.8
3 Daniel Faris, New Mexico	10.7
4 Luke Nevill, Utah	10.2

5 Joseph Taylor, Wyoming	9.7	
6 Billy White, San Diego St.	9.4	
7 Trent Plaisted, BYU	9.2	
8 Rene Rougeau, UNLV	9.1	
9 Roman Martinez, New Mexico	8.7	
10 Tyson Johnson, Wyoming	8.4	
11 Ryan Amoroso, San Diego St.	8.3	
12 Matt Shaw, UNLV	7.7	
13 Lee Cummard, BYU	7.3	
14 Kevin Langford, TCU	7.3	
15 Corey Bailey, UNLV	6.7	

Defensive Rebounding Percentage

1 J.R. Giddens, New Mexico	27.6
2 Joseph Taylor, Wyoming	24.6
3 Trent Plaisted, BYU	21.0
4 Andrew Henke, Air Force	20.0
5 Luke Nevill, Utah	19.8
6 Henry Salter, TCU	18.5
7 Ryan Amoroso, San Diego St.	18.4
8 John Ortiz, TCU	18.3
9 Alvarado Parker, TCU	16.9
10 Carlon Brown, Utah	16.8
11 Billy White, San Diego St.	16.4
12 Matt Shaw, UNLV	16.3
13 Rene Rougeau, UNLV	16.3
14 Jonathan Tavernari, BYU	16.1
15 Shaun Green, Utah	16.0

Steal Rate

1 Jason Ebie, TCU	4.92
2 Rene Rougeau, UNLV	4.65
3 Tim Anderson, Air Force	4.16
4 Richie Williams, San Diego St.	4.03
5 Kelvin Davis, San Diego St.	3.71
6 Dairese Gary, New Mexico	3.41
7 Brent Hackett, TCU	3.17
8 Billy White, San Diego St.	3.02
9 Jonathan Tavernari, BYU	2.82
10 Wink Adams, UNLV	2.79
11 Keith Maren, Air Force	2.71
12 J.R. Giddens, New Mexico	2.66
13 Joseph Taylor, Wyoming	2.65
14 John Ortiz, TCU	2.61
15 Jimmer Fredette, BYU	2.37

Pct. of Possible Minutes Played

1 Brandon Ewing, Wyoming	93.8
2 Tim Anderson, Air Force	90.1
3 Brad Jones, Wyoming	85.8
4 Marcus Walker, Colorado St.	83.2
5 Evan Washington, Air Force	83.1
6 Ryan Dermody, Wyoming	82.9
7 Curtis Terry, UNLV	80.9
8 Wink Adams, UNLV	80.0
9 Lorrenzo Wade, San Diego St.	79.6
10 J.R. Giddens, New Mexico	78.7

NEC INDIVIDUAL STATISTICS

Offensive Rating

(Pct. of possessions used in parenthesis)

At least 28% of possessions used

1 Tony Lee, Robert Morris	104.5	(29.5)
2 DeMario Anderson, Quinnipiac	99.9	(35.5)
3 Kellen Allen, Long Island	97.4	(30.6)
4 Robert Hines, St. Francis NY	88.0	(28.3)
5 Jhamar Youngblood, Monmouth	81.6	(29.9)

At least 24% of possessions used

1 Manny Ubilla, F. Dickinson	109.2	(28.0)
2 Tristan Blackwood, CCSU	107.8	(25.9)
3 Jaytornah Wisseh, Long Island	105.1	(24.4)
4 Tony Lee, Robert Morris	104.5	(29.5)
5 Jeremy Goode, Mount St. Mary's	102.4	(27.4)
6 Mark Porter, Wagner	100.1	(25.9)
7 DeMario Anderson, Quinnipiac	99.9	(35.5)
8 Kellen Allen, Long Island	97.4	(30.6)
9 Durell Vinson, Wagner	94.0	(25.7)
10 Whitney Coleman, Monmouth	88.2	(24.8)
11 Robert Hines, St. Francis NY	88.0	(28.3)
12 Cale Nelson, St. Francis PA	86.6	(24.1)
13 Jhamar Youngblood, Monmouth	81.6	(29.9)

At least 20% of possessions used

1 Ken Horton, Central Conn.	115.5	(20.6)
2 Sean Baptiste, F. Dickinson	115.0	(23.7)
3 Jeremy Chappell, Robert Morris	114.0	(20.2)
4 Chris Vann, Mount St. Mary's	110.4	(22.0)
5 Manny Ubilla, F. Dickinson	109.2	(28.0)
6 Tristan Blackwood, CCSU	107.8	(25.9)
7 Marcus Palmer, Central Conn.	107.1	(21.8)
8 Jaytornah Wisseh, Long Island	105.1	(24.4)
9 Kyle Johnson, Long Island	104.8	(20.5)
10 Evann Baker, Quinnipiac	104.5	(21.0)
11 Tony Lee, Robert Morris	104.5	(29.5)
12 A.J. Jackson, Robert Morris	103.5	(23.8)
13 Chris Berry, St. Francis PA	103.2	(22.7)
14 Jeremy Goode, Mount St. Mary's	102.4	(27.4)
15 Brice Brooks, Sacred Heart	101.5	(22.4)
16 Chauncey Hardy, Sacred Heart	100.9	(20.1)
17 Corey Hassan, Sacred Heart	100.4	(22.2)
18 Mark Porter, Wagner	100.1	(25.9)
19 Drew Shubik, Sacred Heart	100.1	(22.1)
20 DeMario Anderson, Quinnipiac	99.9	(35.5)

ALL PLAYERS

1 Jimmy Langhurst, Robert Morris	118.3	(16.5)
2 Ken Horton, Central Conn.	115.5	(20.6)
3 Sean Baptiste, F. Dickinson	115.0	(23.7)
4 Jeremy Chappell, Robert Morris	114.0	(20.2)
5 Ryon Howard, Sacred Heart	112.5	(16.2)
6 Bryan Geffen, Quinnipiac	112.5	(17.2)
7 James Feldeine, Quinnipiac	111.2	(15.5)
8 Chris Vann, Mount St. Mary's	110.4	(22.0)
9 Manny Ubilla, F. Dickinson	109.2	(28.0)
10 Tristan Blackwood, CCSU	107.8	(25.9)
11 Marcus Palmer, Central Conn.	107.1	(21.8)
12 Eugene Kotorobai, Long Island	106.5	(17.3)
13 Justin Rutty, Quinnipiac	106.0	(18.1)
14 Jaytornah Wisseh, Long Island	105.1	(24.4)
15 Kyle Johnson, Long Island	104.8	(20.5)
16 Joe Seymore, Central Conn.	104.7	(18.6)
17 Tony Lee, Robert Morris	104.5	(29.5)
18 Evann Baker, Quinnipiac	104.5	(21.0)
19 Jamal Smith, Wagner	104.3	(17.0)
20 A.J. Jackson, Robert Morris	103.5	(23.8)

Turnover Rate

(Pct. of possessions used in parenthesis)

At least 28% of possessions used

1 Kellen Allen, Long Island	17.9	(30.6)
2 DeMario Anderson, Quinnipiac	20.5	(35.5)
3 Jhamar Youngblood, Monmouth	20.6	(29.9)
4 Robert Hines, St. Francis NY	23.6	(28.3)
5 Tony Lee, Robert Morris	28.0	(29.5)

At least 24% of possessions used

1 Kellen Allen, Long Island	17.9	(30.6)
2 Manny Ubilla, F. Dickinson	19.9	(28.0)
3 DeMario Anderson, Quinnipiac	20.5	(35.5)
4 Jhamar Youngblood, Monmouth	20.6	(29.9)
5 Jaytornah Wisseh, Long Island	20.6	(24.4)
6 Jeremy Goode, Mount St. Mary's	21.3	(27.4)
7 Whitney Coleman, Monmouth	21.7	(24.8)
8 Tristan Blackwood, CCSU	23.3	(25.9)
9 Robert Hines, St. Francis NY	23.6	(28.3)
10 Durell Vinson, Wagner	23.6	(25.7)
11 Mark Porter, Wagner	23.9	(25.9)
12 Cale Nelson, St. Francis PA	26.7	(24.1)
13 Tony Lee, Robert Morris	28.0	(29.5)

At least 20% of possessions used

1 Sean Baptiste, F. Dickinson	11.0	(23.7)
2 Chris Vann, Mount St. Mary's	11.6	(22.0)

3 Corey Hassan, Sacred Heart	14.9	(22.2)
4 A.J. Jackson, Robert Morris	15.4	(23.8)
5 Kyle Johnson, Long Island	15.8	(20.5)
6 Jeremy Chappell, Robert Morris	16.0	(20.2)
7 Ryan Litke, Sacred Heart	16.4	(23.3)
8 Chris Berry, St. Francis PA	16.5	(22.7)
9 Marcus Palmer, Central Conn.	17.1	(21.8)
10 Ken Horton, Central Conn.	17.4	(20.6)
11 Kellen Allen, Long Island	17.9	(30.6)
12 James Ulrich, Wagner	18.9	(20.2)
13 Manny Ubilla, F. Dickinson	19.9	(28.0)
14 Bass Dieng, St. Francis PA	20.0	(21.1)
15 Brice Brooks, Sacred Heart	20.2	(22.4)
16 DeMario Anderson, Quinnipiac	20.5	(35.5)
17 Jaytornah Wisseh, Long Island	20.6	(24.4)
18 Jhamar Youngblood, Monmouth	20.6	(29.9)
19 Chauncey Hardy, Sacred Heart	20.7	(20.1)
20 B. Yessoufou, St. Francis NY	21.3	(20.2)

ALL PLAYERS

1 Sean Baptiste, F. Dickinson	11.0	(23.7)
2 Chris Vann, Mount St. Mary's	11.6	(22.0)
3 Eugene Kotorobai, Long Island	12.5	(17.3)
4 Jamaal Womack, St. Francis NY	13.8	(18.7)
5 Ryon Howard, Sacred Heart	13.9	(16.2)
6 R.J. Rutledge, Monmouth	14.3	(19.3)
7 James Feldeine, Quinnipiac	14.7	(15.5)
8 Joey Mundweiler, Wagner	14.9	(16.8)
9 Corey Hassan, Sacred Heart	14.9	(22.2)
10 A.J. Jackson, Robert Morris	15.4	(23.8)
11 Jamal Smith, Wagner	15.8	(17.0)
12 Kyle Johnson, Long Island	15.8	(20.5)
13 Bryan Geffen, Quinnipiac	15.8	(17.2)
14 Alex Nunner, Monmouth	16.0	(16.0)
15 Jeremy Chappell, Robert Morris	16.0	(20.2)
16 Ryan Litke, Sacred Heart	16.4	(23.3)
17 Chris Berry, St. Francis PA	16.5	(22.7)
18 Justin Rutty, Quinnipiac	16.7	(18.1)
19 David Hicks, Long Island	17.0	(16.1)
20 Marcus Palmer, Central Conn.	17.1	(21.8)

Usage (Pct. of Possessions Used)

1 DeMario Anderson, Quinnipiac	35.5
2 Kellen Allen, Long Island	30.6
3 Jhamar Youngblood, Monmouth	29.9
4 Tony Lee, Robert Morris	29.5
5 Robert Hines, St. Francis NY	28.3
6 Manny Ubilla, F. Dickinson	28.0
7 Jeremy Goode, Mount St. Mary's	27.4
8 Mark Porter, Wagner	25.9

9 Tristan Blackwood, CCSU	25.9
10 Durell Vinson, Wagner	25.7
11 Whitney Coleman, Monmouth	24.8
12 Jaytornah Wisseh, Long Island	24.4
13 Cale Nelson, St. Francis PA	24.1
14 A.J. Jackson, Robert Morris	23.8
15 Sean Baptiste, F. Dickinson	23.7
16 Ryan Litke, Sacred Heart	23.3
17 Chris Berry, St. Francis PA	22.7
18 Kayode Ayeni, St. Francis NY	22.4
19 Brice Brooks, Sacred Heart	22.4
20 Corey Hassan, Sacred Heart	22.2
21 Devin Sweetney, St. Francis PA	22.2
22 Drew Shubik, Sacred Heart	22.1
23 Chris Vann, Mount St. Mary's	22.0
24 Marcus Palmer, Central Conn.	21.8
25 Bass Dieng, St. Francis PA	21.1

Assist Rate

1 Tony Lee, Robert Morris	43.5
2 Jeremy Goode, Mount St. Mary's	35.0
3 Jaytornah Wisseh, Long Island	30.5
4 Drew Shubik, Sacred Heart	30.2
5 Manny Ubilla, F. Dickinson	30.1
6 Tristan Blackwood, CCSU	29.8
7 Cale Nelson, St. Francis PA	29.1
8 Mark Porter, Wagner	28.9
9 James Hett, Monmouth	23.5
10 DeMario Anderson, Quinnipiac	23.5
11 Bryan Geffen, Quinnipiac	23.0
12 Marquis Ford, St. Francis PA	22.1
13 Casey Cosgrove, Quinnipiac	20.6
14 Jhamar Youngblood, Monmouth	20.1
15 Shemik Thompson, Central Conn.	19.9

Block Rate

1 Ken Horton, Central Connecticut	8.0
2 Sam Atupem, Mount St. Mary's	6.0
3 DeJuan Pursley, F. Dickinson	4.9
4 Dutch Gaitley, Monmouth	4.4
5 Durell Vinson, Wagner	4.1
6 Kayode Ayeni, St. Francis NY	4.0
7 Bass Dieng, St. Francis PA	3.6
8 A.J. Jackson, Robert Morris	3.4
9 Eugene Kotorobai, Long Island	3.2
10 Markus Mitchell, Mount St. Mary's	2.7
11 Mark Porter, Wagner	2.6
12 Karl Anderson, Quinnipiac	2.6

13 Brice Brooks, Sacred Heart	2.4
14 Nick DelTufo, Monmouth	2.4
15 Ryan Litke, Sacred Heart	2.2

Offensive Rebounding Percentage

1 Durell Vinson, Wagner	15.6
2 Karl Anderson, Quinnipiac	12.4
3 Justin Rutty, Quinnipiac	12.4
4 Kayode Ayeni, St. Francis NY	11.9
5 Bassith Yessoufou, St. Francis NY	11.8
6 Louis Brookins, Quinnipiac	11.8
7 Chris Berry, St. Francis PA	11.2
8 Markus Mitchell, Mount St. Mary's	10.1
9 Tony Lee, Robert Morris	9.8
10 Aaron Hall, Central Connecticut	9.7
11 James Ulrich, Wagner	9.2
12 Ken Horton, Central Connecticut	8.8
13 Kellen Allen, Long Island	8.7
14 Ron Manigault, Long Island	8.3
15 Ryon Howard, Sacred Heart	8.3

Defensive Rebounding Percentage

1 Durell Vinson, Wagner	24.2
2 Bass Dieng, St. Francis PA	21.0
3 Marcus Palmer, Central Connecticut	20.6
4 Bassith Yessoufou, St. Francis NY	19.7
5 Kayode Ayeni, St. Francis NY	19.1
6 Eugene Kotorobai, Long Island	19.0
7 DeMario Anderson, Quinnipiac	18.5
8 Markus Mitchell, Mount St. Mary's	18.4
9 Ryon Howard, Sacred Heart	18.0
10 Tony Lee, Robert Morris	16.9
11 Chris Berry, St. Francis PA	16.3
12 James Ulrich, Wagner	16.1
13 Drew Shubik, Sacred Heart	16.1
14 Ron Manigault, Long Island	16.0
15 A.J. Jackson, Robert Morris	16.0

Steal Rate

1 Tony Lee, Robert Morris	5.34
2 Jeremy Chappell, Robert Morris	4.31
3 Drew Shubik, Sacred Heart	3.88
4 Jhamar Youngblood, Monmouth	3.47
5 Jeremy Goode, Mount St. Mary's	3.44
6 Marcus Williams, St. Francis NY	3.33
7 Chauncey Hardy, Sacred Heart	2.98
8 Whitney Coleman, Monmouth	2.96
9 Mark Porter, Wagner	2.90
10 Markus Mitchell, Mount St. Mary's	2.87
11 DeMario Anderson, Quinnipiac	2.70
12 Bateko Francisco, Robert Morris	2.63
13 Jamaal Womack, St. Francis NY	2.58
14 Ryan Litke, Sacred Heart	2.55
15 Jaytornah Wisseh, Long Island	2.54

Pct. of Possible Minutes Played

1 Manny Ubilla, Fairleigh Dickinson	95.5
2 Mark Porter, Wagner	91.0
3 Jaytornah Wisseh, Long Island	89.3
4 Tristan Blackwood, Central Conn.	88.4
5 Jamaal Womack, St. Francis NY	85.3
6 Drew Shubik, Sacred Heart	82.9
7 Whitney Coleman, Monmouth	82.0
8 Eric Hazard, Fairleigh Dickinson	82.0
9 Sean Baptiste, Fairleigh Dickinson	81.7
10 Devin Sweetney, St. Francis PA	81.7

OVC INDIVIDUAL STATISTICS

Offensive Rating

(Pct. of possessions used in parenthesis)

At least 28% of possessions used

1 Lester Hudson, UT-Martin	116.2	(32.4)
2 Bruce Price, Tennessee St.	101.0	(30.4)
3 Kenneth Faried, Morehead St.	100.8	(29.2)

At least 24% of possessions used

1 Lester Hudson, UT-Martin	116.2	(32.4)
2 Bruce Carter, Murray St.	115.3	(25.3)
3 Travis Peterson, Samford	110.7	(26.6)
4 Anthony Fisher, Tennessee Tech	104.9	(26.0)
5 Bruce Price, Tennessee St.	101.0	(30.4)
6 Kenneth Faried, Morehead St.	100.8	(29.2)
7 Gerald Robinson, UT-Martin	100.4	(25.6)
8 Mike Rose, Eastern Kentucky	99.9	(25.8)
9 Drake Reed, Austin Peay	99.1	(26.7)
10 Jerrell Houston, Tennessee St.	95.5	(25.8)
11 Romain Martin, Eastern Illinois	95.4	(26.5)
12 Roderick Pearson, SEMO	89.5	(24.6)
13 Ray George, Murray St.	87.5	(26.8)

At least 20% of possessions used

1 Lester Hudson, UT-Martin	116.2	(32.4)
2 Bruce Carter, Murray St.	115.3	(25.3)
3 Leon Buchanan, Morehead St.	114.5	(21.5)
4 Amadi McKenzie, Tennessee Tech	110.8	(22.9)
5 Derek Wright, Austin Peay	110.8	(20.1)
6 Travis Peterson, Samford	110.7	(26.6)
7 Gerald Robinson, Tennessee St.	106.7	(23.6)
8 Joe Ross Merritt, Samford	106.6	(20.3)
9 Maze Stallworth, Morehead St.	106.2	(20.8)
10 Jaycen Herring, SE Missouri St	106.0	(22.6)
11 Darnell Dialls, E. Kentucky	105.1	(23.5)
12 Anthony Fisher, Tennessee Tech	104.9	(26.0)
13 Marquis Weddle, UT-Martin	103.8	(23.3)
14 Julio Anthony, E. Illinois	103.4	(21.8)
15 Daniel Northern, Tenn. Tech	102.4	(21.5)
16 Bobby Catchings, E. Illinois	101.8	(22.1)
17 Bruce Price, Tennessee St.	101.0	(30.4)
18 Nick Murphy, Jacksonville St.	100.9	(23.9)
19 Kenneth Faried, Morehead St.	100.8	(29.2)
20 Danero Thomas, Murray St.	100.7	(23.9)

ALL PLAYERS

1 Tyler Holloway, Murray St.	128.2	(15.8)
2 Tony Easley, Murray St.	127.4	(17.1)
3 Darius Cox, Tennessee St.	124.9	(14.3)

4 Djero Riedewald, UT-Martin	120.8	(13.2)
5 LaDarious Weaver, Tennessee St	118.8	(17.0)
6 Olajide Hay, UT-Martin	116.3	(10.2)
7 Lester Hudson, UT-Martin	116.2	(32.4)
8 Bruce Carter, Murray St.	115.3	(25.3)
9 Kyle Duncan, Austin Peay	114.8	(13.9)
10 Leon Buchanan, Morehead St.	114.5	(21.5)
11 Jake Byrne, Eastern Illinois	114.4	(18.1)
12 Todd Babington, Austin Peay	113.5	(17.4)
13 Fernandez Lockett, Austin Peay	112.2	(19.0)
14 J.J. Wesley, Jacksonville St.	111.4	(19.1)
15 Kenard Moore, SE Missouri St.	111.3	(19.1)
16 Derek Wright, Austin Peay	110.8	(20.1)
17 Amadi McKenzie, Tennessee Tech	110.8	(22.9)
18 Travis Peterson, Samford	110.7	(26.6)
19 Jamaal Douglas, E. Kentucky	110.3	(16.8)
20 Adam Leonard, Eastern Kentucky	109.1	(18.5)

Turnover Rate

(Pct. of possessions used in parenthesis)

At least 28% of possessions used

1 Kenneth Faried, Morehead St.	16.6	(29.2)
2 Lester Hudson, UT-Martin	18.0	(32.4)
3 Bruce Price, Tennessee St.	21.9	(30.4)

At least 24% of possessions used

1 Bruce Carter, Murray St.	15.2	(25.3)
2 Gerald Robinson, UT-Martin	15.5	(25.6)
3 Mike Rose, Eastern Kentucky	16.0	(25.8)
4 Kenneth Faried, Morehead St.	16.6	(29.2)
5 Travis Peterson, Samford	17.5	(26.6)
6 Lester Hudson, UT-Martin	18.0	(32.4)
7 Romain Martin, Eastern Illinois	19.5	(26.5)
8 Drake Reed, Austin Peay	19.9	(26.7)
9 Anthony Fisher, Tennessee Tech	21.6	(26.0)
10 Bruce Price, Tennessee St.	21.9	(30.4)
11 Jerrell Houston, Tennessee St.	25.0	(25.8)
12 Roderick Pearson, SEMO	28.8	(24.6)
13 Ray George, Murray St.	29.9	(26.8)

At least 20% of possessions used

1 Gerald Robinson, Tennessee St.	14.0	(23.6)
2 Bruce Carter, Murray St.	15.2	(25.3)
3 Gerald Robinson, UT-Martin	15.5	(25.6)
4 Wes Channels, Austin Peay	15.7	(23.5)
5 Mike Rose, Eastern Kentucky	16.0	(25.8)
6 Daniel Northern, Tennessee Tech	16.1	(21.5)
7 Marquis Weddle, UT-Martin	16.2	(23.3)
8 Kenneth Faried, Morehead St.	16.6	(29.2)

9 Leon Buchanan, Morehead St.	17.2	(21.5)
10 Joe Ross Merritt, Samford	17.3	(20.3)
11 Travis Peterson, Samford	17.5	(26.6)
12 Maze Stallworth, Morehead St.	17.6	(20.8)
13 Nick Murphy, Jacksonville St.	17.8	(23.9)
14 Lester Hudson, UT-Martin	18.0	(32.4)
15 Bobby Catchings, E. Illinois	18.6	(22.1)
16 Derek Wright, Austin Peay	19.1	(20.1)
17 Amadi McKenzie, Tennessee Tech	19.4	(22.9)
18 Darnell Dialls, E. Kentucky	19.4	(23.5)
19 Romain Martin, Eastern Illinois	19.5	(26.5)
20 Drake Reed, Austin Peay	19.9	(26.7)

ALL PLAYERS

1 J.J. Wesley, Jacksonville St.	11.4	(19.1)
2 Fernandez Lockett, Austin Peay	12.8	(19.0)
3 Todd Babington, Austin Peay	13.0	(17.4)
4 Adam Leonard, Eastern Kentucky	13.5	(18.5)
5 Tyler Holloway, Murray St.	13.7	(15.8)
6 Kenard Moore, SE Missouri St.	13.8	(19.1)
7 Gerald Robinson, Tennessee St.	14.0	(23.6)
8 LaDarious Weaver, Tennessee St.	14.2	(17.0)
9 Jamyron Steward, Morehead St.	14.2	(19.5)
10 Darius Cox, Tennessee St.	14.3	(14.3)
11 Jake Byrne, Eastern Illinois	14.4	(18.1)
12 Bruce Carter, Murray St.	15.2	(25.3)
13 Tony Easley, Murray St.	15.3	(17.1)
14 Gerald Robinson, UT-Martin	15.5	(25.6)
15 Wes Channels, Austin Peay	15.7	(23.5)
16 Mike Rose, Eastern Kentucky	16.0	(25.8)
17 Daniel Northern, Tennessee Tech	16.1	(21.5)
18 Marquis Weddle, UT-Martin	16.2	(23.3)
19 Kenneth Faried, Morehead St.	16.6	(29.2)
20 Olajide Hay, UT-Martin	17.2	(10.2)

Usage (Pct. of Possessions Used)

1 Lester Hudson, UT-Martin	32.4
2 Bruce Price, Tennessee St.	30.4
3 Kenneth Faried, Morehead St.	29.2
4 Ray George, Murray St.	26.8
5 Drake Reed, Austin Peay	26.7
6 Travis Peterson, Samford	26.6
7 Romain Martin, Eastern Illinois	26.5
8 Anthony Fisher, Tennessee Tech	26.0
9 Mike Rose, Eastern Kentucky	25.8
10 Jerrell Houston, Tennessee St.	25.8
11 Gerald Robinson, UT-Martin	25.6
12 Bruce Carter, Murray St.	25.3
13 Roderick Pearson, SEMO	24.6
14 Nick Murphy, Jacksonville St.	23.9

15 Danero Thomas, Murray St.	23.9
16 Gerald Robinson, Tennessee St.	23.6
17 Wes Channels, Austin Peay	23.5
18 Darnell Dialls, E. Kentucky	23.5
19 Marquis Weddle, UT-Martin	23.3
20 Amadi McKenzie, Tennessee Tech	22.9
21 Calvin Williams, SE Missouri St	22.8
22 Jaycen Herring, SE Missouri St.	22.6
23 Jon'Tee Willhite, E. Illinois	22.1
24 Bobby Catchings, E. Illinois	22.1
25 Julio Anthony, Eastern Illinois	21.8

Assist Rate

1 DeAndre Bray, Jacksonville St.	39.8
2 Nikola Stojakovic, Morehead St.	39.2
3 Travis Peterson, Samford	32.1
4 Derek Wright, Austin Peay	29.9
5 Jon'Tee Willhite, E. Illinois	29.1
6 Kevin Thomas, Murray St.	28.6
7 Lester Hudson, UT-Martin	28.4
8 Bruce Price, Tennessee St.	27.9
9 Carlos Wright, UT-Martin	27.6
10 Will Barnes, Tennessee Tech	23.3
11 Ray George, Murray St.	22.6
12 Jamaal Douglas, E. Kentucky	22.6
13 Reiley Ervin, Tennessee St.	22.2
14 Anthony Fisher, Tennessee Tech	21.7
15 Jonathan Toles, Jacksonville St	20.5

Block Rate

1 Daniel Northern, Tennessee Tech	9.3
2 Amadou Mbodji, Jacksonville St.	9.0
3 Calvin Williams, SE Missouri St.	5.8
4 Travis Peterson, Samford	5.7
5 Kenneth Faried, Morehead St.	5.4
6 Darius Cox, Tennessee St.	5.2
7 Jerrell Houston, Tennessee St.	5.0
8 Tony Easley, Murray St.	4.6
9 Jamaal Douglas, Eastern Kentucky	4.1
10 Marvin Williams, Murray St.	4.1
11 Ray George, Murray St.	3.9
12 Ousmane Cisse, Eastern Illinois	3.6
13 Michael Rembert, SE Missouri St.	3.4
14 Darnell Dialls, Eastern Kentucky	2.8
15 Danero Thomas, Murray St.	2.7

Offensive Rebounding Percentage

1	Kenneth Faried, Morehead St.	20.2
2	Ousmane Cisse, Eastern Illinois	13.7
3	Tony Easley, Murray St.	12.5
4	Marvin Williams, Murray St.	12.4
5	Djero Riedewald, UT-Martin	11.8
6	Amadi McKenzie, Tennessee Tech	11.7
7	Darius Cox, Tennessee St.	11.5
8	Daniel Northern, Tennessee Tech	10.9
9	Calvin Williams, SE Missouri St.	10.6
10	Michael Rembert, SE Missouri St.	10.4
11	Amadou Mbodji, Jacksonville St.	9.8
12	Leon Buchanan, Morehead St.	9.6
13	Fernandez Lockett, Austin Peay	9.4
14	Gerald Robinson, UT-Martin	9.2
15	Jamaal Douglas, Eastern Kentucky	8.7

Steal Rate

1	Derek Wright, Austin Peay	4.63
2	Lester Hudson, UT-Martin	4.33
3	Kenneth Faried, Morehead St.	3.74
4	Bruce Price, Tennessee St.	3.68
5	DeAndre Bray, Jacksonville St.	3.60
6	Trey Montgomery, Samford	3.57
7	Wes Channels, Austin Peay	3.37
8	Reiley Ervin, Tennessee St.	3.35
9	Nick Murphy, Jacksonville St.	3.32
10	Jerrell Houston, Tennessee St.	3.20
11	Mike Rose, Eastern Kentucky	3.17
12	Gerald Robinson, Tennessee St.	3.17
13	Danero Thomas, Murray St.	3.10
14	Rashaud Nixon, Tennessee Tech	3.00
15	Will Barnes, Tennessee Tech	2.85

Defensive Rebounding Percentage

1	Kenneth Faried, Morehead St.	31.0
2	Daniel Northern, Tennessee Tech	23.1
3	Gerald Robinson, UT-Martin	21.7
4	Marvin Williams, Murray St.	20.5
5	Calvin Williams, SE Missouri St.	20.2
6	Darnell Dialls, Eastern Kentucky	19.7
7	Amadi McKenzie, Tennessee Tech	19.6
8	Amadou Mbodji, Jacksonville St.	19.4
9	Ousmane Cisse, Eastern Illinois	19.0
10	Jerrell Houston, Tennessee St.	18.5
11	Fernandez Lockett, Austin Peay	17.3
12	Lester Hudson, UT-Martin	17.0
13	Bruce Carter, Murray St.	16.8
14	Michael Rembert, SE Missouri St.	16.5
15	Leon Buchanan, Morehead St.	16.2

Pct. of Possible Minutes Played

1	Lester Hudson, UT-Martin	91.0
2	Mike Rose, Eastern Kentucky	90.1
3	Adam Leonard, Eastern Kentucky	87.0
4	Marquis Weddle, UT-Martin	85.8
5	Joe Ross Merritt, Samford	85.6
6	Bruce Price, Tennessee St.	85.1
7	Nikola Stojakovic, Morehead St.	84.1
8	Anthony Fisher, Tennessee Tech	82.7
9	Jamyron Steward, Morehead St.	82.2
10	Trey Montgomery, Samford	81.0

PAC 10 INDIVIDUAL STATISTICS

Offensive Rating

(Pct. of possessions used in parenthesis)

At least 28% of possessions used

1 Ryan Anderson, Cal	121.1	(28.4)
2 James Harden, Arizona St.	115.7	(28.3)
3 Jerryd Bayless, Arizona	112.5	(28.8)
4 Brook Lopez, Stanford	109.9	(32.3)
5 Jon Brockman, Washington	107.3	(28.2)
6 O.J. Mayo, USC	105.2	(30.8)

At least 24% of possessions used

1 Kevin Love, UCLA	126.6	(27.7)
2 Ryan Anderson, Cal	121.1	(28.4)
3 James Harden, Arizona St.	115.7	(28.3)
4 Jerryd Bayless, Arizona	112.5	(28.8)
5 Aron Baynes, Washington St.	110.1	(24.2)
6 Brook Lopez, Stanford	109.9	(32.3)
7 Jon Brockman, Washington	107.3	(28.2)
8 Chase Budinger, Arizona	105.6	(26.5)
9 O.J. Mayo, USC	105.2	(30.8)
10 Kyle Weaver, Washington St.	104.8	(26.0)
11 Marcel Jones, Oregon St.	89.7	(24.7)

At least 20% of possessions used

1 Kevin Love, UCLA	126.6	(27.7)
2 Ryan Anderson, Cal	121.1	(28.4)
3 Malik Hairston, Oregon	120.6	(23.5)
4 Darren Collison, UCLA	118.6	(20.8)
5 James Harden, Arizona St.	115.7	(28.3)
6 Jeff Pendergraph, Arizona St.	113.7	(23.3)
7 Jerryd Bayless, Arizona	112.5	(28.8)
8 Jordan Hill, Arizona	111.0	(22.8)
9 Derrick Low, Washington St.	110.7	(22.0)
10 Aron Baynes, Washington St.	110.1	(24.2)
11 Brook Lopez, Stanford	109.9	(32.3)
12 Russell Westbrook, UCLA	109.6	(22.7)
13 Patrick Christopher, Cal	108.0	(21.4)
14 Jon Brockman, Washington	107.3	(28.2)
15 Joevan Catron, Oregon	107.2	(21.1)
16 Justin Dentmon, Washington	106.6	(21.2)
17 Lawrence Hill, Stanford	106.6	(21.1)
18 Quincy Pondexter, Washington	106.2	(22.4)
19 Robin Lopez, Stanford	106.1	(22.8)
20 Chase Budinger, Arizona	105.6	(26.5)

ALL PLAYERS

1 Maarty Leunen, Oregon	134.4	(19.1)
2 Kevin Love, UCLA	126.6	(27.7)

3 Taj Finger, Stanford	122.9	(16.5)
4 Ryan Anderson, Cal	121.1	(28.4)
5 Malik Hairston, Oregon	120.6	(23.5)
6 Taylor Rochestie, Wash. St.	119.2	(18.7)
7 Darren Collison, UCLA	118.6	(20.8)
8 Ryan Appleby, Washington	116.9	(16.6)
9 James Harden, Arizona St.	115.7	(28.3)
10 Robbie Cowgill, Washington St.	114.1	(15.3)
11 Jeff Pendergraph, Arizona St.	113.7	(23.3)
12 Jerryd Bayless, Arizona	112.5	(28.8)
13 Bryce Taylor, Oregon	112.1	(18.8)
14 Daven Harmeling, Washington St	111.0	(14.3)
15 Jordan Hill, Arizona	111.0	(22.8)
16 Derrick Low, Washington St.	110.7	(22.0)
17 Nic Wise, Arizona	110.7	(19.3)
18 Josh Shipp, UCLA	110.2	(18.9)
19 Aron Baynes, Washington St.	110.1	(24.2)
20 Brook Lopez, Stanford	109.9	(32.3)

Turnover Rate

(Pct. of possessions used in parenthesis)

At least 28% of possessions used

1 Brook Lopez, Stanford	13.4	(32.3)
2 Ryan Anderson, Cal	14.0	(28.4)
3 Jon Brockman, Washington	15.3	(28.2)
4 Jerryd Bayless, Arizona	17.6	(28.8)
5 James Harden, Arizona St.	17.7	(28.3)
6 O.J. Mayo, USC	18.8	(30.8)

At least 24% of possessions used

1 Marcel Jones, Oregon St.	12.7	(24.7)
2 Brook Lopez, Stanford	13.4	(32.3)
3 Ryan Anderson, Cal	14.0	(28.4)
4 Kevin Love, UCLA	14.9	(27.7)
5 Jon Brockman, Washington	15.3	(28.2)
6 Chase Budinger, Arizona	15.4	(26.5)
7 Aron Baynes, Washington St.	17.4	(24.2)
8 Jerryd Bayless, Arizona	17.6	(28.8)
9 James Harden, Arizona St.	17.7	(28.3)
10 O.J. Mayo, USC	18.8	(30.8)
11 Kyle Weaver, Washington St.	21.5	(26.0)

At least 20% of possessions used

1 Derrick Low, Washington St.	11.2	(22.0)
2 Marcel Jones, Oregon St.	12.7	(24.7)
3 Brook Lopez, Stanford	13.4	(32.3)
4 Ryan Anderson, Cal	14.0	(28.4)
5 Malik Hairston, Oregon	14.1	(23.5)
6 Kevin Love, UCLA	14.9	(27.7)

7 Lawrence Hill, Stanford	15.0	(21.1)
8 Patrick Christopher, Cal	15.1	(21.4)
9 Jon Brockman, Washington	15.3	(28.2)
10 Seth Tarver, Oregon St.	15.3	(20.1)
11 Chase Budinger, Arizona	15.4	(26.5)
12 Aron Baynes, Washington St.	17.4	(24.2)
13 Jerryd Bayless, Arizona	17.6	(28.8)
14 James Harden, Arizona St.	17.7	(28.3)
15 Justin Dentmon, Washington	17.9	(21.2)
16 Tajuan Porter, Oregon	17.9	(23.9)
17 Quincy Pondexter, Washington	18.7	(22.4)
18 O.J. Mayo, USC	18.8	(30.8)
19 Darren Collison, UCLA	19.1	(20.8)
20 Jordan Hill, Arizona	19.3	(22.8)

ALL PLAYERS

1 Derrick Low, Washington St.	11.2	(22.0)
2 Robbie Cowgill, Washington St.	11.5	(15.3)
3 Daven Harmeling, Washington St.	11.8	(14.3)
4 Marcel Jones, Oregon St.	12.7	(24.7)
5 Brook Lopez, Stanford	13.4	(32.3)
6 Maarty Leunen, Oregon	13.9	(19.1)
7 Ryan Anderson, Cal	14.0	(28.4)
8 Malik Hairston, Oregon	14.1	(23.5)
9 Taj Finger, Stanford	14.2	(16.5)
10 Ryan Appleby, Washington	14.6	(16.6)
11 Kevin Love, UCLA	14.9	(27.7)
12 Jerren Shipp, Arizona St.	15.0	(13.7)
13 Lawrence Hill, Stanford	15.0	(21.1)
14 Ty Abbott, Arizona St.	15.0	(17.3)
15 Patrick Christopher, Cal	15.1	(21.4)
16 Bryce Taylor, Oregon	15.2	(18.8)
17 Seth Tarver, Oregon St.	15.3	(20.1)
18 Jon Brockman, Washington	15.3	(28.2)
19 Roeland Schaftenaar, Oregon St.	15.3	(14.6)
20 Chase Budinger, Arizona	15.4	(26.5)

Usage (Pct. of Possessions Used)

1 Brook Lopez, Stanford	32.3
2 O.J. Mayo, USC	30.8
3 Jerryd Bayless, Arizona	28.8
4 Ryan Anderson, Cal	28.4
5 James Harden, Arizona St.	28.3
6 Jon Brockman, Washington	28.2
7 Kevin Love, UCLA	27.7
8 Chase Budinger, Arizona	26.5
9 Kyle Weaver, Washington St.	26.0
10 Marcel Jones, Oregon St.	24.7
11 Aron Baynes, Washington St.	24.2
12 Tajuan Porter, Oregon	23.9

13 Calvin Haynes, Oregon St.	23.7
14 Malik Hairston, Oregon	23.5
15 Davon Jefferson, USC	23.4
16 Jeff Pendergraph, Arizona St.	23.3
17 Jordan Hill, Arizona	22.8
18 Robin Lopez, Stanford	22.8
19 Russell Westbrook, UCLA	22.7
20 Quincy Pondexter, Washington	22.4
21 Derrick Low, Washington St.	22.0
22 Josh Tarver, Oregon St.	21.6
23 Kamyron Brown, Oregon	21.5
24 Patrick Christopher, Cal	21.4
25 Justin Dentmon, Washington	21.2

Assist Rate

1 Mitch Johnson, Stanford	30.3
2 Derek Glasser, Arizona St.	30.1
3 Kamyron Brown, Oregon	29.6
4 Nic Wise, Arizona	29.2
5 Kyle Weaver, Washington St.	28.5
6 Taylor Rochestie, Washington St	28.2
7 Venoy Overton, Washington	25.6
8 Jerryd Bayless, Arizona	25.0
9 James Harden, Arizona St.	24.7
10 Russell Westbrook, UCLA	24.4
11 Josh Tarver, Oregon St.	21.9
12 Jerome Randle, Cal	21.5
13 O.J. Mayo, USC	21.4
14 Darren Collison, UCLA	21.0
15 Rickey Claitt, Oregon St.	19.8

Block Rate

1 Robin Lopez, Stanford	9.5
2 Taj Gibson, USC	8.4
3 Jeff Pendergraph, Arizona St.	7.9
4 Brook Lopez, Stanford	6.8
5 DeVon Hardin, Cal	5.9
6 Jordan Hill, Arizona	5.6
7 Kevin Love, UCLA	5.0
8 Aron Baynes, Washington St.	3.7
9 Davon Jefferson, USC	3.7
10 Robbie Cowgill, Washington St.	3.6
11 Malik Hairston, Oregon	2.9
12 Roeland Schaftenaar, Oregon St.	2.8
13 Kyle Weaver, Washington St.	2.6
14 James Harden, Arizona St.	2.3
15 Joevan Catron, Oregon	1.9

Offensive Rebounding Percentage

1 Kevin Love, UCLA	15.4
2 Jon Brockman, Washington	15.0
3 Taj Finger, Stanford	14.8
4 Robin Lopez, Stanford	12.4
5 Ryan Anderson, Cal	11.6
6 Jordan Hill, Arizona	11.4
7 Brook Lopez, Stanford	10.9
8 Jeff Pendergraph, Arizona St.	10.9
9 Aron Baynes, Washington St.	10.8
10 Taj Gibson, USC	10.2
11 Davon Jefferson, USC	9.9
12 Joevan Catron, Oregon	9.9
13 Roeland Schaftenaar, Oregon St.	9.8
14 Luc Richard Mbah a Moute, UCLA	9.5
15 Quincy Pondexter, Washington	9.5

Steal Rate

1 Nic Wise, Arizona	4.17
2 James Harden, Arizona St.	4.11
3 Venoy Overton, Washington	3.81
4 Kyle Weaver, Washington St.	3.46
5 Darren Collison, UCLA	3.27
6 Josh Tarver, Oregon St.	2.95
7 Russell Westbrook, UCLA	2.93
8 Derrick Low, Washington St.	2.87
9 Justin Dentmon, Washington	2.58
10 O.J. Mayo, USC	2.53
11 Josh Shipp, UCLA	2.51
12 Kamyron Brown, Oregon	2.39
13 Daniel Hackett, USC	2.30
14 Ty Abbott, Arizona St.	2.29
15 Tim Morris, Washington	2.22

Defensive Rebounding Percentage

1 Kevin Love, UCLA	28.5
2 Jon Brockman, Washington	28.1
3 DeVon Hardin, Cal	26.1
4 Ryan Anderson, Cal	23.5
5 Maarty Leunen, Oregon	23.4
6 Aron Baynes, Washington St.	22.5
7 Jordan Hill, Arizona	22.3
8 Brook Lopez, Stanford	19.3
9 Jeff Pendergraph, Arizona St.	18.6
10 Taj Gibson, USC	18.5
11 Marcel Jones, Oregon St.	17.2
12 Joevan Catron, Oregon	16.8
13 Davon Jefferson, USC	16.7
14 Kyle Weaver, Washington St.	16.4
15 Luc Richard Mbah a Moute, UCLA	15.7

Pct. of Possible Minutes Played

1 O.J. Mayo, USC	91.1
2 Chase Budinger, Arizona	87.3
3 Patrick Christopher, Cal	87.0
4 Jawann McClellan, Arizona	86.8
5 Taylor Rochestie, Washington St.	86.4
6 Maarty Leunen, Oregon	85.7
7 Russell Westbrook, UCLA	84.2
8 James Harden, Arizona St.	83.6
9 Derrick Low, Washington St.	82.3
10 Kyle Weaver, Washington St.	81.9
11 Josh Shipp, UCLA	81.1
12 Ryan Anderson, Cal	81.0
13 Dwight Lewis, USC	80.7
14 Ty Abbott, Arizona St.	80.3
15 Tajuan Porter, Oregon	80.0

PATRIOT LEAGUE
INDIVIDUAL STATISTICS

Offensive Rating

(Pct. of possessions used in parenthesis)

At least 28% of possessions used

1 Greg Sprink, Navy	101.7	(31.5)
2 Marquis Hall, Lehigh	100.7	(28.3)

At least 24% of possessions used

1 Tim Clifford, Holy Cross	114.9	(27.3)
2 Garrison Carr, American	114.5	(25.0)
3 Andrew Brown, Lafayette	109.4	(26.4)
4 Jarell Brown, Army	106.0	(24.7)
5 Kyle Roemer, Colgate	104.3	(25.7)
6 Greg Sprink, Navy	101.7	(31.5)
7 Marquis Hall, Lehigh	100.7	(28.3)
8 Zahir Carrington, Lehigh	98.8	(27.9)
9 Kaleo Kina, Navy	90.7	(27.0)

At least 20% of possessions used

1 Brian Gilmore, American	117.2	(22.1)
2 Tim Clifford, Holy Cross	114.9	(27.3)
3 Garrison Carr, American	114.5	(25.0)
4 Kendall Chones, Colgate	112.9	(21.6)
5 Bilal Abdullah, Lafayette	110.2	(23.8)
6 Andrew Brown, Lafayette	109.4	(26.4)
7 Matt Betley, Lafayette	108.3	(20.5)
8 Chris Harris, Navy	108.3	(21.4)
9 Jarell Brown, Army	106.0	(24.7)
10 Kyle Roemer, Colgate	104.3	(25.7)
11 Bryan White, Lehigh	103.3	(20.4)
12 Greg Sprink, Navy	101.7	(31.5)
13 John Griffin, Bucknell	101.3	(23.9)
14 Marquis Hall, Lehigh	100.7	(28.3)
15 Justin Castleberry, Bucknell	99.4	(23.4)
16 Zahir Carrington, Lehigh	98.8	(27.9)
17 Derrick Mercer, American	97.8	(23.1)
18 Pat Doherty, Holy Cross	93.2	(21.2)
19 Kaleo Kina, Navy	90.7	(27.0)
20 Everest Schmidt, Lafayette	90.3	(20.6)

ALL PLAYERS

1 Brian Gilmore, American	117.2	(22.1)
2 Jordan Nichols, American	115.7	(13.3)
3 Tim Clifford, Holy Cross	114.9	(27.3)
4 Garrison Carr, American	114.5	(25.0)
5 Kendall Chones, Colgate	112.9	(21.6)
6 Bilal Abdullah, Lafayette	110.2	(23.8)
7 Alex Vander Baan, Holy Cross	109.7	(17.6)
8 Andrew Brown, Lafayette	109.4	(26.4)
9 Chris Harris, Navy	108.3	(21.4)
10 Matt Betley, Lafayette	108.3	(20.5)
11 Adam Teague, Navy	107.5	(14.2)
12 Mike Gruner, Lafayette	107.0	(14.6)
13 Jarell Brown, Army	106.0	(24.7)
14 Doug Williams, Army	105.1	(16.1)
15 Romeo Garcia, Navy	104.9	(11.7)
16 Kyle Roemer, Colgate	104.3	(25.7)
17 Stephen Tyree, Bucknell	103.4	(17.0)
18 Bryan White, Lehigh	103.3	(20.4)
19 Dave Buchberger, Lehigh	103.2	(13.1)
20 Greg Sprink, Navy	101.7	(31.5)

Turnover Rate

(Pct. of possessions used in parenthesis)

At least 28% of possessions used

1 Greg Sprink, Navy	16.8	(31.5)
2 Marquis Hall, Lehigh	16.9	(28.3)

At least 24% of possessions used

1 Jarell Brown, Army	11.6	(24.7)
2 Garrison Carr, American	15.9	(25.0)
3 Greg Sprink, Navy	16.8	(31.5)
4 Marquis Hall, Lehigh	16.9	(28.3)
5 Kyle Roemer, Colgate	17.5	(25.7)
6 Tim Clifford, Holy Cross	18.8	(27.3)
7 Andrew Brown, Lafayette	20.5	(26.4)
8 Zahir Carrington, Lehigh	21.0	(27.9)
9 Kaleo Kina, Navy	23.9	(27.0)

At least 20% of possessions used

1 Jarell Brown, Army	11.6	(24.7)
2 Bryan White, Lehigh	13.9	(20.4)
3 Garrison Carr, American	15.9	(25.0)
4 Kendall Chones, Colgate	16.6	(21.6)
5 Greg Sprink, Navy	16.8	(31.5)
6 Marquis Hall, Lehigh	16.9	(28.3)
7 Kyle Roemer, Colgate	17.5	(25.7)
8 Brian Gilmore, American	17.9	(22.1)
9 Tim Clifford, Holy Cross	18.8	(27.3)
10 Justin Castleberry, Bucknell	18.8	(23.4)
11 Andrew Brown, Lafayette	20.5	(26.4)
12 Zahir Carrington, Lehigh	21.0	(27.9)
13 Matt Betley, Lafayette	21.2	(20.5)
14 John Griffin, Bucknell	21.6	(23.9)
15 Derrick Mercer, American	21.7	(23.1)
16 Josh Miller, Army	22.0	(22.8)
17 Chris Harris, Navy	22.6	(21.4)

18 Bilal Abdullah, Lafayette	23.1	(23.8)
19 Kaleo Kina, Navy	23.9	(27.0)
20 Patrick Behan, Bucknell	24.7	(22.8)

ALL PLAYERS

1 Jarell Brown, Army	11.6	(24.7)
2 Doug Williams, Army	13.5	(16.1)
3 Bryan White, Lehigh	13.9	(20.4)
4 Garrison Carr, American	15.9	(25.0)
5 Kendall Chones, Colgate	16.6	(21.6)
6 Greg Sprink, Navy	16.8	(31.5)
7 Mike Venezia, Colgate	16.9	(17.1)
8 Marquis Hall, Lehigh	16.9	(28.3)
9 Kyle Roemer, Colgate	17.5	(25.7)
10 Dave Buchberger, Lehigh	17.9	(13.1)
11 Brian Gilmore, American	17.9	(22.1)
12 Matt Szalachowski, Lehigh	18.7	(11.1)
13 Justin Castleberry, Bucknell	18.8	(23.4)
14 Tim Clifford, Holy Cross	18.8	(27.3)
15 Alex Vander Baan, Holy Cross	19.2	(17.6)
16 Romeo Garcia, Navy	19.4	(11.7)
17 Travis Lay, American	19.6	(19.2)
18 Mark Veazey, Navy	19.7	(13.2)
19 Mike Gruner, Lafayette	20.3	(14.6)
20 Andrew Brown, Lafayette	20.5	(26.4)

Usage (Pct. of Possessions Used)

1 Greg Sprink, Navy	31.5
2 Marquis Hall, Lehigh	28.3
3 Zahir Carrington, Lehigh	27.9
4 Tim Clifford, Holy Cross	27.3
5 Kaleo Kina, Navy	27.0
6 Andrew Brown, Lafayette	26.4
7 Kyle Roemer, Colgate	25.7
8 Garrison Carr, American	25.0
9 Jarell Brown, Army	24.7
10 John Griffin, Bucknell	23.9
11 Bilal Abdullah, Lafayette	23.8
12 Justin Castleberry, Bucknell	23.4
13 Derrick Mercer, American	23.1
14 Patrick Behan, Bucknell	22.8
15 Josh Miller, Army	22.8
16 Daniel Waddy, Colgate	22.4
17 Brian Gilmore, American	22.1
18 Kendall Chones, Colgate	21.6
19 Chris Harris, Navy	21.4
20 Pat Doherty, Holy Cross	21.2
21 Ted Detmer, Lafayette	20.7
22 Everest Schmidt, Lafayette	20.6
23 Matt Betley, Lafayette	20.5

24 Bryan White, Lehigh	20.4
25 Rob Keefer, Lehigh	19.3

Assist Rate

1 Marquis Hall, Lehigh	34.8
2 Pat Doherty, Holy Cross	33.0
3 Josh Miller, Army	30.6
4 Derrick Mercer, American	25.4
5 Kaleo Kina, Navy	24.7
6 Andrew Brown, Lafayette	24.3
7 Chris Harris, Navy	23.7
8 Stephen Tyree, Bucknell	23.2
9 Marcus Nelson, Army	21.6
10 John Griffin, Bucknell	20.7
11 Daniel Waddy, Colgate	20.6
12 Brian Gilmore, American	19.4
13 Darryl Shazier, Bucknell	19.3
14 Greg Sprink, Navy	18.9
15 Justin Castleberry, Bucknell	17.8

Block Rate

1 Tim Clifford, Holy Cross	9.8
2 Alex Woodhouse, Colgate	9.7
3 Mark Veazey, Navy	7.6
4 Jordan Nichols, American	6.4
5 Ted Detmer, Lafayette	4.8
6 Zahir Carrington, Lehigh	4.6
7 Bryan White, Lehigh	3.9
8 Everest Schmidt, Lafayette	3.4
9 Romeo Garcia, Navy	2.9
10 Doug Williams, Army	2.5
11 Cleveland Richard, Army	2.3
12 Bilal Abdullah, Lafayette	1.9
13 Marcus Nelson, Army	1.8
14 Alex Vander Baan, Holy Cross	1.5
15 Daniel Waddy, Colgate	1.5

Offensive Rebounding Percentage

1 Everest Schmidt, Lafayette	12.7
2 Tim Clifford, Holy Cross	12.2
3 Jordan Nichols, American	10.3
4 Alex Woodhouse, Colgate	10.0
5 Travis Lay, American	9.9
6 Doug Williams, Army	9.9
7 Kendall Chones, Colgate	9.8
8 Alex Vander Baan, Holy Cross	9.3

9 Mark Veazey, Navy	8.8
10 Matt Betley, Lafayette	8.4
11 Ted Detmer, Lafayette	8.2
12 Zahir Carrington, Lehigh	7.8
13 Bryan White, Lehigh	7.7
14 Dave Buchberger, Lehigh	7.6
15 Brian Gilmore, American	7.2

Defensive Rebounding Percentage

1 Bryan White, Lehigh	25.1
2 Alex Woodhouse, Colgate	21.0
3 Doug Williams, Army	17.4
4 Mark Veazey, Navy	17.3
5 Alex Vander Baan, Holy Cross	16.7
6 Matt Betley, Lafayette	15.9
7 Greg Sprink, Navy	15.6
8 Ted Detmer, Lafayette	15.5
9 Adam Teague, Navy	15.5
10 Bryce Simon, American	15.2
11 Jordan Nichols, American	15.1
12 Patrick Behan, Bucknell	14.9
13 Travis Lay, American	14.9
14 Stephen Tyree, Bucknell	14.9
15 Brian Gilmore, American	14.9

Steal Rate

1 Ted Detmer, Lafayette	4.41
2 Josh Miller, Army	3.84
3 Pat Doherty, Holy Cross	3.82
4 Kyle Cruze, Holy Cross	3.77
5 Marcus Nelson, Army	3.22
6 Chris Harris, Navy	3.18
7 Kaleo Kina, Navy	3.11
8 Bryan White, Lehigh	3.11
9 Cleveland Richard, Army	3.04
10 John Griffin, Bucknell	2.93
11 Marquis Hall, Lehigh	2.91
12 Darryl Shazier, Bucknell	2.85
13 Everest Schmidt, Lafayette	2.79
14 Jarell Brown, Army	2.70
15 Daniel Waddy, Colgate	2.66

Pct. of Possible Minutes Played

1 Derrick Mercer, American	94.7
2 Jarell Brown, Army	90.2
3 Garrison Carr, American	89.9
4 Greg Sprink, Navy	84.9
5 Kyle Roemer, Colgate	81.8
6 Chris Harris, Navy	79.4
7 Tim Clifford, Holy Cross	79.3
8 John Griffin, Bucknell	78.8
9 Colin Cunningham, Holy Cross	76.8
10 Marquis Hall, Lehigh	76.4

SUN BELT
INDIVIDUAL STATISTICS

Offensive Rating

(Pct. of possessions used in parenthesis)

At least 28% of possessions used

1	Bo McCalebb, New Orleans	117.0	(32.5)
2	Courtney Lee, Western Kentucky	116.9	(30.5)
3	O'Darien Bassett, Troy	106.7	(28.3)
4	Carlos Monroe, Fla. Atlantic	98.8	(28.6)
5	Paul Graham, Fla. Atlantic	98.5	(31.2)
6	Tony Hooper, UL-Monroe	95.2	(30.7)
7	Elijah Millsap, UL-Lafayette	84.1	(31.5)

At least 24% of possessions used

1	Demetric Bennett, S. Alabama	120.3	(24.9)
2	Bo McCalebb, New Orleans	117.0	(32.5)
3	Courtney Lee, Western Kentucky	116.9	(30.5)
4	Adrian Banks, Arkansas St.	113.3	(27.8)
5	Collin Dennis, North Texas	109.4	(27.3)
6	Tyrone Brazelton, W. Kentucky	108.4	(27.9)
7	O'Darien Bassett, Troy	106.7	(28.3)
8	Jordan Payne, UL-Monroe	104.2	(26.0)
9	Russell Hicks, Fla. Int'l	103.5	(25.8)
10	Rob Lewis, Denver	101.9	(25.3)
11	Carlos Monroe, Fla. Atlantic	98.8	(28.6)
12	Paul Graham, Fla. Atlantic	98.5	(31.2)
13	David Dees, UL-Lafayette	95.6	(27.6)
14	Tony Hooper, UL-Monroe	95.2	(30.7)
15	Elijah Millsap, UL-Lafayette	84.1	(31.5)

At least 20% of possessions used

1	Demetric Bennett, S. Alabama	120.3	(24.9)
2	Desmond Yates, Middle Tenn.	119.6	(22.6)
3	Bo McCalebb, New Orleans	117.0	(32.5)
4	Courtney Lee, Western Kentucky	116.9	(30.5)
5	Brandon Davis, South Alabama	115.2	(21.5)
6	Ryan Wedel, Arkansas St.	114.3	(21.7)
7	Adrian Banks, Arkansas St.	113.3	(27.8)
8	Domonic Tilford, South Alabama	111.9	(20.7)
9	Collin Dennis, North Texas	109.4	(27.3)
10	Justin Jonus, Troy	109.1	(21.6)
11	Daon Merritt, South Alabama	109.1	(21.8)
12	Tyrone Brazelton, W. Kentucky	108.4	(27.9)
13	Kyndall Dykes, New Orleans	107.2	(22.6)
14	O'Darien Bassett, Troy	106.7	(28.3)
15	Randell Daigle, UL-Lafayette	106.2	(20.1)
16	Chris Gradnigo, UL-Lafayette	105.9	(22.7)
17	Jonas Brown, UL-Monroe	105.7	(21.7)
18	Quincy Williams, North Texas	104.9	(20.7)
19	Shawn Morgan, Arkansas St.	104.6	(21.5)
20	Keith Wooden, North Texas	104.6	(23.7)

ALL PLAYERS

1	Demetric Bennett, S. Alabama	120.3	(24.9)
2	Desmond Yates, Middle Tenn.	119.6	(22.6)
3	Ty Rogers, Western Kentucky	118.8	(13.4)
4	Jeremy Evans, Western Kentucky	118.6	(13.7)
5	Jerome Odem, Troy	118.2	(16.9)
6	Bo McCalebb, New Orleans	117.0	(32.5)
7	Courtney Lee, Western Kentucky	116.9	(30.5)
8	Josh White, North Texas	116.7	(19.3)
9	Brandon Davis, South Alabama	115.2	(21.5)
10	Ryan Wedel, Arkansas St.	114.3	(21.7)
11	Adrian Banks, Arkansas St.	113.3	(27.8)
12	Domonic Tilford, South Alabama	111.9	(20.7)
13	Jeff Parmer, Fla. Atlantic	111.4	(19.9)
14	Michael Vogler, Troy	111.0	(18.2)
15	Sean Alarcon, Fla. Atlantic	110.0	(11.1)
16	Carderro Nwoji, Fla. Atlantic	109.8	(17.1)
17	Collin Dennis, North Texas	109.4	(27.3)
18	Ronald Douglas, South Alabama	109.2	(17.5)
19	Daon Merritt, South Alabama	109.1	(21.8)
20	Justin Jonus, Troy	109.1	(21.6)

Turnover Rate

(Pct. of possessions used in parenthesis)

At least 28% of possessions used

1	Bo McCalebb, New Orleans	12.3	(32.5)
2	O'Darien Bassett, Troy	12.9	(28.3)
3	Courtney Lee, Western Kentucky	14.6	(30.5)
4	Carlos Monroe, Fla. Atlantic	16.2	(28.6)
5	Paul Graham, Fla. Atlantic	20.9	(31.2)
6	Tony Hooper, UL-Monroe	23.7	(30.7)
7	Elijah Millsap, UL-Lafayette	23.9	(31.5)

At least 24% of possessions used

1	Bo McCalebb, New Orleans	12.3	(32.5)
2	O'Darien Bassett, Troy	12.9	(28.3)
3	Courtney Lee, Western Kentucky	14.6	(30.5)
4	Russell Hicks, Fla. Int'l	16.1	(25.8)
5	Carlos Monroe, Fla. Atlantic	16.2	(28.6)
6	Demetric Bennett, South Alabama	16.9	(24.9)
7	Adrian Banks, Arkansas St.	17.4	(27.8)
8	Collin Dennis, North Texas	17.9	(27.3)
9	Jordan Payne, UL-Monroe	19.6	(26.0)
10	Paul Graham, Fla. Atlantic	20.9	(31.2)
11	Tyrone Brazelton, W. Kentucky	21.0	(27.9)
12	David Dees, UL-Lafayette	21.1	(27.6)

13 Rob Lewis, Denver	23.3	(25.3)
14 Tony Hooper, UL-Monroe	23.7	(30.7)
15 Elijah Millsap, UL-Lafayette	23.9	(31.5)

At least 20% of possessions used

1 Kyndall Dykes, New Orleans	12.0	(22.6)
2 Bo McCalebb, New Orleans	12.3	(32.5)
3 O'Darien Bassett, Troy	12.9	(28.3)
4 Desmond Yates, Middle Tennessee	13.2	(22.6)
5 Chris Gradnigo, UL-Lafayette	14.0	(22.7)
6 Domonic Tilford, South Alabama	14.4	(20.7)
7 Courtney Lee, Western Kentucky	14.6	(30.5)
8 Justin Jonus, Troy	14.9	(21.6)
9 Ryan Wedel, Arkansas St.	15.3	(21.7)
10 Russell Hicks, Fla. Int'l	16.1	(25.8)
11 Carlos Monroe, Fla. Atlantic	16.2	(28.6)
12 Demetric Bennett, South Alabama	16.9	(24.9)
13 Yima Chia-Kur, Arkansas St.	17.4	(23.4)
14 Adrian Banks, Arkansas St.	17.4	(27.8)
15 Collin Dennis, North Texas	17.9	(27.3)
16 Quincy Williams, North Texas	19.0	(20.7)
17 Kechan Myers, New Orleans	19.5	(21.9)
18 Jordan Payne, UL-Monroe	19.6	(26.0)
19 Joe Jackson, Denver	19.7	(20.5)
20 Demetrius Green, Middle Tenn.	19.8	(23.2)

ALL PLAYERS

1 Kyndall Dykes, New Orleans	12.0	(22.6)
2 Bo McCalebb, New Orleans	12.3	(32.5)
3 Jarvis Acker, Troy	12.6	(14.9)
4 O'Darien Bassett, Troy	12.9	(28.3)
5 Desmond Yates, Middle Tennessee	13.2	(22.6)
6 Chris Gradnigo, UL-Lafayette	14.0	(22.7)
7 Ty Rogers, Western Kentucky	14.3	(13.4)
8 Domonic Tilford, South Alabama	14.4	(20.7)
9 Courtney Lee, Western Kentucky	14.6	(30.5)
10 Lance Brasher, UL-Monroe	14.9	(14.6)
11 Justin Jonus, Troy	14.9	(21.6)
12 Ryan Wedel, Arkansas St.	15.3	(21.7)
13 James Parlow, New Orleans	15.9	(18.2)
14 Russell Hicks, Fla. Int'l	16.1	(25.8)
15 Carlos Monroe, Fla. Atlantic	16.2	(28.6)
16 Demetric Bennett, South Alabama	16.9	(24.9)
17 Adrian Banks, Arkansas St.	17.4	(27.8)
18 Yima Chia-Kur, Arkansas St.	17.4	(23.4)
19 Jerome Odem, Troy	17.7	(16.9)
20 Collin Dennis, North Texas	17.9	(27.3)

Usage (Pct. of Possessions Used)

1 Bo McCalebb, New Orleans	32.5
2 Elijah Millsap, UL-Lafayette	31.5
3 Paul Graham, Fla. Atlantic	31.2
4 Tony Hooper, UL-Monroe	30.7
5 Courtney Lee, Western Kentucky	30.5
6 Carlos Monroe, Fla. Atlantic	28.6
7 O'Darien Bassett, Troy	28.3
8 Tyrone Brazelton, W. Kentucky	27.9
9 Adrian Banks, Arkansas St.	27.8
10 David Dees, UL-Lafayette	27.6
11 Collin Dennis, North Texas	27.3
12 Jordan Payne, UL-Monroe	26.0
13 Russell Hicks, Fla. Int'l	25.8
14 Rob Lewis, Denver	25.3
15 Demetric Bennett, South Alabama	24.9
16 Keith Wooden, North Texas	23.7
17 Steven Moore, UALR	23.4
18 Yima Chia-Kur, Arkansas St.	23.4
19 Demetrius Green, Middle Tenn.	23.2
20 Chris Gradnigo, UL-Lafayette	22.7
21 Alex Galindo, Fla. Int'l	22.7
22 Desmond Yates, Middle Tennessee	22.6
23 Kyndall Dykes, New Orleans	22.6
24 De'Andre Eggins, UALR	22.2
25 Tremayne Russell, Fla. Int'l	22.2

Assist Rate

1 Michael Vogler, Troy	32.6
2 Steven Moore, UALR	32.3
3 Daon Merritt, South Alabama	32.3
4 Tyrone Brazelton, W. Kentucky	26.7
5 Randell Daigle, UL-Lafayette	23.7
6 Carderro Nwoji, Fla. Atlantic	22.9
7 Bo McCalebb, New Orleans	22.8
8 Adam Tanner, Denver	22.7
9 Nigel Johnson, Middle Tennessee	22.6
10 Tony Hooper, UL-Monroe	21.9
11 Ifeanyi Koggu, Arkansas St.	21.8
12 Terrance Akins, UALR	20.9
13 Xander McNally, Denver	20.3
14 Tremayne Russell, Fla. Int'l	20.3
15 Jerome Odem, Troy	20.2

Block Rate

1	Russell Hicks, Fla. International	9.3
2	Jeremy Evans, Western Kentucky	8.2
3	Jarvis Acker, Troy	7.5
4	Brandon Davis, South Alabama	6.3
5	Tyren Johnson, UL-Lafayette	5.8
6	Ronald Douglas, South Alabama	5.7
7	Kewain Gant, Arkansas St.	5.4
8	Xander McNally, Denver	4.4
9	Theryn Hudson, Middle Tennessee	4.2
10	Quincy Williams, North Texas	3.9
11	Rob Lewis, Denver	3.9
12	Ben Elias, New Orleans	3.3
13	Shane Edwards, UALR	3.0
14	Courtney Lee, Western Kentucky	3.0
15	Keith Wooden, North Texas	2.9

Offensive Rebounding Percentage

1	Ronald Douglas, South Alabama	14.7
2	Shawn Morgan, Arkansas St.	14.1
3	Brandon Davis, South Alabama	12.8
4	Russell Hicks, Fla. International	12.6
5	Boris Siakam, Western Kentucky	11.9
6	Quincy Williams, North Texas	11.8
7	Afam Nweke, UL-Monroe	11.0
8	Theryn Hudson, Middle Tennessee	10.5
9	DeAndre Coleman, South Alabama	10.5
10	Elijah Millsap, UL-Lafayette	10.1
11	Jeremy Evans, Western Kentucky	9.9
12	De'Andre Eggins, UALR	9.8
13	Shane Edwards, UALR	9.7
14	Ben Elias, New Orleans	9.3
15	John Fowler, UALR	9.3

Defensive Rebounding Percentage

1	Carlos Monroe, Fla. Atlantic	31.4
2	DeAndre Coleman, South Alabama	25.8
3	Keith Wooden, North Texas	23.1
4	Rob Lewis, Denver	21.4
5	Afam Nweke, UL-Monroe	20.6

6	Quincy Williams, North Texas	20.4
7	Alex Galindo, Fla. International	20.1
8	Elijah Millsap, UL-Lafayette	19.4
9	Jeremy Evans, Western Kentucky	19.4
10	Kewain Gant, Arkansas St.	18.6
11	Mike Smith, UALR	18.0
12	Ben Elias, New Orleans	17.7
13	Theryn Hudson, Middle Tennessee	17.3
14	Russell Hicks, Fla. International	17.2
15	Brandon Davis, South Alabama	16.9

Steal Rate

1	Xander McNally, Denver	5.98
2	Michael Vogler, Troy	4.63
3	Bo McCalebb, New Orleans	4.10
4	Shawn Morgan, Arkansas St.	4.05
5	Elijah Millsap, UL-Lafayette	4.04
6	Courtney Lee, Western Kentucky	3.45
7	A.J. Slaughter, Western Kentucky	3.39
8	Tony Hooper, UL-Monroe	3.22
9	Jerome Odem, Troy	3.15
10	Orlando Mendez-Valdez, W. Kentucky	3.10
11	Tyren Johnson, UL-Lafayette	3.01
12	John Fowler, UALR	3.01
13	James Parlow, New Orleans	2.90
14	Erick Nsangou, Fla. International	2.55
15	Adrian Banks, Arkansas St.	2.47

Pct. of Possible Minutes Played

1	Kevin Kanaskie, Middle Tennessee	87.6
2	Demetric Bennett, South Alabama	86.2
3	Adam Tanner, Denver	84.5
4	Jonas Brown, UL-Monroe	83.6
5	Bo McCalebb, New Orleans	82.9
6	Carderro Nwoji, Fla. Atlantic	82.7
7	Daon Merritt, South Alabama	80.8
8	Alex Galindo, Fla. International	80.8
9	Nate Rohnert, Denver	79.7
10	Ryan Wedel, Arkansas St.	79.6

SEC INDIVIDUAL STATISTICS

Offensive Rating

(Pct. of possessions used in parenthesis)

At least 28% of possessions used

1 A.J. Ogilvy, Vanderbilt	113.4	(28.3)
2 Devan Downey, South Carolina	104.5	(28.4)
3 Jamont Gordon, Mississippi St.	99.5	(30.0)

At least 24% of possessions used

1 Marreese Speights, Florida	118.6	(26.1)
2 Richard Hendrix, Alabama	117.1	(26.4)
3 A.J. Ogilvy, Vanderbilt	113.4	(28.3)
4 Nick Calathes, Florida	111.2	(27.6)
5 Marcus Thornton, Louisiana St.	110.6	(27.7)
6 Charles Rhodes, Mississippi St.	110.0	(26.2)
7 Chris Warren, Mississippi	107.4	(25.5)
8 Joe Crawford, Kentucky	107.3	(27.4)
9 Sonny Weems, Arkansas	105.8	(24.7)
10 Ramel Bradley, Kentucky	105.1	(25.7)
11 Devan Downey, South Carolina	104.5	(28.4)
12 Alonzo Gee, Alabama	104.2	(25.6)
13 Sundiata Gaines, Georgia	103.6	(26.8)
14 Frank Tolbert, Auburn	103.0	(25.5)
15 Jamont Gordon, Mississippi St.	99.5	(30.0)
16 Zam Fredrick, South Carolina	98.7	(24.1)
17 Anthony Randolph, Louisiana St.	96.6	(27.8)

At least 20% of possessions used

1 Dwayne Curtis, Mississippi	125.7	(20.3)
2 Shan Foster, Vanderbilt	124.6	(21.7)
3 Marreese Speights, Florida	118.6	(26.1)
4 Darian Townes, Arkansas	118.2	(23.4)
5 Chris Lofton, Tennessee	118.1	(21.0)
6 JaJuan Smith, Tennessee	117.7	(21.4)
7 Mykal Riley, Alabama	117.1	(20.4)
8 Quan Prowell, Auburn	117.1	(20.6)
9 Richard Hendrix, Alabama	117.1	(26.4)
10 Tyler Smith, Tennessee	116.3	(23.6)
11 Patrick Patterson, Kentucky	116.0	(23.1)
12 A.J. Ogilvy, Vanderbilt	113.4	(28.3)
13 Mike Holmes, South Carolina	112.0	(21.6)
14 Nick Calathes, Florida	111.2	(27.6)
15 Marcus Thornton, Louisiana St.	110.6	(27.7)
16 Charles Rhodes, Mississippi St.	110.0	(26.2)
17 David Huertas, Mississippi	108.3	(20.1)
18 Wayne Chism, Tennessee	108.2	(20.6)
19 Chris Warren, Mississippi	107.4	(25.5)
20 Joe Crawford, Kentucky	107.3	(27.4)

ALL PLAYERS

1 Dwayne Curtis, Mississippi	125.7	(20.3)
2 Shan Foster, Vanderbilt	124.6	(21.7)
3 Marreese Speights, Florida	118.6	(26.1)
4 Darian Townes, Arkansas	118.2	(23.4)
5 Chris Lofton, Tennessee	118.1	(21.0)
6 B. Raley-Ross, South Carolina	117.7	(14.6)
7 JaJuan Smith, Tennessee	117.7	(21.4)
8 Richard Hendrix, Alabama	117.1	(26.4)
9 Quan Prowell, Auburn	117.1	(20.6)
10 Mykal Riley, Alabama	117.1	(20.4)
11 Tyler Smith, Tennessee	116.3	(23.6)
12 Walter Hodge, Florida	116.3	(16.6)
13 Patrick Patterson, Kentucky	116.0	(23.1)
14 Jermaine Beal, Vanderbilt	114.7	(16.7)
15 Chandler Parsons, Florida	114.3	(19.7)
16 Evaldas Baniulis, S. Carolina	114.0	(13.0)
17 Ben Hansbrough, Mississippi St.	113.8	(15.5)
18 A.J. Ogilvy, Vanderbilt	113.4	(28.3)
19 Jarvis Varnado, Mississippi St.	112.8	(13.7)
20 Mike Holmes, South Carolina	112.0	(21.6)

Turnover Rate

(Pct. of possessions used in parenthesis)

At least 28% of possessions used

1 Devan Downey, South Carolina	15.0	(28.4)
2 A.J. Ogilvy, Vanderbilt	18.6	(28.3)
3 Jamont Gordon, Mississippi St.	22.4	(30.0)

At least 24% of possessions used

1 Richard Hendrix, Alabama	12.2	(26.4)
2 Marcus Thornton, Louisiana St.	13.7	(27.7)
3 Alonzo Gee, Alabama	14.3	(25.6)
4 Devan Downey, South Carolina	15.0	(28.4)
5 Marreese Speights, Florida	15.9	(26.1)
6 Zam Fredrick, South Carolina	16.1	(24.1)
7 Charles Rhodes, Mississippi St.	16.6	(26.2)
8 Sundiata Gaines, Georgia	17.2	(26.8)
9 Joe Crawford, Kentucky	18.2	(27.4)
10 A.J. Ogilvy, Vanderbilt	18.6	(28.3)
11 Nick Calathes, Florida	18.8	(27.6)
12 Anthony Randolph, Louisiana St.	19.0	(27.8)
13 Frank Tolbert, Auburn	19.3	(25.5)
14 Chris Warren, Mississippi	20.5	(25.5)
15 Sonny Weems, Arkansas	21.0	(24.7)
16 Jamont Gordon, Mississippi St.	22.4	(30.0)
17 Ramel Bradley, Kentucky	22.4	(25.7)

1 Mike Holmes, South Carolina	7.9	(21.6)
2 Chris Lofton, Tennessee	11.9	(21.0)
3 Richard Hendrix, Alabama	12.2	(26.4)
4 Shan Foster, Vanderbilt	13.0	(21.7)
5 Wayne Chism, Tennessee	13.2	(20.6)
6 Marcus Thornton, Louisiana St.	13.7	(27.7)
7 Darian Townes, Arkansas	14.1	(23.4)
8 Alonzo Gee, Alabama	14.3	(25.6)
9 Dwayne Curtis, Mississippi	14.6	(20.3)
10 Devan Downey, South Carolina	15.0	(28.4)
11 Patrick Patterson, Kentucky	15.3	(23.1)
12 Mykal Riley, Alabama	15.7	(20.4)
13 Rasheem Barrett, Auburn	15.8	(22.6)
14 JaJuan Smith, Tennessee	15.8	(21.4)
15 Marreese Speights, Florida	15.9	(26.1)
16 Zam Fredrick, South Carolina	16.1	(24.1)
17 David Huertas, Mississippi	16.4	(20.1)
18 Quan Prowell, Auburn	16.5	(20.6)
19 Charles Rhodes, Mississippi St.	16.6	(26.2)
20 Terry Martin, Louisiana St.	17.1	(20.4)

ALL PLAYERS

1 Mike Holmes, South Carolina	7.9	(21.6)
2 Chris Lofton, Tennessee	11.9	(21.0)
3 Richard Hendrix, Alabama	12.2	(26.4)
4 Shan Foster, Vanderbilt	13.0	(21.7)
5 Wayne Chism, Tennessee	13.2	(20.6)
6 Marcus Thornton, Louisiana St.	13.7	(27.7)
7 Darian Townes, Arkansas	14.1	(23.4)
8 Alonzo Gee, Alabama	14.3	(25.6)
9 Chandler Parsons, Florida	14.4	(19.7)
10 Dwayne Curtis, Mississippi	14.6	(20.3)
11 Devan Downey, South Carolina	15.0	(28.4)
12 Patrick Patterson, Kentucky	15.3	(23.1)
13 Dwayne Day, South Carolina	15.5	(14.4)
14 Mykal Riley, Alabama	15.7	(20.4)
15 Rasheem Barrett, Auburn	15.8	(22.6)
16 JaJuan Smith, Tennessee	15.8	(21.4)
17 Dominique Archie, S. Carolina	15.8	(18.0)
18 Marreese Speights, Florida	15.9	(26.1)
19 Zam Fredrick, South Carolina	16.1	(24.1)
20 Walter Hodge, Florida	16.3	(16.6)

Usage (Pct. of Possessions Used)

1 Jamont Gordon, Mississippi St.	30.0
2 Devan Downey, South Carolina	28.4
3 A.J. Ogilvy, Vanderbilt	28.3
4 Anthony Randolph, Louisiana St.	27.8
5 Marcus Thornton, Louisiana St.	27.7
6 Nick Calathes, Florida	27.6
7 Joe Crawford, Kentucky	27.4
8 Sundiata Gaines, Georgia	26.8
9 Richard Hendrix, Alabama	26.4
10 Charles Rhodes, Mississippi St.	26.2
11 Marreese Speights, Florida	26.1
12 Ramel Bradley, Kentucky	25.7
13 Alonzo Gee, Alabama	25.6
14 Frank Tolbert, Auburn	25.5
15 Chris Warren, Mississippi	25.5
16 Sonny Weems, Arkansas	24.7
17 Zam Fredrick, South Carolina	24.1
18 Charles Thomas, Arkansas	23.7
19 Tyler Smith, Tennessee	23.6
20 Darian Townes, Arkansas	23.4
21 Patrick Patterson, Kentucky	23.1
22 Ramar Smith, Tennessee	22.8
23 Rasheem Barrett, Auburn	22.6
24 Eniel Polynice, Mississippi	22.2
25 Jeremy Price, Georgia	21.8

Assist Rate

1 Nick Calathes, Florida	33.4
2 Jamont Gordon, Mississippi St.	29.7
3 Devan Downey, South Carolina	28.7
4 Jermaine Beal, Vanderbilt	28.7
5 Sundiata Gaines, Georgia	27.1
6 Rico Pickett, Alabama	26.9
7 Ramar Smith, Tennessee	25.3
8 Chris Warren, Mississippi	25.1
9 Eniel Polynice, Mississippi	24.1
10 Gary Ervin, Arkansas	23.8
11 Tyler Smith, Tennessee	22.3
12 Ramel Bradley, Kentucky	21.3
13 Brandon Hollinger, Alabama	20.9
14 Dewayne Reed, Auburn	20.4
15 Zac Swansey, Georgia	19.1

Block Rate

1 Jarvis Varnado, Mississippi St.	16.1
2 Steven Hill, Arkansas	14.3
3 Chris Johnson, Louisiana St.	8.6
4 Richard Hendrix, Alabama	7.2
5 Perry Stevenson, Kentucky	6.8
6 Anthony Randolph, Louisiana St.	6.7
7 Wayne Chism, Tennessee	6.6
8 Marreese Speights, Florida	5.9

9 A.J. Ogilvy, Vanderbilt	5.5	
10 Darian Townes, Arkansas	5.2	
11 Dave Bliss, Georgia	4.5	
12 Charles Rhodes, Mississippi St.	4.3	
13 Patrick Patterson, Kentucky	3.9	
14 Kenny Williams, Mississippi	3.5	
15 Derrick Jasper, Kentucky	3.2	

Offensive Rebounding Percentage

1 Dwayne Curtis, Mississippi	14.9
2 Mike Holmes, South Carolina	13.2
3 Richard Hendrix, Alabama	12.9
4 Marreese Speights, Florida	12.8
5 Darian Townes, Arkansas	11.5
6 Patrick Patterson, Kentucky	10.6
7 Charles Rhodes, Mississippi St.	10.4
8 Alonzo Gee, Alabama	10.1
9 Lucas Hargrove, Auburn	10.0
10 Perry Stevenson, Kentucky	9.7
11 Dan Werner, Florida	9.7
12 Tyler Smith, Tennessee	9.6
13 Demetrius Jemison, Alabama	9.5
14 Anthony Randolph, Louisiana St.	9.5
15 A.J. Ogilvy, Vanderbilt	9.4

Defensive Rebounding Percentage

1 Marreese Speights, Florida	26.4
2 Richard Hendrix, Alabama	23.6
3 A.J. Ogilvy, Vanderbilt	19.7
4 Jarvis Varnado, Mississippi St.	18.8
5 Wayne Chism, Tennessee	18.8
6 Anthony Randolph, Louisiana St.	18.5
7 Patrick Beverley, Arkansas	18.3
8 Derrick Jasper, Kentucky	18.2
9 Kenny Williams, Mississippi	18.1

10 Dan Werner, Florida	18.0
11 Dwayne Curtis, Mississippi	18.0
12 Mike Holmes, South Carolina	17.9
13 Darian Townes, Arkansas	16.5
14 Quan Prowell, Auburn	16.4
15 Dave Bliss, Georgia	16.3

Steal Rate

1 Devan Downey, South Carolina	5.03
2 Dewayne Reed, Auburn	3.57
3 JaJuan Smith, Tennessee	3.37
4 Quantez Robertson, Auburn	3.29
5 Sundiata Gaines, Georgia	3.16
6 Eniel Polynice, Mississippi	3.04
7 Mykal Riley, Alabama	2.99
8 Frank Tolbert, Auburn	2.97
9 Alonzo Gee, Alabama	2.95
10 Nick Calathes, Florida	2.90
11 Zac Swansey, Georgia	2.90
12 Ramar Smith, Tennessee	2.85
13 Ramel Bradley, Kentucky	2.77
14 Tyler Smith, Tennessee	2.69
15 Walter Hodge, Florida	2.66

Pct. of Possible Minutes Played

1 Quantez Robertson, Auburn	93.8
2 Devan Downey, South Carolina	93.2
3 Barry Stewart, Mississippi St.	88.3
4 Zam Fredrick, South Carolina	87.8
5 Jamont Gordon, Mississippi St.	85.7
6 Garrett Temple, Louisiana St.	85.6
7 Patrick Beverley, Arkansas	84.2
8 Marcus Thornton, Louisiana St.	83.8
9 Sundiata Gaines, Georgia	83.5
10 Ramel Bradley, Kentucky	83.5

SOUTHLAND
INDIVIDUAL STATISTICS

1 Josh Alexander, S. F. Austin	118.0	(23.3)
2 Jeremy Thomas, Sam Houston St.	116.3	(16.0)
3 Kenny Dawkins, Lamar	114.6	(19.9)
4 Matt Kingsley, S. F. Austin	114.0	(28.7)
5 Brent Benson, Texas St.	113.2	(22.0)
6 Anthony Vereen, UT-Arlington	111.5	(28.2)
7 Chris Daniels, Texas A&M-CC	110.7	(22.1)
8 Gerald Fonzie, S. F. Austin	110.0	(15.9)
9 Justin Nabors, Lamar	109.6	(22.7)
10 Currye Todd, Lamar	109.5	(23.1)
11 S. McDaniel, Sam Houston St.	108.2	(16.8)
12 JohnMark Ludwick, UTSA	108.1	(16.6)
13 Jermaine Griffin, UTA	107.6	(23.3)
14 Lamar Sanders, Lamar	107.4	(21.1)
15 Brent Holder, Texas St.	106.8	(17.5)
16 Kleon Penn, McNeese St.	106.7	(14.2)
17 Dekyron Nicks, SE Louisiana	106.3	(15.9)
18 Trey Gilder, Northwestern St.	105.5	(28.5)
19 Nate Bowie, Central Arkansas	105.3	(26.9)
20 Colby Bargeman, NW St.	104.4	(20.4)

Offensive Rating

(Pct. of possessions used in parenthesis)

At least 28% of possessions used

1 Matt Kingsley, S. F. Austin	114.0	(28.7)
2 Anthony Vereen, UT-Arlington	111.5	(28.2)
3 Trey Gilder, Northwestern St.	105.5	(28.5)
4 Devin Gibson, UT-San Antonio	99.5	(28.4)

At least 24% of possessions used

1 Matt Kingsley, S. F. Austin	114.0	(28.7)
2 Anthony Vereen, UT-Arlington	111.5	(28.2)
3 Trey Gilder, Northwestern St.	105.5	(28.5)
4 Nate Bowie, Central Arkansas	105.3	(26.9)
5 Brandon Bush, Texas St.	104.3	(24.1)
6 Kevyn Green, SE Louisiana	102.9	(24.2)
7 Devin Gibson, UT-San Antonio	99.5	(28.4)
8 Justin Reynolds, Texas A&M-CC	99.2	(24.9)
9 Ryan Bathie, Nicholls St.	95.8	(26.6)
10 Jarvis Bradley, McNeese St.	92.4	(25.0)
11 Ryan Bright, Sam Houston St.	90.5	(25.1)
12 York Sims, Central Arkansas	90.2	(25.9)
13 Kevin Perkins, Texas A&M-CC	87.5	(25.0)
14 Ryan White, Texas St.	85.3	(24.4)

At least 20% of possessions used

1 Josh Alexander, S. F. Austin	118.0	(23.3)
2 Matt Kingsley, S. F. Austin	114.0	(28.7)
3 Brent Benson, Texas St.	113.2	(22.0)
4 Anthony Vereen, UT-Arlington	111.5	(28.2)
5 Chris Daniels, Texas A&M-CC	110.7	(22.1)
6 Justin Nabors, Lamar	109.6	(22.7)
7 Currye Todd, Lamar	109.5	(23.1)
8 Jermaine Griffin, UT-Arlington	107.6	(23.3)
9 Lamar Sanders, Lamar	107.4	(21.1)
10 Trey Gilder, Northwestern St.	105.5	(28.5)
11 Nate Bowie, Central Arkansas	105.3	(26.9)
12 Colby Bargeman, NW St.	104.4	(20.4)
13 Brandon Bush, Texas St.	104.3	(24.1)
14 Kevyn Green, SE Louisiana	102.9	(24.2)
15 Diego Kapelan, McNeese St.	101.9	(20.2)
16 Anatoly Bose, Nicholls St.	101.4	(22.5)
17 Warrell Span, SE Louisiana	100.3	(22.0)
18 Adonis Gray, Nicholls St.	100.3	(22.2)
19 Larry Posey, UT-Arlington	100.0	(20.2)
20 Devin Gibson, UT-San Antonio	99.5	(28.4)

Turnover Rate

(Pct. of possessions used in parenthesis)

At least 28% of possessions used

1 Matt Kingsley, S. F. Austin	13.9	(28.7)
2 Trey Gilder, Northwestern St.	18.4	(28.5)
3 Anthony Vereen, UT-Arlington	20.6	(28.2)
4 Devin Gibson, UT-San Antonio	25.3	(28.4)

At least 24% of possessions used

1 Matt Kingsley, S. F. Austin	13.9	(28.7)
2 Kevyn Green, SE Louisiana	17.6	(24.2)
3 Brandon Bush, Texas St.	18.0	(24.1)
4 Trey Gilder, Northwestern St.	18.4	(28.5)
5 York Sims, Central Arkansas	18.4	(25.9)
6 Nate Bowie, Central Arkansas	19.2	(26.9)
7 Anthony Vereen, UT-Arlington	20.6	(28.2)
8 Ryan Bathie, Nicholls St.	20.6	(26.6)
9 Justin Reynolds, Texas A&M-CC	21.0	(24.9)
10 Jarvis Bradley, McNeese St.	21.7	(25.0)
11 Ryan Bright, Sam Houston St.	24.7	(25.1)
12 Devin Gibson, UT-San Antonio	25.3	(28.4)
13 Kevin Perkins, Texas A&M-CC	28.3	(25.0)
14 Ryan White, Texas St.	29.8	(24.4)

1 Colby Bargeman, NW St.	10.1	(20.4)
2 Josh Alexander, S. F. Austin	12.0	(23.3)
3 Brent Benson, Texas St.	12.4	(22.0)
4 Matt Kingsley, S. F. Austin	13.9	(28.7)
5 Diego Kapelan, McNeese St.	14.0	(20.2)
6 Currye Todd, Lamar	17.3	(23.1)
7 Kevyn Green, SE Louisiana	17.6	(24.2)
8 Brandon Bush, Texas St.	18.0	(24.1)
9 York Sims, Central Arkansas	18.4	(25.9)
10 Trey Gilder, Northwestern St.	18.4	(28.5)
11 Jermaine Griffin, UT-Arlington	18.9	(23.3)
12 Nate Bowie, Central Arkansas	19.2	(26.9)
13 Chris Daniels, Texas A&M-CC	19.8	(22.1)
14 Justin Nabors, Lamar	19.9	(22.7)
15 Warrell Span, SE Louisiana	19.9	(22.0)
16 Ryan Bathie, Nicholls St.	20.6	(26.6)
17 Marcus Pillow, Central Arkansas	20.6	(23.0)
18 Anthony Vereen, UT-Arlington	20.6	(28.2)
19 Larry Posey, UT-Arlington	20.8	(20.2)
20 Justin Reynolds, Texas A&M-CC	21.0	(24.9)

ALL PLAYERS

1 Colby Bargeman, NW St.	10.1	(20.4)
2 Josh Alexander, S. F. Austin	12.0	(23.3)
3 Brent Benson, Texas St.	12.4	(22.0)
4 Matt Kingsley, S. F. Austin	13.9	(28.7)
5 Jeremy Thomas, Sam Houston St.	13.9	(16.0)
6 Diego Kapelan, McNeese St.	14.0	(20.2)
7 Brent Holder, Texas St.	14.6	(17.5)
8 Keithan Hancock, NW St.	16.4	(19.1)
9 Gerald Fonzie, S. F. Austin	16.4	(15.9)
10 Joey Shank, UT-San Antonio	16.9	(16.2)
11 Currye Todd, Lamar	17.3	(23.1)
12 John Gardiner, Sam Houston St.	17.4	(17.9)
13 Kevyn Green, SE Louisiana	17.6	(24.2)
14 Tommy Moffitt, UT-Arlington	17.7	(15.9)
15 Brandon Bush, Texas St.	18.0	(24.1)
16 Shamir McDaniel, Sam Houston St	18.1	(16.8)
17 York Sims, Central Arkansas	18.4	(25.9)
18 Durrell Nevels, C. Arkansas	18.4	(19.6)
19 Trey Gilder, Northwestern St.	18.4	(28.5)
20 Darren Hopkins, Lamar	18.5	(20.0)

Usage (Pct. of Possessions Used)

1 Matt Kingsley, S. F. Austin	28.7
2 Trey Gilder, Northwestern St.	28.5
3 Devin Gibson, UT-San Antonio	28.4
4 Anthony Vereen, UT-Arlington	28.2
5 Nate Bowie, Central Arkansas	26.9

6 Ryan Bathie, Nicholls St.	26.6
7 York Sims, Central Arkansas	25.9
8 Ryan Bright, Sam Houston St.	25.1
9 Jarvis Bradley, McNeese St.	25.0
10 Kevin Perkins, Texas A&M-CC	25.0
11 Justin Reynolds, Texas A&M-CC	24.9
12 Ryan White, Texas St.	24.4
13 Kevyn Green, SE Louisiana	24.2
14 Brandon Bush, Texas St.	24.1
15 Tim Green, Texas A&M-CC	23.6
16 Josh Alexander, S. F. Austin	23.3
17 Jermaine Griffin, UT-Arlington	23.3
18 Patrick Sullivan, SE Louisiana	23.1
19 Currye Todd, Lamar	23.1
20 Marcus Pillow, Central Arkansas	23.0
21 Justin Nabors, Lamar	22.7
22 Anatoly Bose, Nicholls St.	22.5
23 Ty Gough, Texas St.	22.2
24 Adonis Gray, Nicholls St.	22.2
25 Chris Daniels, Texas A&M-CC	22.1

Assist Rate

1 Devin Gibson, UT-San Antonio	36.6
2 Eric Bell, S. F. Austin	34.6
3 Ashton Mitchell, Sam Houston St	33.2
4 Ryan White, Texas St.	30.9
5 Michael McConathy, NW St.	29.0
6 Corey Jefferson, Texas St.	27.0
7 Dekyron Nicks, SE Louisiana	24.8
8 Ryan Bright, Sam Houston St.	24.7
9 Nate Bowie, Central Arkansas	24.1
10 Tim Green, Texas A&M-CC	24.1
11 Cardell Hunter, UT-Arlington	22.0
12 Kenny Dawkins, Lamar	21.9
13 Justin Payne, Nicholls St.	21.7
14 John Ford, McNeese St.	21.6
15 Ryan Bathie, Nicholls St.	19.8

Block Rate

1 Kleon Penn, McNeese St.	17.4
2 Patrick Sullivan, SE Louisiana	7.8
3 Chris Daniels, Texas A&M-CC	6.9
4 John Gardiner, Sam Houston St.	6.7
5 Durrell Nevels, Central Arkansas	6.7
6 Landrell Brewer, Central Arkansas	6.3
7 Jermaine Griffin, UT-Arlington	4.9
8 Demond Watt, Texas A&M-CC	4.8
9 Lamar Sanders, Lamar	4.7

10 Brian Marks, Central Arkansas	3.9
11 Matt Kingsley, S. F. Austin	3.9
12 King Cannon, Central Arkansas	3.7
13 Trey Gilder, Northwestern St.	2.6
14 John Pichon, McNeese St.	2.4
15 Jarvis Bradley, McNeese St.	2.4

Offensive Rebounding Percentage

1 Demond Watt, Texas A&M-CC	14.7
2 Brian Marks, Central Arkansas	14.5
3 Justin Nabors, Lamar	14.0
4 Justin Reynolds, Texas A&M-CC	13.1
5 Ty Gough, Texas St.	12.7
6 Jermaine Griffin, UT-Arlington	11.8
7 Keith Spencer, UT-San Antonio	11.5
8 Brandon Thomas, Texas St.	11.0
9 Landrell Brewer, Central Arkansas	10.9
10 Lamar Sanders, Lamar	10.9
11 Larry Posey, UT-Arlington	10.7
12 Ryan Bright, Sam Houston St.	10.5
13 Kleon Penn, McNeese St.	10.1
14 John Gardiner, Sam Houston St.	9.4
15 Durrell Nevels, Central Arkansas	9.4

Defensive Rebounding Percentage

1 Ryan Bright, Sam Houston St.	26.2
2 Brian Marks, Central Arkansas	23.5
3 Jermaine Griffin, UT-Arlington	20.0
4 Ty Gough, Texas St.	19.9
5 Durrell Nevels, Central Arkansas	19.7
6 Tommy Moffitt, UT-Arlington	19.6
7 Patrick Sullivan, SE Louisiana	19.0
8 Chris Daniels, Texas A&M-CC	18.5
9 Jarvis Bradley, McNeese St.	18.4
10 Kleon Penn, McNeese St.	18.2
11 Lamar Sanders, Lamar	18.1
12 Larry Posey, UT-Arlington	17.9
13 Brandon Bush, Texas St.	17.9
14 Justin Reynolds, Texas A&M-CC	17.8
15 Demond Watt, Texas A&M-CC	17.7

Steal Rate

1 Devin Gibson, UT-San Antonio	5.97
2 Gil Verner, Nicholls St.	4.67
3 Ashton Mitchell, Sam Houston St.	4.01
4 Tavaris Nance, SE Louisiana	3.90
5 Brandon Thomas, Texas St.	3.86
6 Colby Bargeman, Northwestern St.	3.49
7 Eric Bell, Stephen F. Austin	3.45
8 Corey Jefferson, Texas St.	3.28
9 Ryan White, Texas St.	3.28
10 Nate Bowie, Central Arkansas	3.19
11 Kenny Dawkins, Lamar	3.10
12 Ryan Bright, Sam Houston St.	3.10
13 Lamar Sanders, Lamar	2.97
14 Rorey Lawrence, McNeese St.	2.94
15 Josh Alexander, Stephen F. Austin	2.80

Pct. of Possible Minutes Played

1 Nate Bowie, Central Arkansas	86.3
2 Kenny Dawkins, Lamar	86.2
3 Shamir McDaniel, Sam Houston St.	82.2
4 Josh Alexander, S. F. Austin	79.5
5 Eric Bell, S. F. Austin	78.8
6 Rog'er Guignard, UT-Arlington	78.4
7 Ryan Bright, Sam Houston St.	77.6
8 Dekyron Nicks, SE Louisiana	77.6
9 Devin Gibson, UT-San Antonio	77.2
10 John Ford, McNeese St.	76.1

SUMMIT LEAGUE
INDIVIDUAL STATISTICS

1 Gary Patterson, IUPUI	126.3	(17.3)
2 George Hill, IUPUI	125.4	(28.8)
3 Erik Kangas, Oakland	122.1	(19.6)
4 Austin Montgomery, IUPUI	117.7	(21.3)
5 Mike Nelson, North Dakota St.	116.5	(19.4)
6 Jon Avery, IUPUI	116.3	(22.8)
7 Ben Woodside, North Dakota St.	116.2	(27.2)
8 Dane Brumagin, UMKC	115.6	(25.8)
9 DeWitt Scott, IPFW	114.8	(16.1)
10 Brett Winkelman, N. Dakota St.	114.0	(28.5)
11 Moses Ehambe, Oral Roberts	112.5	(20.2)
12 Kai Williams, South Dakota St.	111.9	(20.3)
13 Geoff Payne, Southern Utah	111.3	(28.3)
14 Johnathon Jones, Oakland	111.0	(23.1)
15 Shawn King, Oral Roberts	110.8	(23.5)
16 Robert Jarvis, Oral Roberts	110.5	(26.1)
17 Jaraun Burrows, IPFW	110.3	(23.7)
18 David Marek, Southern Utah	109.5	(14.3)
19 James Washington, W. Illinois	109.3	(20.6)
20 Dan Waterstradt, Oakland	108.3	(16.1)

Offensive Rating

(Pct. of possessions used in parenthesis)

At least 28% of possessions used

1 George Hill, IUPUI	125.4	(28.8)
2 Brett Winkelman, N. Dakota St.	114.0	(28.5)
3 Geoff Payne, Southern Utah	111.3	(28.3)

At least 24% of possessions used

1 George Hill, IUPUI	125.4	(28.8)
2 Ben Woodside, North Dakota St.	116.2	(27.2)
3 Dane Brumagin, UMKC	115.6	(25.8)
4 Brett Winkelman, N. Dakota St.	114.0	(28.5)
5 Geoff Payne, Southern Utah	111.3	(28.3)
6 Robert Jarvis, Oral Roberts	110.5	(26.1)
7 Lance Hill, Centenary	108.0	(25.5)
8 Derick Nelson, Oakland	104.1	(27.3)
9 Ben Beran, South Dakota St.	99.9	(25.6)
10 Nick Stallings, Centenary	99.1	(25.5)
11 David Jackson, Western Illinois	98.8	(25.7)
12 Marcus Lewis, Oral Roberts	95.4	(25.0)
13 Tyrone Hamilton, Centenary	92.9	(27.7)
14 David Carson, IPFW	91.2	(25.3)
15 Demetrius Johnson, IPFW	89.3	(24.5)
16 Jerryck Owens-Murray, W. Ill.	88.6	(27.1)

At least 20% of possessions used

1 George Hill, IUPUI	125.4	(28.8)
2 Austin Montgomery, IUPUI	117.7	(21.3)
3 Jon Avery, IUPUI	116.3	(22.8)
4 Ben Woodside, North Dakota St.	116.2	(27.2)
5 Dane Brumagin, UMKC	115.6	(25.8)
6 Brett Winkelman, N. Dakota St.	114.0	(28.5)
7 Moses Ehambe, Oral Roberts	112.5	(20.2)
8 Kai Williams, South Dakota St.	111.9	(20.3)
9 Geoff Payne, Southern Utah	111.3	(28.3)
10 Johnathon Jones, Oakland	111.0	(23.1)
11 Shawn King, Oral Roberts	110.8	(23.5)
12 Robert Jarvis, Oral Roberts	110.5	(26.1)
13 Jaraun Burrows, IPFW	110.3	(23.7)
14 James Washington, W. Illinois	109.3	(20.6)
15 Lance Hill, Centenary	108.0	(25.5)
16 Billy Pettiford, IUPUI	106.8	(20.2)
17 Garrett Callahan, S. Dakota St	105.5	(21.0)
18 Brandon Cassise, Oakland	105.3	(20.4)
19 Derick Nelson, Oakland	104.1	(27.3)
20 Brent Stephens, UMKC	101.2	(23.3)

Turnover Rate

(Pct. of possessions used in parenthesis)

At least 28% of possessions used

1 George Hill, IUPUI	17.3	(28.8)
2 Geoff Payne, Southern Utah	17.7	(28.3)
3 Brett Winkelman, N. Dakota St.	17.9	(28.5)

At least 24% of possessions used

1 Dane Brumagin, UMKC	14.6	(25.8)
2 David Carson, IPFW	15.4	(25.3)
3 Robert Jarvis, Oral Roberts	15.7	(26.1)
4 Nick Stallings, Centenary	16.9	(25.5)
5 Lance Hill, Centenary	16.9	(25.5)
6 George Hill, IUPUI	17.3	(28.8)
7 Derick Nelson, Oakland	17.5	(27.3)
8 David Jackson, Western Illinois	17.5	(25.7)
9 Ben Woodside, N. Dakota St.	17.7	(27.2)
10 Geoff Payne, Southern Utah	17.7	(28.3)
11 Brett Winkelman, N. Dakota St.	17.9	(28.5)
12 Ben Beran, South Dakota St.	18.4	(25.6)
13 Marcus Lewis, Oral Roberts	21.3	(25.0)
14 Tyrone Hamilton, Centenary	23.2	(27.7)
15 Jerryck Owens-Murray, W. Ill.	23.7	(27.1)
16 Demetrius Johnson, IPFW	31.4	(24.5)

1 Moses Ehambe, Oral Roberts	11.2	(20.2)
2 Dane Brumagin, UMKC	14.6	(25.8)
3 Brent Stephens, UMKC	14.8	(23.3)
4 David Carson, IPFW	15.4	(25.3)
5 Robert Jarvis, Oral Roberts	15.7	(26.1)
6 Austin Montgomery, IUPUI	16.9	(21.3)
7 Lance Hill, Centenary	16.9	(25.5)
8 Nick Stallings, Centenary	16.9	(25.5)
9 Shawn King, Oral Roberts	17.1	(23.5)
10 George Hill, IUPUI	17.3	(28.8)
11 David Jackson, Western Illinois	17.5	(25.7)
12 Derick Nelson, Oakland	17.5	(27.3)
13 Ben Woodside, North Dakota St.	17.7	(27.2)
14 David Dubois, Western Illinois	17.7	(20.6)
15 Geoff Payne, Southern Utah	17.7	(28.3)
16 Jon Avery, IUPUI	17.9	(22.8)
17 Brett Winkelman, N. Dakota St.	17.9	(28.5)
18 Jaraun Burrows, IPFW	18.2	(23.7)
19 Kai Williams, South Dakota St.	18.4	(20.3)
20 Ben Beran, South Dakota St.	18.4	(25.6)

ALL PLAYERS

1 DeWitt Scott, IPFW	7.9	(16.1)
2 Moses Ehambe, Oral Roberts	11.2	(20.2)
3 Gary Patterson, IUPUI	12.0	(17.3)
4 Dane Brumagin, UMKC	14.6	(25.8)
5 Dan Waterstradt, Oakland	14.6	(16.1)
6 Brent Stephens, UMKC	14.8	(23.3)
7 Erik Kangas, Oakland	15.0	(19.6)
8 Ben Botts, IPFW	15.1	(16.0)
9 David Carson, IPFW	15.4	(25.3)
10 Robert Jarvis, Oral Roberts	15.7	(26.1)
11 Brian Gettinger, UMKC	16.5	(18.0)
12 Austin Montgomery, IUPUI	16.9	(21.3)
13 Nick Stallings, Centenary	16.9	(25.5)
14 Lance Hill, Centenary	16.9	(25.5)
15 Chris Perkins, IPFW	17.1	(18.4)
16 Shawn King, Oral Roberts	17.1	(23.5)
17 George Hill, IUPUI	17.3	(28.8)
18 Mike Nelson, North Dakota St.	17.3	(19.4)
19 Derick Nelson, Oakland	17.5	(27.3)
20 David Jackson, Western Illinois	17.5	(25.7)

Usage (Pct. of Possessions Used)

1 George Hill, IUPUI	28.8
2 Brett Winkelman, N. Dakota St.	28.5
3 Geoff Payne, Southern Utah	28.3
4 Tyrone Hamilton, Centenary	27.7

5 Derick Nelson, Oakland	27.3
6 Ben Woodside, North Dakota St.	27.2
7 Jerryck Owens-Murray, W. Ill.	27.1
8 Robert Jarvis, Oral Roberts	26.1
9 Dane Brumagin, UMKC	25.8
10 David Jackson, Western Illinois	25.7
11 Ben Beran, South Dakota St.	25.6
12 Nick Stallings, Centenary	25.5
13 Lance Hill, Centenary	25.5
14 David Carson, IPFW	25.3
15 Marcus Lewis, Oral Roberts	25.0
16 Demetrius Johnson, IPFW	24.5
17 Reggie Hamilton, UMKC	24.0
18 Jaraun Burrows, IPFW	23.7
19 Shawn King, Oral Roberts	23.5
20 Brent Stephens, UMKC	23.3
21 Johnathon Jones, Oakland	23.1
22 Nurudeen Adepoju, Southern Utah	23.0
23 Jon Avery, IUPUI	22.8
24 Austin Montgomery, IUPUI	21.3
25 Jakari Johnson, IPFW	21.2

Assist Rate

1 Demetrius Johnson, IPFW	39.4
2 Johnathon Jones, Oakland	31.7
3 Ben Woodside, North Dakota St.	28.5
4 Chase Adams, Centenary	26.6
5 Reggie Hamilton, UMKC	25.4
6 George Hill, IUPUI	24.2
7 David Marek, Southern Utah	22.1
8 Adam Liberty, Oral Roberts	20.3
9 James Washington, W. Ill.	20.3
10 Brandon Cassise, Oakland	19.7
11 Garrett Callahan, S. Dakota St.	18.6
12 Tyrone Hamilton, Centenary	18.6
13 Nurudeen Adepoju, Southern Utah	18.2
14 Tim Blackwell, UMKC	17.9
15 Clint Sargent, South Dakota St.	17.8

Block Rate

1 Shawn King, Oral Roberts	9.6
2 Justin Glenn, Centenary	5.3
3 Jaraun Burrows, IPFW	5.2
4 James Humphrey, UMKC	5.0
5 Jeremiah Hartsock, UMKC	4.7
6 Brian Gettinger, UMKC	4.3
7 Demetrius Johnson, IPFW	3.5

8 Billy Pettiford, IUPUI	2.9	
9 Jerrald Bonham, Centenary	2.8	
10 Yemi Ogunoye, Oral Roberts	2.7	
11 Dan Waterstradt, Oakland	2.7	
12 Jon Avery, IUPUI	2.6	
13 Lucas Moormann, North Dakota St.	2.3	
14 Rick Roberts, Southern Utah	2.1	
15 Drew Conner, IUPUI	2.0	

Offensive Rebounding Percentage

1 Shawn King, Oral Roberts	14.1
2 Derick Nelson, Oakland	10.4
3 Tyler Quinney, Southern Utah	10.2
4 Jerryck Owens-Murray, W. Ill.	10.2
5 Dan Waterstradt, Oakland	10.0
6 Marcus Lewis, Oral Roberts	9.9
7 Geoff Payne, Southern Utah	9.8
8 Jon Avery, IUPUI	9.8
9 Brett Winkelman, North Dakota St.	9.5
10 Lucas Moormann, North Dakota St.	9.5
11 Billy Pettiford, IUPUI	8.9
12 Lance Hill, Centenary	8.7
13 Kai Williams, South Dakota St.	8.4
14 Jerrald Bonham, Centenary	8.4
15 Drew Conner, IUPUI	8.2

Defensive Rebounding Percentage

1 Brett Winkelman, North Dakota St.	21.4
2 Jaraun Burrows, IPFW	20.7
3 Shawn King, Oral Roberts	20.7
4 James Humphrey, UMKC	19.1
5 Rick Roberts, Southern Utah	19.0
6 Marcus Lewis, Oral Roberts	18.5
7 Kai Williams, South Dakota St.	18.3
8 Dan Waterstradt, Oakland	18.1
9 Lucas Moormann, North Dakota St.	17.9

10 Jerryck Owens-Murray, W. Illinois	17.8
11 George Hill, IUPUI	17.7
12 Billy Pettiford, IUPUI	16.5
13 Justin Glenn, Centenary	16.5
14 Jon Avery, IUPUI	15.9
15 Derick Nelson, Oakland	15.3

Steal Rate

1 Chase Adams, Centenary	4.08
2 Jakari Johnson, IPFW	3.48
3 George Hill, IUPUI	3.01
4 Derick Nelson, Oakland	2.98
5 Geoff Payne, Southern Utah	2.97
6 Billy Pettiford, IUPUI	2.77
7 Drew Conner, IUPUI	2.65
8 Brandon Cassise, Oakland	2.61
9 Jeremiah Hartsock, UMKC	2.54
10 David Dubois, Western Illinois	2.52
11 Dane Brumagin, UMKC	2.51
12 Johnathon Jones, Oakland	2.48
13 Nick Stallings, Centenary	2.40
14 Ben Woodside, North Dakota St.	2.35
15 Chris Perkins, IPFW	2.28

Pct. of Possible Minutes Played

1 Ben Woodside, North Dakota St.	91.2
2 Johnathon Jones, Oakland	89.9
3 George Hill, IUPUI	89.0
4 Geoff Payne, Southern Utah	87.7
5 Kai Williams, South Dakota St.	86.9
6 Gary Patterson, IUPUI	85.7
7 Tim Blackwell, UMKC	85.4
8 Nick Stallings, Centenary	85.0
9 Derick Nelson, Oakland	84.3
10 Chase Adams, Centenary	83.3

SWAC INDIVIDUAL STATISTICS

Offensive Rating

(Pct. of possessions used in parenthesis)

At least 28% of possessions used

1 Anthony Williams, Grambling	95.9	(29.9)
2 Trant Simpson, Alabama A&M	93.9	(28.6)

At least 24% of possessions used

1 Darrion Griffin, Jackson St.	106.9	(25.1)
2 Grant Maxey, Jackson St.	105.2	(26.2)
3 Chris Davis, Southern	103.2	(25.4)
4 Carl Lucas, Miss. Valley St.	99.6	(24.8)
5 Alex Owumi, Alcorn St.	98.1	(25.0)
6 Anthony Williams, Grambling	95.9	(29.9)
7 Larry Cox, Miss. Valley St.	94.3	(26.4)
8 Trant Simpson, Alabama A&M	93.9	(28.6)
9 Brian Ezeh, Prairie View A&M	90.8	(25.6)
10 Steffon Wiley, Southern	85.1	(24.6)

At least 20% of possessions used

1 Andrew Hayles, Alabama St.	115.4	(21.3)
2 Brandon Brooks, Alabama St.	108.5	(21.5)
3 Darrion Griffin, Jackson St.	106.9	(25.1)
4 Grant Maxey, Jackson St.	105.2	(26.2)
5 Chris Davis, Southern	103.2	(25.4)
6 Jeremy Caldwell, Jackson St.	102.5	(23.1)
7 Carl Lucas, Miss. Valley St.	99.6	(24.8)
8 Alex Owumi, Alcorn St.	98.1	(25.0)
9 Troy Jackson, Alcorn St.	98.0	(24.0)
10 Anthony Ford, Alcorn St.	97.8	(20.4)
11 Larry Williams, Ark.-Pine Bluff	97.6	(22.1)
12 Andrew Prestley, Grambling	96.9	(21.2)
13 Anthony Williams, Grambling	95.9	(29.9)
14 Sollie Norwood, Texas Southern	95.5	(22.7)
15 Jonathan Belt, Alabama A&M	95.0	(20.9)
16 Anthony Ike, Texas Southern	94.7	(20.1)
17 Larry Cox, Miss. Valley St.	94.3	(26.4)
18 Trant Simpson, Alabama A&M	93.9	(28.6)
19 William Byrd, Ark.-Pine Bluff	93.6	(23.0)
20 Evan Hilton, Alabama A&M	93.0	(23.7)

ALL PLAYERS

1 Andrew Hayles, Alabama St.	115.4	(21.3)
2 Brandon Brooks, Alabama St.	108.5	(21.5)
3 Darrion Griffin, Jackson St.	106.9	(25.1)
4 Joel Bosh, Alabama St.	106.1	(15.6)
5 Grant Maxey, Jackson St.	105.2	(26.2)
6 Aaron Smith, Prairie View A&M	105.0	(18.2)
7 Duran Diaz, Grambling	105.0	(16.7)

8 Brandon Gordon, Alabama St.	104.7	(19.7)
9 Joseph Jack, Southern	104.2	(17.7)
10 Chris Davis, Southern	103.2	(25.4)
11 Jeremy Caldwell, Jackson St.	102.5	(23.1)
12 Joe Holliday, Southern	101.2	(15.9)
13 Michael Clark, Miss. Valley St	101.2	(13.7)
14 James Kendrick, Alcorn St.	100.6	(19.0)
15 Carl Lucas, Miss. Valley St.	99.6	(24.8)
16 Jamar Sanders, Alabama St.	99.5	(19.1)
17 Alex Owumi, Alcorn St.	98.1	(25.0)
18 Jamal Breaux, Grambling	98.1	(18.2)
19 Troy Jackson, Alcorn St.	98.0	(24.0)
20 Anthony Ford, Alcorn St.	97.8	(20.4)

Turnover Rate

(Pct. of possessions used in parenthesis)

At least 28% of possessions used

1 Anthony Williams, Grambling	21.4	(29.9)
2 Trant Simpson, Alabama A&M	23.1	(28.6)

At least 24% of possessions used

1 Grant Maxey, Jackson St.	18.4	(26.2)
2 Darrion Griffin, Jackson St.	18.8	(25.1)
3 Carl Lucas, Miss. Valley St.	18.8	(24.8)
4 Chris Davis, Southern	18.9	(25.4)
5 Larry Cox, Miss. Valley St.	19.1	(26.4)
6 Alex Owumi, Alcorn St.	19.6	(25.0)
7 Anthony Williams, Grambling	21.4	(29.9)
8 Trant Simpson, Alabama A&M	23.1	(28.6)
9 Brian Ezeh, Prairie View A&M	25.7	(25.6)
10 Steffon Wiley, Southern	29.7	(24.6)

At least 20% of possessions used

1 Andrew Hayles, Alabama St.	13.1	(21.3)
2 Larry Williams, Ark.-Pine Bluff	15.1	(22.1)
3 Sollie Norwood, Texas Southern	16.1	(22.7)
4 Evan Hilton, Alabama A&M	16.8	(23.7)
5 Anthony Ike, Texas Southern	17.4	(20.1)
6 Anthony Ford, Alcorn St.	17.9	(20.4)
7 Marcelle Goins, Ark.-Pine Bluff	18.1	(22.9)
8 Grant Maxey, Jackson St.	18.4	(26.2)
9 Darrion Griffin, Jackson St.	18.8	(25.1)
10 Carl Lucas, Miss. Valley St.	18.8	(24.8)
11 Chris Davis, Southern	18.9	(25.4)
12 Larry Cox, Miss. Valley St.	19.1	(26.4)
13 William Byrd, Ark.-Pine Bluff	19.4	(23.0)
14 Alex Owumi, Alcorn St.	19.6	(25.0)
15 Barry Honoré, Southern	19.7	(22.0)
16 Troy Jackson, Alcorn St.	20.0	(24.0)

17 Stanford Speech, MVSU	20.4	(22.1)
18 Eric Petty, Miss. Valley St.	20.4	(20.6)
19 Matthew Miller, Texas Southern	21.1	(23.0)
20 Jeremy Caldwell, Jackson St.	21.4	(23.1)

ALL PLAYERS

1 Joseph Jack, Southern	12.4	(17.7)
2 Andrew Hayles, Alabama St.	13.1	(21.3)
3 Aaron Smith, Prairie View A&M	14.4	(18.2)
4 Larry Williams, Ark.-Pine Bluff	15.1	(22.1)
5 Brandon Gordon, Alabama St.	15.7	(19.7)
6 Joel Bosh, Alabama St.	15.9	(15.6)
7 Duran Diaz, Grambling	15.9	(16.7)
8 Sollie Norwood, Texas Southern	16.1	(22.7)
9 Evan Hilton, Alabama A&M	16.8	(23.7)
10 Anthony Ike, Texas Southern	17.4	(20.1)
11 Garrison Johnson, Jackson St.	17.4	(17.9)
12 Anthony Ford, Alcorn St.	17.9	(20.4)
13 Marcelle Goins, Ark.-Pine Bluff	18.1	(22.9)
14 Michael Clark, Miss. Valley St.	18.3	(13.7)
15 Grant Maxey, Jackson St.	18.4	(26.2)
16 Joe Holliday, Southern	18.5	(15.9)
17 Darrion Griffin, Jackson St.	18.8	(25.1)
18 Carl Lucas, Miss. Valley St.	18.8	(24.8)
19 Chris Davis, Southern	18.9	(25.4)
20 Larry Cox, Miss. Valley St.	19.1	(26.4)

Usage (Pct. of Possessions Used)

1 Anthony Williams, Grambling	29.9
2 Trant Simpson, Alabama A&M	28.6
3 Larry Cox, Miss. Valley St.	26.4
4 Grant Maxey, Jackson St.	26.2
5 Brian Ezeh, Prairie View A&M	25.6
6 Chris Davis, Southern	25.4
7 Darrion Griffin, Jackson St.	25.1
8 Alex Owumi, Alcorn St.	25.0
9 Carl Lucas, Miss. Valley St.	24.8
10 Steffon Wiley, Southern	24.6
11 Troy Jackson, Alcorn St.	24.0
12 Evan Hilton, Alabama A&M	23.7
13 Jeremy Caldwell, Jackson St.	23.1
14 William Byrd, Ark.-Pine Bluff	23.0
15 Matthew Miller, Texas Southern	23.0
16 Marcelle Goins, Ark.-Pine Bluff	22.9
17 Sollie Norwood, Texas Southern	22.7
18 David Burrell, Texas Southern	22.6
19 Stanford Speech, MVSU	22.1
20 Larry Williams, Ark.-Pine Bluff	22.1
21 Barry Honoré, Southern	22.0
22 Brandon Brooks, Alabama St.	21.5

23 Andrew Hayles, Alabama St.	21.3
24 Derek Johnson, Prairie View A&M	21.3
25 Andrew Prestley, Grambling	21.2

Assist Rate

1 Brandon Brooks, Alabama St.	37.5
2 Trant Simpson, Alabama A&M	28.0
3 David Burrell, Texas Southern	25.9
4 Steffon Wiley, Southern	25.5
5 Catraiva Givens, Jackson St.	24.4
6 Dwayne Harmason, MVSU	23.8
7 Derek Johnson, Prairie View A&M	23.4
8 J. Frazier, Texas Southern	20.7
9 André Ratliff, Grambling	20.5
10 Jumane Reed, Alcorn St.	20.0
11 Darrion Griffin, Jackson St.	19.8
12 Geri Guillory, Southern	19.4
13 Stanford Speech, MVSU	18.7
14 Brian Ezeh, Prairie View A&M	18.5
15 Chris Davis, Southern	18.3

Block Rate

1 Mickell Gladness, Alabama A&M	15.1
2 Larry Cox, Miss. Valley St.	8.9
3 William Byrd, Arkansas-Pine Bluff	8.1
4 Joseph Jack, Southern	8.0
5 Jarvis Gunter, Arkansas-Pine Bluff	6.5
6 Jeremy Caldwell, Jackson St.	4.8
7 Jarred Riley, Grambling	4.2
8 Kevin Abanobi, Texas Southern	3.1
9 Joel Bosh, Alabama St.	3.1
10 Grant Maxey, Jackson St.	2.8
11 Brandon Gordon, Alabama St.	2.3
12 Barry Honoré, Southern	2.1
13 Anthony Williams, Grambling	2.0
14 James Kendrick, Alcorn St.	1.7
15 Jamar Sanders, Alabama St.	1.5

Offensive Rebounding Percentage

1 Larry Cox, Miss. Valley St.	12.3
2 Jeremy Caldwell, Jackson St.	10.4
3 Jamal Breaux, Grambling	10.1
4 Anthony Williams, Grambling	9.9
5 Eric Petty, Miss. Valley St.	9.9
6 James Kendrick, Alcorn St.	9.5
7 Carl Lucas, Miss. Valley St.	9.2

8 Anthony Ike, Texas Southern 9.1
9 Joel Bosh, Alabama St. 8.8
10 Grant Maxey, Jackson St. 8.5
11 Douglas Scott, Southern 8.5
12 Jonathan Belt, Alabama A&M 7.8
13 Mickell Gladness, Alabama A&M 7.4
14 Joseph Jack, Southern 7.3
15 Brian Ezeh, Prairie View A&M 7.3

Defensive Rebounding Percentage

1 Jarvis Gunter, Arkansas-Pine Bluff 27.1
2 Mickell Gladness, Alabama A&M 24.0
3 Anthony Williams, Grambling 23.8
4 Larry Cox, Miss. Valley St. 22.9
5 Jeremy Caldwell, Jackson St. 20.1
6 Jamal Breaux, Grambling 19.1
7 Grant Maxey, Jackson St. 18.8
8 William Byrd, Arkansas-Pine Bluff 18.8
9 Joseph Jack, Southern 18.3
10 Alex Owumi, Alcorn St. 17.4
11 Brandon Gordon, Alabama St. 16.9
12 Barry Honoré, Southern 16.1
13 Brian Ezeh, Prairie View A&M 16.0
14 Jonathan Belt, Alabama A&M 14.7
15 James Kendrick, Alcorn St. 14.5

Steal Rate

1 Steffon Wiley, Southern 4.06
2 David Burrell, Texas Southern 3.95
3 Johnathan Frazier, Texas Southern 3.48
4 Derek Johnson, Prairie View A&M 3.31
5 Geri Guillory, Southern 3.11
6 Chris Davis, Southern 3.02
7 Grant Maxey, Jackson St. 2.95
8 Troy Jackson, Alcorn St. 2.90
9 Brian Ezeh, Prairie View A&M 2.71
10 Catraiva Givens, Jackson St. 2.62
11 Trant Simpson, Alabama A&M 2.49
12 Dwayne Harmason, Miss. Valley St. 2.41
13 Stanford Speech, Miss. Valley St. 2.40
14 Brandon Brooks, Alabama St. 2.35
15 Andrew Hayles, Alabama St. 2.13

Pct. of Possible Minutes Played

1 Sollie Norwood, Texas Southern 85.2
2 Stanford Speech, Miss. Valley St. 81.5
3 Larry Williams, Ark.-Pine Bluff 80.3
4 William Byrd, Arkansas-Pine Bluff 79.1
5 Andrew Hayles, Alabama St. 78.8
6 Derek Johnson, Prairie View A&M 78.6
7 Brian Ezeh, Prairie View A&M 77.4
8 Trant Simpson, Alabama A&M 76.7
9 Michael Clark, Miss. Valley St. 76.4
10 Mickell Gladness, Alabama A&M 76.2

WAC INDIVIDUAL STATISTICS

Offensive Rating

(Pct. of possessions used in parenthesis)

At least 28% of possessions used

1 Marcelus Kemp, Nevada	114.3	(29.6)
2 Kevin Bell, Fresno St.	100.7	(29.7)
3 Jordan Brooks, Idaho	92.2	(31.5)

At least 24% of possessions used

1 Jaycee Carroll, Utah St.	128.8	(24.4)
2 Marcelus Kemp, Nevada	114.3	(29.6)
3 Justin Hawkins, New Mexico St.	114.0	(25.1)
4 Reggie Larry, Boise St.	110.5	(26.1)
5 Kyle Gibson, Louisiana Tech	102.7	(24.9)
6 Matt Gibson, Hawaii	102.6	(27.7)
7 Kevin Bell, Fresno St.	100.7	(29.7)
8 JaVale McGee, Nevada	100.1	(26.9)
9 Jordan Brooks, Idaho	92.2	(31.5)
10 Dwayne Lathan, Louisiana Tech	89.4	(25.4)

At least 20% of possessions used

1 Jaycee Carroll, Utah St.	128.8	(24.4)
2 Gary Wilkinson, Utah St.	118.8	(22.5)
3 Matt Nelson, Boise St.	117.8	(23.8)
4 Tai Wesley, Utah St.	115.8	(23.1)
5 Marcelus Kemp, Nevada	114.3	(29.6)
6 Justin Hawkins, New Mexico St.	114.0	(25.1)
7 Brandon Fields, Nevada	111.9	(20.5)
8 Reggie Larry, Boise St.	110.5	(26.1)
9 Chris Oakes, San Jose St.	108.2	(21.0)
10 C.J. Webster, San Jose St.	106.5	(21.9)
11 Riley Luettgerodt, Hawaii	105.1	(20.5)
12 Kyle Gibson, Louisiana Tech	102.7	(24.9)
13 Matt Gibson, Hawaii	102.6	(27.7)
14 Tim Pierce, San Jose St.	101.4	(21.9)
15 Kevin Bell, Fresno St.	100.7	(29.7)
16 JaVale McGee, Nevada	100.1	(26.9)
17 DaShawn Wright, San Jose St.	96.5	(21.0)
18 Jordan Brooks, Idaho	92.2	(31.5)
19 Dwayne Lathan, Louisiana Tech	89.4	(25.4)
20 Justin Graham, San Jose St.	85.0	(22.8)

ALL PLAYERS

1 Jaycee Carroll, Utah St.	128.8	(24.4)
2 Matt Bauscher, Boise St.	121.6	(13.9)
3 Tyler Newbold, Utah St.	120.7	(12.1)
4 Gary Wilkinson, Utah St.	118.8	(22.5)
5 Hatila Passos, New Mexico St.	118.3	(19.6)
6 Tyler Tiedeman, Boise St.	117.8	(19.2)

7 Matt Nelson, Boise St.	117.8	(23.8)
8 Tai Wesley, Utah St.	115.8	(23.1)
9 Mike Hall, Idaho	114.5	(18.9)
10 Marcelus Kemp, Nevada	114.3	(29.6)
11 Fred Peete, New Mexico St.	114.2	(17.9)
12 Justin Hawkins, New Mexico St.	114.0	(25.1)
13 Jonathan Gibson, New Mexico St	113.8	(18.9)
14 Brandon Fields, Nevada	111.9	(20.5)
15 Reggie Larry, Boise St.	110.5	(26.1)
16 Stephen DuCharme, Utah St.	110.4	(19.7)
17 Eddie Miller, Fresno St.	109.7	(19.6)
18 Bobby Nash, Hawaii	109.4	(19.7)
19 Chris Oakes, San Jose St.	108.2	(21.0)
20 Michael Crowell, Idaho	108.1	(16.2)

Turnover Rate

(Pct. of possessions used in parenthesis)

At least 28% of possessions used

1 Marcelus Kemp, Nevada	14.7	(29.6)
2 Kevin Bell, Fresno St.	17.1	(29.7)
3 Jordan Brooks, Idaho	27.7	(31.5)

At least 24% of possessions used

1 Jaycee Carroll, Utah St.	13.4	(24.4)
2 Kyle Gibson, Louisiana Tech	13.8	(24.9)
3 Marcelus Kemp, Nevada	14.7	(29.6)
4 Reggie Larry, Boise St.	16.2	(26.1)
5 Kevin Bell, Fresno St.	17.1	(29.7)
6 Justin Hawkins, New Mexico St.	18.4	(25.1)
7 JaVale McGee, Nevada	18.8	(26.9)
8 Dwayne Lathan, Louisiana Tech	19.5	(25.4)
9 Matt Gibson, Hawaii	24.6	(27.7)
10 Jordan Brooks, Idaho	27.7	(31.5)

At least 20% of possessions used

1 Jaycee Carroll, Utah St.	13.4	(24.4)
2 Kyle Gibson, Louisiana Tech	13.8	(24.9)
3 Tim Pierce, San Jose St.	14.6	(21.9)
4 Riley Luettgerodt, Hawaii	14.7	(20.5)
5 Marcelus Kemp, Nevada	14.7	(29.6)
6 Reggie Larry, Boise St.	16.2	(26.1)
7 C.J. Webster, San Jose St.	16.4	(21.9)
8 Chris Oakes, San Jose St.	16.7	(21.0)
9 Brandon Fields, Nevada	16.8	(20.5)
10 Kevin Bell, Fresno St.	17.1	(29.7)
11 Gary Wilkinson, Utah St.	17.5	(22.5)
12 Matt Nelson, Boise St.	17.6	(23.8)
13 Justin Hawkins, New Mexico St.	18.4	(25.1)
14 JaVale McGee, Nevada	18.8	(26.9)

15 Dwayne Lathan, Louisiana Tech	19.5	(25.4)
16 Tai Wesley, Utah St.	22.9	(23.1)
17 DaShawn Wright, San Jose St.	23.1	(21.0)
18 Matt Gibson, Hawaii	24.6	(27.7)
19 Jordan Brooks, Idaho	27.7	(31.5)
20 Justin Graham, San Jose St.	36.1	(22.8)

ALL PLAYERS

1 Bobby Nash, Hawaii	9.6	(19.7)
2 Eddie Miller, Fresno St.	10.3	(19.6)
3 Mike Hall, Idaho	11.5	(18.9)
4 Bryan Harvey, Fresno St.	12.7	(19.9)
5 Jaycee Carroll, Utah St.	13.4	(24.4)
6 Hector Hernandez, Fresno St.	13.6	(18.2)
7 Jonathan Clark, Louisiana Tech	13.7	(17.6)
8 Kyle Gibson, Louisiana Tech	13.8	(24.9)
9 Matt Bauscher, Boise St.	13.8	(13.9)
10 Tim Pierce, San Jose St.	14.6	(21.9)
11 Riley Luettgerodt, Hawaii	14.7	(20.5)
12 Marcelus Kemp, Nevada	14.7	(29.6)
13 Darin Nagle, Idaho	16.1	(17.9)
14 Reggie Larry, Boise St.	16.2	(26.1)
15 Drew Washington, La. Tech	16.2	(13.3)
16 Clyde Johnson, Idaho	16.3	(17.3)
17 C.J. Webster, San Jose St.	16.4	(21.9)
18 Chris Oakes, San Jose St.	16.7	(21.0)
19 Brandon Fields, Nevada	16.8	(20.5)
20 Kevin Bell, Fresno St.	17.1	(29.7)

Usage (Pct. of Possessions Used)

1 Jordan Brooks, Idaho	31.5
2 Kevin Bell, Fresno St.	29.7
3 Marcelus Kemp, Nevada	29.6
4 Matt Gibson, Hawaii	27.7
5 JaVale McGee, Nevada	26.9
6 Reggie Larry, Boise St.	26.1
7 Dwayne Lathan, Louisiana Tech	25.4
8 Justin Hawkins, New Mexico St.	25.1
9 Kyle Gibson, Louisiana Tech	24.9
10 Jaycee Carroll, Utah St.	24.4
11 Matt Nelson, Boise St.	23.8
12 Tai Wesley, Utah St.	23.1
13 Justin Graham, San Jose St.	22.8
14 Gary Wilkinson, Utah St.	22.5
15 C.J. Webster, San Jose St.	21.9
16 Tim Pierce, San Jose St.	21.9
17 Chris Oakes, San Jose St.	21.0
18 DaShawn Wright, San Jose St.	21.0
19 Riley Luettgerodt, Hawaii	20.5
20 Brandon Fields, Nevada	20.5

21 Armon Johnson, Nevada	20.0
22 Bryan Harvey, Fresno St.	19.9
23 Bobby Nash, Hawaii	19.7
24 Stephen DuCharme, Utah St.	19.7
25 Eddie Miller, Fresno St.	19.6

Assist Rate

1 Kris Clark, Utah St.	37.2
2 Jordan Brooks, Idaho	36.5
3 Kevin Bell, Fresno St.	36.1
4 Matt Gibson, Hawaii	30.5
5 Anthony Thomas, Boise St.	23.9
6 Fred Peete, New Mexico St.	22.1
7 Marcelus Kemp, Nevada	21.8
8 Armon Johnson, Nevada	19.5
9 James Loe, Louisiana Tech	19.2
10 Tai Wesley, Utah St.	18.6
11 Justin Graham, San Jose St.	18.6
12 Tyler Tiedeman, Boise St.	17.1
13 C.J. Webster, San Jose St.	17.0
14 Matt Bauscher, Boise St.	16.9
15 Jamon Hill, San Jose St.	16.5

Block Rate

1 JaVale McGee, Nevada	9.5
2 Darin Nagle, Idaho	6.7
3 Bill Amis, Hawaii	6.1
4 Tai Wesley, Utah St.	4.4
5 Chris Oakes, San Jose St.	4.3
6 Demarshay Johnson, Nevada	4.0
7 Alex Blair, Fresno St.	4.0
8 Clyde Johnson, Idaho	3.7
9 Reggie Larry, Boise St.	3.0
10 Dwayne Lathan, Louisiana Tech	2.7
11 Gary Wilkinson, Utah St.	2.4
12 Wendell McKines, New Mexico St.	2.3
13 C.J. Webster, San Jose St.	2.1
14 Hector Hernandez, Fresno St.	1.7
15 Justin Hawkins, New Mexico St.	1.6

Offensive Rebounding Percentage

1 Wendell McKines, New Mexico St.	15.6
2 Chris Oakes, San Jose St.	14.2
3 Hatila Passos, New Mexico St.	14.0
4 Tai Wesley, Utah St.	11.3
5 Gary Wilkinson, Utah St.	11.1

6 JaVale McGee, Nevada	11.0	
7 Matt Nelson, Boise St.	10.6	
8 Demarshay Johnson, Nevada	9.3	
9 Bill Amis, Hawaii	9.2	
10 Reggie Larry, Boise St.	9.0	
11 C.J. Webster, San Jose St.	8.8	
12 Jordan Brooks, Idaho	8.4	
13 Alex Blair, Fresno St.	8.4	
14 Mike Kale, Idaho	8.3	
15 Justin Hawkins, New Mexico St.	8.3	

Defensive Rebounding Percentage

1 Reggie Larry, Boise St.	21.7
2 Gary Wilkinson, Utah St.	20.4
3 Stephen DuCharme, Utah St.	19.8
4 C.J. Webster, San Jose St.	19.1
5 Hector Hernandez, Fresno St.	19.0
6 JaVale McGee, Nevada	18.7
7 Wendell McKines, New Mexico St.	18.5
8 Matt Nelson, Boise St.	18.1
9 Chris Oakes, San Jose St.	17.9
10 Alex Blair, Fresno St.	17.7
11 Jordan Brooks, Idaho	17.6
12 Hatila Passos, New Mexico St.	17.4
13 Darin Nagle, Idaho	16.9
14 Nedeljko Golubovic, Fresno St.	16.3
15 Bryan Harvey, Fresno St.	16.3

Steal Rate

1 Jordan Brooks, Idaho	3.47
2 Matt Gibson, Hawaii	3.17
3 DaShawn Wright, San Jose St.	2.98
4 Justin Graham, San Jose St.	2.82
5 Anthony Thomas, Boise St.	2.78
6 Fred Peete, New Mexico St.	2.57
7 Drew Washington, Louisiana Tech	2.45
8 Bryan Harvey, Fresno St.	2.42
9 Dwayne Lathan, Louisiana Tech	2.38
10 Mike Hall, Idaho	2.28
11 Reggie Larry, Boise St.	2.26
12 Clyde Johnson, Idaho	2.24
13 Jared Dillinger, Hawaii	2.14
14 Kris Clark, Utah St.	2.09
15 Matt Bauscher, Boise St.	2.08

Pct. of Possible Minutes Played

1 Jaycee Carroll, Utah St.	93.1
2 Kevin Bell, Fresno St.	92.6
3 Kyle Gibson, Louisiana Tech	89.7
4 Bobby Nash, Hawaii	88.4
5 Riley Luettgerodt, Hawaii	87.6
6 Eddie Miller, Fresno St.	85.9
7 Reggie Larry, Boise St.	84.1
8 Michael Crowell, Idaho	82.0
9 Drew Washington, Louisiana Tech	81.3
10 Marcelus Kemp, Nevada	80.2

WCC INDIVIDUAL STATISTICS

Offensive Rating

(Pct. of possessions used in parenthesis)

At least 28% of possessions used

1 John Bryant, Santa Clara	107.7	(33.3)
2 Dior Lowhorn, San Francisco	103.8	(28.4)
3 Brandon Johnson, San Diego	96.8	(28.5)
4 Tyrone Shelley, Pepperdine	95.8	(29.3)
5 Orlando Johnson, Loy. Marymount	93.3	(28.1)

At least 24% of possessions used

1 Austin Daye, Gonzaga	108.7	(27.3)
2 John Bryant, Santa Clara	107.7	(33.3)
3 Patrick Mills, St. Mary's	104.3	(24.7)
4 Dior Lowhorn, San Francisco	103.8	(28.4)
5 Nik Raivio, Portland	99.7	(24.8)
6 Brandon Johnson, San Diego	96.8	(28.5)
7 Tyrone Shelley, Pepperdine	95.8	(29.3)
8 Manny Quezada, San Francisco	95.0	(28.0)
9 Orlando Johnson, Loy. Marymount	93.3	(28.1)
10 Rico Tucker, Pepperdine	87.4	(27.3)
11 Jon Ziri, Loyola Marymount	76.7	(24.7)

At least 20% of possessions used

1 Gyno Pomare, San Diego	116.0	(23.9)
2 Omar Samhan, St. Mary's	110.3	(24.0)
3 Austin Daye, Gonzaga	108.7	(27.3)
4 Diamon Simpson, St. Mary's	108.5	(22.2)
5 John Bryant, Santa Clara	107.7	(33.3)
6 Matt Bouldin, Gonzaga	107.0	(21.0)
7 Jeremy Pargo, Gonzaga	104.7	(22.7)
8 Patrick Mills, St. Mary's	104.3	(24.7)
9 Dior Lowhorn, San Francisco	103.8	(28.4)
10 Nik Raivio, Portland	99.7	(24.8)
11 Brody Angley, Santa Clara	98.9	(24.0)
12 Mitch Henke, Santa Clara	98.1	(20.1)
13 Robin Smeulders, Portland	97.9	(22.5)
14 Malcolm Thomas, Pepperdine	97.7	(22.8)
15 Brandon Johnson, San Diego	96.8	(28.5)
16 Sherrard Watson, Portland	96.6	(23.0)
17 Luke Sikma, Portland	96.0	(20.2)
18 Tyrone Shelley, Pepperdine	95.8	(29.3)
19 Manny Quezada, San Francisco	95.0	(28.0)
20 Tron Smith, St. Mary's	94.0	(23.2)

ALL PLAYERS

1 Todd Golden, St. Mary's	141.4	(11.1)
2 David Pendergraft, Gonzaga	123.8	(15.8)
3 Steven Gray, Gonzaga	118.8	(13.9)
4 Jonathan Gunderson, S. Clara	116.1	(12.8)
5 Gyno Pomare, San Diego	116.0	(23.9)
6 Danny Cavic, San Francisco	114.6	(14.1)
7 Omar Samhan, St. Mary's	110.3	(24.0)
8 Austin Daye, Gonzaga	108.7	(27.3)
9 Ian O'Leary, St. Mary's	108.7	(19.2)
10 Micah Downs, Gonzaga	108.7	(17.5)
11 Diamon Simpson, St. Mary's	108.5	(22.2)
12 Jared Stohl, Portland	108.0	(17.6)
13 John Bryant, Santa Clara	107.7	(33.3)
14 Matt Bouldin, Gonzaga	107.0	(21.0)
15 Calvin Johnson, Santa Clara	106.1	(10.9)
16 Carlin Hughes, St. Mary's	105.2	(19.8)
17 Jeremy Pargo, Gonzaga	104.7	(22.7)
18 Patrick Mills, St. Mary's	104.3	(24.7)
19 Dior Lowhorn, San Francisco	103.8	(28.4)
20 Mychel Thompson, Pepperdine	102.5	(16.4)

Turnover Rate

(Pct. of possessions used in parenthesis)

At least 28% of possessions used

1 Dior Lowhorn, San Francisco	16.9	(28.4)
2 Tyrone Shelley, Pepperdine	18.5	(29.3)
3 John Bryant, Santa Clara	19.2	(33.3)
4 Orlando Johnson, Loy. Marymount	19.9	(28.1)
5 Brandon Johnson, San Diego	20.0	(28.5)

At least 24% of possessions used

1 Dior Lowhorn, San Francisco	16.9	(28.4)
2 Nik Raivio, Portland	18.0	(24.8)
3 Tyrone Shelley, Pepperdine	18.5	(29.3)
4 John Bryant, Santa Clara	19.2	(33.3)
5 Austin Daye, Gonzaga	19.5	(27.3)
6 Orlando Johnson, Loy. Marymount	19.9	(28.1)
7 Brandon Johnson, San Diego	20.0	(28.5)
8 Patrick Mills, St. Mary's	20.8	(24.7)
9 Manny Quezada, San Francisco	25.0	(28.0)
10 Jon Ziri, Loyola Marymount	28.0	(24.7)
11 Rico Tucker, Pepperdine	30.4	(27.3)

At least 20% of possessions used

1 Gyno Pomare, San Diego	12.7	(23.9)
2 Omar Samhan, St. Mary's	13.8	(24.0)
3 Dior Lowhorn, San Francisco	16.9	(28.4)
4 Robin Smeulders, Portland	17.4	(22.5)
5 Nik Raivio, Portland	18.0	(24.8)
6 Tyrone Shelley, Pepperdine	18.5	(29.3)
7 Diamon Simpson, St. Mary's	19.1	(22.2)
8 John Bryant, Santa Clara	19.2	(33.3)

9 Austin Daye, Gonzaga	19.5	(27.3)
10 Orlando Johnson, Loy. Marymount	19.9	(28.1)
11 Brandon Johnson, San Diego	20.0	(28.5)
12 Patrick Mills, St. Mary's	20.8	(24.7)
13 Matt Bouldin, Gonzaga	21.4	(21.0)
14 Malcolm Thomas, Pepperdine	21.5	(22.8)
15 Rob Jones, San Diego	24.0	(22.9)
16 Shawn Deadwiler, Loy. Marymount	24.3	(21.2)
17 Sherrard Watson, Portland	24.4	(23.0)
18 Brody Angley, Santa Clara	25.0	(24.0)
19 Manny Quezada, San Francisco	25.0	(28.0)
20 Jeremy Pargo, Gonzaga	25.5	(22.7)

ALL PLAYERS

1 Gyno Pomare, San Diego	12.7	(23.9)
2 David Pendergraft, Gonzaga	12.8	(15.8)
3 Omar Samhan, St. Mary's	13.8	(24.0)
4 Todd Golden, St. Mary's	14.5	(11.1)
5 Ian O'Leary, St. Mary's	15.5	(19.2)
6 Dior Lowhorn, San Francisco	16.9	(28.4)
7 Robin Smeulders, Portland	17.4	(22.5)
8 Nik Raivio, Portland	18.0	(24.8)
9 Mychel Thompson, Pepperdine	18.2	(16.4)
10 Danny Cavic, San Francisco	18.4	(14.1)
11 Tyrone Shelley, Pepperdine	18.5	(29.3)
12 De'Jon Jackson, San Diego	18.5	(15.2)
13 Diamon Simpson, St. Mary's	19.1	(22.2)
14 John Bryant, Santa Clara	19.2	(33.3)
15 Austin Daye, Gonzaga	19.5	(27.3)
16 Orlando Johnson, Loy. Marymount	19.9	(28.1)
17 Mike Hornbuckle, Pepperdine	19.9	(13.6)
18 Brandon Johnson, San Diego	20.0	(28.5)
19 Micah Downs, Gonzaga	20.4	(17.5)
20 Steven Gray, Gonzaga	20.5	(13.9)

Usage (Pct. of Possessions Used)

1 John Bryant, Santa Clara	33.3
2 Tyrone Shelley, Pepperdine	29.3
3 Brandon Johnson, San Diego	28.5
4 Dior Lowhorn, San Francisco	28.4
5 Orlando Johnson, Loy. Marymount	28.1
6 Manny Quezada, San Francisco	28.0
7 Austin Daye, Gonzaga	27.3
8 Rico Tucker, Pepperdine	27.3
9 Nik Raivio, Portland	24.8
10 Jon Ziri, Loyola Marymount	24.7
11 Patrick Mills, St. Mary's	24.7
12 Omar Samhan, St. Mary's	24.0
13 Brody Angley, Santa Clara	24.0

14 Gyno Pomare, San Diego	23.9
15 Tron Smith, St. Mary's	23.2
16 Sherrard Watson, Portland	23.0
17 Rob Jones, San Diego	22.9
18 Malcolm Thomas, Pepperdine	22.8
19 Jeremy Pargo, Gonzaga	22.7
20 Robin Smeulders, Portland	22.5
21 Diamon Simpson, St. Mary's	22.2
22 Shawn Deadwiler, Loy. Marymount	21.2
23 Matt Bouldin, Gonzaga	21.0
24 Luke Sikma, Portland	20.2
25 Mitch Henke, Santa Clara	20.1

Assist Rate

1 Brody Angley, Santa Clara	34.2
2 Jeremy Pargo, Gonzaga	33.4
3 Manny Quezada, San Francisco	30.8
4 Rico Tucker, Pepperdine	26.8
5 Carlin Hughes, St. Mary's	25.7
6 Corey Counts, Loyola Marymount	25.2
7 Brandon Johnson, San Diego	23.5
8 Taishi Ito, Portland	22.0
9 Orlando Johnson, Loy. Marymount	21.9
10 Patrick Mills, St. Mary's	21.8
11 Jon Ziri, Loyola Marymount	21.1
12 Trumaine Johnson, San Diego	20.5
13 Shawn Deadwiler, Loy. Marymount	20.1
14 Luke Sikma, Portland	20.0
15 Myron Strong, San Francisco	19.6

Block Rate

1 John Bryant, Santa Clara	10.5
2 Austin Daye, Gonzaga	10.0
3 Malcolm Thomas, Pepperdine	6.6
4 Hyman Taylor, San Francisco	5.8
5 Diamon Simpson, St. Mary's	5.5
6 Omar Samhan, St. Mary's	5.4
7 Gyno Pomare, San Diego	5.1
8 Luke Sikma, Portland	4.8
9 Dior Lowhorn, San Francisco	2.9
10 Robin Smeulders, Portland	2.6
11 Rob Jones, San Diego	2.3
12 Kramer Knutson, Portland	2.1
13 Marko Deric, Loyola Marymount	2.1
14 Tyrone Shelley, Pepperdine	2.0
15 Jon Ziri, Loyola Marymount	1.8

Offensive Rebounding Percentage

1 Omar Samhan, St. Mary's   15.4
2 John Bryant, Santa Clara   13.5
3 Luke Sikma, Portland   13.0
4 Gyno Pomare, San Diego   12.0
5 Ian O'Leary, St. Mary's   11.3
6 Malcolm Thomas, Pepperdine   10.6
7 Rob Jones, San Diego   10.0
8 Diamon Simpson, St. Mary's   9.8
9 Kramer Knutson, Portland   9.7
10 Dior Lowhorn, San Francisco   9.2
11 Orlando Johnson, Loyola Marymount 8.9
12 Robin Smeulders, Portland   8.6
13 David Pendergraft, Gonzaga   8.2
14 Tyrone Shelley, Pepperdine   8.0
15 Hyman Taylor, San Francisco   7.8

Steal Rate

1 Jon Ziri, Loyola Marymount   5.40
2 Rico Tucker, Pepperdine   4.78
3 Brandon Johnson, San Diego   3.79
4 Mychel Thompson, Pepperdine   3.55
5 Tyrone Shelley, Pepperdine   3.28
6 Patrick Mills, St. Mary's   3.22
7 Myron Strong, San Francisco   3.18
8 Brody Angley, Santa Clara   2.82
9 Carlin Hughes, St. Mary's   2.79
10 Manny Quezada, San Francisco 2.69
11 Matt Bouldin, Gonzaga   2.56
12 Jeremy Pargo, Gonzaga   2.45
13 Mike Hornbuckle, Pepperdine   2.42
14 Trumaine Johnson, San Diego   2.41
15 Rob Jones, San Diego   2.39

Defensive Rebounding Percentage

1 John Bryant, Santa Clara   31.4
2 Luke Sikma, Portland   26.9
3 Diamon Simpson, St. Mary's   24.7
4 Austin Daye, Gonzaga   23.5
5 Jon Ziri, Loyola Marymount   23.0
6 Hyman Taylor, San Francisco   22.1
7 Malcolm Thomas, Pepperdine   21.8
8 Robin Smeulders, Portland   21.7
9 Gyno Pomare, San Diego   19.6
10 Omar Samhan, St. Mary's   18.9
11 Rob Jones, San Diego   17.6
12 Tyrone Shelley, Pepperdine   16.7
13 Chris Lewis, San Diego   16.6
14 Dior Lowhorn, San Francisco   15.7
15 Ian O'Leary, St. Mary's   13.8

Pct. of Possible Minutes Played

1 Dior Lowhorn, San Francisco   91.2
2 Brody Angley, Santa Clara   86.9
3 Brandon Johnson, San Diego   84.5
4 Jeremy Pargo, Gonzaga   83.6
5 Manny Quezada, San Francisco   80.4
6 Myron Strong, San Francisco   79.8
7 Patrick Mills, St. Mary's   79.3
8 Danny Cavic, San Francisco   77.8
9 Mitch Henke, Santa Clara   77.8
10 De'Jon Jackson, San Diego   77.2

Author Biographies

Ken Pomeroy and **John Gasaway** write on college basketball for Basketball Prospectus (basketballprospectus.com). During the site's first year, Ken and John's work was cited on the Web by ESPN, *Sports Illustrated*, *The Sporting News*, MSNBC, the *New York Times*, the *Wall Street Journal*, *Newsweek*, and the *New Republic*.

Kevin Pelton covers NBA hoops for Basketball Prospectus. Previously, his NBA analysis appeared on SI.com, 82games.com, and Hoopsworld.com. Kevin also covers the WNBA's Seattle Storm for storm.wnba.com and served as beat writer for supersonics.com for four years. A graduate of the University of Washington, he believes that East Coast bias has blinded fans and the media to the superiority of the Pac-10.

Will Carroll was described as "Bo Jackson" when he wrote for Football Prospectus after coming over from Baseball Prospectus. There's not nearly as good a comparison for this book, especially considering he's short and has no outside jump shot. Will writes about injuries and sports medicine, is a three-time Fantasy Sports Writers Association award winner, and lives in Indiana, which would have given him some hoops cred about a decade ago.

John Perrotto has covered Major League Baseball, and the Pittsburgh Pirates in particular, for the *Beaver County (Pa.) Times* and other publications for twenty years. He began writing for Basketball Prospectus last year. He graduated from Geneva College, birthplace of college basketball, and lives in Beaver Falls, Pennsylvania, birthplace of Joe Willie Namath, with his wife, Brenda.

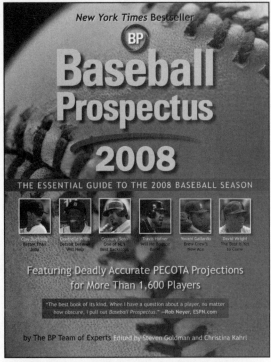
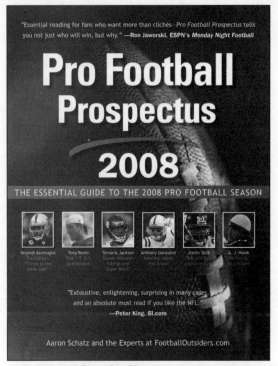